T0093294

R

ALL-IN-ONE

by Joseph Schmuller

A Wiley Brand

R All-in-One For Dummies®

Published by: **John Wiley & Sons, Inc.,** 111 River Street, Hoboken, NJ 07030-5774, www.wiley.com

Copyright © 2023 by John Wiley & Sons, Inc., Hoboken, New Jersey

Published simultaneously in Canada

For general information on our other products and services, please contact our Customer Care Department within the U.S. at 877-762-2974, outside the U.S. at 317-572-3993, or fax 317-572-4002. For technical support, please visit https://hub.wiley.com/community/support/dummies.

Wiley publishes in a variety of print and electronic formats and by print-on-demand. Some material included with standard print versions of this book may not be included in e-books or in print-on-demand. If this book refers to media such as a CD or DVD that is not included in the version you purchased, you may download this material at http://booksupport.wiley.com. For more information about Wiley products, visit www.wiley.com.

Library of Congress Control Number: 2022950749

ISBN: 978-1-119-98369-9 (pbk); 978-1-119-98370-5 (ebk); 978-1-119-98371-2 (ebk)

Printed and bound by CPI Group (UK) Ltd, Croydon, CR0 4YY

C004611_030123

Contents at a Glance

Table of Contents

Introduction

n this book, I've brought together all the information you need to hit the ground running with R. It's heavy on statistics, of course, because R's creators built this language to analyze data.

So it's necessary that you learn the foundations of statistics. Let me tell you at the outset: This *All-in-One* is not a cookbook. I've never taught statistics that way and I never will. Before I show you how to use R to work with a statistical concept, I give you a strong grounding in what that concept is all about.

In fact, Books 2 and 3 of this 5-book compendium are something like an introductory statistics text that happens to use R as a way of explaining statistical ideas.

Book 4 follows that path by teaching the ideas behind machine learning before you learn how to use R to implement them. Book 5 gives you a set of projects that give you a chance to exercise your newly minted R skill set.

Want some more details? Read on.

About This All-in-One

The volume you're holding (or the e-book you're viewing) consists of five books that cover a lot of the length and breadth of R.

Book 1: Introducing R

As I said earlier in this introduction, R is a language that deals with statistics. Accordingly, Book 1 introduces you to the fundamental concepts of statistics that you just *have* to know in order to progress with R.

You then learn about R and RStudio, a widely used development environment for working with R. I begin by describing the rudiments of R code, and I discuss R functions and structures.

R truly comes alive when you use its specialized packages, which you learn about early on.

Book 2: Describing Data

Part of working with statistics is to summarize data in meaningful ways. In Book 2, you find out how to do just that.

Most people know about averages and how to compute them. But that's not the whole story. In Book 2, I tell you about additional descriptive statistics that fill in the gaps, and I show you how to use R to calculate and work with those statistics. You also learn to create graphics that visualize the data descriptions and analyses you encounter in Books 2 and 3.

Book 3: Analyzing Data

Book 3 addresses the fundamental aim of statistical analysis: to go beyond the data and help you make decisions. Usually, the data are measurements of a sample taken from a large population. The goal is to use these data to figure out what's going on in the population.

This opens a wide range of questions: What does an average mean? What does the difference between two averages mean? Are two things associated? These are only a few of the questions I address in Book 3, and you learn to use the R tools that help you answer them.

Book 4: Learning from Data

Effective machine learning model creation comes with experience. Accordingly, in Book 4 you gain experience by completing machine learning projects. In addition to the projects you complete along with me, I suggest additional projects for you to try on your own.

I begin by telling you about the University of California-Irvine Machine Learning Repository, which provides the data sets for most of the projects you encounter in Book 4.

To give you a gentle on-ramp into the field, I show you the `Rattle` package for creating machine learning applications. It's a friendly interface to R's machine learning functionality. I like `Rattle` a lot, and I think you will, too. You use it to learn about and work with decision trees, random forests, support vector machines, k-means clustering, and neural networks.

You also work with fairly large data sets — not the terabytes and petabytes data scientists work with, but large enough to get you started. In one project, you analyze a data set of more than 500,000 airline flights. In another, you complete a customer segmentation analysis of over 300,000 customers of an online retailer.

Book 5: Harnessing R: Some Projects to Keep You Busy

As its title suggests, Book 5 is also organized around projects.

In these projects, you create applications that respond to users. I show you the `shiny` package for working with web browsers and the `shinydashboard` package for creating dashboards.

All this is a little far afield from R's original mission in life, but you get an idea of R's potential to expand in new directions.

After you've worked with R for a while, maybe you can discover some of those new directions!

What You Can Safely Skip

Any reference book throws a lot of information at you, and this one is no exception. I intended it all to be useful, but I didn't aim it all at the same level. So if you're not deeply into the subject matter, you can avoid paragraphs marked with the Technical Stuff icon, and you can also skip the sidebars.

Foolish Assumptions

I'm assuming that you

>> Know how to work with Windows or the Mac. I don't go through the details of pointing, clicking, selecting, and so forth.

>> Can install R and RStudio (I show you how in Book 1) and follow along with the examples. I use the Windows version of RStudio, but you should have no problem if you're working on a Mac.

Icons Used in This Book

As is the case in all *For Dummies* books, icons help guide you through your journey. Each one is a little picture in the margin that lets you know something special about the paragraph it's next to.

TIP

This icon points out a hint or a shortcut that helps you in your work and makes you an all-around better person.

REMEMBER

This one points out timeless wisdom to take with you as you continue on the path to enlightenment.

WARNING

Pay attention to this icon. It's a reminder to avoid something that might gum up the works for you.

TECHNICAL STUFF

As I mention in "What You Can Safely Skip," this icon indicates material you can blow past if it's just too technical. (I've kept this content to a minimum.)

Beyond This Book

In addition to what you're reading right now, this book comes with a free, access-anywhere Cheat Sheet that will help you quickly use the tools I discuss. To find this Cheat Sheet, visit www.dummies.com and search for *R All-in-One For Dummies Cheat Sheet* in the Search box.

If you've read any of my earlier books, welcome back!

Where to Go from Here

Time to hit the books! You can start from anywhere, but here are a couple of hints. Want to introduce yourself to R and packages? Book 1 is for you. Has it been a while (or maybe never?) since your last statistics course? Hit Book 2. For anything else, find it in the table of contents or in the index and go for it.

If you prefer to read from cover to cover, just turn the page. . . .

1
Introducing R

Contents at a Glance

Chapter **1**

R: What It Does and How It Does It

So you're ready to journey into the wonderful world of R! Designed by and for statisticians and data scientists, R has a short but illustrious history.

In the 1990s, Ross Ihaka and Robert Gentleman developed R at the University of Auckland, New Zealand. The R Core Team and the R Foundation for Statistical Computing support R, which has a huge worldwide user base.

Before I tell you about R, however, I have to introduce you to the world that R lives in — the world of data and statistics.

The Statistical (and Related) Ideas You Just Have to Know

The analytical tools that R provides are based on statistical concepts I help you explore in this section. As you'll see, these concepts are based on common sense.

Samples and populations

If you watch TV on election night, you know that one of the main events is the prediction of the outcome immediately after the polls close (and before all the votes are counted). How is it that pundits almost always get it right?

The idea is to talk to a *sample* of voters right after they vote. If they're truthful about how they marked their ballots, and if the sample is representative of the *population* of voters, analysts can use the sample data to draw conclusions about the population.

That, in a nutshell, is what statistics is all about — using the data from samples to draw conclusions about populations.

Here's another example. Imagine that your job is to find the average height of 10-year-old children in the United States. Because you probably wouldn't have the time or the resources to measure every child, you'd measure the heights of a representative sample. Then you'd average those heights and use that average as the estimate of the population average.

Estimating the population average is one kind of *inference* that statisticians make from sample data. I discuss inference in more detail in the later section "Inferential Statistics: Testing Hypotheses."

REMEMBER

Here's some important terminology: Properties of a population (like the population average) are called *parameters*, and properties of a sample (like the sample average) are called *statistics*. If your only concern is the sample properties (like the heights of the children in your sample), the statistics you calculate are *descriptive*. (I discuss descriptive statistics in Book 2.) If you're concerned about estimating the population properties, your statistics are *inferential*. (I discuss inferential statistics in Book 3.)

REMEMBER

Now for an important convention about notation: Statisticians use Greek letters (μ, σ, ρ) to stand for parameters, and English letters ($\bar{X}$, s, r) to stand for statistics. Figure 1-1 summarizes the relationship between populations and samples, and between parameters and statistics.

Variables: Dependent and independent

A *variable* is something that can take on more than one value — like your age, the value of the dollar against other currencies, or the number of games your favorite sports team wins. Something that can have only one value is a *constant*. Scientists tell us that the speed of light is a constant, and we use the constant π to calculate the area of a circle.

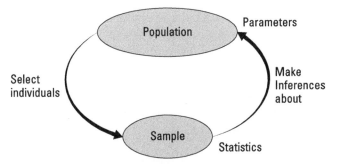

FIGURE 1-1:
The relationship
between
populations,
samples,
parameters, and
statistics.

Statisticians work with *independent* variables and *dependent* variables. In any study or experiment, you'll find both kinds. Statisticians assess the relationship between them.

For example, imagine a computerized training method designed to increase a person's IQ. How would a researcher find out whether this method does what it's supposed to do? First, the researcher would randomly assign a sample of people to one of two groups. One group would receive the training method, and the other would complete another kind of computer-based activity — like reading text on a website. Before and after each group completes its activities, the researcher measures each person's IQ. What happens next? I discuss that topic in the later section "Inferential Statistics: Testing Hypotheses."

For now, understand that the independent variable here is Type of Activity. The two possible values of this variable are IQ Training and Reading Text. The dependent variable is the change in IQ from Before to After.

REMEMBER

A dependent variable is what a researcher *measures*. In an experiment, an independent variable is what a researcher *manipulates*. In other contexts, a researcher can't manipulate an independent variable. Instead, they note naturally occurring values of the independent variable and how they affect a dependent variable.

REMEMBER

In general, the objective is to find out whether changes in an independent variable are associated with changes in a dependent variable.

In examples that appear throughout this book, I show you how to use R to calculate characteristics of groups of scores, or to compare groups of scores. Whenever I show you a group of scores, I'm talking about the values of a dependent variable.

Types of data

When you do statistical work, you can run into four kinds of data. And when you work with a variable, the way you work with it depends on what kind of data it is:

The first kind is *nominal* data. If a set of numbers happens to be nominal data, the numbers are labels — their values don't signify anything. On a sports team, the jersey numbers are nominal. They just identify the players.

The next kind is *ordinal* data. In this data type, the numbers are more than just labels. As the name *ordinal* might tell you, the order of the numbers is important. If I ask you to rank ten foods from the one you like best (1) to the one you like least (10), we'd have a set of ordinal data.

But the difference between your third-favorite food and your fourth-favorite food might not be the same as the difference between your ninth-favorite and your tenth-favorite. So this type of data lacks equal intervals and equal differences.

Interval data gives us equal differences. The Fahrenheit scale of temperature is a good example. The difference between 30° and 40° is the same as the difference between 90° and 100°. So each degree is an interval.

People are sometimes surprised to find out that on the Fahrenheit scale a temperature of 80° is not twice as hot as 40°. For ratio statements ("twice as much as," "half as much as") to make sense, *zero* has to mean the complete absence of the thing you're measuring. A temperature of 0° F doesn't mean the complete absence of heat — it's just an arbitrary point on the Fahrenheit scale. (The same holds true for Celsius.)

The fourth kind of data, *ratio*, provides a meaningful zero point. On the Kelvin scale of temperature, *zero* means absolute zero, where all molecular motion (the basis of heat) stops. So 200° Kelvin is twice as hot as 100° Kelvin. Another example is length. Eight inches is twice as long as 4 inches. *Zero inches* means a complete absence of length.

An independent variable or a dependent variable can be either nominal, ordinal, interval, or ratio. The analytical tools you use depend on the type of data you work with.

A little probability

When statisticians make decisions, they use probability to express their confidence about those decisions. They can never be absolutely certain about what they decide. They can tell you only how probable their conclusions are.

What do we mean by *probability?* Mathematicians and philosophers might give you complex definitions. In my experience, however, the best way to understand probability is in terms of examples.

Here's a simple example: If you toss a coin, what's the probability that it turns up heads? If the coin is fair, you might figure that you have a 50-50 chance of heads and a 50-50 chance of tails. And you'd be right. In terms of the kinds of numbers associated with probability, that's ½.

Think about rolling a fair die (one member of a pair of dice). What's the probability that you roll a 4? Well, a die has six faces and one of them is 4, so that's ⅙.

Still another example: Select one card at random from a standard deck of 52 cards. What's the probability that it's a diamond? A deck of cards has four suits, so that's ¼.

These examples tell you that if you want to know the probability that an event occurs, count how many ways that event can happen and divide by the total number of events that can happen. In the first two examples (heads, 4), the event you're interested in happens only one way. For the coin, we divide 1 by 2. For the die, we divide 1 by 6. In the third example (diamond), the event can happen 13 ways (Ace through King), so we divide 13 by 52 (to get ¼).

Now for a slightly more complicated example. Toss a coin and roll a die at the same time. What's the probability of tails and a 4? Think about all the possible events that can happen when you toss a coin and roll a die at the same time. You could have tails and 1 through 6, or heads and 1 through 6. That adds up to 12 possibilities. The tails-and-4 combination can happen only one way. So the probability $\frac{1}{12}$.

In general, the formula for the probability that a particular event occurs is

$$Pr(event) = \frac{\text{Number of ways the event can occur}}{\text{Total number of possible events}}$$

At the beginning of this section, I say that statisticians express their confidence about their conclusions in terms of probability, which is why I brought all this up in the first place. This line of thinking leads to *conditional* probability — the probability that an event occurs given that some other event occurs. Suppose that I roll a die, look at it (so that you don't see it), and tell you that I rolled an odd number. What's the probability that I've rolled a 5? Ordinarily, the probability of a 5 is ⅙, but "I rolled an odd number" narrows it down. That piece of information eliminates the three even numbers (2, 4, 6) as possibilities. Only the three odd numbers (1, 3, 5) are possible, so the probability is ⅓.

What's the big deal about conditional probability? What role does it play in statistical analysis? Read on.

Inferential statistics: Testing hypotheses

Before a statistician does a study, they draw up a tentative explanation — a *hypothesis* that tells why the data might come out a certain way. After gathering all the data, the statistician has to decide whether to reject the hypothesis.

That decision is the answer to a conditional probability question — what's the probability of obtaining the data, given that this hypothesis is correct? Statisticians have tools that calculate the probability. If the probability turns out to be low, the statistician rejects the hypothesis.

Back to coin-tossing for an example: Imagine that you're interested in whether a particular coin is fair — whether it has an equal chance of heads or tails on any toss. Let's start with "The coin is fair" as the hypothesis.

To test the hypothesis, you'd toss the coin a number of times — let's say 100. These 100 tosses are the sample data. If the coin is fair (as per the hypothesis), you'd expect 50 heads and 50 tails.

If it's 99 heads and 1 tail, you'd surely reject the fair-coin hypothesis: The conditional probability of 99 heads and 1 tail given a fair coin is very low. Of course, the coin could still be fair and you could, quite by chance, get a 99–1 split, right? Sure. You never really know. You have to gather the sample data (the 100 toss results) and then decide. Your decision might be right, or it might not.

Juries make these types of decisions. In the United States, the starting hypothesis is that the defendant is not guilty ("innocent until proven guilty"). Think of the evidence as data. Jury members consider the evidence and answer a conditional probability question: What's the probability of the evidence, given that the defendant is not guilty? Their answer determines the verdict.

Null and alternative hypotheses

Think again about that coin-tossing study I just mentioned. The sample data are the results from the 100 tosses. I said that we can start with the hypothesis that the coin is fair. This starting point is called the *null hypothesis*. The statistical notation for the null hypothesis is H_0. According to this hypothesis, any heads–tails split in the data is consistent with a fair coin. Think of it as the idea that nothing in the sample data is out of the ordinary.

An alternative hypothesis is possible — that the coin isn't a fair one and it's biased to produce an unequal number of heads and tails. This hypothesis says that any heads-tails split is consistent with an unfair coin. This alternative hypothesis is called, believe it or not, the *alternative hypothesis.* The statistical notation for the alternative hypothesis is H_1.

Now toss the coin 100 times and note the number of heads and tails. If the results are something like 90 heads and 10 tails, it's a good idea to reject H_0. If the results are around 50 heads and 50 tails, don't reject H_0.

Similar ideas apply to the IQ example I gave earlier. One sample receives the computer-based IQ training method, and the other participates in a different computer-based activity — like reading text on a website. Before and after each group completes its activities, the researcher measures each person's IQ. The null hypothesis, H_0, is that one group's improvement isn't different from the other. If the improvements are greater with the IQ training than with the other activity — so much greater that it's unlikely that the two aren't different from one another — reject H_0. If they're not, don't reject H_0.

REMEMBER

Notice that I did *not* say "accept H_0." The way the logic works, you *never* accept a hypothesis. You either reject H_0 or don't reject H_0. In a jury trial, the verdict is either "guilty" (reject the null hypothesis of "not guilty") or "not guilty" (don't reject H_0). "Innocent" (acceptance of the null hypothesis) is not a possible verdict.

Notice also that in the coin-tossing example, I said "around 50 heads and 50 tails." What does *around* mean? Also, I said that if it's 90-10, reject H_0. What about 85-15? 80-20? 70-30? Exactly how much different from 50-50 does the split have to be for you to reject H_0? In the IQ training example, how much greater does the IQ improvement have to be to reject H_0?

I don't answer these questions now. Statisticians have formulated decision rules for situations like this, and I'll explore those rules in Book 3.

Two types of error

Whenever you evaluate data and decide to reject H_0 or to not reject H_0, you can never be absolutely sure. You never really know the "true" state of the world. In the coin-tossing example, that means you can't be certain whether the coin is fair. All you can do is make a decision based on the sample data. If you want to know for sure about the coin, you have to have the data for the entire population of tosses — which means you have to keep tossing the coin until the end of time.

Because you're never certain about your decisions, you can make an error either way you decide. As I mention earlier, the coin could be fair and you just happen to get 99 heads in 100 tosses. That's not likely, and that's why you reject H_0 if that happens. It's also possible that the coin is biased, yet you just happen to toss 50 heads in 100 tosses. Again, that's not likely and you don't reject H_o in that case.

Although those errors are not likely, they are possible. They lurk in every study that involves inferential statistics. Statisticians have named them Type I errors and Type II errors.

If you reject H_o and you shouldn't, that's a *Type I* error. In the coin example, that's rejecting the hypothesis that the coin is fair, when in reality it is a fair coin.

If you don't reject H_o and you should have, that's a *Type II* error. It happens if you don't reject the hypothesis that the coin is fair, and in reality it's biased.

How do you know if you've made either type of error? You don't — at least not right after you make the decision to reject or not reject H_o. (If it's possible to know, you wouldn't make the error in the first place!) All you can do is gather more data and see whether the additional data is consistent with your decision.

If you think of H_o as a tendency to maintain the status quo and not interpret anything as being out of the ordinary (no matter how it looks), a Type II error means you've missed out on something big. In fact, some iconic mistakes are Type II errors.

Here's what I mean. On New Year's Day in 1962, a rock group consisting of three guitarists and a drummer auditioned in the London studio of a major recording company. Legend has it that the recording executives didn't like what they heard, didn't like what they saw, and believed that guitar groups were on the way out. Although the musicians played their hearts out, the group failed the audition.

Who was that group? The Beatles!

And *that's* a Type II error.

Getting R

Now that I've taken you through the world that R lives in, let's dive into R.

If you don't already have R on your computer, the first thing to do is to download R and install it.

You'll find the appropriate software on the website of the Comprehensive R Archive Network (CRAN). In your browser, type this web address:

```
https://cran.rstudio.com
```

Click the appropriate link to download R for your computer.

Getting RStudio

Working with R is a lot easier if you do it through an application called RStudio. Computer honchos refer to RStudio as an IDE (Integrated Development Environment). Think of it as a tool that helps you write, edit, run, and keep track of your R code, and as an environment that connects you to a world of helpful hints about R.

Here's the web address for this terrific tool:

```
www.rstudio.com/products/rstudio/download
```

Click the link for the installer for your flavor of computer and again follow the usual installation procedures. (You'll want RStudio Desktop.)

TIP

In this book, I work with R version 4.2.0 and RStudio version 2022.02.3 Build 492. By the time you read this, later versions of both might be available. Incidentally, each version of R has its own whimsical nickname. Version 4.2.0 is called Vigorous Calisthenics. Why? I have no idea. Perhaps it reflects an evolution from the previous version, One Push-Up.

After you finish installing R and RStudio, click your brand-new RStudio icon to open the window that looks very much like the window shown in Figure 1-2. It won't be an exact match, because my history with RStudio — reflected in the upper right pane — is probably different from yours.

The large Console pane on the left runs R code. One way to run R code is to type it directly into the Console pane. I show you another in a moment.

The other two panes provide helpful information as you work with R. The Environment and History pane is in the upper right. The Environment tab keeps track of the things you create (which R calls *objects*) as you work with R. The History tab tracks R code that you enter.

TIP

Get used to the word *object*. Everything in R is an object.

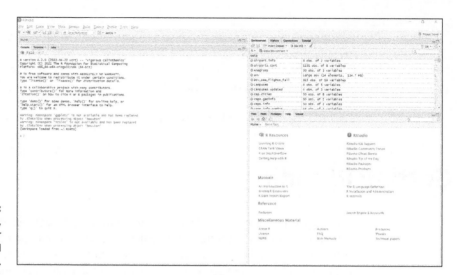

FIGURE 1-2:
RStudio,
immediately after
you install it and
click its icon.

The Files, Plots, Packages, and Help pane is in the lower right. The Files tab shows files you create. The Plots tab holds graphs you create from your data. The Packages tab shows add-ons (called *packages*) that have downloaded with R. Bear in mind that *downloaded* doesn't mean "ready to use." To use a package's capabilities, one more step is necessary — and trust me — you'll want to use packages.

Figure 1-3 shows the Packages tab. I discuss packages later in this chapter.

The Help tab, shown in Figure 1-4, links you to a wealth of information about R and RStudio.

To tap into the full power of RStudio as an IDE, click the icon in the rightmost upper corner of the Console pane. (It looks like a tall folder with a gray band across the top.) That changes the appearance of RStudio so that it looks like Figure 1-5.

The Console pane relocates to the lower left. The new pane in the upper left is the Scripts pane. You type and edit code in the Scripts pane, press Ctrl+Enter (Command+Enter on the Mac), and then the code executes in the Console pane.

TIP

You can also highlight lines of code in the Scripts pane and choose Code⇨Run Selected Line(s) from RStudio's main menu.

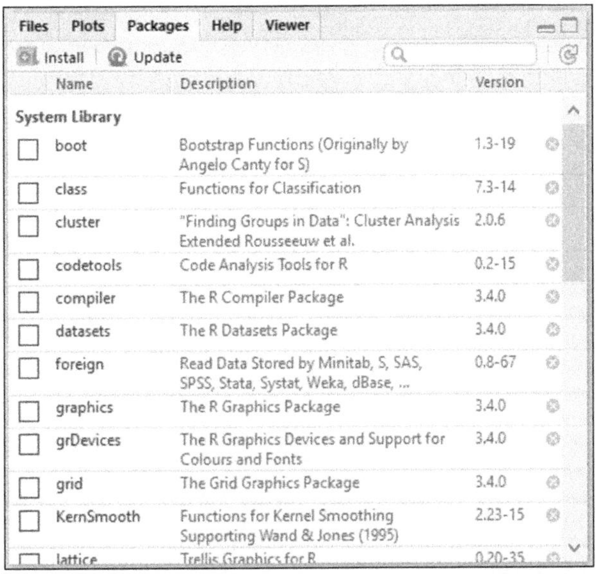

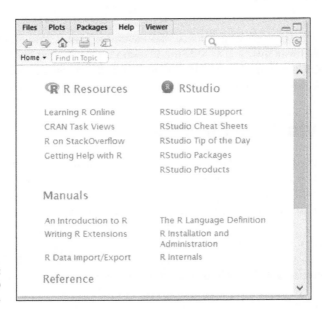

FIGURE 1-3:
The RStudio
Packages tab.

FIGURE 1-4:
The RStudio
Help tab.

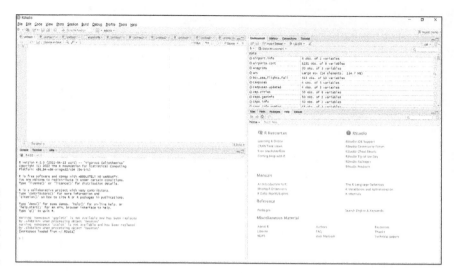

FIGURE 1-5:
RStudio, after you
click the icon in
the upper right
corner of the
Console pane.

A Session with R

Before you start working, choose File ⇨ Save As from RStudio's main menu and then save the blank pane as My First R Session. This relabels the tab in the Scripts pane with the name of the file and adds the .R extension. This also causes the filename (along with the .R extension) to appear on the Files tab.

The working directory

When you follow my advice and save something called My First R Session, what exactly is R saving and where does R save it? What R saves is called the *workspace*, which is the environment you're working in. R saves the workspace in the *working directory*. In Windows, the default working directory is

```
C:\Users\<User Name>\Documents
```

If you ever forget the path to your working directory, type

```
> getwd()
```

in the Console pane, and R returns the path onscreen.

TIP

In the Console pane, you don't have to type the right-pointing arrowhead at the beginning of the line. That's a prompt, and it's there by default.

My working directory looks like this:

```
> getwd()
[1] "C:/Users/Joseph Schmuller/Documents"
```

Note the direction in which the slashes are slanted. They're opposite to what you typically see in Windows file paths. This is because R uses \ as an *escape character*, meaning that whatever follows the \ means something different from what it usually means. For example, \t in R means *Tab key.*

TIP

You can also write a Windows file path in R as

```
C:\\Users\\<User Name>\\Documents
```

If you like, you can change the working directory:

```
> setwd(<file path>)
```

Another way to change the working directory is to choose Session⇨Set Working Directory⇨Choose Directory from R Studio's main menu.

Getting started

Let's get down to business and start writing R code. In the Scripts pane, type

```
x <- c(5,10,15,20,25,30,35,40)
```

and then press Ctrl+Enter.

That puts this line into the Console pane:

```
> x <- c(5,10,15,20,25,30,35,40)
```

As I said in an earlier Tip, the right-pointing arrowhead (the greater-than sign) is a prompt that R puts in the Console pane. You don't see it in the Scripts pane.

Here's what R just did: The arrow sign says that x gets assigned whatever is to the right of the arrow sign. Think of the arrow sign as R's *assignment operator.*

So the set of numbers 5, 10, 15, 20 . . . 40 is now assigned to x.

REMEMBER

In R-speak, a set of numbers like this is a *vector*. I tell you more about this topic in the later section "R Structures." That *c* in front of the parentheses is what does the actual vector-creating.

You can read that line of code as "x gets the vector 5, 10, 15, 20."

Type **x** into the Scripts pane and press Ctrl+Enter, and here's what you see in the Console pane:

```
> x
[1]   5 10 15 20 25 30 35 40
```

The 1 in square brackets is the label for the first line of output. So this signifies that 5 is the first value.

Here you have only one line, of course. What happens when R outputs many values over many lines? Each line gets a bracketed numeric label, and the number corresponds to the first value in the line. For example, if the output consists of 23 values and the 18th value is the first one on the second line, the second line begins with [18].

Creating the vector x adds the line in Figure 1-6 to the Environment tab.

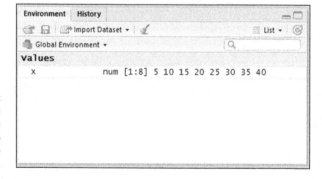

FIGURE 1-6:
A line in
the RStudio
Environment tab
after creating the
vector x.

TIP

Another way to see the objects in the environment is to type

```
ls()
```

into the Scripts pane and then press Ctrl+Enter. Or you can type

```
> ls()
```

directly into the Console pane and press Enter. Either way, the result in the
Console pane is

```
[1] "x"
```

Now you can work with x. First, add all the numbers in the vector. Typing

```
sum(x)
```

in the Scripts pane (be sure to follow with pressing Ctrl+Enter) executes the
following line in the Console pane:

```
> sum(x)
[1] 180
```

How about the average of the numbers in vector x?

That would be

```
mean(x)
```

in the Scripts pane, which (when followed by pressing Ctrl+Enter) executes

```
> mean(x)
[1] 22.5
```

in the Console pane.

TIP

As you type in the Scripts pane or in the Console pane, you see that helpful information pops up. As you become experienced with RStudio, you learn how to use
that information.

Variance is a measure of how much a set of numbers differ from their mean. Here's
how to use R to calculate variance:

```
> var(x)
[1] 150
```

What exactly is variance and what does it mean? I tell you all about it in Book 2.

After R executes all these commands, the History tab looks like the one in
Figure 1-7.

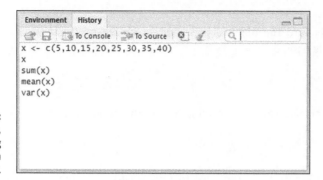

FIGURE 1-7:
The History tab,
after creating
and working with
a vector.

To end a session, choose File⇨Quit Session from R Studio's main menu or press Ctrl+Q. As Figure 1-8 shows, a dialog box opens and asks what you want to save from the session. Saving the selections enables you, the next time you open RStudio, to reopen the session where you left off (although the Console pane doesn't save your work).

FIGURE 1-8:
The Quit
R Session
dialog box.

REMEMBER

Moving forward, most of the time I don't say "Type this code into the Scripts pane and press Ctrl+Enter" whenever I take you through an example. I just show you the code and its output, as in the var() example.

REMEMBER

Also, sometimes I show code with the > prompt, and sometimes without. Generally, I show the prompt when I want you to see R code and its results. I don't show the prompt when I just want you to see R code that I create in the Scripts pane.

R Functions

The examples in the preceding section use c(), sum(), and var(). These are three *functions* built into R. Each one consists of a function name immediately followed by parentheses. Inside the parentheses are *arguments*. In the context of a function, *argument* doesn't mean "debate" or "disagreement" or anything like that. It's the math term for whatever a function operates on.

REMEMBER

Sometimes a function takes no arguments (as is the case with ls()). You still include the parentheses.

The functions in the examples I showed you are pretty simple: Supply an argument, and each one gives you a result. Some R functions, however, take more than one argument.

R has a couple of ways for you to deal with multiargument functions. One way is to list the arguments in the order that they appear in the function's definition. R calls this *positional mapping.*

Here's an example. Remember when I created the vector x?

```
x <- c(5,10,15,20,25,30,35,40)
```

Another way to create a vector of those numbers is with the function seq():

```
> y <- seq(5,40,5)
> y
[1]  5 10 15 20 25 30 35 40
```

Think of seq() as creating a "sequence." The first argument to seq() is the number to start the sequence *from* (5). The second argument is the number that ends the sequence — the number the sequence goes *to* (40). The third argument is the increment of the sequence — the amount the sequence increases *by* (5, in this case).

If you *name* the arguments, it doesn't matter how you order them:

```
> z <- seq(to=40,by=5,from=5)
> z
[1]  5 10 15 20 25 30 35 40
```

So if you name a function when using it, you can place the function's arguments out of order. R calls this *keyword matching.* This comes in handy when you use an R function that has many arguments. If you can't remember their order, use their names and the function works.

TIP

For help with a particular function — seq(), for example — type **?seq** and press Ctrl+Enter to open helpful information on the Help tab.

User-Defined Functions

R enables you to create your own functions, and here are the fundamentals on how to do it.

The form of an R function is

```
myfunction <- function(argument1, argument2, ...){
  statements
  return(object)
}
```

Here's a function for dealing with right triangles. Remember them? A right triangle has two sides that form a right angle and a third side called a *hypotenuse*. You might also remember that a guy named Pythagoras showed that if one side has length a, and the other side has length b, the length of the hypotenuse, c, is

$$c = \sqrt{a^2 + b^2}$$

So here's a simple function called hypotenuse() that takes two numbers a and b, (the lengths of the two sides of a right triangle) and returns c, the length of the hypotenuse.

```
hypotenuse <- function(a,b){
  hyp <- sqrt(a^2+b^2)
  return(hyp)
}
```

Type that code snippet into the Scripts pane and highlight it. Then press Ctrl+Enter. Here's what appears in the Console pane:

```
> hypoteneuse <- function(a,b){
+    hyp <- sqrt(a^2+b^2)
+    return(hyp)
+ }
```

Each plus sign is a *continuation prompt*. It just indicates that a line continues from the preceding line.

And here's how to use the function:

```
> hypoteneuse(3,4)
[1] 5
```

Comments

A *comment* is a way of annotating code. Begin a comment with the # symbol, which, as everyone knows, is called an *octothorpe*. (Wait. What? "Hashtag?" Getattahere!) This symbol tells R to ignore everything to the right of it.

Comments help someone who has to read the code you've written. For example:

```
hypoteneuse <- function(a,b){ # list the arguments
  hyp <- sqrt(a^2+b^2) # perform the computation
  return(hyp) # return the value
}
```

Here's a heads-up: I don't typically add comments to lines of code in this book. Instead, I provide detailed descriptions. In a book like this, I feel it's the best way to get the message across.

R Structures

As I mention in the "R Functions" section, earlier in this chapter, an R function can have many arguments. An R function can also have many outputs. To understand the possible inputs and outputs, you must understand the structures that R works with.

Vectors

The *vector* is the fundamental structure in R. I show it to you in earlier examples. It's an array of elements of the same type. The data elements in a vector are called *components*.

To create a vector, use the function c( ), as I did in the earlier example:

```
x <- c(5,10,15,20,25,30,35,40)
```

In the vector x, of course, the components are numbers.

In a *character vector*, the components are quoted text strings:

```
> beatles <- c("john","paul","george","ringo")
```

It's also possible to have a *logical vector*, whose components are TRUE and FALSE, or the abbreviations T and F:

```
> w <- c(T,F,F,T,T,F)
```

To refer to a specific component of a vector, follow the vector name with a bracketed number:

```
> beatles[2]
[1] "paul"
```

Within the brackets, you can use a colon (:) to refer to two consecutive components:

```
> beatles[2:3]
[1] "paul"   "george"
```

Want to refer to non-consecutive components? That's a bit more complicated, but doable via c():

```
> beatles[c(2,4)]
[1] "paul"  "ringo"
```

Numerical vectors

In addition to c(), R provides two shortcut functions for creating numerical vectors. One, seq(), I showed you earlier:

```
> y <- seq(5,40,5)
> y
[1]  5 10 15 20 25 30 35 40
```

Without the third argument, the sequence increases by 1:

```
> y <- seq(5,40)
> y
 [1]  5  6  7  8  9 10 11 12 13 14 15 16 17 18 19 20 21 22 23
[20] 24 25 26 27 28 29 30 31 32 33 34 35 36 37 38 39 40
```

REMEMBER

On my screen, and probably on yours too, all the elements in y appear on one line. The printed page, however, is not as wide as the Console pane. Accordingly, I separated the output into two lines and added the R-style bracketed number [20]. I do that throughout the book where necessary.

TIP

R has a special syntax for creating a numerical vector whose elements increase by 1:

```
> y <- 5:40
> y
 [1]  5  6  7  8  9 10 11 12 13 14 15 16 17 18 19 20 21 22 23
[20] 24 25 26 27 28 29 30 31 32 33 34 35 36 37 38 39 40
```

Another function, rep( ), creates a vector of repeating values:

```
> quadrifecta <- c(7,8,4,3)
> repeated_quadrifecta <- rep(quadrifecta,3)
> repeated_quadrifecta
 [1] 7 8 4 3 7 8 4 3 7 8 4 3
```

You can also supply a vector as the second argument:

```
> rep_vector <-c(1,2,3,4)
> repeated_quadrifecta <- rep(quadrifecta,rep_vector)
```

The vector specifies the number of repetitions for each element. So here's what happens:

```
> repeated_quadrifecta
 [1] 7 8 8 4 4 4 3 3 3 3
```

The first element repeats once; the second, twice; the third, three times; and the fourth, four times.

You can use append( ) to add an item at the end of a vector:

```
> xx <- c(3,4,5)
> xx
[1] 3 4 5
> xx <- append(xx,6)
> xx
[1] 3 4 5 6
```

How many items are in a vector? That's

```
> length(xx)
[1] 4
```

Matrices

A *matrix* is a two-dimensional array of data elements of the same type. You can have a matrix of numbers:

```
5    30  55   80

10   35  60   85

15   40  65   90

20   45  70   95

25   50  75  100
```

or a matrix of character strings:

```
"john"      "paul"    "george"    "ringo"

"groucho"   "harpo"   "chico"     "zeppo"

"levi"      "duke"    "larry"     "obie"
```

The numbers are a 5 (rows) X 4 (columns) matrix. The character strings matrix is 3 X 4.

To create this particular 5 X 4 numerical matrix, first create the vector of numbers from 5 to 100 in steps of 5:

```
> num_matrix <- seq(5,100,5)
```

Then you use R's dim( ) function to turn the vector into a two-dimensional matrix:

```
> dim(num_matrix) <- c(5,4)
> num_matrix
     [,1] [,2] [,3] [,4]
[1,]    5   30   55   80
[2,]   10   35   60   85
[3,]   15   40   65   90
[4,]   20   45   70   95
[5,]   25   50   75  100
```

Note how R displays the bracketed row numbers along the side and the bracketed column numbers along the top.

Transposing a matrix interchanges the rows with the columns. The t() function takes care of that:

```
> t(num_matrix)
      [,1] [,2] [,3] [,4] [,5]
[1,]     5   10   15   20   25
[2,]    30   35   40   45   50
[3,]    55   60   65   70   75
[4,]    80   85   90   95  100
```

The function matrix() give you another way to create matrices:

```
> num_matrix <- matrix(seq(5,100,5),nrow=5)
> num_matrix
      [,1] [,2] [,3] [,4]
[1,]     5   30   55   80
[2,]    10   35   60   85
[3,]    15   40   65   90
[4,]    20   45   70   95
[5,]    25   50   75  100
```

If you add the argument byrow=T, R fills the matrix by rows, like this:

```
> num_matrix <- matrix(seq(5,100,5),nrow=5,byrow=T)
> num_matrix
      [,1] [,2] [,3] [,4]
[1,]     5   10   15   20
[2,]    25   30   35   40
[3,]    45   50   55   60
[4,]    65   70   75   80
[5,]    85   90   95  100
```

How do you refer to a specific matrix component? You type the matrix name and then, in brackets, the row number, a comma, and the column number:

```
> num_matrix[5,4]
[1] 100
```

To refer to a whole row (like the third one):

```
> num_matrix[3,]
[1] 45 50 55 60
```

and to a whole column (like the second one):

```
> num_matrix[,2]
[1] 10 30 50 70 90
```

Although it's a column, R displays it as a row in the Console pane.

BUT BEAR IN MIND . . .

As I mention, a matrix is a two-dimensional array. In R, however, an array can have more than two dimensions. One well-known set of data (which I use as an example in Chapter 1 of Book 3) has three dimensions: Hair Color (Black, Brown, Red, Blond), Eye Color (Brown, Blue, Hazel, Green), and Gender (Male, Female). So this particular array is 4 X 4 X 2. It's called HairEyeColor and it looks like this:

```
> HairEyeColor
, , Sex = Male

       Eye
Hair    Brown Blue Hazel Green
   Black    32   11    10     3
   Brown    53   50    25    15
   Red      10   10     7     7
   Blond     3   30     5     8

, , Sex = Female

       Eye
Hair    Brown Blue Hazel Green
   Black    36    9     5     2
   Brown    66   34    29    14
   Red      16    7     7     7
   Blond     4   64     5     8
```

Each number represents the number of people in this group who have a particular combination of hair color, eye color, and gender — 16 brown-eyed red-haired females, for example. (Why did I choose brown-eyed red-haired females? Because I have the pleasure of looking at an extremely beautiful one every day!)

How would I refer to all the females? That's

```
HairEyeColor[,,2]
```

Lists

In R, a *list* is a collection of objects that aren't necessarily the same type. Suppose you're putting together some information on the Beatles:

```
> beatles <- c("john","paul","george","ringo")
```

One piece of important information might be each Beatle's age when he joined the group. John and Paul started singing together when they were 17 and 15, respectively, and 14 year-old George joined them soon after. Ringo, a late arriver, became a Beatle when he was 22. So

```
> ages <- c(17,15,14,22)
```

To combine the information into a list, you use the `list()` function:

```
> beatles_info <-list(names=beatles,age_joined=ages)
```

Naming each argument (`names`, `age_joined`) causes R to use those names as the names of the list components.

And here's what the list looks like:

```
> beatles_info
$names
[1] "john"   "paul"   "george" "ringo"

$age_joined
[1] 17 15 14 22
```

R uses the dollar sign ($) to indicate each component of the list. If you want to refer to a list component, you type the name of the list, the dollar sign, and the component name:

```
> beatles_info$names
[1] "john"   "paul"   "george" "ringo"
```

And to zero in on a particular Beatle, like the fourth one? You can probably figure out that it's

```
> beatles_info$names[4]
[1] "ringo"
```

R also allows you to use criteria inside the brackets. For example, to refer to members of the Fab Four who were older than 16 when they joined:

```
> beatles_info$names[beatles_info$age_joined > 16]
[1] "john"  "ringo"
```

Data frames

A list is a good way to collect data. A *data frame* is even better. Why? When you think about data for a group of individuals, you typically think in terms of rows that represent the individuals and columns that represent the data variables. And that's a data frame. If the terms *data set* or *data matrix* come to mind, you have the right idea.

Suppose I have a set of six people:

```
> name <- c("al","barbara","charles","donna","ellen","fred")
```

and I have each person's height (in inches) and weight (in pounds):

```
> height <- c(72,64,73,65,66,71)
> weight <- c(195,117,205,122,125,199)
```

I also tabulate each person's gender:

```
> gender <- c("M","F","M","F","F","M")
```

Before I show you how to combine all these vectors into a data frame, I have to show you one more thing. The components of the gender vector are character strings. For purposes of data summary and analysis, it's a good idea to turn them into categories — the Male category and the Female category. To do this, I use the factor() function:

```
> factor_gender <-factor(gender)
> factor_gender
[1] M F M F F M
Levels: F M
```

In the last line of output, *Levels* is the term that R uses for categories.

The function data.frame() works with the vectors to create a data frame:

```
> d <- data.frame(name,factor_gender,height,weight)
> d
```

```
    name factor_gender height weight
1     al              M     72    195
2 barbara             F     64    117
3 charles             M     73    205
4  donna              F     65    122
5  ellen              F     66    125
6   fred              M     71    199
```

Want to know the height of the third person?

```
> d[3,3]
[1] 73
```

How about all the information for the fifth person:

```
> d[5,]
    name factor_gender height weight
5 ellen             F     66    125
```

Like lists, data frames use the dollar sign. In this context, the dollar sign identifies a column:

```
> d$height
[1] 72 64 73 65 66 71
```

You can calculate statistics, like the average height:

```
> mean(d$height)
[1] 68.5
```

As is the case with lists, you can put criteria inside the brackets. This is often done with data frames in order to summarize and analyze data within categories. To find the average height of the females:

```
> mean(d$height[d$factor_gender == "F"])
[1] 65
```

The double equal sign (==) in the brackets is a *logical operator*. Think of it as "if d$factor_gender is equal to 'F'".

REMEMBER

The double equal sign (a == b) distinguishes the logical operator ("if a equals b") from the assignment operator (a = b; "set a equal to b").

TIP

Yes, I know — I went through an involved explanation about `factor()` and how it's better to have categories (levels) than character strings, and then I had to put quote marks around F inside the brackets. R is quirky that way.

TIP

If you'd like to eliminate $ signs from your R code, you can use the function `with()`. You put your code inside the parentheses after the first argument, which is the data you're using.

For example,

```
> with(d,mean(height[factor_gender == "F"]))
```

is equivalent to

```
> mean(d$height[d$factor_gender == "F"])
```

How many rows are in a data frame?

```
> nrow(d)
[1] 6
```

And how many columns?

```
> ncol(d)
[1] 4
```

To add a column to a data frame, I use `cbind()`. Begin with a vector of scores

```
> aptitude <- c(35,20,32,22,18,15)
```

Then add that vector as a column:

```
> d.apt <- cbind(d,aptitude)
> d.apt
    name factor_gender height weight aptitude
1     al             M     72    195       35
2 barbara            F     64    117       20
3 charles            M     73    205       32
4   donna            F     65    122       22
5   ellen            F     66    125       18
6    fred            M     71    199       15
```

for Loops and if Statements

Like many programming languages, R provides a way of iterating through its structures to get things done. R's way is called the *for* loop. And, like many languages, R gives you a way to test against a criterion — the *if* statement.

The general format of a `for` loop is

```
for counter in start:end{
        statement 1
              .
              .
              .
        statement n
}
```

As you might imagine, `counter` tracks the iterations.

The simplest general format of an `if` statement is

```
if(test){statement to execute if test is TRUE}
else{statement to execute if test is FALSE}
```

Here is an example that incorporates both. I have one vector xx:

```
> xx
[1] 2 3 4 5 6
```

And another vector yy with nothing in it at the moment:

```
> yy <-NULL
```

I want the components of yy to reflect the components of xx: If a number in xx is an odd number, I want the corresponding component of yy to be "ODD" and if the xx number is even, I want the yy component to be "EVEN".

How do I test a number to see whether it's odd or even? Mathematicians have developed *modular arithmetic*, which is concerned with the remainder of a division operation. If you divide *a* by *b* and the result has a remainder of *r*, mathematicians say that "a *modulo* b is r." So 10 divided by 3 leaves a remainder of 1, and 10 modulo 3 is 1. Typically, *modulo* gets shortened to *mod*, so that would be "10 mod 3 = 1."

Most computer languages write 10 mod 3 as mod(10,3). (Excel does that, in fact.) R does it differently: R uses the double percent sign (%%) as its *mod operator*:

```
> 10 %% 3
[1] 1
> 5 %% 2
[1] 1
> 4 %% 2
[1] 0
```

I think you're getting the picture: if xx[i] %% 2 == 0, then xx[i] is even. Otherwise, it's odd.

Here, then, is the for loop and the if statement:

```
for(i in 1:length(xx)){
if(xx[i] %% 2 == 0){yy[i]<- "EVEN"}
else{yy[i] <- "ODD"}
}

> yy
[1] "EVEN" "ODD"  "EVEN" "ODD"  "EVEN"
```

Chapter **2**

Working with Packages, Importing, and Exporting

A *package* is a collection of functions and data that augments R. If you're looking for data to work with, you'll find many data frames in R packages. If you're looking for a specialized function that's not in the basic R installation, you can probably find it in a package.

Installing Packages

As the Packages tab (in the Files/Plots/Packages/Help/Viewer pane of RStudio) shows, many packages come with the basic R installation, but if you want to work with them, you have to install them. This means putting them in a directory called the *library*. To get one of these comes-with-basic-R packages into the library, you click the Packages tab. Figure 2-1 shows this tab.

Scroll down until you find the package you're looking for. For this example, I work with the datasets package.

Files	Plots	Packages	Help	Viewer		
Install	Update					
Name		Description			Version	
System Library						
☑ base		The R Base Package			4.2.0	
☐ boot		Bootstrap Functions (Originally by Angelo Canty for S)			1.3-28	
☐ class		Functions for Classification			7.3-20	
☐ cluster		"Finding Groups in Data": Cluster Analysis Extended Rousseeuw et al.			2.1.3	
☐ codetools		Code Analysis Tools for R			0.2-18	
☐ compiler		The R Compiler Package			4.2.0	
☑ datasets		The R Datasets Package			4.2.0	
☐ foreign		Read Data Stored by 'Minitab', 'S', 'SAS', 'SPSS', 'Stata', 'Systat', 'Weka', 'dBase', ...			0.8-82	
☑ graphics		The R Graphics Package			4.2.0	
☑ grDevices		The R Graphics Devices and Support for Colours and Fonts			4.2.0	
☐ grid		The Grid Graphics Package			4.2.0	
☐ KernSmooth		Functions for Kernel Smoothing Supporting Wand & Jones (1995)			2.23-20	
☐ lattice		Trellis Graphics for R			0.20-45	
☐ MASS		Support Functions and Datasets for Venables and Ripley's MASS			7.3-56	
☐ Matrix		Sparse and Dense Matrix Classes and Methods			1.4-1	
☑ methods		Formal Methods and Classes			4.2.0	
☐ mgcv		Mixed GAM Computation Vehicle with Automatic Smoothness Estimation			1.8-40	
☐ nlme		Linear and Nonlinear Mixed Effects Models			3.1-157	
☐ nnet		Feed-Forward Neural Networks and Multinomial Log-Linear Models			7.3-17	
☐ parallel		Support for Parallel computation in R			4.2.0	
☐ rpart		Recursive Partitioning and Regression Trees			4.1.16	
☐ spatial		Functions for Kriging and Point Pattern Analysis			7.3-15	
☐ splines		Regression Spline Functions and Classes			4.2.0	
☑ stats		The R Stats Package			4.2.0	
☐ stats4		Statistical Functions using S4 Classes			4.2.0	
☐ survival		Survival Analysis			3.3-1	
☐ tcltk		Tcl/Tk Interface			4.2.0	

FIGURE 2-1:
The Packages tab in RStudio.

I click the check box next to `datasets`, and this line appears in the Console pane:

```
> library(datasets, lib.loc = "C:/Program Files/R/R-4.2.0/library")
```

This tells you the `datasets` package is installed. For information on what's in this package, click `datasets` on the Packages tab. (You can do this before you install or afterward.) Information about the package appears on the Help tab, as Figure 2-2 shows.

TIP

If you have a package downloaded but not installed, you can use `library()` to put it in the library:

```
> library(MASS)
```

This is also called *attaching* the package, and it's equivalent to selecting the package's check box on the Packages tab.

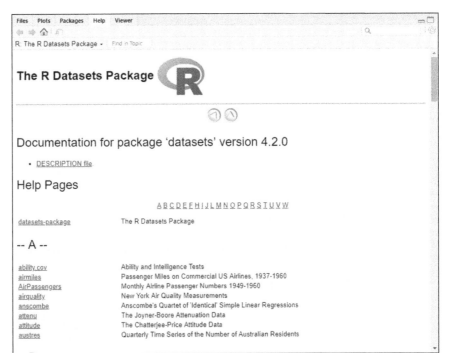

FIGURE 2-2:
The Help tab,
after clicking
datasets on
the Packages tab.

Examining Data

Let's take a look at one of the data frames in datasets. The data frame airquality provides measurements of four aspects of air quality (ozone, solar radiation, temperature, and velocity) in New York City over the 153 days from May 1, 1973, to September 30, 1973.

Heads and tails

To get an idea of what the data looks like, I can use the function head() to show the first six rows of the data frame:

```
> head(airquality)
  Ozone Solar.R Wind Temp Month Day
1    41     190  7.4   67     5   1
2    36     118  8.0   72     5   2
3    12     149 12.6   74     5   3
4    18     313 11.5   62     5   4
5    NA      NA 14.3   56     5   5
6    28      NA 14.9   66     5   6
```

and then `tail()` to show the final six:

```
> tail(airquality)
    Ozone Solar.R Wind Temp Month Day
148    14      20 16.6   63     9  25
149    30     193  6.9   70     9  26
150    NA     145 13.2   77     9  27
151    14     191 14.3   75     9  28
152    18     131  8.0   76     9  29
153    20     223 11.5   68     9  30
```

Missing data

Notice the `NA` in each output. This means that a particular data entry is missing, a common occurrence in data frames. If you try to find the average of, say, `Ozone`, here's what happens:

```
> mean(airquality$Ozone)
[1] NA
```

You have to remove the NAs before you calculate, and you do that by adding an argument to `mean()`:

```
> mean(airquality$Ozone, na.rm=TRUE)
[1] 42.12931
```

The `rm` in `na.rm` means "remove," and `= TRUE` means "get it done."

Subsets

Sometimes you're interested in part of a data frame. For example, in `airquality`, you might want to work only with `Month`, `Day`, and `Ozone`. To isolate those columns into a data frame, use `subset()`:

```
> Month.Day.Ozone <- subset(airquality, select = c(Month,Day,Ozone))
> head(Month.Day.Ozone)
  Month Day Ozone
1     5   1    41
2     5   2    36
3     5   3    12
4     5   4    18
5     5   5    NA
6     5   6    28
```

The second argument, `select`, is the vector of columns you want to work with. You have to name that argument because it's not the second argument in the definition of `subset()`.

The `subset()` function also allows you to select rows. To work with the ozone data from August, add Month == 8 as the second argument the criterion for selecting the rows:

```
> August.Ozone <- subset(airquality, Month == 8, select = c(Month,Day,Ozone))
> head(August.Ozone)
   Month Day Ozone
93     8   1    39
94     8   2     9
95     8   3    16
96     8   4    78
97     8   5    35
98     8   6    66
```

R Formulas

Suppose I'm interested in how the temperature varies with the month. Having lived through many Mays through Septembers in my hometown, my guess is that the temperature generally increases in this data frame from month to month. Is that the case?

This gets into the area of statistical analysis, and at a fairly esoteric level. In Books 3 and 4, I delve more deeply into statistics. Here, I just touch on the basics to show you another R capability — the *formula*.

In this example, we would say that Temperature depends on Month. Another way to say this is that Temperature is the *dependent variable* and Month is the *independent variable*.

An R formula incorporates these concepts and serves as the basis of many of R's statistical functions and graphing functions. This is the basic structure of an R formula:

```
function(dependent_var ~ independent_var, data = data.frame)
```

Read the tilde operator (~) as "depends on."

Here's how I address the relationship between `Temp` and `Month`:

```
> analysis <- lm(Temp ~ Month, data=airquality)
```

The name of the function `lm()` is an abbreviation of *linear model*. This means that I expect the temperature to increase linearly (at a constant rate) from month to month. To see the results of the analysis, I use `summary()`:

```
> summary(analysis)

Call:
lm(formula = Temp ~ Month, data = airquality)

Residuals:
    Min      1Q  Median      3Q     Max
-20.5263 -6.2752  0.9121  6.2865  17.9121

Coefficients:
            Estimate Std. Error t value Pr(>|t|)
(Intercept)  58.2112     3.5191  16.541  < 2e-16 ***
Month         2.8128     0.4933   5.703 6.03e-08 ***
---
Signif. codes:  0 '***' 0.001 '**' 0.01 '*' 0.05 '.' 0.1 ' ' 1

Residual standard error: 8.614 on 151 degrees of freedom
Multiple R-squared:  0.1772,	Adjusted R-squared:  0.1717
F-statistic: 32.52 on 1 and 151 DF,  p-value: 6.026e-08
```

Whoa! What does all that mean? For the complete answer, see Book 4. Right now, I'll just tell you that the `Estimate` for `Month` indicates temperature increases at a rate of 2.8128 degrees per month between May and September. Along with the `Estimate` for `(Intercept)`, I can summarize the relationship between `Temp` and `Month` as

$$Temp = 58.2112 + (2.8128 \times Month)$$

where *Month* is a number from 5 to 9.

You might remember from algebra class that when you graph this kind of equation, you get a straight line — hence the term *linear model*. Is the linear model a good way to summarize this data? The numbers in the bottom line of the output say that it is, but I won't go into the details. (Again, see Book 4.)

More Packages

Members of the R community create and contribute useful new packages to the Comprehensive R Archive Network (CRAN) all the time. So you won't find every R package on the RStudio Packages tab.

When you find out about a package that you think might be helpful, you can easily install it in your library. I illustrate by installing tidyverse, a package (consisting of other packages!) created by R megastar Hadley Wickham to help you manage your data.

One way to install it is via the Packages tab. (Refer to Figure 2-1.) Click the Install icon in the upper left corner of the tab. This opens the Install Packages dialog box, shown in Figure 2-3.

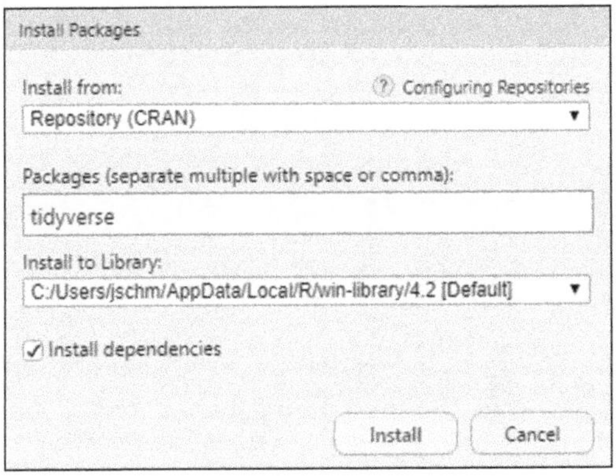

Working with Packages, Importing, and Exporting

FIGURE 2-3:
The Install
Packages
dialog box.

In the Packages field, I've typed tidyverse. Click Install, and the following line appears in the Console pane:

```
> install.packages("tidyverse")
```

This line is difficult to see because lots and lots of other things happen immediately in the Console pane and on onscreen status bars. The process might seem to stall temporarily, but be patient.

When the downloading is finished, tidyverse and a number of other packages appear on the Packages tab. This downloads the packages, but you still have to install them. Select the check box next to tidyverse, and R installs most of them in the library.

Exploring the tidyverse

Let's take a look at some of the wonders of the `tidyverse`. One component package is `tidyr`. One of its extremely useful functions is called `drop_na()`. The name tells you it deletes data frame rows that have missing data.

Here, I'll show you:

```
> aq.no.missing <-drop_na(airquality)
> head(aq.no.missing)
  Ozone Solar.R Wind Temp Month Day
1    41     190  7.4   67     5   1
2    36     118  8.0   72     5   2
3    12     149 12.6   74     5   3
4    18     313 11.5   62     5   4
7    23     299  8.6   65     5   7
8    19      99 13.8   59     5   8
```

Compare this with

```
> head(airquality)
  Ozone Solar.R Wind Temp Month Day
1    41     190  7.4   67     5   1
2    36     118  8.0   72     5   2
3    12     149 12.6   74     5   3
4    18     313 11.5   62     5   4
5    NA      NA 14.3   56     5   5
6    28      NA 14.9   66     5   6
```

You can see that `drop_na()` has deleted rows 5 and 6, which had missing data.

Another `tidyverse` package is called `tibble`. This package has functions that help you modify data frames. For example, in Chapter 3 of Book 2, I create a data frame that shows the revenue in millions of dollars for five industries connected with outer space. The data are for the years 1990–1994:

```
> space.revenues
                                1990 1991 1992 1993 1994
Commercial Satellites Delivered 1000 1300 1300 1100 1400
Satellite Services               800 1200 1500 1850 2330
Satellite Ground Equipment       860 1300 1400 1600 1970
Commercial Launches              570  380  450  465  580
Remote Sensing Data              155  190  210  250  300
```

The first column has the row names (rather than row numbers) as the identifiers for the rows. You can do something like this:

```
> space.revenues["Satellite Services",2]
[1] 1200
```

which is equivalent to this:

```
> space.revenues[2,2]
[1] 1200
```

But it's more productive (for analysis and graphing) to turn those identifiers into a named column. The tibble function rownames_to_column() does just that:

```
> revenues.industry <- rownames_to_column(space.revenues, var="Industry")
```

Now I have a column called Industry:

```
> revenues.industry
                        Industry 1990 1991 1992 1993 1994
1 Commercial Satellites Delivered 1000 1300 1300 1100 1400
2               Satellite Services  800 1200 1500 1850 2330
3         Satellite Ground Equipment  860 1300 1400 1600 1970
4               Commercial Launches  570  380  450  465  580
5               Remote Sensing Data  155  190  210  250  300
```

Why did I do that? Glad you asked. That little trick enables me to *reshape* the data.

Here's what I mean. The revenues.industry data frame is in *wide format*. The revenues are in multiple columns. Many R analysis functions and graphics functions prefer to see the data in *long format*, in which all revenues are stacked into one column.

Think of revenue as a dependent variable. If the revenue values are stacked into one column, it's easy to see how each revenue value depends on the combination of the other variables (Industry and Year) in its row. Long format looks like this:

```
> long.revenues
                        Industry Year Million_Dollars
1 Commercial Satellites Delivered 1990            1000
2               Satellite Services 1990             800
3         Satellite Ground Equipment 1990             860
4               Commercial Launches 1990             570
5               Remote Sensing Data 1990             155
6 Commercial Satellites Delivered 1991            1300
```

```
7                       Satellite Services 1991            1200
8               Satellite Ground Equipment 1991            1300
9                      Commercial Launches 1991             380
10                      Remote Sensing Data 1991             190
11 Commercial Satellites Delivered 1992            1300
12                      Satellite Services 1992            1500
13              Satellite Ground Equipment 1992            1400
14                     Commercial Launches 1992             450
15                      Remote Sensing Data 1992             210
16 Commercial Satellites Delivered 1993            1100
17                      Satellite Services 1993            1850
18              Satellite Ground Equipment 1993            1600
19                     Commercial Launches 1993             465
20                      Remote Sensing Data 1993             250
21 Commercial Satellites Delivered 1994            1400
22                      Satellite Services 1994            2330
23              Satellite Ground Equipment 1994            1970
24                     Commercial Launches 1994             580
25                      Remote Sensing Data 1994             300
```

How do I accomplish this format change? A `tidyr` function called `gather()` does the trick. Here's how to reshape `revenues.industry` into `long.revenues`:

```
long.revenues <- gather(revenues.industry,Year,Million_Dollars,2:6)
```

The first argument to `gather()` is the data frame to reshape, the second is the name of the new column in which to *gather* existing columns, the third is the new name for the dependent variable, and the fourth is the sequence of columns to gather from.

Had I not used `rownames_to_column()` earlier, all of this would have been difficult to do.

If it's ever necessary to go in the opposite direction (from long format to wide format), the `tidyr` function `spread()` handles it:

```
> spread(long.revenues,Year,Million_Dollars)
                          Industry 1990 1991 1992 1993 1994
1                Commercial Launches  570  380  450  465  580
2 Commercial Satellites Delivered 1000 1300 1300 1100 1400
3                Remote Sensing Data  155  190  210  250  300
4        Satellite Ground Equipment  860 1300 1400 1600 1970
5                 Satellite Services  800 1200 1500 1850 2330
```

Another prominent package in the tidyverse is called dplyr. This one is also for data manipulation. One of its functions, filter(), returns rows that meet a condition or a set of conditions. For example, if I want to have just the rows in long. revenue that hold information for Satellite Services, I write:

```
> filter(long.revenues,Industry == "Satellite Services")
           Industry Year Million_Dollars
1 Satellite Services 1990             800
2 Satellite Services 1991            1200
3 Satellite Services 1992            1500
4 Satellite Services 1993            1850
5 Satellite Services 1994            2330
```

Suppose I want the data for the first day of each month in the airquality data frame:

```
  Ozone Solar.R Wind Temp Month Day
1    41     190  7.4   67     5   1
2    NA     286  8.6   78     6   1
3   135     269  4.1   84     7   1
4    39      83  6.9   81     8   1
5    96     167  6.9   91     9   1
```

How would I do that?

I've given you only a taste of the tidyverse. Possibly the most widely used tidyverse package is ggplot2, and I tell you about that one in Chapter 1 of Book 2.

TIP

To search for R packages and functions that might suit your needs, visit www. rdocumentation.org.

Importing and Exporting

Before I close out this chapter on R's capabilities, I have to let you know how to import data from other formats as well as how to export data to those formats.

The general form of an R function for reading a file is

```
> read.<format>("File Name", arg1, arg2, ...)
```

The general form of an R function for writing data to a file is

```
> write.<format>(dataframe, "File Name", arg1, arg2, ...)
```

In this section, I cover spreadsheets, comma-separated value (CSV) files, and text files. The ‹format› is either xlsx, csv, or table. The arguments after "File Name" are optional arguments that vary for the different formats.

Spreadsheets

The information in this section will be important to you if you've read my timeless classic *Statistical Analysis with Excel For Dummies* (published by Wiley). (Okay, so that was a shameless plug for my timeless classic.) If you have data on spreadsheets that you want to analyze with R, pay close attention.

The first order of business is to download the xlsx package and put it in the library. Check out the section "More Packages," earlier in this chapter, for more on how to do this.

On my drive C, I have a spreadsheet called Scores in a folder called Spreadsheets. The data, on Sheet1 of the worksheet, is a set of math quiz scores and science quiz scores for ten students.

To read the Scores spreadsheet into R, the code is

```
> scores_frame <- read.xlsx("C:/Spreadsheets/Scores.xlsx", sheetName="Sheet1")
```

Here's that data frame:

```
> scores_frame
   Student Math_Score Science_Score
1        1         85            90
2        2         91            87
3        3         78            75
4        4         88            78
5        5         93            99
6        6         82            89
7        7         67            71
8        8         79            84
9        9         89            88
10      10         98            97
```

As is the case with any data frame, if you want the math score for the fourth student, it's just

```
> scores_frame$Math_Score[4]
[1] 88
```

The xlsx package enables writing to a spreadsheet, too. Here's an example. The MASS package (which I use in Chapter 1 of Book 2) has a data frame called anorexia. (It deals with treatments for this eating disorder.) If you want your Excel-centric friends to look at the anorexia data frame, here's what you do (after you install the MASS package):

```
> write.xlsx(anorexia,"C:/Spreadsheets/anorexia.xlsx")
```

This line puts the data frame into a spreadsheet in the indicated folder on drive C.

CSV files

The functions for reading and writing CSV files and text files are in the R installation, so no additional packages are necessary. A CSV file looks just like a spreadsheet when you open it in Excel. In fact, I created a CSV file for the Scores spreadsheet by saving the spreadsheet as a CSV file in the folder CSVFiles on drive C. (To see all the commas, you have to open it in a text editor, like Notepad++.)

Here's how to read that csv file into R:

```
> read.csv("C:/CSVFiles/Scores.csv")
   Student Math_Score Science_Score
1        1         85            90
2        2         91            87
3        3         78            75
4        4         88            78
5        5         93            99
6        6         82            89
7        7         67            71
8        8         79            84
9        9         89            88
10      10         98            97
```

To write the anorexia data frame to a CSV file:

```
> write.csv(anorexia,"C:/CSVFiles/anorexia.csv")
```

Text files

If you have some data stored in text files, R can import them into data frames. The read.table() function gets it done. I stored the Scores data as a text file in a directory called TextFiles. Here's how R turns it into a data frame:

```
> read.table("C:/TextFiles/ScoresText.txt", header=TRUE)
   Student Math_Score Science_Score
1        1        85            90
2        2        91            87
3        3        78            75
4        4        88            78
5        5        93            99
6        6        82            89
7        7        67            71
8        8        79            84
9        9        89            88
10      10        98            97
```

The second argument (header=TRUE) lets R know that the first row of the file contains column headers.

You use write.table() to write the anorexia data frame to a text file:

```
> write.table(anorexia, "C:/TextFiles/anorexia.txt", quote = FALSE, sep = "\t")
```

This puts the file anorexia.txt in the TextFiles folder on the drive C. The second argument (quote = FALSE) ensures that no quotes appear, and the third argument (sep = "\t") makes the file tab-delimited.

REMEMBER

In each of these examples, you use the full file path for each file. That's not necessary if the files are in the working directory. If, for example, you put the Scores spreadsheet in the working directory, here's all you have to do to read it into R:

```
> read.xlsx("Scores.xlsx","Sheet1")
```

2

Describing Data

Contents at a Glance

Chapter **1**

Getting Graphic

D ata visualization is an important part of statistics. A good graph enables you to spot trends and relationships you might otherwise miss if you look only at numbers. Graphics are valuable for another reason: They help you present your ideas to groups.

This concept is especially important in the field of data science. Organizations rely on data scientists to make sense of huge amounts of data so that decision-makers can formulate strategy. Graphics enable data scientists to explain patterns in the data to managers and to nontechnical personnel.

Finding Patterns

Data often resides in long, complex tables. Often, you have to visualize only a portion of the table to find a pattern or a trend. A number of good examples reside in the MASS package, so download this package into your R library by selecting the check box next to MASS on the Packages tab. (Chapter 2 of Book 1 tells you how to install a package.)

I work with the Cars93 data frame, which holds data on 27 variables for 93 car models that were available in 1993.

Figure 1-1 shows part of the data frame in the Data Editor window that opens after you type

```
> edit(Cars93)
```

Close the Data Editor window and we'll move on to visualizing the data.

	Manufacturer	Model	Type	Min.Price	Price	Max.Price	MPG.city
1	Acura	Integra	Small	12.9	15.9	18.8	25
2	Acura	Legend	Midsize	29.2	33.9	38.7	18
3	Audi	90	Compact	25.9	29.1	32.3	20
4	Audi	100	Midsize	30.8	37.7	44.6	19
5	BMW	535i	Midsize	23.7	30	36.2	22
6	Buick	Century	Midsize	14.2	15.7	17.3	22
7	Buick	LeSabre	Large	19.9	20.8	21.7	19
8	Buick	Roadmaster	Large	22.6	23.7	24.9	16
9	Buick	Riviera	Midsize	26.3	26.3	26.3	19
10	Cadillac	DeVille	Large	33	34.7	36.3	16
11	Cadillac	Seville	Midsize	37.5	40.1	42.7	16
12	Chevrolet	Cavalier	Compact	8.5	13.4	18.3	25
13	Chevrolet	Corsica	Compact	11.4	11.4	11.4	25
14	Chevrolet	Camaro	Sporty	13.4	15.1	16.8	19
15	Chevrolet	Lumina	Midsize	13.4	15.9	18.4	21
16	Chevrolet	Lumina_APV	Van	14.7	16.3	18	18
17	Chevrolet	Astro	Van	14.7	16.6	18.6	15
18	Chevrolet	Caprice	Large	18	18.8	19.6	17
19	Chevrolet	Corvette	Sporty	34.6	38	41.5	17

FIGURE 1-1: Part of the Cars93 data frame.

Graphing a distribution

One pattern that might be of interest is the distribution of the prices of all cars listed in the Cars93 data frame. If you had to examine the entire data frame to determine this, it would be a tedious task. A graph, however, provides the information immediately. Figure 1-2, a *histogram*, shows what I mean.

The histogram is appropriate when the variable on the x-axis is an interval variable or a ratio variable. (See Chapter 1 of Book 1 for more on these variables.) With interval and ratio variables, the numbers have meaning (as opposed to nominal variables where numbers are just labels).

You can distinguish between independent variables and dependent variables. Here, Price is the independent variable, and Frequency is the dependent variable. In most (but not all) graphs, the independent variable is on the x-axis, and the dependent variable is on the y-axis.

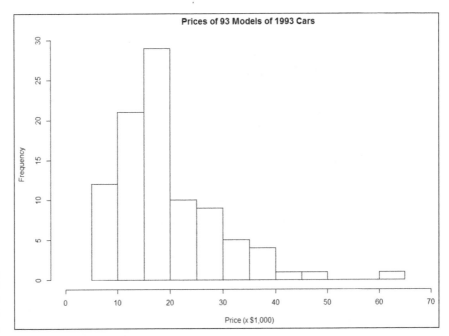

FIGURE 1-2:
Histogram of
prices of cars in
the Cars93 data
frame.

Bar-hopping

For nominal variables (again, see Chapter 1 of Book 1), numbers are just labels. In fact, the levels of a nominal variable (also called a *factor*) can be names. Case in point: Another possible point of interest is the frequencies of the different types of cars (sporty, midsize, van, and so on) in the data frame. So "Type" is a nominal variable. If you looked at every entry in the data frame and created a table of these frequencies, it would look like Table 1-1.

The table shows some trends — more midsize and small car models than large cars and vans. Compact cars and sporty cars are in the middle.

Figure 1-3 shows this information in graphical form. This type of graph is a *bar graph*. The spaces between the bars emphasize that Type, on the *x*-axis, is a nominal variable.

Although the table is pretty straightforward, I think we'd agree that an audience would prefer to see the picture. As I'm fond of saying, eyes that glaze over when looking at numbers often shine brighter when looking at pictures.

TABLE 1-1

Types and Frequencies of Cars in the Cars93 Data Frame

Type	Frequency
Compact	16
Large	11
Midsize	22
Small	21
Sporty	14
Van	9

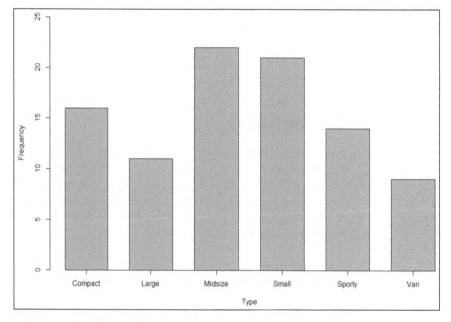

FIGURE 1-3:
Table 1-1 as a
bar graph.

Slicing the pie

The *pie graph* is another type of picture that shows the same data in a slightly different way. Each frequency appears as a slice of a pie. Figure 1-4 shows what I mean. In a pie graph, the area of the slice represents the frequency.

PIE GRAPH GUIDELINES

Pardon me if you've heard this one before. It's a cute anecdote that serves as a rule of thumb for pie graphs.

The late, great Yogi Berra often made loveable misstatements that became part of the popular culture. He once reputedly walked into a pizzeria and ordered a whole pizza.

"Should I cut that into four slices or eight?" asked the waitress.

"Better make it four," said Yogi. "I'm not hungry enough to eat eight."

The takeaway: If a nominal variable has a lot of levels, resulting in a pie graph with a lot of slices, it's probably information overload. The message would come across better in a bar graph.

(Did that Yogi incident really happen? It's not clear. Summarizing a lifetime of sayings attributed to him, Mr. Berra said: "Half the lies they tell about me aren't true.")

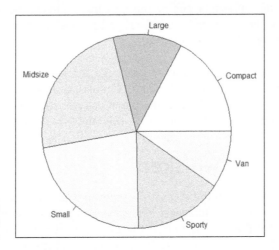

FIGURE 1-4:
Table 1-1 as a
pie graph.

The plot of scatter

Another potential pattern of interest is the relationship between miles per gallon for city driving and horsepower. One type of graph well-suited to demonstrating the nature of this relationship is a *scatter plot*. Figure 1-5 shows the scatter plot for these two variables.

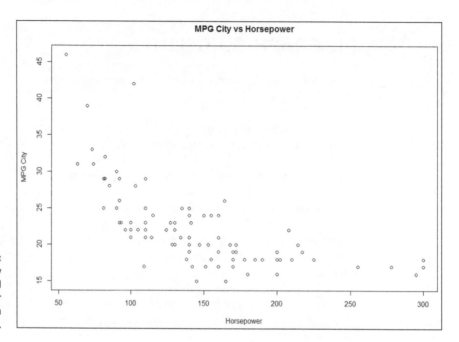

FIGURE 1-5:
MPG in city
driving and
horsepower
for the data in
Cars93.

Each small circle represents one of the 93 cars. A circle's position along the x-axis (its *x-coordinate*) is its horsepower, and its position along the y-axis (its *y-coordinate*) is its MPG for city driving.

A quick look at the shape of the scatter plot suggests a relationship: As horsepower increases, MPG-city seems to decrease. (Statisticians would say "MPG-city decreases with horsepower.") Is it possible to use statistics to analyze this relationship and perhaps make predictions? Absolutely! (See Book 4.)

Of boxes and whiskers

What about the relationship between horsepower and the number of cylinders in a car's engine? You would expect horsepower to increase with cylinders, and Figure 1-6 shows that this is indeed the case. Invented by famed statistician John Tukey, this type of graph is called a *box plot*, and it's a nice, quick way to visualize data.

Each box represents a group of numbers. The leftmost box, for example, represents the horsepower of cars with three cylinders. The black solid line inside the box is the *median* — the horsepower-value that falls between the lower half of the numbers and the upper half. The lower and upper edges of the box are called *hinges*. The lower hinge is the *lower quartile*, the number below which 25 percent of the numbers fall. The upper hinge is the *upper* quartile, the number that exceeds 75 percent of the numbers. (I discuss medians in Chapter 2 of Book 2 and percentiles in Chapter 4 of Book 2.)

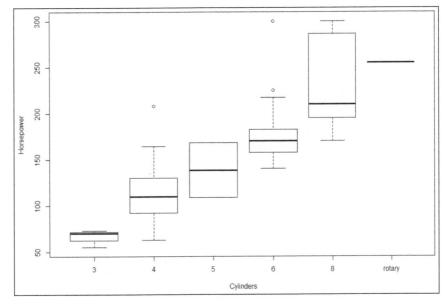

The elements sticking out of the hinges are called *whiskers* (so you sometimes see this type of graph referred to as a *box-and-whiskers* plot). The whiskers include data values outside the hinges. The upper whisker boundary is either the maximum value or the upper hinge plus 1.5 times the length of the box, whichever is *smaller*. The lower whisker boundary is either the minimum value or the lower hinge minus 1.5 times the length of the box, whichever is *larger*. Data points outside the whiskers are *outliers*. The box plot shows that the data for four cylinders and for six cylinders have outliers.

Note that the graph shows only a solid line for "rotary," an engine type that occurs just once in the data.

Doing the Basics: Base R Graphics, That Is

The capability to create the graphs like the ones I show you in earlier sections of this chapter comes with your R installation, which makes these graphs part of *base R graphics*. I start with that. Then, in the next section, I show you the very useful ggplot2 package.

In base R, the general format for creating graphics is

```
graphics_function(data, arg1, arg2, ...)
```

After you create a graph in RStudio, click Zoom on the RStudio Plots tab to open the graph in a larger window. The graph is clearer in the Zoom window than it is on the Plots tab.

Histograms

Time to take another look at that Cars93 data frame I introduce in the "Finding Patterns" section, at the beginning of this chapter. To create a histogram of the distribution of prices in that data frame, you'd enter

```
> hist(Cars93$Price)
```

which produces Figure 1-7, the histogram in the Plots pane.

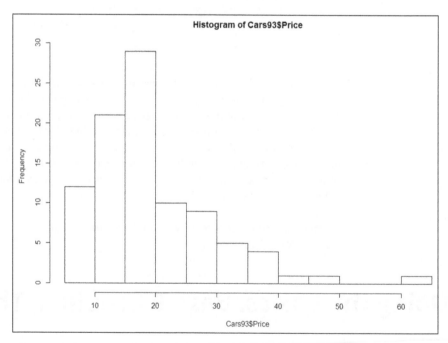

FIGURE 1-7:
Initial histogram of the distribution of prices in Cars93.

You'll note that this isn't quite as spiffy-looking as Figure 1-2. How do you spruce it up? By adding arguments.

One often-used argument in base R graphics changes the label of the x-axis from R's default into something more meaningful. It's called xlab. For the x-axis in Figure 1-2, I added

```
xlab= "Price (x $1,000)"
```

to the arguments. You can use ylab to change the y-axis label, but I left that alone here.

I wanted the x-axis to extend from a lower limit of 0 to an upper limit of 70, and that's the province of the argument xlim. Because this argument works with a vector, I added

```
xlim = c(0,70)
```

I also wanted a different title, and for that I used main:

```
main = "Prices of 93 Models of 1993 Cars"
```

To produce the histogram in Figure 1-2, the whole megillah is

```
> hist(Cars93$Price, xlab="Price (x $1,000)", xlim = c(0,70), main = "Prices of
    93 Models of 1993 Cars")
```

TIP

When creating a histogram, R figures out the best number of columns for a nice-looking appearance. Here, R decided that 12 is a pretty good number. You can vary the number of columns by adding an argument called breaks and setting its value. R doesn't always give you the value you set. Instead, it provides something close to that value and tries to maintain a nice-looking appearance. Add this argument, set its value (breaks =4, for example), and you'll see what I mean.

Graph features

An important aspect of base R graphics is the ability to add features to a graph after you create it. To show you what I mean, I have to start with a slightly different type of graph.

Another way of showing histogram information is to think of the data as *probabilities* rather than frequencies. So, instead of the frequency of a particular price range, you graph the probability that a car selected from the data is in that price range. To do this, you add

```
probability = TRUE
```

to the arguments. Now the R code looks like this:

```
> hist(Cars93$Price, xlab="Price (x $1,000)", xlim = c(0,70), main = "Prices of
    93 Models of 1993 Cars",probability = TRUE)
```

The result appears in Figure 1-8. The *y*-axis measures *density* — a concept related to probability, which I discuss in Chapter 2 of Book 2. The graph is called a *density plot.*

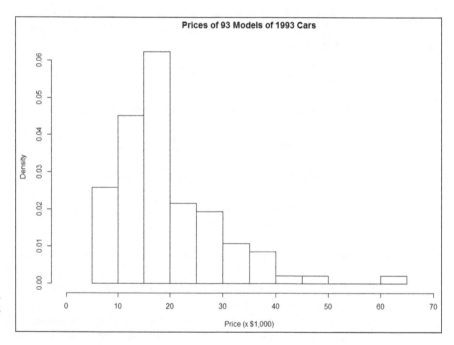

FIGURE 1-8:
Density plot of
the distribution of
prices in Cars93.

The point of all this is what you do next. After you create the graph, you can use an additional function called lines() to add a line to the density plot:

```
> lines(density(Cars93$Price))
```

The graph now looks like Figure 1-9.

So, in base R graphics, you can create a graph and then start adding to it after you see what the initial graph looks like. It's something like painting a picture of a lake and then adding mountains and trees as you see fit.

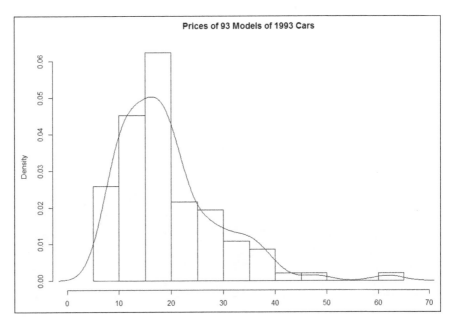

FIGURE 1-9:
Density plot with
an added line.

Bar plots

In the "Finding Patterns" section, at the beginning of this chapter, I show you a bar graph illustrating the types and frequencies of cars, I also show you Table 1-1. As it turns out, you have to make this kind of a table before you can use barplot() to create the bar graph.

To put Table 1-1 together, the R code is (appropriately enough)

```
> table(Cars93$Type)

Compact  Large Midsize  Small Sporty   Van
     16     11      22     21     14     9
```

For the bar graph, then, it's

```
> barplot(table(Cars93$Type))
```

which creates the graph in Figure 1-10.

Again, it's not as jazzy as the final product shown in Figure 1-3. Additional arguments do the trick. To put 0 through 25 on the y-axis, you use ylim, which, like xlim, works with a vector:

```
ylim = c(0,25)
```

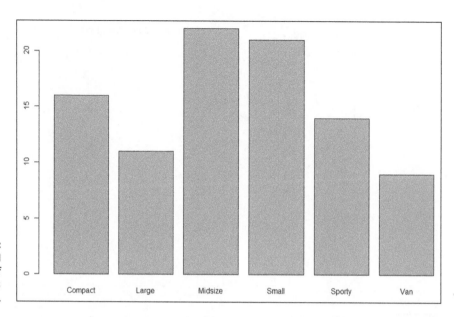

FIGURE 1-10:
The initial
bar plot of
table(Cars93$
Type).

For the *x*-axis label and *y*-axis label, you use

```
xlab = "Type"
ylab = "Frequency"
```

To draw a solid axis, you work with `axis.lty`. Think of this as "axis linetype" which you set to `solid` by typing

```
axis.lty = "solid"
```

The values `dashed` and `dotted` for `axis.lty` result in different looks for the *x*-axis.

Finally, you use `space` to increase the spacing between bars:

```
space = .05
```

Here's the entire function for producing the graph shown earlier, in Figure 1-3:

```
> barplot(table(Cars93$Type),ylim=c(0,25), xlab="Type", ylab="Frequency", axis.
  lty = "solid", space = .05)
```

Pie graphs

The pie graph couldn't be more straightforward. The line

```
> pie(table(Cars93$Type))
```

takes you directly to Figure 1-4.

Dot charts

Wait. What? Where did the dot chart come from? This is yet another way of visualizing the data in Table 1-1. Noted graphics honcho William Cleveland believes that people perceive values along a common scale (as in a bar plot) better than they perceive areas (as in a pie graph). So he came up with the *dot chart*, which I show you in Figure 1-11.

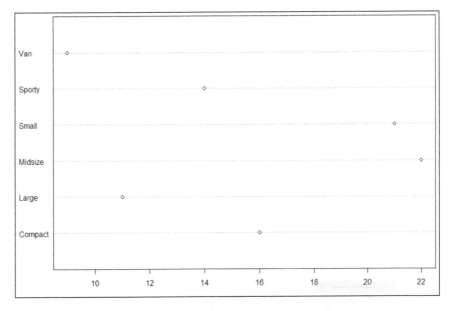

FIGURE 1-11:
Dot chart for the
data in Table 1-1.

Looks a little like an abacus laid on its side, doesn't it? This is one of those infrequent cases where the independent variable is on the *y*-axis and the dependent variable is on the *x*-axis.

The format for the function that creates a dot chart is

```
> dotchart(x, labels, arg1, arg2 ...)
```

The first two arguments are vectors, and the others are optional arguments for modifying the appearance of the dot chart. The first vector is the vector of values (the frequencies). The second is pretty self-explanatory — in this case, it's labels for the types of vehicles.

To create the two necessary vectors (one for the type of car, the other for the frequency), you have to turn the table (which is a single vector) into a data frame:

```
> type.frame <- data.frame(table(Cars93$Type))
> type.frame
     Var1 Freq
1 Compact   16
2   Large   11
3 Midsize   22
4   Small   21
5  Sporty   14
6     Van    9
```

(For more on data frames, see Chapter 2 of Book 1.)

After you have the data frame, this line produces the dot chart:

```
> dotchart(type.frame$Freq,type.frame$Var1)
```

The `type.frame$Freq` specifies that the Frequency column in the data frame is the *x*-axis, and `type.frame$Var1` specifies that the `Var1` column (which holds the car types) is the *y*-axis.

This line works, too:

```
> dotchart(type.frame[,2],type.frame[,1])
```

You might remember from Chapter 2 of Book 1 that [,2] means "column 2" and [,1] means "column 1."

Bar plots revisited

In all the preceding graphs in this chapter, the dependent variable has been frequency. Many times, however, the dependent variable is a data point rather than a frequency. Here's what I mean.

Table 1-2 shows the data for commercial space revenues for the early 1990s. (The data, by the way, is from the US Department of Commerce, via the Statistical Abstract of the US; I touch on this topic in Chapter 2 of Book 1.)

TABLE 1-2

US Commercial Space Revenues 1990–1994 (in Millions of Dollars)

Industry	1990	1991	1992	1993	1994
Commercial satellites delivered	1,000	1,300	1,300	1,100	1,400
Satellite services	800	1,200	1,500	1,850	2,330
Satellite ground equipment	860	1,300	1,400	1,600	1,970
Commercial launches	570	380	450	465	580
Remote sensing data	155	190	210	250	300

The data are the numbers in the cells, which represent revenue in thousands of dollars. A base R bar plot of the data in this table appears in Figure 1-12.

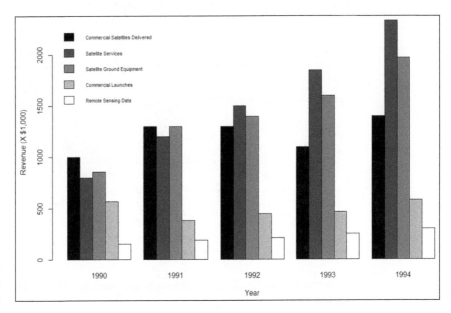

FIGURE 1-12:
Bar plot of the
data in Table 1-2.

If you had to make a presentation about these data, I think you'd agree that your audience would prefer the graph to the table. Although the table is informative, it doesn't hold people's attention. It's easier to see trends in the graph — satellite services rose fastest while commercial launches stayed fairly level, for example.

This graph is called a *grouped bar plot*. How do you create a plot like this one in base R?

The first thing to do is create a vector of the values in the cells:

```
rev.values <- c(1000,1300,1300,1100,1400,800,1200,1500,1850,2330,860,1300,1400,
    1600,1970,570,380,450,465,580,155,190,210,250,300)
```

Although commas appear in the values in the table (for values greater than a thousand), you can't have commas in the values in the vector! (For the obvious reason: Commas separate consecutive values in the vector.)

Next, you turn this vector into a matrix. You have to let R know how many rows (or columns) will be in the matrix, and that the values load into the matrix row-by-row:

```
space.rev <- matrix(rev.values,nrow=5,byrow = T)
```

Finally, you supply column names and row names to the matrix:

```
colnames(space.rev) <- c("1990","1991","1992","1993","1994")
rownames(space.rev) <- c("Commercial Satellites Delivered","Satellite Services",
    "Satellite Ground Equipment","Commercial Launches","Remote Sensing Data")
```

Let's have a look at the matrix:

```
> space.rev
                                1990 1991 1992 1993 1994
Commercial Satellites Delivered 1000 1300 1300 1100 1400
Satellite Services               800 1200 1500 1850 2330
Satellite Ground Equipment       860 1300 1400 1600 1970
Commercial Launches              570  380  450  465  580
Remote Sensing Data              155  190  210  250  300
```

Perfect. It looks just like Table 1-2.

With the data in hand, you move on to the bar plot. You create a vector of colors for the bars:

```
color.names = c("black","grey25","grey50","grey75","white")
```

A word about those color names: You can join any number from 0 to 100 with "grey" and get a color: "grey0" is equivalent to "black" and "grey100" is equivalent to "white".

And now for the plot:

```
> barplot(space.rev, beside = T, xlab= "Year",ylab= "Revenue (X $1,000)",
    col=color.names)
```

beside = T means the bars will be, well, beside each other. (You ought to try this without that argument and see what happens.) The col=color.names argument supplies the colors you specified in the vector.

The resulting plot is shown in Figure 1-13.

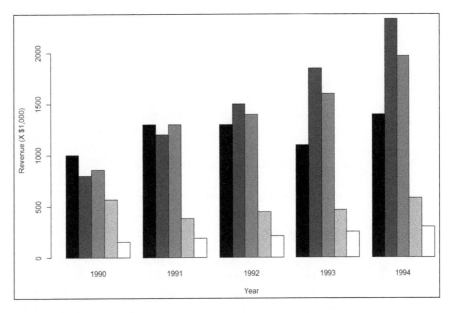

FIGURE 1-13:
Initial bar plot of the data shown in Table 1-2.

What's missing, of course, is the legend. You add that with the legend() function to produce Figure 1-12:

```
> legend(1,2300,rownames(space.rev), cex=0.7, fill = color.names, bty = "n")
```

The first two values are the *x*- and *y*-coordinates for locating the legend. (That took a *lot* of tinkering!) The next argument shows what goes into the legend (the names of the industries). The cex argument specifies the size of the characters in the legend. The value, 0.7, indicates that you want the characters to be 70 percent of the size they would normally be. That's the only way to fit the legend on the graph. (Think of cex as "character expansion," although in this case it's "character contraction.") fill = color.names puts the color swatches in the legend, next to the row names. Setting bty (the "border type") to "n" ("none") is another little trick to fit the legend into the graph.

Scatter plots

To visualize the relationship between horsepower and MPG for city driving (as shown earlier, in Figure 1-5), you use the plot( ) function:

```
> plot(Cars93$Horsepower, Cars93$MPG.city, xlab="Horsepower",ylab="MPG City",
    main ="MPG City vs Horsepower")
```

As you can see, I added the arguments for labeling the axes, and for the title.

Another way to do this is to use the tilde operator (~) I show you in Chapter 2 of Book 1. So, if you want the R code to show that MPG-city depends on horsepower, you type

```
> plot(Cars93$MPG.city ~ Cars93$Horsepower, xlab="Horsepower",ylab="MPG City",
    main ="MPG City vs Horsepower")
```

to produce the same scatter plot.

The tilde operator (~) means "depends on."

A plot twist

R enables you to change the symbol that depicts the points in the graph. Figure 1-5 shows that the default symbol is an empty circle. To change the symbol, which is called the *plotting character*, set the argument pch. R has a set of built-in numerical values (0–25) for pch that correspond to a set of symbols. The values 0–15 correspond to unfilled shapes, and 16–25 are filled.

The default value is 1. To change the plotting character to squares, set pch to 0. For triangles, it's 2, and for filled circles, it's 16:

```
> plot(Cars93$Horsepower,Cars93$MPG.city, xlab="Horsepower", ylab="MPG City",
    main = "MPG City vs Horsepower",pch=16)
```

Figure 1-14 shows the plot with the filled circles.

You can also set the argument col to change the color from "black" to "blue" or to a variety of other colors (which wouldn't show up well on the black-and-white page you're looking at).

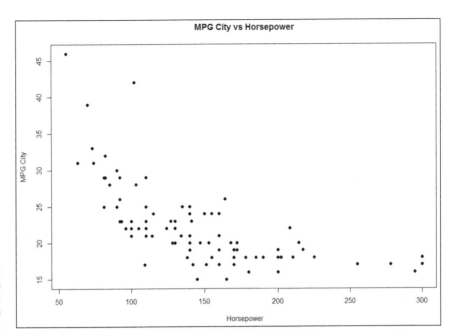

Scatter plot matrix

Base R provides a nice way of visualizing relationships among more than two variables. If you add price into the mix and you want to show all the pairwise relationships among MPG-city, price, and horsepower, you'd need multiple scatter plots. R can plot them all together in a matrix, as Figure 1-15 shows.

The names of the variables are in the cells of the main diagonal. Each off-diagonal cell shows the scatter plot for its row variable (on the *y*-axis) and its column variable (on the *x*-axis). For example, the scatter plot in the first row, second column, shows MPG-city on the *y*-axis and price on the *x*-axis. In the second row, first column, the axes are reversed: MPG city is on the *x*-axis, and price is on the *y*-axis.

The R function for plotting this matrix is pairs(). To calculate the coordinates for all scatter plots, this function works with numerical columns from a matrix or a data frame.

For convenience, you create a data frame that's a subset of the Cars93 data frame. This new data frame consists of just the three variables to plot. The function subset() handles that nicely:

```
> cars.subset <- subset(Cars93, select = c(MPG.city,Price,Horsepower))
```

Getting Graphic

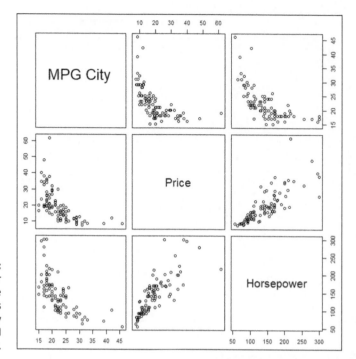

FIGURE 1-15:
Multiple scatter
plots for the
relationships
among city
MPG, price, and
horsepower.

The second argument to subset creates a vector of exactly what to select out of
Cars93. Just to make sure the new data frame is the way you want it, use the
head() function to take look at the first six rows:

```
> head(cars.subset)
  MPG.city Price Horsepower
1       25  15.9        140
2       18  33.9        200
3       20  29.1        172
4       19  37.7        172
5       22  30.0        208
6       22  15.7        110
```

And now,

```
> pairs(cars.subset)
```

creates the plot in Figure 1-15.

This capability isn't limited to three variables, nor to continuous ones. To see
what happens with a different type of variable, add Cylinders to the vector for
select and then use the pairs() function on cars.subset.

Box plots

To draw a box plot like the one shown earlier, in Figure 1-6, you use a formula to show that Horsepower is the dependent variable and Cylinders is the independent variable:

```
> boxplot(Cars93$Horsepower ~ Cars93$Cylinders, xlab="Cylinders",
    ylab="Horsepower")
```

If you get tired of typing the $ signs, here's another way:

```
> boxplot(Horsepower ~ Cylinders, data = Cars93, xlab="Cylinders",
    ylab="Horsepower")
```

TIP

With the arguments laid out as in either of the two preceding code examples, plot() works exactly like boxplot().

Kicking It Up a Notch to ggplot2

The base R graphics toolset will get you started, but if you really want to shine at visualization, it's a good idea to learn ggplot2. Created by R megastar Hadley Wickham, the *gg* in the package name stands for "grammar of graphics," and that's a good indicator of what's ahead. That's also the title of the book (by Leland Wilkinson) that is the source of the concepts for this package.

In general, a *grammar* is a set of rules for combining things. In the grammar that people are most familiar with, the things happen to be words, phrases, and clauses: The grammar of our language tells you how to combine these components to produce valid sentences.

So a "grammar of graphics" is a set of rules for combining graphics components to produce graphs. Wilkinson proposed that all graphs have underlying common components — like data, a coordinate system (the *x*- and *y*-axes you know so well, for example), statistical transformations (like frequency counts), and objects within the graph (dots, bars, lines, or pie slices, for example — to name just a few).

Just as combining words and phrases produces grammatical sentences, combining graphics components produces graphs. And just as some sentences are grammatical but make no sense ("Colorless green ideas sleep furiously"), some ggplot2 creations are beautiful graphs that aren't always useful. It's up to the speaker/writer to make sense for their audiences, and it's up to the graphics developer to create useful graphs for people who use them.

Histograms

In `ggplot2`, Wickham's implementation of Wilkinson's grammar is an easy-to-learn structure for R graphics code. To learn that structure, make sure you have `ggplot2` in the library so that you can follow what comes next. (Find `ggplot2` on the Packages tab and select its check box.)

A graph starts with `ggplot()`, which takes two arguments. The first argument is the source of the data. The second argument maps the data components of interest into components of the graph. The function that does the job is `aes()`.

To begin a histogram for `Price` in `Cars93`, the function is

```
> ggplot(Cars93, aes(x=Price))
```

The `aes()` function associates `Price` with the *x*-axis. In `ggplot`-world, this is called an *aesthetic mapping*. In fact, each argument to `aes()` is called an *aesthetic*.

This line of code draws Figure 1-16, which is just a grid with a gray background and `Price` on the *x*-axis.

Well, what about the *y*-axis? Does anything in the data map into it? No. That's because this is a histogram and nothing explicitly in the data provides a *y*-value for each *x*. So you can't say "y=" in `aes()`. Instead, you let R do the work to calculate the heights of the bars in the histogram.

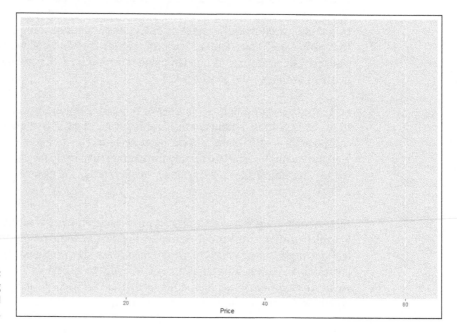

FIGURE 1-16:
Applying
`ggplot()` and
nothing else.

And what about that histogram? How do you put it into this blank grid? You have to add something indicating that you want to plot a histogram and let R take care of the rest. What you add is a geom function. (*Geom* is short for "geometric object.")

These geom functions come in a variety of types. ggplot2 supplies one for almost every graphing need and provides the flexibility to work with special cases. To draw a histogram, the geom function to use is called geom_histogram().

How do you add geom_histogram() to ggplot()? With a plus sign, that's how:

```
ggplot(Cars93, aes(x=Price)) +
    geom_histogram()
```

This snippet produces Figure 1-17. The grammar rules tell ggplot2 that when the geometric object is a histogram, R does the necessary calculations on the data and produces the appropriate plot.

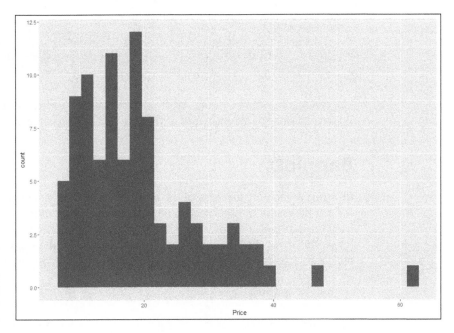

FIGURE 1-17:
The initial
histogram for
Price in Cars93.

At the bare minimum, ggplot2 graphics code has to have data, aesthetic mappings, and a geometric object. It's like answering a logical sequence of questions: What's the source of the data? What parts of the data are you interested in? Which parts of the data correspond to which parts of the graph? How do you want the graph to look?

Beyond those minimum requirements, you can modify the graph. Each bar is called a *bin*, and by default, ggplot() uses 30 of them. After plotting the histogram, ggplot() displays an onscreen message that advises experimenting with binwidth (which, unsurprisingly, specifies the width of each bin) to change the graph's appearance. Accordingly, you use binwidth = 5 as an argument in geom_histogram().

Additional arguments modify the way the bars look:

```
geom_histogram(binwidth=5, color = "black", fill = "white")
```

With another function, labs(), you modify the labels for the axes and supply a title for the graph:

```
labs(x = "Price (x $1000)", y="Frequency",title="Prices of 93 Models of 1993
    Cars")
```

Altogether now:

```
ggplot(Cars93, aes(x=Price)) +
   geom_histogram(binwidth=5,color="black",fill="white") +
   labs(x = "Price (x $1000)", y="Frequency", title="Prices of 93 Models of 1993
    Cars")
```

The result is shown in Figure 1-18. (Note that it's a little different from Figure 1-2. I'd have to tinker a bit with both of them to make them come out the same.)

Bar plots

Drawing a bar plot in ggplot2 is a little easier than drawing one in base R: It's not necessary to first create a table like Table 1-1 in order to draw the graph. As in the example in the preceding section, you don't specify an aesthetic mapping for y. This time, the geom function is geom_bar(), and the rules of the grammar tell ggplot2 to do the necessary work with the data and then draw the plot:

```
ggplot(Cars93, aes(x=Type))+
   geom_bar() +
   labs(y="Frequency", title="Car Type and Frequency in Cars93")
```

Figure 1-19 shows the resulting bar plot.

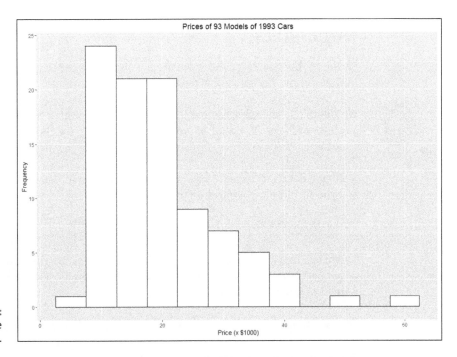

FIGURE 1-18:
The finished Price
histogram.

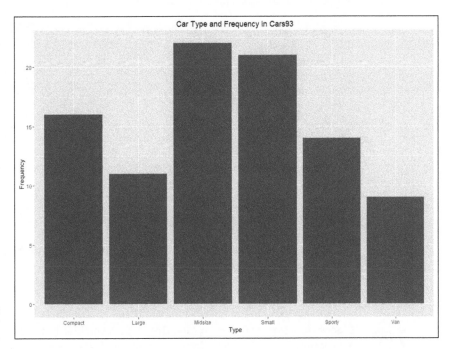

FIGURE 1-19:
Bar plot for
Car Type.

Dot charts

Earlier in this chapter, I show you the dot chart as an alternative to the pie graph. In this section, I tell you how to use ggplot() to draw one.

TIP

Why didn't I lead with the pie graph and show you how to create one with the ggplot2 package? It's a lot of work, and little bang for the buck. If you want to create one, the base R pie() function is much easier to work with.

Making a dot chart begins much the same as in base R: You create a table for ype, and you turn the table into a data frame:

```
type.frame <- data.frame(table(Cars$93.Type))
```

To ensure that you have meaningful variable names for the aesthetic mapping, you apply the colnames() function to name the columns in this data frame (that's a step I didn't do in base R):

```
colnames(type.frame)<- c("Type","Frequency")
```

Now type.frame looks just like Table 1-1:

```
> type.frame
      Type Frequency
1 Compact        16
2   Large        11
3 Midsize        22
4   Small        21
5  Sporty        14
6     Van         9
```

On to the graph. To orient the dot chart as shown earlier, in Figure 1-11, you map Frequency to the x-axis and Type to the y-axis:

```
ggplot(type.frame, aes(x=Frequency,y= Type))
```

Again, usually the independent variable is on the x-axis and the dependent variable is on the y-axis, but that's not the case in this graph.

Next, you add a geom function.

WARNING

A geom function called geom_dotplot() is available, but surprisingly, it's not appropriate here. That one draws something else. In ggplot-world, a dot *plot* is different from a dot *chart*. Go figure.

The geom function for the dot chart is geom_point(). So this code:

```
ggplot(type.frame, aes(x=Frequency,y=Type)) +
   geom_point()
```

results in Figure 1-20.

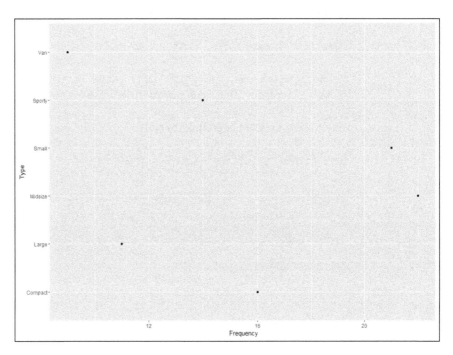

FIGURE 1-20:
The initial dot
chart for Type.

A couple of modifications are in order. First, with a graph like this, it's a nice touch to rearrange the categories on the y-axis with respect to how they order on what you're measuring on the x-axis. That necessitates a slight change in the aesthetic mapping to the y-axis:

```
ggplot(type.frame,
   aes(x=Frequency,y=reorder(Type,Frequency)))
```

Larger dots would make the chart look a little nicer:

```
geom_point(size =4)
```

Additional functions modify the graph's overall appearance. One family of these functions is called *themes*. One member of this family, theme_bw(), removes the gray background. Adding theme() with appropriate arguments a) removes the vertical lines in the grid and b) blackens the horizontal lines and makes them dotted:

```
theme_bw() +
theme(panel.grid.major.x=element_blank(),
        panel.grid.major.y=element_line(color = "black", linetype = "dotted"))
```

Finally, labs() changes the *y*-axis label:

```
labs(y= "Type")
```

Without that change, the *y*-axis label would be reorder(Type,Frequency). Though picturesque, that label makes little sense to the average viewer.

Here's the code from beginning to end:

```
ggplot(type.frame, aes(x=Frequency,y=reorder(Type,Frequency))) +
  geom_point(size = 4) +
  theme_bw() +
  theme(panel.grid.major.x=element_blank(),
        panel.grid.major.y=element_line(color = "black",linetype = "dotted"))+
  labs(y="Type")
```

Figure 1-21 shows the dot chart.

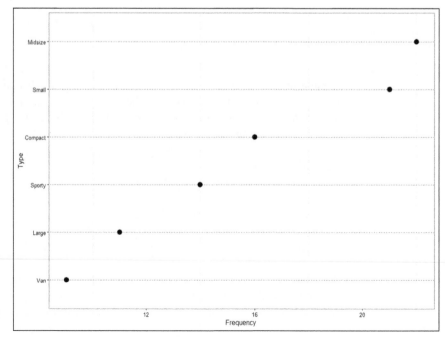

FIGURE 1-21:
The modified dot
chart for Type.

Bar plots re-revisited

As was the case with the first few graphs in base R, the graphs I've shown so far in this section have frequencies (or "counts") as the dependent variable. And, of course, as Table 1-2 shows, that's not always the case.

In the section on base R, I show you how to create a grouped bar plot. Here, I show you how to use ggplot() to create one from space.rev, the data set I created from the data in Table 1-2. The finished product will look like Figure 1-22.

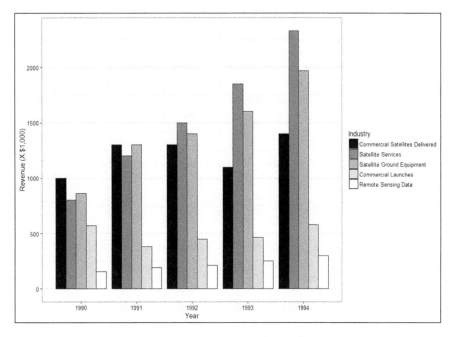

FIGURE 1-22: Bar plot for the data in Table 1-2, created with ggplot().

The first order of business is to get the data ready. It's not in the format that ggplot() uses. This format

```
> space.rev
                               1990 1991 1992 1993 1994
Commercial Satellites Delivered 1000 1300 1300 1100 1400
Satellite Services               800 1200 1500 1850 2330
Satellite Ground Equipment       860 1300 1400 1600 1970
Commercial Launches              570  380  450  465  580
Remote Sensing Data              155  190  210  250  300
```

is called *wide* format. `ggplot()`, however, works with *long* format, which looks like this:

```
                              Industry Year Revenue
1 Commercial Satellites Delivered 1990    1000
2               Satellite Services 1990     800
3        Satellite Ground Equipment 1990     860
4               Commercial Launches 1990     570
5                Remote Sensing Data 1990     155
6 Commercial Satellites Delivered 1991    1300
```

Those are just the first six rows for this data set. The total number of rows is 25 (because 5 rows and 5 columns are in the wide format).

Hadley Wickham (there's that name again!) created a package called `reshape2` that provides everything for a seamless transformation. The function `melt()` turns wide format into long. Another function, `cast()`, does the reverse. These functions are a huge help because they eliminate the need to go schlepping around in spreadsheets to reshape a data set.

So, with `reshape2` in the library (select its check box on the Packages tab), the code is

```
> space.melt <- melt(space.rev)
```

Yes, that's really all there is to it. Here, I'll prove it to you:

```
> head(space.melt)
                               Var1 Var2 value
1 Commercial Satellites Delivered 1990  1000
2               Satellite Services 1990   800
3        Satellite Ground Equipment 1990   860
4               Commercial Launches 1990   570
5                Remote Sensing Data 1990   155
6 Commercial Satellites Delivered 1991  1300
```

Next, you give meaningful names to the columns:

```
> colnames(space.melt) <- c("Industry","Year","Revenue")
> head(space.melt)
                              Industry Year Revenue
1 Commercial Satellites Delivered 1990    1000
2               Satellite Services 1990     800
3        Satellite Ground Equipment 1990     860
4               Commercial Launches 1990     570
5                Remote Sensing Data 1990     155
6 Commercial Satellites Delivered 1991    1300
```

And now you're ready to roll. You start with `ggplot()`. The aesthetic mappings are straightforward:

```
ggplot(space.melt, aes(x=Year,y=Revenue,fill=Industry))
```

You add the `geom` function for the bar, and you specify three arguments:

```
geom_bar(stat = "identity", position = "dodge", color ="black")
```

The first argument is absolutely necessary for a graph of this type. If left on its own, `geom_bar` defaults to the bar plot I showed you earlier — a graph based on frequencies. Because you defined an aesthetic mapping for y, and that type of graph is incompatible with an aesthetic for y, not setting this argument results in an error message.

Accordingly, you let `ggplot()` know that this is a graph based on explicit data values. So `stat="identity"` means "use the given numbers as the data."

The value for the next argument, `position`, is a cute name that means the bars "dodge" each other and line up side-by-side. (Omit this argument and see what happens.) It's analogous to "`beside =T`" in base R.

The third argument sets the color of the borders for each bar. The fill-color scheme for the bars is the province of the next function:

```
scale_fill_grey(start = 0,end = 1)
```

As its name suggests, this function fills the bars with shades of gray (excuse me — "grey"). The `start` value, 0, is black, and the `end` value, 1, is white. (Reminiscent of "grey0" = "black" and "grey100" = "white.") The effect is to fill the five bars with five shades from black to white.

You'd like to relabel the *y*-axis, so that's

```
labs(y="Revenue (X $1,000)")
```

and then remove the gray background

```
theme_bw()
```

and, finally, remove the vertical lines from the grid

```
theme(panel.grid.major.x = element_blank())
```

The whole chunk for producing Figure 1-23 is

```
ggplot(space.melt, aes(x=Year,y=Revenue,fill=Industry)) +
  geom_bar(stat = "identity", position = "dodge", color="black") +
  scale_fill_grey(start = 0,end = 1)+
  labs(y="Revenue (X $1,000)")+
  theme_bw()+
  theme(panel.grid.major.x = element_blank())
```

Scatter plots

As I describe earlier, a scatter plot is a great way to show the relationship between two variables, like horsepower and miles per gallon for city driving. And ggplot() is a great way to draw the scatter plot. If you've been following along, the grammar of this will be easy for you:

```
ggplot(Cars93,aes(x=Horsepower,y=MPG.city))+
  geom_point()
```

Figure 1-23 shows the scatter plot. I'll leave it to you to change the y-axis label to "Miles per Gallon (City)" and to add a descriptive title.

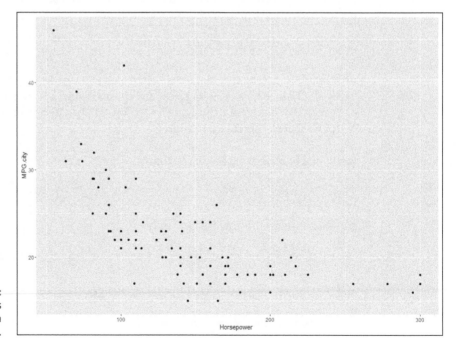

FIGURE 1-23: MPG.city versus Horsepower in Cars93.

About that plot twist . . .

Take another look at Figure 1-15, the relationship between MPG.city and Horsepower. In that one, the points in the plot aren't dots. Instead, each data point is the number of cylinders, which is a label that appears as a text character.

How do you make that happen in ggplot-world? First, you need an additional aesthetic mapping in aes(). That mapping is label, and you set it to Cylinders:

```
ggplot(Cars93, aes(x=Horsepower, y=MPG.city, label = Cylinders))
```

You add a geometric object for text and — voilà:

```
ggplot(Cars93, aes(x = Horsepower,y = MPG.city,label = Cylinders)) +
                    geom_text()
```

Figure 1-24 shows the graph this code produces. One difference from base R is "rotary" rather than "r" as a data point label.

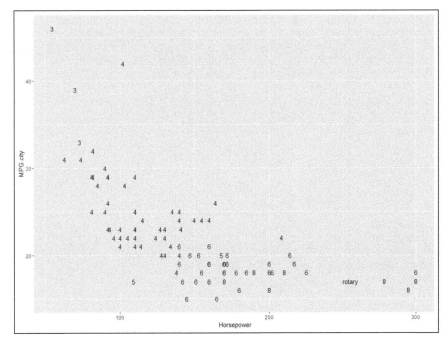

FIGURE 1-24:
The initial ggplot2 scatter plot for MPG.city vs. Horsepower with Cylinders as the data point label.

Just for the heck of it, I used theme functions (see the earlier "Dot charts" section) to make the graph's appearance look more like the one shown in Figure 1-15.

As in the dot chart example, theme_bw() eliminates the gray background. The theme() function (with a specific argument) eliminates the grid:

```
theme(panel.grid=element_blank())
```

element_blank() is a function that draws a blank element.

Putting it all together:

```
ggplot(Cars93, aes(x=Horsepower, y=MPG.city, label=Cylinders)) +
    geom_text() +
    theme_bw() +
    theme(panel.grid=element_blank())
```

produces Figure 1-25. Once again, I leave it to you to use labs() to change the y-axis label and to add a descriptive title.

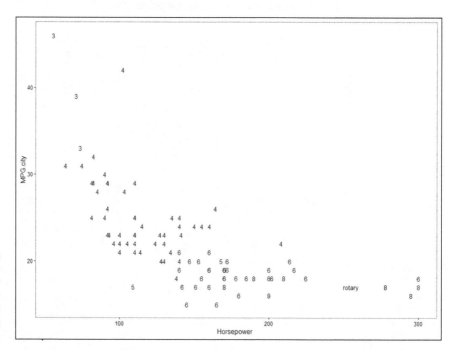

FIGURE 1-25: Modified scatter plot for MPG.city vs Horsepower with Cylinders as the data point label.

Scatter plot matrix

A matrix of scatter plots shows the pairwise relationships among more than two variables. Figure 1-15 shows how the base R pairs() function draws this kind of matrix.

The ggplot2 package once had a function called plotpairs() that did something similar, but not anymore. GGally, a package built on ggplot2, provides ggpairs() to draw scatter plot matrices, and it does this in a flamboyant way.

TIP

The GGally package isn't on the Packages tab. You have to select Install and type **GGally** in the Install Packages dialog box. When it appears on the Packages tab, select the check box next to it.

Earlier, I created a subset of Cars93 that includes MPG.city, Price, and Horsepower:

```
> cars.subset <- subset(Cars93, select = c(MPG.city,Price,Horsepower))
```

With the GGally package in your library, this code creates the scatter plot matrix in Figure 1-26:

```
> ggpairs(cars.subset)
```

As Figure 1-26 shows, this one's a beauty. The cells along the main diagonal present density plots of the variables. (See the earlier subsection "Graph features," and also see Chapter 6 of Book 2.) One drawback is that the *y*-axis is visible for the variable MPG.city only in the first row and first column.

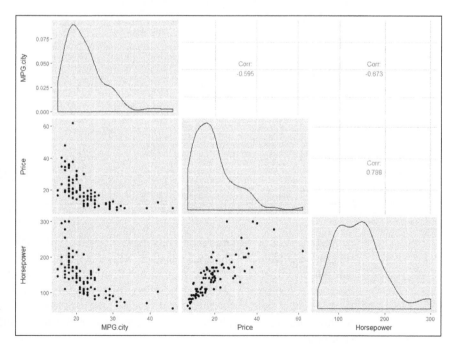

FIGURE 1-26: Scatter plot matrix for MPG. city, Price, and Horsepower.

The three scatter plots are in the cells below the main diagonal. Rather than show the same scatter plots with the axes reversed in the cells above the main diagonal (like pairs() does), each above-the-diagonal cell shows a *correlation coefficient* that summarizes the relationship between the cell's row variable and its column variable. (Correlation coefficients? No, I'm not going to explain them now. See Chapter 7 of Book 3.)

For a real visual treat, add Cylinders to cars.subset and then apply ggpairs():

```
> cars.subset <- subset(Cars93, select = c(MPG.city,Price,Horsepower,Cylinders))
> ggpairs(cars.subset)
```

Figure 1-27 shows the new scatter plot matrix, in all its finery.

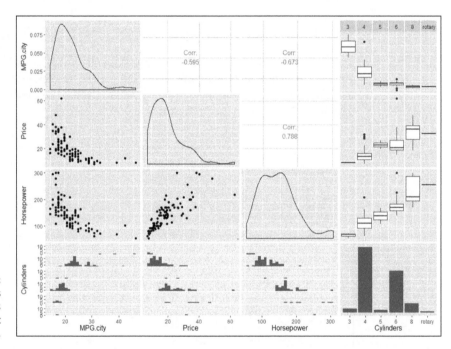

FIGURE 1-27:
Adding Cylinders
produces this
scatter plot
matrix.

Cylinders is not a variable that lends itself to scatter plots, density plots, or correlation coefficients. (Thought question: Why not?) Thus, the cell in the fourth column, fourth row, has a bar plot rather than a density plot. Bar plots relating Cylinders (on each *y*-axis) to the other three variables (on the *x*-axes) are in the remaining three cells in row 4. Box plots relating Cylinders (on each *x*-axis) to the other three variables (on the *y*-axes) are in the remaining three cells in column 4.

Which brings me to the next graph type. . . .

Box plots

Statisticians use box plots to quickly show how groups differ from one another. As in the base R example, I show you the box plot for Cylinders and Horsepower. This is a replication of the graph in row 3, column 4 of Figure 1-27.

At this point, you can probably figure out the ggplot() function:

```
ggplot(Cars93, aes(x=Cylinders, y= Horsepower))
```

What's the geom function? If you guessed geom_boxplot(), you're right!

So the code is

```
ggplot(Cars93, aes(x=Cylinders,y=Horsepower)) +
    geom_boxplot()
```

And that gives you Figure 1-28.

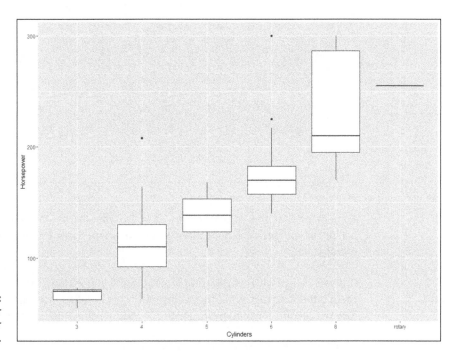

FIGURE 1-28:
Box plot for
Horsepower
versus Cylinders.

Want to show all the data points in addition to the boxes? Add the geom function for points:

```
ggplot(Cars93, aes(x=Cylinders,y=Horsepower)) +
    geom_boxplot()+
    geom_point()
```

to produce the graph shown in Figure 1-29.

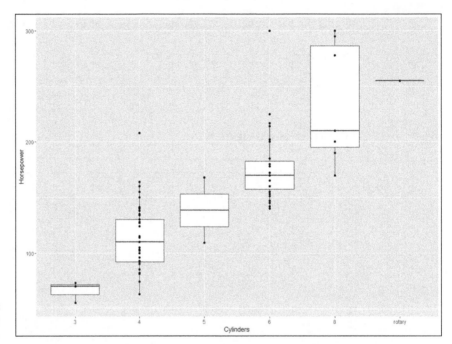

FIGURE 1-29:
Box plot with
data points.

Remember that this is data for 93 cars. Do you see 93 data points? Neither do I. This, of course, is because many points overlap. Graphics gurus refer to this as *overplotting*.

One way to deal with overplotting is to randomly reposition the points so as to reveal them but not change what they represent. This is called *jittering*. And ggplot2 has a geom function for that: geom_jitter(). Adding this function to the code

```
gplot(Cars93, aes(x=Cylinders,y=Horsepower)) +
    geom_boxplot()+
    geom_point()+
    geom_jitter()
```

draws Figure 1-30.

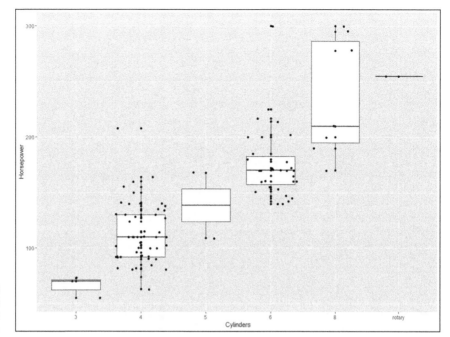

FIGURE 1-30:
Boxplot with
jittered data
points.

Putting a Bow On It

As far as graphics goes, I've just scratched the surface. R has a rich set of graphics tools and packages — way more than I could show you in this chapter. In the
chapters to come, every time I show you an analytic technique, I also show you
how to visualize its results. I'll use what you've read in this chapter to get started,
adding new tools and packages as necessary.

Chapter **2**

Finding Your Center

I f you've ever worked with a set of numbers and had to figure out how to summarize them with a single number, you've faced a situation that statisticians deal with all the time. Where would this ideal "single number" come from?

A good idea might be to select a number from somewhere in the middle of the set. That number could then represent the entire set of numbers. When you're looking around in the middle of the set, you're looking at *central tendency*. We can address central tendency in a variety of ways.

Means: The Lure of Averages

Almost everyone has used averages. Statisticians refer to the average as the *mean*. The mean is an easy way to summarize your spending, your school grades, your performance in a sport over time.

In the course of their work, scientists calculate means. When a researcher creates a study, they apply some kind of treatment or procedure to a small sample of people or things. Then they measure the results and estimate the effects of the procedure on the population that produced the sample. Statisticians have shown that the sample mean is the estimate of the mean of the population.

Calculating the Mean

I think you know how to calculate the mean, but I'll walk you through it anyway. Then I show you the statistical formula. My objective is that you understand statistical formulas in general, and then I show you how R calculates means.

A *mean* is just the sum of a set of numbers divided by how many numbers you added up. Suppose that you measure the heights (in inches) of six 5-year-old children and find that their heights are

36, 42, 43, 37, 40, 45

The average height of these six children is

$$\frac{36 + 42 + 43 + 37 + 40 + 45}{6} = 40.5$$

The mean of this sample, then, is 40.5 inches.

A first attempt at a formula for the mean might be

$$\text{Mean} = \frac{\text{Sum of Numbers}}{\text{Amount of Numbers You Added Up}}$$

Formulas, though, usually involve abbreviations. A common abbreviation of *number* is X. Statisticians usually abbreviate *amount of numbers you added up* as N. So the formula becomes

$$\text{Mean} = \frac{\text{Sum of } X}{N}$$

Statisticians also use an abbreviation for *Sum of* — the uppercase Greek letter for S. Pronounced "sigma," it looks like this: Σ. So the formula with the sigma is

$$\text{Mean} = \frac{\sum X}{N}$$

I'm not done yet. Statisticians abbreviate *mean*, too. You might think that M would be the abbreviation, and some statisticians agree with you, but most prefer a symbol that's related to X. For this reason, the most popular abbreviation for the mean is $\bar{X}$, which is pronounced "x bar." And here's the formula:

$$\bar{X} = \frac{\sum X}{N}$$

I have to tie up one more loose end. In Chapter 1 of Book 1, I discuss samples and populations. Symbols in formulas have to reflect the distinction between the two. The convention is that English letters, like $\bar{X}$, stand for characteristics of samples, and Greek letters stand for characteristics of populations. For the population mean, the symbol is the Greek equivalent of m, which is μ. It's pronounced like "you" but with "m" in front of it. The formula for the population mean, then, is

$$\mu = \frac{\sum X}{N}$$

The Average in R: mean()

R provides an extremely straightforward way of calculating the mean of a set of numbers: mean(). I apply it to the example of the heights of six children.

First, I create a vector of the heights:

```
> heights <- c(36, 42, 43, 37, 40, 45)
```

Then I apply the function:

```
> mean(heights)
[1] 40.5
```

And there you have it.

What's your condition?

When you work with a data frame, sometimes you want to calculate the mean of just the cases (rows) that meet certain conditions rather than the mean of all the cases. This is easy to do in R.

For the discussion that follows, I use the same Cars93 data frame that I use in Chapter 1 of Book 2. That's the one that has data for a sample of 93 cars from 1993. It's in the MASS package. So make sure you have the MASS package in your library. (Find MASS on the Packages tab and select its check box.)

Suppose I'm interested in the average horsepower of the cars made in the USA. First, I select those cars and put their horsepower values into a vector:

```
Horsepower.USA <- Cars93$Horsepower[Cars93$Origin == "USA"]
```

(If the righthand part of that line looks strange to you, reread Chapter 2 of Book 1.)

The average horsepower is then

```
> mean(Horsepower.USA)
[1] 147.5208
```

Hmmm . . . I wonder what that average is for cars not made in the USA:

```
Horsepower.NonUSA <- Cars93$Horsepower[Cars93$Origin == "non-USA"]

> mean(Horsepower.NonUSA)
[1] 139.8889
```

So the averages differ a bit. (Can we examine that difference more closely? Yes we can, which is just what I do in Chapter 3 of Book 3.)

Eliminate $ signs for with()

In the preceding R code, the $ signs denote variables in the Cars93 data frame. R provides a way out of using the name of the data frame (and, hence, the $ sign) each time you refer to one of its variables.

In Chapter 1 of Book 2, I show that graphics functions take as their first argument the data source. Then, in the argument list, it's not necessary to repeat the source along with the $ sign to denote a variable to plot.

The function with() does this for other R functions. The first argument is the data source, and the second argument is the function to apply to a variable in that data source.

To find the mean horsepower of US cars in Cars93:

```
> with(Cars93, mean(Horsepower[Origin == "USA"]))
[1] 147.5208
```

This also skips the step of creating the Horsepower.USA vector.

How about multiple conditions, like the average horsepower of US 4-cylinder cars?

```
> with(Cars93, mean(Horsepower[Origin == "USA" & Cylinders ==4]))
[1] 104.0909
```

R also provides the `attach()` function as a way of eliminating $ signs and keystrokes. Attach the data frame (`attach(Cars93)`, for example) and you don't have to refer to it again when you use its variables. Numerous R authorities recommend against this, however, because it can lead to errors.

Explore the data

Now that I've examined the horsepower means of USA and non-USA cars, how about the overall distributions?

That calls for a little data exploration. I use the `ggplot2` package (see Chapter 1 of Book 2) to create side-by-side histograms from the `Cars93` data frame so that I can compare them. (Make sure you have `ggplot2` in the library.) Figure 2-1 shows what I mean.

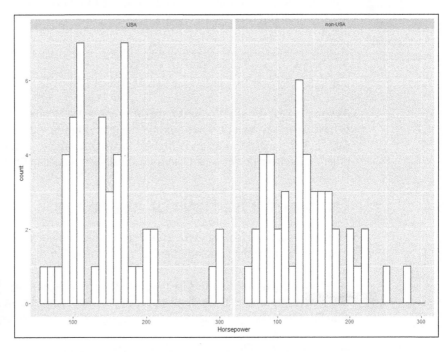

FIGURE 2-1:
Horsepower histograms for USA and non-USA cars in Cars93.

To create the histograms in the figure, I begin in the usual way:

```
ggplot(Cars93, aes(x=Horsepower))
```

and then add a geom

```
geom_histogram(color="black", fill="white",binwidth = 10)
```

I tinkered around a little to arrive at that binwidth value.

The code so far creates an ordinary histogram with Horsepower on the x-axis. How can I create Figure 2-1? To do that, I add a ggplot capability called *faceting*. Simply put, faceting splits the data according to a nominal variable — like Origin, which is either "USA" or "non-USA." A couple of faceting functions are available. The one I use here is called facet_wrap(). To split the data according to Origin, it's

```
facet_wrap(~Origin)
```

REMEMBER

The tilde operator (~) means "depends on," so think of Origin as an independent variable. The full code for Figure 2-1 is

```
ggplot(Cars93, aes(x=Horsepower)) +
  geom_histogram(color="black", fill="white",binwidth = 10)+
  facet_wrap(~Origin)
```

As you can see, the distributions have different overall shapes. The USA cars seem to have a gap between the low 200s and the next-highest values, and the non-USA cars, not so much. You also see higher maximum values for the USA cars. What other differences do you see? (I address those differences in Chapter 5 of Book 2.)

Outliers: The flaw of averages

An *outlier* is an extreme value in a data set. If the data set is a sample and you're trying to estimate the population mean, then the outlier might bias the estimate.

Statisticians deal with outliers by *trimming* the mean — eliminating extreme values at the low end and the high end before calculating the sample mean. The amount of trim is a percentage, like the upper and lower 5 percent of the scores.

For example, the histogram on the left side of Figure 2-1 shows some extreme values. To trim the upper and lower 5 percent, I add the trim argument to mean():

```
> mean(Horsepower.USA, trim =.05)
[1] 144.1818
```

The result is a bit lower than the untrimmed mean.

REMEMBER

What's the appropriate percentage for `trim`? That's up to you. It depends on what you're measuring, how extreme your scores can be, and how well you know the area you're studying. When you report a trimmed mean, let your audience know that you've done this and tell them the percentage you've trimmed.

In the upcoming section on the median, I show you another way to deal with extreme scores.

Medians: Caught in the Middle

The mean is a useful way to summarize a group of numbers. One drawback ("the flaw of averages") is that it's sensitive to extreme values. If one number is out of whack, the mean is out of whack, too. When that happens, the mean may not be a good representative of the group.

Here, for example, are the reading speeds (in words per minute) for a group of children:

56, 78, 45, 49, 55, 62

The mean is

```
> reading.speeds <- c(56, 78, 45, 49, 55, 62)
> mean(reading.speeds)
[1] 57.5
```

Suppose the child who reads at 78 words per minute leaves the group and an exceptionally fast reader replaces him. Her reading speed is a phenomenal 180 words per minute:

```
> reading.speeds.new <- replace(reading.speeds,reading.speeds == 78,180)
> reading.speeds.new
[1] 56 180 45 49 55 62
```

Now the mean is

```
> mean(reading.speeds.new)
[1] 74.5
```

The new average is misleading. Except for the new child, no one else in the group reads nearly that fast. In a case like this, it's a good idea to use a different measure of central tendency — the *median*.

Median is a fancy name for a simple concept: It's the middle value in a group of numbers. Arrange the numbers in order and the median is the value below which half the scores fall and above which half the scores fall:

```
> sort(reading.speeds)
[1] 45 49 55 56 62 78
> sort(reading.speeds.new)
[1] 45 49 55 56 62 180
```

In each case, the median is halfway between 55 and 56, or 55.5.

The Median in R: `median( )`

It's no big mystery how to use R to find the median:

```
> median(reading.speeds)
[1] 55.5
> median(reading.speeds.new)
[1] 55.5
```

With larger data sets, you might encounter replication of scores. In any case, the median is still the middle value. For example, here are the horsepowers for 4-cylinder cars in `Cars93`:

```
> Horsepower.Four <- with(Cars93, Horsepower[Cylinders == 4])
> sort(Horsepower.Four)
 [1] 63 74 81 81 82 82 85 90 90 92 92 92 92 92
[15] 93 96 100 100 100 102 103 105 110 110 110 110 110 110
[29] 110 114 115 124 127 128 130 130 130 134 135 138 140 140
[43] 140 141 150 155 160 164 208
```

You see quite a bit of duplication in these numbers — particularly around the middle. Count through the sorted values and you'll see that 24 scores are equal to or less than 110 and that 24 scores are greater than or equal to 110, which makes the median

```
> median(Horsepower.Four)
[1] 110
```

Statistics à la Mode

One more measure of central tendency, the *mode*, is important. It's the score that occurs most frequently in a group of scores.

Sometimes, the mode is the most best measure of central tendency to use. Imagine a small company that consists of 30 consultants and two high-ranking officers. Each consultant has an annual salary of $40,000. Each officer has an annual salary of $250,000. The mean salary in this company is $53,125.

Does the mean give you a clear picture of the company's salary structure? If you were looking for a job with that company, would the mean influence your expectations? You're probably better off if you consider the mode, which in this case is $40,000 (unless you happen to be high-priced executive talent!).

Nothing is complicated about finding the mode. Look at the scores find the one that occurs most frequently, and you've found the mode. Two scores tie for that honor? In that case, your set of scores has two modes. (The technical name is *bimodal.*)

Can you have more than two modes? Absolutely.

If every score occurs equally often, you have no mode.

The Mode in R

Base R does not provide a function for finding the mode. It does have a function called mode( ), but it's for something *way* different. Instead, you need a package called modeest in your library. (On the Packages tab, select Install and then, in the Install dialog box, type **modeest** in the Packages box and click Install. Then select its check box when it appears on the Packages tab.)

One function in the modeest package is called mfv( ) ("most frequent value"), and that's the one we need. Here's a vector with two modes (2 and 4):

```
> scores <- c(1,2,2,2,3,4,4,4,5,6)
> mfv(scores)
[1] 2 4
```

Chapter **3**

Deviating from the Average

Here's a well-known statistician joke: Three statisticians go deer hunting with bows and arrow. They spot a deer and take aim. One shoots and his arrow flies off ten feet to the left. The second shoots and his arrow goes ten feet to the right. The third statistician happily yells out, "We got him!"

Moral of the story: Calculating the mean is a great way to summarize a set of numbers, but the mean might mislead you. How? By not giving you all the information you typically need. If you rely only on the mean, you might miss something important about the set of numbers.

To avoid missing important information, another type of statistic is necessary — a statistic that measures variation. Think of *variation* as a kind of average of how much each number in a group of numbers differs from the group mean. Several statistics are available for measuring variation. They all work the same way: The larger the value of the statistic, the more the numbers differ from their mean. The smaller the value, the less they differ.

Measuring Variation

Suppose you measure the heights of a group of children and you find that their heights (in inches) are

48, 48, 48, 48, and 48

Then you measure another group and find that their heights are

50, 47, 52, 46, and 45

If you calculate the mean of each group, you'll find they're the same — 48 inches. Just looking at the numbers tells you the two groups of heights are different: The heights in the first group are all the same, and the heights in the second vary quite a bit.

Averaging squared deviations: Variance and how to calculate it

One way to show the dissimilarity between the two groups is to examine the deviations in each one. Think of a *deviation* as the difference between a score and the mean of all scores in a group.

Here's what I'm talking about. Table 3-1 shows the first group of heights and their deviations.

TABLE 3-1

The First Group of Heights and Their Deviations

Height	Height-Mean	Deviation
48	48-48	0
48	48-48	0
48	48-48	0
48	48-48	0
48	48-48	0

One way to proceed is to average the deviations. Clearly, the average of the numbers in the Deviation column is zero.

Table 3-2 shows the second group of heights and their deviations.

TABLE 3-2

The Second Group of Heights and Their Deviations

Height	Height-Mean	Deviation
50	50-48	2
47	47-48	–1
52	52-48	4
46	46-48	–2
45	45-48	–3

What about the average of the deviations in Table 5-2? That's . . . zero!

So now what?

Averaging the deviations doesn't help you see a difference between the two groups, because the average of deviations from the mean in any group of numbers is *always* zero. In fact, veteran statisticians will tell you that's a defining property of the mean.

The joker in the deck here is the negative numbers. How do statisticians deal with them?

The trick is to use something you might recall from algebra: A minus times a minus is a plus. Sound familiar?

So . . . does this mean that you multiply each deviation times itself and then average the results? Absolutely. Multiplying a deviation times itself is called *squaring a deviation*. The average of the squared deviations is so important that it has a special name: *variance*.

Table 3-3 shows the group of heights from Table 3-2, along with their deviations and squared deviations.

The variance — the average of the squared deviations for this group — is (4 + 1 + 16 + 4 + 9)/5 = 34/5 = 6.8. This, of course, is quite different from the first group, whose variance is zero.

To develop the variance formula for you and show you how all this works, I use symbols. X represents the Height heading in Column 1 of the table, and $\bar{X}$ represents the mean.

TABLE 3-3

The Second Group of Heights and Their Squared Deviations

Height	Height-Mean	Deviation	Squared Deviation
50	50-48	2	4
47	47-48	–1	1
52	52-48	4	16
46	46-48	–2	4
45	45-48	–3	9

A deviation is the result of subtracting the mean from each number, so

$$\left(X - \bar{X}\right)$$

symbolizes a deviation. How about multiplying a deviation by itself? That's

$$\left(X - \bar{X}\right)^2$$

To calculate variance, you square each deviation, add them up, and find the average of the squared deviations. If N represents the number of squared deviations you have (in this example, five), then the formula for calculating the variance is

$$\frac{\sum\left(X - \bar{X}\right)^2}{N}$$

Σ is the uppercase Greek letter *sigma,* and it means "the sum of."

What's the symbol for variance? As I mention in Chapter 1 of Book 1, Greek letters represent population parameters, and English letters represent sample statistics. Imagine that our little group of five numbers is an entire population. Does the Greek alphabet have a letter that corresponds to V in the same way that μ (the symbol for the population mean) corresponds to M?

Nope. Instead, you use the *lowercase* sigma! It looks like this: σ. And on top of that, because you're talking about squared quantities, the symbol for population variance is σ^2.

Bottom line: The formula for calculating population variance is

$$\sigma^2 = \frac{\sum\left(X - \bar{X}\right)^2}{N}$$

REMEMBER

A large value for the variance tells you that the numbers in a group vary greatly from their mean. A small value for the variance tells you that the numbers are similar to their mean.

Sample variance

The variance formula I show you in the preceding section is appropriate if the group of five measurements is a population. Does this mean that variance for a sample is different? It does, and here's why.

If your set of numbers is a sample drawn from a large population, your objective is most likely to use the variance of the sample to estimate the variance of the population.

The formula in the preceding section doesn't work as an estimate of the population variance. Although the mean calculated in the usual way is an accurate estimate of the population mean, that's not the case for the variance, for reasons far beyond the scope of this book.

REMEMBER

It's pretty easy to calculate an accurate estimate of the population variance. All you have to do is use $N-1$ in the denominator rather than N. (Again, for reasons way beyond this book's scope.)

And because you're working with a characteristic of a sample (rather than of a population), you use the English equivalent of the Greek letter — s rather than σ. This means that the formula for the sample variance (as an estimate of the population variance) is

$$s^2 = \frac{\sum \left(X - \bar{X} \right)^2}{N-1}$$

The value of s^2, given the squared deviations in the set of five numbers, is

$(4 + 1 + 16 + 4 + 9)/4 = 34/4 = 8.5$

So, if these numbers

50, 47, 52, 46, and 45

are an entire population, their variance is 6.8. If they're a sample drawn from a larger population, the best estimate of that population's variance is 8.5.

Deviating from the Average

Variance in R

Calculating variance in R is simplicity itself. You use the var() function. But which variance does it give you? The one with N in the denominator or the one with $N-1$? Let's find out:

```
> heights <- c(50, 47, 52, 46, 45)
> var(heights)
[1] 8.5
```

It calculates the estimated variance (with $N-1$ in the denominator). To calculate that first variance I showed you (with N in the denominator), I have to multiply this number by $(N-1)/N$. Using length() to calculate N, that's

```
> var(heights)*(length(heights)-1)/length(heights)
[1] 6.8
```

If I were going to work with this kind of variance frequently, I'd define a function var.p():

```
var.p = function(x){var(x)*(length(x)-1)/length(x)}
```

and here's how to use it:

```
> var.p(heights)
[1] 6.8
```

For reasons that will become clear later, I'd like you to think of the denominator of a variance estimate (like $N-1$) as *degrees of freedom*. Why? Stay tuned. (Chapter 4 of Book 3 reveals all!)

Back to the Roots: Standard Deviation

After you calculate the variance of a set of numbers, you have a value whose units are different from your original measurements. For example, if your original measurements are in inches, their variance is in *square* inches. This is because you square the deviations before you average them. So the variance in the five-score population in the preceding example is 6.8 square inches.

It might be hard to grasp what that means. Often, it's more intuitive if the variation statistic is in the same units as the original measurements. It's easy to turn variance into that kind of statistic. All you have to do is take the square root of the variance.

Like the variance, this square root is so important that it is has a special name: standard deviation.

Population standard deviation

The *standard deviation* of a population is the square root of the population variance. The symbol for the population standard deviation is σ (sigma). Its formula is

$$\sigma = \sqrt{\sigma^2} = \sqrt{\frac{\sum(X - \bar{X})^2}{N}}$$

For this five-score population of measurements (in inches)

50, 47, 52, 46, and 45

the population variance is 6.8 square inches, and the population standard deviation is 2.61 inches (rounded off).

Sample standard deviation

The standard deviation of a sample — an estimate of the standard deviation of a population — is the square root of the sample variance. Its symbol is *s* and its formula is

$$s = \sqrt{s^2} = \sqrt{\frac{\sum(X - \bar{X})^2}{N-1}}$$

For this sample of measurements (in inches)

50, 47, 52, 46, and 45

the estimated population variance is 8.5 square inches, and the estimated population standard deviation is 2.92 inches (rounded off).

Standard Deviation in R

As is the case with variance, using R to compute the standard deviation is *easy* — you use the sd() function. And like its variance counterpart, sd() calculates *s*, not σ:

```
> sd(heights)
[1] 2.915476
```

For σ — treating the five numbers as a self-contained population, in other words — you have to multiply the sd() result by the square root of $(N-1)/N$:

```
> sd(heights)*(sqrt((length(heights)-1)/length(heights)))
[1] 2.607681
```

Again, if you're going to use this one frequently, defining a function is a good idea:

```
sd.p=function(x){sd(x)*sqrt((length(x)-1)/length(x))}
```

And here's how you use this function:

```
> sd.p(heights)
[1] 2.607681
```

Conditions, conditions, conditions . . .

In Chapter 2 of Book 2, I point out that with larger data frames, you sometimes want to calculate statistics on cases (rows) that meet certain conditions rather than on all the cases.

As in Book 2, Chapter 1 and Book 2, Chapter 2, I use the Cars93 data frame for the discussion that follows. That data frame has data for a sample of 93 cars from 1993. You'll find it in the MASS package, so be sure you have the MASS package in your library. (Find MASS on the Packages tab and select its check box.)

I calculate the variance of the horsepowers of cars that originated in the US. Using the with() function I show you in Chapter 2 of Book 2, that's

```
> with(Cars93, var(Horsepower[Origin == "USA"]))
[1] 2965.319
```

How many of those cars are in this group?

```
> with(Cars93, length(Horsepower[Origin == "USA"]))
[1] 48
```

How about the non-USA cars?

```
> with(Cars93, var(Horsepower[Origin == "non-USA"]))
[1] 2537.283
> with(Cars93, length(Horsepower[Origin == "non-USA"]))
[1] 45
```

Can we compare those variances? Sure — but not until Chapter 3 of Book 3.

I'll leave it as an exercise for you to compute the standard deviations for the USA cars and for the non-USA cars.

Chapter **4**

Meeting Standards and Standings

I n my left hand I hold 100 Philippine pesos. In my right, I hold 1,000 Colombian pesos. Which is worth more? Both are called *pesos*, right? So shouldn't the 1,000 be greater than the 100? Not necessarily. *Peso* is just a coincidence of names. Each one comes from a different country, and each country has its own economy.

To compare the two amounts of money, you have to convert each currency into a standard unit. The most intuitive standard for US residents is our own currency. How much is each amount worth in dollars and cents? As I write this chapter, 100 Philippine pesos are worth $1.82. One thousand Colombian pesos are worth 24 cents.

So, when we compare numbers, context is important. To make valid comparisons across contexts, we often have to convert numbers into standard units. In this chapter, I show you how to use statistics to do just that. Standard units show you where a score stands in relation to other scores within a group. I also show you other ways to determine a score's standing within a group.

Catching Some Zs

A number in isolation doesn't provide much information. To fully understand what a number means, you have to take into account the process that produced it. To compare one number to another, the numbers have to be on the same scale.

When you're converting currency, it's easy to figure out a standard. When you convert temperatures from Fahrenheit to Celsius, or lengths from feet to meters, a formula guides you.

When it's not so clear-cut, you can use the mean and standard deviation to standardize scores that come from different processes. The idea is to take a set of scores and use its mean as a zero-point and its standard deviation as a unit of measure. Then you make comparisons: You calculate the deviation of each score from the mean and then you compare that deviation to the standard deviation. You're asking, "How big is a particular deviation relative to (something like) an average of all the deviations?"

To make a comparison, you divide the score's deviation by the standard deviation. This transforms the score into another kind of score. The transformed score is called a *standard score*, or a *z-score*.

The formula for this is

$$z = \frac{X - \bar{X}}{s}$$

if you're dealing with a sample, and it's

$$z = \frac{X - \mu}{\sigma}$$

if you're dealing with a population. In either case, x represents the score you're transforming into a z-score.

Characteristics of z-scores

A z-score can be positive, negative, or zero. A negative z-score represents a score that's less than the mean, and a positive z-score represents a score that's greater than the mean. When the score is equal to the mean, its z-score is zero.

When you calculate the z-score for every score in the set, the mean of the z-scores is 0, and the standard deviation of the z-scores is 1.

After you do this for several sets of scores, you can legitimately compare a score from one set to a score from another. If the two sets have different means and different standard deviations, comparing without standardizing is like comparing apples with kumquats.

In the examples that follow, I show you how to use z-scores to make comparisons.

Bonds versus the Bambino

Here's an important question that often comes up in the context of serious meta-physical discussions: Who is the greatest home run hitter of all time: Barry Bonds or Babe Ruth? Although this question is a difficult one to answer, one way to get your hands around it is to look at each player's best season and compare the two. Bonds hit 73 home runs in 2001, and Ruth hit 60 in 1927. On the surface, Bonds appears to be the more productive hitter.

The year 1927 was quite different from 2001, however. Baseball (and everything else) went through huge, long-overdue changes in the intervening years, and player statistics reflect those changes. A home run was harder to hit in the 1920s than in the 2000s. Still, 73 versus 60? Hmm. . . .

Standard scores can help decide whose best season was better. To standardize, I took the top 50 home run hitters of 1927 and the top 50 from 2001. I calculated the mean and standard deviation of each group and then turned Ruth's 60 and Bonds' 73 into z-scores.

The average from 1927 is 12.68 homers with a standard deviation of 10.49. The average from 2001 is 37.02 homers with a standard deviation of 9.64. Although the means differ greatly, the standard deviations are pretty close.

And the z-scores? Ruth's is

$$z = \frac{60 - 12.68}{10.49} = 4.51$$

Bonds' is

$$z = \frac{73 - 37.02}{9.64} = 3.73$$

The clear winner in the z-score best-season home run derby is Babe Ruth. Period.

Just to show you how times have changed, Lou Gehrig hit 47 home runs in 1927 (finishing second to Ruth) for a z-score of 3.27. In 2001, 47 home runs amounted to a z-score of 1.04.

Exam scores

Moving away from sports debates, one practical application of z-scores is the assignment of grades to exam scores. Based on percentage scoring, instructors traditionally evaluate a score of 90 points or higher (out of 100) as an A, 80–89 points as a B, 70–79 points as a C, 60–69 points as a D, and fewer than 60 points as an F. Then they average together scores from several exams to assign a course grade.

Is that fair? Just as a peso from the Philippines is worth more than a peso from Colombia, and a home run was harder to hit in 1927 than in 2001, is a "point" on one exam worth the same as a "point" on another? Like "pesos," isn't "points" just a coincidence?

Absolutely. A point on a difficult exam is, by definition, harder to come by than a point on an easy exam. Because points might not mean the same thing from one exam to another, the fairest thing to do is convert scores from each exam into z-scores before averaging them. That way, you're averaging numbers on a level playing field.

I do that in the courses I teach. I often find that a lower numerical score on one exam results in a higher z-score than a higher numerical score from another exam. For example, on an exam where the mean is 65 and the standard deviation is 12, a score of 71 results in a z-score of .5. On another exam, with a mean of 69 and a standard deviation of 14, a score of 75 is equivalent to a z-score of .429. (Yes, it's like Ruth's 60 home runs versus Bonds' 73.) The moral of the story: Numbers in isolation tell you very little. You have to understand the process that produces them.

Standard Scores in R

The R function for calculating standard scores is called scale(). Supply a vector of scores, and scale() returns a vector of z-scores along with, helpfully, the mean and the standard deviation.

To show scale() in action, I isolate a subset of the Cars93 data frame. (It's in the MASS package. On the Packages tab, select the check box next to MASS if it's deselected.)

Specifically, I create a vector of the horsepowers of 8-cylinder cars from the US:

```
> Horsepower.USA.Eight <- with(Cars93, Horsepower[Origin == "USA" & Cylinders
    == 8])
> Horsepower.USA.Eight
[1] 200 295 170 300 190 210
```

And now for the z-scores:

```
> scale(Horsepower.USA.Eight)
           [,1]
[1,] -0.4925263
[2,]  1.2089283
[3,] -1.0298278
[4,]  1.2984785
[5,] -0.6716268
[6,] -0.3134259
attr(,"scaled:center")
[1] 227.5
attr(,"scaled:scale")
[1] 55.83458
```

That last value is s, not σ. If you have to base your z-scores on σ, divide each element in the vector by the square root of $(N-1)/N$:

```
> N <- length(Horsepower.USA.Eight)
> scale(Horsepower.USA.Eight)/sqrt((N-1)/N)
           [,1]
[1,] -0.5395356
[2,]  1.3243146
[3,] -1.1281198
[4,]  1.4224120
[5,] -0.7357303
[6,] -0.3433408
attr(,"scaled:center")
[1] 227.5
attr(,"scaled:scale")
[1] 55.83458
```

Notice that scale() still returns s.

CACHING SOME ZS

Because negative z-scores might have connotations that are, well, negative, educators sometimes change the z-score when they evaluate students. In effect, they're hiding the z-score, but the concept is the same — standardization with the standard deviation as the unit of measure.

One popular transformation is called the T-score. The T-score eliminates negative scores because a set of T-scores has a mean of 50 and a standard deviation of 10. The idea is to give an exam, grade all the tests, and calculate the mean and standard deviation. Next, turn each score into a z-score. Then follow this formula:

$$T = (z)(10) + 50$$

People who use the T-score often like to round to the nearest whole number.

Here's how to transform the vector from the example into a set of T-scores:

```
T.Hp.USA.Eight <- round((10*scale(Horsepower.USA.Eight)+50),
    digits = 0)
```

The `digits=0` argument in the `round()` function rounds off the result to the nearest whole number.

SAT scores are another transformation of the z-score. (Some refer to the SAT as a C-score.) Under the old scoring system, the SAT has a mean of 500 and a standard deviation of 100. After the exams are graded, and their mean and standard deviation are calculated, each exam score becomes a z-score in the usual way. This formula converts the z-score into a SAT score:

$$SAT = (z)(100) + 50$$

Rounding to the nearest whole number is part of the procedure here, too.

The IQ score is still another transformed z. Its mean is 100, and its standard deviation is 15. What's the procedure for computing an IQ score? You guessed it. In a group of IQ scores, calculate the mean and standard deviation and then calculate the z-score. Then it's

$$IQ = (z)(15) + 100$$

As with the other two, IQ scores are rounded to the nearest whole number.

Where Do You Stand?

Standard scores show you how a score stands in relation to other scores in the same group. To do this, they use the standard deviation as a unit of measure.

If you don't want to use the standard deviation, you can show a score's relative standing in a simpler way. You can determine the score's rank within the group: In ascending order, the lowest score has a rank of 1, the second lowest has a rank of 2, and so on. In descending order, the highest score is ranked 1; the second highest, 2; and so on.

Ranking in R

Unsurprisingly, the rank() function ranks the scores in a vector. The default order is ascending:

```
> Horsepower.USA.Eight
[1] 200 295 170 300 190 210
> rank(Horsepower.USA.Eight)
[1] 3 5 1 6 2 4
```

For descending order, put a minus sign (–) in front of the vector name:

```
> rank(-Horsepower.USA.Eight)
[1] 4 2 6 1 5 3
```

Tied scores

R handles tied scores by including the optional ties.method argument in rank(). To show you how this works, I create a new vector that replaces the sixth value (210) in Horsepower.USA.Eight with 200:

```
> tied.Horsepower <- replace(Horsepower.USA.Eight,6,200)
> tied.Horsepower
[1] 200 295 170 300 190 200
```

One way to deal with tied scores is to give each tied score the average of the ranks they would have attained. So the two scores of 200 would have been ranked 3 and 4, and their average 3.5 is what this method assigns to both of them:

```
> rank(tied.Horsepower, ties.method = "average")
[1] 3.5 5.0 1.0 6.0 2.0 3.5
```

Another method assigns the minimum of the ranks:

```
> rank(tied.Horsepower, ties.method = "min")
[1] 3 5 1 6 2 3
```

And still another assigns the maximum of the ranks:

```
> rank(tied.Horsepower, ties.method = "max")
[1] 4 5 1 6 2 4
```

A couple of other methods are available. Type **?rank** into the console window for the details (which appear on the Help tab).

Nth smallest, Nth largest

You can turn the ranking process inside out by supplying a rank (like second-lowest) and asking which score has that rank. This procedure begins with the sort() function, which arranges the scores in increasing order:

```
> sort(Horsepower.USA.Eight)
[1] 170 190 200 210 295 300
```

For the second-lowest score, supply the index-value 2:

```
> sort(Horsepower.USA.Eight)[2]
[1] 190
```

How about from the other end? Start by assigning the length of the vector to *N*:

```
> N <- length(Horsepower.USA.Eight)
```

Then, to find the second-highest score, it's

```
> sort(Horsepower.USA.Eight)[N-1]
[1] 295
```

Percentiles

Closely related to rank is the *percentile*, which represents a score's standing in the group as the percent of scores below it. If you've taken standardized tests like the SAT, you've encountered percentiles. An SAT score in the 80th percentile is higher than 80 percent of the other SAT scores.

Sounds simple, doesn't it? Not so fast. *Percentile* can have a couple of definitions, and hence a couple of ways (or more) to calculate it. Some define percentile as "greater than" (as in the preceding paragraph), and some define percentile as "greater than or equal to." *Greater than* equates to *exclusive. Greater than or equal to* equates to *inclusive.*

The function `quantile()` calculates percentiles. If left to its own devices, it a) calculates the 0th, 25th, 50th, 75th, and 100th percentiles and b) calculates the percentiles in a manner that's consistent with *inclusive* and (if necessary) interpolates values for the percentiles.

I begin by sorting the `Horsepower.USA.Eight` vector so that you can see the scores in order and compare them with the percentiles:

```
> sort(Horsepower.USA.Eight)
[1] 170 190 200 210 295 300
```

And now the percentiles:

```
>   quantile(Horsepower.USA.Eight)
    0%     25%     50%     75%    100%
170.00 192.50 205.00 273.75 300.00
```

Notice that the 25th, 50th, and 75th percentiles are values that aren't in the vector.

To calculate percentiles consistent with *exclusive,* add the `type` argument and set it equal to 6:

```
> quantile(Horsepower.USA.Eight, type = 6)
    0%     25%     50%     75%    100%
170.00 185.00 205.00 296.25 300.00
```

The default `type` (the first type I showed you) is 7, by the way. Seven other types (ways of calculating percentiles) are available. To take a look at them, type **?quantile** into the Console window (and then read the documentation on the Help tab).

Moving forward, I use the default type for percentiles.

The 25th, 50th, 75th, and 100th percentiles are often used to summarize a group of scores. Because they divide a group of scores into fourths, they're called *quartiles.*

You're not stuck with quartiles, however. You can get `quantile()` to return any percentile. Suppose you want to find the 54th, 68th, and 91st percentiles. Include a vector of those numbers (expressed as proportions) and you're in business:

```
> quantile(Horsepower.USA.Eight, c(.54, .68, .91))
    54%    68%    91%
 207.00 244.00 297.75
```

Percent ranks

The `quantile()` function gives you the scores that correspond to given percentiles. You can also work in the reverse direction — find the percent ranks that correspond to given scores in a data set. For example, in `Horsepower.USA.Eight`, 170 is lowest in the list of six, so its rank is 1 and its percent rank is 1/6, or 16.67%.

Base R doesn't provide a function for this, but it's easy enough to create one:

```
percent.ranks <- function(x){round((rank(x)/length(x))*100, digits = 2)}
```

The `round()` function with `digits = 2` rounds the results to two decimal places.

Applying this function returns the percent ranks of the values in `Horsepower. USA.Eight`:

```
> percent.ranks(Horsepower.USA.Eight)
[1]  50.00  83.33  16.67 100.00  33.33  66.67
```

A NEAT TRICK

Sometimes, you might just want to know the percent rank of a single score in a set of scores — even if that score isn't in the data set. For example, what would the percent rank of 273 be in `Horsepower.USA.Eight`?

To answer this question, you can harness `mean()`. Using this function along with logical operators yields interesting results. Here's what I mean:

```
xx <- c(15,20,25,30,35,40,45,50)
```

Here's a result you'd expect:

```
> mean(xx)
[1] 32.5
```

But here's one you might not:

```
> mean(xx > 15)
[1] 0.875
```

The result is the proportion of scores in xx that are greater than 15.

Here are a few more:

```
> mean(xx < 25)
[1] 0.25
> mean(xx <= 25)
[1] 0.375
> mean(xx <= 28)
[1] 0.375
```

That <= operator, of course, means "less than or equal to," so that last one gives the proportion of scores in xx that are less than or equal to 28.

Are you catching my drift? To find the percent rank of a score (or a potential score) in a vector like Horsepower.USA.Eight, it's

```
> mean(Horsepower.USA.Eight <= 273)*100
[1] 66.66667
```

Summarizing

In addition to the functions for calculating percentiles and ranks, R provides a couple of functions that quickly summarize data and do a lot of the work I discuss in this chapter.

One is called fivenum(). This function, unsurprisingly, yields five numbers. They're the five numbers that John Tukey used to summarize a data set. Then he used those numbers in his box plots (for more on Tukey and his box plots, see Book 2, Chapter 1):

```
> fivenum(Horsepower.USA.Eight)
[1] 170 190 205 295 300
```

From left to right, that's the minimum, lower hinge, median, upper hinge, and maximum. Remember the quantile() function and the nine available ways (types) to calculate quantiles? This function's results are what type = 2 yields in quantile().

Another function, summary(), is more widely used:

```
> summary(Horsepower.USA.Eight)
  Min. 1st Qu.  Median   Mean 3rd Qu.    Max.
 170.0   192.5   205.0  227.5   273.8   300.0
```

It provides the mean along with the quantiles (as the default type in quantile() calculates them).

The function summary() is a versatile one. You can use it to summarize a wide variety of objects, and the results can look very different from object to object. I use it quite a bit in upcoming chapters.

Chapter **5**

Summarizing It All

The measures of central tendency and variability I discuss in previous chapters aren't the only ways to summarize a set of scores. These measures are a subset of descriptive statistics. Some descriptive statistics — like maximum, minimum, and range — are easy to understand. Some — like skewness and kurtosis — are not.

This chapter covers descriptive statistics, and shows you how to calculate them in R.

How Many?

Perhaps the fundamental descriptive statistic is the number of scores in a set of data. In previous chapters, I work with length(), the R function that calculates this number. As in those chapters, I work with the Cars93 data frame, which is in the MASS package. (If it's unchecked, select the check box next to MASS on the Packages tab.)

Cars93 holds data on 27 variables for 93 cars available in 1993. What happens when I apply length() to the data frame?

```
> length(Cars93)
[1] 27
```

So `length()` returns the number of variables in the data frame. The function `ncol()` does the same thing:

```
> ncol(Cars93)
[1] 27
```

I already know the number of cases (rows) in the data frame, but if I had to find that number, `nrow()` would get it done:

```
> nrow(Cars93)
[1] 93
```

If I want to know how many cases in the data frame meet a particular condition — like how many cars originated in the USA — I have to take into account the way R treats conditions: R attaches the label TRUE to cases that meet a condition and attaches FALSE to cases that don't. Also, R assigns the value 1 to TRUE and 0 to FALSE.

To count the number of USA-originated cars, then, I state the condition and then add up all the 1's:

```
> sum(Cars93$Origin == "USA")
[1] 48
```

To count the number of non-USA cars in the data frame, I can change the condition to "non-USA", of course, or I can use the not-equal-to operator:

```
> sum(Cars93$Origin != "USA")
[1] 45
```

More complex conditions are possible. For the number of 4-cylinder USA cars:

```
> sum(Cars93$Origin == "USA" & Cars93$Cylinders == 4)
[1] 22
```

Or, if you prefer no $-signs:

```
> with(Cars93, sum(Origin == "USA" & Cylinders == 4))
[1] 22
```

To calculate the number of elements in a vector, `length()`, as I show you earlier, is the function to use. Here is a vector of horsepower values for 4-cylinder US cars:

```
> Horsepower.USA.Four <- with(Cars93, Horsepower[Origin == "USA"
  & Cylinders == 4])
```

and here's the number of horsepower values in that vector:

```
> length(Horsepower.USA.Four)
[1] 22
```

The High and the Low

Two descriptive statistics that need no introduction are the maximum and minimum value in a set of scores:

```
> max(Horsepower.USA.Four)
[1] 155
> min(Horsepower.USA.Four)
[1] 63
```

If you happen to need both values at the same time:

```
> range(Horsepower.USA.Four)
[1]   63 155
```

Living in the Moments

In statistics, *moments* are quantities related to the shape of a set of numbers. By "shape of a set of numbers," I mean "what a histogram based on the numbers looks like."

A *raw moment* of order k is the average of all numbers in the set, with each number raised to the kth power before you average it. So the *first* raw moment is the arithmetic mean. The *second* raw moment is the average of the squared scores. The *third* raw moment is the average of the cubed scores, and so on.

A *central moment* is based on the average of *deviations* of numbers from their mean. (Beginning to sound vaguely familiar?) If you square the deviations before you average them, you have the *second* central moment. If you cube the deviations before you average them, that's the *third* central moment. Raise each one to the fourth power before you average them, and you have the *fourth* central moment. I could go on and on, but you get the idea.

Two quick questions:

>> What's the first central moment?

>> By what other name do we know the second central moment?

Two quick answers:

>> Zero

>> Population variance

Check out Chapter 3 of Book 2 if you don't believe me.

A teachable moment

Before I proceed, I think it's a good idea to translate into R everything I say in this main section, "Living in the Moments." That way, when you get to the next R package to install (which calculates moments), you'll know what's going on behind the scenes.

I create a function for calculating a central moment of a vector:

```
cen.mom <-function(x,y){mean((x - mean(x))^y)}
```

The first argument, x, is the vector. The second argument, y, is the order (second, third, or fourth, for example).

Here's a vector to try it out on:

```
Horsepower.USA <- with(Cars93, Horsepower[Origin == "USA"])
```

And here are the second, third, and fourth central moments:

```
> cen.mom(Horsepower.USA,2)
[1] 2903.541
> cen.mom(Horsepower.USA,3)
[1] 177269.5
> cen.mom(Horsepower.USA,4)
[1] 37127741
```

Back to descriptives

What does all this have to do with descriptive statistics? As I said, well, a moment ago, think of a histogram based on a set of numbers. The first raw moment (the mean) locates the *center* of the histogram. The second central moment indicates the *spread* of the histogram. The third central moment is involved in the *symmetry* of the histogram, which is called *skewness*. The fourth central moment figures into how fat or thin the tails (extreme ends) of the histogram are. This is called *kurtosis*. Getting into moments of higher order than that is way beyond where we are.

But let's get into symmetry and "tailedness."

Skewness

Figure 5-1 shows three histograms. The first is symmetric; the other two are not. The symmetry and the asymmetry are reflected in the skewness statistic.

For the symmetric histogram, the skewness is 0. For the second histogram — the one that tails off to the right — the value of the skewness statistic is *positive*. It's also said to be "skewed to the right." For the third histogram (which tails off to the left), the value of the skewness statistic is *negative*. It's also said to be "skewed to the left."

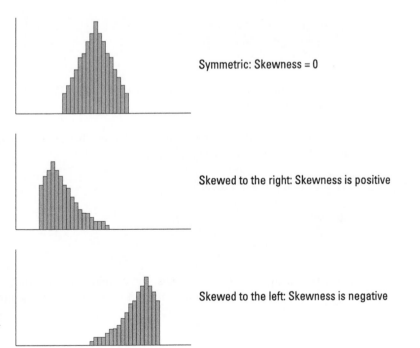

Symmetric: Skewness = 0

Skewed to the right: Skewness is positive

Skewed to the left: Skewness is negative

FIGURE 5-1: Three histograms, showing three kinds of skewness.

Now for a formula. I'll let M_k represent the kth central moment. To calculate skewness, it's

$$skewness = \frac{M_3}{M_2^{3/2}}$$

In English, the skewness of a set of numbers is the third central moment divided by the second central moment raised to the three-halves power. In R, it's easier done than said:

```
> cen.mom(Horsepower.USA,3)/cen.mom(Horsepower.USA,2)^1.5
[1] 1.133031
```

With the moments package, it's easier still. On the Packages tab, click Install, type **moments** into the Install Packages dialog box, and click Install. Then, on the Packages tab, select the check box next to moments.

Here's its skewness() function in action:

```
> skewness(Horsepower.USA)
[1] 1.133031
```

So the skew is positive. How does that compare with the horsepower for non-USA cars?

```
> Horsepower.NonUSA <- with(Cars93, Horsepower[Origin == "non-USA"])>
    skewness(Horsepower.NonUSA)
[1] 0.642995
```

The skew is more positive for USA cars than for non-USA cars. What do the two histograms look like?

I produced them side-by-side in Figure 2-1. (See Chapter 2 of Book 2.) For convenience, I show them here as Figure 5-2.

The code that produces them is

```
ggplot(Cars93, aes(x=Horsepower)) +
  geom_histogram(color="black", fill="white",binwidth = 10)+
  facet_wrap(~Origin)
```

Consistent with the skewness values, the histograms show that in the USA cars, the scores are more bunched up on the left than they are in the non-USA cars.

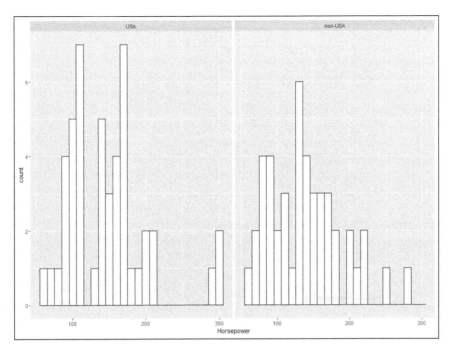

FIGURE 5-2:
Horsepower
histograms for
USA cars and
non-USA cars.

It's sometimes easier to see trends in a density plot than in a histogram. A *density plot* shows the proportions of scores between a given lower boundary and a given upper boundary (like the proportion of cars with horsepower between 100 and 140). I discuss density in more detail in Chapter 6 of Book 2.

Changing one line of code produces the density plots:

```
ggplot(Cars93, aes(x=Horsepower)) +
    geom_density() +
    facet_wrap(~Origin)
```

Figure 5-3 shows the two density plots.

With the density plots, it seems to be easier (for me, anyway) to see the more left-ward tilt (and hence more positive skew) in the plot on the left.

Kurtosis

Figure 5-4 shows two histograms. The first has fatter tails than the second. The first is said to be *leptokurtic.* The second is *platykurtic.* The kurtosis for the first histogram is greater than for the second.

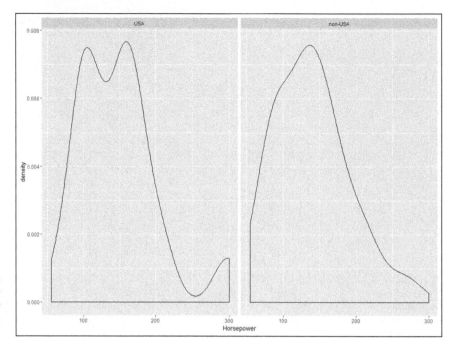

FIGURE 5-3:
Horsepower
density plots for
USA cars and
non-USA cars.

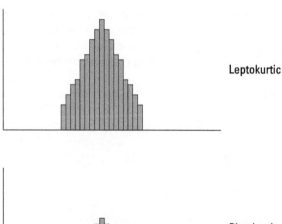

Leptokurtic

Platykurtic

FIGURE 5-4:
Two histograms,
showing two
kinds of kurtosis.

The formula for kurtosis is

$$kurtosis = \frac{M_4}{M_2^2}$$

where M_4 is the fourth central moment and M_2 is the second central moment. So kurtosis is the fourth central moment divided by the square of the second central moment.

TIP

Many statisticians subtract 3 from the result of the kurtosis formula. They refer to that value as *excess kurtosis*. By *excess*, they mean kurtosis that differs from the kurtosis of something called the *standard normal distribution*, which I discuss in Chapter 6 of Book 2. Because of the subtraction, excess kurtosis can be negative. Why does 3 represent the kurtosis of the standard normal distribution? Don't ask.

Using the function I defined earlier, the kurtosis of horsepower for USA cars is

```
> cen.mom(Horsepower.USA,4)/cen.mom(Horsepower.USA,2)^2
[1] 4.403952
```

Of course, the kurtosis() function in the moments package makes this a snap:

```
> kurtosis(Horsepower.USA)
[1] 4.403952
```

The fatter tail in the left-side density plot shown in Figure 5-3 suggests that the USA cars have a higher kurtosis than the non-USA cars. Is this true?

```
> kurtosis(Horsepower.NonUSA)
[1] 3.097339
```

Yes, it is!

TIP

In addition to skewness() and kurtosis(), the moments package provides a function called moment() that does everything cen.mom() does and a bit more. I just thought it would be a good idea to show you a user-defined function that illustrates what goes into calculating a central moment. Was I being momentous — or did I just seize the moment? (Okay. I'll stop.)

Tuning in the Frequency

A good way of exploring data is to find out the frequencies of occurrence for each category of a nominal variable, and for each interval of a numerical variable.

Nominal variables: table() et al.

For nominal variables, like the type of automobile in `Cars93`, the easiest way to get the frequencies is the `table()` function I use earlier:

```
> car.types <-table(Cars93$Type)
> car.types

Compact  Large Midsize  Small Sporty    Van
     16     11      22     21     14      9
```

Another function, `prop.table()`, expresses these frequencies as proportions of the whole amount:

```
> prop.table(car.types)

   Compact       Large     Midsize       Small      Sporty         Van
0.17204301  0.11827957  0.23655914  0.22580645  0.15053763  0.09677419
```

The values appear out of whack because the page isn't as wide as the Console window. If I round off the proportions to two decimal places, the output looks much better on the page:

```
> round(prop.table(car.types),2)

Compact  Large Midsize  Small Sporty    Van
   0.17   0.12    0.24   0.23   0.15   0.10
```

Another function, `margin.table()`, adds up the frequencies:

```
> margin.table(car.types)
[1] 93
```

Numerical variables: hist()

Tabulating frequencies for intervals of numerical data is part and parcel of creating histograms. (See Chapter 1 of Book 2.) To create a table of frequencies, use the graphic function `hist()`, which produces a list of components when the `plot` argument is `FALSE`:

```
> prices <- hist(Cars93$Price, plot=F, breaks=5)
> prices
$breaks
[1]  0 10 20 30 40 50 60 70
```

```
$counts
[1] 12 50 19  9  2  0  1

$density
[1] 0.012903226 0.053763441 0.020430108 0.009677419 0.002150538 0.000000000
[7] 0.001075269

$mids
[1]  5 15 25 35 45 55 65

$xname
[1] "Cars93$Price"

$equidist
[1] TRUE
attr(,"class")
[1] "histogram"
```

(In Cars93, remember, each price is in thousands of dollars.)

Although I specified five breaks, hist() uses a number of breaks that makes everything look prettier. From here, I can use mids (the interval-midpoints) and counts to make a matrix of the frequencies, and then a data frame:

```
> prices.matrix <- matrix(c(prices$mids,prices$counts), ncol = 2)
> prices.frame <- data.frame(prices.matrix)
> colnames(prices.frame) <- c("Price Midpoint (X $1,000)","Frequency")
> prices.frame
  Price Midpoint (X $1,000) Frequency
1                         5        12
2                        15        50
3                        25        19
4                        35         9
5                        45         2
6                        55         0
7                        65         1
```

Cumulative frequency

Another way of looking at frequencies is to examine *cumulative frequencies*: Each interval's cumulative frequency is the sum of its own frequency and all the frequencies in the preceding intervals.

The cumsum( ) function does the arithmetic on the vector of frequencies:

```
> prices$counts
[1] 12 50 19  9  2  0  1
> cumsum(prices$counts)
[1] 12 62 81 90 92 92 93
```

To plot a cumulative frequency histogram, I substitute the cumulative frequencies vector for the original one:

```
> prices$counts <- cumsum(prices$counts)
```

and then apply plot( ):

```
> plot(prices, main = "Cumulative Histogram", xlab = "Price", ylab = "Cumulative
  Frequency")
```

The result is shown in Figure 5-5.

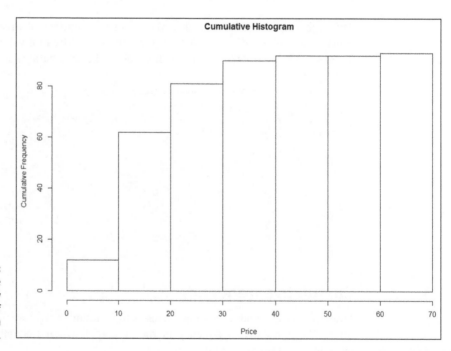

FIGURE 5-5:
Cumulative
frequency
histogram of
the price data in
Cars93.

Step by step: The empirical cumulative distribution function

The *empirical cumulative distribution function* (ecdf) is closely related to cumulative frequency. Rather than show the frequency in an interval, however, the ecdf shows the proportion of scores that are less than or equal to each score. If this sounds familiar, it's probably because I tell you about percentiles in Chapter 4 of Book 2.

In base R, it's easy to plot the ecdf:

```
> plot(ecdf(Cars93$Price), xlab = "Price", ylab = "Fn(Price)")
```

This produces what you see in Figure 5-6.

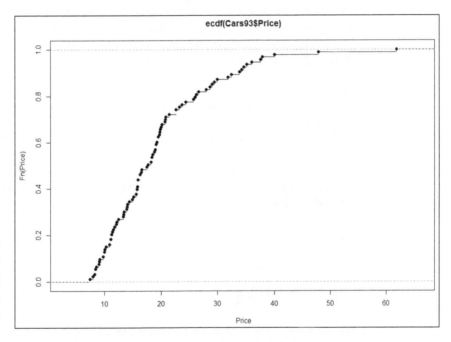

FIGURE 5-6: Empirical cumulative distribution function for the price data in Cars93.

The uppercase *F* in the *Fn* you see on the *y*-axis is a notational convention for a cumulative distribution. The *Fn* means, in effect, "cumulative function," as opposed to *f* or *fn*, which just means "function." (The *y*-axis label could also be "Percentile(Price)".)

Look closely at the plot. When consecutive points are far apart (like the two in the upper right), you can see a horizontal line extending rightward out of a point. (A line extends out of every point, but the lines aren't visible when the points are bunched up.) Think of this line as a step, and then the next dot is a step higher than the previous one. How much higher? That would be 1/*N*, where *N* is the number of scores in the sample. For `Cars93`, that would be 1/93, which rounds off to .011. (Now reconsider the title of this subsection. See what I did there?)

Why is this called an *empirical* cumulative distribution function? Something that's empirical is based on observations, like sample data. Is it possible to have a non-empirical cumulative distribution function (cdf)? Yes — and that's the cdf of the population that the sample comes from. (See Chapter 1 of Book 1.) One important use of the ecdf is as a tool for estimating the population cdf.

So the plotted ecdf is an estimate of the cdf for the population, and the estimate is based on the sample data. To create an estimate, we assign a probability to each point and then add up the probabilities point-by-point, from the minimum value to the maximum value. This strategy produces the cumulative probability for each point. The probability assigned to a sample value is the estimate of the proportion of times that value occurs in the population. What is the estimate? That's the aforementioned 1/*N* for each point — .011, for this sample. For any given value, that might not be the exact proportion in the population. It's just the best estimate from the sample.

I prefer to use `ggplot()` to visualize the ecdf. Because I base the plot on a vector (`Cars93$Price`), the data source is `NULL`:

```
ggplot(NULL, aes(x=Cars93$Price))
```

To emphasize the step-by-step nature of this function, the plot will consist of steps, so the geom is `geom_step`. The statistic that locates each step on the plot is the ecdf, so that's

```
geom_step(stat="ecdf")
```

and I'll label the axes this way:

```
labs(x= "Price X $1,000",y = "Fn(Price)")
```

Putting those three lines of code together, like this:

```
ggplot(NULL, aes(x=Cars93$Price)) +
  geom_step(stat="ecdf") +
    labs(x= "Price X $1,000",y = "Fn(Price)")
```

gives you what you see in Figure 5-7.

To put a little pizzazz in the graph, I add a dashed vertical line at each quartile. Before I add the geom for a vertical line, I put the quartile information in a vector:

```
price.q <-quantile(Cars93$Price)
```

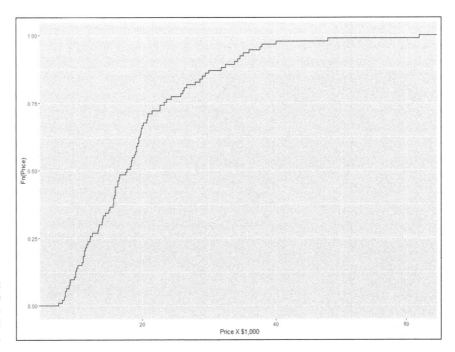

FIGURE 5-7:
The ecdf for the price data in Cars93, plotted with ggplot().

And now

```
geom_vline(aes(xintercept=price.q),linetype = "dashed")
```

adds the vertical lines. The aesthetic mapping sets the *x*-intercept of each line at a quartile value.

So these lines of code

```
ggplot(NULL, aes(x=Cars93$Price)) +
  geom_step(stat="ecdf") +
  labs(x= "Price X $1,000",y = "Fn(Price)") +
  geom_vline(aes(xintercept=price.q),linetype = "dashed")
```

result in Figure 5-8.

A nice finishing touch is to put the quartile values on the *x*-axis. The function scale_x_continuous() gets that done. It uses one argument called breaks (which sets the location of values to put on the axis) and another called labels (which puts the values on those locations). Here's where that price.q vector comes in handy:

```
scale_x_continuous(breaks = price.q,labels = price.q)
```

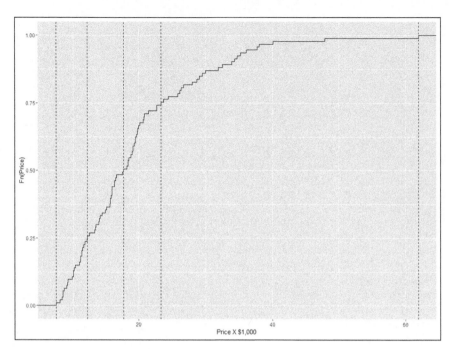

FIGURE 5-8:
The ecdf for price data, with a dashed vertical line at each quartile.

And here's the R code that creates what you see in Figure 5-9:

```
ggplot(NULL, aes(x=Cars93$Price)) +
  geom_step(stat="ecdf") +
  labs(x= "Price X $1,000",y = "Fn(Price)") +
  geom_vline(aes(xintercept=price.q),linetype = "dashed")+
  scale_x_continuous(breaks = price.q,labels = price.q)
```

Numerical variables: stem()

Boxplot creator John Tukey popularized the *stem-and-leaf plot* as a way to quickly visualize a distribution of numbers. It's not a plot in the usual sense of a graph in the Plot window. Instead, it's an arrangement of numbers in the Console window. With each score rounded off to the nearest whole number, each "leaf" is a score's rightmost digit. Each "stem" consists of all the other digits.

An example will help. Here are the prices of the cars in Cars93, arranged in ascending order and rounded off to the nearest whole number (remember, each price is in thousands of dollars):

```
> rounded <- (round(sort(Cars93$Price),0))
```

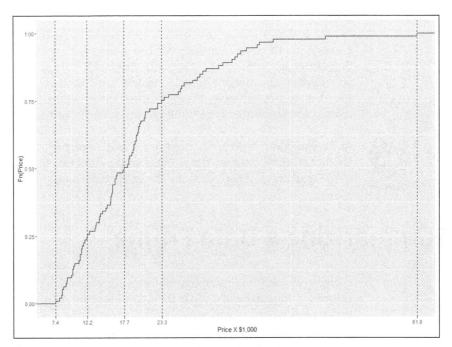

FIGURE 5-9:
The ecdf for
price data, with
quartile values on
the x-axis.

I use cat() to display the rounded values on this page. (Otherwise, it would look like a mess.) The value of its fill argument limits the number of characters (including spaces) on each line:

```
> cat(rounded, fill = 50)
7 8 8 8 8 9 9 9 9 10 10 10 10 10 11 11 11 11 11
11 12 12 12 12 12 13 13 14 14 14 14 14 15 15 16
16 16 16 16 16 16 16 16 16 17 18 18 18 18 18 18
19 19 19 19 19 20 20 20 20 20 20 20 21 21 21 22
23 23 23 24 24 26 26 26 27 28 29 29 30 30 32 32
34 34 35 35 36 38 38 40 48 62
```

The stem() function produces a stem-and-leaf plot of these values:

```
> stem(Cars93$Price)

  The decimal point is 1 digit(s) to the right of the |

  0 | 788889999
  1 | 0000011111122223334444455666666666677788888999999
  2 | 0000000011112333446667899
  3 | 00234455688
  4 | 08
  5 |
  6 | 2
```

In each row, the number to the left of the vertical bar is the stem. The remaining numbers are the leaves for that row. The message about the decimal point means "multiply each stem by 10." Then add each leaf to that stem. So the bottom row tells you that one rounded score in the data is 62. The next row up reveals that no rounded score is between 50 and 59. The row above that one indicates that one score is 40 and another is 48. I'll leave it to you to figure out (and verify) the rest.

WARNING

As I reviewed the leaves, I noticed that the stem plot shows one score of 32 and another of 33. By contrast, the rounded scores show two scores of 32 and no score of 33. Apparently, stem( ) rounds differently than round( ) does.

Summarizing a Data Frame

If you're looking for descriptive statistics for the variables in a data frame, the summary( ) function will do that for you. I illustrate with a subset of the Cars93 data frame:

```
> autos <- subset(Cars93, select = c(MPG.city,Type, Cylinders, Price,
    Horsepower))
> summary(autos)
   MPG.city            Type      Cylinders        Price
 Min.   :15.00   Compact:16   3     : 3   Min.    : 7.40
 1st Qu.:18.00   Large  :11   4     :49   1st Qu.:12.20
 Median :21.00   Midsize:22   5     : 2   Median :17.70
 Mean   :22.37   Small  :21   6     :31   Mean   :19.51
 3rd Qu.:25.00   Sporty :14   8     : 7   3rd Qu.:23.30
 Max.   :46.00   Van    : 9   rotary: 1   Max.   :61.90
   Horsepower
 Min.   : 55.0
 1st Qu.:103.0
 Median :140.0
 Mean   :143.8
 3rd Qu.:170.0
 Max.   :300.0
```

Notice the maxima, minima, and quartiles for the numerical variables and the frequency tables for Type and for Cylinders.

Two functions from the Hmisc package also summarize data frames. To use these functions, you need Hmisc in your library. (On the Packages tab, click Install and type **Hmisc** into the Packages box in the Install dialog box. Then click Install, and after installing select the check box next to Hmisc on the Packages tab.)

One function, describe(), provides output that's a bit more extensive than what you get from summary(). (See Figure 5-10.)

```
> describe(autos)
autos

 5  variables      93  observations
--------------------------------------------------------------------------------
MPG.city
      n  missing distinct     Info     Mean      Gmd      .05      .10      .25      .50      .75      .90      .95
     93        0       21    0.993    22.37      5.8     16.6     17.0     18.0     21.0     25.0     29.0     31.4

lowest : 15 16 17 18 19, highest: 32 33 39 42 46
--------------------------------------------------------------------------------
Type
      n  missing distinct
     93        0        6

lowest : Compact Large  Midsize Small   Sporty , highest: Large   Midsize Small    Sporty  Van

value        Compact    Large Midsize    Small   Sporty      van
Frequency         16       11      22       21       14        9
Proportion     0.172    0.118   0.237    0.226    0.151    0.097
--------------------------------------------------------------------------------
Cylinders
      n  missing distinct
     93        0        6

lowest : 3       4       5       6       8   , highest: 4      5       6       8      rotary

value          3        4        5        6        8 rotary
Frequency      3       49        2       31        7        1
Proportion 0.032    0.527    0.022    0.333    0.075    0.011
--------------------------------------------------------------------------------
Price
      n  missing distinct     Info     Mean      Gmd      .05      .10      .25      .50      .75      .90      .95
     93        0       81        1    19.51    10.17     8.52     9.84    12.20    17.70    23.30    33.62    36.74

lowest :  7.4  8.0  8.3  8.4  8.6, highest: 37.7 38.0 40.1 47.9 61.9
--------------------------------------------------------------------------------
Horsepower
      n  missing distinct     Info     Mean      Gmd      .05      .10      .25      .50      .75      .90      .95
     93        0       57    0.999    143.8    57.44     78.2     86.0    103.0    140.0    170.0    206.8    237.0

lowest :  55  63  70  73  74, highest: 225 255 278 295 300
--------------------------------------------------------------------------------
```

FIGURE 5-10:
Chart created by
datadensity
(autos).

A value labeled Info appears in the summaries of the numerical variables. That value is related to the number of tied scores — the greater the number of ties, the lower the value of Info. (The calculation of the value is fairly complicated.)

Another Hmisc function, datadensity(), gives graphical summaries, as in Figure 5-11:

```
> datadensity(autos)
```

WARNING

If you plan to use the datadensity() function, arrange for the first data frame variable to be numerical. If the first variable is categorical (and thus appears at the top of the chart), longer bars in its plot are cut off at the top.

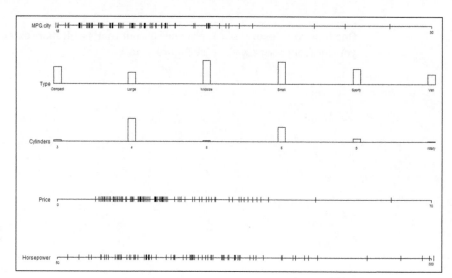

FIGURE 5-11:
Chart created by
datadensity
(autos).

Chapter **6**

What's Normal?

O ne of the main jobs of a statistician is to estimate characteristics of a population. The job becomes easier if the statistician can make some assumptions about the populations they study.

Here's an assumption that works over and over again: A specific attribute, ability, or trait is distributed throughout a population so that (1) most people have an average or near-average amount of the attribute and (2) progressively fewer people have increasingly extreme amounts of the attribute. In this chapter, I discuss this assumption and its implications for statistics. I also discuss R functions related to this assumption.

Hitting the Curve

Attributes in the physical world, like length or weight, are all about objects we can see and touch. It's not that easy in the world of social scientists, statisticians, market researchers, and businesspeople. They have to be creative when they measure traits they can't put their arms around — like "intelligence," "musical ability", or "willingness to buy a new product."

That assumption I just mentioned — most people are around the average, and progressively fewer people are toward the extremes — seems to work out well for those intangible traits. Because this happens so often, it's become an assumption about how most traits are distributed.

It's possible to capture this assumption in a graphical way. Figure 6-1 shows the well-known *bell curve*, which describes the distribution of a wide variety of attributes. The horizontal axis represents measurements of the ability under consideration. A vertical line drawn down the center of the curve would correspond to the average of the measurements.

Assuming that it's possible to measure a trait like intelligence and assuming that this curve represents the distribution of intelligence in the population, we can say this: The bell curve shows that most people have about average intelligence, very few have very little intelligence, and very few are geniuses. That seems to fit nicely with what we know about people, doesn't it?

Digging deeper

On the horizontal axis of Figure 6-1, you see x, and on the vertical axis, $f(x)$. What do these symbols mean? The horizontal axis, as I mention, represents measurements, so think of each measurement as an x.

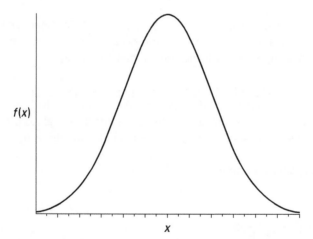

$f(x)$

x

FIGURE 6-1:
The bell curve.

The explanation of $f(x)$ is a little more involved. A mathematical relationship between x and $f(x)$ creates the bell curve and enables us to visualize it. The relationship is rather complex, and I won't burden you with it right now. (I discuss it a little later in this chapter.) Just understand that $f(x)$ represents the height of the curve for a specified value of x. This means that you supply a value for x (and for a couple of other things), and then that complex relationship returns a value of $f(x)$.

Let's get into specifics. The formal name for the bell curve is *normal distribution*. The term $f(x)$ is called *probability density*, so a normal distribution is an example of a *probability density function*. Rather than give you a technical definition of probability density, I ask you to think of probability density as a concept that allows you to think about area under the curve as probability. Probability of . . . what? That explanation is coming up in the next subsection.

Parameters of a normal distribution

You often hear people talk about "*the* normal distribution." That's a misnomer. It's really a family of distributions. The members of the family differ from one another in terms of two parameters — yes, *parameters,* because I'm talking about populations. Those two parameters are the mean (μ) and the standard deviation (σ). The *mean* tells you where the center of the distribution is, and the *standard deviation* tells you how spread out the distribution is around the mean. The mean is in the middle of the distribution. Every member of the normal distribution family is *symmetric:* The left side of the distribution is a mirror image of the right. (If you checked out Chapter 3 of Book 2, you'll remember skewness. *Symmetric* means that skewness of a normal distribution is zero.)

How? This brings me back to probability. You can find some useful probabilities if you can do these four things:

>> Lay out a line that represents the scale of the attribute you're measuring (the *x*-axis, in other words).

>> Indicate on the line where the mean of the measurements is.

>> Know the standard deviation.

>> Know (or assume) that the attribute is normally distributed throughout the population.

I'll work with IQ scores to show you what I mean. Scores on the IQ test follow a normal distribution. The mean of the distribution of these scores is 100, and the standard deviation is 15. Figure 6-2 shows this distribution.

TECHNICAL
STUFF

You might have read elsewhere that the standard deviation for IQ is 16 rather than 15. That's the case for the Stanford-Binet version of the IQ test. For other versions, the standard deviation is 15.

As Figure 6-2 shows, I've laid out a line for the IQ scale (the *x*-axis). Each point on the line represents an IQ score. With the mean (100) as the reference point, I've marked off every 15 points (the standard deviation). I've drawn a dashed line from the mean up to *f(100)* (the height of the distribution where x = 100) and a dashed line from each standard deviation point.

What's Normal?

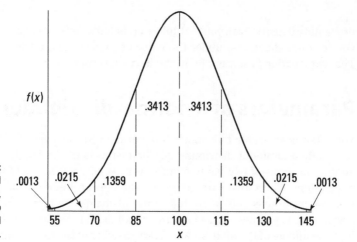

FIGURE 6-2:
The normal
distribution of IQ,
divided into
standard
deviations.

.3413 .3413

f(x)

.0013 .0215 .1359 .1359 .0215 .0013

55   70   85   100   115   130   145

x

The figure also shows the proportion of the area bounded by the curve and the horizontal axis, and by successive pairs of standard deviations. It also shows the proportion beyond three standard deviations on either side (55 and 145). Note that the curve never touches the horizontal. It gets closer and closer, but it never touches. (Mathematicians say the curve is *asymptotic* to the horizontal.)

So, between the mean and one standard deviation — between 100 and 115 — are .3413 (or 34.13 percent) of the scores in the population. Here's another way to say this: The probability that an IQ score is between 100 and 115 is .3413. At the extremes, in the tails of the distribution, .0013 (.13 percent) of the scores are on each side (less than 55 or greater than 145).

REMEMBER

The proportions in Figure 6-2 hold for every member of the normal distribution family, not just for IQ scores. For example, in the sidebar "Caching some zs" in Chapter 4 of Book 2, I mention SAT scores, which (under the old scoring system) have a mean of 500 and a standard deviation of 100. They're normally distributed, too. That means 34.13 percent of SAT scores are between 500 and 600, 34.13 percent are between 400 and 500, and . . . well, you can use Figure 6-2 as a guide for other proportions.

Working with Normal Distributions

The complex relationship I told you about between x and f(x) is

$$f(x) = \frac{1}{\sigma\sqrt{2\pi}} e^{-\left[\frac{(x-\mu)^2}{2\sigma^2}\right]}$$

If you supply values for μ (the mean), σ (the standard deviation), and *x* (a score), the equation gives you back a value for *f(x)*, the height of the normal distribution at *x*. The constants π and e are important in mathematics: π is approximately 3.1416 (the ratio of a circle's circumference to its diameter), and e is approximately 2.71828. It's related to the concept of natural logarithms (described in Chapter 7 of Book 3) and to numerous other mathematical concepts.

Distributions in R

The normal distribution family is one of many distribution families baked into R. Dealing with these families is intuitive:

» Begin with the distribution family's name in R (norm for the normal family, for example).

» To the beginning of the family name, add d to work with the probability density function. For the probability density function for the normal family, then, it's dnorm( ) — which is equivalent to the equation I just showed you.

» For the cumulative density function (cdf), add p (pnorm( ), for example).

» For quantiles, add q (qnorm( ), which in mathematical terms is the *inverse* of the cdf).

» To generate random numbers from a distribution, add r. So rnorm( ) generates random numbers from a member of the normal distribution family.

Normal density function

When working with any normal distribution function, you have to let the function know which member of the normal distribution family you're interested in. You do that by specifying the mean and the standard deviation.

So, if you happen to need the height of the IQ distribution for IQ = 100, here's how to find it:

```
> dnorm(100,m=100,s=15)
[1] 0.02659615
```

REMEMBER

This does *not* mean that the probability of finding an IQ score of 100 is .027. Probability density is *not* the same as probability. With a probability density function, it only makes sense to talk about the probability of a score between two boundaries — like the probability of a score between 100 and 115.

Plotting a normal curve

dnorm( ) is useful as a tool for plotting a normal distribution. I use it along with ggplot( ) to draw a graph for IQ that looks a lot like Figure 6-2.

Before I set up a ggplot( ) statement, I create three helpful vectors. The first

```
x.values <- seq(40,160,1)
```

is the vector I'll give to ggplot( ) as an aesthetic mapping for the x-axis. This statement creates a sequence of 121 numbers beginning with 40 (four standard deviations below the mean) to 160 (four standard deviations above the mean).

The second

```
sd.values <- seq(40,160,15)
```

is a vector of the nine standard deviation values from 40 to 160. This figures into the creation of the vertical dashed lines at each standard deviation in Figure 6-2.

The third vector

```
zeros9 <- rep(0,9)
```

will also be part of creating the vertical dashed lines. It's just a vector of nine zeros.

On to ggplot( ). Because the data is a vector, the first argument is NULL. The aesthetic mapping for the x-axis is, as I mention earlier, the x.values vector. What about the mapping for the y-axis? Well, this is a plot of a normal density function for mean = 100 and standard deviation =15, so you'd expect the y-axis mapping to be dnorm(x.values, m=100, s=15), wouldn't you? And you'd be right! Here's the ggplot( ) statement:

```
ggplot(NULL,aes(x=x.values,y=dnorm(x.values,m=100,s=15)))
```

Add a line geom for the plot and labels for the axes, and here's what I have:

```
ggplot(NULL,aes(x=x.values,y=dnorm(x.values,m=100,s=15))) +
  geom_line() +
  labs(x="IQ",y="f(IQ)")
```

And that draws Figure 6-3.

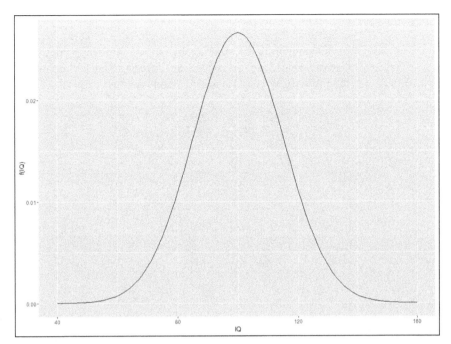

FIGURE 6-3:
Initial plot of the
normal density
function for IQ.

As you can see, ggplot() has its own ideas about the values to plot on the *x*-axis. Instead of the defaults, I want the sd.values on the *x*-axis. To change those values, I use scale_x_continuous() to rescale the *x*-axis. One of its arguments, breaks, sets the points on the *x*-axis for the values, and the other, labels, supplies the values. For each one, I supply sd.values:

```
scale_x_continuous(breaks=sd.values,labels = sd.values)
```

Now the code is

```
ggplot(NULL,aes(x=x.values,y=dnorm(x.values,m=100,s=15))) +
  geom_line() +
  labs(x="IQ",y="f(IQ)")+
  scale_x_continuous(breaks=sd.values,labels = sd.values)
```

and the result is Figure 6-4.

In ggplot world, vertical lines that start at the *x*-axis and end at the curve are called *segments*. So the appropriate geom to draw them is geom_segment. This geom requires a starting point for each segment and an endpoint for each segment. I specify those points in an aesthetic mapping within the geom. The *x*-coordinates for the starting points for the nine segments are in sd.values. The segments start at the *x*-axis, so the nine *y*-coordinates are all zeros — which happens to be the contents of the zeros9 vector. The segments end at the curve, so the x-coordinates for the endpoints are, once again, sd.values. The y-coordinates? Those would be dnorm(sd.values, m=100,s=15). After adding a statement about dashed lines, the rather busy geom_segment() statement is

```
geom_segment((aes(x=sd.values,y=zeros9,xend = sd.values,yend=dnorm(sd.
    values,m=100,s=15))), linetype = "dashed")
```

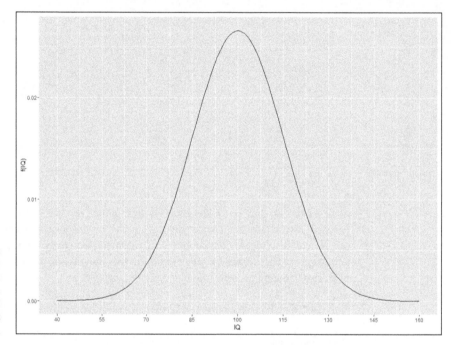

FIGURE 6-4:
The normal density function for IQ with standard deviations on the x-axis.

The code now becomes

```
ggplot(NULL,aes(x=x.values,y=dnorm(x.values,m=100,s=15))) +
    geom_line() +
    labs(x="IQ",y="f(IQ)")+
    scale_x_continuous(breaks=sd.values,labels = sd.values) +
    geom_segment((aes(x=sd.values,y=zeros9,xend = sd.values,yend=dnorm(sd.
        values,m=100,s=15))), linetype = "dashed")
```

which produces Figure 6-5.

One more little touch and I'm done. I'm not all that crazy about the space between the x-values and the x-axis. I'd like to remove that little slice of the graph and move the values up closer to where (at least I think) they should be.

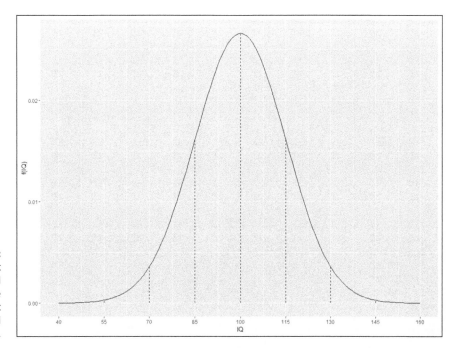

FIGURE 6-5:
The IQ plot
with vertical
dashed-line
segments at
the standard
deviations.

To do that, I use `scale_y_continuous()`, whose `expand` argument controls the space between the *x*-values and the *x*-axis. It's a 2-element vector with defaults that set the amount of space you see in Figure 6-5. Without going too deeply into it, setting that vector to `c(0,0)` removes the spacing.

So these lines of code let you draw the aesthetically pleasing Figure 6-6:

```
ggplot(NULL,aes(x=x.values,y=dnorm(x.values,m=100,s=15))) +
  geom_line() +
  labs(x="IQ",y="f(IQ)")+
  scale_x_continuous(breaks=sd.values,labels = sd.values) +
  geom_segment((aes(x=sd.values,y=zeros9,xend = sd.values,yend=dnorm(sd.
    values,m=100,s=15))), linetype = "dashed")+
  scale_y_continuous(expand = c(0,0))
```

Cumulative density function

The cumulative density function `pnorm(x,m,s)` returns the probability of a score less than x in a normal distribution with mean m and standard deviation s.

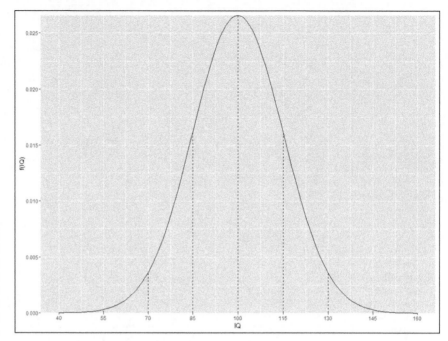

FIGURE 6-6:
The finished
product:
The IQ plot
with no
spacing between
the x-values
and the x-axis.

As you'd expect from Figure 6-2 (and the subsequent plots I created),

```
> pnorm(100,m=100,s=15)
[1] 0.5
```

How about the probability of less than 85?

```
> pnorm(85,m=100,s=15)
[1] 0.1586553
```

If you want to find the probability of a score greater than 85, pnorm() can handle that, too. It has an argument called lower.tail argument whose default value, TRUE, returns the probability of "less than." For "greater than,"set the value to FALSE:

```
> pnorm(85,m=100,s=15, lower.tail = FALSE)
[1] 0.8413447
```

It's often the case that you want the probability of a score between a lower bound and an upper bound — like the probability of an IQ score between 85 and 100. Multiple calls to pnorm() combined with a little arithmetic will get that done.

That's not necessary, however. A function called pnormGC() in a terrific package called tigerstats does that and more. The letters *GC* stand for *graphical calculator*, but they could also stand for Georgetown College (in Georgetown, Kentucky), the school from which this package originates. (On the Packages tab, click Install and then, in the Install Packages dialog box, type **tigerstats** and click Install. When you see tigerstats on the Packages tab, select its check box.)

Now watch closely:

```
> pnormGC(c(85,100),region="between",m=100,s=15,graph=TRUE)
[1] 0.3413447
```

In addition to the answer, the graph=TRUE argument produces what you see in Figure 6-7.

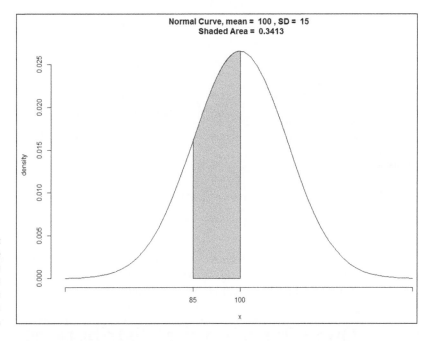

FIGURE 6-7:
Visualizing the
probability of an
IQ score between
85 and 100 (in
the tigerstats
package).

Plotting the cdf

Given that I've already done the heavy lifting when I plotted the density function, the R code for the cumulative density function is a snap:

```
ggplot(NULL,aes(x=x.values,y=pnorm(x.values,m=100,s=15))) +
  geom_line() +
  labs(x="IQ",y="Fn(IQ)")+
```

```
scale_x_continuous(breaks=sd.values,labels = sd.values) +
geom_segment((aes(x=sd.values,y=zeros9,xend = sd.values,yend=pnorm(sd.values,
  mean=100,sd=15))),linetype = "dashed")+
scale_y_continuous(expand=c(0,0))
```

Yes, all I did was change dnorm to pnorm and edit the *y*-axis label. Code reuse —
it's a beautiful thing. And so (I hope you agree) is Figure 6-8.

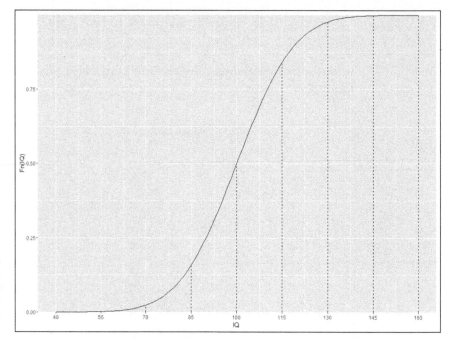

FIGURE 6-8:
Cumulative
density
function of
the IQ
distribution.

The line segments shooting up from the *x*-axis clearly show that 100 is at the
50th percentile (.50 of the scores are below 100) — which brings me to quantiles
of normal distributions, the topic of the next section.

Quantiles of normal distributions

The qnorm( ) function is the inverse of pnorm( ). Give qnorm( ) an area and it returns
the score that cuts off that area (to the left) in the specified normal distribution:

```
> qnorm(0.1586553,m=100,s=15)
[1] 85
```

The area (to the left), of course, is a percentile. (See Chapter 2 of Book 2.)

To find a score that cuts off an indicated area to the right:

```
> qnorm(0.1586553,m=100,s=15, lower.tail = FALSE)
[1] 115
```

Here's how qnormGC() (in the tigerstats package) handles the task:

```
> qnormGC(.1586553, region = "below",m=100,s=15, graph=TRUE)
[1] 85
```

This function also creates Figure 6-9.

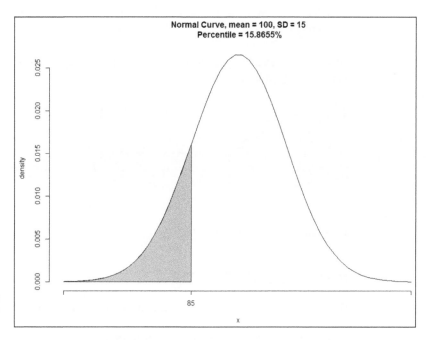

FIGURE 6-9:
Plot created by
qnormGC().

You're typically not concerned with the 15.86553rd percentile. Usually, it's quartiles that attract your attention:

```
> qnorm(c(0,.25,.50,.75,1.00),m=100,s=15)
[1]      -Inf  89.88265 100.00000 110.11735        Inf
```

The 0th and 100th percentiles (−Infinity and Infinity) show that the cdf never completely touches the x-axis nor reaches an exact maximum. The middle quartiles are of greatest interest, and best if rounded:

```
> round(qnorm(c(.25,.50,.75),m=100,s=15))
[1]  90 100 110
```

Plotting the cdf with quartiles

The objective here is to replace the standard deviation values in Figure 6-8 with the three quartile values. Begin by creating two new vectors:

```
> q.values <-round(qnorm(c(.25,.50,.75),m=100,s=15))
> zeros3 <- c(0,0,0)
```

Now, all you have to do is put those vectors in the appropriate places in scale_x_continuous() and in geom_segment():

```
ggplot(NULL,aes(x=x.values,y=pnorm(x.values,m=100,s=15))) +
  geom_line() +
  labs(x="IQ",y="Fn(IQ)")+
  scale_x_continuous(breaks=q.values,labels = q.values) +
  geom_segment((aes(x=q.values,y=zeros3,xend = q.values,yend=pnorm(q.
    values,mean=100,sd=15))), linetype = "dashed")+
  scale_y_continuous(expand=c(0,0))
```

The code produces Figure 6-10.

Random sampling

The rnorm() function generates random numbers from a normal distribution.

Here are five of them from the IQ distribution:

```
> rnorm(5,m=100,s=15)
[1] 127.02944  75.18125  66.49264 113.98305 103.39766
```

Here's what happens when you run that again:

```
> rnorm(5,m=100,s=15)
[1] 73.73596 91.79841 82.33299 81.59029 73.40033
```

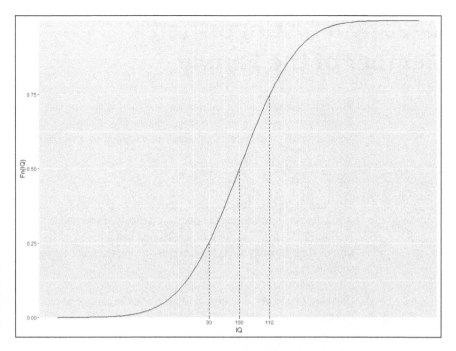

FIGURE 6-10:
The normal cumulative density function with quartile values.

Yes, the numbers are all different. The function generated a new set of random numbers. The randomization process starts with a number called a *seed*. If you want to reproduce randomization results, use the set.seed() function to set the seed to a particular number before randomizing:

```
> set.seed(7637060)
> rnorm(5,m=100,s=15)
[1]  71.99120  98.67231  92.68848 103.42207  99.61904
```

If you set the seed to that same number the next time you randomize, you get the same results:

```
> set.seed(7637060)
> rnorm(5,m=100,s=15)
[1]  71.99120  98.67231  92.68848 103.42207  99.61904
```

If you don't, you won't.

Meeting a Distinguished Member of the Family

To standardize a set of scores so that you can compare them to other sets of scores, you convert each one to a z-score. (See Chapter 4 of Book 2.) The formula for converting a score to a z-score (also known as a *standard* score) is

$$z = \frac{x - \mu}{\sigma}$$

The idea is to use the standard deviation as a unit of measure. For example, the Wechsler version (among others) has a mean of 100 and a standard deviation of 15. The Stanford-Binet version of the IQ test has a mean of 100 and a standard deviation of 16. How does a Wechsler score of, say, 110 stack up against a Stanford-Binet score of 110?

One way to answer this question is to put the two versions on a level playing field by standardizing both scores. For the Wechsler:

$$z = \frac{110 - 100}{15} = .667$$

For the Stanford-Binet:

$$z = \frac{110 - 100}{16} = .625$$

So 110 on the Wechsler is a slightly higher score than 110 on the Stanford-Binet.

Now, if you standardize all the scores in a normal distribution (such as either version of the IQ), you have a normal distribution of z-scores. Any set of z-scores (normally distributed or not) has a mean of 0 and a standard deviation of 1. If a normal distribution has those parameters, it's a *standard normal distribution* — a normal distribution of standard scores. Its equation is

$$f(z) = \frac{1}{\sqrt{2\pi}} e^{\left[\frac{-z^2}{2}\right]}$$

Figure 6-11 shows the standard normal distribution. It looks like Figure 6-2, except that I've substituted 0 for the mean and I've standard deviation units in the appropriate places.

 WARNING
This is the member of the normal distribution family that most people are familiar with. It's the one they remember most from statistics courses, and the one they have in mind when they (mistakenly) say *the* normal distribution. It's also what people think of when they hear the term *z-scores*. This distribution leads many

people to the mistaken idea that converting to *z*-scores somehow transforms a set of scores into a normal distribution.

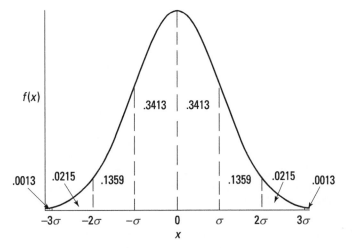

FIGURE 6-11:
The standard normal distribution, divided up by standard deviations.

The standard normal distribution in R

Working with the standard normal distribution in R couldn't be easier. The only change you make to the four norm functions is to *not* specify a mean and a standard deviation — the defaults are zero and one.

Here are some examples:

```
> dnorm(0)
[1] 0.3989423
> pnorm(0)
[1] 0.5
> qnorm(c(.25,.50,.75))
[1] -0.6744898  0.0000000  0.6744898
> rnorm(5)
[1] -0.4280188 -0.9085506  0.6746574  1.0728058 -1.2646055
```

This also applies to the tigerstats functions:

```
> pnormGC(c(-1,0),region="between")
[1] 0.3413447
> qnormGC(.50, region = "below")
[1] 0
```

Plotting the standard normal distribution

To plot the standard normal distribution, you create a couple of new vectors:

```
z.values <-seq(-4,4,.01)
z.sd.values <- seq(-4,4,1)
```

and make a few changes to the code I show you how to use earlier to plot the IQ distribution:

```
ggplot(NULL,aes(x=z.values,y=dnorm(z.values))) +
  geom_line() +
  labs(x="z",y="f(z)")+
  scale_x_continuous(breaks=z.sd.values,labels=z.sd.values) +
  geom_segment((aes(x=z.sd.values,y=zeros9,xend = z.sd.values,yend=dnorm(z.
    sd.values))),linetype = "dashed")+
  scale_y_continuous(expand=c(0,0))
```

In addition to putting the new vectors into scale_x_continuous() and geom_segment(), the notable change you make is to drop the mean and standard deviation arguments from dnorm(). The code creates what you see in Figure 6-12.

I leave it to you as an exercise to plot the cumulative density function for the standard normal distribution.

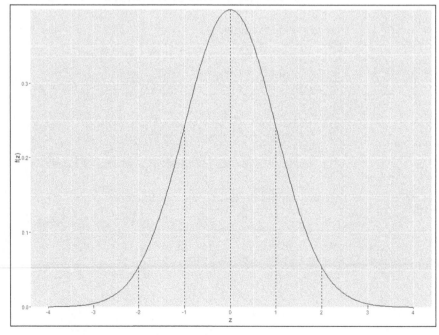

FIGURE 6-12: The standard normal distribution, divided by standard deviations, plotted in ggplot().

3 Analyzing Data

Contents at a Glance

Chapter **1**

The Confidence Game: Estimation

opulation and *sample* are pretty easy to understand. A *population* is a huge collection of individuals, and a *sample* is a group of individuals you draw from a population. Measure the sample-members on some trait or attribute, calculate statistics that summarize that sample, and you're off and running.

In addition to those summary statistics, you can use the statistics to estimate the population parameters. This is a big deal: Just on the basis of a small percentage of individuals from the population, you can draw a picture of the entire population.

How definitive is that picture? In other words, how much confidence can you have in your estimates? To answer this question, you have to have a context for your estimates. How probable are they? How likely is the true value of a parameter to be within a particular lower bound and upper bound?

In this chapter, I introduce the context for estimates, show how that plays into confidence in those estimates, and show you how to use R to calculate confidence levels.

Understanding Sampling Distributions

So you have a population, and you pull a sample out of this population. You measure the sample-members on some attribute and calculate the sample mean. You return the sample-members to the population, draw another sample, assess the new sample-members, and then calculate *their* mean. You repeat this process again and again, always with same number of individuals as in the original sample. If you could do this an infinite amount of times (with the same-size sample each time), you'd have an infinite amount of means. Those sample means form a distribution of their own. This distribution is called *the sampling distribution of the mean.*

For a sample mean, this is the "context" I mention at the beginning of this chapter. Like any other number, a statistic makes no sense by itself. You have to know where it comes from in order to understand it. Of course, a statistic *comes from* a calculation performed on sample data. In another sense, a statistic is part of a sampling distribution.

REMEMBER

In general, *a sampling distribution is the distribution of all possible values of a statistic for a given sample size.*

I italicize that definition for a reason: It's extremely important. After many years of teaching statistics, I can tell you that this concept usually sets the boundary line between people who understand statistics and people who don't.

So . . . if you understand what a sampling distribution is, you'll understand what the field of statistics is all about. If you don't, you won't. It's almost that simple.

If you don't know what a sampling distribution is, statistics will be a cookbook type of subject for you: Whenever you have to apply statistics, you'll find yourself plugging numbers into formulas and hoping for the best. On the other hand, if you're comfortable with the idea of a sampling distribution, you'll grasp the big picture of inferential statistics.

To help clarify the idea of a sampling distribution, take a look at Figure 1-1. It summarizes the steps in creating a sampling distribution of the mean.

A sampling distribution — like any other group of scores — has a mean and a standard deviation. The symbol for the mean of the sampling distribution of the mean (yes, I know that's a mouthful) is

$$\mu_{\bar{x}}$$

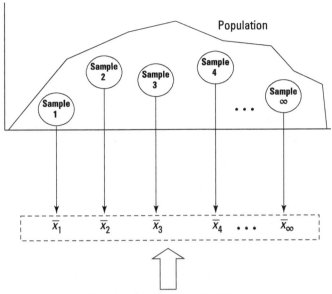

FIGURE 1-1:
Creating the sampling distribution of the mean.

Sampling Distribution of the Mean

REMEMBER

The standard deviation of a sampling distribution is a pretty hot item. It has a special name — *standard error.* For the sampling distribution of the mean, the standard deviation is called *the standard error of the mean.* Its symbol is

$$\sigma_{\bar{x}}$$

An EXTREMELY Important Idea: The Central Limit Theorem

The situation I ask you to imagine in my "Understanding Sampling Distributions" section, earlier in this chapter, never happens in the real world. You never take an infinite amount of samples and calculate their means, and you never actually create a sampling distribution of the mean. Typically, you draw one sample and calculate its statistics.

So, if you have only one sample, how can you ever know anything about a sampling distribution — a theoretical distribution that encompasses an infinite number of samples? Is this all just a wild goose chase?

No, it's not. You can figure out a lot about a sampling distribution because of a great gift from mathematicians to the field of statistics. This gift is called the *central limit theorem*.

According to the central limit theorem:

>> The sampling distribution of the mean is approximately a normal distribution — if the sample size is large enough.

   Large enough means about 30 or more.

>> The mean of the sampling distribution of the mean is the same as the population mean.

   In equation form, that's

   $$\mu_{\bar{x}} = \mu$$

>> The standard deviation of the sampling distribution of the mean (also known as the standard error of the mean) is equal to the population standard deviation divided by the square root of the sample size.

   The equation for the standard error of the mean is

   $$\sigma_{\bar{x}} = \sigma / \sqrt{N}$$

Notice that the central limit theorem says nothing about the population. All it says is that if the sample size is large enough, the sampling distribution of the mean is a normal distribution, with the indicated parameters. The population that supplies the samples doesn't have to be a normal distribution for the central limit theorem to hold.

What if the population is a normal distribution? In that case, the sampling distribution of the mean is a normal distribution regardless of the sample size.

Figure 1-2 shows a general picture of the sampling distribution of the mean, partitioned into standard error units.

(Approximately) simulating the central limit theorem

It almost doesn't sound right. How can a population that's not normally distributed produce a normally distributed sampling distribution?

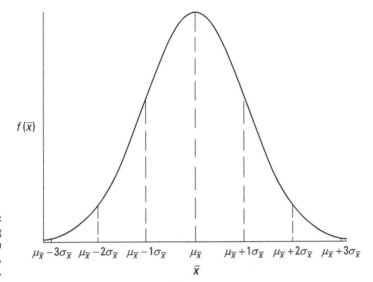

$\mu_{\bar{x}}-3\sigma_{\bar{x}} \quad \mu_{\bar{x}}-2\sigma_{\bar{x}} \quad \mu_{\bar{x}}-1\sigma_{\bar{x}} \qquad \mu_{\bar{x}} \qquad \mu_{\bar{x}}+1\sigma_{\bar{x}} \quad \mu_{\bar{x}}+2\sigma_{\bar{x}} \quad \mu_{\bar{x}}+3\sigma_{\bar{x}}$

$\bar{x}$

To give you an idea of how the central limit theorem works, I work through a simulation. This simulation creates something like a sampling distribution of the mean for a very small sample, based on a population that's not normally distributed. As you'll see, even though the population is not a normal distribution, and even though the sample is small, the sampling distribution of the mean looks quite a bit like a normal distribution.

Imagine a huge population that consists of just three scores — 1, 2, and 3, and each one is equally likely to appear in a sample. That kind of population is definitely *not* a normal distribution.

Imagine also that you can randomly select a sample of three scores from this population. Table 1-1 shows all the possible samples and their means.

If you look closely at the table, you can almost see what's about to happen in the simulation. The sample mean that appears most frequently is 2.00. The sample means that appear least frequently are 1.00 and 3.00. Hmmm . . . .

In the simulation, I randomly select a score from the population and then randomly select two more. That group of three scores is a sample. Then I calculate the mean of that sample. I repeat this process for a total of 600 samples, resulting in 600 sample means. Finally, I graph the distribution of the sample means.

TABLE 1-1

All Possible Samples of Three Scores (and Their Means) from a Population Consisting of the Scores 1, 2, and 3

Sample	Mean	Sample	Mean	Sample	Mean
1,1,1	1.00	2,1,1	1.33	3,1,1	1.67
1,1,2	1.33	2,1,2	1.67	3,1,2	2.00
1,1,3	1.67	2,1,3	2.00	3,1,3	2.33
1,2,1	1.33	2,2,1	1.67	3,2,1	2.00
1,2,2	1.67	2,2,2	2.00	3,2,2	2.33
1,2,3	2.00	2,2,3	2.33	3,2,3	2.67
1,3,1	1.67	2,3,1	2.00	3,3,1	2.33
1,3,2	2.00	2,3,2	2.33	3,3,2	2.67
1,3,3	2.33	2,3,3	2.67	3,3,3	3.00

What does the simulated sampling distribution of the mean look like? I work through it in R. I begin by creating a vector for the possible scores, and another for the probability of sampling each score:

```
values <- c(1,2,3)
probabilities <- c(1/3,1/3,1/3)
```

One more vector will hold the 600 sample means:

```
smpl.means <- NULL
```

To draw a sample, I use the `sample()` function:

```
smpl <-sample(x=values,prob = probabilities, size=3,replace=TRUE)
```

The first two arguments, of course, provide the scores to sample and the probability of each score. The third is the sample size. The fourth indicates that after I select a score for the sample, I replace it. This procedure (unsurprisingly called "sampling with replacement") simulates a huge population from which I can select any score at any time.

Each time I draw a sample, I take its mean and *append* it (add it to the end of) the `smpl.means` vector:

```
smpl.means <- append(smpl.means, mean(smpl))
```

I don't want to have to manually repeat this whole process 600 times. Fortunately, like all computer languages, R has a way of handling this: Its for loop does all the work. To do the sampling, the calculation, and the appending 600 times, the for loop looks like this:

```
for(i in 1:600){
    smpl <-sample(x = values,prob = probabilities,
        size = 3,replace=TRUE)
    smpl.means <- append(smpl.means, mean(smpl))
    }
```

As you can see, the curly brackets enclose what happens in each iteration of the loop, and i is a counter for how many times the loop occurs.

If you'd like to run this, here's all the code before the for loop, including the seed so that you can replicate my results:

```
> values <- c(1,2,3)
> probabilities <- c(1/3,1/3,1/3)
> smpl.means <- NULL
> set.seed(7637060)
```

Then run the for loop. If you want to run the loop over and over again, make sure you reset smpl.means to NULL each time. If you want to get different results each time, don't set the seed to the same number (or don't set it at all).

What does the sampling distribution look like? I use ggplot() to do the honors. (To follow along, make sure you load ggplot2.) The data values (the 600 sample means) are in a vector, so the first argument is NULL. The smpl.means vector maps to the x-axis. And I'm creating a histogram, so the geom is geom_histogram:

```
ggplot(NULL,aes(x=smpl.means)) +
    geom_histogram()
```

Figure 1-3 shows the histogram for the sampling distribution of the mean.

Looks a lot like the beginnings of a normal distribution, right? I explore the distribution further in a moment, but first I'll make the graph a bit more informative. I'd like the labeled points on the x-axis to reflect the values of the mean in the smpl.means vector. I can't just specify the vector values for the x-axis because the vector has 600 of them. Instead, I'll list the *unique* values:

```
> unique(smpl.means)
[1] 2.333333 1.666667 1.333333 2.000000 2.666667 3.000000
[7] 1.000000
```

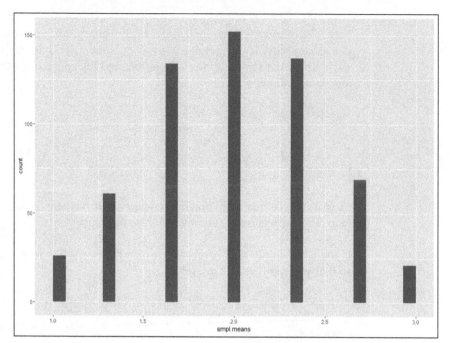

FIGURE 1-3:
Sampling
distribution of
the mean based
on 600 samples
of size 3 from
a population
consisting of the
equally probable
scores 1, 2, and 3.

They look better if I round them to two decimal places:

```
> round(unique(smpl.means),2)
[1] 2.33 1.67 1.33 2.00 2.67 3.00 1.00
```

Finally, I store these values in a vector called m.values, which I'll use to rescale the x-axis.

```
> m.values <-round(unique(smpl.means),2)
```

For the rescaling, I use a trick that I show you in Chapter 6 of Book 2:

```
scale_x_continuous(breaks=m.values,label=m.values)
```

Another trick from Chapter 6 of Book 2 eliminates the space between the x-axis values and the x-axis:

```
scale_y_continuous(expand = c(0,0))
```

One more trick uses R's expression syntax to display $\bar{X}$ as the x-axis label and *frequency*$(\bar{X})$ as the y-axis label:

```
labs(x=expression(bar(X)),y=expression(frequency(bar(X))))
```

Putting it all together gives the sampling distribution shown in Figure 1-4:

```
ggplot(NULL,aes(x=smpl.means)) +
  geom_histogram()+
  scale_x_continuous(breaks=m.values,label=m.values)+
  scale_y_continuous(expand = c(0,0)) +
  labs(x=expression(bar(X)),y=expression(frequency(bar(X))))
```

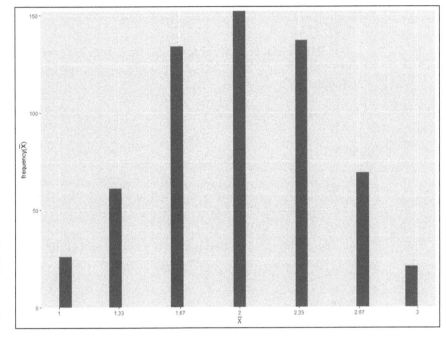

FIGURE 1-4:
The sampling
distribution of the
mean with the
x-axis rescaled
and cool axis
labels.

Predictions of the central limit theorem

How do the characteristics of the sampling distribution match up with what the central limit theorem predicts?

To derive the predictions, I have to start with the population. Think of each population value (1, 2, or 3) as an X, and think of each probability as $pr(X)$. Mathematicians would refer to X as a *discrete random variable*.

The mean of a discrete random variable is called its *expected value*. The notation for the expected value of X is $E(X)$.

To find $E(X)$, you multiply each X by its probability and then add all those products together. So, for this example, that's

$$E(X) = \sum X(pr(X)) = 1\left(\frac{1}{3}\right) + 2\left(\frac{1}{3}\right) + 3\left(\frac{1}{3}\right) = 2$$

Or, if you prefer R:

```
> E.values<-sum(values*probabilities)
> E.values
[1] 2
```

To find the variance of X, subtract $E(X)$ from each X, square each deviation, multiply each squared deviation by the probability of X, and add the products. For this example:

$$\text{var}(X) = \sum(X - E(X))^2 pr(x) = (1-2)^2\left(\frac{1}{3}\right) + (2-2)^2\left(\frac{1}{3}\right) + (3-2)^2\left(\frac{1}{3}\right) = .67$$

In R:

```
> var.values <- sum((values-E.values)^2*probabilities)
> var.values
[1] 0.6666667
```

As always, the standard deviation is the square root of the variance:

$$\sigma = \sqrt{\text{var}(X)} = \sqrt{.67} = .82$$

Again, in R:

```
> sd.values<-sqrt(var.values)
> sd.values
[1] 0.8164966
```

So the population has a mean of 2 and a standard deviation of .82.

According to the central limit theorem, the mean of the sampling distribution should be

$$\mu_{\bar{x}} = \mu = 2$$

and the standard deviation should be

$$\sigma_{\bar{x}} = \sigma \big/ \sqrt{N} = .82 \big/ \sqrt{3} = .4714$$

How do these predicted values match up with the characteristics of the sampling distribution?

```
> mean(smpl.means)
[1] 2.002222
> sd(smpl.means)
[1] 0.4745368
```

Pretty close! So, even with a non-normally distributed population and a small sample size, the central limit theorem gives you an accurate picture of the sampling distribution of the mean.

Confidence: It Has Its Limits!

I tell you about sampling distributions because they help answer the question I pose at the beginning of this chapter: How much confidence can you have in the estimates you create?

The procedure is to calculate a statistic and then use that statistic to establish upper and lower bounds for the population parameter with, say, 95 percent confidence. (The interpretation of confidence limits is a bit more involved than that, as you'll see.) You can only do this if you know the sampling distribution of the statistic and the standard error of the statistic. In the next section, I show how to do this for the mean.

Finding confidence limits for a mean

The FarBlonJet Corporation manufactures navigation systems. (Corporate motto: "Taking a trip? Get FarBlonJet.") The company has developed a new battery to power its portable model. To help market the system, FarBlonJet wants to know how long, on average, each battery lasts before it burns out.

Company leaders like to estimate that average with 95 percent confidence. They test a sample of 100 batteries and find that the sample mean is 60 hours, with a standard deviation of 20 hours. The central limit theorem, remember, says that with a large enough sample (30 or more), the sampling distribution of the mean approximates a normal distribution. The standard error of the mean (the standard deviation of the sampling distribution of the mean) is

$$\sigma_{\bar{x}} = \sigma / \sqrt{N}$$

The sample size, N, is 100. What about σ? That's unknown, so you have to estimate it. If you know σ, that would mean you know μ and establishing confidence limits would be unnecessary.

The best estimate of σ is the standard deviation of the sample. In this case, that's 20. This leads to an estimate of the standard error of the mean:

$$s_{\bar{x}} = \frac{s}{\sqrt{N}} = \frac{20}{\sqrt{100}} = \frac{20}{10} = 2$$

The best estimate of the population mean is the sample mean, 60. Armed with this information — estimated mean, estimated standard error of the mean, normal distribution — you can envision the sampling distribution of the mean, which is shown in Figure 1-5. Consistent with Figure 1-2, each standard deviation is a standard error of the mean.

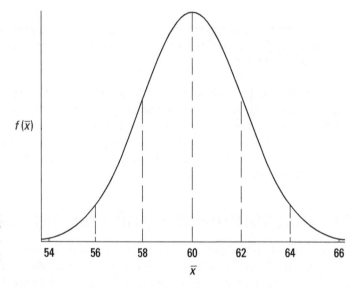

FIGURE 1-5:
The sampling distribution of the mean for the FarBlonJet battery.

$f(\bar{x})$

54   56   58   60   62   64   66

$\bar{x}$

Now that you have the sampling distribution, you can establish the 95 percent confidence limits for the mean. This means that, starting at the center of the distribution, how far out to the sides do you have to extend until you have 95 percent of the area under the curve? (For more on the area under a normal distribution and what it means, see Chapter 2 of Book 2.)

One way to answer this question is to work with the standard normal distribution and find the z-score that cuts off 2.5 percent of the area in the upper tail. Then multiply that z-score by the standard error. Add the result to the sample mean to get the upper confidence limit, and then subtract the same result from the mean to get the lower confidence limit.

Using R to find the confidence limits for a mean

Here's how to do all that in R. First, the setup:

```
> mean.battery <- 60
> sd.battery <- 20
> N <- 100
> error <- qnorm(.025,lower.tail=FALSE)*sd.battery/sqrt(N)
```

Then the limits:

```
> lower <- mean.battery - error
> upper <- mean.battery + error
> lower
[1] 56.08007
> upper
[1] 63.91993
```

Figure 1-6 shows these bounds on the sampling distribution.

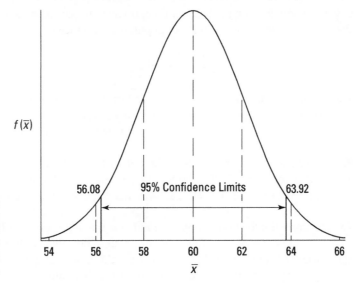

FIGURE 1-6:
The 95%
confidence limits
on the FarBlonJet
sampling
distribution.

What does this tell you, exactly? One interpretation is that if you repeat this sampling and estimation procedure many times, the confidence intervals you calculate (which would be different each time you do it) would include the population mean 95 percent of the time.

Fit to a t

The central limit theorem specifies (approximately) a normal distribution for large samples. In the real world, however, you deal with smaller samples, and the normal distribution isn't appropriate. What do you do?

First of all, you pay a price for using a smaller sample — you have a larger standard error. Suppose the FarBlonJet Corporation found a mean of 60 and a standard deviation of 20 in a sample of 25 batteries. The estimated standard error is

$$s_{\bar{x}} = {}^{s}\!\!\diagup\!\!{}_{\sqrt{N}} = {}^{20}\!\!\diagup\!\!{}_{\sqrt{25}} = {}^{20}\!\!\diagup\!\!{}_{5} = 4$$

which is twice as large as the standard error for $N=100$.

Second, you don't get to use the standard normal distribution to characterize the sampling distribution of the mean. For small samples, the sampling distribution of the mean is a member of a family of distributions called the *t-distribution*. The parameter that distinguishes members of this family from one another is called *degrees of freedom*.

REMEMBER

As I say in Chapter 3 of Book 2, think of "degrees of freedom" as the denominator of your variance estimate. For example, if your sample consists of 25 individuals, the sample variance that estimates population variance is

$$s^2 = \frac{\sum(x-\bar{x})^2}{N-1} = \frac{\sum(x-\bar{x})^2}{25-1} = \frac{\sum(x-\bar{x})^2}{24}$$

The number in the denominator is 24, and that's the value of the degrees of freedom parameter. In general, degrees of freedom (df) = $N-1$ (N is the sample size) when you use the t-distribution the way I'm about to in this section.

Figure 1-7 shows two members of the t-distribution family (df = 3 and df = 10), along with the normal distribution for comparison. As the figure shows, the greater the df, the more closely t approximates a normal distribution.

To determine the lower and upper bounds for the 95 percent confidence level for a small sample, work with the member of the t-distribution family that has the appropriate df. Find the value that cuts off the upper 2.5 percent of the area in the upper tail of the distribution. Then multiply that value by the standard error.

Add the result to the mean to get the upper confidence limit, and then subtract the same result from the mean to get the lower confidence limit.

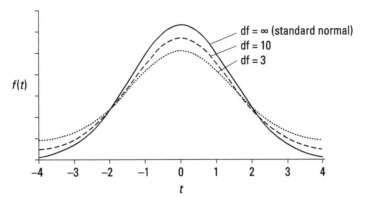

FIGURE 1-7:
Some
members of the
t-distribution
family.

df = ∞ (standard normal)
df = 10
df = 3

f(*t*)

R provides dt() (density function), pt() (cumulative density function), qt() (quantile), and rt() (random number generation) for working with the *t*-distribution. For the confidence intervals, I use qt().

In the FarBlonJet batteries example:

```
> mean.battery <- 60
> sd.battery <- 20
> N <- 25
> error <- qt(.025,N-1,lower.tail=FALSE)*sd.battery/sqrt(N)
> lower <- mean.battery - error
> upper <- mean.battery + error
> lower
[1] 51.74441
> upper
[1] 68.25559
```

So the lower and upper limits are 51.74 and 68.26. Notice that with the smaller sample, the range is wider than in the previous example.

If you have the raw data, you can use t.test() to generate confidence intervals:

```
> battery.data <- c(82,64,68,44,54,47,50,85,51,41,61,84, 53,83,91,43,35,36,33,
    87,90,86,49,37,48)
```

Here's how to use t.test() to generate the lower and upper bounds for 90 percent confidence — the default value is .95:

```
> t.test(battery.data, conf.level=.90)

    One Sample t-test

data:  c(82, 64, 68, 44, 54, 47, 50, 85, 51, 41, 61, 84, 53, 83, 91,  ...
t = 15, df = 24, p-value = 1.086e-13
```

```
alternative hypothesis: true mean is not equal to 0
90 percent confidence interval:
 53.22727 66.93273
sample estimates:
mean of x
    60.08
```

The t.test() function is really more appropriate for Chapter 2 of Book 3.

Chapter **2**

One-Sample Hypothesis Testing

Whatever your occupation, you often have to assess whether something new and different has happened. Sometimes you start with a population that you know a lot about (like its mean and standard deviation) and you draw a sample. Is that sample like the rest of the population, or does it represent something out of the ordinary?

To answer that question, you measure each individual in the sample and calculate the sample's statistics. Then you compare those statistics with the population's parameters. Are they the same? Are they different? Is the sample extraordinary in some way? The proper use of statistics helps you make the decision.

Sometimes, though, you don't know the parameters of the population that the sample came from. What happens then? In this chapter, I discuss statistical techniques and R functions for dealing with both cases.

Hypotheses, Tests, and Errors

A *hypothesis* is a guess about the way the world works. It's a tentative explanation of some process, whether that process occurs in nature or in a laboratory.

Before studying and measuring the individuals in a sample, a researcher formulates hypotheses that predict what the data should look like.

Generally, one hypothesis predicts that the data won't show anything new or out of the ordinary. This is called the *null hypothesis* (abbreviated H_0). According to the null hypothesis, if the data deviates from the norm in any way, that deviation is due strictly to chance. Another hypothesis, the *alternative hypothesis* (abbreviated H_1), explains things differently. According to the alternative hypothesis, the data show something important.

After gathering the data, it's up to the researcher to make a decision. The way the logic works, the decision centers around the null hypothesis. The researcher must decide to either reject the null hypothesis or to not reject the null hypothesis.

In *hypothesis testing*, you

» Formulate null and alternative hypotheses

» Gather data

» Decide whether to reject or not reject the null hypothesis

Nothing in the logic involves *accepting* either hypothesis. Nor does the logic involve making any decisions about the alternative hypothesis. It's all about rejecting or not rejecting H_0.

Regardless of the reject-don't-reject decision, an error is possible. One type of error occurs when you believe that the data shows something important and you reject H_0, but in reality, the data are due just to chance. This is called a *Type I error*. At the outset of a study, you set the criteria for rejecting H_0. In so doing, you set the probability of a Type I error. This probability is called *alpha* (α).

The other type of error occurs when you don't reject H_0 and the data is really due to something out of the ordinary. For one reason or another, you happened to miss it. This is called a *Type II error*. Its probability is called *beta* (β). Table 2-1 summarizes the possible decisions and errors.

Note that you never know the true state of the world. (If you do, it's not necessary to do the study!) All you can ever do is measure the individuals in a sample, calculate the statistics, and make a decision about H_0. (I discuss hypotheses and hypothesis testing in Chapter 1 of Book 1.)

TABLE 2-1

Decisions and Errors in Hypothesis Testing

		"True State" of the World	
		H_0 Is True	H_1 Is True
	Reject H_0	Type I Error	Correct Decision
Decision			
	Do Not Reject H_0	Correct Decision	Type II Error

Hypothesis Tests and Sampling Distributions

In Chapter 1 of Book 3, I discuss sampling distributions. A sampling distribution, remember, is the set of all possible values of a statistic for a given sample size.

Also in Chapter 1 of Book 3, I discuss the central limit theorem. This theorem tells you that the sampling distribution of the mean approximates a normal distribution if the sample size is large (for practical purposes, at least 30). This works whether or not the population is normally distributed. If the population is a normal distribution, the sampling distribution is normal for any sample size. Here are two other points from the central limit theorem:

>> The mean of the sampling distribution of the mean is equal to the population mean.

The equation for this is

$\mu_{\bar{x}} = \mu$

>> The standard error of the mean (the standard deviation of the sampling distribution) is equal to the population standard deviation divided by the square root of the sample size.

This equation is

$$\sigma_{\bar{x}} = \sigma \big/ \sqrt{N}$$

The sampling distribution of the mean figures prominently into the type of hypothesis testing I discuss in this chapter. Theoretically, when you test a null hypothesis versus an alternative hypothesis, each hypothesis corresponds to a separate sampling distribution.

Figure 2-1 shows what I mean. The figure shows two normal distributions. I placed them arbitrarily. Each normal distribution represents a sampling distribution of the mean. The one on the left represents the distribution of possible sample means if the null hypothesis is truly how the world works. The one on the right represents the distribution of possible sample means if the alternative hypothesis is truly how the world works.

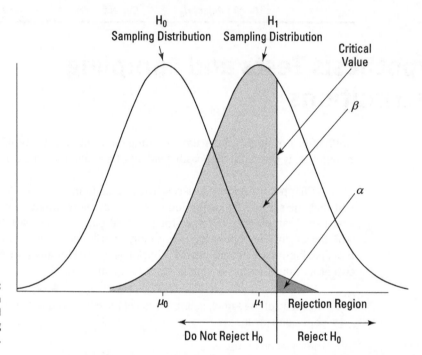

H_0
Sampling Distribution

H_1
Sampling Distribution

Critical Value

β

α

μ_0

μ_1 Rejection Region

Do Not Reject H_0 Reject H_0

FIGURE 2-1:
H_0 and H_1 each correspond to a sampling distribution.

Of course, when you do a hypothesis test, you never know which distribution produces the results. You work with a sample mean — a point on the horizontal axis. The reject-or-don't reject decision boils down to deciding which distribution the sample mean is part of. You set up a *critical value* — a decision criterion. If the sample mean is on one side of the critical value, you reject H_0. If not, you don't.

In this vein, the figure also shows α and β. These, as I mention earlier in this chapter, are the probabilities of decision errors. The area that corresponds to α is in the H_0 distribution. I've shaded it in dark gray. It represents the probability that a sample mean comes from the H_0 distribution, but it's so extreme that you reject H_0.

REMEMBER

Where you set the critical value determines α. In most hypotheses testing, you set α at .05. This means that you're willing to tolerate a Type I error (rejecting H_0 when you shouldn't) 5 percent of the time. Graphically, the critical value cuts off 5 percent of the area of the sampling distribution. By the way, if you're talking about the 5 percent of the area that's in the right tail of the distribution (refer to Figure 2-1), you're talking about the *upper* 5 percent. If it's the 5 percent in the left tail you're interested in, that's the *lower* 5 percent.

The area that corresponds to β is in the H_1 distribution. I've shaded it in light gray. This area represents the probability that a sample mean comes from the H_1 distribution, but it's close enough to the center of the H_0 distribution that you don't reject H_0 (but you should have). You don't get to set β. The size of this area depends on the separation between the means of the two distributions, and that's up to the world we live in — not up to you.

These sampling distributions are appropriate when your work corresponds to the conditions of the central limit theorem: if you know that the population you're working with is a normal distribution or if you have a large sample.

Catching Some Z's Again

Here's an example of a hypothesis test that involves a sample from a normally distributed population. Because the population is normally distributed, any sample size results in a normally distributed sampling distribution. Because it's a normal distribution, you use z-scores in the hypothesis test:

$$z = \frac{\bar{x} - \mu}{\sigma / \sqrt{N}}$$

One more "because": Because you use the z-score in the hypothesis test, the z-score here is called the *test statistic.*

Suppose you think that people living in a particular zip code have higher-than-average IQs. You take a sample of nine people from that zip code, give them IQ tests, tabulate the results, and calculate the statistics. For the population of IQ scores, $\mu = 100$ and $\sigma = 15$.

The hypotheses are

$$H_0: \mu_{\text{ZIP code}} \leq 100$$

$$H_1: \mu_{\text{ZIP code}} > 100$$

Assume that α = .05. That's the shaded area in the tail of the H_0 distribution in Figure 2-1.

Why the ≤ in H_0? You use that symbol because you'll reject H_0 only if the sample mean is larger than the hypothesized value. Anything else is evidence in favor of not rejecting H_0.

Suppose the sample mean is 108.67. Can you reject H_0?

The test involves turning 108.67 into a standard score in the sampling distribution of the mean:

$$z = \frac{\bar{x} - \mu}{\sigma / \sqrt{N}} = \frac{108.67 - 100}{\left(15 / \sqrt{9}\right)} = \frac{8.67}{\left(15 / 3\right)} = \frac{8.67}{5} = 1.73$$

Is the value of the test statistic large enough to enable you to reject H_0 with α = .05? It is. The critical value — the value of z that cuts off 5 percent of the area in a standard normal distribution — is 1.645. (After years of working with the standard normal distribution, I happen to know this. Read Chapter 6 of Book 2 to find out about R's qnorm( ) function and you can have information like that at your fingertips, too.) The calculated value, 1.73, exceeds 1.645, so it's in the rejection region. The decision is to reject H_0.

This means that if H_0 is true, the probability of getting a test statistic value that's at least this large is less than .05. That's strong evidence in favor of rejecting H_0.

REMEMBER

In statistical parlance, any time you reject H_0, the result is said to be *statistically significant*.

This type of hypothesis testing is called *one-tailed* because the rejection region is in one tail of the sampling distribution.

A hypothesis test can be one-tailed in the other direction. Suppose you have reason to believe that people in that zip code have lower-than-average IQs. In that case, the hypotheses are

$H_0\text{: } \mu_{ZIP\ code} \geq 100$

$H_1\text{: } \mu_{ZIP\ code} < 100$

For this hypothesis test, the critical value of the test statistic is −1.645 if α=.05.

A hypothesis test can be *two-tailed*, meaning that the rejection region is in both tails of the H_0 sampling distribution. That happens when the hypotheses look like this:

$$H_0: \mu_{\text{ZIP code}} = 100$$

$$H_1: \mu_{\text{ZIP code}} \neq 100$$

In this case, the alternative hypothesis just specifies that the mean is different from the null-hypothesis value, without saying whether it's greater or whether it's less. Figure 2-2 shows what the two-tailed rejection region looks like for $\alpha = .05$. The 5 percent is divided evenly between the left tail (also called the *lower tail*) and the right tail (the *upper tail*).

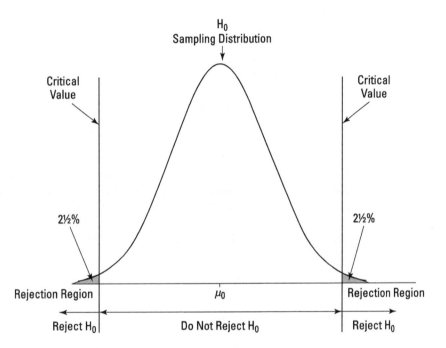

FIGURE 2-2:
The two-tailed rejection region for $\alpha = .05$.

For a standard normal distribution, incidentally, the z-score that cuts off 2.5 percent in the right tail is 1.96. The z-score that cuts off 2.5 percent in the left tail is –1.96. (Again, I happen to know these values after years of working with the standard normal distribution.) The z-score in the preceding example, 1.73, does not exceed 1.96. The decision, in the two-tailed case, is to *not* reject H_0.

TIP

This brings up an important point. A one-tailed hypothesis test can reject H_0, while a two-tailed test on the same data might not. A two-tailed test indicates that you're looking for a difference between the sample mean and the null-hypothesis mean, but you don't know in which direction. A one-tailed test shows that you have a pretty good idea of how the difference should come out. For practical purposes, this means you should try to have enough knowledge to be able to specify a one-tailed test: That gives you a better chance of rejecting H_0 when you should.

Z Testing in R

An R function called z.test() would be useful for doing the kind of testing I discuss in the previous section. One problem: That function does not exist in base R. Although you can find one in other packages, it's easy enough to create one and learn a bit about R programming in the process.

The function will work like this:

```
> IQ.data <- c(100,101,104,109,125,116,105,108,110)
> z.test(IQ.data,100,15)
z = 1.733
one-tailed probability = 0.042
two-tailed probability = 0.084
```

Begin by creating the function name and its arguments:

```
z.test = function(x,mu,popvar){
```

The first argument is the vector of data, the second is the population mean, and the third is the population variance. The left curly bracket signifies that the remainder of the code is what happens inside the function.

Next, create a vector that will hold the one-tailed probability of the z-score you'll calculate:

```
one.tail.p <- NULL
```

Then you calculate the z-score and round it to three decimal places:

```
z.score <- round((mean(x)-mu)/(popvar/sqrt(length(x))),3)
```

Without the rounding, R might calculate many decimal places, and the output would look messy.

Finally, you calculate the one-tailed probability (the proportion of area beyond the calculated z-score), and again round to three decimal places:

```
one.tail.p <- round(pnorm(abs(z.score),lower.tail = FALSE),3)
```

Why put abs() (absolute value) in the argument to pnorm? Remember that an alternative hypothesis can specify a value below the mean, and the data might result in a negative z-score.

The next order of business is to set up the output display. For this, you use the cat() function. I use this function in Chapter 5 of Book 2 to display a fairly sizable set of numbers in an organized way. The name *cat* is short for *concatenate and print*, which is exactly what I want you to do here: Concatenate (put together) strings (like one-tailed probability =) with expressions (like one.tail.p), and then show that whole thing onscreen. I also want you to start a new line for each concatenation, and \n is R's way of making that happen.

Here's the cat statement:

```
cat(" z =",z.score,"\n",
    "one-tailed probability =", one.tail.p,"\n",
    "two-tailed probability =", 2*one.tail.p )}
```

The space between the left quote and z lines up the first line with the next two onscreen. The right curly bracket closes off the function.

Here it is, all together:

```
z.test = function(x,mu,popvar){
  one.tail.p <- NULL
  z.score <- round((mean(x)-mu)/(popvar/sqrt(length(x))),3)
  one.tail.p <- round(pnorm(abs(z.score),lower.tail = FALSE),3)
  cat(" z =",z.score,"\n",
      "one-tailed probability =", one.tail.p,"\n",
      "two-tailed probability =", 2*one.tail.p )}
```

Running this function produces what you see at the beginning of this section.

t for One

In the preceding example, you work with IQ scores. The population of IQ scores is a normal distribution with a well-known mean and standard deviation. Thus, you can work with the central limit theorem and describe the sampling distribution of the mean as a normal distribution. You can then use z as the test statistic.

In the real world, however, you usually don't have the luxury of working with well-defined populations. You usually have small samples, and you're typically measuring something that isn't as well-known as IQ. The bottom line is that you often don't know the population parameters, nor do you know whether the population is normally distributed.

When that's the case, you use the sample data to estimate the population standard deviation, and you treat the sampling distribution of the mean as a member of a family of distributions called the t-distribution. You use t as a test statistic. In Chapter 1 of Book 3, I introduce this distribution and mention that you distinguish members of this family by a parameter called *degrees of freedom* (df).

The formula for the test statistic is

$$t = \frac{\bar{x} - \mu}{s / \sqrt{N}}$$

Think of df as the denominator of the estimate of the population variance. For the hypothesis tests in this section, that's $N-1$, where N is the number of scores in the sample. The higher the df, the more closely the t-distribution resembles the normal distribution.

Here's an example. FarKlempt Robotics, Inc., markets microrobots. The company claims that its product averages four defects per unit. A consumer group believes this average is higher. The consumer group takes a sample of nine FarKlempt microrobots and finds an average of seven defects, with a standard deviation of 3.12. The hypothesis test is

$H_0: \mu \leq 4$

$H_1: \mu > 4$

$\alpha = .05$

The formula is

$$t = \frac{\bar{x} - \mu}{s / \sqrt{N}} = \frac{7 - 4}{\left(3.12 / \sqrt{9}\right)} = \frac{3}{\left(3.12 / 3\right)} = 2.88$$

Can you reject H_0? The R function in the next section tells you.

t Testing in R

I talk about the t.test() function in Chapter 1 of Book 3. Here, you use it to test hypotheses.

Start with the data for FarKlempt Robotics:

```
> FarKlempt.data <- c(3,6,9,9,4,10,6,4,12)
```

Then apply t.test(). For the example, it looks like this:

```
t.test(FarKlempt.data,mu=4, alternative="greater")
```

The second argument specifies that you're testing against a hypothesized mean of 4, and the third argument indicates that the alternative hypothesis is that the true mean is greater than 4.

Here it is in action:

```
> t.test(FarKlempt.data,mu=4, alternative="greater")

        One Sample t-test
data:  c(3, 6, 9, 9, 4, 10, 6, 4, 12)
t = 2.8823, df = 8, p-value = 0.01022
alternative hypothesis: true mean is greater than 4
95 percent confidence interval:
 5.064521       Inf
sample estimates:
mean of x
        7
```

The output provides the t-value, and the low p-value shows that you can reject the null hypothesis with $\alpha = .05$.

This t.test() function is versatile. I work with it again in Chapter 3 of Book 3, when I test hypotheses about two samples.

Working with t-Distributions

Just as you can use d, p, q, and r prefixes for the normal distribution family, you can use dt() (density function), pt() (cumulative density function), qt() (quantiles), and rt() (random number generation) for the t-distribution family.

Here are dt() and rt() at work for a t-distribution with 12 df:

```
> t.values <- seq(-4,4,1)
> round(dt(t.values,12),2)
[1] 0.00 0.01 0.06 0.23 0.39 0.23 0.06 0.01 0.00
> round(pt(t.values,12),2)
[1] 0.00 0.01 0.03 0.17 0.50 0.83 0.97 0.99 1.00
```

I show you more about how to use dt() in the next section. (Way more. Trust me.)

For quantile information about the *t*-distribution with 12 df:

```
> quartiles <- c(0,.25,.50,.75,1)
> qt(quartiles,12)
[1]      -Inf -0.6954829  0.0000000  0.6954829       Inf
```

the `-Inf` and `Inf` tell you that the curve never touches the *x*-axis at either tail.

To generate eight (rounded) random numbers from the *t*-distribution with 12 df:

```
> round(rt(8,12),2)
[1]  0.73  0.13 -1.32  1.33 -1.27  0.91 -0.48 -0.83
```

All these functions give you the option of working with *t*-distributions not centered around zero. You do this by entering a value for ncp (the *noncentrality* parameter). In most applications of the *t*-distribution, noncentrality doesn't come up.

Visualizing t-Distributions

Visualizing a distribution often helps you understand it. The process can be a bit involved in R, but it's worth the effort. Over in Chapter 1 of Book 3, Figure 1-7 shows three members of the *t*-distribution family on the same graph. The first has df=3, the second has df=10, and the third is the standard normal distribution (df=infinity).

In this section, I show you how to create that graph in base R graphics and in ggplot2.

With either method, the first step is to set up a vector of the values that the density functions will work with:

```
t.values <- seq(-4,4,.1)
```

One more thing and I'll get you started. After the graphs are complete, you'll put the infinity symbol, ∞ on the legends to denote the df for the standard normal distribution. To do that, you have to install a package called grDevices (if it isn't already loaded and installed as part of an earlier installation): On the Packages tab, click Install and then, in the Install Packages dialog box, type **grDevices** and click Install. When grDevices appears on the Packages tab, select its check box.

With grDevices installed, this adds the infinity symbol to a legend:

```
expression(infinity)
```

But I digress. . . .

Plotting t in base R graphics

Begin with the plot() function, and plot the *t*-distribution with 3 df:

```
plot(x = t.values,y = dt(t.values,3),  type = "l", lty = "dotted", ylim =
    c(0,.4), xlab = "t", ylab = "f(t)")
```

The first two arguments are pretty self-explanatory. The next two establish the type of plot — type = "l" means *line plot* (that's a lowercase *L*, not the number 1), and lty = "dotted" indicates the type of line. The ylim argument sets the lower and upper limits of the *y*-axis — ylim = c(0,.4). A little tinkering shows that if you don't do this, subsequent curves get chopped off at the top. The final two arguments label the axes. Figure 2-3 shows the graph so far.

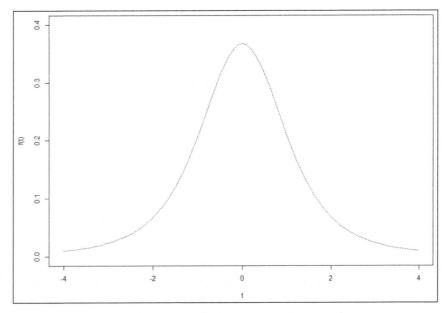

FIGURE 2-3:
t-distribution with
3 df, base R.

The next two lines add the *t*-distribution for df=10, and for the standard normal (df = infinity):

```
lines(t.values,dt(t.values,10),lty = "dashed")
lines(t.values,dnorm(t.values))
```

The line for the standard normal is solid (the default value for `lty`). Figure 2-4 shows the progress. All that's missing is the legend that explains which curve is which.

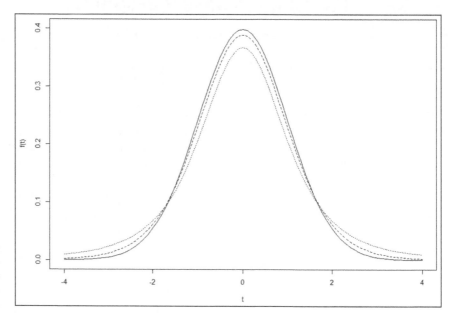

FIGURE 2-4:
Three
distributions
in search
of a legend.

One advantage of base R is that positioning and populating the legend is not difficult:

```
legend("topright", title = "df",legend = c(expression(infinity),"10","3"), lty =
    c("solid","dashed","dotted"), bty = "n")
```

The first argument positions the legend in the upper right corner. The second gives the legend its title. The third argument is a vector that specifies what's in the legend. As you can see, the first element is that infinity expression I showed you earlier, corresponding to the df for the standard normal. The second and third elements are the df for the remaining two t-distributions. You order them this way because that's the order in which the curves appear at their centers. The `lty` argument is the vector that specifies the order of the linetypes. (They correspond with the df.) The final argument `bty="n"` removes the border from the legend.

And this produces Figure 2-5.

Plotting t in ggplot2

The grammar-of-graphics approach takes considerably more effort than base R. But follow along and you'll learn a lot about `ggplot2`.

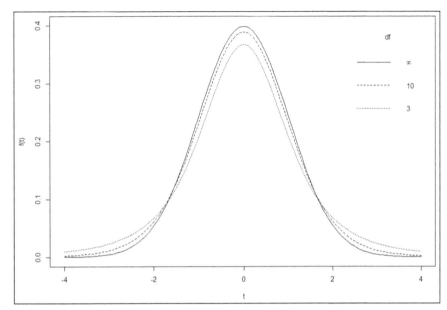

FIGURE 2-5:
The final graph,
including the
legend.

You start by putting the relevant numbers into a data frame:

```
t.frame = data.frame(t.values,
                     df3 = dt(t.values,3),
                     df10 = dt(t.values,10),
                     std_normal = dnorm(t.values))
```

The first six rows of the data frame look like this:

```
> head(t.frame)
  t.values         df3        df10    std_normal
1     -4.0 0.009163361 0.002031034 0.0001338302
2     -3.9 0.009975671 0.002406689 0.0001986555
3     -3.8 0.010875996 0.002854394 0.0002919469
4     -3.7 0.011875430f 0.003388151 0.0004247803
5     -3.6 0.012986623 0.004024623 0.0006119019
6     -3.5 0.014224019 0.004783607 0.0008726827
```

That's a pretty good-looking data frame, but it's in wide format. As I point out in Chapter 1 of Book 2, ggplot() prefers long format — which is the three columns of density-numbers stacked into a single column. To get to that format — it's called *reshaping* the data — make sure you have the reshape2 package installed. Select its check box on the Packages tab and you're ready to go.

Reshaping from wide format to long format is called *melting* the data, so the function is

```
t.frame.melt <- melt(t.frame,id="t.values")
```

The id argument specifies that t.values is the variable whose numbers *don't* get stacked with the rest. Think of it as the variable that stores the data. The first six rows of t.frame.melt are

```
> head(t.frame.melt)
  t.values variable      value
1     -4.0      df3 0.009163361
2     -3.9      df3 0.009975671
3     -3.8      df3 0.010875996
4     -3.7      df3 0.011875430
5     -3.6      df3 0.012986623
6     -3.5      df3 0.014224019
```

It's always a good idea to have meaningful column names, so . . .

```
> colnames(t.frame.melt)= c("t","df","density")
> head(t.frame.melt)
     t  df      density
1 -4.0 df3 0.009163361
2 -3.9 df3 0.009975671
3 -3.8 df3 0.010875996
4 -3.7 df3 0.011875430
5 -3.6 df3 0.012986623
6 -3.5 df3 0.014224019
```

Now, one more thing before I have you start on the graph. This is a vector that will be useful when you lay out the x-axis:

```
x.axis.values <- seq(-4,4,2)
```

Begin with ggplot():

```
ggplot(t.frame.melt, aes(x=t,y=f(t),group =df))
```

The first argument is the data frame. The aesthetic mappings tell you that t is on the x-axis, density is on the y-axis, and the data falls into groups specified by the df variable.

This is a line plot, so the appropriate geom function to add is geom_line:

```
geom_line(aes(linetype=df))
```

Geom functions can work with aesthetic mappings. The aesthetic mapping here maps df to the type of line.

Rescale the x-axis so that it goes from −4 to 4, by twos. Here's where to use that x.axis.values vector:

```
scale_x_continuous(breaks=x.axis.values,labels=x.axis.values)
```

The first argument sets the breakpoints for the x-axis, and the second provides the labels for those points. Putting these three statements together:

```
ggplot(t.frame.melt, aes(x=t,y=density,group =df)) +
  geom_line(aes(linetype=df)) +
  scale_x_continuous(breaks = x.axis.values,labels = x.axis.values)
```

results in Figure 2-6. One of the benefits of ggplot2 is that the code automatically produces a legend.

You still have some work to do. First of all, the default linetype assignments are not what you want, so you have to redo them:

```
scale_linetype_manual(values = c("dotted","dashed","solid"),
  labels = c("3","10", expression(infinity)))
```

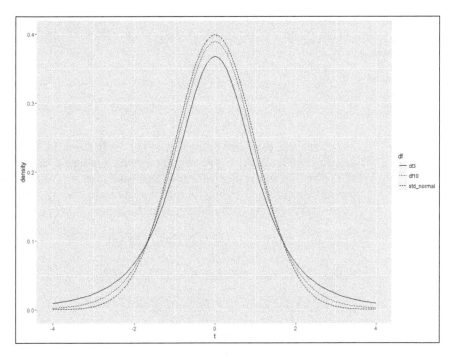

FIGURE 2-6:
Three
t-distribution
curves, plotted
in ggplot2.

The four statements

```
ggplot(t.frame.melt, aes(x=t,y=density,group =df)) +
   geom_line(aes(linetype=df)) +
   scale_x_continuous(breaks = x.axis.values,labels = x.axis.values)+
   scale_linetype_manual(values = c("dotted","dashed","solid"),
   labels = c("3","10", expression(infinity)))
```

produce Figure 2-7.

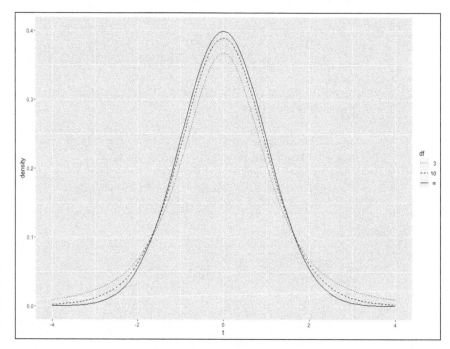

FIGURE 2-7:
Three
t-distribution
curves, with
the linetypes
reassigned.

As you can see, the items in the legend are not in the order that the curves appear at their centers. I'm a stickler for that. I think it makes a graph more comprehensible when the graph elements and the legend elements are in sync. The ggplot2 package provides guide functions that enable you to control the legend's details. To reverse the order of the linetypes in the legend, here's what you do:

```
guides(linetype=guide_legend(reverse = TRUE))
```

Putting all the code together, finally, yields Figure 2-8.

```
ggplot(t.frame.melt, aes(x=t,y=density,group =df)) +
   geom_line(aes(linetype=df)) +
   scale_x_continuous(breaks = x.axis.values,labels = x.axis.values)+
```

```
  scale_linetype_manual(values = c("dotted","dashed","solid"),
labels = c("3","10", expression(infinity)))+
  guides(linetype=guide_legend(reverse = TRUE))
```

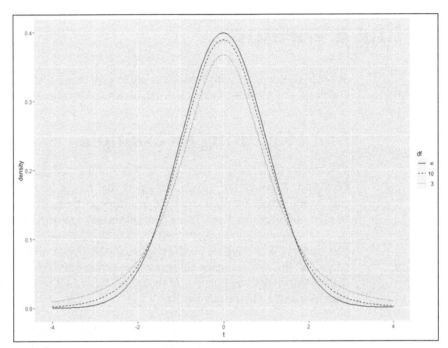

FIGURE 2-8:
The final product,
with the legend
rearranged.

I leave it to you as an exercise to relabel the *y*-axis `f(t)`.

Base R graphics versus `ggplot2`: It's like driving a car with a standard transmission versus driving with an automatic transmission — but I'm not always sure which is which!

One more thing about ggplot2

I could have had you plot all this without creating and reshaping a data frame. An alternative approach is to set `NULL` as the data source, map `t.values` to the *x*-axis, and then add three `geom_line` statements. Each of those statements would map a vector of densities (created on the fly) to the *y*-axis, and each one would have its own `linetype`.

The problem with that approach? When you do it that way, the grammar does not automatically create a legend. Without a dataframe, it has nothing to create a legend from. It's something like using `ggplot()` to create a base R graph.

Is it ever a good idea to use this approach? Yes, it is — when you don't want to include a legend but you want to annotate the graph in some other way. I provide an example in the later section "Visualizing Chi-Square Distributions."

Testing a Variance

So far in this chapter, I discuss one-sample hypothesis testing for means. All well and good, but it turns out that you can also test hypotheses about *variances*.

Manufacturing an Example

This topic sometimes comes up in the context of manufacturing. Suppose FarKlempt Robotics, Inc., produces a part that has to be a certain length with a very small variability. You can take a sample of parts, measure them, find the sample variability, and perform a hypothesis test against the desired variability.

The family of distributions for the test is called *chi-square*. Its symbol is χ^2. I won't go into all the mathematics. I'll just tell you that, once again, df is the parameter that distinguishes one member of the family from another. Figure 2-9 shows two members of the chi-square family.

As the figure shows, chi-square is not like the previous distribution families I showed you. Members of this family can be skewed, and none of them can take a value less than zero.

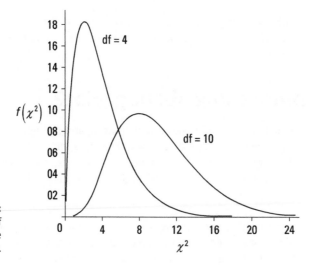

FIGURE 2-9:
Two members of
the chi-square
family.

The formula for the test statistic is

$$\chi^2 = \frac{(N-1)s^2}{\sigma^2}$$

N is the number of scores in the sample, s^2 is the sample variance, and σ^2 is the population variance specified in H_0.

With this test, you have to assume that what you're measuring has a normal distribution.

Suppose the process for the FarKlempt part has to have, at most, a standard deviation of 1.5 inches for its length. (Notice that I use *standard deviation.* This allows me to speak in terms of inches. If I use *variance*, the units would be square inches.) After measuring a sample of ten parts, you find a standard deviation of 1.80 inches.

The hypotheses are

H_0: $\sigma^2 \leq 2.25$ (remember to square the "at-most" standard deviation of 1.5 inches)

H_1: $\sigma^2 > 2.25$

$\alpha = .05$

Working with the formula,

$$\chi^2 = \frac{(N-1)s^2}{\sigma^2} = \frac{(10-1)(1.80)^2}{(1.5)^2} = \frac{(9)(3.25)}{2.25} = 12.96$$

can you reject H_0? Read on.

Testing in R

At this point, you might think that the function `chisq.test()` would answer the question. Although base R provides this function, it's not appropriate here. (Statisticians use this function to test other kinds of hypotheses, but that topic is beyond the scope of this book.)

Instead, turn to a function called `varTest`, which is in the EnvStats package. On the Packages tab, click Install. Then type **EnvStats** into the Install Packages dialog box and click Install. When EnvStats appears on the Packages tab, select its check box.

Before you use the test, you create a vector to hold the ten measurements described in the example in the preceding section:

```
FarKlempt.data2 <- c(12.43, 11.71, 14.41, 11.05, 9.53, 11.66,
  9.33,11.71,14.35,13.81)
```

And now, the test:

```
varTest(FarKlempt.data2,alternative="greater",conf.level = 0.95,sigma.squared =
    2.25)
```

The first argument is the data vector. The second specifies the alternative hypothesis that the true variance is greater than the hypothesized variance, the third gives the confidence level $(1-\alpha)$, and the fourth is the hypothesized variance.

Running that line of code produces these results:

```
Results of Hypothesis Test
--------------------------

Null Hypothesis:          variance = 2.25

Alternative Hypothesis:   True variance is greater than 2.25

Test Name:                Chi-Squared Test on Variance

Estimated Parameter(s):   variance = 3.245299

Data:                     FarKlempt.data2

Test Statistic:           Chi-Squared = 12.9812

Test Statistic Parameter: df = 9

P-value:                  0.163459

95% Confidence Interval:  LCL = 1.726327
                          UCL =     Inf
```

Among other statistics, the output shows the chi-square (12.9812) and the p-value (0.163459). (The chi-square value in the previous section is a bit lower because of rounding.) The p-value is greater than .05. Therefore, you cannot reject the null hypothesis.

How high would chi-square (with df=9) have to be in order to reject? Hmmm . . . .

Working with Chi-Square Distributions

As is the case for the distribution families I discuss earlier in this chapter, R provides functions for working with the chi-square distribution family: dchisq() (for the density function), pchisq() (for the cumulative density function), `qchisq()` (for quantiles), and `rchisq()` (for random-number generation).

To answer the question I pose at the end of the previous section, I use `qchisq()`:

```
> qchisq(.05,df=9,lower.tail = FALSE)
[1] 16.91898
```

The observed value missed that critical value by quite a bit.

Here are examples of the other `chisq` functions with df=9. For this set of values,

```
> chisq.values <- seq(0,16,2)
```

here are the densities

```
> round(dchisq(chisq.values,9),3)
[1] 0.000 0.016 0.066 0.100 0.101 0.081 0.056 0.036 0.021
```

and here are the cumulative densities

```
> round(pchisq(chisq.values,9),3)
[1] 0.000 0.009 0.089 0.260 0.466 0.650 0.787 0.878 0.933
```

Here are six random numbers selected from this chi-square distribution:

```
> round(rchisq(n=6,df=9),3)
[1] 13.231  5.674  7.396  6.170 11.806  7.068
```

Visualizing Chi-Square Distributions

Figure 2-9 nicely shows a couple of members of the chi-square family, with each member annotated with its degrees of freedom. In this section, I show you how to use base R graphics and `ggplot2` to re-create that picture. You'll learn some more about graphics, and you'll know how to visualize any member of this family.

Plotting chi-square in base R graphics

To get started, you create a vector of values from which `dchisq()` calculates densities:

```
chi.values <- seq(0,25,.1)
```

Start the graphing with a `plot` statement:

```
plot(x=chi.values,
    y=dchisq(chi.values,df=4),
    type = "l",
    xlab=expression(chi^2),
      ylab="")
```

The first two arguments indicate what you're plotting — the chi-square distribution with four degrees of freedom versus the `chi.values` vector. The third argument specifies a line (that's a lowercase *L*, not the number 1). The third argument labels the *x*-axis with the Greek letter *chi* (χ) raised to the second power. The fourth argument gives the *y*-axis a blank label.

Why did I have you do that? When I first created the graph, I found that `ylab` locates the *y*-axis label too far to the left, and the label was cut off slightly. To fix that, I blank out `ylab` and then use `mtext()`:

```
mtext(side = 2, text = expression(f(chi^2)), line = 2.5)
```

The `side` argument specifies the side of the graph to insert the label: bottom = 1, left = 2, top = 3, and right = 4. The `text` argument sets $f\left(\chi^2\right)$ as the label for the axis. The `line` argument specifies the distance from the label to the *y*-axis: The distance increases with the value.

Next, you add the curve for chi-square with ten degrees of freedom:

```
lines(x=chi.values,y=dchisq(chi.values,df= 10))
```

Rather than add a legend, follow Figure 2-9 and add an annotation for each curve. Here's how:

```
text(x=6,y=.15, label="df=4")
text(x=16, y=.07, label = "df=10")
```

The first two arguments locate the annotation, and the third one provides the content.

Putting it all together:

```
plot(x=chi.values,
    y=dchisq(chi.values,df=4),
    type = "l",
    xlab=expression(chi^2),
      ylab="")
```

```
mtext(side = 2, expression(f(chi^2)), line = 2.5)
lines(x=chi.values,y=dchisq(chi.values,df= 10))
text(x=6,y=.15, label="df=4")
text(x=16, y=.07, label = "df=10")
```

creates Figure 2-10.

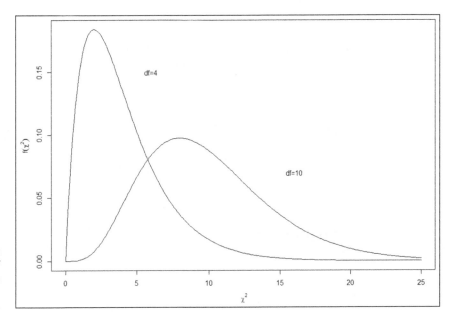

FIGURE 2-10:
Two members of
the chi-square
family, plotted in
base R graphics.

Plotting chi-square in ggplot2

In this plot, I again have you use annotations rather than a legend, so you set NULL
as the data source and work with a vector for each line. The first aesthetic maps
chi.values to the x-axis:

```
ggplot(NULL, aes(x=chi.values))
```

Then you add a geom_line for each chi-square curve, with the mapping to the
y-axis as indicated:

```
geom_line(aes(y=dchisq(chi.values,4)))
geom_line(aes(y=dchisq(chi.values,10)))
```

As I point out earlier in this chapter, this is like using ggplot2 to create a base R
graph, but in this case, it works (because it doesn't create an unwanted legend).

Next, you label the axes:

```
labs(x=expression(chi^2),y=expression(f(chi^2)))
```

And finally, the aptly named `annotate()` function adds the annotations:

```
annotate(geom = "text",x=6,y=.15,label="df=4")
annotate(geom = "text",x=16,y=.07,label="df=10")
```

The first argument specifies that the annotation is a text object. The next two locate the annotation in the graph, and the fourth provides the label.

So all of this

```
ggplot(NULL, aes(x=chi.values))+
  geom_line(aes(y=dchisq(chi.values,4))) +
  geom_line(aes(y=dchisq(chi.values,10))) +
  labs(x=expression(chi^2),y=expression(f(chi^2)))+
  annotate(geom = "text",x=6,y=.15,label = "df=4")+
  annotate(geom = "text",x=16,y=.07,label = "df=10")
```

draws Figure 2-11.

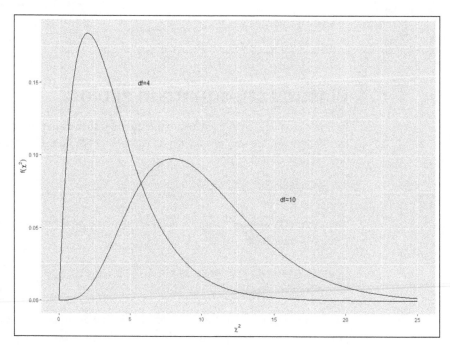

FIGURE 2-11: Two members of the chi-square family, plotted in ggplot2.

Chapter **3**

Two-Sample Hypothesis Testing

I n a variety of fields, the need often arises to compare one sample with another. Sometimes the samples are independent and sometimes they're matched in some way. Given that each sample comes from a separate population, the objective here is to decide whether these populations are different from one another.

Usually, this involves tests of hypotheses about population means. You can also test hypotheses about population variances. In this chapter, I show you how to carry out these tests, and how to use R to get the job done.

Hypotheses Built for Two

As in the one-sample case (see Chapter 2 of Book 3), hypothesis testing with two samples starts with a null hypothesis (H_0) and an alternative hypothesis (H_1). The *null hypothesis* specifies that any differences you see between the two samples are due strictly to chance. The alternative hypothesis says, in effect, that any differences you see are real and not due to chance.

It's possible to have a *one-tailed test*, in which the alternative hypothesis specifies the direction of the difference between the two means, or a *two-tailed test*, in which the alternative hypothesis does not specify the direction of the difference.

For a one-tailed test, the hypotheses look like this:

$H_0: \mu_1 - \mu_2 = 0$

$H_1: \mu_1 - \mu_2 > 0$

or like this:

$H_0: \mu_1 - \mu_2 = 0$

$H_1: \mu_1 - \mu_2 < 0$

For a two-tailed test, the hypotheses are

$H_0: \mu_1 - \mu_2 = 0$

$H_1: \mu_1 - \mu_2 \neq 0$

The zero in these hypotheses is the typical case. It's possible, however, to test for any value — just substitute that value for zero.

To carry out the test, you first set α, the probability of a Type I error that you're willing to live with. (See Chapter 2 of Book 3.) Then you calculate the mean and standard deviation of each sample, subtract one mean from the other and use a formula to convert the result into a test statistic. Compare the test statistic to a sampling distribution of test statistics. If it's in the rejection region that α specifies (again, see Chapter 2 of Book 3), reject H_0. If it's not, don't reject H_0.

Sampling Distributions Revisited

In Chapter 1 of Book 3, I introduce the idea of a sampling distribution — a distribution of all possible values of a statistic for a particular sample size. In that chapter, I describe the sampling distribution of the mean. In Chapter 2 of Book 3, I show its connection with one-sample hypothesis testing.

For two-sample hypothesis testing, another sampling distribution is necessary This one is the sampling distribution of the difference between means.

The *sampling distribution of the difference between means* is the distribution of all possible values of differences between pairs of sample means with the sample sizes held constant from pair to pair. (Yes, that's a mouthful.) *Held constant from pair to pair* means that the first sample in the pair always has the same size, and the second sample in the pair always has the same size. The two sample sizes are not necessarily equal.

Within each pair, each sample comes from a different population. All samples are independent of one another so that picking individuals for one sample has no effect on picking individuals for another.

Figure 3-1 shows the steps in creating this sampling distribution. This is something you never do in practice. It's all theoretical. As the figure shows, the idea is to take a sample out of one population and a sample out of another, calculate their means, and subtract one mean from the other. Return the samples to the populations and repeat over and over and over. The result of the process is a set of differences between means. This set of differences is the sampling distribution.

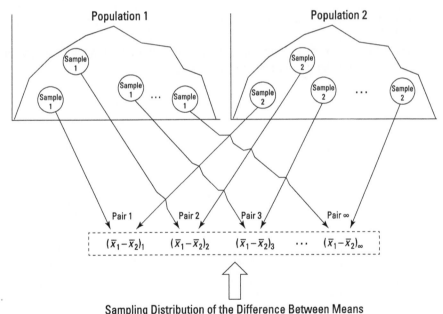

FIGURE 3-1:
Creating the sampling distribution of the difference between means.

Applying the central limit theorem

Like any other set of numbers, this sampling distribution has a mean and a standard deviation. As is the case with the sampling distribution of the mean (see Chapters 1 and 2 of Book 3), the central limit theorem applies here.

According to the central limit theorem, if the samples are large, the sampling distribution of the difference between means is approximately a normal distribution. If the populations are normally distributed, the sampling distribution is a normal distribution even if the samples are small.

The central limit theorem also has something to say about the mean and standard deviation of this sampling distribution. Suppose that the parameters for the first population are μ_1 and σ_1, and the parameters for the second population are μ_2 and σ_2. The mean of the sampling distribution is

$$\mu_{\bar{x}_1-\bar{x}_2} = \mu_1 - \mu_2$$

The standard deviation of the sampling distribution is

$$\sigma_{\bar{x}_1-\bar{x}_2} = \sqrt{\frac{\sigma_1^2}{N_1} + \frac{\sigma_2^2}{N_2}}$$

N_1 is the number of individuals in the sample from the first population, and N_2 is the number of individuals in the sample from the second.

This standard deviation is called *the standard error of the difference between means.*

Figure 3-2 shows the sampling distribution along with its parameters, as specified by the central limit theorem.

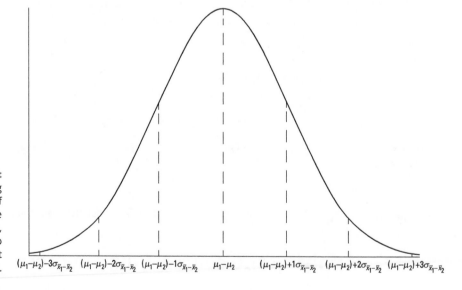

FIGURE 3-2:
The sampling distribution of the difference between means, according to the central limit theorem.

$(\mu_1-\mu_2)-3\sigma_{\bar{x}_1-\bar{x}_2}$ $(\mu_1-\mu_2)-2\sigma_{\bar{x}_1-\bar{x}_2}$ $(\mu_1-\mu_2)-1\sigma_{\bar{x}_1-\bar{x}_2}$ $\mu_1-\mu_2$ $(\mu_1-\mu_2)+1\sigma_{\bar{x}_1-\bar{x}_2}$ $(\mu_1-\mu_2)+2\sigma_{\bar{x}_1-\bar{x}_2}$ $(\mu_1-\mu_2)+3\sigma_{\bar{x}_1-\bar{x}_2}$

Zs once more

Because the central limit theorem says that the sampling distribution is approximately normal for large samples (or for small samples from normally distributed populations), you use the z-score as your test statistic. Another way to say "use the z-score as your test statistic" is "perform a z-test." Here's the formula:

$$z = \frac{(\bar{x}_1 - \bar{x}_2) - (\mu_1 - \mu_2)}{\sigma_{\bar{x}_1 - \bar{x}_2}}$$

The term $(\mu_1 - \mu_2)$ represents the difference between the means in H_0.

This formula converts the difference between sample means into a standard score. Compare the standard score against a standard normal distribution — a normal distribution with $\mu = 0$ and $\sigma = 1$. If the score is in the rejection region defined by α, reject H_0. If it's not, don't reject H_0.

You use this formula when you know the value of σ_1^2 and σ_2^2.

Here's an example. Imagine a new training technique designed to increase IQ. Take a sample of nine people and train them under the new technique. Take another sample of nine people and give them no special training. Suppose that the sample mean for the new technique sample is 110.222, and for the no-training sample it's 101. The hypothesis test is

$$H_0: \mu_1 - \mu_2 \leq 0$$

$$H_1: \mu_1 - \mu_2 > 0$$

I'll set α at .05.

The IQ is known to have a standard deviation of 15, and I assume that standard deviation would be the same in the population of people trained on the new technique. Of course, that population doesn't exist. The assumption is that if it did, it should have the same value for the standard deviation as the regular population of IQ scores. Does the mean of that (theoretical) population have the same value as the regular population? H_0 says it does. H_1 says it's larger.

The test statistic is

$$z = \frac{(\bar{x}_1 - \bar{x}_2) - (\mu_1 - \mu_2)}{\sigma_{\bar{x}_1 - \bar{x}_2}} = \frac{(\bar{x}_1 - \bar{x}_2) - (\mu_1 - \mu_2)}{\sqrt{\frac{\sigma_1^2}{N_1} + \frac{\sigma_2^2}{N_2}}} = \frac{(107 - 101.2)}{\sqrt{\frac{16^2}{25} + \frac{16^2}{25}}} = \frac{5.8}{4.53} = 1.28$$

With $\alpha = .05$, the critical value of z — the value that cuts off the upper 5 percent of the area under the standard normal distribution — is 1.645. (You can use the qnorm( ) function from Chapter 6 of Book 2 to verify this.) The calculated value of the test statistic is less than the critical value, so the decision is to not reject H_0. Figure 3-3 summarizes.

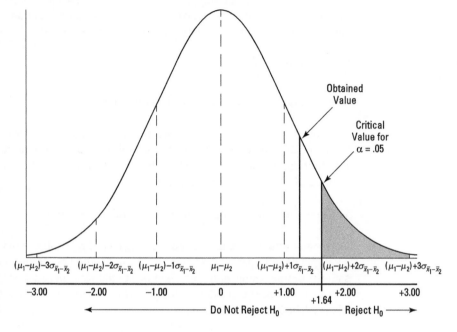

FIGURE 3-3: The sampling distribution of the difference between means, along with the critical value for $\alpha = .05$ and the obtained value of the test statistic in the IQ example.

Z-testing for two samples in *R*

As is the case for one-sample testing (explained in Chapter 2 of Book 3), base R provides no function for a two-sample z-test. If this function existed, you'd probably want it to work like this for the example:

```
> sample1 <-c(100,118,97,92,118,125,136,95,111)
> sample2 <-c(91,109,83,88,115,108,127,102,86)
> z.test2(sample1,sample2,15,15)
mean1 = 110.2222      mean2 = 101
standard error = 7.071068
z = 1.304
one-tailed probability = 0.096
two-tailed probability = 0.192
```

Because this function isn't available, I'll show you how to create one.

Begin with the function name and the arguments:

```
z.test2 = function(x,y,popsd1,popsd2){
```

The first two arguments are data vectors and the second two are the population standard deviations. The left curly bracket indicates that subsequent statements are what occurs inside the function.

Next, you initialize a vector that will hold the one-tailed probability:

```
one.tail.p <- NULL
```

Then you calculate the standard error of the difference between means:

```
std.error <- sqrt((popsd1^2/length(x) + popsd2^2/length(y)))
```

and then the (rounded) z-score:

```
z.score <- round((mean(x)-mean(y))/std.error,3)
```

Finally, you calculate the rounded one-tailed probability:

```
one.tail.p <- round(pnorm(abs(z.score),lower.tail = FALSE),3)
```

The abs() function (absolute value) ensures the appropriate calculation for a negative z-score.

Last but not least, a cat() (concatenate-and-print) statement displays this output:

```
cat(" mean1 =", mean(x)," ", "mean2 =", mean(y), "\n",
    "standard error =", std.error, "\n",
    "z =", z.score,"\n",
    "one-tailed probability =", one.tail.p,"\n",
    "two-tailed probability =", 2*one.tail.p )}
```

I use a cat() function like this one for the one-sample case in Chapter 2 of Book 3. The right curly bracket closes off the function.

Here's the newly defined function:

```
z.test2 = function(x,y,popsd1,popsd2){
  one.tail.p <- NULL
  std.error <- sqrt((popsd1^2/length(x) + popsd2^2/length(y)))
  z.score <- round((mean(x)-mean(y))/std.error,3)
  one.tail.p <- round(pnorm(abs(z.score),lower.tail = FALSE),3)
  cat(" mean1 =", mean(x)," ", "mean2 =", mean(y), "\n",
      "standard error =", std.error, "\n",
      "z =", z.score,"\n",
      "one-tailed probability =", one.tail.p,"\n",
      "two-tailed probability =", 2*one.tail.p )}
```

t for Two

The example in the preceding section involves a situation you rarely encounter — known population variances. If you know a population's variance, you're likely to know the population mean. If you know the mean, you probably don't have to perform hypothesis tests about it.

Not knowing the variances takes the central limit theorem out of play. This means that you can't use the normal distribution as an approximation of the sampling distribution of the difference between means. Instead, you use the *t*-distribution, a family of distributions I introduce in Chapter 1 of Book 3 and apply to one-sample hypothesis testing in Chapter 2 of Book 3. The members of this family of distributions differ from one another in terms of a parameter called *degrees of freedom (df)* — think of df as the denominator of the variance estimate you use when you calculate a value of *t* as a test statistic. Another way to say "calculate a value of *t* as a test statistic" is "perform a *t*-test."

Unknown population variances lead to two possibilities for hypothesis testing. One possibility is that although the variances are unknown, you have reason to assume they're equal. The other possibility is that you cannot assume they're equal. In the sections that follow, I discuss these possibilities.

Like Peas in a Pod: Equal Variances

When you don't know a population variance, you use the sample variance to estimate it. If you have two samples, you average (sort of) the two sample variances to arrive at the estimate.

REMEMBER

Putting sample variances together to estimate a population variance is called *pooling*. With two sample variances, here's how you do it:

$$s_p{}^2 = \frac{(N_1 - 1)s_1^2 + (N_2 - 1)s_2^2}{(N_1 - 1) + (N_2 - 1)}$$

In this formula, $s_p{}^2$ stands for the pooled estimate. Notice that the denominator of this estimate is $(N_1 - 1) + (N_2 - 1)$. Is this the df? Absolutely!

The formula for calculating *t* is

$$t = \frac{(\bar{x}_1 - \bar{x}_2) - (\mu_1 - \mu_2)}{s_p \sqrt{\frac{1}{N_1} + \frac{1}{N_2}}}$$

On to an example. FarKlempt Robotics is trying to choose between two machines to produce a component for its new microrobot. Speed is of the essence, so the company has each machine produce ten copies of the component and time each production run. The hypotheses are

$$H_0: \mu_1 - \mu_2 = 0$$
$$H_1: \mu_1 - \mu_2 \neq 0$$

They set α at .05. This is a two-tailed test because they don't know in advance which machine might be faster.

Table 3-1 presents the data for the production times in minutes.

TABLE 3-1

Sample Statistics from the FarKlempt Machine Study

	Machine 1	Machine 2
Mean production time	23.00	20.00
Standard deviation	2.71	2.79
Sample size	10	10

The pooled estimate of σ^2 is

$$s_p^{\,2} = \frac{(N_1-1)s_1^2 + (N_2-1)s_2^2}{(N_1-1)+(N_2-1)} = \frac{(10-1)(2.71)^2 + (10-1)(2.79)^2}{(10-1)+(10-1)}$$

$$= \frac{(9)(2.71)^2 + (9)(2.79)^2}{(9)+(9)} = \frac{66+70}{18} = 7.56$$

The estimate of σ is 2.75, the square root of 7.56.

The test statistic is

$$t = \frac{(\bar{x}_1 - \bar{x}_2)-(\mu_1 - \mu_2)}{s_p\sqrt{\dfrac{1}{N_1}+\dfrac{1}{N_2}}} = \frac{(23-20)}{2.75\sqrt{\dfrac{1}{10}+\dfrac{1}{10}}} = \frac{3}{1.23} = 2.44$$

For this test statistic, df = 18, the denominator of the variance estimate. In a t-distribution with 18 df, the critical value is 2.10 for the right-side (upper) tail and −2.10 for the left-side (lower) tail. If you don't believe me, apply qt(). (See Chapter 2 of Book 3.) The calculated value of the test statistic is greater than 2.10, so the decision is to reject H_0. The data provide evidence that Machine 2 is significantly faster than Machine 1. (You can use the word *significant* whenever you reject H_0.)

t-Testing in *R*

Here are a couple of vectors for the sample data in the example in the preceding section:

```
machine1 <-c(24.58, 22.09, 23.70, 18.89, 22.02, 28.71, 24.44, 20.91, 23.83,
   20.83)
machine2 <- c(21.61, 19.06, 20.72, 15.77, 19, 25.88, 21.48, 17.85, 20.86, 17.77)
```

R provides two ways for performing the *t*-test. Both involve t.test(), which I use in Chapters 1 and 2 of Book 3.

Working with two vectors

Here's how to test the hypotheses with two vectors and the equal variances assumption:

```
t.test(machine1,machine2,var.equal = TRUE, alternative="two.sided", mu=0)
```

The alternative=two-sided argument reflects the type of alternative hypothesis specified in the example, and the last argument indicates the hypothesized difference between means.

Running that function produces this output:

```
Two Sample t-test

data:  machine1 and machine2          t = 2.4396, df = 18, p-value = 0.02528
alternative hypothesis: true difference in means is not equal to 0
95 percent confidence interval:
 0.4164695 5.5835305
sample estimates:
mean of x mean of y
      23        20
```

The *t*-value and the low *p*-value indicate that you can reject the null hypothesis. Machine 2 is significantly faster than Machine 1.

Working with a data frame and a formula

The other way of carrying out the test in the preceding section is to create a data frame and then use a formula that looks like this:

```
prod.time ~ machine
```

The formula expresses the idea that production time depends on the machine you use. Although it's not necessary to do the test this way, it's a good idea to get accustomed to formulas. I show you how to use them quite a bit in later chapters.

The first thing to do is create a data frame in long format. First you create a vector for the 20 production times — machine1's times first and then machine2's:

```
prod.time <- c(machine1,machine2)
```

Next, you create a vector of the two machine names:

```
machine <-c("machine1","machine2")
```

Then you turn that vector into a vector of ten repetitions of "machine1" followed by ten repetitions of "machine2". It's a little tricky, but here's how:

```
machine <- rep(machine, times = c(10,10))
```

And the data frame is

```
FarKlempt.frame <-data.frame(machine,prod.time)
```

Its first six rows are

```
> head(FarKlempt.frame)
  machine prod.time
1 machine1     24.58
2 machine1     22.09
3 machine1     23.70
4 machine1     18.89
5 machine1     22.02
6 machine1     28.71
```

The t.test() function is then

```
with (FarKlempt.frame,t.test(prod.time~machine,
                    var.equal = TRUE,
                    alternative="two.sided",
                    mu=0))
```

This produces the same output as the 2-vector version.

Visualizing the results

In studies like in the preceding section, two ways of presenting the results are box plots and bar graphs.

Box plots

Box plots depict the data in each sample along with the sample median, as explained in Chapter 1 of Book 3. They're easy to create in base R and in ggplot2. For base R graphics, the code looks quite a bit like the formula method for t.test():

```
with (FarKlempt.frame,boxplot(prod.time~machine, xlab = "Machine",
    ylab="Production Time (minutes)"))
```

The plot looks like Figure 3-4.

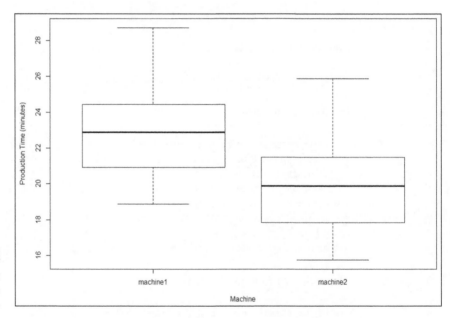

FIGURE 3-4:
Box plot of
FarKlempt
Machines data
in base R.

Figure 3-5 shows the box plot rendered in ggplot2. The code that produces that box plot is

```
ggplot(FarKlempt.frame, aes(x=machine, y=prod.time))+
    stat_boxplot(geom="errorbar", width =.5) +
    geom_boxplot()
```

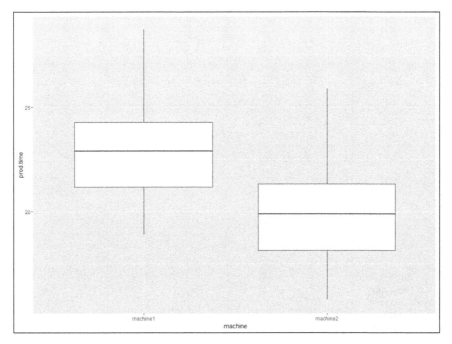

FIGURE 3-5:
Box plot of
FarKlempt
Machines data
in ggplot2.

The only new function is stat_boxplot(), which adds the perpendicular line to the end of each whisker. The default width of those lines is the width of the box. I added width =.5 to cut that width in half.

**TECHNICAL
STUFF**

In ggplot2, stat is a way of summarizing the data so that a geom function can use it. The stat function used here calculates the components for the box plot. You use it to override the default appearance of the box plot — which is without the perpendicular line at the end of each whisker. In earlier examples (and in the next one), you use stat="identity" to instruct geom_bar() to use table data rather than counts.

Bar graphs

Traditionally, researchers report and plot sample means and standard errors. It's easy to do that in ggplot2. Figure 3-6 shows what I mean.

The *t*-shaped bars that extend above and below the top of each bar are the *error bars* that denote the standard error of the mean.

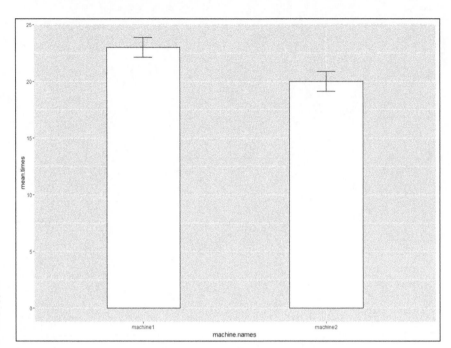

FIGURE 3-6:
FarKlempt
Machine means
and standard
errors.

To use `ggplot2`, you have to create a data frame of machine names, mean times, and standard errors. The three vectors that will constitute the data frame are

```
machine.names <-c("machine1","machine2")
mean.times <- c(mean(machine1),mean(machine2))
se.times <- c(sd(machine1)/sqrt(length(machine1)),     sd(machine2)/
   sqrt(length(machine2)))
```

The data frame is then

```
FKmeans.frame <-data.frame(machine.names,mean.times,se.times)
```

It looks like this:

```
> FKmeans.frame
  machine.names mean.times  se.times
1      machine1         23 0.8570661
2      machine2         20 0.8818339
```

The code to create Figure 3-6 is

```
ggplot(FKmeans.frame, aes(x=machine.names, y=mean.times))+
  geom_bar(stat="identity", width=.4,color="black",fill="white")+
  geom_errorbar(aes(ymin=mean.times-se.times, ymax=mean.times+se.times),width=.1)
```

The first function sets the stage with the aesthetic mappings, and the second plots the bars. The `stat = identity` argument instructs `geom_bar` to use the tabled statistics rather than to count instances of `machine1` and `machine2`. The other arguments set the appearance of the bars.

The third function is the `geom` that plots the error bars. The aesthetic mappings set the minimum point and maximum point for each error bar. The `width` argument sets the width for the perpendicular line at the end of each error bar.

TIP

In most scientific publications, you see graphs like this one with only the positive error bar — the one extending above the mean. To graph it that way in this example, set `ymin=mean.times` rather than `ymin=mean.times-se.times`.

Like ps and qs: Unequal variances

The case of unequal variances presents a challenge. As it happens, when variances are not equal, the t-distribution with $(N_1-1) + (N_2-1)$ degrees of freedom is not as close an approximation to the sampling distribution as statisticians would like.

Statisticians meet this challenge by reducing the degrees of freedom. To accomplish the reduction, they use a fairly involved formula that depends on the sample standard deviations and the sample sizes.

Because the variances aren't equal, a pooled estimate isn't appropriate. So you calculate the t-test in a different way:

$$t = \frac{(\bar{x}_1 - \bar{x}_2) - (\mu_1 - \mu_2)}{\sqrt{\dfrac{s_1^2}{N_1} + \dfrac{s_2^2}{N_2}}}$$

You evaluate the test statistic against a member of the t-distribution family that has the reduced degrees of freedom.

Here's what `t.test()` produces for the FarKlempt example if you assume that the variances are not equal:

```
with (FarKlempt.frame,t.test(prod.time~machine,
                             var.equal = FALSE,
                             alternative="two.sided",
                             mu=0))

Welch Two Sample t-test

data:  prod.time by machine
t = 2.4396, df = 17.985, p-value = 0.02529
```

```
alternative hypothesis: true difference in means between group machine1 and
    group machine2 is not equal to 095 percent confidence interval:
  0.4163193 5.5836807
sample estimates:
mean in group machine1 mean in group machine2
                  23                      20
```

You can see the slight reduction in degrees of freedom. The variances are so close that little else changes.

A Matched Set: Hypothesis Testing for Paired Samples

In the hypothesis tests I describe so far, the samples are independent of one another. Choosing an individual for one sample has no bearing on the choice of an individual for the other.

Sometimes, the samples are matched. The most obvious case is when the same individual provides a score under each of two conditions — as in a before-after study. Suppose ten people participate in a weight-loss program. They weigh in before they start the program and again after one month on the program. The important data is the set of before-after differences. Table 3-2 shows the data

The idea is to think of these differences as a sample of scores and treat them as you would if you were doing a one-sample t-test. (See Chapter 2 of Book 3.)

You carry out a test on these hypotheses:

$H_0: \mu_d \leq 0$

$H_1: \mu_d > 0$

The d in the subscripts stands for "difference." Set $\alpha = .05$.

The formula for this kind of t-test is

$$t = \frac{\bar{d} - \mu_d}{s_d}$$

TABLE 3-2

Data for the Weight-Loss Example

Person	Weight Before Program	Weight After One Month	Difference
1	198	194	4
2	201	203	–2
3	210	200	10
4	185	183	2
5	204	200	4
6	156	153	3
7	167	166	1
8	197	197	0
9	220	215	5
10	186	184	2
Mean			2.9
Standard deviation			3.25

In this formula, $\bar{d}$ is the mean of the differences. To find $s_{\bar{d}}$, you calculate the standard deviation of the differences and divide by the square root of the number of pairs:

$$s_{\bar{d}} = \frac{s}{\sqrt{N}}$$

The df is N–1 (where N is the number of pairs).

From Table 3-2,

$$t = \frac{\bar{d} - \mu_d}{s_d} = \frac{2.9}{\left(3.25 / \sqrt{10}\right)} = 2.82$$

With df = 9 (Number of pairs – 1), the critical value for α = .05 is 1.83. (Use qt() to verify.) The calculated value exceeds this value, so the decision is to reject H_0.

Paired Sample t-testing in R

For paired sample t-tests, it's the same formula as for independent-samples t-tests. As you'll see, you add an argument. Here's the data from Table 3-2:

```
before <-c(198,201,210,185,204,156,167,197,220,186)
after <- c(194,203,200,183,200,153,166,197,215,184)
```

And the t-test:

```
t.test(before,after,alternative = "greater",paired=TRUE)
```

That last argument, of course, specifies a paired-samples test. The default value for that one is FALSE.

Running that test yields

```
        Paired t-test

data:  before and after
t = 2.8241, df = 9, p-value = 0.009956
alternative hypothesis: true difference in means is greater than 0
95 percent confidence interval:
 1.017647      Inf
sample estimates:
mean of the differences
              2.9
```

Because of the very low p-value, you reject the null hypothesis.

Testing Two Variances

The two-sample hypothesis testing I describe in this chapter pertains to means. It's also possible to test hypotheses about variances.

In this section, I extend the one-variance manufacturing example I use in Chapter 2 of Book 3. FarKlempt Robotics, Inc., produces a part that has to be a certain length with little variability. Company leaders are considering two machines to produce this part, and they want to choose the one that results in the least variability. FarKlempt Robotics takes a sample of parts from each machine, measures them, finds the variance for each sample, and performs a hypothesis test to see whether one machine's variance is significantly greater than the other's.

The hypotheses are

$$H_{0:}\ \sigma_1^2 = \sigma_2^2$$
$$H_{1:}\ \sigma_1^2 \neq \sigma_2^2$$

As always, an α is a must-have item. As usual, I set it to .05.

When you test two variances, you don't subtract one from the other. Instead, you divide one by the other to calculate the test statistic. Sir Ronald Fisher was the famous statistician who worked out the mathematics and the family of distributions for working with variances in this way. The test statistic is named in his honor. It's called an *F-ratio,* and the test is the *F test.* The family of distributions for the test is called the *F-distribution.*

Without going into all the mathematics, I'll just tell you that, once again, df is the parameter that distinguishes one member of the family from another. What's different about this family is that two variance estimates are involved, so each member of the family is associated with two values of df, rather than one as in the *t*-test. Another difference between the *F*-distribution and the others you've seen is that the *F* cannot have a negative value. Figure 3-7 shows two members of the *F*-distribution family.

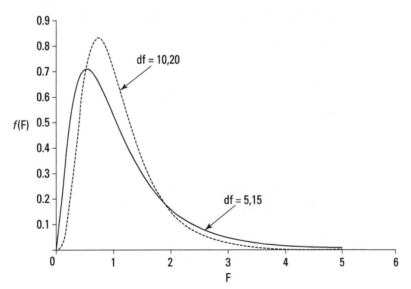

FIGURE 3-7:
Two members of
the *F*-distribution
family.

The test statistic is

$$F = \frac{\text{larger } s^2}{\text{smaller } s^2}$$

Suppose FarKlempt Robotics produces 10 parts with Machine 1 and finds a sample variance of .81 square inches. It produces 15 parts with Machine 2 and finds a sample variance of .64 square inches. Can the company reject H_0?

Calculating the test statistic,

$$F = \frac{.81}{.64} = 1.27$$

the dfs are 9 and 14: The variance estimate in the numerator of the F ratio is based on 10 cases, and the variance estimate in the denominator is based on 15 cases.

When the dfs are 9 and 14 and it's a two-tailed test at $\alpha = .05$, the critical value of F is 3.21. (In a moment, I show you an R function that calculates this.) The calculated value is less than the critical value, so the decision is to not reject H_0.

REMEMBER

It makes a difference which df is in the numerator and which df is in the denominator. The F-distribution for df = 9 and df = 14 is different from the F-distribution for df = 14 and df = 9. For example, the critical value in the latter case is 3.80, not 3.21.

F testing in R

R provides a function for testing hypotheses like the one in the FarKlempt Robotics 2-machines example. It's called var.test(). Should it have been called F.test()? Well, maybe.

The important point is to not confuse this function with varTest(), which I use in Chapter 2 of Book 3 to test hypotheses about a single sample variance (with chi-square). That function is in the EnvStats package.

To apply var.test(), you first create the vectors that hold the data for the parts that Machine 1 and Machine 2 produce:

```
> m1.parts <-c(3.8,2.5,2.3,2.1,3.5,3.9,2.0,3.8,4.0,4.4)
> m2.parts <-c(2.9,3.5,2.2,4.5,3.1,3.8,4.3,2.4,2.7,2.6,3.6,4.1,4.8,3.0,3.0)
```

The vectors are the first two arguments to var.test(). The third is the ratio of their variances under the null hypothesis, and the fourth is the nature of the alternative hypothesis:

```
> var.test(m1.parts,m2.parts,ratio=1,alternative="two.sided")
F test to compare two variances

data:  m1.parts and m2.parts
F = 1.2805, num df = 9, denom df = 14, p-value = 0.6544
```

```
alternative hypothesis: true ratio of variances is not equal to 1
95 percent confidence interval:
 0.3990074 4.8634101
sample estimates:
ratio of variances
          1.280535
```

The low F-ratio and high p-value indicate that you cannot reject the null hypothesis. (The slight discrepancy between this F-ratio and the one calculated in the example is caused by rounding.)

F in conjunction with *t*

One use of the F-distribution is in conjunction with the t-test for independent samples. Before you do the t-test, you use F to help decide whether to assume equal variances or unequal variances in the samples.

In the equal variances t-test example I show you earlier, the standard deviations are 2.71 and 2.79. The variances are 7.34 and 7.78. The F-ratio of these variances is

$$F = \frac{7.78}{7.34} = 1.06$$

Each sample is based on ten observations, so df = 9 for each sample variance. An F-ratio of 1.06 cuts off the upper 47 percent of the F-distribution whose df are 9 and 9, so it's safe to use the equal variances version of the t-test for these data.

How does all this play out in the context of hypothesis testing? On rare occasions, H_0 is a desirable outcome and you'd rather not reject it. In that case, you stack the deck against *not* rejecting by setting α at a high level so that small differences cause you to reject H_0.

This is one of those rare occasions. It's more desirable to use the equal variances t-test, which typically provides more degrees of freedom than the unequal variances t-test. Setting a high value of α (.20 is a good one) for the F-test enables you to be confident when you assume equal variances.

Working with *F* Distributions

Just like the other distribution families I cover earlier (normal, t, chi-square), R provides functions for dealing with F distributions: `qf()` gives quantile information, `df()` provides the density function, `pf()` provides the cumulative density function, and `rf()` generates random numbers.

TIP

Note that throughout this section, I spell out *degrees of freedom* rather than use the abbreviation *df*, as I do elsewhere. That's to avoid confusion with the density function `df()`.

That critical value I refer to earlier for a two-tailed *F*-test with 9 and 14 degrees of freedom is

```
> qf(.025,9,14,lower.tail = FALSE)
[1] 3.2093
```

It's a two-tailed test at $\alpha = .05$, so .025 is in each tail.

To watch `df()` and `pf()` in action, you create a vector for them to operate on:

```
F.scores <-seq(0,5,1)
```

With 9 and 14 degrees of freedom, the (rounded) densities for these values are

```
> round(df(F.scores,9,14),3)
[1] 0.000 0.645 0.164 0.039 0.011 0.004
```

The (rounded) cumulative densities are

```
> round(pf(F.scores,9,14),3)
[1] 0.000 0.518 0.882 0.968 0.990 0.996
```

To generate five random numbers from this member of the *F*-family:

```
> rf(5,9,14)
[1] 0.6409125 0.4015354 1.1601984 0.6552502 0.8652722
```

Visualizing *F* Distributions

As I say elsewhere, visualizing distributions helps you learn them. *F* distributions are no exception, and with density functions and `ggplot2`, it's easy to plot them. My objective in this section is to show you how to use `ggplot2` to create a graph that looks like Figure 3-7, which depicts an *F*-distribution with 5 and 15 degrees of freedom and another with 10 and 20 degrees of freedom. To make the graph look like the figure, I have to add annotations with arrows pointing to the appropriate curves.

Begin with a vector of values for df( ) to do its work on:

```
F.values <-seq(0,5,.05)
```

Then create a vector of densities for an *F* distribution with 5 and 15 degrees of freedom:

```
F5.15 <- df(F.values,5,15)
```

and another for an *F* distribution with 10 and 20 degrees of freedom:

```
F10.20 <- df(F.values,10,20)
```

Now for a data frame for ggplot2:

```
F.frame <- data.frame(F.values,F5.15,F10.20)
```

This is what the first six rows of F.frame look like:

```
> head(F.frame)
  F.values      F5.15      F10.20
1     0.00 0.00000000 0.000000000
2     0.05 0.08868702 0.001349914
3     0.10 0.21319965 0.015046816
4     0.15 0.33376038 0.053520748
5     0.20 0.43898395 0.119815721
6     0.25 0.52538762 0.208812406
```

This is in wide format. As I point out earlier, ggplot( ) prefers long format, in which the data values are stacked on top of one another in one column. This is called *melting* the data and is part and parcel of the reshape2 package. (On the Packages tab, find the check box next to reshape2. If it's deselected, click on it.)

To appropriately reshape the data,

```
F.frame.melt <- melt(F.frame,id="F.values")
```

The id argument tells melt( ) what *not* to include in the stack. (F.values is the identifier, in other words.) Next, assign meaningful column names:

```
colnames(F.frame.melt)=c("F","deg.fr","density")
```

The first six rows of the melted data frame are

```
> head(F.frame.melt)
     F  deg.fr    density
1 0.00  F5.15  0.00000000
2 0.05  F5.15  0.08868702
3 0.10  F5.15  0.21319965
4 0.15  F5.15  0.33376038
5 0.20  F5.15  0.43898395
6 0.25  F5.15  0.52538762
```

To begin the visualizing, the first statement, as always, is ggplot():

```
ggplot(F.frame.melt,aes(x=F,y=density,group=deg.fr))
```

The first argument is the data frame. The first two aesthetic mappings associate *F* with the *x*-axis, and density with the *y*-axis. The third mapping forms groups based on the deg.fr variable.

Next, you add a geom_line:

```
geom_line(stat="identity",aes(linetype=deg.fr),show.legend = FALSE)
```

The stat argument tells the geom function to use the tabled data. The aesthetic mapping associates the linetype ("solid" and "dotted" are the default values) with deg.fr. I include show.legend = FALSE because I don't want ggplot2 to draw a legend on this graph — I want it to look like Figure 3-7.

TIP

If you prefer "solid" and "dashed", as in Figure 3-7, you have to change things manually:

```
scale_linetype_manual(values = c("solid","dashed"),)
```

Here's the code so far:

```
ggplot(F.frame.melt,aes(x=F,y=density,group=deg.fr)) +
   geom_line(stat="identity",aes(linetype=deg.fr),show.legend = FALSE)+
   scale_linetype_manual(values = c("solid","dashed"))
```

Figure 3-8 shows the progress.

Finally, add a couple of annotations that show the degrees of freedom for each curve. The annotation for the curve with 10 and 20 degrees of freedom is

```
annotate(geom="text",x=1.98,y=.78,label="df=10,20")
```

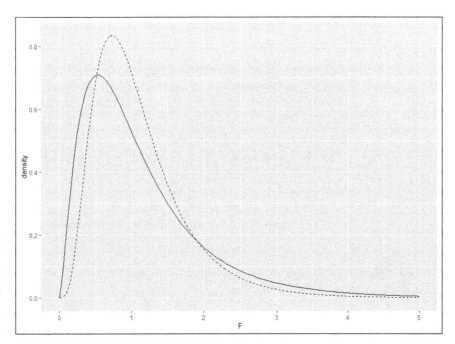

FIGURE 3-8:
Two members
of the
F-distribution
family in
ggplot2 —
intermediate
graph.

The first argument specifies a `text` geom, the next two position the `text` geom within the graph (centered on the indicated coordinates), and the fourth sets what the annotation says.

Now for the arrow that points from the annotation to the curve. It consists of a line segment and an arrowhead. The line segment part of the arrow is a `segment` geom. The arrowhead part of the arrow is the product of a function called `arrow()`, which is in the `grid` package. Once upon a time, you had to download and install this package. Now, it comes with R, but to use it you have to type

```
> library(grid)
```

Another `annotate()` function sets the arrow:

```
annotate(geom="segment",x=2.0,xend=1.15,y=0.75,yend = .6, arrow=arrow())
```

The four arguments after the `geom` function locate the start point and the end point for the line segment. The final argument plots the arrowhead.

TIP

Finding the values for the start point and the end point can involve some trial and error. It's not a bad idea to plot the arrow first and then the text.

Here's the code for everything, including the two `annotate()` functions for the other curve:

```
ggplot(F.frame.melt,aes(x=F,y=density,group=deg.fr)) +
  geom_line(stat="identity",aes(linetype=deg.fr),show.legend = FALSE)+
  scale_linetype_manual(values = c("solid","dashed")) +
  annotate(geom="text",x=1.98,y=.78,label="df=10,20")+
  annotate(geom="segment",x = 2.00, xend=1.15,y =0.75, yend=0.6,arrow=arrow()) +
  annotate(geom="text",x=3.3,y=.28,label="df=5,15") +
  annotate(geom="segment",x = 3.35, xend=2.45,y =0.25, yend=0.1,arrow=arrow())
```

And Figure 3-9 is the result.

Experiment with other values for degrees of freedom and see what the curves look like.

TIP

You can clean up your code a bit by omitting `geom=` from the `annotate()` functions. This line of code:

```
annotate(geom="text",x=1.98,y=.78,label="df=10,20")
```

is equivalent to

```
annotate("text",x=1.98,y=.78,label="df=10,20")
```

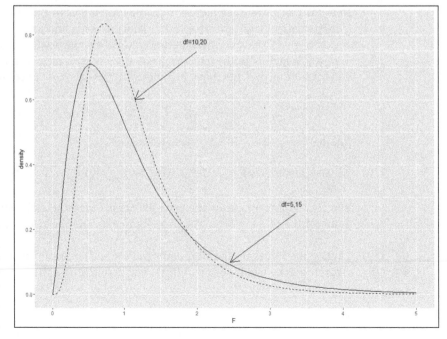

FIGURE 3-9:
Two members
of the
F-distribution
family in
ggplot2 — final
product.

» Analyzing variance

» Taking the next step after an ANOVA

» Working with repeated measures

» Performing a trend analysis

Chapter **4**

Testing More than Two Samples

Statistics would be limited if you could only make inferences about one or two samples. In this chapter, I discuss the procedures for testing hypotheses about three or more samples. I show what to do when samples are independent of one another, and what to do when they're not. In both cases, I discuss what to do after you test the hypotheses. I also discuss R functions that do the work for you.

Testing More than Two

Imagine this situation. Your company asks you to evaluate three different methods for training its employees to do a particular job. You randomly assign 30 employees to one of the three methods, resulting in 10 employees in the Method 1 group, 10 different employees in the Method 2 group, and 10 more in the Method 3 group. Your plan is to train and test the employees, tabulate the results, and form some conclusions. Before you can finish the study, three people leave the company — one from the Method 1 group and two from the Method 3 group.

Table 4-1 shows the data.

TABLE 4-1

Data from Three Training Methods

	Method 1	Method 2	Method 3
	95	83	68
	91	89	75
	89	85	79
	90	89	74
	99	81	75
	88	89	81
	96	90	73
	98	82	77
	95	84	
		80	
Mean	93.44	85.20	75.25
Variance	16.28	14.18	15.64
Standard Deviation	4.03	3.77	3.96

Do the three methods provide different results, or are they so similar that you can't distinguish among them? To decide, you have to carry out a hypothesis test

$H_0: \mu_1 = \mu_2 = \mu_3$

H_1: Not H_0

with $\alpha = .05$.

A thorny problem

Finding differences among three groups sounds pretty easy, particularly if you read Chapter 3 in Book 3. Take the mean of the scores from Method 1 and the mean of the scores from Method 2, and then do a t-test to see whether they're different. Follow the same procedure for Method 1 versus Method 3 and for Method 2 versus Method 3. If at least one of those t-tests shows a significant difference, reject H_0. Nothing to it, right? Wrong.

If your α is .05 for each t-test, you're setting yourself up for a Type I error with a probability higher than you planned on. The probability that at least one of the three t-tests results in a significant difference is way above .05. In fact, it's .14, which is way beyond acceptable. (The mathematics behind calculating that number is a little involved, so I won't elaborate.)

With more than three samples, the situation gets even worse. Four groups require six t-tests, and the probability that at least one of them is significant is .26. Table 4-2 shows what happens with increasing numbers of samples.

TABLE 4-2

The Incredible Increasing Alpha

Number of Samples t	Number of Tests	Pr (At Least One Significant t)
3	3	.14
4	6	.26
5	10	.40
6	15	.54
7	21	.66
8	28	.76
9	36	.84
10	45	.90

Carrying out multiple t-tests is clearly not the answer. What do you do?

A solution

It's necessary to take a different approach. The idea is to think in terms of variances rather than means.

I'd like you to think of variance in a slightly different way. The formula for estimating population variance, remember, is

$$s^2 = \frac{\sum (x - \bar{x})^2}{N - 1}$$

Because the variance is almost a mean of squared deviations from the mean, statisticians also refer to it as *mean square*. In a way, that's an unfortunate nickname: It leaves out "deviation from the mean," but there you have it.

The numerator of the variance — excuse me, mean square — is the sum of squared deviations from the mean. This leads to another nickname, *sum of squares*.

The denominator, as I say in Chapter 2 of Book 3, is *degrees of freedom* (df). So the slightly different way to think of variance is

$$\text{Mean Square} = \frac{\text{Sum of Squares}}{\text{df}}$$

You can abbreviate this as

$$\text{MS} = \frac{\text{SS}}{\text{df}}$$

Now, on to solving the thorny problem. One important step is to find the mean squares hiding in the data. Another is to understand that you use these mean squares to estimate the variances of the populations that produced these samples. In this case, assume that those variances are equal, so you're really estimating one variance. The final step is to understand that you use these estimates to test the hypotheses I show you at the beginning of this chapter.

Three different mean squares are inside the data in Table 4-1. Start with the whole set of 27 scores, forgetting for the moment that they're divided into three groups. Suppose that you want to use those 27 scores to calculate an estimate of the population variance. (A dicey idea, but humor me.) The mean of those 27 scores is 85. I'll call that mean the *grand mean* because it's the average of everything.

So the mean square would be

$$\frac{(95-85)^2 + (91-85)^2 + \ldots + (73-85)^2 + (77-85)^2}{(27-1)} = 68.08$$

The denominator has 26 (27−1) degrees of freedom. I refer to that variance as the *total variance* or, in the new way of thinking about this concept, the MS_{Total}. It's often abbreviated as MS_{T}.

Here's another variance to consider. In Chapter 3 of Book 3, I describe the *t*-test for two samples with equal variances. For that test, you put together the two sample variances to create a *pooled* estimate of the population variance. The data in Table 4-1 provides three sample variances for a pooled estimate: 16.28, 14.18, and 15.64. Assuming that these numbers represent equal population variances, the pooled estimate is

$$s_p^2 = \frac{(N_1-1)s_1^2 + (N_2-1)s_2^2 + (N_3-1)s_3^2}{(N_1-1) + (N_2-1) + (N_3-1)}$$

$$= \frac{(9-1)(16.28) + (10-1)(14.18) + (8-1)(15.64)}{(9-1) + (10-1) + (8-1)} = 15.31$$

Because this pooled estimate comes from the variance within the groups, it's called $\text{MS}_{\text{Within}}$, or MS_{W}.

One more mean square to go — the variance of the sample means around the grand mean. In this example, that means the variance in the numbers 93.44, 85.20, and 75.25 — sort of. I say "sort of" because these are means, not scores. When you deal with means, you have to take into account the number of scores that produced each mean. To do that, you multiply each squared deviation by the number of scores in that sample.

So this variance is

$$\frac{(9)(93.44 - 85)^2 + (10)(85.20 - 85)^2 + (8)(75.25 - 85)^2}{3 - 1} = 701.34$$

The df for this variance is 2 (Number of Samples (3, in this case)−1).

Statisticians, not known for their crispness of usage, refer to this as the variance *between* sample means. (*Among* is the correct word when you're talking about more than two items.) This variance is known as $MS_{Between}$, or MS_B.

So you now have three estimates of population variance: MS_T, MS_W, and MS_B. What do you do with them?

Remember that the original objective is to test a hypothesis about three means. According to H_0, any differences you see among the three sample means are due strictly to chance. The implication is that the variance among those means is the same as the variance of any three numbers selected at random from the population.

If you could somehow compare the variance among the means (that's MS_B, remember) with the population variance, you could see whether that holds up. If only you had an estimate of the population variance that's independent of the differences among the groups, you'd be in business.

Ah . . . but you do have that estimate. You have MS_W, an estimate based on pooling the variances within the samples. Assuming that those variances represent equal population variances, this is a solid estimate. In this example, it's based on 24 degrees of freedom.

The reasoning now becomes: If MS_B is about the same as MS_W, you have evidence consistent with H_0. If MS_B is significantly larger than MS_W, you have evidence that's inconsistent with H_0. In effect, you transform these hypotheses

$H_0: \mu_1 = \mu_2 = \mu_3$

$H_1:$ Not H_0

into these

$$H_0: \sigma_B^2 \leq \sigma_W^2$$
$$H_1: \sigma_B^2 > \sigma_W^2$$

Rather than perform multiple t-tests among sample means, you perform a test of the difference between two variances.

What is that test? In Chapter 3 of Book 3, I show you the test for hypotheses about two variances. It's called the F-test. To perform this test, you divide one variance by the other and then evaluate the result against a family of distributions called the F-distribution. Because two variances are involved, two values for degrees of freedom define each member of the family.

For this example, F has df = 2 (for the MS_B) and df = 24 (for the MS_W). Figure 4-1 shows what this member of the F family looks like. For our purposes, it's the distribution of possible F values if H_0 is true. (See the section in Chapter 3 of Book 3 about visualizing F-distributions.)

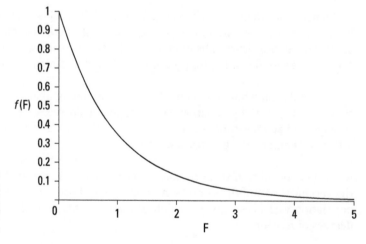

FIGURE 4-1:
The F-distribution with 2 and 24 degrees of freedom.

The test statistic for the example is

$$F = \frac{701.34}{15.31} = 45.82$$

What proportion of area does this value cut off in the upper tail of the F-distribution? From Figure 4-1, you can see that this proportion is microscopic, as the values on the horizontal axis only go up to 5. (And the proportion of area beyond 5 is tiny.) It's way less than .05.

This means that it's highly unlikely that differences among the means are due to chance. It means that you reject H_0.

REMEMBER

This whole procedure for testing more than two samples is called the *analysis of variance,* often abbreviated as ANOVA. In the context of an ANOVA, the denominator of an F-ratio has the generic name *error term.* The independent variable is sometimes called a *factor.* So this is a single-factor, or (1-factor), ANOVA.

In this example, the factor is Training Method. Each instance of the independent variable is called a *level.* The independent variable in this example has three levels.

More complex studies have more than one factor, and each factor can have many levels.

Meaningful relationships

Take another look at the mean squares in this example, each with its sum of squares and degrees of freedom. Before, when I calculated each mean square for you, I didn't explicitly show you each sum of squares, but here I include them:

$$MS_B = \frac{SS_B}{df_B} = \frac{1402.68}{2} = 701.34$$

$$MS_W = \frac{SS_W}{df_W} = \frac{367.32}{24} = 15.31$$

$$MS_T = \frac{SS_T}{df_T} = \frac{1770}{26} = 68.08$$

Start with the degrees of freedom: $df_B = 2$, $df_W = 24$, and $df_T = 26$. Is it a coincidence that the first two add up to the third? Hardly. It's always the case that

$$df_B + df_W = df_T$$

How about those sums of squares?

$$1402.68 + 367.32 = 1770$$

Again, this is no coincidence. In the analysis of variance, this always happens:

$$SS_B + SS_W = SS_T$$

In fact, statisticians who work with the analysis of variance speak of partitioning (read: "breaking down into non-overlapping pieces") the SS_T into one portion for the SS_B and another for the SS_W and partitioning the df_T into one amount for the df_B and another for the df_W.

ANOVA in R

In this section, I walk you through the previous section's example and show you how straightforward an analysis of variance is in R. In fact, I start at the finish line so that you can see where I'm heading.

The R function for ANOVA is `aov()`. Here's how it looks generically:

```
aov(Dependent_variable ~ Independent_variable, data)
```

In the example, the scores are the dependent variable, and the method is the independent variable. In ANOVA-speak, an independent variable is also called a *factor*. The different values of the independent variable (in this case, Method 1, Method 2, and Method 3) are called *levels* of the factor.

To proceed, you need a 2-column data frame with *Method* in the first column and *Score* in the second. (This is equivalent to the long-form data format, which I discuss in Chapters 2 and 3 of Book 3.)

Start with a vector for each column in Table 4-1:

```
method1.scores <- c(95,91,89,90,99,88,96,98,95)
method2.scores <- c(83,89,85,89,81,89,90,82,84,80)
method3.scores <- c(68,75,79,74,75,81,73,77)
```

Then create a single vector that consists of all these scores:

```
Score <- c(method1.scores, method2.scores, method3.scores)
```

Next, create a vector consisting of the names of the methods, matched up against the scores. In other words, this vector has to consist of "method1" repeated nine times, followed by "method2" repeated ten times, followed by "method3" repeated eight times:

```
Method <- rep(c("method1", "method2", "method3"), times=c(length(method1.
   scores), length(method2.scores), length(method3.scores)))
```

The data frame is then

```
Training.frame <- data.frame(Method,Score)
```

And the ANOVA is

```
analysis <-aov(Score ~ Method,data = Training.frame)
```

For a table of the analysis, use `summary()`:

```
> summary(analysis)
          Df Sum Sq Mean Sq F value   Pr(>F)
Method     2 1402.7   701.3   45.82 6.38e-09 ***
Residuals 24  367.3    15.3
---
Signif. codes: 0 '***' 0.001 '**' 0.01 '*' 0.05 '.' 0.1 ' ' 1
```

The first column consists of Method and Residuals, which map correspond to Between and Within from the preceding section. A *residual*, in this context, is a score's deviation from its group mean. (I have more to say about residuals in Chapter 6 of Book 3.) The next columns provide degrees of freedom, SS, MS, F, and p.

The high value of F and the tiny value of p (listed here as `Pr(>F)`) tell you to reject the null hypothesis. The significance codes tell you that F is so high that you can reject the null hypothesis even if α is .0001.

Plotting a boxplot to visualize the data

One way of plotting the findings is to show them as a boxplot. Here's how to plot one in `ggplot2`.

Start out with the following statement, which maps variables to the axes:

```
ggplot(Training.frame, aes(x=Method, y=Score))
```

Your next statements set up the crossbars for the whiskers:

```
stat_boxplot(geom="errorbar", width =.5)
```

And the last one plots the appropriate `geom` function:

```
geom_boxplot()
```

So these lines of R code

```
ggplot(Training.frame, aes(x=Method, y=Score))+
  stat_boxplot(geom="errorbar", width =.5) +
  geom_boxplot()
```

produce Figure 4-2.

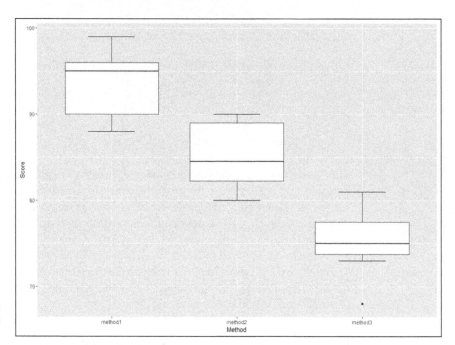

FIGURE 4-2:
Boxplot of the
sample results.

After the ANOVA

The ANOVA enables you to decide whether to reject H_0. After you decide to reject, then what? All you can say is that somewhere within the set of means, something is different from something else. The analysis doesn't specify what those "somethings" are.

Planned comparisons

For decisions that are more specific, you have to do some further tests. Not only that, you have to plan those tests in advance of carrying out the ANOVA.

These post-ANOVA tests are called *planned comparisons.* Some statisticians refer to them as *a priori tests* or *contrasts.* I illustrate by following through with the example. Suppose that, before you gathered the data, you had reason to believe that Method 2 would result in higher scores than Method 3 and that Method 1 would result in higher scores than Method 2 and Method 3 averaged together. In that case, you plan in advance to compare the means of those samples in the event that your ANOVA-based decision is to reject H_0.

As I mention earlier, the overall analysis partitions the SS_T into the SS_B and the SS_W, and the df_T into the df_B and the df_W. Planned comparisons further partition the SS_B and the df_B. Each contrast (remember, that's another name for *planned comparison*) has its own SS along with 1 df. I refer to Method 2 versus Method 3 as *Contrast1* and Method 1 versus the average of Method 2 and 3 as *Contrast2*. For this example,

$$SS_{Contrast1} + SS_{Contrast2} = SS_B$$

and

$$df_{Contrast1} + df_{Contrast2} = df_B$$

Because each SS has 1 df, it's equal to its corresponding MS. Dividing the SS for the contrast by MS_W yields an F-ratio for the contrast. The F has df=1 and df_W. If that F cuts off less than .05 in the upper tail of its F-distribution, reject the null hypothesis for that contrast (and you can refer to the contrast as "statistically significant").

It's possible to set up a contrast between two means as an expression that involves all three of the sample means. For example, to compare Method 2 versus Method 3, I can write the difference between them as

$$(0)\bar{x}_1 + (+1)\bar{x}_2 + (-1)\bar{x}_3$$

The 0, +1, and −1 are *comparison coefficients*. I refer to them, in a general way, as c_1, c_2, and c_3. To compare Method 1 versus the average of Method 2 and Method 3, it's

$$(+2)\bar{x}_1 + (-1)\bar{x}_2 + (-1)\bar{x}_3$$

The important point is that the coefficients add up to 0. How do you use the comparison coefficients and the means to calculate an SS for a contrast? For this example, here's $SS_{Contrast1}$:

$$SS_{Contrast1} = \frac{((0)(93.44) + (+1)(85.20) + (-1)(75.25))^2}{\frac{(0)^2}{9} + \frac{(+1)^2}{10} + \frac{(-1)^2}{8}} = 358.5$$

And here's $SS_{Contrast2}$:

$$SS_{Contrast2} = \frac{((+2)(93.44) + (-1)(85.20) + (-1)(75.25))^2}{\frac{(2)^2}{9} + \frac{(-1)^2}{10} + \frac{(-1)^2}{8}} = 1044.2$$

In general, the formula is

$$SS_{Contrast} = \frac{\sum c_j \bar{x}_j}{\sum \left(\frac{c_j^2}{n_j}\right)}$$

in which the j subscript stands for "level of the independent variable" (for Method 1, $j=1$, for example).

For Contrast 1:

$$F_{1,24} = \frac{SS_{Contrast1}}{MS_{Within}} = \frac{358.5}{15.3} = 23.42$$

And for Contrast 2:

$$F_{1,24} = \frac{SS_{Contrast2}}{MS_{Within}} = \frac{1044.2}{15.3} = 68.22$$

Are these contrasts significant? Yes, they are — meaning that Method 2 yields significantly higher learning than Method 3, and that Method 1 results in significantly higher learning than the average of Methods 2 and 3. You can use pf() to verify (or see the upcoming subsection "Contrasts in R").

Another word about contrasts

Earlier, I say that the important thing about a contrast is that its coefficients add up to 0. Another important thing is the relationship between the coefficients in a set of contrasts. In the two contrasts I show you, the sum of the products of corresponding coefficients is 0:

$$((0)(+2)) + ((+1)(-1)) + ((-1)(-1)) = 0$$

When this happens, the contrasts are *orthogonal* — this means they have no overlapping information. It doesn't mean that other contrasts aren't possible. It's just that other contrasts would be part of a different set (or sets) of orthogonal contrasts.

The two other sets of orthogonal contrasts for this example are (1) Method 1 versus Method 2, and Method 3 versus the average of Method 1 and Method 2 and (2) Method 1 versus Method 3, and Method 2 versus the average of Method 1 and Method 3.

Contrasts in R

The objective here is to create a table of the ANOVA that shows the contrasts partitioning the SS_B and also shows the associated F-ratios and p-values. It will look like this:

```
                    Df Sum Sq Mean Sq F value   Pr(>F)
Method               2 1402.7   701.3   45.82 6.38e-09 ***
  Method: 2 vs 3     1  358.5   358.5   23.42 6.24e-05 ***
  Method: 1 vs 2 & 3 1 1044.2  1044.2   68.22 1.78e-08 ***
Residuals           24  367.3    15.3
---
Signif. codes:  0 '***' 0.001 '**' 0.01 '*' 0.05 '.' 0.1 ' ' 1
```

To set up for the contrasts, you first create a matrix of the coefficients in the set of orthogonal contrasts:

```
contrasts(Training.frame$Method) <- matrix(c(0,1,-1,2,-1,-1),3,2)
```

Next, you explicitly define `Training.frame$Method` as a factor:

```
Training.frame$Method <- as.factor(Training.frame$Method)
```

On the left, the term inside the parentheses specifies what to contrast — the levels of the independent variable `Method` in the `Training.frame`. On the right, the `matrix()` function creates a matrix with the coefficients in the columns:

```
> contrasts(Training.frame$Method)
        [,1] [,2]
method1    0    2
method2    1   -1
method3   -1   -1
```

Next, you run the analysis of variance, but this time with a `contrasts` argument:

```
Anova.w.Contrasts <-aov(Score ~ Method,data=Training.frame,
contrasts = contrasts(Training.frame$Method))
```

TIP

If you see a warning message, you can safely ignore it.How do you create the table at the beginning of this subsection? With a `summary()` statement that adds a little twist:

```
summary(Anova.w.Contrasts,split=list(Method=list("2 vs 3"= 1,
   "1 vs 2 & 3" = 2)))
```

The little twist (a little "split," actually) is in the second argument. The goal is to partition `Method` into two pieces — one that corresponds to the first contrast and one that corresponds to the second. You do that with `split`, which divides a list into the indicated number of components and reassembles the list with a name assigned to each component. In this case, the list is `Method` split into a list with two components. The name of each component corresponds to what's in the contrast.

Running that `summary` statement produces the table at the top of this subsection.

Unplanned comparisons

Things would get boring if your post-ANOVA testing is limited to comparisons you have to plan in advance. Sometimes, you want to snoop around your data and see whether anything interesting reveals itself. Sometimes, something jumps out at you that you didn't anticipate.

When this happens, you can make comparisons you didn't plan on. These comparisons are called *a posteriori tests, post hoc tests,* or simply *unplanned comparisons.* Statisticians have come up with a wide variety of these tests, many of them with exotic names and many of them dependent on special sampling distributions.

The idea behind these tests is that you pay a price for not having planned them in advance. That price has to do with stacking the deck against rejecting H_0 for the particular comparison.

One of the best-known members of the post-hoc world is Tukey's HSD (Honest Significant Difference) test. This test performs all possible pairwise comparisons among the sample means.

Wait. What? In the earlier section "A thorny problem," I discuss why multiple pairwise *t*-tests don't work — if each test has $\alpha = .05$, the overall probability of a Type I error increases with the number of means.

So, what's the story? The story is that Tukey's test adjusts for the number of sample means and compares the differences not to the *t*-distribution but rather to the *Studentized Range* distribution. The overall effect is to make it more difficult to reject the null hypothesis about any pairwise comparison than it would be if you compare the difference against the t-distribution. (I haven't heard multiple *t*-tests referred to as Dishonestly Significant Differences, but maybe someday . . . .)

This test is easy to do in R:

```
> TukeyHSD(analysis)
  Tukey multiple comparisons of means
    95% family-wise confidence level

Fit: aov(formula = Score ~ Method, data = Training.frame)

$Method
                      diff       lwr        upr     p adj
method2-method1  -8.244444 -12.73337  -3.755523 0.0003383
method3-method1 -18.194444 -22.94172 -13.447166 0.0000000
method3-method2  -9.950000 -14.58423  -5.315769 0.0000481
```

The table shows each pairwise comparison along with the difference, lower and upper 95 percent confidence limits, and adjusted probability. Each probability is way lower than .05, so the conclusion is that each difference is statistically significant.

Another Kind of Hypothesis, Another Kind of Test

The preceding ANOVA works with independent samples. As Chapter 3 of Book 3 explains, sometimes you work with matched samples. For example, sometimes a person provides data in a number of different conditions. In this section, I introduce the ANOVA you use when you have more than two matched samples.

This type of ANOVA is called *repeated measures*. You'll see it called other names, too, like *randomized blocks* or *within subjects*.

Working with repeated measures ANOVA

To show how this works, I extend the example from Chapter 3 of Book 3. In that example, ten men participate in a weight loss program. Table 4-3 shows their data over a 3-month period.

Is the program effective? This question calls for a hypothesis test:

H_0: $\mu_{Before} = \mu_1 = \mu_2 = \mu_3$

H_1: Not H_0

TABLE 4-3   **Data for the Weight Loss Example**

Person	Before	One Month	Two Months	Three Months	Mean
Al	198	194	191	188	192.75
Bill	201	203	200	196	200.00
Charlie	210	200	192	188	197.50
Dan	185	183	180	178	181.50
Ed	204	200	195	191	197.50
Fred	156	153	150	145	151.00
Gary	167	166	167	166	166.50
Harry	197	197	195	192	195.25
Irv	220	215	209	205	212.25
Jon	186	184	179	175	181.00
Mean	192.4	189.5	185.8	182.4	187.525

Once again, you set $\alpha = .05$

As in the previous ANOVA, start with the variances in the data. The MS_T is the variance in all 40 scores from the grand mean, which is 187.525:

$$MS_T = \frac{(198-187.525)^2 + (201-187.525)^2 + \dots + (175-187.525)^2}{(40-1)} = 318.20$$

The people participating in the weight loss program also supply variance. Each one's overall mean (his average over the four measurements) varies from the grand mean. Because these data are in the rows, I call this MS_{Rows}:

$$MS_{Rows} = \frac{(192.75-187.525)^2 + (200-187.525)^2 + \dots + (181-187.525)^2}{(10-1)} = 1292.41$$

The means of the columns also vary from the grand mean:

$$MS_{Columns} = \frac{\begin{array}{c}(192.4-187.525)^2 + (189.5-187.525)^2 + \\ (185.8-187.525)^2 + (182.4-187.525)^2\end{array}}{(4-1)} = 189.69$$

One more source of variance is in the data. Think of it as the variance left over after you pull out the variance in the rows and the variance in the columns from the total variance. Actually, it's more correct to say that it's the sum of squares that's left over when you subtract the SS_{Rows} and the $SS_{Columns}$ from the SS_T.

This variance is called MS_{Error}. As I say earlier, in the ANOVA the denominator of an F is called an *error term*. So the word *error* here gives you a hint that this MS is a denominator for an F.

To calculate MS_{Error}, you use the relationships among the sums of squares and among the df.

$$MS_{Error} = \frac{SS_{Error}}{df_{Error}} = \frac{SS_T - SS_{Rows} - SS_{Columns}}{df_T - df_{Rows} - df_{Columns}} = \frac{209.175}{27} = 7.75$$

Here's another way to calculate the df_{Error}:

$$df_{Error} = (\text{number of rows - 1})(\text{number of columns - 1})$$

To perform the hypothesis test, you calculate the F:

$$F = \frac{MS_{Columns}}{MS_{Error}} = \frac{189.69}{7.75} = 24.49$$

With 3 and 27 degrees of freedom, the critical F for $\alpha = .05$ is 2.96. (Use qf( ) to verify.) The calculated F is larger than the critical F, so the decision is to reject H_0.

What about an F involving MS_{Rows}? That one doesn't figure into H_0 for this example. If you find a significant F, all it shows is that people are different from one another with respect to weight and that doesn't tell you much.

Repeated measures ANOVA in R

To set the stage for the repeated measures analysis, put the columns of Table 4-3 into vectors:

```
Person <-c("Al", "Bill", "Charlie", "Dan", "Ed", "Fred",
    "Gary","Harry","Irv","Jon")
Before <- c(198,201,210,185,204,156,167,197,220,186)
OneMonth <- c(194,203,200,183,200,153,166,197,215,184)
TwoMonths <- c(191,200,192,180,195,150,167,195,209,179)
ThreeMonths <- c(188,196,188,178,191,145,166,192,205,175)
```

Then create a data frame:

```
Weight.frame <- data.frame(Person, Before, OneMonth,  TwoMonths, ThreeMonths)
```

The data frame looks like this:

```
> Weight.frame
    Person Before OneMonth TwoMonths ThreeMonths
1       Al    198      194       191         188
2     Bill    201      203       200         196
3  Charlie    210      200       192         188
4      Dan    185      183       180         178
5       Ed    204      200       195         191
6     Fred    156      153       150         145
7     Gary    167      166       167         166
8    Harry    197      197       195         192
9      Irv    220      215       209         205
10     Jon    186      184       179         175
```

It's in wide format, and you have to reshape it. With the reshape2 package installed (on the Packages tab, select the check box next to reshape2), melt the data into long format:

```
Weight.frame.melt <- melt(Weight.frame,id="Person")
```

Next, assign column names to the melted data frame:

```
colnames(Weight.frame.melt) = c("Person","Time","Weight")
```

And now, the first six rows of the new data frame are

```
> head(Weight.frame.melt)
    Person   Time Weight
1       Al Before    198
2     Bill Before    201
3  Charlie Before    210
4      Dan Before    185
5       Ed Before    204
6     Fred Before    156
```

In addition to Person, you now have Time as an independent variable.

I'm going to use R as a teaching tool: To give you an idea of how this analysis works, I'll start by pretending that it's an independent samples analysis, like the first one in this chapter. Then I'll run it as a repeated measures analysis so that you can see the differences and perhaps better understand what a repeated measures analysis does.

As independent samples:

```
> ind.anova <- aov(Weight ~ Time, data=Weight.frame.melt)
> summary(ind.anova)
            Df Sum Sq Mean Sq F value Pr(>F)
Time         3    569   189.7   0.577  0.634
Residuals   36  11841   328.9
```

This analysis shows no significant differences among the levels of Time. The key is to tease out the effects of having each row represent the data from one person. That will break down the SS for Residuals into two components: one SS for Person (which has nine degrees of freedom) and another SS that has the remaining 27 degrees of freedom. Divide that second SS by its degrees of freedom, and you have the MS_{Error} I mention earlier (although R doesn't refer to it that way).

Here's how to get that done:

```
rm.anova <- aov(Weight ~ Time + Error(Person/Time),
         data = Weight.frame.melt)
```

The new term indicates that Weight depends not only on Time but also on Person and that each Person experiences all levels of Time. The effect of Time — decreasing body weight over the four levels of Time — is evident within each Person. (It's easier to see that in the wide format than in the long.)

REMEMBER

In some fields, the word *subject* means *person:* That's why a repeated measures analysis is also called a *within-subjects* analysis, as I point out earlier.

And now for the table:

```
> summary(rm.anova)

Error: Person
          Df Sum Sq Mean Sq F value Pr(>F)
Residuals  9  11632    1292

Error: Person:Time
          Df Sum Sq Mean Sq F value  Pr(>F)
Time       3  569.1  189.69   24.48 7.3e-08 ***
Residuals 27  209.2    7.75

---
Signif. codes: 0 '***' 0.001 '**' 0.01 '*' 0.05 '.' 0.1 ' ' 1
```

Now the analysis shows the significant effect of `Time`.

Visualizing the results

One way to visualize the results is to plot the mean weight loss on the *y*-axis and the month (0, 1, 2, 3) on the *x*-axis. Notice I use 0-3 to represent the levels of `Time` (Before, OneMonth, TwoMonths, ThreeMonths).

Figure 4-3 shows the plot, along with the standard error of the mean (reflected in the error bars).

The foundation of the plot is a data frame that holds time (for convenience, as a numerical variable), mean weight, and standard error:

```
time <- c(0,1,2,3)

mean.weight <- c(mean(Before),mean(OneTime), mean(TwoTimes),mean(ThreeTimes))
se.weight <- c(sd(Before), sd(OneTime), sd(TwoTimes), sd(ThreeTimes))/
    sqrt(length(Person))
wt.means.frame <- data.frame(time,mean.weight,se.weight)
> wt.means.frame
  time mean.weight se.weight
1    0       192.4  6.144917
2    1       189.5  5.856146
3    2       185.8  5.466667
4    3       182.4  5.443038
```

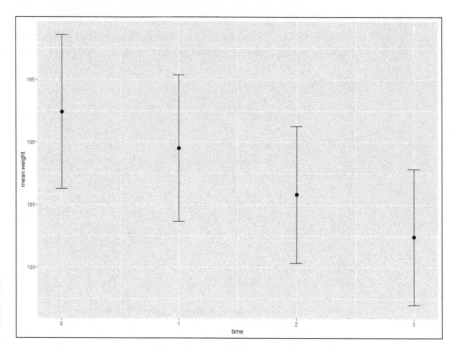

Here's what the plotting in `ggplot2` looks like:

```
ggplot(wt.means.frame,aes(x=time,y=mean.weight)) +
  geom_point(size=3)+
  geom_errorbar(aes(ymin=mean.weight-se.weight,
    ymax=mean.weight+se.weight),width=.1)
```

The first statement maps the independent variable into the x-axis, and the dependent variable into the y-axis. The second statement specifies a point as the geometric object and sets its size. The third statement gives the boundaries and size for the error bars.

Getting Trendy

In situations like the one in the weight loss example, you have an independent variable that's quantitative — its levels are numbers (0 months, 1 month, 2 months, 3 months). Not only that, but in this case, the intervals are equal.

With that kind of an independent variable, it's often a good idea to look for trends in the data rather than just plan comparisons among means. As Figure 4-3 shows, the means in the weight loss example seem to fall along a line.

Trend analysis is the statistical procedure that examines that pattern. The objective is to see whether the pattern contributes to the significant differences among the means.

A trend can be linear, as it apparently is in this example, or nonlinear (in which the means fall on a curve). The two nonlinear types of curves for four means are called *quadratic* and *cubic*. If the means show a quadratic trend, they align in a pattern that shows one change of direction. Figure 4-4 shows what I mean.

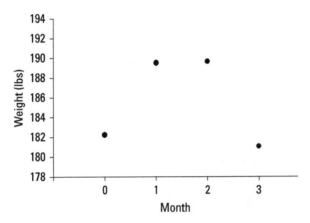

FIGURE 4-4: A quadratic trend with four means.

If the means show a cubic trend, they align in a pattern that shows two changes of direction. Figure 4-5 shows what a cubic trend looks like.

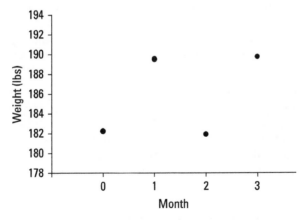

FIGURE 4-5: A cubic trend with four means.

The three components are orthogonal, so

$$SS_{Linear} + SS_{Quadratic} + SS_{Cubic} = SS_{Time}$$

and

$$df_{Linear} + df_{Quadratic} + df_{Cubic} = df_{Time}$$

To analyze a trend, you use comparison coefficients — those numbers you use in contrasts. You use them in a slightly different way than you did before. The formula for computing an SS for a trend component is

$$SS_{Component} = \frac{N\left(\sum c\bar{x}\right)^2}{\sum c^2}$$

In this formula, N is the number of people, and c represents the coefficients.

So you start by using comparison coefficients to find a sum of squares for linear trend. I abbreviate that as SS_{Linear}.

The comparison coefficients are different for different numbers of samples. For four samples, the linear coefficients are -3, -1, 1, and 3.

TIP

The easiest way to get the coefficients is to look them up in a stat textbook or on the Internet!

For this example, the SS_{Linear} is

$$SS_{Linear} = \frac{N\left(\sum c\bar{x}\right)^2}{\sum c^2} = \frac{10[(-3)(192.4)+(-1)(189.5)+(1)(185.8)+(3)(182.4)]^2}{(-3)^2+(-1)^2+(3)^2+(1)^2}$$
$$= 567.845$$

After you calculate SS_{Linear}, you divide it by df_{Linear} to produce MS_{Linear}. This is extremely easy because $df_{Linear} = 1$. Divide MS_{Linear} by MS_{Error} and you have an F. If that F is higher than the critical value of F with df = 1 and df_{Error} at your α, then weight is decreasing in a linear way over the period of the weight loss program. The F-ratio here is

$$F = \frac{MS_{Linear}}{MS_{Error}} = \frac{567.85}{7.75} = 73.30$$

The critical value for F with 1 and 27 degrees of freedom and $\alpha = .05$ is 4.21. Because the calculated value is larger than the critical value, statisticians would say the data shows a *significant linear component*. This, of course, verifies what you see in Figure 4-3.

The linear component of SS_{Time} is so large that the other two components are very small. I'll walk you through the computations anyway.

The coefficients for the quadratic component are $1, -1, -1, 1$. So the $SS_{Quadratic}$ is

$$SS_{Quadratic} = \frac{N\left(\sum c\bar{x}\right)^2}{\sum c^2} = \frac{10[(1)(192.4) + (-1)(189.5) + (-1)(185.8) + (1)(182.4)]^2}{(1)^2 + (-1)^2 + (-1)^2 + (1)^2}$$
$$= 0.6$$

The coefficients for the cubic component are $-1, 3, -3, 1$, and the SS_{Cubic} is

$$SS_{Cubic} = \frac{N\left(\sum c\bar{x}\right)^2}{\sum c^2} = \frac{10[(-1)(192.4) + (3)(189.5) + (-3)(185.8) + (1)(182.4)]^2}{(-1)^2 + (3)^2 + (-3)^2 + (1)^2}$$
$$= 0.6$$

Rather than complete the final calculations to get the microscopic F-ratios, I'll let R do the work for you in the next subsection.

A LITTLE MORE ON TREND

Linear, quadratic, and cubic are as far as you can go with four means. With five means, you can look for those three plus a *quartic component* (three direction changes), and with six you can try to scope out all the preceding plus a *quintic component* (four direction changes). What do the coefficients look like?

For five means, they're

- Linear: -2, -1, 0, 1, 2
- Quadratic: 2, -1, -2, -1, 2
- Cubic: -1, 2, 0, -2, 1
- Quartic: 1, -4, 6, -4, 1

And for six means, they're

- Linear: -5, -3, -1, 1, 3, 5
- Quadratic: 5, -1, -4, -4, -1, 5
- Cubic: -5, 7, 4, -4, -7, 5
- Quartic: 1, -3, 2, 2, -3, 1
- Quintic: -1, 5, -10, 10, -5, 1

I could go on with more means, coefficients, and exotic component names (hextic? septic?), but enough already. This should hold you for a while.

Trend Analysis in R

I treat this analysis pretty much the same way as contrasts for the independent samples example. I begin by creating a matrix of the coefficients for the three trend components:

```
contrasts(Weight.frame.melt$Time) <- matrix(c(-3,-1,1,3,1,-1, -1,1,-1,3,-3,1),
    4, 3)
```

Then I run the ANOVA, adding the contrasts argument:

```
rm.anova <- aov(Weight ~ Time + Error(factor(Person)/Time), data=Weight.frame.
    melt,
contrasts = contrasts(Weight.frame.melt$Time))
```

TIP As in the previous example with contrasts, if you see a warning message, you can safely ignore it.

Finally, I apply summary( ) (including the split of Time into three components) to print the table of the analysis:

```
summary(rm.anova,split=list(Time=list("Linear" =1, "Quadratic"=2,"Cubic" =3)))
```

Running this statement produces this table:

```
Error: factor(Person)
          Df Sum Sq Mean Sq F value Pr(>F)
Residuals  9  11632    1292


Error: factor(Person):Time
                Df Sum Sq Mean Sq F value    Pr(>F)
Time             3  569.1   189.7  24.485 7.30e-08 ***
  Time: Linear   1  567.8   567.8  73.297 3.56e-09 ***
  Time: Quadratic 1   0.6     0.6   0.081    0.779
  Time: Cubic    1    0.6     0.6   0.078    0.782
Residuals       27  209.2     7.7
---
Signif. codes: 0 '***' 0.001 '**' 0.01 '*' 0.05 '.' 0.1 ' ' 1
```

Once again, you can see the overwhelming linearity of the trend — just as you would expect from Figure 4-3.

» Working with replications

» Understanding interactions

» Mixing variable types

» Working with multiple dependent variables

Chapter **5**

More Complicated Testing

I n Chapter 3 of Book 3, I show you how to test hypotheses with two samples. In Chapter 4 of Book 3, I show you how to test hypotheses when you have more than two samples. The common thread in both chapters is one independent variable (also called a *factor*).

Many times, you have to test the effects of more than one factor. In this chapter, I show how to analyze two factors within the same set of data. Several types of situations are possible, and I describe R functions that deal with each one.

Cracking the Combinations

Imagine that a company has two methods of presenting its training information: One is via a person who presents the information orally, and the other is via a text document. Imagine also that the information is presented in either a humorous way or a technical way. I refer to the first factor as Presentation Method and to the second as Presentation Style.

Combining the two levels of Presentation Method with the two levels of Presentation Style gives four combinations. The company randomly assigns 4 people to each combination, for a total of 16 people. After providing the training, they test the 16 people on their comprehension of the material.

Figure 5-1 shows the combinations, the four comprehension scores within each combination, and summary statistics for the combinations, rows, and columns.

Presentation Style

		Humorous		Technical		
	Spoken	Spoken and Humorous	57 56 60 64	Spoken and Technical	22 21 29 25	
Presentation Method		Mean = 59.25 Variance = 12.92		Mean = 24.25 Variance = 12.92		Mean = 41.75
	Text	Text and Humorous	33 25 28 31	Text and Technical	66 65 71 72	
		Mean = 29.25 Variance = 12.25		Mean = 68.50 Variance = 12.33		Mean = 48.88
		Mean = 44.25		Mean = 46.38		Grand Mean = 44.31

FIGURE 5-1: Combining the levels of Presentation Method with the levels of Presentation Style.

REMEMBER

With each of two levels of one factor combined with each of two levels of the other factor, this kind of study is called a 2 X 2 *factorial* design.

Here are the hypotheses:

$H_0: \mu_{Spoken} = \mu_{Text}$

$H_1:$ Not H_0

and

$H_0: \mu_{Humorous} = \mu_{Technical}$

$H_1:$ Not H_0

Because the two presentation methods (Spoken and Text) are in the rows, I refer to Presentation Type as the *row factor*. The two presentation styles (Humorous and Technical) are in the columns, so Presentation Style is the *column factor*.

Interactions

When you have rows and columns of data and you're testing hypotheses about the row factor and the column factor, you have an additional consideration. Namely, you have to be concerned about the row-column combinations. Do the combinations result in peculiar effects?

For the example I present, it's possible that combining Spoken and Text with Humorous and Technical yields an unexpected result. In fact, you can see that in the data in Figure 5-1: For Spoken presentation, the Humorous style produces a higher average than the Technical style. For Text presentation, the Humorous style produces a lower average than the Technical style.

REMEMBER

A situation like this one is called an interaction. In formal terms, an *interaction* occurs when the levels of one factor affect the levels of the other factor differently. The label for the interaction is row factor × column factor, so for this example it's Method × Type.

The hypotheses for this are

H_0: Presentation Method does not interact with Presentation Style

H_1: Not H_0

The analysis

The statistical analysis is, once again, an analysis of variance (ANOVA). As is the case with the ANOVAs I show you earlier in this book, it depends on the variances in the data. It's called a *two-factor* ANOVA, or a *two-way* ANOVA.

The first variance is the total variance, labeled MS_T. That's the variance of all 16 scores around their mean (the grand mean), which is 44.81:

$$MS_T = \frac{(57-45.31)^2 + (56-45.31)^2 + \ldots + (72-45.31)^2}{16-1} = \frac{5885.43}{15} = 392.36$$

The denominator tells you that df = 15 for MS_T.

The next variance comes from the row factor. That's MS_{Method}, and it's the variance of the row means around the grand mean:

$$MS_{Method} = \frac{(8)(41.75-45.31)^2 + (8)(48.88-45.31)^2}{2-1} = \frac{203.06}{1} = 203.06$$

The 8 in the equation multiplies each squared deviation because you have to take into account the number of scores that produced each row mean. The df for MS_{Method} is the number of rows − 1, which is 1.

Similarly, the variance for the column factor is

$$MS_{Style} = \frac{(8)(43.25-45.31)^2 + (8)(46.38-45.31)^2}{2-1} = \frac{18.06}{1} = 18.06$$

The df for MS_{Style} is 1 (the number of columns − 1).

Another variance is the pooled estimate based on the variances within the four row-column combinations. It's called the MS_{Within}, or MS_w. (For details on MS_w and pooled estimates, see Chapter 4 of Book 3.). For this example:

$$MS_W = \frac{(4-1)(12.92)+(4-1)(12.92)+(4-1)(12.25)+(4-1)(12.33)}{(4-1)+(4-1)+(4-1)+(4-1)} = \frac{151.25}{12} = 12.60$$

This one is the *error term* (the denominator) for each F you calculate. Its denominator tells you that df = 12 for this Mean Square.

The last variance comes from the interaction between the row factor and the column factor. In this example, it's labeled $MS_{Method \times Type}$. You can calculate this in a couple of ways. The easiest way is to take advantage of this general relationship:

$$SS_{Row\ X\ Column} = SS_T - SS_{Row\ Factor} - SS_{Column\ Factor} - SS_W$$

And this one:

$$df_{Row\ X\ Column} = df_T - df_{Row\ Factor} - df_{Column\ Factor} - df_W$$

Another way to calculate this is

$$df_{Row\ X\ Column} = (\text{number of rows - 1})(\text{number of columns - 1})$$

The MS is

$$MS_{Row\ X\ Column} = \frac{SS_{Row\ X\ Column}}{df_{Row\ X\ Column}}$$

For this example:

$$MS_{Method\ X\ Style} = \frac{SS_{Method\ X\ Style}}{df_{Method\ X\ Style}} = \frac{5885.43 - 203.06 - 18.06 - 151.25}{15 - 12 - 1 - 1} = \frac{5513.06}{1} = 5513.06$$

To test the hypotheses, you calculate three Fs:

$$F = \frac{MS_{Style}}{MS_W} = \frac{18.06}{12.60} = 1.43$$

$$F = \frac{MS_{Method}}{MS_W} = \frac{203.06}{12.60} = 16.12$$

$$F = \frac{MS_{Method\ X\ Style}}{MS_W} = \frac{5513.06}{12.60} = 437.54$$

For df = 1 and 12, the critical F at α = .05 is 4.75. (You can use $qf()$ to verify.) The decision is to reject H_0 for the Presentation Method and the Method $\times$ Style interaction, and to not reject H_0 for the Presentation Style.

REMEMBER

It's possible, of course, to have more than two levels of each factor. It's also possible to have more than two factors. In that case, things (like interactions) become way more complex.

Two-Way ANOVA in R

As in any analysis, the first step is to get the data in shape, and in R that means getting the data into long format.

Start with vectors for the scores in each of the columns in Figure 5-1:

```
humorous <- c(57,56,60,64,33,25,28,31)
technical <- c(22,21,29,25,66,65,71,72)
```

Then combine them to produce a vector of all scores:

```
Score = c(humorous,technical)
```

Next, create vectors for Method and for Style:

```
Method =rep(c("spoken","text"),each=4,2)
Style =rep(c("humorous","technical"),each=8)
```

And then put everything into a data frame:

```
pres.frame <-data.frame(Method,Style,Score)
```

which looks like this:

```
> pres.frame
   Method      Style Score
1  spoken   humorous    57
2  spoken   humorous    56
3  spoken   humorous    60
4  spoken   humorous    64
5    text   humorous    33
6    text   humorous    25
7    text   humorous    28
8    text   humorous    31
9  spoken  technical    22
10 spoken  technical    21
11 spoken  technical    29
12 spoken  technical    25
13   text  technical    66
14   text  technical    65
15   text  technical    71
16   text  technical    72
```

And here's the two-way analysis of variance:

```
> two.way <- aov(Score ~ Style*Method,  data = pres.frame)
```

The `Style*Method` expression indicates that all levels of `Style` (humorous and technical) combine with all levels of `Method` (spoken and text).

Here's the ANOVA table:

```
> summary(two.way)
             Df Sum Sq Mean Sq F value   Pr(>F)
Style         1     18      18   1.433  0.25438
Method        1    203     203  16.111  0.00172 **
Style:Method  1   5513    5513 437.400 8.27e-11 ***
Residuals    12    151      13
---
Signif. codes: 0 '***' 0.001 '**' 0.01 '*' 0.05 '.' 0.1 ' ' 1
```

Again, the F-values and p-values indicate rejection of the null hypothesis for `Method` and for the `Style X Method` interaction, but not for `Style`.

With just two levels of each factor, no post-analysis tests are necessary to explore a significant result.

Visualizing the two-way results

The best way to show the results of a study like this one is with a grouped bar plot that shows the means and the standard errors. The foundation for the plot is a data frame that holds these statistics for each combination of levels of the independent variables:

```
> mse.frame
  Method     Style  Mean       SE
1 spoken  humorous 59.25 1.796988
2   text  humorous 29.25 1.750000
3 spoken technical 24.25 1.796988
4   text technical 68.50 1.755942
```

To create this data frame, start by creating four vectors:

```
Score.spk.hum <- with(pres.frame, Score[Method=="spoken" & Style=="humorous"])
Score.txt.hum <- with(pres.frame, Score[Method=="text" & Style=="humorous"])
Score.spk.tec <- with(pres.frame, Score[Method=="spoken" & Style=="technical"])
Score.txt.tec <- with(pres.frame, Score[Method=="text" & Style=="technical"])
```

Then concatenate the vector means into another vector:

```
mean.Scores <- c(mean(Score.spk.hum), mean(Score.txt.hum), mean(Score.spk.tec),
    mean(Score.txt.tec))
```

Concatenate the standard errors into still another vector:

```
se.Scores <- c(sd(Score.spk.hum), sd(Score.txt.hum), sd(Score.spk.tec),
    sd(Score.txt.tec))/2
```

In dividing by 2, I cheated a bit on that last one. Each combination consists of four scores, and the square root of 4 is 2.

Create a vector for the levels of Method and another for the levels of Style:

```
mse.Method =rep(c("spoken","text"),2)
mse.Style =rep(c("humorous","technical"),each=2)
```

Then create the data frame:

```
mse.frame <- data.frame(mse.Method,mse.Style,mean.Scores,se.Scores)
```

Finally, make the column names a little nicer-looking:

```
colnames(mse.frame)=c("Method","Style","Mean","SE")
```

At this point, run the `mse.frame` statement to see the data frame.

On to the visualization. In `ggplot2`, begin with a `ggplot()` statement that maps the components of the data to the components of the graph:

```
ggplot(mse.frame,aes(x=Method,y=Mean,fill=Style))
```

Now use a `geom_bar` that takes the given mean as its statistic:

```
geom_bar(stat = "identity", position = "dodge",
     color = "black", width = .5)
```

The `position` argument sets up this plot as a grouped bar plot, the `color` argument specifies `"black"` as the border color, and `width` sets up a size for nice-looking bars. You might experiment a bit to see whether another width is more to your liking.

If you don't change the colors of the bars, they appear as light red and light blue, which are pleasant enough but would be indistinguishable on a black-and-white page. Here's how to change the colors:

```
scale_fill_grey(start = 0,end = .8)
```

In the grey scale, 0 corresponds to black and 1 to white. Finally, the `geom_errobar` adds the bars for the standard errors:

```
geom_errorbar(aes(ymin=Mean,ymax=Mean+SE), width=.2,
    position=position_dodge(width=.5))
```

Using `Mean` as the value of `ymin` ensures that you plot only the upper error bar, which is what you typically see in published bar plots. The `position` argument uses the `position_dodge()` function to center the error bars.

So these lines of code

```
ggplot(mse.frame,aes(x=Method,y=Mean,fill=Style)) +
  geom_bar(stat = "identity", position = "dodge",
         color = "black", width = .5)+
  scale_fill_grey(start = 0,end = .8)+
```

```
geom_errorbar(aes(ymin=Mean,ymax=Mean+SE), width=.2,
    position=position_dodge(width=.5))
```

produce Figure 5-2.

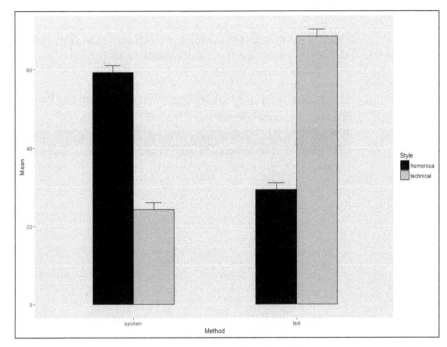

This graph clearly shows the Method × Style interaction. For the spoken presentation, humorous is more effective than technical, and it's the reverse for the text presentation.

Two Kinds of Variables . . . at Once

What happens when you have a Between Groups variable and a Within Groups variable . . . in the same study? How can that happen?

Very easily. Here's an example. Suppose you want to study the effects of presentation media on the reading speeds of fourth-graders. You randomly assign the fourth-graders (I'll call them *subjects*) to read either books or e-readers. So "Medium" is the Between Groups variable.

Let's say you're also interested in the effects of font. So you assign each subject to read each of these fonts: Haettenschweiler, Arial, and Calibri. (I've never seen a document in Haettenschweiler, but it's my favorite font because "Haettenschweiler" is fun to say. Try it. Am I right?) Because each subject reads all the fonts, "Font" is the Within Groups variable. For completeness, you have to randomly order the fonts for each subject.

Table 5-1 shows data that might result from a study like this. The dependent variable is the score on a reading comprehension test.

TABLE 5-1   ## Data for a Study of Presentation Media (between Groups Variable) and Font (within Groups Variable)

Medium	Subject	Haettenschweiler	Arial	Calibri
Book	Alice	48	40	38
	Brad	55	43	45
	Chris	46	45	44
	Donna	61	53	53
E-reader	Eddie	43	45	47
	Fran	50	52	54
	Gil	56	57	57
	Harriet	53	53	55

REMEMBER

Because this kind of analysis mixes a Between Groups variable with a Within Groups variable, it's called a *mixed ANOVA*.

To show you how the analysis works, I present the kind of table that results from a mixed ANOVA. It's a bit more complete than the output of an ANOVA in R, but bear with me. Table 5-2 shows it to you in a generic way. It's categorized into a set of sources that make up Between Groups variability and a set of sources that make up Within Groups (also known as Repeated Measures) variability.

In the Between category, A is the name of the Between Groups variable. (In the example, that's Medium.) Read "S/A" as "Subjects within A." This just says that the people in one level of A are different from the people in the other levels of A.

TABLE 5-2

The ANOVA Table for the Mixed ANOVA

Source	SS	df	MS	F
Between	$SS_{Between}$	$df_{Between}$		
A	SS_A	df_A	SS_A/df_A	$MS_A/MS_{S/A}$
S/A	$SS_{S/A}$	$df_{S/A}$	$SS_{S/A}/df_{S/A}$	
Within	SS_{Within}	df_{Within}		
B	SS_B	df_B	SS_B/df_B	$MS_B/MS_{B \times S/A}$
A × B	$SS_{A \times B}$	$df_{A \times B}$	$SS_{A \times B}/df_{A \times B}$	$MS_{A \times B}/MS_{B \times S/A}$
B × S/A	$SS_{B \times S/A}$	$df_{B \times S/A}$	$SS_{B \times S/A}/df_{B \times S/A}$	
Total	SS_{Total}	df_{Total}		

In the Within category, B is the name of the Within Groups variable. (In the example, that's Font.) A × B is the interaction of the two variables. B × S/A is something like the B variable interacting with subjects within A. As you can see, anything associated with B falls into the Within Groups category.

The first thing to note is the three F-ratios. The first one tests for differences among the levels of A; the second, for differences among the levels of B; and the third, for the interaction of the two. Notice also that the denominator for the first F-ratio is different from the denominator for the other two. This happens more and more as ANOVAs increase in complexity.

Next, it's important to be aware of some relationships. At the top level:

$$SS_{Between} + SS_{Within} = SS_{Total}$$

$$df_{Between} + df_{Within} = df_{Total}$$

The Between component breaks down further:

$$SS_A + SS_{S/A} = SS_{Between}$$

$$df_A + df_{S/A} = df_{Between}$$

The Within component breaks down, too:

$$SS_B + SS_{A \times B} + SS_{B \times S/A} = SS_{Within}$$

$$df_B + df_{A \times B} + df_{B \times S/A} = df_{Within}$$

REMEMBER

It's possible to have more than one Between Groups factor and more than one repeated measure in a study.

On to the analysis . . . .

Mixed ANOVA in R

First, I show you how to use the data from Table 5-1 to build a data frame in long format. When finished, it looks like this:

```
> mixed.frame
      Medium              Font Subject Score
1       Book Haettenschweiler   Alice    48
2       Book Haettenschweiler    Brad    55
3       Book Haettenschweiler   Chris    46
4       Book Haettenschweiler   Donna    61
5       Book               Arial   Alice    40
6       Book               Arial    Brad    43
7       Book               Arial   Chris    45
8       Book               Arial   Donna    53
9       Book             Calibri   Alice    38
10      Book             Calibri    Brad    45
11      Book             Calibri   Chris    44
12      Book             Calibri   Donna    53
13  E-reader Haettenschweiler   Eddie    43
14  E-reader Haettenschweiler    Fran    50
15  E-reader Haettenschweiler     Gil    56
16  E-reader Haettenschweiler Harriet    53
17  E-reader               Arial   Eddie    45
18  E-reader               Arial    Fran    52
19  E-reader               Arial     Gil    57
20  E-reader               Arial Harriet    53
21  E-reader             Calibri   Eddie    47
22  E-reader             Calibri    Fran    54
23  E-reader             Calibri     Gil    57
24  E-reader             Calibri Harriet    55
```

I begin with a vector for the Book scores and a vector for the E-reader scores:

```
BkScores <- c(48,55,46,61,40,43,45,53,38,45,44,53)
ErScores <- c(43,50,56,53,45,52,57,53,47,54,57,55)
```

Then I combine them into a vector:

```
Score <-c(BkScores,ErScores)
```

I complete a similar process for the subjects: one vector for the Book subjects and another for the E-reader subjects. Note that I have to repeat each list three times:

```
BkSubjects <- rep(c("Alice","Brad","Chris","Donna"),3)
ErSubjects <- rep(c("Eddie","Fran","Gil","Harriet"),3)
```

Then I combine the two:

```
Subject <- c(BkSubjects,ErSubjects)
```

Next up is a vector for Book versus E-reader, and note that I repeat that list 12 times:

```
Medium <- rep(c("Book","E-reader"),each=12)
```

The vector for Font is a bit tricky. I have to repeat each font name four times and then repeat *that* again:

```
Font <- rep(c("Haettenschweiler","Arial","Calibri"), each=4,2)
```

I can now create the data frame:

```
mixed.frame <-data.frame(Medium,Font,Subject,Score)
```

The analysis is

```
mixed.anova <- aov(Score ~ Medium*Font + Error(Subject/Font), data=mixed.frame)
```

The arguments show that Score depends on Medium and Font and that Font is repeated throughout each Subject.

To see the table:

```
> summary(mixed.anova)

Error: Subject
          Df Sum Sq Mean Sq F value Pr(>F)
Medium     1  108.4  108.37   1.227   0.31
Residuals  6  529.9   88.32

Error: Subject:Font
            Df Sum Sq Mean Sq F value  Pr(>F)
Font         2  40.08   20.04   5.681 0.018366 *
Medium:Font  2 120.25   60.13  17.043 0.000312 ***
Residuals   12  42.33    3.53
---
Signif. codes:  0 '***' 0.001 '**' 0.01 '*' 0.05 '.' 0.1 ' ' 1
```

You can reject the null hypothesis about Font and about the interaction of Medium and Font, but not about Medium.

Visualizing the mixed ANOVA results

You use ggplot() to create a barplot of the means and standard errors. Begin by creating this data frame, which contains the necessary information:

```
> mse.frame
    Medium            Font  Mean       SE
1     Book Haettenschweiler 52.50 3.427827
2     Book            Arial 45.25 2.780138
3     Book           Calibri 45.00 3.082207
4 E-reader Haettenschweiler 50.50 2.783882
5 E-reader            Arial 51.75 2.495830
6 E-reader          Calibri 53.25 2.174665
```

To create this data frame, follow the same steps as in the earlier "Visualizing the two-way results" section, with appropriate changes. The ggplot code is also the same as in that earlier section, with changes to variable names:

```
ggplot(mse.frame,aes(x=Medium,y=Mean,fill=Font)) +
  geom_bar(stat = "identity", position = "dodge",color="black",width = .5) +
  scale_fill_grey(start = 0,end = .8) +
  geom_errorbar(aes(ymin=Mean,ymax=Mean+SE),
    width=.2,position=position_dodge(width=.5))
```

The result is Figure 5-3. The figure shows the Between Groups variable on the x-axis and levels of the repeated measure in the bars — but that's just my preference. You might prefer vice versa. In this layout, the different ordering of the heights of the bars from Book to E-reader reflects the interaction.

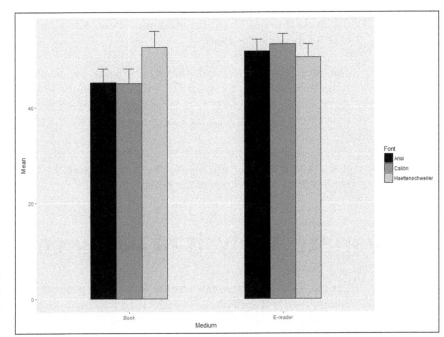

FIGURE 5-3: Means and standard errors for the Book-versus-E-reader study.

After the Analysis

As I point out in Chapter 4 of Book 3, a significant result in an ANOVA tells you that an effect is lurking somewhere in the data. Post-analysis tests tell you where. Two types of tests are possible: planned or unplanned. Chapter 4 of Book 3 provides the details.

In this example, the Between Groups variable has only two levels. For this reason, if the result is statistically significant, no further test would be necessary. The Within Groups variable, Font, is significant. Ordinarily, the test would proceed as described in Chapter 4 of Book 3. In this case, however, the interaction between Media and Font necessitates a different path.

With the interaction, post-analysis tests can proceed in either (or both) of two ways. You can examine the effects of each level of the A variable (the Between

Groups variable) on the levels of the B variable (the repeated measure), or you can examine the effects of each level of the B variable on the levels of the A variable. Statisticians refer to these as *simple main effects.*

For this example, the first way examines the means for the three fonts in a book and the means for the three fonts in the e-reader. The second way examines the means for the book versus the mean for the e-reader with Haettenschweiler font, with Arial, and with Calibri.

Statistics texts provide complicated formulas for calculating these analyses. R makes them easy. To analyze the three fonts in the book, do a repeated measures ANOVA for Subjects 1–4. To analyze the three fonts in the e-reader, do a repeated measures ANOVA for Subjects 5–8.

For the analysis of the book versus the e-reader in the Haettenschweiler font, that's a single-factor ANOVA for the Haettenschweiler data. You'd complete a similar procedure for each of the other fonts.

Multivariate Analysis of Variance

The examples thus far in this chapter involve a dependent variable and more than one independent variable. Is it possible to have more than one dependent variable? Absolutely! That gives you MANOVA — the abbreviation for the title of this section.

When might you encounter this type of situation? Suppose you're thinking of adopting one of three textbooks for a basic science course. You have 12 students and you randomly assign 4 of them to read Book 1, another 4 to read Book 2, and the remaining 4 to read Book 3. You're interested in how each book promotes knowledge in physics, chemistry, and biology, so after the students read the books, they take a test of fundamental knowledge in each of those three sciences.

The independent variable is Book, and the dependent variable is multivariate — it's a vector that consists of Physics score, Chemistry score, and Biology score. Table 5-3 shows the data.

The dependent variable for the first student in the Book 1 sample is a vector consisting of 50, 66, and 71.

TABLE 5-3

Data for the Science Textbook MANOVA Study

Student	Book	Physics	Chemistry	Biology
Art	Book 1	50	66	71
Brenda	Book 1	53	45	56
Cal	Book 1	52	48	65
Dan	Book 1	54	51	68
Eva	Book 2	75	55	88
Frank	Book 2	72	58	85
Greg	Book 2	64	59	79
Hank	Book 2	76	59	82
Iris	Book 3	68	67	55
Jim	Book 3	61	56	59
Kendra	Book 3	62	66	63
Lee	Book 3	64	78	61

What are the hypotheses in a case like this? The null hypothesis has to take all components of the vector into account, so here are the null and the alternative:

$$H_0 : \begin{pmatrix} \mu_{Book1,Phys} \\ \mu_{Book1,Chem} \\ \mu_{Book1,Bio} \end{pmatrix} = \begin{pmatrix} \mu_{Book2,Phys} \\ \mu_{Book2,Chem} \\ \mu_{Book2,Bio} \end{pmatrix} = \begin{pmatrix} \mu_{Book3,Phys} \\ \mu_{Book3,Chem} \\ \mu_{Book3,Bio} \end{pmatrix}$$

$$H_1 : Not\ H_0$$

I don't go into the same depth on MANOVA in this chapter as I did on ANOVA. I don't discuss SS, MS, and df. That would require knowledge of math (matrix algebra) and other material that's beyond the scope of this chapter. Instead, I dive right in and show you how to get the analysis done.

MANOVA in R

The data frame for the MANOVA looks just like Table 5-3:

```
> Textbooks.frame
  Student  Book Physics Chemistry Biology
1     Art Book1      50        66      71
2  Brenda Book1      53        45      56
3     Cal Book1      52        48      65
```

4	Dan	Book1	54	51	68
5	Eva	Book2	75	55	88
6	Frank	Book2	72	58	85
7	Greg	Book2	64	59	79
8	Hank	Book2	76	59	82
9	Iris	Book3	68	67	55
10	Jim	Book3	61	56	59
11	Kendra	Book3	62	66	63
12	Lee	Book3	64	78	61

In ANOVA, the dependent variable for the analysis is a single column. In MANOVA, the dependent variable for the analysis is a matrix. In this case, it's a matrix with 12 rows (one for each student) and three columns (Physics, Chemistry, and Biology).

To create the matrix, use the cbind() function to *bind* the appropriate columns together. You can do this inside the manova() function that performs the analysis:

```
m.analysis <- manova(cbind(Physics,Chemistry,Biology) ~ Book,
    data = Textbooks.frame)
```

The formula inside the parentheses shows the 12 × 3 matrix (the result of cbind()) depending on Book, with Textbooks.frame as the source of the data.

As always, apply summary() to see the table:

```
> summary(m.analysis)
          Df Pillai approx F num Df den Df    Pr(>F)
Book       2 1.7293   17.036      6     16 3.922e-06 ***
Residuals  9

---
Signif. codes: 0 '***' 0.001 '**' 0.01 '*' 0.05 '.' 0.1 ' ' 1
```

The only new item is Pillai, a test statistic that results from a MANOVA. It's a little complicated, so I'll leave it alone. Suffice to say that R turns Pillai into an F-ratio (with 6 and 16 df) and that's what you use as the test statistic. The high F and exceptionally low p-value indicate rejection of the null hypothesis.

Pillai is the default test. In the summary statement, you can specify other MANOVA test statistics. They're called "Wilks", "Hotelling-Lawley", and "Roy". For example:

```
> summary(m.analysis, test = "Roy")
          Df   Roy approx F num Df den Df    Pr(>F)
Book       2 10.926   29.137      3      8 0.0001175 ***
```

```
Residuals  9
---
Signif. codes: 0 '***' 0.001 '**' 0.01 '*' 0.05 '.' 0.1 ' ' 1
```

The different tests result in different values for F and df, but the overall decision is the same.

REMEMBER

This example is a MANOVA extension of an ANOVA with just one factor. It's possible to have multiple dependent variables with more complex designs (like the ones I discuss earlier in this chapter).

Visualizing the MANOVA results

The objective of the study is to show how the distribution of Physics, Chemistry, and Biology scores differs from book to book. A separate set of boxplots for each book visualizes the differences. Figure 5-4 shows what I'm talking about.

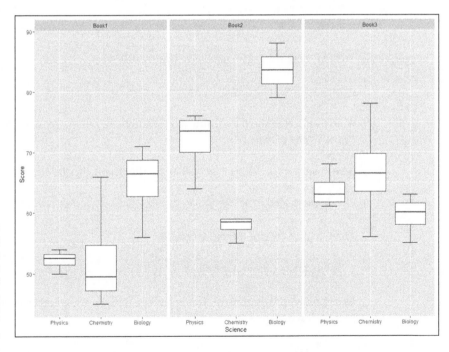

FIGURE 5-4:
Three boxplots show the distribution of scores for physics, chemistry, and biology for each book.

The ggplot2 *faceting* capability splits the data by Book and creates the three side-by-side graphs. Each graph is called a *facet*. (I discuss faceting in the "Explore the data" section in Chapter 2 of Book 2.)

To set this all up, you have to reshape the `Textbooks.frame` into long format. With the `reshape2` package installed (on the Packages tab, select the check box next to `reshape2`), apply the `melt()` function:

```
Textbooks.frame.melt = melt(Textbooks.frame)
```

After assigning column names:

```
colnames(Textbooks.frame.melt) = c("Student", "Book", "Science", "Score")
```

the first six rows of the melted frame are

```
> head(Textbooks.frame.melt)
  Student  Book Science Score
1     Art Book1 Physics    50
2  Brenda Book1 Physics    53
3     Cal Book1 Physics    52
4     Dan Book1 Physics    54
5     Eva Book2 Physics    75
6   Frank Book2 Physics    72
```

To create Figure 5-4 in `ggplot2`, begin with

```
ggplot(Textbooks.frame.melt,(aes(x=Science,y=Score)))
```

which indicates the data frame and aesthetically maps `Science` to the *x*-axis and `Score` to the *y*-axis.

Next, use `stat_boxplot()` to calculate the perpendicular lines for the whiskers:

```
stat_boxplot(geom="errorbar", width =.5)
```

Then, a `geom` function for the boxplot:

```
geom_boxplot()
```

And, finally, the statement that splits the data by `Book` and creates a row of three graphs (excuse me — *facets*):

```
facet_grid(. ~ Book)
```

The dot followed by the tilde (~) followed by Book arranges the facets side by side. To put the three graphs in a column, it's

```
facet_grid(Book ~ .)
```

Putting it all together, the code for creating Figure 5-4 is

```
ggplot(Textbooks.frame.melt,(aes(x=Science,y=Score)))+
  stat_boxplot(geom="errorbar", width =.5) +
  geom_boxplot() +
  facet_grid(. ~ Book)
```

After the MANOVA

When a MANOVA results in rejection of the null hypothesis, one way to proceed is to perform an ANOVA on each component of the dependent variable. The results tell you which components contribute to the significant MANOVA.

The summary.aov() function does this for you. Remember that m.analysis holds the results of the MANOVA in this section's example:

```
> summary.aov(m.analysis)
 Response Physics :
          Df Sum Sq Mean Sq F value    Pr(>F)
Book       2 768.67  384.33  27.398 0.0001488 ***
Residuals  9 126.25   14.03
---
Signif. codes: 0 '***' 0.001 '**' 0.01 '*' 0.05 '.' 0.1 ' ' 1


 Response Chemistry :
          Df Sum Sq Mean Sq F value  Pr(>F)
Book       2  415.5 207.750  3.6341 0.06967 .
Residuals  9  514.5  57.167
---
Signif. codes: 0 '***' 0.001 '**' 0.01 '*' 0.05 '.' 0.1 ' ' 1


 Response Biology :
          Df Sum Sq Mean Sq F value    Pr(>F)
Book       2 1264.7  632.33  27.626 0.0001441 ***
Residuals  9  206.0   22.89
---
Signif. codes: 0 '***' 0.001 '**' 0.01 '*' 0.05 '.' 0.1 ' ' 1
```

These analyses show that Physics and Biology contribute to the overall effect, and Chemistry just misses significance.

TIP

Notice the word Response in these tables. This is R terminology for "dependent variable."

TECHNICAL
STUFF

This separate-ANOVAs procedure doesn't consider the relationships among pairs of components. The relationship is called *correlation*, which I discuss in Chapter 7 of Book 3.

Chapter **6**

Regression: Linear, Multiple, and the General Linear Model

One of the main things you do when you work with statistics is make predictions. The idea is to use data from one or more variables to predict the value of another variable. To do this, you have to understand how to summarize relationships among variables, and to test hypotheses about those relationships.

In this chapter, I introduce *regression*, a statistical way to do just that. Regression also enables you to use the details of relationships to make predictions. First, I show you how to analyze the relationship between one variable and another. Then I show you how to analyze the relationship between a variable and two others. Finally, I let you in on the connection between regression and ANOVA.

The Plot of Scatter

FarMisht Consulting, Inc., is a consulting firm with a wide range of specialties. It receives numerous applications from people interested in becoming FarMisht consultants. Accordingly, the FarMisht Human Resources department has to be able to predict which applicants will succeed and which ones will not. The team has developed a Performance measure that they use to assess current employees. The scale is 0–100, where 100 indicates top performance.

What's the best prediction for a new applicant? Without knowing anything about an applicant, and knowing only their own employees' Performance scores, the answer is clear: It's the average Performance score among their employees. Regardless of who the applicant is, that's all the Human Resources team can say if its members' knowledge is limited.

With more knowledge about the employees and about the applicants, a more accurate prediction becomes possible. For example, if FarMisht develops an aptitude test and assesses its employees, Human Resources can match up every employee's Performance score with their Aptitude score and see whether the two pieces of data are somehow related. If they are, an applicant can take the FarMisht aptitude test, and Human Resources can use that score (and the relationship between Aptitude and Performance) to help make a prediction.

Figure 6-1 shows the Aptitude-Performance matchup in a graphical way. Because the points are scattered, it's called a *scatterplot.* By convention, the vertical axis (the *y*-axis) represents what you're trying to predict. That's also called the *dependent variable,* or the *y-variable.* In this case, that's Performance. Also by convention, the horizontal axis (the *x*-axis) represents what you're using to make your prediction. That's also called the *independent variable,* or *x-variable.* Here, that's Aptitude.

Each point in the graph represents an individual's Performance and Aptitude. In a scatterplot for a real-life corporation, you'd see many more points than I show here. The general tendency of the set of points seems to be that high Aptitude scores are associated with high Performance scores and that low Aptitude scores are associated with low Performance scores.

I've singled out one of the points. It shows a FarMisht employee with an Aptitude score of 54 and a Performance score of 68. I also show the average Performance score, to give you a sense that knowing the Aptitude-Performance relationship provides an advantage over knowing only the mean.

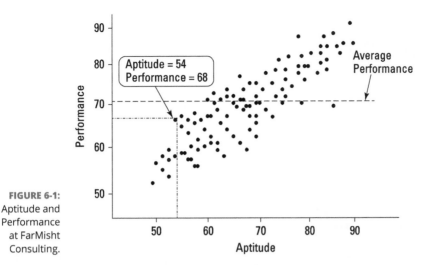

FIGURE 6-1:
Aptitude and
Performance
at FarMisht
Consulting.

How do you make that advantage work for you? You start by summarizing the relationship between Aptitude and Performance. The summary is a line through the points. How and where do you draw the line?

I get to that in a minute. First, I have to tell you about lines in general.

Graphing Lines

In the world of mathematics, a line is a way to picture a relationship between an independent variable *(x)* and a dependent variable *(y)*. In this relationship,

$$y = 4 + 2x$$

If you supply a value for *x*, you can figure out the corresponding value for *y*. The equation says to multiply the *x*-value by 2 and then add 4.

If *x* = 1, for example, *y* = 6. If *x* =2, *y* = 8. Table 6-1 shows a number of *x-y* pairs in this relationship, including the pair in which *x* = 0.

Figure 6-2 shows these pairs as points on a set of *x-y* axes, along with a line through the points. Each time I list an *x-y* pair in parentheses, the *x-value* is first.

As the figure shows, the points fall neatly onto the line. The line *graphs* the equation *y* = 4 + 2*x*. In fact, whenever you have an equation like this, where *x* isn't squared or cubed or raised to any power higher than 1, you have what mathematicians call a *linear* equation. (If *x* is raised to a higher power than 1, you connect the points with a curve, not a line.)

TABLE 6-1 ***x-y* Pairs in *y* = 4 + 2*x***

x	y
0	4
1	6
2	8
3	10
4	12
5	14
6	16

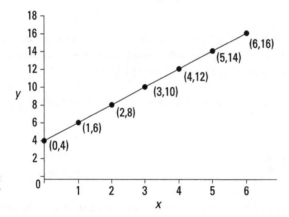

FIGURE 6-2:
The graph for
$y = 4 + 2x$.

REMEMBER

A couple of things to keep in mind about a line: You can describe a line in terms of how slanted it is, and where it runs into the y-axis.

The how-slanted-it-is part is the slope. The *slope* tells you how much y changes when x changes by 1 unit. In the line shown in Figure 6-2, when x changes by 1 (from 4 to 5, for example), y changes by 2 (from 12 to 14).

The where-it-runs-into-the-y-axis part is called the y-*intercept* (or sometimes just the *intercept*). That's the value of y when $x = 0$. In Figure 6-2, the y-intercept is 4.

You can see these numbers in the equation. The slope is the number that multiplies x, and the intercept is the number you add to x. In general,

$$y = a + bx$$

where a represents the intercept and b represents the slope.

The slope can be a positive number, a negative number, or 0. In Figure 6-2, the slope is positive. If the slope is negative, the line is slanted in a direction opposite to what you see in Figure 6-2. A negative slope means that y *decreases* as x increases. If the slope is 0, the line is parallel to the horizontal axis. In other words, if the slope is 0, y doesn't change as x changes.

The same applies to the intercept — it can be a positive number, a negative number, or 0. If the intercept is positive, the line cuts off the y-axis *above* the x-axis. If the intercept is negative, the line cuts off the y-axis *below* the x-axis. If the intercept is 0, it intersects with the y-axis and the x-axis at the point called the *origin*.

And now, back to what I was originally talking about.

Regression: What a Line!

I mention earlier that a line is the best way to summarize the relationship in the scatterplot in Figure 6-1. It's possible to draw an infinite number of straight lines through the scatterplot. Which one best summarizes the relationship?

Intuitively, the *best-fitting* line ought to be the one that passes through the maximum number of points and isn't too far away from the points it doesn't pass through. For statisticians, that line has a special property: If you draw that line through the scatterplot and then draw distances (in the vertical direction) between the points and the line and then square those distances and add them up, the sum of the squared distances is a minimum.

Statisticians call this line the *regression line,* and they indicate it as

$$y' = a + bx$$

Each y' is a point on the line. It represents the best prediction of y for a given value of x.

To figure out exactly where this line is, you calculate its slope and its intercept. For a regression line, the slope and intercept are called *regression coefficients.*

The formulas for the regression coefficients are pretty straightforward. For the slope, the formula is

$$b = \frac{\sum(x - \bar{x})(y - \bar{y})}{\sum(x - \bar{x})^2}$$

The intercept formula is

$$a = \bar{y} - b\bar{x}$$

I illustrate with an example. To keep the numbers manageable and comprehensible, I use a small sample instead of the hundreds (or perhaps thousands) of employees you'd find in a scatterplot for a corporation. Table 6-2 shows a sample of data from 16 FarMisht consultants.

TABLE 6-2 **Aptitude Scores and Performance Scores for 16 FarMisht Consultants**

Consultant	Aptitude	Performance
1	45	56
2	81	74
3	65	56
4	87	81
5	68	75
6	91	84
7	77	68
8	61	52
9	55	57
10	66	82
11	82	73
12	93	90
13	76	67
14	83	79
15	61	70
16	74	66
Mean	72.81	70.63
Variance	181.63	126.65
Standard Deviation	13.48	11.25

For this set of data, the slope of the regression line is

$$b = \frac{(45-72.81)(56-70.63)+(81-72.81)(74-70.63)+...+(74-72.81)(66-70.63)}{(45-72.81)^2+(81-72.81)^2+...+(74-72.81)^2} = 0.654$$

The intercept is

$$a = \bar{y} - b\bar{x} = 70.63 - 0.654(72.81) = 23.03$$

So the equation of the best-fitting line through these 16 points is

$$y' = 23.03 + 0.654x$$

Or, in terms of Performance and Aptitude, it's

Predicted Performance = $23.03 + 0.654(Aptitude)$

REMEMBER

The slope and the intercept of a regression line are generically called *regression coefficients*.

Using regression for forecasting

Based on this sample and this regression line, you can take an applicant's Aptitude score — say, 85 — and predict the applicant's Performance:

Predicted Performance = $23.03 + 0.654(85) = 78.59$

Without this regression line, the only prediction is the mean Performance, 70.63.

Variation around the regression line

In Chapter 3 of Book 2, I describe how the mean doesn't tell the whole story about a set of data. You have to show how the scores vary around the mean. For that reason, I introduce the variance and standard deviation.

You have a similar situation here. To form the full picture of the relationship in a scatterplot, you have to show how the scores vary around the regression line. Here, I introduce the *residual variance* and *standard error of estimate*, which are analogous to the variance and the standard deviation.

The residual variance is sort of an average of the squared deviations of the observed y-values around the predicted y-values. Each deviation of a data point from a predicted point ($y - y'$) is called a *residual*; hence, the name. The formula is

$$s_{yx}^2 = \frac{\sum(y - y')^2}{N - 2}$$

I say "sort of" because the denominator is $N-2$ rather than N. Telling you the reason for the -2 is beyond the scope of this discussion. As I mention earlier, the denominator of a variance estimate is *degrees of freedom* (df), and that concept comes in handy in a little while.

The standard error of estimate is

$$s_{yx} = \sqrt{s_{yx}^2} = \sqrt{\frac{\sum(y - y')^2}{N - 2}}$$

To show you how the residual error and the standard error of estimate play out for the data in the example, here's Table 6-3. This table extends Table 6-2 by showing the predicted Performance score for each given Aptitude score:

TABLE 6-3

Aptitude Scores, Performance Scores, and Predicted Performance Scores for 16 FarMisht Consultants

Consultant	Aptitude	Performance	Predicted Performance
1	45	56	52.44
2	81	74	75.98
3	65	56	65.52
4	87	81	79.90
5	68	75	67.48
6	91	84	82.51
7	77	68	73.36
8	61	52	62.90
9	55	57	58.98
10	66	82	66.17
11	82	73	76.63
12	93	90	83.82
13	76	67	72.71
14	83	79	77.28

Consultant	Aptitude	Performance	Predicted Performance
15	61	70	62.90
16	74	66	71.40
Mean	72.81	70.63	
Variance	181.63	126.65	
Standard Deviation	13.48	11.25	

As the table shows, sometimes the predicted Performance score is pretty close, and sometimes it's not.

For these data, the residual variance is

$$s_{yx}^2 = \frac{\sum(y-y')^2}{N-2} = \frac{(56-52.44)^2 + (74-75.98)^2 + \ldots + (66-71.40)^2}{16-2} = \frac{735.65}{14} = 52.54$$

The standard error of estimate is

$$s_{yx} = \sqrt{s_{yx}^2} = \sqrt{52.54} = 7.25$$

If the residual variance and the standard error of estimate are small, the regression line is a good fit to the data in the scatterplot. If the residual variance and the standard error of estimate are large, the regression line is a poor fit.

What's "small"? What's "large"? What's a "good" fit?

Keep reading.

Testing hypotheses about regression

The regression equation you are working with:

$$y' = a + bx$$

summarizes a relationship in a scatterplot of a sample. The regression coefficients a and b are sample statistics. You can use these statistics to test hypotheses about population parameters, and that's what you do in this section.

The regression line through the population that produces the sample (like the entire set of FarMisht consultants) is the graph of an equation that consists of parameters rather than statistics. By convention, remember, Greek letters stand for parameters, so the regression equation for the population is

$$y' = \alpha + \beta x + \varepsilon$$

The first two Greek letters on the right are α (alpha) and β (beta), the equivalents of a and b. What about that last one? It looks something like the Greek equivalent of e. What's it doing there?

That last term is the Greek letter *epsilon*. It represents "error" in the population. In a way, *error* is an unfortunate term. It's a catchall for "things you don't know or things you have no control over." Error is reflected in the residuals — the deviations from the predictions. The more you understand about what you're measuring, the more you decrease the error.

You can't measure the error in the relationship between Aptitude and Performance, but it's lurking there. Someone might score low on Aptitude, for example, and then go on to have a wonderful consulting career with a higher-than-predicted Performance. On a scatterplot, this person's Aptitude-Performance point looks like an error in prediction. As you find out more about that person, you might discover she was sick on the day of the Aptitude test, and that explains the "error."

You can test hypotheses about α, β, and ε, and that's what you do in the upcoming subsections.

Testing the fit

You begin with a test of how well the regression line fits the scatterplot. This is a test of ε, the error in the relationship.

The objective is to decide whether the line really represents a relationship between the variables. It's possible that what looks like a relationship is just due to chance and that the equation of the regression line doesn't mean anything (because the amount of error is overwhelming) — or it's possible that the variables are strongly related.

These possibilities are testable, and you set up hypotheses to test them:

H_0: No real relationship

H_1: Not H_0

Although those hypotheses make nice light reading, they don't set up a statistical test. To set up the test, you have to consider the variances. To consider the variances, you start with the deviations. Figure 6-3 focuses on one point in a scatterplot and its deviation from the regression line (the residual) and from the mean of the y-variable. It also shows the deviation between the regression line and the mean.

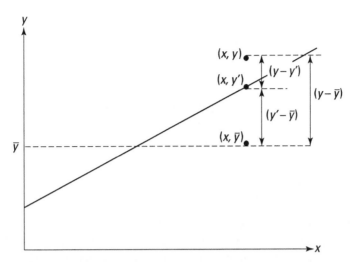

FIGURE 6-3:
The deviations in
a scatterplot.

As the figure shows, the distance between the point and the regression line and the distance between the regression line and the mean add up to the distance between the point and the mean:

$$(y - y') + (y' - \bar{y}) = (y - \bar{y})$$

This sets the stage for other important relationships.

Start by squaring each deviation. That gives you $(y - y')^2$, $(y' - \bar{y})^2$, and $(y - \bar{y})^2$. If you add up each of the squared deviations, you have

$$\sum (y - y')^2$$

You just saw this one. That's the numerator for the residual variance. It represents the variability around the regression line — the "error" I mention earlier. In the terminology of Chapter 4 of Book 3, the numerator of a variance is called a *sum of squares*, or *SS*. So this is $SS_{Residual}$.

$$\sum (y' - \bar{y})^2$$

This one is new. The deviation $(y' - \bar{y})$ represents the gain in prediction due to using the regression line rather than the mean. The sum reflects this gain and is called $SS_{Regression}$.

$$\sum (y - \bar{y})^2$$

I show you this one in Chapter 3 of Book 2 — although in that chapter I use x rather than y. That's the numerator of the variance of y. In Chapter 4 of Book 3 terms, it's the numerator of *total variance*. This one is SS_{Total}.

This relationship holds among these three sums:

$$SS_{Residual} + SS_{Regression} = SS_{Total}$$

Each one is associated with a value for degrees of freedom — the denominator of a variance estimate. As I point out in the preceding section, the denominator for $SS_{Residual}$ is $N-2$. The df for SS_{Total} is $N-1$. (See Chapter 3 of Book 2 and Chapter 4 of Book 3.) As with the SS, the degrees of freedom add up:

$$df_{Residual} + df_{Regression} = df_{Total}$$

This leaves one degree of freedom for regression.

Where is this all headed, and what does it have to do with hypothesis testing? Well, since you asked, you get variance estimates by dividing SS by df. Each variance estimate is called a *mean square*, abbreviated MS. (Again, see Chapter 4 of Book 3):

$$MS_{Regression} = \frac{SS_{Regression}}{df_{Regression}}$$

$$MS_{Residual} = \frac{SS_{Residual}}{df_{Residual}}$$

$$MS_{Total} = \frac{SS_{Total}}{df_{Total}}$$

Now for the hypothesis part. If H_0 is true and what looks like a relationship between x and y is really no big deal, the piece that represents the gain in prediction because of the regression line ($MS_{Regression}$) should be no greater than the variability around the regression line ($MS_{Residual}$). If H_0 is not true and the gain in prediction is substantial, then $MS_{Regression}$ should be a lot bigger than $MS_{Residual}$.

So the hypotheses now become

$$H_0: \sigma^2_{Regression} \leq \sigma^2_{Residual}$$

$$H_1: \sigma^2_{Regression} > \sigma^2_{Residual}$$

These are hypotheses you can test. How? To test a hypothesis about two variances, you use an F test. (See Chapter 3 of Book 3.) The test statistic here is

$$F = \frac{MS_{Regression}}{MS_{Residual}}$$

To show you how it all works, I apply the formulas to the FarMisht example. The $MS_{Residual}$ is the same as s_{yx}^2 from the preceding section, and that value is 18.61. The $MS_{Regression}$ is

$$MS_{Regression} = \frac{(59.64 - 70.63)^2 + (71.40 - 70.63)^2 + ... + (66.17 - 70.63)^2}{1} = 1164.1$$

This sets up the F:

$$F = \frac{MS_{Regression}}{MS_{Residual}} = \frac{1164.1}{52.55} = 22.15$$

With 1 and 14 df and $\alpha = .05$, the critical value of F is 4.60. (Use $qf()$ to verify.) The calculated F is greater than the critical F, so the decision is to reject H_0. That means the regression line provides a good fit to the data in the sample.

Testing the slope

Another question that arises in linear regression is whether the slope of the regression line is significantly different from zero. If it's not, the mean is just as good a predictor as the regression line.

The hypotheses for this test are

$H_0: \beta \leq 0$

$H_1: \beta > 0$

The statistical test is t, which I discuss in Chapters 1, 2, and 3 of Book 3 in connection with means. The t-test for the slope is

$$t = \frac{b - \beta}{s_b}$$

with df $= N-2$. The denominator estimates the standard error of the slope. This term sounds more complicated than it is. The formula is

$$s_b = \frac{s_{yx}}{s_x \sqrt{(N-1)}}$$

where s_x is the standard deviation of the x-variable. For the data in the example,

$$s_b = \frac{s_{yx}}{s_x \sqrt{(N-1)}} = \frac{7.25}{(13.48)\sqrt{(16-1)}} = .139$$

$$t = \frac{b - \beta}{s_b} = \frac{.654 - 0}{.139} = 4.71$$

This is larger than the critical value of t for 14 df and $\alpha = .05$ (2.14), so the decision is to reject H_o.

Testing the intercept

Finally, here's the hypothesis test for the intercept. The hypotheses are

H_0: $\alpha = 0$

H_1: $\alpha \neq 0$

The test, once again, is a t-test. The formula is

$$t = \frac{a - \alpha}{s_a}$$

The denominator is the estimate of the standard error of the intercept. Without going into detail, the formula for s_a is

$$s_a = s_{yx} \sqrt{\left[\frac{1}{N} + \frac{\bar{x}^2}{(N-1)s_x^2} \right]}$$

where s_x is the standard deviation of the x-variable, s_x^2 is the variance of the x-variable, and $\bar{x}^2$ is the squared mean of the x-variable. Applying this formula to the data in the example,

$$s_a = s_{yx} \sqrt{\left[\frac{1}{N} + \frac{\bar{x}^2}{(N-1)s_x^2} \right]} = 10.27$$

The t-test is

$$t = \frac{a - \alpha}{s_a} = \frac{23.03}{10.27} = 2.24$$

With 15 degrees of freedom and the probability of a Type I error at .05, the critical t is 2.13 for a two-tailed test. (It's a two-tailed test because H_1 is that the intercept doesn't equal zero — it doesn't specify whether the intercept is greater than zero or less than zero.) Because the calculated value is greater than the critical value, the decision is to reject H_0.

Linear Regression in R

Time to see how R handles linear regression. To start the analysis for this example, create a vector for the Aptitude scores and another for the Performance scores:

```
Aptitude <- c(45, 81, 65, 87, 68, 91, 77, 61, 55, 66, 82, 93, 76, 83, 61, 74)
Performance <- c(56, 74, 56, 81, 75, 84, 68, 52, 57, 82, 73, 90, 67, 79, 70, 66)
```

Then use the two vectors to create a data frame

```
FarMisht.frame <- data.frame(Aptitude,Performance)
```

The lm( ) (linear model) function performs the analysis:

```
FM.reg <-lm(Performance ~ Aptitude, data=FarMisht.frame)
```

As always, the tilde (~) operator signifies "depends on," so this is a perfect example of a dependent variable and an independent variable.

Applying summary( ) to FM.reg produces the regression information:

```
> summary(FM.reg)

Call:
lm(formula = Performance ~ Aptitude, data = FarMisht.frame)

Residuals:
     Min      1Q  Median      3Q     Max
 -10.9036 -5.3720 -0.4379  4.2111 15.8281

Coefficients:
            Estimate Std. Error t value Pr(>|t|)
(Intercept) 23.0299    10.2732    2.242 0.041697 *
Aptitude     0.6537     0.1389    4.707 0.000337 ***
---
Signif. codes: 0 '***' 0.001 '**' 0.01 '*' 0.05 '.' 0.1 ' ' 1

Residual standard error: 7.249 on 14 degrees of freedom
Multiple R-squared:  0.6128,   Adjusted R-squared:  0.5851
F-statistic: 22.15 on 1 and 14 DF,  p-value: 0.0003368
```

The first couple of lines provide summary information about the residuals. The coefficients table shows the intercept and slope of the regression line. If you divide each number in the Estimate column by the adjoining number in the Std. Error column, you get the number in the t value column. These t-values, of course, are the significance tests I mention earlier for the intercept and the slope. The extremely low p-values indicate rejection of the null hypothesis (that a coefficient = 0) for each coefficient.

The bottom part of the output shows the info on how well the line fits the scatterplot. It presents the standard error of the residual, followed by `Multiple R-squared` and `Adjusted R-squared`. These last two range from 0 to 1.00 (the higher the value, the better the fit). I discuss them in Chapter 7 of Book 3, but for now I'll leave them alone. The `F-statistic` corresponds to the F-ratio I show you earlier. Its high value (22.15) and low associated p-value (.0003368) indicate that the line is a great fit to the scatterplot.

REMEMBER

I refer to the result of the linear regression analysis as "the linear model."

Features of the linear model

The linear model produced by `lm( )` is an object that provides information, if you ask for it in the right way. As I already showed you, applying `summary( )` gives all the information you need about the analysis.

You can also zero in on the coefficients:

```
> coefficients(FM.reg)
(Intercept)    Aptitude
  23.029869    0.653667
```

and on their confidence intervals:

```
> confint(FM.reg)
                 2.5 %      97.5 %
(Intercept) 0.9961369 45.0636002
Aptitude    0.3558034  0.9515307
```

Applying `fitted(FM.reg)` produces the fitted values, and `residuals(FM.reg)` gives the residuals.

Making predictions

The value of linear regression is that it gives you the ability to predict, and R provides a function that does just that: `predict( )` applies a set of x-values to the linear model and returns the predicted values. Imagine two applicants with Aptitude scores of 85 and 62:

```
predict(FM.reg,data.frame(Aptitude=c(85,62)))
```

The first argument is the linear model, and the second makes a data frame out of the vector of values for the independent variable. Running this function produces these predicted values:

```
      1        2
78.59157 63.55723
```

Visualizing the scatterplot and regression line

With the `ggplot2` package, you can visualize a scatterplot and its regression line in three statements. The first statement, as always, indicates the data source and maps the components of the data to components of the plot:

```
ggplot(FarMisht.frame,aes(x=Aptitude,y=Performance))
```

The second statement plots points in the graph:

```
geom_point()
```

And the third specifies a `geom` function that adds the regression line (as indicated by the `method = lm` argument):

```
geom_smooth(method=lm)
```

Putting all three together

```
ggplot(FarMisht.frame,aes(x=Aptitude,y=Performance)) +
  geom_point()+
  geom_smooth(method=lm)
```

produces Figure 6-4.

The shaded area represents the 95 percent confidence interval around the regression line.

Plotting the residuals

After a regression analysis, it's a good idea to plot the residuals against the predicted values. If the residuals form a random pattern around a horizontal line at 0, that's evidence in favor of a linear relationship between the independent variable and the dependent variable.

Figure 6-5 shows the residual plot for the example. The pattern of residuals around the line is consistent with a linear model.

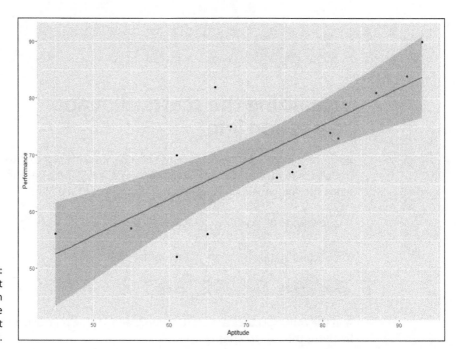

FIGURE 6-4:
Scatterplot
and regression
line for the
16 FarMisht
consultants.

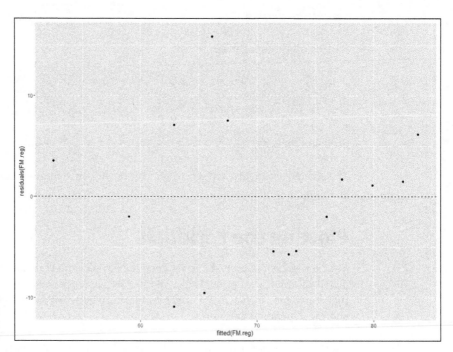

FIGURE 6-5:
Residuals plot
for the FarMisht
example.

The plot is based on `FM.reg`, the linear model. Here's the `ggplot()` statement:

```
ggplot(FM.reg, aes(x=fitted(FM.reg), y=residuals(FM.reg)))
```

The *x* and *y* mappings are based on information from the analysis. As you might guess, `fitted(FM.reg)` retrieves the predicted values, and `residuals(FM.reg)` retrieves the residuals.

To plot points, add the appropriate `geom` function:

```
geom_point()
```

and then a `geom` function for the dashed horizontal line whose *y*-intercept is 0:

```
geom_hline(yintercept = 0, linetype = "dashed" )
```

So the code for Figure 6-5 is

```
ggplot(FM.reg, aes(x=fitted(FM.reg), y=residuals(FM.reg)))+
  geom_point() +
  geom_hline(yintercept = 0, linetype = "dashed" )
```

Juggling Many Relationships at Once: Multiple Regression

Linear regression is a useful tool for making predictions. When you know the slope and the intercept of the line that relates two variables, you can take a new *x*-value and predict a new *y*-value. In the example you work through in this chapter, you take an Aptitude score and predict a Performance score for a FarMisht applicant.

What if you know more than just the Aptitude score for each applicant? Imagine that the FarMisht management team decides that a particular personality type is ideal for their consultants. So they develop the FarMisht Personality Inventory, a 20-point scale in which a higher score indicates greater compatibility with the FarMisht corporate culture and, presumably, predicts better performance. The idea is to use that data along with Aptitude scores to predict performance.

Table 6-4 shows the Aptitude, Performance, and Personality scores for the 16 current consultants. Of course, in a real-life corporation, you might have many more employees in the sample.

TABLE 6-4

Aptitude, Performance, and Personality Scores for 16 FarMisht Consultants

Consultant	Aptitude	Performance	Personality
1	45	56	9
2	81	74	15
3	65	56	11
4	87	81	15
5	68	75	14
6	91	84	19
7	77	68	12
8	61	52	10
9	55	57	9
10	66	82	14
11	82	73	15
12	93	90	14
13	76	67	16
14	83	79	18
15	61	70	15
16	74	66	12
Mean	72.81	70.63	13.63
Variance	181.63	126.65	8.65
Standard Deviation	13.48	11.25	2.94

When you work with more than one independent variable, you're in the realm of *multiple regression.* As in linear regression, you find regression coefficients. In the case of two independent variables, you're looking for the best-fitting *plane* through a 3-dimensional scatterplot. Once again, *best-fitting* means that the sum of the squared distances from the data points to the plane is a minimum.

Here's the equation of the regression plane:

$$y' = a + b_1 x_1 + b_2 x_2$$

For this example, that translates to

$$Predicted\ Performance = a + b_1(Aptitude) + b_2(Personality)$$

You can test hypotheses about the overall fit and about all three of the regression coefficients.

I don't walk you through all the formulas for finding the coefficients, because that gets *really* complicated. Instead, I go right to the R analysis.

Here are a few things to bear in mind before I proceed:

>> You can have any number of *x*-variables. (I use two in this example.)

>> Expect the coefficient for Aptitude to change from linear regression to multiple regression. Expect the intercept to change, too.

>> Expect the standard error of estimate to decrease from linear regression to multiple regression. Because multiple regression uses more information than linear regression, it reduces the error.

Multiple regression in R

I begin by adding a vector for the personality scores in column 4 of Table 6-4:

```
Personality <- c(9, 15, 11, 15, 14, 19, 12, 10, 9, 14, 15, 14, 16, 18, 15, 12)
```

And then I add that vector to the data frame:

```
FarMisht.frame["Personality"] = Personality
```

Applying lm() produces the analysis:

```
FM.multreg <- lm(Performance ~ Aptitude + Personality, data = FarMisht.frame)
```

And applying summary() gives the information:

```
> summary(FM.multreg)

Call:
lm(formula = Performance ~ Aptitude + Personality, data = FarMisht.frame)
```

```
Residuals:
   Min     1Q Median    3Q    Max
 -8.689 -2.834 -1.840  2.886 13.432


Coefficients:
             Estimate Std. Error t value Pr(>|t|)
(Intercept)  20.2825     9.6595   2.100    0.0558 .
Aptitude      0.3905     0.1949   2.003    0.0664 .
Personality   1.6079     0.8932   1.800    0.0951 .
---
Signif. codes:  0 '***' 0.001 '**' 0.01 '*' 0.05 '.' 0.1 ' ' 1


Residual standard error: 6.73 on 13 degrees of freedom
Multiple R-squared:   0.69,    Adjusted R-squared:  0.6423
F-statistic: 14.47 on 2 and 13 DF,  p-value: 0.0004938
```

So the equation for the best-fitting regression plane through these 16 points is

$$y' = 20.2825 + .3905x_1 + 1.6079x_2$$

Or, in terms of Performance, Aptitude, and Personality, its

$$Predicted\ Performance = 20.2825 + .3905(Aptitude) + 1.6079(Personality)$$

As in the linear example, the high F-value (14.47) and low p-value (.0004938) indicate that the regression plane is an excellent fit for the scatterplot.

Making predictions

Once again, predict() enables predictions of Performance. This time, I use it with the multiple regression model: FM.multreg. Imagine two applicants: One has Aptitude and Personality scores of 85 and 14, and the other has Aptitude and Personality scores of 62 and 17. This requires two vectors — one for the Aptitude scores and one for the Personality scores:

```
> predict(FM.multreg, data.frame(Aptitude = c(85,62), Personality=c(14,17)))
        1        2
 75.98742 71.82924
```

Visualizing the 3d scatterplot and regression plane

The ggplot2 package, for all its wonderful features, does not provide a way to draw 3-dimensional graphics — like a scatterplot for a dependent variable and two independent variables. Never fear, however: R has a number of other ways to do this. In this section, I show you two of them.

The scatterplot3d package

If you want to make a nifty 3-dimensional scatterplot like the one shown in Figure 6-6 — a figure that looks darn good on a printed page — the scatterplot3d() function is for you.

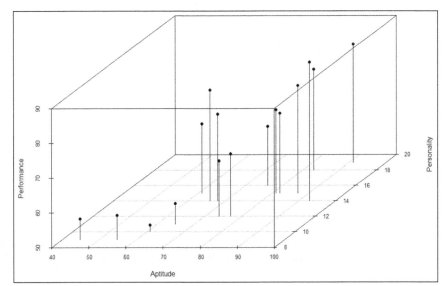

FIGURE 6-6:
Scatterplot for the FarMisht multiple regression example, rendered in scatterplot3d().

First, install the scatterplot3d package. On the Packages tab, find scatterplot3d and select its check box.

Next, write a statement that creates the plot:

```
with (FarMisht.frame,
(splot <- scatterplot3d(Performance ~ Aptitude + Personality,
    type = "h", pch = 19)))
```

If you use with, you don't have to repeat the name of the data frame three times. The first argument to scatterplot3d() is the formula for setting up the linear model. The second argument adds the vertical lines from the x-y plane to the data points. Those vertical lines aren't absolutely necessary, but I think they help the viewer understand where the points are in the plot. The third argument specifies what the plot characters look like.

The function produces an object that you can use to embellish the plot. For example, here's how to add the regression plane and produce Figure 6-7:

```
splot$plane3d(FM.multreg,lty="dashed")
```

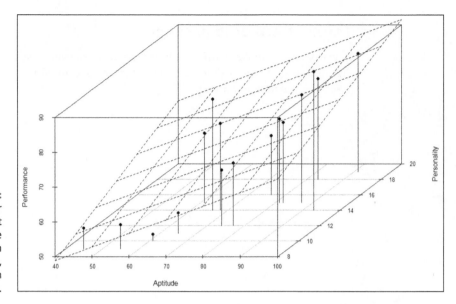

FIGURE 6-7:
Scatterplot for
the FarMisht
multiple
regression
example,
complete with
regression plane.

car and rgl: A package deal

If you have to present a 3D scatterplot to an audience and you want to dazzle them
with an interactive plot, the next method is for you.

The plot-creating function is called scatter3d(), and it lives in the car package.
On the Packages tab, click Install. In the Install Packages dialog box, type **car** and
click Install. When car appears on the Packages tab, select its check box.

This function works with the rgl package, which uses tools from the Open Graphics Library (OpenGL), a toolset for creating 2D and 3D graphics. You'll find OpenGL
tools at work in virtual reality, computer-aided design, flight simulation, and a
number of other applications In the Install Packages dialog box, type **rgl** and click
Install. When rgl appears on the Packages tab, select its check box.

With those two packages installed, run this function:

```
scatter3d(Performance ~ Aptitude + Personality, data=FarMisht.frame)
```

This opens an RGL window with the 3D scatterplot shown in Figure 6-8. As you
can see, the scatterplot shows the regression plane and the residuals.

You can move the mouse inside this plot, press the left mouse button, and rotate
the plot to present different angles. You can also use the scroll wheel to zoom in
or out of the plot. Try it!

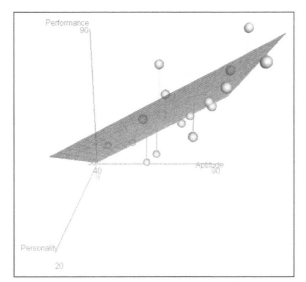

FIGURE 6-8:
Scatterplot for the FarMisht multiple regression example, rendered in scatter3d().

ANOVA: Another Look

Here's a statement you might find radical: Analysis of variance and linear regression *are the same thing.*

They're both part of what's called the general linear model (GLM). In linear regression, the objective is to predict a value of a dependent variable given a value of an independent variable. In ANOVA, the objective is to decide whether several sample means differ enough from one another to enable you to reject the null hypothesis about levels of the independent variable.

How are they similar? It's easier to see the connection if you rethink ANOVA: Given the data, imagine that the objective is to predict the dependent variable, given the level of the independent variable. What would be the best prediction? For any level of the independent variable, that would be the mean of the sample for that level — also known as the *group mean.* This means that deviations from the group mean (the best predicted value) are residuals, and this is why, in an R ANOVA, the MS_{Error} is called $MS_{Residuals}$.

It goes deeper than that. To show you how, I revisit the ANOVA example from Chapter 4 of Book 3. For convenience, here's Table 4-1 from that same chapter, reproduced as this chapter's Table 6-5.

TABLE 6-5

Data from Three Training Methods (ANOVA Example from Chapter 4 of Book 3)

	Method 1	Method 2	Method 3
	95	83	68
	91	89	75
	89	85	79
	90	89	74
	99	81	75
	88	89	81
	96	90	73
	98	82	77
	95	84	
		80	
Mean	93.44	85.20	75.25
Variance	16.28	14.18	15.64
Standard Deviation	4.03	3.77	3.96

You have to test

$H_0: \mu_1 = \mu_2 = \mu_3$

$H_1:$ Not H_0

To use the aov() function to produce an analysis of variance, set up the data in long format. Here are the first six rows:

```
> head(Training.frame)
  Method Score
1 method1    95
2 method1    91
3 method1    89
4 method1    90
5 method1    99
6 method1    88
```

The result of the analysis is

```
> analysis <-aov(Score~Method,data = Training.frame)
> summary(analysis)
            Df Sum Sq Mean Sq F value   Pr(>F)
Method       2 1402.7   701.3   45.82 6.38e-09 ***
Residuals   24  367.3    15.3
---
Signif. codes: 0 '***' 0.001 '**' 0.01 '*' 0.05 '.' 0.1 ' ' 1
```

What if you tried a linear regression analysis on the data?

```
> reg.analysis <-lm(Score~Method,data = Training.frame)
> summary(reg.analysis)

Call:
lm(formula = Score ~ Method, data = Training.frame)

Residuals:
    Min     1Q Median     3Q    Max
 -7.250 -2.822 -0.250  3.775  5.750

Coefficients:
              Estimate Std. Error t value Pr(>|t|)
(Intercept)     93.444      1.304  71.657  < 2e-16 ***
Methodmethod2   -8.244      1.798  -4.587 0.000119 ***
Methodmethod3  -18.194      1.901  -9.571 1.15e-09 ***
---
Signif. codes: 0 '***' 0.001 '**' 0.01 '*' 0.05 '.' 0.1 ' ' 1

Residual standard error: 3.912 on 24 degrees of freedom
Multiple R-squared:  0.7925,   Adjusted R-squared:  0.7752
F-statistic: 45.82 on 2 and 24 DF,  p-value: 6.381e-09
```

You see a good bit more information than in the ANOVA table, but the bottom line shows the same F-ratio and associated information as the analysis of variance. Also, the coefficients provide the group means: The intercept (93.444) is the mean of Method 1, the intercept plus the second coefficient (−8.244) is the mean of Method 2 (85.20), and the intercept plus the third coefficient (−18.194) is the mean of Method 3 (75.25). Check the means in Table 6-5, if you don't believe me.

A bit more on the coefficients: The Intercept represents Method 1, which is a baseline against which to compare each of the others. The t-value for Method 2 (along with its associated probability, which is much less than .05) shows that Method 2 differs significantly from Method 1. It's the same story for Method 3, which also differs significantly from Method 1.

Here's a question that should be forming in your mind: How can you perform a linear regression when the independent variable (Method) is categorical rather than numerical?

Glad you asked.

REMEMBER

To form a regression analysis with categorical data, R (and other statistical software packages) recode the levels of a variable like Method into combinations of numeric *dummy variables*. The only values a dummy variable can take are 0 or 1: 0 indicates the *absence* of a categorical value; 1 indicates the *presence* of a categorical value.

I'll do this manually. For the three levels of Method (Method 1, Method 2, and Method 3), I need two dummy variables. I'll call them D1 and D2. Here's how I (arbitrarily) assign the values:

» For Method 1, D1 = 0 and D2 = 0

» For Method 2, D1 = 1, and D2 = 0

» For Method 3, D1 = 0, and D2 = 1

To illustrate further, here's a data frame called Training.frame.w.Dummies. Ordinarily, I wouldn't show you all 27 rows of a data frame, but here I think it's instructive:

```
> Training.frame.w.Dummies
    Method D1 D2 Score
1  method1  0  0    95
2  method1  0  0    91
3  method1  0  0    89
4  method1  0  0    90
5  method1  0  0    99
6  method1  0  0    88
7  method1  0  0    96
8  method1  0  0    98
9  method1  0  0    95
10 method2  1  0    83
11 method2  1  0    89
12 method2  1  0    85
13 method2  1  0    89
14 method2  1  0    81
15 method2  1  0    89
16 method2  1  0    90
17 method2  1  0    82
18 method2  1  0    84
19 method2  1  0    80
20 method3  0  1    68
```

```
21  method3  0  1  75
22  method3  0  1  79
23  method3  0  1  74
24  method3  0  1  75
25  method3  0  1  81
26  method3  0  1  73
27  method3  0  1  77
```

These lines of code

```
model.w.Dummies <- lm(Score ~ D1 + D2, data= Training.frame.w.Dummies)
summary(model.w.Dummies)
```

produce the same result as the analysis of variance and the linear regression I show you earlier. The only difference is that the coefficients are expressed in terms of the dummy variables:

```
Coefficients:
             Estimate Std. Error t value Pr(>|t|)
(Intercept)    93.444       1.304  71.657  < 2e-16 ***
D1             -8.244       1.798  -4.587 0.000119 ***
D2            -18.194       1.901  -9.571 1.15e-09 ***
```

So dummy variables enable a linear regression model with categorical independent variables. In fact, linear regression with categorical independent variables *is* the analysis of variance.

Analysis of Covariance: The Final Component of the GLM

In this chapter, I've shown you how linear regression works with a numeric independent (predictor) variable, and with a categorical independent (predictor) variable. Is it possible to have a study with both a numeric predictor variable and a categorical predictor variable?

Absolutely! The analytical tool for this type of study is called the *analysis of covariance (ANCOVA)*. It's the third and final component of the general linear model. (Linear regression and ANOVA are the first two.) The easiest way to describe it is with an example.

Make sure you have the MASS package installed. On the Packages tab, find its check box and select it, if it isn't already. In the MASS package, you'll find a data frame called `anorexia`. (I use it in Chapter 2 of Book 1.) This data frame contains data for 72 young women randomly selected for one of three types of treatment for anorexia: `Cont` (a control condition with no therapy), `CBT` (cognitive behavioral therapy), or `FT` (family treatment).

Here are the first six rows:

```
> head(anorexia)
  Treat Prewt Postwt
1  Cont  80.7   80.2
2  Cont  89.4   80.1
3  Cont  91.8   86.4
4  Cont  74.0   86.3
5  Cont  78.1   76.1
6  Cont  88.3   78.1
```

`Prewt` is the weight before treatment, and `Postwt` is the weight after treatment. What you need, of course, is a variable that indicates the amount of weight gained during treatment. I'll call it `WtGain`, and here's how to add it to the data frame:

```
anorexia["WtGain"]=anorexia["Postwt"]-anorexia["Prewt"]
```

Now:

```
> head(anorexia)
  Treat Prewt Postwt WtGain
1  Cont  80.7   80.2   -0.5
2  Cont  89.4   80.1   -9.3
3  Cont  91.8   86.4   -5.4
4  Cont  74.0   86.3   12.3
5  Cont  78.1   76.1   -2.0
6  Cont  88.3   78.1  -10.2
```

Figure 6-9 plots the data points for this data frame.

Here's the code for this plot, in case you're curious:

```
ggplot(anorexia,aes(x=Treat,y=WtGain))+
  geom_point()
```

An analysis of variance or a linear regression analysis would be appropriate to test these:

$H_0: \mu_{Cont} = \mu_{CBT} = \mu_{FT}$

$H_1:$ Not H_0

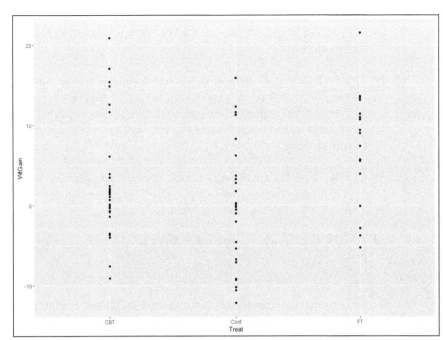

FIGURE 6-9:
Weight Gain
versus Treat in
the anorexia data
frame.

Here's the linear regression model:

```
> anorexia.linreg <-lm(WtGain ~ Treat, data=anorexia)
> summary(anorexia.linreg)

Call:
lm(formula = WtGain ~ Treat, data = anorexia)

Residuals:
    Min      1Q  Median      3Q     Max
-12.565  -4.543  -1.007   3.846  17.893

Coefficients:
            Estimate Std. Error t value Pr(>|t|)
(Intercept)    3.007      1.398   2.151   0.0350 *
TreatCont     -3.457      2.033  -1.700   0.0936 .
TreatFT        4.258      2.300   1.852   0.0684 .
---
Signif. codes: 0 '***' 0.001 '**' 0.01 '*' 0.05 '.' 0.1 ' ' 1

Residual standard error: 7.528 on 69 degrees of freedom
Multiple R-squared:  0.1358,   Adjusted R-squared:  0.1108
F-statistic: 5.422 on 2 and 69 DF,  p-value: 0.006499
```

The F-ratio and p-value on the bottom line tell you that you can reject the null hypothesis.

Let's look at the coefficients. The intercept represents cognitive behavioral therapy (CBT). This is the baseline against which you compare the other treatments. The t-values and associated probabilities (greater than .05) tell you that neither of those levels differs from CBT. The significant F-ratio must result from other comparisons.

Also, check the coefficients against the treatment means. Here's a quick and easy way to find the treatment means: Use the function `tapply()` to apply `mean()` and find the mean `WtGain` in the levels of `Treat`:

```
> with (anorexia, tapply(WtGain,Treat,mean))
      CBT       Cont        FT
3.006897 -0.450000  7.264706
```

The intercept, remember, is the mean for `CBT`. Add the intercept to the next coefficient to calculate the mean for `Cont` (the control condition with no therapy) and add the intercept to the final coefficient to calculate the mean for `FT` (family treatment).

If you prefer to see the F-ratio and associated statistics in an ANOVA table, you can apply the `anova()` function to the model:

```
> anova(anorexia.linreg)
Analysis of Variance Table

Response: WtGain
          Df Sum Sq Mean Sq F value   Pr(>F)
Treat      2  614.6 307.322  5.4223 0.006499 **
Residuals 69 3910.7  56.677
---
Signif. codes: 0 '***' 0.001 '**' 0.01 '*' 0.05 '.' 0.1 ' ' 1
```

You can dig a little deeper. Suppose weight gain depends only not only the type of treatment but also a person's initial weight (which is called a *covariate*). Taking `PreWt` into consideration might yield a more accurate picture. `Treat` is a categorical variable, and `Prewt` is a numerical variable. Figure 6-10 shows a plot based on the two variables.

The code for this plot is

```
ggplot(anorexia, aes(x=Prewt,y=WtGain, shape = Treat)) +
  geom_point(size=2.5)
```

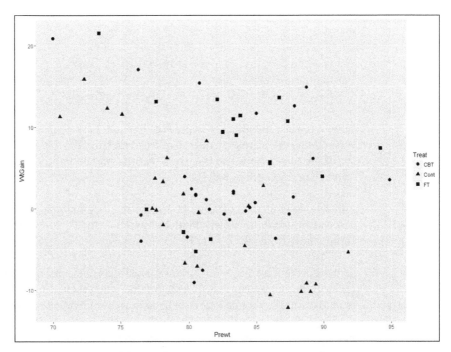

FIGURE 6-10:
Weight Gain
versus Treat
and Prewt in
the anorexia
data frame.

The first statement maps Prewt to the *x*-axis, WtGain to the *y*-axis, and Treat to Shape. Thus, the shape of a data point reflects its treatment group. The second statement specifies that points appear in the plot. Its size argument enlarges the data points and makes them easier to see.

For the analysis of covariance, I use the lm() function to create a model based on both Treat and Prewt:

```
> anorexia.T.and.P <- lm(WtGain ~ Treat + Prewt, data=anorexia)
> summary(anorexia.T.and.P)

Call:
lm(formula = WtGain ~ Treat + Prewt, data = anorexia)

Residuals:
    Min      1Q   Median      3Q     Max
-14.1083  -4.2773  -0.5484  5.4838  15.2922

Coefficients:
            Estimate Std. Error t value Pr(>|t|)
(Intercept)  49.7711    13.3910   3.717 0.000410 ***
TreatCont    -4.0971     1.8935  -2.164 0.033999 *
TreatFT       4.5631     2.1333   2.139 0.036035 *
Prewt        -0.5655     0.1612  -3.509 0.000803 ***
---
```

CHAPTER 6 Regression: Linear, Multiple, and the General Linear Model   311

```
Signif. codes: 0 '***' 0.001 '**' 0.01 '*' 0.05 '.' 0.1 ' ' 1

Residual standard error: 6.978 on 68 degrees of freedom
Multiple R-squared:  0.2683,   Adjusted R-squared:  0.236
F-statistic: 8.311 on 3 and 68 DF,  p-value: 8.725e-05
```

Note in the last line that the degrees of freedom have changed from the first analysis: Adding Prewt takes a degree of freedom from the df Residual and adds it to the df for Treat. Note also that the F-ratio is higher and the p-value considerably lower than in the first analysis.

And now look at the coefficients. Unlike the original analysis, the t-values and associated probabilities (less than .05) for Cont and FT show that each one differs significantly from CBT.

So it seems that adding Prewt to the analysis has helped uncover treatment differences. Bottom line: The ANCOVA shows that when evaluating the effect of an anorexia treatment, it's important to also know an individual's pretreatment weight.

But the phrase "it seems" is not enough for statisticians. Can you really be sure that the ANCOVA adds value? To find out, you have to compare the linear regression model with the ANCOVA model. To make the comparison, use the anova() function, which does double-duty: In addition to creating an ANOVA table for a model (as in the preceding section), you can use it to compare models. Here's how:

```
> anova(anorexia.linreg,anorexia.T.and.P)
Analysis of Variance Table

Model 1: WtGain ~ Treat
Model 2: WtGain ~ Treat + Prewt
  Res.Df    RSS Df Sum of Sq      F    Pr(>F)
1     69 3910.7
2     68 3311.3  1    599.48 12.311 0.0008034 ***
---
Signif. codes: 0 '***' 0.001 '**' 0.01 '*' 0.05 '.' 0.1 ' ' 1
```

What do the numbers in the table mean? The RSS indicates the residual sums of squares from each model. They're next to their degrees of freedom in the Res.Df column. In the Df column, 1 is the difference between the two instances of Res.Df. In the Sum of Sq column, 599.48 is the difference between the two instances of RSS. The F-ratio is the result of dividing two mean squares: The mean square for the numerator is 599.48 divided by its df (1), and the mean square for the denominator is 3311.3 divided by its df (68). The high F-ratio and low Pr(>F) (probability of a Type 1 error) tell you that adding Prewt significantly lowered the residual sum of squares. In English, that means it was a good idea to add Prewt to the mix.

TECHNICAL STUFF

Statisticians would say that this analysis statistically controls for the effects of the covariate (`Prewt`).

But Wait — There's More

In an analysis of covariance, it's important to ask whether the relationship between the dependent variable and the numerical predictor variable is the same across the levels of the categorical variable. In this example, that's the same as asking whether the slope of the regression line between `WtGain` and `Prewt` is the same for the scores in `Cont` as it is for the scores in `CBT` and for the scores in `FT`. If the slopes are the same, that's called *homogeneity of regression*. If not, you have an interaction of `Prewt` and `Treat` and you have to be careful about how you state your conclusions.

Adding the regression lines to the plot in Figure 6-10 is helpful. To do this, I add this line to the code that produced Figure 6-10:

```
geom_smooth(method = lm,se = FALSE, aes(linetype=Treat))
```

This instructs `ggplot` to add a separate line that "smoothes" the data within each treatment group. The `method` argument specifies `lm` (linear modeling) so that each line is a regression line. The next argument, `se=FALSE`, prevents the plotting of the confidence interval around each line. Finally, the aesthetic mapping indicates that the line for each level of `Treat` will look different. So the full code is

```
ggplot(anorexia, aes(x=Prewt,y=WtGain, shape = Treat)) +
  geom_point(size=2.5) +
  geom_smooth(method = lm,se = FALSE, aes(linetype=Treat))
```

and the result is Figure 6-11.

As you can see, the three negatively sloped regression lines are not parallel. The line for `CBT` parallels the line for `FT`, but the line for `Cont` (the control condition) has a much greater negative slope. Assuming that patients in the control group received no treatment, this sounds fairly intuitive: Because they received no treatment, many of these anorexic patients (the heavier ones) continued to lose weight (rather than gain weight), resulting in the highly negative slope for that line.

Apparently, we have a `Treat` × `Prewt` interaction. Does analysis bear this out?

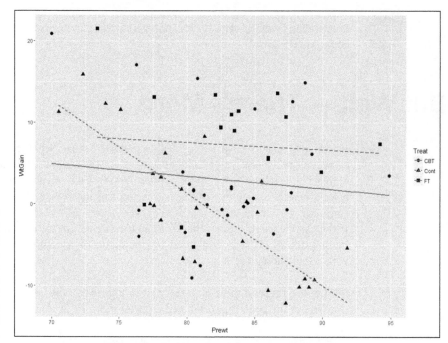

FIGURE 6-11:
Weight Gain
versus Treat
and Prewt in the
anorexia data
frame, with a
regression line
for the scores in
each level
of Treat.

To include the interaction in the model, I have to add `Treat*Prewt` to the formula:

```
anorexia.w.interaction <- lm(WtGain ~ Treat + Prewt + Treat*Prewt,
    data=anorexia)
```

Does adding the interaction make a difference?

```
> anova(anorexia.T.and.P,anorexia.w.interaction)
Analysis of Variance Table

Model 1: WtGain ~ Treat + Prewt
Model 2: WtGain ~ Treat + Prewt + Treat * Prewt
  Res.Df    RSS Df Sum of Sq      F   Pr(>F)
1     68 3311.3
2     66 2844.8  2    466.48 5.4112 0.006666 **
---
Signif. codes: 0 '***' 0.001 '**' 0.01 '*' 0.05 '.' 0.1 ' ' 1
```

It sure does! In your conclusions about this study, you have to include the caveat that the relationship between pre-weight and weight gain is different for the control than it is for the cognitive–behavioral treatment and for the family treatment.

Correlation: The Rise and Fall of Relationships

I n Chapter 6 of Book 3, I introduce the concept of regression, a tool for summarizing and testing relationships between (and among) variables. In this chapter, I introduce you to the ups and downs of correlation, another tool for looking at relationships.

I use the example of employee aptitude and performance from Chapter 6 of Book 3 and show how to think about the data in a slightly different way. The new concepts connect to what I show you in Chapter 6 of Book 3 and you'll see how those connections work. I also show you how to test hypotheses about relationships and how to use R functions for correlation.

Understanding Correlation

A *scatterplot* is a graphical way of showing a relationship between two variables. In Chapter 6 of Book 3, I show you a scatterplot of the data for employees at FarMisht Consulting, Inc. I reproduce that scatterplot here as Figure 7-1. Each point represents one employee's score on a measure of Aptitude (on the *x*-axis) and on a measure of Performance (on the *y*-axis).

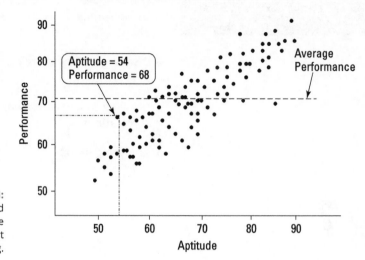

FIGURE 7-1:
Aptitude and
Performance
at FarMisht
Consulting.

In Chapter 6 of Book 3, I refer to Aptitude as the *independent variable* and to Performance as the *dependent variable.* The objective in Chapter 6 of Book 3 is to use Aptitude to predict Performance.

REMEMBER

Although I use scores on one variable to *predict* scores on the other, I do *not* mean that the score on one variable *causes* a score on the other. *Relationship* doesn't necessarily mean *causality.*

Correlation is a statistical way of looking at a relationship. When two things are correlated, it means that they vary together. *Positive* correlation means that high scores on one are associated with high scores on the other, and that low scores on one are associated with low scores on the other. The scatterplot in Figure 7-1 is an example of positive correlation.

Negative correlation, on the other hand, means that high scores on the first thing are associated with *low* scores on the second. Negative correlation also means that low scores on the first are associated with high scores on the second. An example is the correlation between body weight and the time spent on a weight loss program. If the program is effective, the higher the amount of time spent on the program, the lower the body weight. Also, the lower the amount of time spent on the program, the higher the body weight.

Table 7-1, a repeat of this Book's Table 6-2, shows the data for 16 FarMisht consultants.

In keeping with the way I use Aptitude and Performance in Chapter 6 of Book 3, Aptitude is the *x*-variable and Performance is the *y*-variable.

TABLE 7-1

Aptitude Scores and Performance Scores for 16 FarMisht Consultants

Consultant	Aptitude	Performance
1	45	56
2	81	74
3	65	56
4	87	81
5	68	75
6	91	84
7	77	68
8	61	52
9	55	57
10	66	82
11	82	73
12	93	90
13	76	67
14	83	79
15	61	70
16	74	66
Mean	72.81	70.63
Variance	181.63	126.65
Standard deviation	13.48	11.25

The formula for calculating the correlation between the two is

$$r = \frac{\left[\frac{1}{N-1}\right]\sum(x-\bar{x})(y-\bar{y})}{s_x s_y}$$

The term on the left, r, is called the *correlation coefficient*. It's also called *Pearson's product-moment correlation coefficient*, after its creator, Karl Pearson.

The two terms in the denominator on the right are the standard deviation of the x-variable and the standard deviation of the y-variable. The term in the numerator is called the *covariance*. Another way to write this formula is

$$r = \frac{\text{cov}(x,y)}{s_x s_y}$$

The covariance represents x and y varying together. Dividing the covariance by the product of the two standard deviations imposes some limits. The lower limit of the correlation coefficient is −1.00, and the upper limit is +1.00.

A correlation coefficient of −1.00 represents perfect negative correlation (low x-scores associated with high y-scores, and high x-scores associated with low y-scores). A correlation of +1.00 represents perfect positive correlation (low x-scores associated with low y-scores and high x-scores associated with high y-scores). A correlation of 0.00 means that the two variables are not related.

Applying the formula to the data in Table 7-1,

$$r = \frac{\left[\frac{1}{N-1}\right]\sum(x-\bar{x})(y-\bar{y})}{s_x s_y}$$

$$= \frac{\left[\frac{1}{16-1}\right]\left[(45-72.81)(56-70.63)+\ldots+(74-72.81)(66-70.83)\right]}{(13.48)(11.25)} = .783$$

What, exactly, does this number mean? I'm about to tell you.

Correlation and Regression

Figure 7-2 shows the scatterplot of just the 16 employees in Table 7-1 with the line that *best fits* the points. It's possible to draw an infinite number of lines through these points. Which one is best?

To be the best, a line has to meet a specific standard: If you draw the distances in the vertical direction between the points and the line and you square those distances and then you add those squared distances, the best-fitting line is the one that makes the sum of those squared distances as small as possible. This line is called the *regression line*.

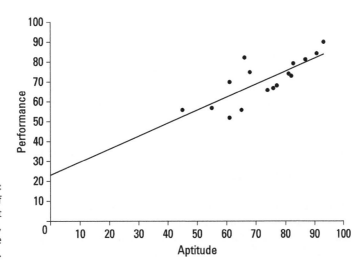

FIGURE 7-2:
Scatterplot of
16 FarMisht
consultants,
including the
regression line.

The regression line's purpose in life is to enable you to make predictions. As I mention in Chapter 6 of Book 3, without a regression line, the best predicted value of the y-variable is the mean of the y's. A regression line takes the x-variable into account and delivers a more precise prediction. Each point on the regression line represents a predicted value for y. In the symbology of regression, each predicted value is a y'.

Why do I tell you all this? Because correlation is closely related to regression. Figure 7-3 focuses on one point in the scatterplot, and on its distance to the regression line and to the mean. (This is a repeat of this Book's Figure 6-3.)

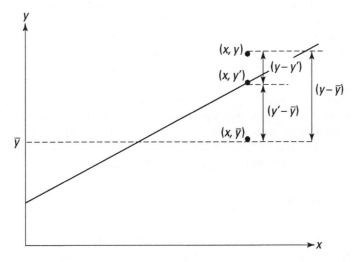

FIGURE 7-3:
One point in the
scatterplot and
its associated
distances.

Notice the three distances laid out in the figure. The distance labeled $(y - y')$ is the difference between the point and the regression line's prediction for where the point should be. (In Chapter 6 of Book 3, I call that a *residual*.) The distance labeled $(y - \bar{y})$ is the difference between the point and the mean of the y's. The distance labeled $(y' - \bar{y})$ is the gain in prediction capability you get from using the regression line to predict the point rather than using the mean to predict the point.

Figure 7-3 shows that the three distances are related like this:

$$(y - y') + (y' - \bar{y}) = (y - \bar{y})$$

As I point out in Chapter 6 of Book 3, you can square all the residuals and add them, square all the deviations of the predicted points from the mean and add them, and square all deviations of the actual points from the mean and add them, too.

It turns out that these sums of squares are related in the same way as the deviations I just showed you:

$$SS_{Residual} + SS_{Regression} = SS_{Total}$$

If $SS_{Regression}$ is large in comparison to $SS_{Residual}$, the relationship between the x-variable and the y-variable is a strong one. It means that, throughout the scatterplot, the variability around the regression line is small.

On the other hand, if $SS_{Regression}$ is small in comparison to $SS_{Residual}$, the relationship between the x-variable and the y-variable is weak. In this case, the variability around the regression line is large throughout the scatterplot.

One way to test $SS_{Regression}$ against $SS_{Residual}$ is to divide each by its degrees of freedom (1 for $SS_{Regression}$ and $N-2$ for $SS_{Residual}$) to form variance estimates (also known as *mean squares*, or *MS*), and then divide one by the other to calculate an F. If $MS_{Regression}$ is significantly larger than $MS_{Residual}$, you have evidence that the x-y relationship is strong. (See Chapter 6 of Book 3 for details.)

Here's the clincher, as far as correlation is concerned: Another way to assess the size of $SS_{Regression}$ is to compare it with SS_{Total}. Divide the first by the second. If the ratio is large, this tells you the x-y relationship is strong. This ratio has a name: It's called the *coefficient of determination*. Its symbol is r^2. Take the square root of this coefficient, and you have . . . the correlation coefficient!

$$r = \pm\sqrt{r^2} = \pm\sqrt{\frac{SS_{Regression}}{SS_{Total}}}$$

The plus-or-minus sign ($\pm$) means that r is either the positive or negative square root, depending on whether the slope of the regression line is positive or negative.

So, if you calculate a correlation coefficient and you quickly want to know what its value signifies, just square it. The answer — the coefficient of determination — lets you know the proportion of the SS_{Total} that's tied up in the relationship between the x-variable and the y-variable. If it's a large proportion, the correlation coefficient signifies a strong relationship. If it's a small proportion, the correlation coefficient signifies a weak relationship.

In the Aptitude-Performance example, the correlation coefficient is .783. The coefficient of determination is

$$r^2 = (.783)^2 = .613$$

In this sample of 16 consultants, the $SS_{Regression}$ is 61.3 percent of the SS_{Total}. Sounds like a large proportion, but what's large? What's small? Those questions scream out for hypothesis tests.

Testing Hypotheses about Correlation

In this section, I show you how to answer important questions about correlation. Like any other kind of hypothesis testing, the idea is to use sample statistics to make inferences about population parameters. Here, the sample statistic is r, the correlation coefficient. By convention, the population parameter is ρ (rho), the Greek equivalent of r. (Yes, it does look like the letter p, but it really is the Greek equivalent of r.)

Two kinds of questions are important in connection with correlation:

1. Is a correlation coefficient greater than 0?
2. Are two correlation coefficients different from one another?

Is a correlation coefficient greater than zero?

Returning once again to the Aptitude-Performance example, you can use the sample r to test hypotheses about the population ρ — the correlation coefficient for all consultants at FarMisht Consulting.

Assuming that you know in advance (before you gather any sample data) that any correlation between Aptitude and Performance should be positive, the hypotheses are

$$H_0: \rho \leq 0$$

$$H_1: \rho > 0$$

Set $\alpha = .05$.

The appropriate statistical test is a t-test. The formula is

$$t = \frac{r - \rho}{s_r}$$

This test has $N-2$ df.

For the example, the values in the numerator are set: r is .783 and ρ (in H_0) is 0. What about the denominator? I won't burden you with the details. I'll just tell you that's

$$\sqrt{\frac{1 - r^2}{N - 2}}$$

With a little algebra, the formula for the t-test simplifies to

$$t = \frac{r\sqrt{N-2}}{\sqrt{1 - r^2}}$$

For the example,

$$t = \frac{r\sqrt{N-2}}{\sqrt{1-r^2}} = \frac{.783\sqrt{16-2}}{\sqrt{1-.783^2}} = 4.707$$

With df = 14 and $\alpha = .05$ (one-tailed), the critical value of t is 1.76. Because the calculated value is greater than the critical value, the decision is to reject H_0.

Do two correlation coefficients differ?

FarKlempt Robotics has a consulting branch that assesses aptitude and performance with the same measurement tools that FarMisht Consulting uses. In a sample of 20 consultants at FarKlempt Robotics, the correlation between Aptitude and Performance is .695. Is this different from the correlation (.783) at FarMisht Consulting? If you have no way of assuming that one correlation should be higher than the other, the hypotheses are

$H_0: \rho_{FarMisht} = \rho_{FarKlempt}$

$H_1: \rho_{FarMisht} \neq \rho_{FarKlempt}$

Again, $\alpha = .05$.

For highly technical reasons, you can't set up a t-test for this one. In fact, you can't even work with .783 and .695, the two correlation coefficients.

Instead, what you do is *transform* each correlation coefficient into something else and then work with the two something-elses in a formula that gives you — believe it or not — a z-test.

TECHNICAL STUFF

The transformation is called *Fisher's r to z transformation.* Fisher is the statistician who is remembered as the F in F-test. He transforms the r into a z by doing this:

$$z_r = \frac{1}{2}[\log_e(1+r) - \log_e(1-r)]$$

If you know what $\log_e$ means, fine. If not, don't worry about it. (I explain it in Chapter 8 of Book 3.) R takes care of all of this for you, as you see in a moment.

Anyway, for this example

$$z_{.783} = \frac{1}{2}[\log_e(1+.783) - \log_e(1-.783)] = 1.0530$$

$$z_{.695} = \frac{1}{2}[\log_e(1+.695) - \log_e(1-.695)] = 0.8576$$

After you transform r to z, the formula is

$$Z = \frac{z_1 - z_2}{\sigma_{z_1-z_2}}$$

The denominator turns out to be easier than you might think. It's

$$\sigma_{z_1-z_2} = \sqrt{\frac{1}{N_1-3} + \frac{1}{N_2-3}}$$

For this example,

$$\sigma_{z_1-z_2} = \sqrt{\frac{1}{N_1-3} + \frac{1}{N_2-3}} = \sqrt{\frac{1}{16-3} + \frac{1}{20-3}} = .368$$

The whole formula is

$$Z = \frac{z_1 - z_2}{\sigma_{z_1-z_2}} = \frac{1.0530 - 0.8576}{.368} = .531$$

The next step is to compare the calculated value to a standard normal distribution. For a two-tailed test with $\alpha = .05$, the critical values in a standard normal distribution are 1.96 in the upper tail and −1.96 in the lower tail. The calculated value falls between those two, so the decision is to not reject H_0.

Correlation in *R*

In this section, I work with the FarMisht example. The data frame, FarMisht. frame, holds the data points shown in Table 6-4, in Chapter 6 of Book 3. Here's how I created it:

```
Aptitude <- c(45, 81, 65, 87, 68, 91, 77, 61, 55, 66, 82, 93, 76, 83, 61, 74)
Performance <- c(56, 74, 56, 81, 75, 84, 68, 52, 57, 82, 73, 90, 67, 79, 70, 66)
Personality <- c(9, 15, 11, 15, 14, 19, 12, 10, 9, 14, 15, 14, 16, 18, 15, 12)
FarMisht.frame <- data.frame(Aptitude, Performance, Personality)
```

Calculating a correlation coefficient

To find the correlation coefficient for the relationship between Aptitude and Performance, I use the function cor():

```
> with(FarMisht.frame, cor(Aptitude,Performance))
[1] 0.7827927
```

TECHNICAL STUFF

The Pearson product-moment correlation coefficient that cor() calculates in this example is the default for its method argument:

```
cor(FarMisht.frame, method = "pearson")
```

Two other possible values for method are "spearman" and "kendall", which I cover in Chapter 10 of Book 3.

Testing a correlation coefficient

To find a correlation coefficient and test it at the same time, R provides cor. test(). Here is a one-tailed test (specified by alternative = "greater"):

```
> with(FarMisht.frame, cor.test(Aptitude,Performance, alternative = "greater"))

        Pearson's product-moment correlation
```

```
data:  Aptitude and Performance
t = 4.7068, df = 14, p-value = 0.0001684
alternative hypothesis: true correlation is greater than 0
95 percent confidence interval:
 0.5344414 1.0000000
sample estimates:
      cor
0.7827927
```

TECHNICAL STUFF

As is the case with `cor()`, you can specify `"spearman"` or `"kendall"` as the method for `cor.test()`.

Testing the difference between two correlation coefficients

In the earlier section "Do two correlation coefficients differ?" I compare the Aptitude-Performance correlation coefficient (.695) for 20 consultants at FarKlempt Robotics with the correlation (.783) for 16 consultants at FarMisht Consulting.

The comparison begins with Fisher's *r* to *z* transformation for each coefficient. The test statistic (Z) is the difference of the transformed values divided by the standard error of the difference.

A function called `r.test()` does all the work if you provide the coefficients and the sample sizes. This function lives in the psych package, so, on the Packages tab, click Insert. Then, in the Insert Packages dialog box, type **psych**. When psych appears on the Packages tab, select its check box.

Here's the function, and its arguments:

```
r.test(r12=.783, n=16, r34=.695, n2=20)
```

This one is pretty particular about how you state the arguments. The first argument is the first correlation coefficient. The second is its sample size. The third argument is the second correlation coefficient, and the fourth is its sample size. The `12` label for the first coefficient and the `34` label for the second indicate that the two coefficients are independent.

If you run that function, this is the result:

```
Correlation tests
Call:r.test(n = 16, r12 = 0.783, r34 = 0.695, n2 = 20)
Test of difference between two independent correlations
 z value 0.53    with probability  0.6
```

Calculating a correlation matrix

In addition to finding a single correlation coefficient, `cor()` can find all pairwise correlation coefficients for a data frame, resulting in a correlation matrix:

```
> cor(FarMisht.frame)
            Aptitude Performance Personality
Aptitude   1.0000000   0.7827927   0.7499305
Performance 0.7827927   1.0000000   0.7709271
Personality 0.7499305   0.7709271   1.0000000
```

Visualizing correlation matrices

In Chapter 1 of Book 2, I describe a couple of ways to visualize a matrix like the one in the preceding section. Here's how to do it with base R graphics:

```
pairs(FarMisht.frame)
```

This function produces Figure 7-4.

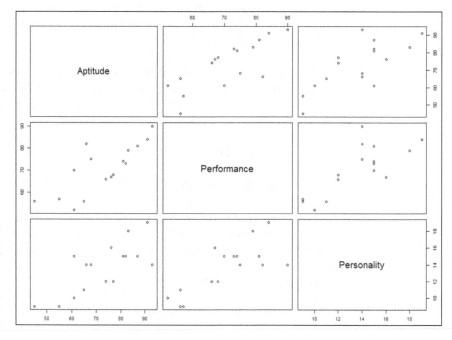

FIGURE 7-4:
The correlation matrix for Aptitude, Performance, and Personality, rendered in base R graphics.

The main diagonal, of course, holds the names of the variables. Each off-diagonal cell is a scatterplot of the pair of variables named in the row and the column. For example, the cell to the immediate right of Aptitude is the scatterplot of Aptitude (*y*-axis) and Performance (*x*-axis). The cell just below Aptitude is the reverse — it's the scatterplot of Performance (*y*-axis) and Aptitude (*x*-axis).

As I also mention in Chapter 1 of Book 2, a package called GGally (built on ggplot2) provides ggpairs(), which produces a bit more. Find GGally on the Packages tab and select its check box. Then

```
ggpairs(FarMisht.frame)
```

draws Figure 7-5.

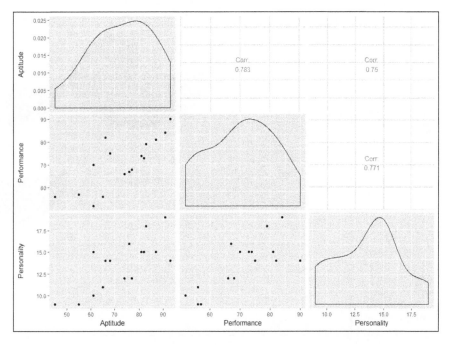

FIGURE 7-5:
The correlation
matrix for
Aptitude,
Performance,
and Personality,
rendered in
GGally (a
ggplot2-based
package).

The main diagonal provides a density function for each variable, the upper off-diagonal cells present the correlation coefficients, and the remaining cells show pairwise scatterplots.

More elaborate displays are possible with the corrgram package. On the Packages tab, click Install and then, in the Install dialog box, type **corrgram** and click Install. (Be patient. This package installs a *lot* of items.) Then, on the Packages tab, find corrgram and select its check box.

The `corrgram()` function works with a data frame and enables you to choose options for what goes into the main diagonal (`diag.panel`) of the resulting matrix, what goes into the cells in the upper half of the matrix (`upper.panel`), and what goes into the cells in the lower half of the matrix (`lower.panel`). For the main diagonal, I chose to show the minimum and maximum values for each variable. For the upper half, I specified a pie chart to show the value of a correlation coefficient: The filled-in proportion represents the value. For the lower half, I'd like a scatterplot in each cell:

```
corrgram(FarMisht.frame, diag.panel=panel.minmax,
                    upper.panel = panel.pie,
                    lower.panel = panel.pts)
```

The result is shown in Figure 7-6.

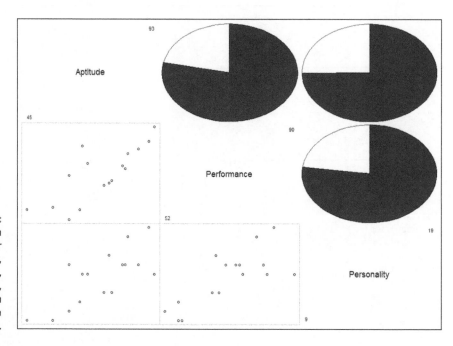

FIGURE 7-6:
The correlation matrix for Aptitude, Performance, and Personality, rendered in the `corrgram` package.

Multiple Correlation

The correlation coefficients in the correlation matrix described in the preceding section combine to produce a *multiple correlation coefficient.* This is a number that summarizes the relationship between the dependent variable — Performance, in this example — and the two independent variables (Aptitude and Personality).

To show you how these correlation coefficients combine, I abbreviate Performance as P, Aptitude as A, and Personality as F (FarMisht Personality Inventory). So r_{PA} is the correlation coefficient for Performance and Aptitude (.7827927), r_{PF} is the correlation coefficient for Performance and Personality (.7709271), and r_{AF} is the correlation coefficient for Aptitude and Personality (.7499305).

Here's the formula that puts them all together:

$$R_{P.AF} = \sqrt{\frac{r_{PA}^2 + r_{PF}^2 - 2r_{PA}r_{PF}r_{AF}}{1 - r_{AF}^2}}$$

The uppercase R on the left indicates that this is a multiple correlation coefficient, as opposed to the lowercase r, which indicates a correlation between two variables. The subscript $P.AF$ means that the multiple correlation is between Performance and the combination of Aptitude and Personality.

For this example,

$$R_{P.AF} = \sqrt{\frac{(.7827927)^2 + (.7709271)^2 - 2(.7827927)(.7709271)(.7499305)}{1 - (.7499305)^2}} = .8306841$$

If you square this number, you get the *multiple coefficient of determination*. In Chapter 6 of Book 3, you met Multiple R-squared, and that's what this is. For this example, that result is

$$R_{P.AF}^2 = (.830641)^2 = .6900361$$

Multiple correlation in *R*

The easiest way to calculate a multiple correlation coefficient is to use `lm( )` and proceed as in multiple regression:

```
> FarMisht.multreg <- lm(Performance ~ Aptitude + Personality, data = FarMisht.
   frame)
> summary(FarMisht.multreg)

Call:
lm(formula = Performance ~ Aptitude + Personality, data = FarMisht.frame)

Residuals:
    Min     1Q Median     3Q    Max
 -8.689 -2.834 -1.840  2.886 13.432
```

```
Coefficients:
              Estimate Std. Error t value Pr(>|t|)
(Intercept)   20.2825     9.6595    2.100    0.0558 .
Aptitude       0.3905     0.1949    2.003    0.0664 .
Personality    1.6079     0.8932    1.800    0.0951 .
---
Signif. codes: 0 '***' 0.001 '**' 0.01 '*' 0.05 '.' 0.1 ' ' 1

Residual standard error: 6.73 on 13 degrees of freedom
Multiple R-squared:   0.69,   Adjusted R-squared:  0.6423
F-statistic: 14.47 on 2 and 13 DF,   p-value: 0.0004938
```

In the next-to-last line, `Multiple R-squared` is right there, waiting for you.

If you have to work with that quantity for some reason, that's

```
> summary(FarMisht.multreg)$r.squared
[1] 0.6900361
```

And to calculate R:

```
> Mult.R.sq <- summary(FarMisht.multreg)$r.squared
> Mult.R <- sqrt(Mult.R.sq)
> Mult.R
[1] 0.8306841
```

Adjusting *R*-squared

In the output of `lm()`, you see *Adjusted R-squared.* Why is it necessary to "adjust" R-squared?

In multiple regression, adding independent variables (like `Personality`) sometimes makes the regression equation less accurate. The multiple coefficient of determination, R-squared, doesn't reflect this. Its denominator is SS_{Total} (for the dependent variable), and that never changes. The numerator can only increase or stay the same. So any decline in accuracy doesn't result in a lower R-squared.

Taking degrees of freedom into account fixes the flaw. Every time you add an independent variable, you change the degrees of freedom, and that makes all the difference. Just so you know, here's the adjustment:

$$Adjusted\ R^2 = 1 - \left(1 - R^2\right)\left[\frac{(N-1)}{(N-k-1)}\right]$$

The k in the denominator is the number of independent variables.

If you ever have to work with this quantity (and I'm not sure why you would), here's how to retrieve it:

```
> summary(FarMisht.multreg)$adj.r.squared
[1] 0.6423494
```

Partial Correlation

Performance and Aptitude are associated with Personality (in the example). Each one's association with Personality might somehow hide the true correlation between them.

What would their correlation be if you could remove that association? Another way to ask this: What would be the Performance–Aptitude correlation if you could hold Personality constant?

One way to hold Personality constant is to find the Performance–Aptitude correlation for a sample of consultants who have one Personality score — 17, for example. In a sample like this, the correlation of each variable with Personality is 0. This usually isn't feasible in the real world, however.

Another way is to find the *partial correlation* between Performance and Aptitude. This is a statistical way of removing each variable's association with Personality in your sample. You use the correlation coefficients in the correlation matrix to do this:

$$r_{PA.F} = \frac{r_{PA} - r_{PF}r_{AF}}{\sqrt{1-r_{PF}^2}\sqrt{1-r_{AF}^2}}$$

Once again, P stands for Performance, A for Aptitude, and F for Personality. The subscript *PA.F* means that the correlation is between Performance and Aptitude with Personality "partialed out."

For this example,

$$r_{PA.F} = \frac{.7827927 - (.7709271)(.7499305)}{\sqrt{1-(.7709271)^2}\sqrt{1-(.7499305)^2}} = .4857198$$

Partial Correlation in *R*

A package called `ppcor` holds the functions for calculating partial correlation and for calculating semipartial correlation, which I cover in the next section.

On the Packages tab, click Install. In the Install Packages dialog box, type **ppcor** and then click Install. Next, find `ppcor` in the Packages dialog box and select its check box.

The function `pcor.test()` calculates the correlation between Performance and Aptitude with Personality partialed out:

```
> with (FarMisht.frame, pcor.test(x=Performance, y=Aptitude, z=Personality))
   estimate    p.value statistic  n gp  Method
1 0.4857199 0.06642269   2.0035 16  1 pearson
```

In addition to the correlation coefficient (shown below `estimate`), it calculates a *t*-test of the correlation with $N-3$ df (shown below `statistic`) and an associated *p*-value.

If you prefer to calculate all possible partial correlations (and associated *p*-values and *t*-statistics) in the data frame, use `pcor()`:

```
> pcor(FarMisht.frame)
$estimate
             Aptitude Performance Personality
Aptitude    1.0000000   0.4857199   0.3695112
Performance 0.4857199   1.0000000   0.4467067
Personality 0.3695112   0.4467067   1.0000000


$p.value
             Aptitude Performance Personality
Aptitude    0.00000000  0.06642269  0.17525219
Performance 0.06642269  0.00000000  0.09506226
Personality 0.17525219  0.09506226  0.00000000


$statistic
             Aptitude Performance Personality
Aptitude    0.000000    2.003500    1.433764
Performance 2.003500    0.000000    1.800222
Personality 1.433764    1.800222    0.000000
```

Each cell under $estimate is the partial correlation of the cell's row variable with the cell's column variable, with the third variable partialed out. If you have more than three variables, each cell is the row-column partial correlation with everything else partialed out.

Semipartial Correlation

It's possible to remove the correlation with Personality from just Aptitude without removing it from Performance. This is called *semipartial correlation.* The formula for this one also uses the correlation coefficients from the correlation matrix:

$$r_{P(A.F)} = \frac{r_{PA} - r_{PF}r_{AF}}{\sqrt{1 - r_{AF}^2}}$$

The subscript $P(A.F)$ means that the correlation is between Performance and Aptitude with Personality partialed out of Aptitude only.

Applying this formula to the example,

$$r_{P(A.F)} = \frac{.7827927 - (.7709271)(.7499305)}{\sqrt{1 - (.7499305)^2}} = .3093663$$

REMEMBER

Some statistics textbooks refer to semipartial correlation as *part correlation.*

Semipartial Correlation in *R*

As I mention earlier in this chapter, the ppcor package has the functions for calculating semipartial correlation. To find the semipartial correlation between Performance and Aptitude with Personality partialed out of Aptitude only, use spcor.test():

```
> with (FarMisht.frame, spcor.test(x=Performance, y=Aptitude, z=Personality))
    estimate   p.value statistic  n gp  Method
1 0.3093664 0.2618492  1.172979 16  1 pearson
```

As you can see, the output is similar to the output for pcor.test(). Again, estimate is the correlation coefficient and statistic is a *t*-test of the correlation coefficient with $N-3$ df.

To find the semipartial correlations for the whole data frame, use spcor():

```
> spcor(FarMisht.frame)
$estimate
             Aptitude Performance Personality
Aptitude    1.0000000   0.3213118   0.2299403
Performance 0.3093664   1.0000000   0.2779778
Personality 0.2353503   0.2955039   1.0000000


$p.value
             Aptitude Performance Personality
Aptitude    0.0000000   0.2429000   0.4096955
Performance 0.2618492   0.0000000   0.3157849
Personality 0.3984533   0.2849315   0.0000000


$statistic
             Aptitude Performance Personality
Aptitude    0.0000000   1.223378    0.8518883
Performance 1.1729794   0.000000    1.0433855
Personality 0.8730923   1.115260    0.0000000
```

Notice that, unlike the matrices in the output for pcor(), in these matrices the numbers above the diagonal are not the same as the numbers below the diagonal.

The easiest way to explain is with an example. In the $estimate matrix, the value in the first column, second row (0.3093664), is the correlation between Performance (the row variable) and Aptitude (the column variable) with Personality partialed out of Aptitude. The value in the second column, first row (0.3213118) is the correlation between Aptitude (which is now the row variable) and Performance (which is now the column variable) with Personality partialed out of Performance.

What happens when you have more than three variables? In that case, each cell value is the row–column correlation with everything else partialed out of the column variable.

Chapter **8**

Curvilinear Regression: When Relationships Get Complicated

I n Chapters 6 and 7 of Book 3, I describe linear regression and correlation — two concepts that depend on the straight line as the best-fitting summary of a scatterplot.

But a line isn't always the best fit. Processes in a variety of areas, from biology to business, conform more to curves than to lines.

For example, think about when you learned a skill — like tying your shoelaces. When you first tried it, it took quite a while, didn't it? And then whenever you tried it again, it took progressively less time for you to finish, right? Until finally, you can tie your shoelaces quickly but you can't really get any faster — you're now doing it as efficiently as you can.

If you plotted shoelace-tying-time (in seconds) on the y-axis and trials (occasions when you tried to tie your shoes) on the x-axis, the graph might look something like Figure 8-1. A straight line is clearly not the best summary of a plot like this one.

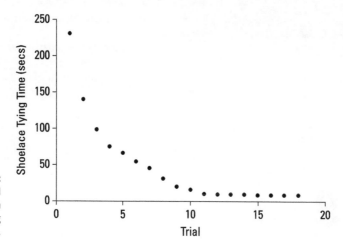

FIGURE 8-1:
Hypothetical
plot of learning a
skill — like tying
your shoelaces.

How do you find the best-fitting curve? (Another way to say this: "How do you formulate a model for these data?") I'll be happy to show you, but first I have to tell you about logarithms, and about an important number called *e*.

Why? Because those concepts form the foundation of three kinds of nonlinear regression.

What Is a Logarithm?

Plainly and simply, a logarithm is an *exponent* — a power to which you raise a number. In the equation

$$10^2 = 100$$

2 is an exponent. Does that mean that 2 is also a logarithm? Well . . . yes. In terms of logarithms,

$$\log_{10} 100 = 2$$

That's really just another way of saying 10^2 = 100. Mathematicians read it as "the logarithm of 100 to the base 10 equals 2." It means that if you want to raise 10 to some power to get 100, that power is 2.

How about 1,000? As you know

$$10^3 = 1000$$

so

$$\log_{10} 1000 = 3$$

How about 763? Uh. . . . Hmm. . . . That's like trying to solve

$$10^x = 763$$

What could that answer possibly be? 10^2 means 10×10 and that gives you 100. 10^3 means $10 \times 10 \times 10$ and that's 1,000. But 763?

Here's where you have to think outside the dialog box. You have to imagine exponents that aren't whole numbers. I know, I know: How can you multiply a number by itself a fraction at a time? If you could, somehow, the number in that 763 equation would have to be between 2 (which gets you to 100) and 3 (which gets you to 1,000).

In the 16th century, mathematician John Napier showed how to do it, and logarithms were born. Why did Napier bother with this? One reason is that it was a great help to astronomers. Astronomers have to deal with numbers that are, well, astronomical. Logarithms ease computational strain in a couple of ways. One way is to substitute small numbers for large ones: The logarithm of 1,000,000 is 6, and the logarithm of 100,000,000 is 8. Also, working with logarithms opens up a helpful set of computational shortcuts. Before calculators and computers appeared on the scene, this was a very big deal.

Incidentally,

$$10^{2.882525} = 763$$

which means that

$$\log_{10} 763 = 2.882525$$

You can use R's log10( ) function to check that out:

```
> log10(763)
[1] 2.882525
```

If you reverse the process, you see that

```
> 10^2.882525
[1] 763.0008
```

So 2.882525 is a *tiny* bit off, but you get the idea.

A bit earlier in this chapter, I mention computational shortcuts that result from logarithms. Here's one: If you want to multiply two numbers, just add their logarithms and then find the number whose logarithm is the sum. That last part is called "finding the antilogarithm." Here's a quick example: To multiply 100 by 1,000:

$$\log_{10}(100) + \log_{10}(1000) = 2 + 3 = 5$$
$$\text{antilog}_{10}(5) = 10^5 = 100,000$$

Here's another computational shortcut: Multiplying the logarithm of a number x by a number b corresponds to raising x to the b power.

Ten, the number that's raised to the exponent, is called the *base*. Because it's also the base of our number system and everyone is familiar with it, logarithms of base 10 are called *common logarithms*. And, as you just saw, a common logarithm in R is log10.

Does that mean you can have other bases? Absolutely. *Any* number (except 0 or 1 or a negative number) can be a base. For example,

$$7.8^2 = 60.84$$

So

$$\log_{7.8} 60.84 = 2$$

And you can use R's log( ) function to check *that* out:

```
> log(60.84,7.8)
[1] 2
```

In terms of bases, one number is special. . . .

What Is e?

Which brings me to *e*, a constant that's all about growth.

Imagine the princely sum of $1 deposited in a bank account. Suppose that the interest rate is 2 percent a year. (Yes, this is just an example!) If it's simple interest, the bank adds $.02 every year, and in 50 years you have $2.

If it's compound interest, at the end of 50 years you have $(1 + .02)^{50}$ — which is just a bit more than $2.68, assuming that the bank compounds the interest once a year.

Of course, if the bank compounds interest twice a year, each payment is $.01, and after 50 years the bank has compounded it 100 times. That gives you $(1 + .01)^{100}$, or just over $2.70. What about compounding it four times a year? After 50 years — 200 compoundings — you have $(1 + .005)^{200}$, which results in the don't-spend-it-all-in-one-place amount of $2.71 and a tiny bit more.

Focusing on "just a bit more" and "a tiny bit more" and taking it to extremes, after 100,000 compoundings, you have $2.718268. After 100 million, you have $2.718282.

If you could get the bank to compound many more times in those 50 years, your sum of money approaches a *limit* — an amount it gets ever so close to but never quite reaches. That limit is *e*.

The way I set up the example, the rule for calculating the amount is

$$\left(1+\left(\frac{1}{n}\right)\right)^{n}$$

where *n* represents the number of payments. Two cents is $\frac{1}{50}$th of a dollar and I specified 50 years — 50 payments. Then I specified two payments a year (and each year's payments have to add up to 2 percent) so that in 50 years you have 100 payments of $\frac{1}{100}$th of a dollar, and so on.

To see this concept in action,

```
x <- c(seq(1,10,1),50,100,200,500,1000,10000,100000000)
> y <- (1+(1/x))^x
> data.frame(x,y)
        x          y
1   1e+00  2.000000
2   2e+00  2.250000
3   3e+00  2.370370
4   4e+00  2.441406
5   5e+00  2.488320
6   6e+00  2.521626
7   7e+00  2.546500
8   8e+00  2.565785
9   9e+00  2.581175
10  1e+01  2.593742
11  5e+01  2.691588
12  1e+02  2.704814
13  2e+02  2.711517
14  5e+02  2.715569
15  1e+03  2.716924
16  1e+04  2.718146
17  1e+08  2.718282
```

So *e* is associated with growth. Its value is 2.718282 . . . The three dots mean that you never quite get to the exact value (like π, the constant that enables you to find the area of a circle).

The number *e* pops up in all kinds of places. It's in the formula for the normal distribution (along with π; see Chapter 6 of Book 2) and it's in distributions I discuss in Chapter 10, later in Book 3). Many natural phenomena are related to *e*.

The number *e* is so important that scientists, mathematicians, and business analysts use it as a base for logarithms. Logarithms to the base *e* are called *natural* logarithms. In many textbooks, a natural logarithm is abbreviated as *ln*. In R, it's log.

Table 8-1 presents some comparisons (rounded to three decimal places) between common logarithms and natural logarithms.

TABLE 8-1

Some Common Logarithms (Log10) and Natural Logarithms (Log)

Number	Log10	Log
e	0.434	1.000
10	1.000	2.303
50	1.699	3.912
100	2.000	4.605
453	2.656	6.116
1000	3.000	6.908

One more thing: In many formulas and equations, it's often necessary to raise *e* to a power. Sometimes, the power is a fairly complicated mathematical expression. Because superscripts are usually printed in a small font, it can be a strain to have to constantly read them. To ease the eyestrain, mathematicians have invented a special notation: *exp*. Whenever you see *exp* followed by something in parentheses, it means to raise *e* to the power of whatever's in the parentheses. For example,

$$\exp(1.6) = e^{1.6} = 4.953032$$

R's exp( ) function does that calculation for you:

```
> exp(1.6)
[1] 4.953032
```

Applying the `exp()` function with natural logarithms is like finding the antilog with common logarithms.

Speaking of raising *e*, when executives at Google, Inc., filed its IPO, they said they wanted to raise $2,718,281,828, which is *e* times a billion dollars rounded to the nearest dollar.

And now . . . back to curvilinear regression.

Power Regression

Biologists have studied the interrelationships between the sizes and weights of parts of the body. One fascinating relationship is the relation between body weight and brain weight. One way to study this is to assess the relationship across different species. Intuitively, it seems like heavier animals should have heavier brains — but what's the exact nature of the relationship?

In the MASS package, you'll find a data frame called Animals that contains the body weights (in kilograms) and brain weights (in grams) of 28 species. (To follow along, click Install on the Package tab. Then, in the Install Packages dialog box, type **MASS**. When MASS appears on the Packages tab, select its check box.)

These are the first six rows of Animals:

```
> head(Animals)
                   body brain
Mountain beaver    1.35   8.1
Cow              465.00 423.0
Grey wolf         36.33 119.5
Goat              27.66 115.0
Guinea pig         1.04   5.5
Diplodocus     11700.00  50.0
```

Have you ever seen a dipliodocus? No? Outside of a natural history museum, no one else has, either. In addition to this dinosaur in Row 6, Animals has triceratops in Row 16 and brachiosaurus in Row 26. Here, I'll show you:

```
> Animals[c(6,16,26),]
                body brain
Dipliodocus    11700  50.0
Triceratops     9400  70.0
Brachiosaurus  87000 154.5
```

To confine your work to living species, create

```
> Animals.living <- Animals[-c(6,16,26),]
```

which causes those three dinosaurs to vanish from the data frame as surely as they have vanished from the face of the earth.

Let's take a look at the data points. This code snippet

```
ggplot(Animals.living, aes(x=body, y=brain))+
    geom_point()
```

produces Figure 8-2. Note that the idea is to use body weight to predict brain weight.

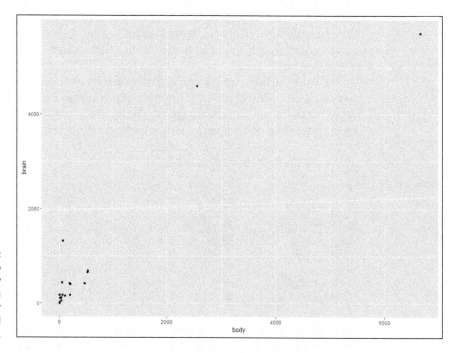

FIGURE 8-2:
The relationship
between body
weight and brain
weight for
25 animal
species.

Doesn't look much like a linear relationship, does it? In fact, it's not. Relationships in this field often take the form

$$y' = ax^b$$

Because the independent (predictor) variable x (body weight, in this case) is raised to a power, this type of model is called *power regression*.

REMEMBER

R has no specific function for creating a power regression model. Its `lm()` function creates linear models, as described in Chapter 6 of Book 3. But you can use `lm()` in this situation if you can somehow transform the data so that the relationship between the transformed body weight and the transformed brain weight is linear.

And this is why I told you about logarithms.

You can "linearize" the scatterplot by working with the logarithm of the body weight and the logarithm of the brain weight. Here's some code to do just that. For good measure, I'll throw in the animal name for each data point:

```
ggplot(Animals.living, aes(x=log(body), y=log(brain)))+
    geom_point()+
    geom_text(aes(label=rownames(Animals.living)))
```

Figure 8-3 shows the result.

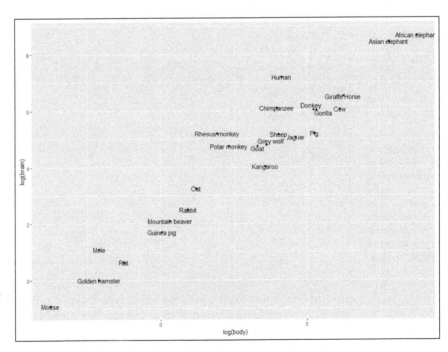

FIGURE 8-3: The relationship between the log of body weight and the log of brain weight for 25 animal species.

I'm surprised by the closeness of donkey and gorilla (to the right of Chimpanzee), but maybe my concept of gorilla comes from *King Kong*. Another surprise is the closeness of horse and giraffe (above Cow).

Anyway, you can fit a regression line through this scatterplot. Here's the code for the plot with the line and without the animal names:

```
ggplot(Animals.living, aes(x=log(body), y=log(brain)))+
  geom_point()+
  geom_smooth(method = "lm",se=FALSE)
```

The first argument in the last statement (`method = "lm"`) fits the regression line to the data points. The second argument (`se=FALSE`) prevents `ggplot` from plotting the 95 percent confidence interval around the regression line. These lines of code produce Figure 8-4.

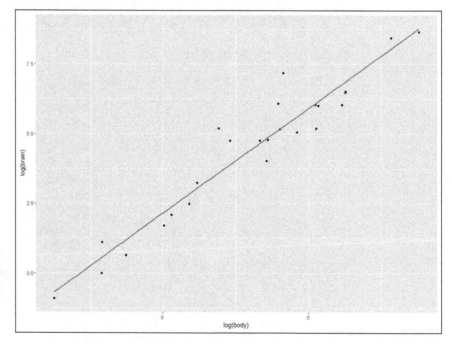

FIGURE 8-4: The relationship between the log of body weight and the log of brain weight for 25 animal species, with a regression line.

This procedure — working with the log of each variable and then fitting a regression line — is exactly what to do in a case like this. Here's the analysis:

```
powerfit <- lm(log(brain) ~ log(body), data = Animals.living)
```

As always, `lm()` indicates a linear model, and the dependent variable is on the left side of the tilde (~) with the predictor variable on the right side. After running the analysis,

```
> summary(powerfit)

Call:
lm(formula = log(brain) ~ log(body), data = Animals.living)

Residuals:
    Min      1Q  Median      3Q     Max
-0.9125 -0.4752 -0.1557  0.1940  1.9303

Coefficients:
            Estimate Std. Error t value Pr(>|t|)
(Intercept)  2.15041    0.20060   10.72 2.03e-10 ***
log(body)    0.75226    0.04572   16.45 3.24e-14 ***
---
Signif. codes:  0 '***' 0.001 '**' 0.01 '*' 0.05 '.' 0.1 ' ' 1

Residual standard error: 0.7258 on 23 degrees of freedom
Multiple R-squared:  0.9217,  Adjusted R-squared:  0.9183
F-statistic: 270.7 on 1 and 23 DF,  p-value: 3.243e-14
```

The high value of F (270.7) and the extremely low p-value let you know that the model is a good fit.

The coefficients tell you that in logarithmic form, the regression equation is

$$\log(y') = \log(a + bx)$$
$$\log(\text{brainweight}') = \log(2.15041 + (.75226 \times \text{bodyweight}))$$

For the power regression equation, you have to take the antilog of both sides. As I mention earlier in this chapter, when you're working with natural logarithms, that's the same as applying the exp( ) function:

$$\exp(\log(y')) = \exp(\log(a + bx))$$
$$y' = \exp(a)x^b$$
$$\text{brainweight}' = \exp(2.15041) \times \text{bodyweight}^{.75226}$$
$$\text{brainweight}' = 8.588397 \times \text{bodyweight}^{.75226}$$

All this is in keeping with what I say earlier in this chapter:

>> Adding the logarithms of numbers corresponds to multiplying the numbers.

>> Multiplying the logarithm of x by b corresponds to raising x to the b power.

Here's how to use R to find the *exp* of the intercept:

```
> a <- exp(powerfit$coefficients[1])
> a
```

```
(Intercept)
  8.588397
```

You can plot the power regression equation as a curve in the original scatterplot:

```
ggplot(Animals.living, aes(x=body, y=brain))+
  geom_point()+
  geom_line(aes(y=exp(powerfit$fitted.values)))
```

That last statement is the business end, of course: `powerfit$fitted.values` contains the predicted brain weights in logarithmic form and applying `exp()` to those values converts those predictions to the original units of measure. You map them to y to position the curve. Figure 8-5 shows the plot.

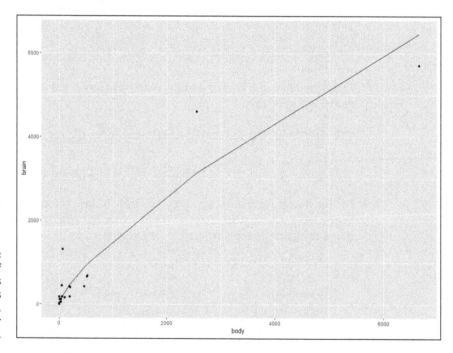

FIGURE 8-5:
Original plot of brain weights and body weights of 25 species, with the power regression curve.

Exponential Regression

As I mention earlier in this chapter, *e* figures into processes in a variety of areas. Some of those processes, like compound interest, involve growth. Others involve decay.

Here's an example. If you've ever poured a glass of beer and let it stand, you might have noticed that the head gets smaller and smaller (it *decays*, in other words) as time passes. You haven't done that? Okay. Go ahead and pour a tall, cool one and watch it for 6 minutes. I'll wait.

... And, we're back. Was I right? Notice that I didn't ask you to measure the height of the head as it decayed. Physicist Arnd Leike did that for us for three brands of beer.

He measured head height every 15 seconds from 0 to 120 seconds after pouring the beer, and then every 30 seconds from 150 seconds to 240 seconds, and, finally, at 300 seconds and 360 seconds. (In the true spirit of science, he then drank the beer.) Here are those intervals as a vector:

```
seconds.after.pour <- c(seq(0,120,15), seq(150,240,30), c(300,360))
```

And here are the measured head heights (in centimeters) for one of those brands:

```
head.cm <- c(17, 16.1, 14.9, 14, 13.2, 12.5, 11.9, 11.2, 10.7, 9.7, 8.9, 8.3,
   7.5, 6.3, 5.2)
```

I combine these vectors into a data frame:

```
beer.head <- data.frame(seconds.after.pour,head.cm)
```

Let's see what the plot looks like. This code snippet

```
ggplot(beer.head, aes(x=seconds.after.pour,y=head.cm))+
   geom_point()
```

produces Figure 8-6.

This one is crying out (in its beer?) for a curvilinear model, isn't it?

One way to linearize the plot (so that you can use lm() to create a model) is to work with the log of the *y*-variable:

```
ggplot(beer.head, aes(x= seconds.after.pour,y=log(head.cm)))+
   geom_point()+
   geom_smooth(method="lm",se=FALSE)
```

The last statement adds the regression line (method = "lm") and doesn't draw the confidence interval around the line (se = FALSE). You can see all this in Figure 8-7.

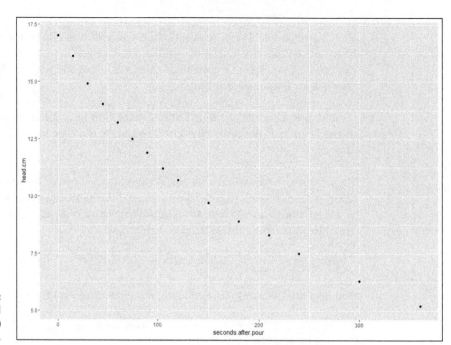

FIGURE 8-6:
How beer head
height (head.cm)
decays over time.

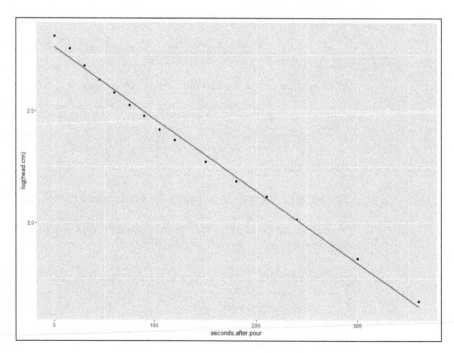

FIGURE 8-7:
How log(head.cm)
decays over time,
including the
regression line.

As in the preceding section, creating this plot points the way for carrying out the analysis. The general equation for the resulting model is

$$y' = ae^{bx}$$

Because the predictor variable appears in an exponent (to which e is raised), this is called *exponential* regression.

And here's how to do the analysis:

```
expfit <- lm(log(head.cm) ~ seconds.after.pour, data = beer.head)
```

Once again, `lm()` indicates a linear model, and the dependent variable is on the left side of the tilde (~), with the predictor variable on the right side. After running the analysis,

```
> summary(expfit)

Call:
lm(formula = log(head.cm) ~ seconds.after.pour, data = beer.head)

Residuals:
      Min        1Q    Median        3Q       Max
-0.031082 -0.019012 -0.001316  0.017338  0.047806

Coefficients:
                     Estimate Std. Error t value Pr(>|t|)
(Intercept)         2.785e+00  1.110e-02  250.99  < 2e-16 ***
seconds.after.pour -3.223e-03  6.616e-05  -48.72  4.2e-16 ***
---
Signif. codes: 0 '***' 0.001 '**' 0.01 '*' 0.05 '.' 0.1 ' ' 1

Residual standard error: 0.02652 on 13 degrees of freedom
Multiple R-squared:  0.9946,  Adjusted R-squared:  0.9941
F-statistic:  2373 on 1 and 13 DF,  p-value: 4.197e-16
```

The F and p-value show that this model is a phenomenally great fit. The R-squared is among the highest you'll ever see. In fact, Arnd did all this to show his students how an exponential process works. If you want to see his data for the other two brands, check out Leike, A. (2002), "Demonstration of the exponential decay law using beer froth," *European Journal of Physics*, 23(1), 21–26.

According to the coefficients, the regression equation in logarithmic form is

$$\log(y') = a + bx$$
$$\log(\text{head.cm}') = 2.785 + ((-.003223) \times \text{seconds.after.pour})$$

For the exponential regression equation, you have to take the exponential of both sides — in other words, you apply the exp( ) function:

$$\exp(\log(y')) = \exp(a + bx)$$
$$y' = \exp(a)e^{bx}$$
$$\text{head.cm}' = \exp(2.785) \times e^{-.003223\text{seconds.after.pour}}$$
$$\text{head.cm}' = 16.20642 \times e^{-.003223\text{seconds.after.pour}}$$

Analogous to what you did in the preceding section, you can plot the exponential regression equation as a curve in the original scatterplot:

```
ggplot(beer.head, aes(x= seconds.after.pour,y=head.cm))+
    geom_point()+
    geom_line(aes(y=exp(expfit$fitted.values)))
```

In the last statement, expfit$fitted.values contains the predicted beer head heights in logarithmic form and applying exp( ) to those values converts those predictions to the original units of measure. Mapping them to y positions the curve. Figure 8-8 shows the plot.

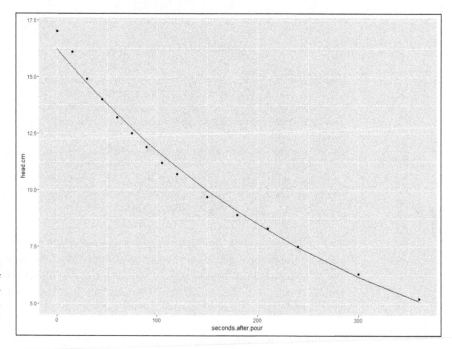

FIGURE 8-8:
The decay of head.cm over time, with the exponential regression curve.

Logarithmic Regression

In the two preceding sections, I explain how power regression analysis works with the log of the *x*-variable and the log of the *y*-variable, and how exponential regression analysis works with the log of just the *y*-variable. As you might imagine, one more analytic possibility is available to you — working with just the log of the *x*-variable. The equation of the model looks like this:

$$y' = a + b \log(x)$$

Because the logarithm is applied to the predictor variable, this is called *logarithmic regression.*

Here's an example that uses the Cars93 data frame in the MASS package. (Make sure you have the MASS package installed. On the Packages tab, find the MASS check box and if it's not selected, click it.)

This data frame, featured prominently in Chapter 1 of Book 2, holds data on a number of variables for 93 cars in the model year 1993. Here, I focus on the relationship between Horsepower (the *x*-variable) and MPG.highway (the *y*-variable).

This is the code to create the scatterplot in Figure 8-9:

```
ggplot(Cars93, aes(x=Horsepower,y=MPG.highway))+
  geom_point()
```

For this example, linearize the plot by taking the log of Horsepower. In the plot, include the regression line: Here's how to draw it:

```
ggplot(Cars93, aes(x=log(Horsepower),y=MPG.highway))+
  geom_point()+
  geom_smooth(method="lm",se=FALSE)
```

Figure 8-10 shows the result.

With log(Horsepower) as the *x*-variable, the analysis is

```
logfit <- lm(MPG.highway ~ log(Horsepower), data=Cars93)
```

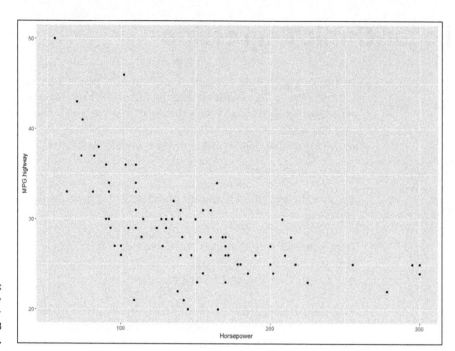

FIGURE 8-9:
MPG.highway
and Horsepower
in the Cars93
data frame.

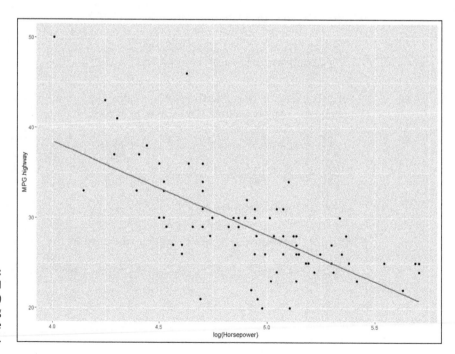

FIGURE 8-10:
MPG.highway and
Log(Horsepower)
in Cars93, along
with the
regression line.

After carrying out that analysis, `summary()` provides the details:

```
> summary(logfit)

Call:
lm(formula = MPG.highway ~ log(Horsepower), data = Cars93)

Residuals:
    Min      1Q  Median      3Q     Max
-10.3109 -2.2066 -0.0707  2.0031 14.0002

Coefficients:
                Estimate Std. Error t value Pr(>|t|)
(Intercept)       80.003      5.520  14.493  < 2e-16 ***
log(Horsepower)  -10.379      1.122  -9.248 9.55e-15 ***
---
Signif. codes:  0 '***' 0.001 '**' 0.01 '*' 0.05 '.' 0.1 ' ' 1

Residual standard error: 3.849 on 91 degrees of freedom
Multiple R-squared:  0.4845,    Adjusted R-squared:  0.4788
F-statistic: 85.53 on 1 and 91 DF,  p-value: 9.548e-15
```

The high value of F and the very low value of p indicate an excellent fit.

From the coefficients, the regression equation is

$$\text{MPG.highway}' = 80.03 - 10.379 \log(\text{Horsepower})$$

As in the preceding sections, I plot the regression curve in the original plot:

```
ggplot(Cars93, aes(x=Horsepower,y=MPG.highway))+
  geom_point()+
  geom_line(aes(y=logfit$fitted.values))
```

Figure 8-11 shows the plot with the regression curve.

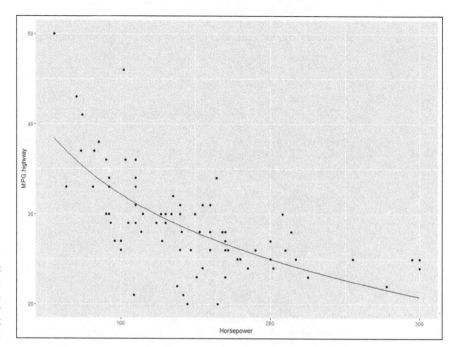

FIGURE 8-11:
MPG.highway
and Horsepower,
with the
logarithmic
regression curve.

Polynomial Regression: A Higher Power

In all the types of regression I describe earlier in this chapter, the model is a line or a curve that doesn't change direction. It's possible, however, to create a model that incorporates a direction-change. This is the province of *polynomial regression*.

I touch on direction-change in Chapter 4 of Book 3, in the context of trend analysis. To model one change of direction, the regression equation has to have an x-term raised to the second power:

$$y' = a + b_1 x + b_2 x^2$$

To model two changes of direction, the regression equation has to have an x-term raised to the third power:

$$y' = a + b_1 x + b_2 x^2 + b_3 x^3$$

and so forth.

I illustrate polynomial regression with another data frame from the MASS package. (On the Packages tab, find MASS. If its check box isn't selected, click it.)

This data frame is called `Boston`. It holds data on housing values in the Boston suburbs. Among its 14 variables are `rm` (the number of rooms in a dwelling) and `medv` (the median value of the dwelling). I focus on those two variables in this example, with `rm` as the predictor variable.

Begin by creating the scatterplot and regression line:

```
ggplot(Boston, aes(x=rm,y=medv))+
  geom_point()+
  geom_smooth(method=lm, se=FALSE)
```

Figure 8-12 shows what this code produces.

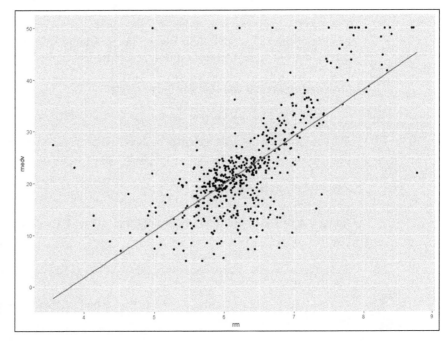

FIGURE 8-12: Scatterplot of median value (medv) versus rooms (rm) in the Boston data frame, with the regression line.

The linear regression model is

```
linfit <- lm(medv ~ rm, data=Boston)
> summary(linfit)

Call:
lm(formula = medv ~ rm, data = Boston)
```

```
Residuals:
    Min     1Q  Median      3Q     Max
-23.346  -2.547   0.090   2.986  39.433

Coefficients:
            Estimate Std. Error t value Pr(>|t|)
(Intercept)  -34.671     2.650  -13.08   <2e-16 ***
rm             9.102     0.419   21.72   <2e-16 ***
---
Signif. codes:  0 '***' 0.001 '**' 0.01 '*' 0.05 '.' 0.1 ' ' 1

Residual standard error: 6.616 on 504 degrees of freedom
Multiple R-squared:  0.4835,   Adjusted R-squared:  0.4825
F-statistic: 471.8 on 1 and 504 DF,  p-value: < 2.2e-16
```

The F and p-value show that this is a good fit. R-squared tells you that about 48 percent of the SS_{Total} for medv is tied up in the relationship between rm and medv. (Check out Chapter 7 of Book 3 if that last sentence sounds unfamiliar.)

The coefficients tell you that the linear model is

$$medv' = -34.671 + 9.102rm$$

But perhaps a model with a change of direction provides a better fit. To set this up in R, create a new variable rm2 — which is just rm squared:

```
rm2 <- Boston$rm^2
```

Now treat this as a multiple regression analysis with two predictor variables: rm and rm2:

```
polyfit2 <-lm(medv ~ rm + rm2, data=Boston)
```

TIP

You can't just go ahead and use rm^2 as the second predictor variable: lm( ) won't work with it in that form.

After you run the analysis, here are the details:

```
> summary(polyfit2)

Call:
lm(formula = medv ~ rm + rm2, data = Boston)

Residuals:
    Min     1Q  Median      3Q     Max
-35.769  -2.752   0.619   3.003  35.464
```

```
Coefficients:
            Estimate Std. Error t value Pr(>|t|)
(Intercept)  66.0588   12.1040   5.458 7.59e-08 ***
rm          -22.6433    3.7542  -6.031 3.15e-09 ***
rm2           2.4701    0.2905   8.502  < 2e-16 ***
---
Signif. codes: 0 '***' 0.001 '**' 0.01 '*' 0.05 '.' 0.1 ' ' 1

Residual standard error: 6.193 on 503 degrees of freedom
Multiple R-squared: 0.5484,  Adjusted R-squared: 0.5466
F-statistic: 305.4 on 2 and 503 DF,  p-value: < 2.2e-16
```

Looks like a better fit than the linear model. The F-statistic here is higher, and this time R-squared tells you that almost 55 percent of the SS_{Total} for medv is due to the relationship between medv and the combination of rm and rm^2. The increase in F and in R-squared comes at a cost — the second model has 1 less df (503 versus 504).

The coefficients indicate that the polynomial regression equation is

$$medv' = 66.0588 - 22.6433rm + 2.4701rm^2$$

Is it worth the effort to add rm^2 to the model? To find out, I use anova() to compare the linear model with the polynomial model:

```
> anova(linfit,polyfit2)
Analysis of Variance Table

Model 1: medv ~ rm
Model 2: medv ~ rm + rm2
  Res.Df   RSS Df Sum of Sq      F    Pr(>F)
1    504 22062
2    503 19290  1    2772.3 72.291 < 2.2e-16 ***
---
Signif. codes: 0 '***' 0.001 '**' 0.01 '*' 0.05 '.' 0.1 ' ' 1
```

The high F-ratio (72.291) and extremely low Pr(>F) indicate that adding rm^2 is a good idea.

Which Model Should You Use?

I present a variety of regression models in this chapter. Deciding on the one that's right for your data is not necessarily straightforward. One superficial answer might be to try each one and see which one yields the highest F and R-squared.

The operative word in that last sentence is *superficial.* The choice of model should depend on your knowledge of the domain from which the data comes and the processes in that domain. Which regression type allows you to formulate a theory about what might be happening in the data?

For instance, in the Boston example, the polynomial model showed that dwelling-value *decreases* slightly as the number of rooms *increases* at the low end, and then value steadily *increases* as the number of rooms increases. The linear model couldn't discern a trend like that. Why would that trend occur? Can you come up with a theory? Does the theory make sense?

I'll leave you with an exercise. Remember the shoelace-tying example at the beginning of this chapter? All I gave you was Figure 8-1, but here are the numbers:

```
trials <-seq(1,18,1)
time.sec <- c(230, 140, 98, 75, 66, 54, 45, 31, 20, 15, 10, 9, 9, 9, 8, 8, 8, 8)
```

What model can *you* come up with? And how does it help you explain the data?

Chapter **9**

In Due Time

I n many fields (science, medicine, business), it's often necessary to take measurements over successive intervals of time. When you have this kind of data, you have yourself a *time series*. This chapter tells you about time series and how to use R to analyze them and use them to make forecasts.

A Time Series and Its Components

Managers often base their decisions on time series — like sales figures — and the numbers in a time series typically show numerous ups and downs.

Let's look at an example. The (totally fictional) FarDrate Timepiece Corporation markets the beautifully designed MeesKyte watch, and they gather the quarterly national sales figures. Table 9-1 shows these quarterly sales figures from 2016–2020.

To work with R's time series capabilities, we first put the numbers in the proper format. We begin by creating a vector of the numbers in the rightmost column:

```
> meeskyte.sales <- c(57,84,68,100,63,81,73,110,70,87,75,112,78,95,88,116,82,
  99,92,122)
```

TABLE 9-1

Quarterly Sales Figures for the MeesKyte watch

Year	Quarter	Sales X 100,000
2016	1	57
	2	84
	3	68
	4	100
2017	1	63
	2	81
	3	73
	4	110
2018	1	70
	2	87
	3	75
	4	112
2019	1	78
	2	95
	3	88
	4	116
2020	1	82
	2	99
	3	92
	4	122

Helpfully, R provides a function called ts() that turns this vector into a time-series object:

```
> meeskyte.ts <- ts(meeskyte.sales, start=c(2016,1), end = c(2020,4),
    frequency=4)
```

The first argument is the vector, the second is the starting point (Quarter 1 of 2016), and the third is the end point (Quarter 4 of 2020). The last argument, frequency, is extremely important: It's the number of observations per unit of time (1 = annual, 4 = quarterly, 12 = monthly). Here's what ts() does for us:

```
> meeskyte.ts
     Qtr1 Qtr2 Qtr3 Qtr4
2016  57   84   68  100
2017  63   81   73  110
2018  70   87   75  112
2019  78   95   88  116
2020  82   99   92  122
```

That's quite a bit of work!

You can begin to see patterns in the numbers. To see them more clearly, however, it's a good idea to create a graph like the one shown in Figure 9-1.

```
> plot(meeskyte.ts, xlab = "Quarter", ylab = "Sales X 1000")
```

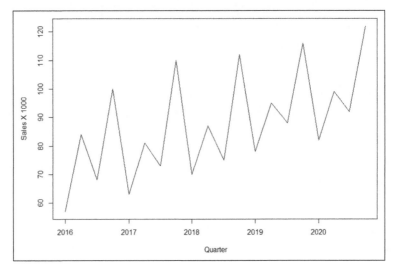

FIGURE 9-1: Visualizing the MeesKyte time series.

As the figure shows, the peaks and valleys seem pretty regular. Sales peak in the last quarter of every year — perhaps people buy these watches as holiday gifts. Sales also peak somewhat (but not as much) in the middle of each year — maybe parents are buying MeesKyte watches as graduation presents. This pattern repeats from year to year, and it's called the *seasonal component* of the time series.

We also see sales moving generally in an upward direction. That might result from an expanding economy, or perhaps increasing awareness of the brand (or both). This is called the *trend component* of the time series. In this example, the trend is linear, but that's not always the case in a time series.

Finally, sporadic nonrecurring influences can affect a time series. This is known as the *random component* of a time series.

The decompose() function allows us to estimate, and then plot, these components. The assumption is that the time series is the sum of the components.

```
> meeskyte.dc <- decompose(meeskyte.ts)
> plot(meeskyte.dc)
```

The plot() function produces Figure 9-2. The time series is in the top panel, the trend component is in the next, and then comes the seasonal component. Finally, the random component is in the bottom panel.

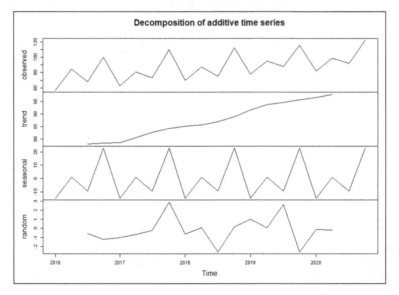

FIGURE 9-2:
Components of
the MeesKyte
time series.

Calculating the component estimates enables you to adjust the time series. For example, a manager might want to see what the seasonally adjusted sales look like. To make this adjustment, subtract the seasonal component from the time series:

```
> meeskyte.adj <- meeskyte.ts - meeskyte.dc$seasonal
> plot(meeskyte.adj)
```

Figure 9-3 shows the plot of the seasonally adjusted data. It's the trend component plus the random component. (The assumption here is that the components are additive.)

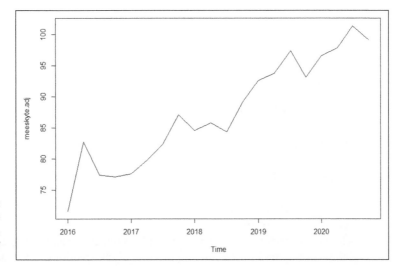

FIGURE 9-3: The MeesKyte time series, seasonally adjusted.

Forecasting: A Moving Experience

To make forecasts from a time series, we try to smooth out the bumps a bit to get a better idea of the underlying process that's generating the data.

One way to smooth out the bumps and still see the big picture is to calculate a *moving average.* This is an average calculated from the most recent scores in the time series. It "moves" because you keep calculating it over the time series. As you add a score to the front end, you delete one from the back end.

So we have the MeesKyte sales figures for 20 quarters, and suppose we decide to keep a moving average for the most recent five quarters. (Another way to say that is that the *interval* is 5.) Start with the average from quarters 1–5 of those 20 quarters, and that will be the estimate for the fifth of the 20 quarters. Then average the prices from quarters 2–6 to estimate the sixth of the quarters. Next, average quarters 3–7, and so on, until you average the final 5 quarters of the time series to estimate the 20th quarter.

REMEMBER

A moving average is a *forecast.* It's a best guess based on averaging the sales figures of the most recent five quarters. (Five just happens to be the number in this example.)

R gives you a function to easily calculate moving averages in a time series. It's called `rollmean()` and it's in a package called zoo. Click the Install icon on R Studio's Package tab to download zoo, and then click the check box next to zoo on the Package tab to finish the installation and show this on the Console tab:

```
> library(zoo)
```

To calculate the moving averages for the most recent five quarters:

```
> movav5 <- rollmean(meeskyte.ts, k=5, align = "right")
```

The first argument is the time series, and the second is the interval — the number of quarters to include in the moving average. The third argument specifies whether the index of the result should be aligned to the left, right, or center (the default) compared to the moving interval of observations. The way I think about moving averages, "right" makes the most sense to me.

What's the result of applying `rollmean()`?

Glad you asked:

```
> movav5
       Qtr1  Qtr2  Qtr3   Qtr4
2017   74.4  79.2  77.0   85.4
2018   79.4  84.2  83.0   90.8
2019   84.4  89.4  89.6   97.8
2020   91.8  96.0  95.4  102.2
```

Compare with `meeskyte.ts` and you'll see that this one begins with Quarter 1 of 2017 rather than Quarter 1 of 2016: The first entry (74.4) is the average of `meeskyte.ts`'s first five quarters.

A graph is the easiest way to compare the two and show how the moving average smooths out the time series. Figure 9-4 shows the graph.

Here's how to create that graph.

```
> plot(meeskyte.ts)
> lines(movav5,lty=2)
```

The second argument in `lines()` specifies a dashed line for the moving average.

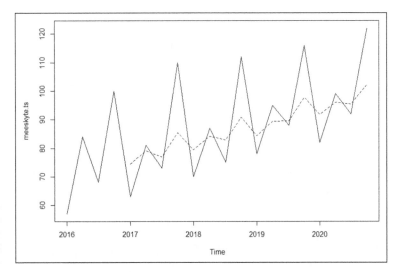

FIGURE 9-4:
The MeesKyte
time series and
the moving
average.

We can use the moving average to forecast the sales figures for future quarters. First, you have to install the `forecast` package. As always, use the Install icon on the Packages tab to download `forecast`, and then click the check box next to `forecast` on the Packages tab so that this appears on the Console tab:

```
> library(forecast)
```

I use the `forecast()` function to create the forecasts for the eight quarters after 2020:

```
> movav5_forecast <- forecast(movav5, level=95, h=2*4)
```

The first argument is the model we're working with to make the forecasts. The second argument specifies the confidence level (95 percent) for each forecast, and the third argument indicates two future years of quarters.

To extract the forecasted values:

```
> movav5_forecast$mean
        Qtr1       Qtr2       Qtr3       Qtr4
2021   96.34825 101.05441 100.10239 107.92256
2022 101.87977 106.58592 105.63391 113.45408
```

Of course, everything looks better in a graph, so here's how I create a graph of the time series and the forecasts:

```
> plot(movav5_forecast, xlab = "Quarter", ylab= "Sales X 1000", main = "Time
   Series and Forecasts from Moving Average")
```

The result is the plot shown in Figure 9-5. The shading around the forecast values depicts the 95 percent confidence interval.

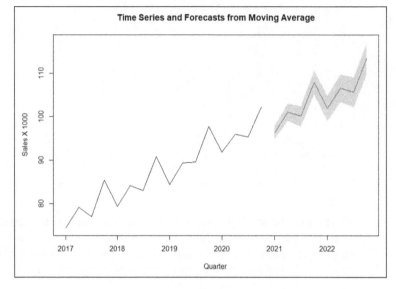

FIGURE 9-5:
The MeesKyte
time series and
forecasts for
eight future
quarters based
on moving
average with
interval = 5.

In general, how many scores should you include in the interval? That's up to you. Include too many and you risk obsolete data influencing your results. Include too few and you risk missing something important. As an exercise, try different values for k and see what their plots and their forecasts look like.

Forecasting: Another Way

We can go beyond the simple moving average and use another technique to forecast values of a time series. The technique is called ARIMA, which stands for *autoregressive integrated moving average*. The name suggests some pretty fancy mathematics, which I avoid as I tell you how to use this technique in R.

The function that gets it done is auto.arima() in the forecast package.

With the forecast package downloaded and installed, here's how to set up the model:

```
> arima_model <- auto.arima(meeskyte.ts)
```

and to forecast values for eight quarters beyond 2020:

```
> arima_forecast <- forecast(arima_model, level= 95, h = 2*4)
```

As in the preceding section, the first argument is the model we're working with, the second argument specifies the confidence level (95 percent), and the third argument indicates two future years of quarters.

To see the forecasted values:

```
> arima_forecast$mean
        Qtr1      Qtr2      Qtr3      Qtr4
2021  87.02490 105.46759  96.26379 128.32255
2022  92.56692 111.00962 101.80581 133.86457
```

The plot, shown in Figure 9-6, shows the time series and the predictions, along with the shaded 95 percent confidence intervals. This is how you create it:

```
> plot(arima_forecast, xlab = "Quarter", ylab= "Sales X 1000", main = "Time
  Series and Forecasts from ARIMA")
```

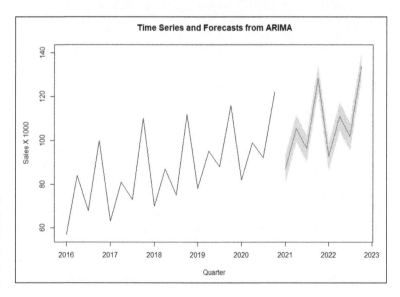

FIGURE 9-6:
The MeesKyte time series and forecasts for eight future quarters based on ARIMA.

Working with Real Data

At this point, you probably want to go beyond the toy problem I explore here and look at some real-world data. I point you to some data sets on which you can try out what you learn in this chapter.

AirPassengers is a frequently used dataset in R. A time series that shows the number of monthly airline passengers in the years 1949–1960, it's in the datasets package that comes with R. AirPassengers is already a time series object, so no need to apply ts(). To see this dataset, it's just:

```
> AirPassengers
     Jan Feb Mar Apr May Jun Jul Aug Sep Oct Nov Dec
1949 112 118 132 129 121 135 148 148 136 119 104 118
1950 115 126 141 135 125 149 170 170 158 133 114 140
1951 145 150 178 163 172 178 199 199 184 162 146 166
1952 171 180 193 181 183 218 230 242 209 191 172 194
1953 196 196 236 235 229 243 264 272 237 211 180 201
1954 204 188 235 227 234 264 302 293 259 229 203 229
1955 242 233 267 269 270 315 364 347 312 274 237 278
1956 284 277 317 313 318 374 413 405 355 306 271 306
1957 315 301 356 348 355 422 465 467 404 347 305 336
1958 340 318 362 348 363 435 491 505 404 359 310 337
1959 360 342 406 396 420 472 548 559 463 407 362 405
1960 417 391 419 461 472 535 622 606 508 461 390 432
```

Go have some fun with this one.

In addition to R's built-in datasets, you'll find a huge trove of time series data in the tsdl (Time Series Data Library) package. When I say *huge,* I'm not kidding: Compiled by Monash University professor Rob Hyndman (who's pretty much the grand poobah of time series), the package offers 648 data sets.

You don't download this package in the usual way. Why? It lives in a GitHub repository, not in CRAN (Comprehensive R Archive Network). So you first install devtools. As always, click the Install icon on the Packages tab to download, and then click the check box next to devtools on the Packages tab.

Then you use the devtools function install_github():

```
> install_github("FinYang/tsdl")
```

After the download is complete, click on the check box next to `tsdl` on the Packages tab so that this appears on the Console tab:

```
> library(tsdl)
```

Let's take a look at what's in the library:

```
> tsdl
Time Series Data Library: 648 time series
                    Frequency
Subject           0.1 0.25   1    4   5   6  12  13  52 365 Total
  Agriculture       0    0  37    0   0   0   3   0   0   0    40
  Chemistry         0    0   8    0   0   0   0   0   0   0     8
  Computing         0    0   6    0   0   0   0   0   0   0     6
  Crime             0    0   1    0   0   0   2   1   0   0     4
  Demography        1    0   9    2   0   0   3   0   0   2    17
  Ecology           0    0  23    0   0   0   0   0   0   0    23
  Finance           0    0  23    5   0   0  20   0   2   1    51
  Health            0    0   8    0   0   0   6   0   1   0    15
  Hydrology         0    0  42    0   0   0  78   1   0   6   127
  Industry          0    0   9    0   0   0   2   0   1   0    12
  Labour market     0    0   3    4   0   0  17   0   0   0    24
  Macroeconomic     0    0  18   33   0   0   5   0   0   0    56
  Meteorology       0    0  18    0   0   0  17   0   0  12    47
  Microeconomic     0    0  27    1   0   0   7   0   1   0    36
  Miscellaneous     0    0   4    0   1   1   3   0   1   0    10
  Physics           0    0  12    0   0   0   4   0   0   0    16
  Production        0    0   4   14   0   0  28   1   1   0    48
  Sales             0    0  10    3   0   0  24   0   9   0    46
  Sport             0    1   1    0   0   0   0   0   0   0     2
  Transport and tourism  0  0  1   1   0   0  12   0   0   0    14
  Tree-rings        0    0  34    0   0   0   1   0   0   0    35
  Utilities         0    0   2    1   0   0   8   0   0   0    11
  Total             1    1 300   64   1   1 240   3  16  21   648
```

Extracting a time series from `tsdl` can be a little tricky, so I'll lay out the procedure for you.

To select a time series, you first create a subset of `tsdl`. The easiest way to do this is by subject. If I'm interested in the time series in Demography, I type

```
> demography <- subset(tsdl, "Demography")
```

The result is a list of the time series in Demography. How do you know what's in the list? You just have to examine each element. You use double brackets to identity a list element, so the first of the 17 time series in this list is

```
> demography[[1]]
```

Quite a few web tutorials use time series from this library as examples, but their directions for extracting a time series from it are either vague or out of date.

TIP

Chapter **10**

Non-Parametric Statistics

The statistical methods I cover in earlier chapters of this *All-in-One* have a couple of things in common. First, you can assume ratio (or at least interval) data. (If you don't know what that means, read the section in Chapter 1 of Book 1 about types of data.) Second, you can use sample statistics to estimate parameters of the sampling distribution, and you use the central limit theorem to characterize the nature of the distribution so that you can test hypotheses.

Sometimes you have to analyze nominal data or ordinal data. (Again, refer to Chapter 1 of Book 1.) And sometimes you can't specify the distribution of the variable you're working with.

To deal with these cases, statisticians have developed *non-parametric* statistical tests. The list of these tests is long and growing. Many of them require special lookup tables for hypothesis tests.

I wanted to avoid those special tables, so I chose six classical non-parametric tests. Five of them have functions built into base R. One of them requires that you install a package.

Let's get started.

Independent Samples

The non-parametric tests I show you in this section are analogous to the independent groups t-test and to the one-factor analysis of variance.

Two samples: Wilcoxon rank-sum test

The Wilcoxon rank-sum test is one of the most popular non-parametric tests. (In fact, it's so popular that it even has an additional name: Mann-Whitney U test. But I digress.) If your data are neither interval nor ratio (and you thus can't use the t-test), you use the Wilcoxon text to test whether two independent samples come from the same population.

When the data are ordinal, statisticians work with the ranks of the data rather than with the original data points, and that's what this test does.

Imagine a study in which eight people are randomly assigned to watch either a horror movie or a comedy. Then they have to rate how stressed they feel on a scale of 1 (least stressed) to 100 (most stressed). Let's assume that subjective ratings are ordinal, at best. (We probably don't carry around in our head a zero-point and an equal interval scale for everything we might have to rate.) So a statistical test that works with ranks sounds like a good idea.

The ratings, along with the rank of each rating (from lowest to highest), appear in Table 10-1. The ranks are for the eight ratings, regardless of which group they happen to be in.

TABLE 10-1   **Stress Ratings (0–100) for Horror versus Comedy, and Rank (from Lowest to Highest) for Each Rating**

Horror Stress Rating	Comedy Stress Rating	Rank Horror Stress Rating	Rank Comedy Stress Rating
87	31	8	3
40	15	5	1
32	55	4	6
56	17	7	2
Sum		24	12

In the bottom row, I've summed the ranks of each group. You can probably guess what's coming: A null hypothesis would imply that the two sums should be about the same — the ranks should be distributed about equally between the two groups. An alternative hypothesis, on the other hand, would imply that the two sums would be different from one another because higher ranks would be in one group and lower ranks in another.

You can go one step further and formulate a one-tailed alternative hypothesis. Before gathering any data, you would expect that a horror-themed movie would cause higher stress levels than a comedy would. A one-tailed alternative hypothesis, then, implies that the sum of ranks for the horror movie is higher than the sum of ranks for the comedy. The null hypothesis in that case implies that the sum of ranks for the horror movie should be about the same or less than the sum of ranks for the comedy.

In conceptual terms, the null hypothesis is that the two come from the same population distribution or from populations where the horror movie causes less stress than the comedy. The alternative hypothesis is that the two samples come from different populations, with the horror movie causing a population shifted toward higher stress.

Let's use the data to test these hypotheses at $\alpha = .05$.

As the bottom row of the table shows, the sum of ranks for the Horror sample is 24. The question becomes: "With two samples of four individuals each, what is the probability of obtaining a rank sum of 24 or higher?" If that probability is less than .05, reject H_0. If it's not, don't reject it.

To answer the question, you have to know how many ways you can divide eight individuals into two sets of four each. It turns out that this number is 70.

**TECHNICAL
STUFF**

I say more in Chapter 11 (later in Book 3) about how to find that number. It's called "the number of combinations of eight things taken four at a time." If you won't take my word for it, you can use the R function choose( ) to verify:

```
> choose(8,4)
[1] 70
```

I also use this function in Chapter 11 of Book 3.

As for the phrase "24 or higher," you already have one set of scores that results in a Horror rank sum of 24 (ranks = 8,5,4,7), and you can form a different set that also results in 24 (ranks = 8,6,3,7). It's possible to rearrange the scores to yield a Horror rank sum of 25 (ranks = 8,7,6,4) and a rank sum of 26 (ranks = 8,7,5,6).

That's four possible ways of arriving at a Horror rank sum of 24 or higher out of 70 possibilities. So the probability of a rank sum of 24 or higher with two groups of four people each is

$$p(rank.sum \geq 24) = \frac{4}{70} = .05714$$

The probability is higher than .05, so you cannot reject the null hypothesis.

In case you're thinking that the set (8,5,4,7) is different from (4,7,8,5) and that should throw all the numbers off . . . well, as they say in my hometown (Brooklyn, New York): "Fuggedaboutit." (English translation: "Forget about it.") These are *combinations*, and order doesn't matter. (I discuss combinations in Chapter 11 of Book 3.)

The usual way of dealing with data like this is to use one of the two rank sums (such as the larger one) to calculate a statistic

$$W = rank.sum - \frac{n(n+1)}{2} = 24 - \frac{4(5)}{2} = 14$$

and then deal with a sampling distribution for W to arrive at the probability I just showed you.

Here's how to do the whole thing in R:

```
> horror <- c(87,40,32,56)
> comedy <- c(31,15,55,17)
> wilcox.test(horror,comedy,alternative = "greater")

          Wilcoxon rank sum test

data:  horror and comedy
W = 14, p-value = 0.05714
alternative hypothesis: true location shift is greater than 0
```

You can also do this test with a long-format data frame:

```
> stress.long
    Type Rating
1 horror     87
2 horror     40
3 horror     32
4 horror     56
5 comedy     31
```

6	comedy	15
7	comedy	55
8	comedy	17

The test, in this form, is

```
> wilcox.test(Rating ~ Type, stress.long, alternative =
  "greater")

        Wilcoxon rank sum test

data:  Rating by Type
W = 14, p-value = 0.05714
alternative hypothesis: true location shift is greater than 0
```

Why bother with long format? It comes in handy if you want to plot the data:

```
ggplot(stress.long, aes(x=Type,y=Rating))+
  geom_boxplot()+
  geom_point(aes(y=Rating))
```

These lines of code draw the box plot with data points in Figure 10-1.

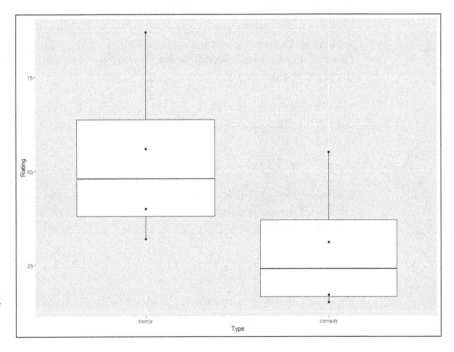

FIGURE 10-1:
Boxplot of
the data in
Table 10-1.

More than two samples: Kruskal-Wallis One-Way ANOVA

FarKlempt Robotics, Inc., surveys its employees about their satisfaction with their jobs. They ask developers, consultants, and tech writers to rate job satisfaction on a scale of 1 (least satisfied) to 100 (most satisfied). Table 10-2 shows the results.

TABLE 10-2 ## Survey Results from FarKlempt Robotics, Inc.

Developer	Consultant	Tech Writer	Rank Developer	Rank Consultant	Rank Tech Writer
25	79	63	1	18	13
58	70	50	10	15	3
57	52	76	9	5	16
51	56	62	4	8	12
42	64	55	2	14	7
59	77	53	11	17	6
	Sum		37	77	57

The appropriate non-parametric test for this particular scenario is the Kruskal-Wallis one-way analysis of variance. As in the Wilcoxon rank-sum test, I start by ranking all 18 scores in ascending order. Again, if the null hypothesis is true, the ranks should be distributed about equally throughout the groups, and the sums of the ranks should be pretty close to one another.

The test statistic is called H — possibly because Kruskal's middle name was Henry, but I don't think anyone really knows why. Here is its formula:

$$H = \left[\frac{12}{N(N+1)} \sum \frac{R^2}{n} \right] - 3(N+1)$$

N is the total number of scores, and n is the number of scores in each group. I specified the same number of scores in each group, but that's not necessary for this test. R is the sum of the ranks in a group. So the math works out to

$$H = \left[\left(\frac{12}{(18)(19)} \right) \left(\frac{37^2}{6} + \frac{77^2}{6} + \frac{57^2}{6} \right) \right] - 3(19) = 4.6784$$

H is distributed approximately as chi-square with df = number of groups – 1, when each n is greater than 5. The probability of a value this high or higher (if the null hypothesis is true) is .096. You can use pchisq() to verify:

```
> pchisq(4.6784,2,lower.tail = FALSE)
[1] 0.09640473
```

Because this value is higher than .05, you cannot reject the null hypothesis.

To do this test in R, I create the data frame FK.survey:

```
> Developer <- c(25,58,57,51,42,59)
> Consultant <- c(79,70,52,56,64,77)
> TechWriter <- c(63,50,76,62,55,53)
> FK.survey <- data.frame(Developer,Consultant,TechWriter)
> FK.survey
  Developer Consultant TechWriter
1        25         79         63
2        58         70         50
3        57         52         76
4        51         56         62
5        42         64         55
6        59         77         53
```

Then the test is just

```
> kruskal.test(FK.survey)

        Kruskal-Wallis rank sum test

data:  FK.survey
Kruskal-Wallis chi-squared = 4.6784, df = 2, p-value =
0.09641
```

The p-value is higher than .05, indicating nonrejection of the null hypothesis.

As is the case with the Wilcoxon rank-sum test, you can also do this test with the data in long format, as in a data frame called FK.survey.long:

```
> head(FK.survey.long)
        Role Rating
1 Developer     25
2 Developer     58
3 Developer     57
4 Developer     51
5 Developer     42
6 Developer     59
```

The test is then

```
> kruskal.test(Rating ~ Role, data=FK.survey.long)

        Kruskal-Wallis rank sum test

data:   Rating by Role
Kruskal-Wallis chi-squared = 4.6784, df = 2, p-value =
0.09641
```

As in the preceding section, you can use the long-format data frame to create a boxplot of the data.

This time, I use the long format to make another point. Notice that the Kruskal-Wallis test resulted in a p-value higher than .05 and that you couldn't reject the null hypothesis. What if you could have performed an analysis of variance on these data?

```
> survey.aov <- aov(Rating ~ Role, data=FK.survey.long)
> summary(survey.aov)
            Df Sum Sq Mean Sq F value Pr(>F)
Role         2  958.1   479.1    3.74 0.0481 *
Residuals   15 1921.5   128.1
---
Signif. codes: 0 '***' 0.001 '**' 0.01 '*' 0.05 '.' 0.1 ' ' 1
```

The analysis of variance tells you to reject the null hypothesis (with the same data!).

This example makes an important point: Most of the time, a non-parametric test is less powerful (has less ability to reject H_0) than its corresponding parametric test.

Another important point: When checking a statistical analysis, make sure the analyst used the right kind of statistic. If the analysis is based on a parametric test, was that test the right one to use? If not, did it result in an inappropriate rejection of the null hypothesis?

Matched Samples

The non-parametric tests I show you in this section are analogous to the matched groups t-test and to the repeated measures analysis of variance.

Two samples: Wilcoxon matched-pairs signed ranks

This test works with the differences between matched pairs. It goes a bit further than that, though. In addition to the direction of the differences, the Wilcoxon test considers the sizes of the differences. So this test is useful when you have ordinal data, and enough precision that you can rank the differences between pairs.

Here's an example. I use a low number of individuals to show the mechanics of how this test works.

A social worker studies three pairs of identical twins. Each child in a twin-pair either attends a public school or is home-schooled. At the end of a school year, the social worker rates all the children on sociability on a scale of 1 (least sociable) to 100 (most sociable). The null hypothesis is that the public-school children have the same or less sociability than the home-school children. The alternative hypothesis is that the public-school children have greater sociability than the home-school children.

The results, along with some other items, are shown in Table 10-3.

As the name of the test implies, it works with signed ranks — specifically, the signed ranks of differences between pairs. So the first two columns are the data for the children. The third column is the Public-Home difference. The fourth column is the absolute value of the difference. The fifth is the rank of the absolute value of the difference (from lowest to highest). Finally, the sixth column is the rank with the sign of the difference attached to it — and that's what Wilcoxon and I mean by a signed rank.

TABLE 10-3 **Sociability of Public-School Children and Home-School Children (with Each Row Reflecting a Pair of Identical Twins)**

Public	Home	Difference	|Difference|	Rank|Diff|	Signed Rank
64	54	10	10	3	3
44	51	–7	7	2	–2
51	48	3	3	1	1
				Sum of positive signed ranks	4

Different sources will show you different ways of proceeding from here. I'll stick to the way that R uses.

In the bottom row, I've provided the sum of the positive ranks (4). Is this sum large enough to enable you to reject the null hypothesis? The idea is to figure out how many ways you can rearrange the + and − signs in the ranks so that the sum of the positive ranks is 4 or higher. Then I divide that number of arrangements by the total number of possible arrangements of signs. That total number, incidentally, is 2^N, where N is the number of pairs. In this case, that's $2^3 = 8$. If the result of the division is less than .05, I reject the null hypothesis.

How can you arrange the signs to come up with a positive rank sum of 4 or more? The data provides one way of getting to 4 (3, −2, 1) and that's the only one. Another arrangement adds up to 5 (3, 2, −1), and one more adds up to 6 (3, 2, 1). That's three ways of getting a positive rank sum of 4 or higher out of a grand total of 8 possibilities. Thus, the probability of positive rank sum of 4 (the obtained value) or higher is 3/8, which is .375. This is way higher than .05, so you can't reject the null hypothesis.

Here it is in R:

```
> Public <- c(64,44,51)
> Home <- c(54,51,48)
> wilcox.test(Public,Home,paired = TRUE,alternative = "greater")

        Wilcoxon signed rank test

data:  Public and Home
V = 4, p-value = 0.375
alternative hypothesis: true location shift is greater than 0
```

In the `wilcox.test()` function, `paired = TRUE` specifies the signed rank test (rather than the rank-sum test I showed you earlier).

Of course, statisticians use this test on *way* more than three matched pairs. I confined the example to three so that you can see where the numbers come from in the output.

More than two samples: Friedman two-way ANOVA

With ordinal data and more than two matched samples, Friedman's two-way ANOVA is the appropriate non-parametric test. In this test, you rank the data within each individual.

Here's an example. Seven students rate their knowledge of economics, geography, and history on a scale of 1 (least knowledge) to 10 (most knowledge). The data are listed in Table 10-4.

TABLE 10-4 **Ratings of Knowledge in Three Courses from 1 (Least Knowledge) to 10 (Most Knowledge) and Ranks within Each Student**

Student	Economics	Geography	History	Rank (Econ)	Rank (Geog)	Rank (Hist)
Al	9	5	7	3	1	2
Brenda	8	7	9	2	1	3
Chris	2	7	8	1	2	3
Dan	4	5	9	1	2	3
Ella	8	2	7	3	1	2
Fran	5	4	6	2	1	3
Gil	1	9	10	1	2	3
			Sum	13	10	19

The null hypothesis is that the three courses yield no differences, and the alternative hypothesis is that they do. If the null hypothesis is true, the sums of the ranks for each area should be about the same.

Friedman referred to the test statistic as χ_r^2, so I will too. The formula is

$$\chi_r^2 = \left[\frac{12}{Nk(k+1)} \sum R^2 \right] - 3N(k+1)$$

N is the number of individuals, and k is the number of groups (economics, geography, and history). With a large enough sample (more than 9), χ_r^2 is distributed as chi-square with $k-1$ degrees of freedom.

For this example, the statistic works out to

$$\chi_r^2 = \left[\frac{12}{7(3)(3+1)} \left(13^2 + 10^2 + 19^2 \right) \right] - 3(7)(3+1) = 6$$

The probability of obtaining a chi-squared value of 6 or higher with two degrees of freedom is just below .05, so I can reject the null hypothesis:

```
> pchisq(6,2,lower.tail = FALSE)
[1] 0.04978707
```

To do this in R, I first create a data frame called School.Subjects in long format. I start with the data in each column:

```
Econ <- c(9,8,2,4,8,5,1)
Geog <- c(5,7,7,5,2,4,9)
Hist <- c(7,9,8,9,7,6,10)
```

Next, I put those data together in a vector:

```
Rating <- c(Econ,Geog,Hist)
```

Then I create a vector of the courses to line up with the ratings:

```
Course <- c(rep("Econ",7),rep("Geog",7),rep("Hist",7))
```

Next is a vector of student names to line up with the courses and the ratings:

```
Student <- c(rep(c("Al", "Brenda", "Chris", "Dan", "Ella",
    "Fran", "Gil"),3))
```

Finally, I put it all together:

```
School.Subjects <- data.frame(Student,Course,Rating)
```

The first six rows of the data frame look like this:

```
> head(School.Subjects)
   Student Course Rating
1       Al   Econ      9
2   Brenda   Econ      8
3    Chris   Econ      2
4      Dan   Econ      4
5     Ella   Econ      8
6     Fran   Econ      5
```

The test is a function called `friedman.test()`. Here's how I set it up:

```
friedman.test(Rating ~ Course|Student, data=School.Subjects)
```

As always, the term on the left of the tilde is the dependent variable (`Rating`). On the right of the tilde, the two variables on either side of the vertical line represent the *grouping* variable (`Course` — think of each course as a group) and the *blocking* variable (`Student` — think of each row in Table 10-4 as a block, and each row in the table corresponds to a student).

Running this analysis gives you

```
> friedman.test(Rating ~ Course|Student, data=School.Subjects)

        Friedman rank sum test

data:  Rating and Course and Student
Friedman chi-squared = 6, df = 2, p-value = 0.04979
```

As you can see, the function does all the ranking as well as the computation, and the *p*-value indicates rejection of the null hypothesis.

More than two samples: Cochran's *Q*

Wait. What? *Another* test for more than two samples? This one's a different animal. The other tests in this chapter work with ordinal data. This one works with nominal data.

Table 10-5 holds the data for a study of ten people solving anagram problems. The anagram difficulty is either Easy, Medium, or Difficult. If a person solves an anagram within 1 minute, that's a success, denoted by 1. If not, it's a failure, denoted by 0. The fourth column holds each row sum, and the bottom row holds each column sum. I use *L* for the row sums and *G* for the column sums because Cochrane uses those letters in his formula.

And here is the formula:

$$Q = \frac{(k-1)\left[k\sum G^2 - \left(\sum G\right)^2\right]}{k\sum L - \sum L^2}$$

As I said, *L* represents row totals, *G* represents column totals, and *k* is the number of groups (3, in this case). *Q* is distributed approximately as chi-squared with $k-1$ degrees of freedom.

TABLE 10-5

Data for Anagrams Study (1 = Anagram Solved within 1 Minute, 0 = Anagram Not Solved within 1 Minute)

Participant	Easy	Medium	Difficult	L (Row Sum)
Alice	1	0	0	1
Betty	1	1	0	2
Carl	0	1	1	2
Dennis	0	0	0	0
Ed	1	0	0	1
Frank	1	1	0	2
Ginny	1	1	0	2
Harry	0	1	0	1
Ina	1	0	0	1
Jane	0	0	0	0
G (Column Sum)	6	5	1	12

For this example, that works out to

$$Q = \frac{(3-1)\left[3\left(6^2 + 5^2 + 1^2\right) - 12^2\right]}{3\left(1^2 + 2^2 + 2^2 + \ldots + 0^2\right) - 12^2} = 5.25$$

The probability of obtaining a chi-squared value of 5.25 or greater if the null hypothesis is true is .0724. This is higher than .05, indicating nonrejection of the null hypothesis. You can use pchisq() to verify this probability:

```
> pchisq(5.25,2,lower.tail = FALSE)
[1] 0.07243976
```

To carry out this test in R, create a long-format data frame called Anagrams. Start with the data in the columns:

```
Easy <- c(1,1,0,0,1,1,1,0,1,0)
Medium <- c(0,1,1,0,0,1,1,1,0,0)
Difficult <- c(0,0,1,0,0,0,0,0,0,0)
Person <- c("Alice", "Betty", "Carl", "Dennis", "Ed", "Frank",
   "Ginny","Harry","Ina","Jane")
```

Next, create a vector for the dependent variable:

```
Performance <- c(Easy,Medium,Difficult)
```

and another for the difficulty level that lines up with the Performance data:

```
Level <- c(rep("Easy",10), rep("Medium",10),
  rep("Difficult",10))
```

and another for the individuals to line up the names appropriately:

```
Participant <- c(rep(Person,3))
```

Here's the data frame:

```
Anagrams <- data.frame(Participant, Level, Performance)
```

Its first six rows are

```
> head(Anagrams)
  Participant Level Performance
1       Alice  Easy           1
2       Betty  Easy           1
3        Carl  Easy           0
4      Dennis  Easy           0
5          Ed  Easy           1
6       Frank  Easy           1
```

The function cochrane.qtest() lives in a package called RVAideMemoire. On the Packages tab, click Install and type **RVAideMemoire** in the Install Packages dialog box; then click Install. This one takes a while, so be patient. When RVAideMemoire appears on the Packages tab, select its check box.

To apply cochrane.qtest():

```
cochran.qtest(Performance ~ Level|Participant, data=Anagrams)
```

As in friedman.test(), the term on the left of the tilde is the dependent variable. To the right of the tilde, the term on the left of the vertical line (Level) is the grouping variable, and the term on the right of the vertical line (Participant) is the blocking variable. Running this test yields

```
> cochran.qtest(Performance ~ Level|Participant, data=Anagrams)
```

```
Cochran's Q test
data:  Performance by Level, block = Participant
Q = 5.25, df = 2, p-value = 0.07244
alternative hypothesis: true difference in probabilities is not
   equal to 0
sample estimates:
proba in group          <NA>              <NA>
0.1            0.6                0.5
```

The value of Q and the p-value indicate that you can't reject the null hypothesis.

TIP

The quantities on the bottom couple of lines don't line up as well on the page as they do onscreen, and the function doesn't label them appropriately. They're the probabilities of successful solutions in each level. They're supposed to be 0.1 for Difficult, 0.6 for Easy, and 0.5 for Medium.

Correlation: Spearman's r_s

Spearman's correlation coefficient, r_s, was the earliest non-parametric test based on ranks. For a sample of individuals, each measured on two variables, the idea is to rank each score within its own variable. Then, for each individual, subtract one rank from the other. If correlation is perfect (in the positive direction), all differences are zero.

Table 10-6 shows an example. An industrial psychologist rated the sociability of ten employees of the FarDrate Timepiece Corporation. The scale ranged from 1 (least sociable) to 100 (most sociable). Each FarDrate employee also rated their job satisfaction on a scale of 1 (least satisfaction) to 80 (most satisfaction). The null hypothesis is that sociability is not correlated with job satisfaction. The alternative hypothesis is that these two variables are correlated.

The formula is

$$r_S = 1 - \frac{6 \sum d^2}{N^3 - N}$$

where d is an interpair rank difference. As is the case with the regular correlation coefficient (described in Chapter 7 of Book 3), if the null hypothesis is true, the value of r_S should be around zero.

TABLE 10-6 Sociability and Job Satisfaction of 12 FarDrate Employees, Ranks of Each Score, and Rank Difference

Employee	Sociability	Job Satisfaction	Rank Sociability	Rank Job Satisfaction	Rank Difference
Abe	84	78	11	11	0
Bill	33	38	1	2	-1
Carla	91	80	12	12	0
Denise	45	52	4	5	-1
Ernie	67	55	8	6	2
Fred	74	60	10	8	2
Grace	54	77	6	10	-4
Helen	34	56	2	7	-5
Inez	59	32	7	1	6
Jim	71	75	9	9	0
Ken	42	42	3	3	0
Len	53	46	5	4	1

Here's the calculation:

$$r_S = 1 - \frac{6\left(0^2 + (-1)^2 + \ldots + 1^2\right)}{12^3 - 12} = .692308$$

A hypothesis test based on t is also familiar if you've read Chapter 7 of Book 3:

$$t = \frac{r_S\sqrt{N-2}}{\sqrt{1-r_S^2}} = \frac{.692308\sqrt{12-2}}{\sqrt{1-(.692308)^2}} = 3.034$$

N is the number of pairs, and the test has $N-2$ degrees of freedom.

You can use pt() to verify that the two-tailed p-value is less than .05:

```
> pt(3.034,10,lower.tail = FALSE)*2
[1] 0.01259087
```

You can reject the null hypothesis that sociability and job satisfaction are not related.

To set up this analysis in R, create a vector for each variable:

```
Sociability <- c(84,33,91,45,67,74,54,34,59,71,42,53)
Job.sat <-c(78,38,80,52,55,60,77,56,32,75,42,46)
```

and then use cor.test() to calculate r_S. The key is to include method="spearman" as an argument:

```
> cor.test(x=Sociability, y=Job.sat, method="spearman",
  alternative= "two.sided")

          Spearman's rank correlation rho

data:  Sociability and Job.sat
S = 88, p-value = 0.01588
alternative hypothesis: true rho is not equal to 0
sample estimates:
      rho
0.6923077
```

Note that the p-value is a bit different from the value that corresponds to the t-test I just showed you. R uses a different test of significance, although the conclusion is the same. It's based on S (the sum of squared rank differences), which appears on the same line as the p-value.

Correlation: Kendall's Tau

Kendall's tau (τ) is another way of assessing the relationship between two variables. Like Spearman's r_S, it's based on ranks, but it uses the ranks in a different way. Rather than work with the differences between ranks, Kendall's tau is based on *concordant* and *discordant* pairs of ranks.

TIP

In this context, the term *pair of ranks* does *not* mean "a pair of ranks on two variables for one individual." Here, a pair of ranks consists of two values for two different individuals on the same variable.

It's easiest to explain with an example. In Table 10-7, I have those 12 FarDrate employees again. Once again, the null hypothesis is that sociability and job satisfaction are not correlated, and the alternative hypothesis is that they are.

To make the table easier to deal with, I left out the sociability scores and job satis-faction scores and present only the ranks of those scores. Notice in the Employee column that the names aren't in alphabetical order, as in the previous table. That's because I reordered everything in terms of rank sociability, which, as you can see, is in numerical order in Column 2.

TABLE 10-7 **Ranks of Sociability and Job Satisfaction of 12 FarDrate Employees, Ordered by Rank Sociability**

Employee	Rank Sociability	Rank Job Satisfaction	Concordant Pairs	Discordant Pairs
Ben	1	2	10	1
Helen	2	7	5	5
Ken	3	3	8	1
Denise	4	5	6	2
Len	5	4	6	1
Grace	6	10	2	4
Inez	7	1	5	0
Ellen	8	6	4	0
Jim	9	9	2	1
Fred	10	8	2	0
Abe	11	11	1	0
Carla	12	12	0	0
		Sum	51	15

The order for Rank Job Satisfaction in Column 3 is not quite the same as the order in Column 2. In the event of perfect positive correlation, Columns 2 and 3 would match up perfectly, but in this example they don't.

From here, I work with Rank Job Satisfaction for each employee. I'll call it RJS, for short. Ben's RJS is 2. Imagine all possible pairs consisting of 2 and each RJS underneath its row in the table. If RJS is positively correlated with rank sociabil-ity, you'd expect most of the scores underneath Ben's in the table to have a *higher* rank than his. All but one of those RJS-pairs involving Ben and another employee are in the order you'd expect — his RJS of 2 is less than the RJS of ten other employees. Those are concordant pairs. One of those is in the opposite order: Inez (in Row 7) has a *lower* RJS, indicating that the Ben-Inez RJS-pair is discordant. So that's ten concordant pairs for Ben and one discordant pair.

In the same way, I can count the number of concordant pairs for Helen — it's the number of RJSs in the rows underneath hers in the table that are *greater* than her RJS (5). And the number of discordant pairs for Helen is the number of RJSs in the rows underneath hers that are *less* than her RJS (also 5, as it turns out). You can verify the concordant and discordant pairs for the rest of the employees.

The formula for the test statistic is

$$\tau = \frac{C - D}{C + D}$$

where C is the number of concordant pairs and D is the number of discordant pairs. In this example

$$\tau = \frac{51 - 15}{51 + 15} = .5454545$$

What does this number mean? Like the other correlation statistics I've shown you, τ can range from –1.00 (perfect negative correlation) to 1.00 (perfect positive correlation). And, like the other ones, you can test it for significance, but not in the same way.

If the number of pairs (N) is greater than 8, the sampling distribution of τ closely approximates the normal distribution with

$$\mu_\tau = 0$$
$$\sigma_\tau = \sqrt{\frac{2(2N + 5)}{9N(N - 1)}}$$

This means you can convert τ to a z-score:

$$z = \frac{\tau}{\sqrt{\dfrac{2(2N + 5)}{9N(N - 1)}}} = \frac{.54545}{\sqrt{\dfrac{2((2)(12) + 5)}{9(12)(12 - 1)}}} = 2.469$$

The two-tailed p-value for this z is less than .05, so you can reject the null hypothesis:

```
> pnorm(2.469,lower.tail = FALSE)*2
[1] 0.01354912
```

Although Kendall's tau produces a different numerical value than r_s for the same data, they lead to the same conclusion about the null hypothesis.

To do this analysis in R, you use cor().test once again and the vectors from the previous example. The only difference is to specify method = "kendall":

```
> cor.test(x = Sociability, y=Job.sat, method="kendall",
  alternative= "two.sided")


          Kendall's rank correlation tau

data:  Sociability and Job.sat
T = 51, p-value = 0.01377
alternative hypothesis: true tau is not equal to 0
sample estimates:
     tau
0.5454545
```

The *p*-value is slightly different from the value I just showed you from the normal distribution. It's based on the sampling distribution of *T*, the number of concordant pairs. With either *p*-value, the conclusion is the same: Reject the null hypothesis.

So, which correlation statistic should you use? Both Spearman's and Kendall's lead to the same decision about the null hypothesis, even though they produce different numbers.

Spearman's r_s is more of an analog of the regular correlation coefficient, if that's a criterion for you. In fact, if you plug the ranks of scores into the correlation coefficient formula I show you in Chapter 7 of Book 3, you'll wind up with r_s.

Kendall's tau has a somewhat esoteric advantage: You can use it as the basis for a partial correlation coefficient — a measure of association between two variables if both are related to a third variable. (I discuss this topic in Chapter 7 of Book 3.) On the other hand, I'm not sure how often you'll require something like that in the non-parametric world.

A Heads-Up

Here are a couple of things to be aware of. First, I didn't put any tied ranks in these examples: Ties present a few wrinkles for the rank-based statistics (except for the Friedman two-way ANOVA), and I wanted to avoid all that. Also, an additional non-parametric test is lurking nearby: In Chapter 11 of Book 3, you find hypothesis testing based on the binomial distribution.

Chapter **11**

Introducing Probability

P robability is the basis of hypothesis testing and inferential statistics, so I use this concept throughout the book. (Seems like a fine time to introduce it!)

Most of the time, I represent probability as the proportion of area under part of a distribution. For example, the probability of a Type I error (also known as α) is the area in a tail of the standard normal distribution, or in a tail of the t distribution.

It's time to examine probability in greater detail, including random variables, permutations, and combinations. I show you some fundamentals and applications of probability, and then I focus on a couple of specific *probability distributions*. I also tell you about some probability-related R functions.

What Is Probability?

Most people have an intuitive idea of probability. Toss a fair coin, and you have a 50–50 chance that it comes up heads. Toss a fair die (one of a pair of dice) and you have a 1-in-6 chance that it comes up displaying a 2.

If you want to be more formal in your definition, you'd most likely say something about all the possible things that could happen, and the proportion of those things you care about. Two things can happen when you toss a coin, and if you care about only one of them (heads), the probability of that event happening is one out of two. Six things can happen when you toss a die, and if you care about only one of them (2), the probability of that event happening is one out of six.

Experiments, trials, events, and sample spaces

Statisticians and others who work with probability refer to a process like tossing a coin or throwing a die as an *experiment.* Each time you go through the process, that's a *trial.*

This might not fit your personal definition of an experiment (or of a trial, for that matter), but for a statistician an *experiment* is any process that produces one of at least two distinct results (like heads or tails).

Here's another piece of the definition of an experiment: You can't predict the result with certainty. Each distinct result is called an *elementary outcome.* Put a bunch of elementary outcomes together and you have an *event.* For example, with a die the elementary outcomes 2, 4, and 6 make up the event "even number."

Put all the possible elementary outcomes together and you've got yourself a *sample space.* The numbers 1, 2, 3, 4, 5, and 6 make up the sample space for a die. Heads and tails make up the sample space for a coin.

Sample spaces and probability

How do events, outcomes, and sample spaces play into probability? If each elementary outcome in a sample space is equally likely, the probability of an event is

$$\text{pr}(\text{Event}) = \frac{\text{Number of Elementary Outcomes in the Event}}{\text{Number of Elementary Outcomes in the Sample Space}}$$

So the probability of tossing a die and getting an even number is

$$\text{pr}(\text{Even Number}) = \frac{\text{Number of Even-Numbered Elementary Outcomes}}{\text{Number of Possible Outcomes of a Die}} = \frac{3}{6} = .5$$

If the elementary outcomes are not equally likely, you find the probability of an event in a different way. First, you have to have some way to assign a probability to each one. Then you add up the probabilities of the elementary outcomes that make up the event.

A couple of things to bear in mind about outcome probabilities:

» Each probability has to be between 0 and 1.

» All the probabilities of elementary outcomes in a sample space have to add up to 1.00.

How do you assign those probabilities? Sometimes you have advance information — such as knowing that a coin is biased toward coming up heads 60 percent of the time. Sometimes, you just have to think through the situation to figure out the probability of an outcome.

Here's a quick example of how to "think through the situation." Suppose a die is biased so that the probability of an outcome is proportional to the numerical label of the outcome: A 6 comes up six times as often as a 1, a 5 comes up five times as often as a 1, and so on. What is the probability of each outcome? All the probabilities have to add up to 1.00, and all the numbers on a die add up to 21 (1+2+3+4+5+6 = 21), so the probabilities are pr(1) = 1/21, pr(2) = 2/21, . . ., pr(6) = $\frac{6}{21}$.

Compound Events

Some rules for dealing with *compound events* help you "think through." A compound event consists of more than one event. It's possible to combine events by either *union* or *intersection* (or both).

Union and intersection

On the toss of a fair die, what's the probability of rolling a 1 or a 4? Mathematicians have a symbol for *or*. It's called *union*, and it looks like this: $\cup$. Using this symbol, the probability of a 1 or a 4 is $pr(1 \cup 4)$.

In approaching this kind of probability, it's helpful to keep track of the elementary outcomes. One elementary outcome is in each event, so the event "1 or 4" has two elementary outcomes. With a sample space of six outcomes, the probability is $\frac{2}{6}$, or $\frac{1}{3}$. Another way to calculate this is

$$pr(1 \cup 4) = pr(1) + pr(4) = \frac{1}{6} + \frac{1}{6} = \frac{2}{6} = \frac{1}{3}$$

Here's a slightly more involved question: What's the probability of rolling a number between 1 and 3 or a number between 2 and 4?

Just adding the elementary outcomes in each event won't get it done this time. Three outcomes are in the event "between 1 and 3" and three are in the event "between 2 and 4." The probability can't be 3 + 3 divided by the six outcomes in the sample space, because that's 1.00, leaving nothing for $pr(5)$ and $pr(6)$. For the same reason, you can't just add the probabilities.

The challenge arises in the overlap of the two events. The elementary outcomes in "between 1 and 3" are 1, 2, and 3. The elementary outcomes in "between 2 and 4" are 2, 3, and 4. Two outcomes overlap: 2 and 3. In order to not count them twice, the trick is to subtract them from the total.

A couple of conventions will make your life easier as I proceed. I abbreviate "between 1 and 3" as A and "between 2 and 4" as B. Also, I use the mathematical symbol for *overlap*. The symbol is $\cap$ and it's called *intersection*.

Using the symbols, the probability of "between 1 and 3" or "between 2 and 4" is

$$pr(A \cup B) = \frac{\text{Number of Outcomes in A} + \text{Number of Outcomes in B} - \text{Number of Outcomes in } (A \cap B)}{\text{Number of Outcomes in the Sample Space}}$$

$$pr(A \cup B) = \frac{3 + 3 - 2}{6} = \frac{4}{6} = \frac{2}{3}$$

You can also work with the probabilities:

$$pr(A \cup B) = \frac{3}{6} + \frac{3}{6} - \frac{2}{6} = \frac{4}{6} = \frac{2}{3}$$

The general formula is

$$pr(A \cup B) = pr(A) + pr(B) - pr(A \cap B)$$

Why was it okay to just add the probabilities together in the earlier example? Because $pr(1 \cap 4)$ is zero: It's impossible to roll a 1 and a 4 in the same toss of a die. Whenever $pr(A \cap B) = 0$, A and B are said to be *mutually exclusive*.

Intersection, again

Imagine throwing a coin and rolling a die at the same time. These two experiments are *independent* because the result of one has no influence on the result of the other.

What's the probability of getting heads and a 4? You use the intersection symbol and write this as $pr(\text{heads} \cap 4)$:

$$pr(\text{Heads} \cap 4) = \frac{\text{Number of Elementary Outcomes in Heads} \cap 4}{\text{Number of Elementary Outcomes in the Sample Space}}$$

Start with the sample space. Table 11-1 lists all the elementary outcomes.

TABLE 11-1

The Elementary Outcomes in the Sample Space for Throwing a Coin and Rolling a Die

Heads, 1	Tails, 1
Heads, 2	Tails, 2
Heads, 3	Tails, 3
Heads, 4	Tails, 4
Heads, 5	Tails, 5
Heads, 6	Tails, 6

As the table shows, 12 outcomes are possible. How many outcomes are in the event "heads and 4"? Just one. So

$$pr(\text{Heads} \cap 4) = \frac{\text{Number of Elementary Outcomes in Heads} \cap 4}{\text{Number of Elementary Outcomes in the Sample Space}} = \frac{1}{12}$$

You can also work with the probabilities:

$$pr(\text{Heads} \cap 4) = pr(\text{Heads}) \times pr(4) = \frac{1}{12}$$

In general, if A and B are independent,

$$pr(A \cap B) = pr(A) \times pr(B)$$

Conditional Probability

In some circumstances, you narrow the sample space. Suppose that I toss a die and I tell you that the result is greater than 2. What's the probability that it's a 5?

Ordinarily, the probability of a 5 would be ⅙. In this case, however, the sample space isn't 1, 2, 3, 4, 5, and 6. When you know the result is greater than 2, the sample space becomes 3, 4, 5, and 6. The probability of a 5 is now 1/4.

This is an example of *conditional probability*. It's *conditional* because I've given a condition — the toss resulted in a number greater than 2. The notation for this is

$$pr(5 \,|\, \text{Greater than 2})$$

The vertical line (|) is shorthand for the word *given*, and you read that notation as "the probability of a 5 given greater than 2."

Working with the probabilities

In general, if you have two events A and B,

$$pr(A|B) = \frac{pr(A \cap B)}{pr(B)}$$

as long as *pr(B)* isn't zero.

For the intersection in the numerator on the right, this is *not* a case where you just multiply probabilities together. In fact, if you could do that, you wouldn't have a conditional probability, because that would mean A and B are independent. If they're independent, one event can't be conditional on the other.

You have to think through the probability of the intersection. In a die, how many outcomes are in the event "5 ∩ Greater than 2"? Just one, so *pr*(5 ∩ Greater than 2) is ⅙, and

$$pr(5 | \text{Greater than 2}) = \frac{pr(5 \cap \text{Greater than 2})}{pr(\text{Greater than 2})} = \frac{\frac{1}{6}}{\frac{4}{6}} = \frac{1}{4}$$

The foundation of hypothesis testing

All the hypothesis testing I discuss in previous chapters involves conditional probability. When you calculate a sample statistic, compute a statistical test, and then compare the test statistic against a critical value, you're looking for a conditional probability. Specifically, you're trying to find

$$pr(\text{obtained test statistic or a more extreme value} | H_0 \text{ is true})$$

If that conditional probability is low (less than .05 in all the examples I show you in hypothesis-testing chapters), you reject H_0.

Large Sample Spaces

When dealing with probability, it's important to understand the sample space. In the examples I've shown you so far in this chapter, the sample spaces are small. With a coin or a die, it's easy to list all the elementary outcomes.

The world, of course, isn't that simple. In fact, even the probability problems that live in statistics textbooks aren't that simple. Most of the time, sample spaces are large and it's not convenient to list every elementary outcome.

Take, for example, rolling a die twice. How many elementary outcomes are in the sample space consisting of both tosses? You can sit down and list them, but it's better to reason it out: six possibilities for the first toss, and each of those six can pair up with six possibilities on the second. So the sample space has $6 \times 6 = 36$ possible elementary outcomes.

This is similar to the coin-and-die sample space in Table 11-1, where the sample space consists of $2 \times 6 = 12$ elementary outcomes. With 12 outcomes, it was easy to list them all in a table. With 36 outcomes, it starts to get, well, dicey. (Sorry.)

Events often require some thought, too. What's the probability of rolling a die twice and totaling 5? You have to count the number of ways the two tosses can total 5 and then divide by the number of elementary outcomes in the sample space (36). You total a 5 by rolling any of these pairs of tosses: 1 and 4, 2 and 3, 3 and 2, or 4 and 1. That totals four ways, and they don't overlap (excuse me — *intersect*), so

$$\text{pr}(5) = \frac{\text{Number of Ways of Rolling a 5}}{\text{Number of Possible Outcomes of Two Tosses}} = \frac{4}{36} = .11$$

Listing all the elementary outcomes for the sample space is often a nightmare. Fortunately, shortcuts are available, as I show in the upcoming subsections. Because each shortcut quickly helps you count a number of items, another name for a shortcut is a *counting rule.*

Believe it or not, I just slipped one counting rule past you. A couple of paragraphs ago, I say that in two tosses of a die, you have a sample space of $6 \times 6 = 36$ possible outcomes. This is the *product rule:* If N_1 outcomes are possible on the first trial of an experiment, and N_2 outcomes are possible on the second trial, the number of possible outcomes is $N_1 N_2$. Each possible outcome on the first trial can associate with all possible outcomes on the second. What about three trials? That's $N_1 N_2 N_3$.

Now for a couple more counting rules.

Permutations

Suppose you have to arrange five objects into a sequence. How many ways can you do that? For the first position in the sequence, you have five choices. After you make that choice, you have four choices for the second position. Then you have three choices for the third, two for the fourth, and one for the fifth. The number of ways is $(5)(4)(3)(2)(1) = 120$.

In general, the number of sequences of N objects is N(N−1)(N−2) . . . (2)(1). This kind of computation occurs fairly frequently in the probability world, and it has its own notation: N! You don't read this by screaming out "N" in a loud voice. Instead, it's "N factorial." By definition, 1! = 1, and 0! = 1.

Now for the good stuff. If you have to order the 26 letters of the alphabet, the number of possible sequences is 26!, a huge number. But suppose the task is to create 5-letter sequences so that no letter repeats in the sequence. How many ways can you do that? You have 26 choices for the first letter, 25 for the second, 24 for the third, 23 for the fourth, 22 for the fifth, and that's it. So that's (26)(25)(24)(23)(22). Here's how that product is related to 26!:

$$\frac{26!}{21!}$$

Each sequence is called a *permutation*. In general, if you take permutations of N things r at a time, the notation is $_NP_r$ (the P stands for *permutation*). The formula is

$$_NP_r = \frac{N!}{(N-r)!}$$

Just for completeness, here's another wrinkle. Suppose that I allow repetitions in these sequences of 5. That is, aabbc is a permissible sequence. In that case, the number of sequences is $26 \times 26 \times 26 \times 26 \times 26$, or, as mathematicians would say, "26 raised to the fifth power." Or, as mathematicians would write, "26^5."

Combinations

In the preceding example, these sequences are different from one another: *abcde, adbce, dbcae,* and on and on and on. In fact, you could come up with 5! = 120 of these different sequences just for the letters *a, b, c, d,* and *e.*

Suppose I add the restriction that one of these sequences is no different from another, and all I'm concerned about is having sets of five nonrepeating letters in no particular order. Each set is called a *combination.* For this example, the number of combinations is the number of permutations divided by 5!:

$$\frac{26!}{5!(21!)}$$

In general, the notation for combinations of N things taken r at a time is $_NC_r$ (the C stands for *combination*). The formula is

$$_NC_r = \frac{N!}{r!(N-r)!}$$

I touch on this topic in Chapter 10 of Book 3. In the context of a statistical test called the Wilcoxon rank-sum test, I use as an example the number of combinations of eight things taken four at a time:

$$_8C_4 = \frac{8!}{4!4!} = 70$$

Now for that completeness wrinkle again. Suppose I allow repetitions in these sequences. How many sequences would I have? It turns out to be equivalent to $N+r-1$ things taken $N-1$ at a time, or $_{N+r-1}C_{N-1}$. For this example, that would be $_{30}C_{25}$.

R Functions for Counting Rules

R provides `factorial()` for finding the factorial of a number:

```
> factorial(6)
[1] 720
```

You can also use this function to find the factorial of each number in a vector:

```
> xx <- c(2,3,4,5,6)
> factorial(xx)
[1]   2   6  24 120 720
```

For combinations, R provides a couple of possibilities. The `choose()` function calculates $_NC_r$ — the number of combinations of N things taken r at a time. So, for eight things taken four at a time (refer to the example from Chapter 10 of Book 3), that's

```
> choose(8,4)
[1] 70
```

To list all the combinations, use `combn()`. I illustrate with $_4C_2$. I have a vector containing the names of four of the Marx Brothers

```
Marx.Bros <- c("Groucho","Chico","Harpo","Zeppo")
```

and I want to list all possible combinations of them taken two at a time:

```
> combn(Marx.Bros,2)
        [,1]      [,2]      [,3]      [,4]    [,5]    [,6]
[1,] "Groucho" "Groucho" "Groucho" "Chico" "Chico" "Harpo"
[2,] "Chico"   "Harpo"   "Zeppo"   "Harpo" "Zeppo" "Zeppo"
```

This matrix tells me that six such combinations are possible, and the two rows in each column show the two names in each combination.

In my view, the best functions for dealing with combinations and permutations are in the `gtools` package. On the Packages tab, click Install and then in the Install Packages dialog box type **gtools** and click Install. After it downloads, on the Packages tab find `gtools` and select its check box.

Here are the `combinations()` and `permutations()` functions from `gtools` at work:

```
> combinations(4,2,v=Marx.Bros)
     [,1]       [,2]
[1,] "Chico"    "Groucho"
[2,] "Chico"    "Harpo"
[3,] "Chico"    "Zeppo"
[4,] "Groucho"  "Harpo"
[5,] "Groucho"  "Zeppo"
[6,] "Harpo"    "Zeppo"

> permutations(4,2,v=Marx.Bros)
      [,1]       [,2]
 [1,] "Chico"    "Groucho"
 [2,] "Chico"    "Harpo"
 [3,] "Chico"    "Zeppo"
 [4,] "Groucho"  "Chico"
 [5,] "Groucho"  "Harpo"
 [6,] "Groucho"  "Zeppo"
 [7,] "Harpo"    "Chico"
 [8,] "Harpo"    "Groucho"
 [9,] "Harpo"    "Zeppo"
[10,] "Zeppo"    "Chico"
[11,] "Zeppo"    "Groucho"
[12,] "Zeppo"    "Harpo"
```

For each function, the first argument is N, the second is r, and the third is the vector containing the items. Without the vector, here's what happens:

```
> combinations(4,2)
     [,1] [,2]
[1,]   1    2
[2,]   1    3
[3,]   1    4
[4,]   2    3
[5,]   2    4
[6,]   3    4
```

If all you want to do is solve for the number of combinations:

```
> nrow(combinations(4,2))
[1] 6
```

Of course, you can do the same for permutations.

Random Variables: Discrete and Continuous

Let me go back to tosses of a fair die, where six elementary outcomes are possible. If I use *x* to refer to the result of a toss, *x* can be any whole number from 1 to 6. Because *x* can take on a set of values, it's a variable. Because *x*'s possible values correspond to the elementary outcomes of an experiment (meaning you can't predict its values with absolute certainty), *x* is called a *random variable.*

Random variables come in two varieties. One variety is discrete, of which die-tossing is a good example. A *discrete* random variable can take on only what mathematicians like to call a *countable* number of values — like the numbers 1 through 6. Values between the whole numbers 1 through 6 (like 1.25 and 3.1416) are impossible for a random variable that corresponds to the outcomes of die tosses.

The other kind of random variable is continuous: A *continuous* random variable can take on an infinite number of values. Temperature is an example. Depending on the precision of a thermometer, having temperatures like 34.516 degrees is possible.

Probability Distributions and Density Functions

Back again to die-tossing. Each value of the random variable *x* (1–6, remember) has a probability. If the die is fair, each probability is ⅙. Pair each value of a discrete random variable like *x* with its probability, and you have a *probability distribution.*

Probability distributions are easy enough to represent in graphs. Figure 11-1 shows the probability distribution for *x.*

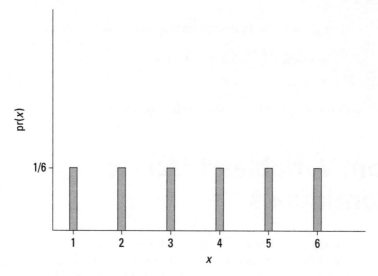

FIGURE 11-1:
The probability
distribution for *x*,
a random
variable based
on the tosses of a
fair die.

A random variable has a mean, a variance, and a standard deviation. Calculating these parameters is pretty straightforward. In the random-variable world, the mean is called the *expected value,* and the expected value of random variable *x* is abbreviated as *E(x).* Here's how you calculate it:

$$E(x) = \sum x(pr(x))$$

For the probability distribution in Figure 11-1, that's

$$E(x) = \sum x(pr(x)) = (1)\left(\frac{1}{6}\right) + (2)\left(\frac{1}{6}\right) + (3)\left(\frac{1}{6}\right) + (4)\left(\frac{1}{6}\right) + (5)\left(\frac{1}{6}\right) + (6)\left(\frac{1}{6}\right) = 3.5$$

The variance of a random variable is often abbreviated as *V(x),* and the formula is

$$V(x) = \sum x^2(pr(x)) - [E(x)]^2$$

Working with the probability distribution in Figure 11-1 once again:

$$V(x) = (1^2)\left(\frac{1}{6}\right) + (2^2)\left(\frac{1}{6}\right) + (3^2)\left(\frac{1}{6}\right) + (4^2)\left(\frac{1}{6}\right) + (5^2)\left(\frac{1}{6}\right) + (6^2)\left(\frac{1}{6}\right) - [3.5]^2 = 2.917$$

The standard deviation is the square root of the variance, which in this case is 1.708.

For continuous random variables, things get a little trickier. You can't pair a value with a probability, because you can't really pin down a value. Instead, you associate a continuous random variable with a mathematical rule (an equation) that generates *probability density,* and the distribution is called a *probability density function.* To calculate the mean and variance of a continuous random variable, you need calculus.

In Chapter 6 of Book 2, I show you a probability density function — the standard normal distribution. I reproduce it here as Figure 11-2.

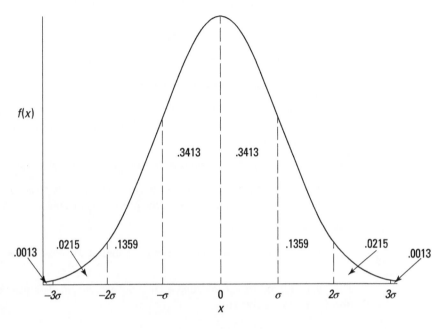

FIGURE 11-2:
The standard
normal
distribution:
a probability
density function.

In the figure, $f(x)$ represents the probability density. Because probability density can involve some heavyweight mathematical concepts, I won't go into it. As I mention in Chapter 6 of Book 2, you can think of probability density as something that turns the area under the curve into probability.

Although you can't speak of the probability of a specific value of a continuous random variable, you can work with the probability of an interval. To find the probability that the random variable takes on a value within an interval, you find the proportion of the total area under the curve that's inside that interval. Figure 11-2 shows this concept. The probability that x is between 0 and 1σ is .3413.

For the rest of this chapter, I deal just with discrete random variables. A specific one is up next.

The Binomial Distribution

Imagine an experiment that has these five characteristics:

» The experiment consists of *N* identical trials.

A trial could be the toss of a die or the toss of a coin.

» Each trial results in one of two elementary outcomes.

It's standard to call one outcome a *success* and the other a *failure.* For die-tossing, a success might be a toss that comes up 3, in which case a failure is any other outcome.

» The probability of a success remains the same from trial to trial.

Again, it's pretty standard to use *p* to represent the probability of a success and to use *1–p* (or *q*) to represent the probability of a failure.

» The trials are independent.

» The discrete random variable *x* is the number of successes in the *N* trials.

This type of experiment is called a *binomial experiment.* The probability distribution for *x* follows this rule:

$$pr(x) = \frac{N!}{x!(n-x)!} p^x (1-p)^{N-x}$$

On the extreme right, $p^x(1-p)^{N-x}$ is the probability of one combination of *x* successes in *N* trials. The term to its immediate left is $_NC_x$, the number of possible combinations of *x* successes in *N* trials.

This is called the *binomial distribution.* You use it to find probabilities like the probability you'll get four 3s in ten tosses of a die:

$$pr(4) = \frac{10!}{4!(6!)}\left(\frac{1}{6}\right)^4\left(\frac{5}{6}\right)^6 = .054$$

The *negative binomial distribution* is closely related. In this distribution, the random variable is the number of trials before the *x*th success. For example, you use the negative binomial to find the probability of five tosses that result in anything but a 3 before the fourth time you roll a 3.

For this to happen, in the eight tosses before the fourth 3, you have to get five non-3s and three successes (tosses when a 3 comes up). Then the next toss results in a 3. The probability of a combination of four successes and five failures is $p^4(1-p)^5$. The number of ways you can have a combination of five failures and four-to-one successes is $_{5+4-1}C_{4-1}$. So the probability is

$$pr(5 \text{ failures before the 4th success}) = \frac{(5+4-1)!}{(4-1)!(5!)}\left(\frac{1}{6}\right)^4\left(\frac{5}{6}\right)^5 = .017$$

In general, the negative binomial distribution (sometimes called the *Pascal distribution*) is

$$pr(f \text{ failures before the } x\text{th success}) = \frac{(f+x-1)!}{(x-1)!(f!)}p^x(1-p)^f$$

The Binomial and Negative Binomial in R

R provides `binom` functions for the binomial distribution, and `nbinom` functions for the negative binomial distribution. For both distributions, I work with die tosses so that p (the probability of a success) = ⅙.

Binomial distribution

As is the case for other built-in distributions, R provides these functions for the binomial distribution: `dbinom()` (density function), `pbinom()` (cumulative distribution function), `qbinom()` (quantiles), and `rbinom()` (random number generation).

To show you a binomial distribution, I use `dbinon()` to plot the density function for the number of successes in ten tosses of a fair die. I begin by creating a vector for the number of successes:

```
successes <- seq(0,10)
```

and then a vector for the associated probabilities:

```
probability <- dbinom(successes,10,1/6)
```

The first argument, of course, is the vector of successes, the second is the number of trials, and the third (⅙) is the probability of a success with a fair 6-sided die.

To plot this density function:

```
ggplot(NULL,aes(x=successes,y=probability))+
  geom_bar(stat="identity",width=1,color="white")
```

The NULL argument in `ggplot()` indicates that I haven't created a data frame — I'm just using the `successes` and `probability` vectors. In `geom_bar()`, the `stat= "identity"` argument indicates that the values in the `probability` vector set the heights of the bars, `width = 1` widens the bars a bit from the default width, and `color = "white"` adds clarity by drawing a white border around each bar. The code creates Figure 11-3.

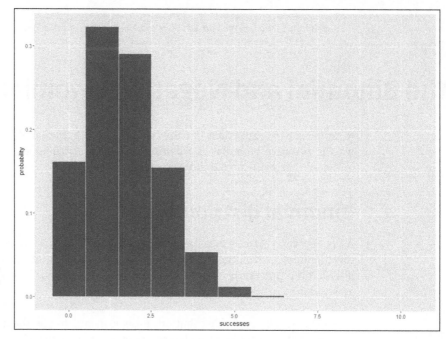

FIGURE 11-3:
Binomial
distribution of
the number of
successes in
ten tosses of a
fair die.

Next, I use `pbinom()` to show you the cumulative distribution for the number of successes in ten tosses of a fair die:

```
cumulative <-pbinom(successes,10,1/6)
```

And here's the code for the plot:

```
ggplot(NULL,aes(x=successes,y=cumulative))+
  geom_step()
```

The second statement produces the stepwise function you see in Figure 11-4.

Each step represents the probability of getting *x* or fewer successes in ten tosses.

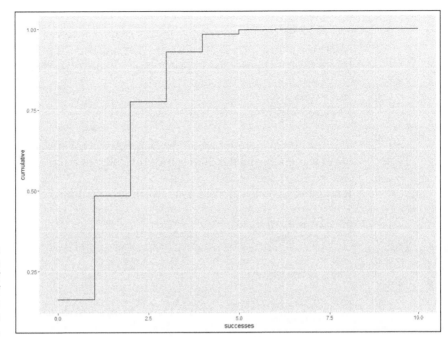

FIGURE 11-4:
Cumulative
distribution of
the number of
successes in
ten tosses of a
fair die.

The qbinom() function computes quantile information. For every fifth quantile from the 10th through the 95th in the binomial distribution with $N = 10$ and $p = \frac{1}{6}$:

```
> qbinom(seq(.10,.95,.05),10,1/6)
 [1] 0 0 1 1 1 1 1 1 2 2 2 2 2 2 3 3 3 4
```

To sample five random numbers from this binomial distribution

```
> rbinom(5, 10, 1/6)
 [1] 4 3 3 0 2
```

Negative binomial distribution

For the negative binomial functions, dnbinom() provides the density function, pnbinom() gives you the cumulative distribution function, qnbinom() gives quantile information, and rnbinom() produces random numbers.

The example I show you earlier in this chapter involves the number of failures before the fourth success of a die toss. That case was the probability of five failures before the fourth toss, and I use dnbinom() to calculate that probability:

```
> dnbinom(5,4,1/6)
[1] 0.01736508
```

The first argument to dnbinom() is the number of failures, the second is the number of successes, and the third is the probability of a success.

If I want to know the probability of five or fewer failures before the fourth success:

```
> pnbinom(5,4,1/6)
[1] 0.04802149
```

which is the same as

```
> sum(dnbinom(seq(0,5),4,1/6))
[1] 0.04802149
```

For every fifth quantile from the 10th through 95th of the number of failures before four successes (with $p = \frac{1}{6}$):

```
> qnbinom(seq(.10,.95,.05),4,1/6)
 [1]  8  9 11 12 13 14 16 17 18 20 21 22 24 26 28 31 35 41
```

And to sample five random numbers from the negative binomial with four successes and $p = \frac{1}{6}$:

```
> rnbinom(5, 4, 1/6)
[1] 10  5  4 23  7
```

Hypothesis Testing with the Binomial Distribution

Hypothesis tests sometimes involve the binomial distribution. Typically, you have some idea about the probability of a success, and you put that idea into a null hypothesis. Then you perform N trials and record the number of successes. Finally, you compute the probability of getting that many successes or a more extreme amount if your H_0 is true. If the probability is low, reject H_0.

When you test in this way, you're using sample statistics to make an inference about a population parameter. Here, that parameter is the probability of a success in the population of trials. By convention, Greek letters represent parameters. Statisticians use π (pi), the Greek equivalent of p, to stand for the probability of a success in the population.

Continuing with the die-tossing example, suppose you have a die and you want to test whether it's fair. You suspect that it's not — it seems to be biased toward 3. Define a toss that results in 3 as a success. You toss it ten times. Five tosses are successes. Casting all this into hypothesis-testing terms:

$H_0: \pi \leq 1/6$

$H_1: \pi > 1/6$

As I usually do, I set $\alpha = .05$.

To test these hypotheses, you have to find the probability of rolling at least four successes in ten tosses with $p = 1/6$. That probability is $pr(5) + pr(6) + pr(7) + pr(8) + pr(9) + pr(10)$. If the total is less than .05, reject H_0.

Once upon a time, that would have been a lot of calculating. With R, not so much. The function `binom.test()` does all the work:

```
binom.test(5,10,1/6, alternative="greater")
```

The first argument is the number of successes, the second is the number of tosses, the third is π, and the fourth is the alternative hypothesis. Running this function produces

```
> binom.test(5,10,1/6, alternative="greater")

        Exact binomial test

data:  5 and 10
number of successes = 5, number of trials = 10,
p-value = 0.01546
alternative hypothesis: true probability of success is greater than 0.1666667
95 percent confidence interval:
 0.2224411 1.0000000
sample estimates:
probability of success
             0.5
```

The p-value (0.01546) is much less than .05, and that tells me to reject the null hypothesis. Also, note the additional information about confidence intervals and the estimated probability of a success (the number of obtained successes divided by number of trials).

If you've been following the discussion about the binomial distribution, you know that two other ways of calculating that p-value are

```
> sum(dbinom(seq(5,10),10,1/6))
[1] 0.01546197
```

and

```
> 1-pbinom(4,10,1/6)
[1] 0.01546197
```

Any way you slice it, the decision is to reject the null hypothesis.

More on Hypothesis Testing: R versus Tradition

When $N \pi \geq 5$ (number of trials × the hypothesized probability of a success) and $N(1-\pi) \geq 5$ (number of trials × the hypothesized probability of a failure) are both greater than 5, the binomial distribution approximates the standard normal distribution. In those cases, statistics textbooks typically tell you to use the statistics of the normal distribution to answer questions about the binomial distribution. For the sake of tradition, let's carry that through and then compare with `binom.test()`.

Those statistics involve z-scores, which means that you have to know the mean and the standard deviation of the binomial. Fortunately, they're easy to compute. If N is the number of trials and π is the probability of a success, the mean is

$$\mu = N\pi$$

the variance is

$$\sigma^2 = N\pi(1-\pi)$$

and the standard deviation is

$$\sigma = \sqrt{N\pi(1-\pi)}$$

When you test a hypothesis, you're making an inference about π and you have to start with an estimate. You run N trials and get x successes. The estimate is

$$P = \frac{x}{N}$$

To create a z-score, you need one more piece of information — the standard error of P. This sounds harder than it is, because this standard error is just

$$\sigma_P = \sqrt{\frac{\pi(1-\pi)}{N}}$$

Now you're ready for a hypothesis test.

Here's an example. The CEO of FarKlempt Robotics, Inc., believes that 50 percent of FarKlempt robots are purchased for home use. A sample of 1,000 FarKlempt customers indicates that 550 of them use their robots at home. Is this significantly different from what the CEO believes? The hypotheses:

$H_0: \pi = .50$

$H_1: \pi \neq .50$

I set $\alpha = .05$, $N\pi = 500$, and $N(1-\pi) = 500$, so the normal approximation is appropriate.

First, calculate P:

$$P = \frac{x}{N} = \frac{550}{1000} = .55$$

Now create a z-score:

$$z = \frac{P - \pi}{\sqrt{\dfrac{\pi(1-\pi)}{N}}} = \frac{.55 - .50}{\sqrt{\dfrac{(.50)(1-.50)}{1000}}} = \frac{.05}{\sqrt{\dfrac{.25}{1000}}} = 3.162$$

With $\alpha = .05$, is 3.162 a large enough z-score to reject H_0?

```
> pnorm(3.162,lower.tail = FALSE)*2
[1] 0.001566896
```

This is much less than .05, so the decision is to reject H_0.

With a little thought, you can see why statisticians recommended this procedure back in the day. To compute the exact probability, you have to calculate the probability of at least 550 successes in 1,000 trials. That would be $pr(550) + pr(551) + \ldots + pr(1000)$, so an approximation based on a well-known distribution was most welcome — particularly in statistics textbooks.

But now

```
> binom.test(550,1000,.5,alternative="two.sided")

    Exact binomial test

data:   550 and 1000
number of successes = 550, number of trials = 1000,
p-value = 0.001731
alternative hypothesis: true probability of success is not equal to 0.5
95 percent confidence interval:
 0.5185565 0.5811483
sample estimates:
probability of success
                  0.55
```

Voilà! The `binom.test()` function calculates the exact probability in the blink of an eye. As you can see, the exact probability (0.001731) differs slightly from the normally approximated p-value, but the conclusion (reject H_0) is the same.

Chapter **12**

Probability Meets Regression: Logistic Regression

In this chapter, I explore a type of regression that's different from any regression analysis I discuss in Chapters 6 and 8 of Book 3. The regression you may have already heard about involves a continuous dependent variable whose value you predict from a continuous independent variable (or from a set of independent variables). You make that prediction on the basis of data on each independent variable.

In this new-and-different type of regression, the dependent variable is the probability of a "success" of a binary event — like, say, if a person decides to buy a product (success) or not (failure) after spending some time looking at an ad for the product. "Time spent looking at the ad" is the independent variable.

The goal is to estimate the probability of buying the product based on how much time the person looks at the ad. The dependent variable is continuous, and because it's probability, it has a minimum value of 0 and a maximum value of 1. (See Chapter 11 of Book 3.)

This is called *logistic regression*.

As with all regression analyses, you start with data. Table 12-1 shows data for 24 people. The first column shows the time each person spent (in seconds) looking at the ad, and the second shows the outcome — whether they bought the product (1) or didn't (0).

TABLE 12-1   **Time (in Seconds) Spent Looking at an Ad and the Outcome (1 = Bought the Product, 0 = Did Not Buy the Product)**

Seconds	Outcome
10	0
12	0
15	0
17	0
22	0
23	0
23	1
24	1
25	0
28	1
30	0
33	1
35	0
36	0
38	1
40	0
42	0
45	1
47	1
50	1
52	1
53	1
55	1
60	1

Because the only possible values for the dependent variable are 0 and 1, the scatterplot is unlike any you've seen. Figure 12-1 shows the scatterplot.

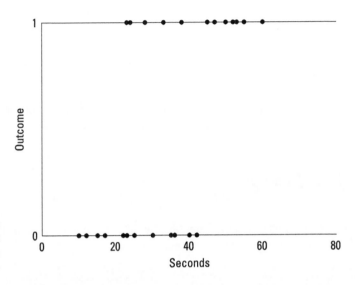

FIGURE 12-1:
The scatterplot
for the data in
Table 12-1.

What would a graph of a logistic regression model look like? Intuitively, you might think it looks something like Figure 12-2, and you'd be right.

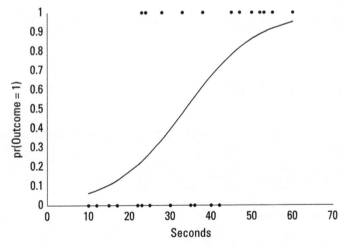

FIGURE 12-2:
Logistic
regression model
for the data in
Table 12-1.

The function (that curved line) in Figure 12-2 is the solution to this equation:

$$\hat{p} = \frac{e^{a+b*Seconds}}{\left(1+e^{a+b*Seconds}\right)}$$

TIP

If you don't know what *e* represents, read the sections "What Is a Logarithm?" and "What Is e?" in Chapter 8 of Book 3.

So logistic regression is all about finding values for *a* and *b* that result in the function that best fits the data. In linear regression, the idea is to find the best-fitting line that minimizes the sum of the squared residuals. By contrast, logistic regression finds the best fit by using an algorithm called *maximum likelihood method* repeatedly on the data to converge on the values for the regression coefficients.

I won't discuss the nuts and bolts of how the maximum likelihood method works. What I will show you is how to do a logistic regression analysis in R.

Getting the Data

I begin by building a data frame for the data in Table 12-1. First, I create a vector for seconds, and another for outcome:

```
> seconds <- c(10,12,15,17,22,23,23,24,25,28,30,33,35,36,38,40,42,45,47,50,52,
  53,55,60)
> outcome <- c(0,0,0,0,0,0,1,1,0,1,0,1,0,0,1,0,0,1,1,1,1,1,1,1)
```

Now for the data frame:

```
ad_frame <- data.frame(seconds, outcome)
```

Doing the Analysis

The analysis is based on the glm() function (general linear model), and it's easy to do:

```
> logistic_model <- glm(outcome ~ seconds, data=ad_frame, family = binomial)
```

To show the results, I use summary():

```
> summary(logistic_model)
```

Running that function causes this to appear:

```
Call:
glm(formula = outcome ~ seconds, family = binomial, data = ad_frame)
```

```
Deviance Residuals:
     Min        1Q    Median        3Q       Max
-1.59143  -0.73781  -0.02316   0.65094   1.71988


Coefficients:
            Estimate Std. Error z value Pr(>|z|)
(Intercept) -3.82981    1.60984  -2.379   0.0174 *
seconds      0.11345    0.04566   2.484   0.0130 *
---
Signif. codes:  0 '***' 0.001 '**' 0.01 '*' 0.05 '.' 0.1 ' ' 1


(Dispersion parameter for binomial family taken to be 1)

    Null deviance: 33.271  on 23  degrees of freedom
Residual deviance: 23.591  on 22  degrees of freedom
AIC: 27.591


Number of Fisher Scoring iterations: 4
```

Quite a bit of complex math is connected to the elements of this output, so I don't discuss them in detail.

The highlights are the two regression coefficients. The intercept coefficient (−3.82891) and the seconds coefficient (0.11345) tell you that the logistic regression equation for this data set is

$$\hat{p} = \frac{e^{-3.82891+0.11345*Seconds}}{\left(1+e^{-3.82891+0.11345*Seconds}\right)}$$

Each coefficient divided by its standard error results in its z-score. As the listing shows, each z-score has a probability less than .05, so you'd conclude that these regression coefficients do a good job of predicting the probabilities.

TIP

The terms *null deviance* and *residual deviance* that show up in the output are additional indicators of how well the model fits the data. *Deviance* is something like *variance*, but because of the associated math, it's more complicated, so I don't dwell on it.

Still, you can draw some analogies with variance in linear regression. Null deviance shows how well the model fits if you just use the intercept as a predictor. It's reminiscent of SS_{Total} in linear regression. Residual deviance shows the fit when you add the independent variable (seconds) to the model. This one is like $SS_{Residual}$ in linear regression — it reflects how much the model *doesn't* account for. Ideally, you want to see a large difference between the two. That difference is analogous to $SS_{Regression}$ in linear regression — the SS that shows how much the model *does* account for. (See Chapters 6 and 7 in Book 3.)

In linear regression, remember (or go back and look), you calculate R² (an indicator of fit) by dividing the $SS_{Regression}$ by the SS_{Total}. The Nobel laureate Daniel McFadden pointed out that you can calculate a Pseudo R-squared for logistic regression, by finding the difference between the null deviance and the residual deviance and then dividing that difference by the null deviance.

It would seem that the difference between the two deviances is important enough conceptually to have its own name. I haven't been able to find one, so I unofficially call it *regression component* from here on out. That way, I can say: You divide the regression component by the null deviance to produce McFadden's Pseudo R-squared:

```
> regression.component <- logistic_model$null.deviance-logistic_model$deviance
```

TIP

Notice that you use $null.deviance to extract the model's null deviance, but you use $deviance to extract the residual deviance:

```
> regression.component
[1] 9.680063
> pseudoR2 <- regression.component/logistic_model$null.deviance
> pseudoR2
[1] 0.2909454
```

So the regression component accounts for 29 percent of the null deviance.

How do you make sense of the size of the regression component? Is a statistical test available?

Absolutely.

In Chapter 2 of Book 3, I discuss the chi-square distribution as a way of testing hypotheses about variances. It turns out (for reasons too technical to go into) that you can treat the regression component as a value in a chi-square distribution with degrees of freedom equal to the number of predictor variables in the model. If the distribution yields a low probability (less than .05) of a regression component as large as the one you observe, you can conclude that the regression component is significant and the model is a good predictor.

The expected value of a chi-square distribution is its degrees of freedom. In this case, df = 1 (because you have one predictor, Seconds). The regression component is 9.680063, so the question becomes "How probable is a value as high as 9.68003 in a chi-square distribution whose expected value is 1?"

Short answer: Not very.

Long answer:

```
> pchisq(regression.component,df=1,lower.tail = FALSE)
[1] 0.001862782
```

That very low probability means it's unlikely that the value of the regression component is due to chance.

So the regression component is a big piece of the pie. Accounting for 29 percent of the null deviance with just one predictor is a pretty good job.

By the way, Fisher scoring (displayed at the bottom of the `glm()` function's output) is the name of the maximum likelihood algorithm I mention earlier in this chapter. It cycles through the data a number of times (4, in this case) to converge on the best estimates for the coefficients. Is this Fisher the same guy that the F-ratio is named after? Yes, he is!

Visualizing the Results

In this section, I show you how to use `ggplot()` to create a graph that looks like the one in Figure 12-2.

To help you in this venture, `glm()` kindly provides a vector of the predicted values. If you want to see them:

```
> logistic_model$fitted.values
```

I'd show you all the values, but the display would look ugly on this page.

So, make sure you have `ggplot2` installed and open for business:

```
> library(ggplot2)
```

Three statements get the job done. The first,

```
ggplot(ad_frame, aes(x=seconds,y=outcome))
```

handles the general layout and labels the axes.

The second,

```
geom_point()
```

adds the data points.

The third,

```
geom_line(aes(y=logistic_model$fitted.values))
```

supplies the logistic regression line according to the model.

Here's how you put them together:

```
> ggplot(ad_frame, aes(x=seconds,y=outcome)) + geom_point() +
    geom_line(aes(y=logistic_model$fitted.values))
```

The result is shown in Figure 12-3, which shows up on R Studio's Plots tab.

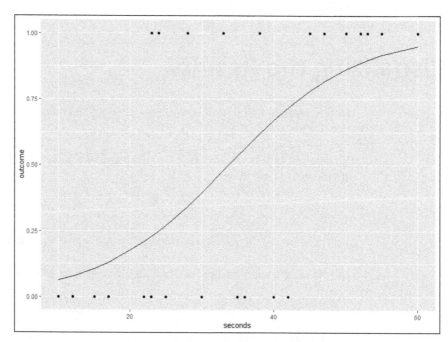

FIGURE 12-3:
Logistic
regression
model plotted
in ggplot().

Logistic regression is a powerful and increasingly popular tool. To acquaint you with its basics, I've just scratched the surface with this simple example.

Ultimately, you'll use it on more complex datasets with much more data and many more predictor variables. When you do, you can use logistic regression to assess which variables aid most in prediction and to filter out the variables that add little value.

4

Learning from Data

Contents at a Glance

Chapter **1**

Tools and Data for Machine Learning Projects

achine learning (ML) is the application of artificial intelligence (AI) to statistics and statistical analysis. ML techniques automate the search for patterns in data. Sometimes, the objective is to figure out a rule for classifying things based on their characteristics: For example, does a particular x-ray mean the x-rayed person is sick or well? Is a particular flower a member of one species or another?

In other efforts, the objective is prediction: Given a sequence of stock market data, will the market go up or down? Given the past three days of weather data, will it rain tomorrow or not?

Think of the characteristics of the x-rays or flowers (or the stock market or weather) as *inputs*. Think of the targets (sick or well, rain or shine) as *outputs*. The learner sees the inputs and their associated outputs and has to come up with some function or rule that characterizes the linkage. Then, when faced with a new input, the learner can apply what it has learned and classify the input (or make a prediction) accordingly.

Learning a function or rule that links inputs with outputs is called *supervised learning*.

If the outputs are categories (sick or well, rain or shine), this is a *classification* problem. If the set of outputs is continuous, it's *regression*.

In another type of learning, the learner receives a set of inputs and the goal is to use the inputs' characteristics to find a structure for the set — to partition the set into subsets, in other words. No specific target outputs are involved.

Early zoologists faced this type of problem. They learned enough about the characteristics of animals to partition "vertebrates" (animals with backbones) into "mammals," "reptiles," "amphibians," "birds," and "fish." Then, whenever they encountered a new animal, they could observe its characteristics and assign it to the appropriate subset. (I'm guessing that assigning whales, bats, dolphins, and duck-billed platypuses to "mammals" might have been a bit dicey at first.)

Discovering the structure in a set of inputs is called *unsupervised learning*.

In any event, a machine learning technique does its work without being explicitly programmed. It changes its behavior on the basis of experience, with the goal of becoming increasingly accurate.

The UCI (University of California-Irvine) ML Repository

For this book's machine learning projects, I work with datasets that reside in the Machine Learning Repository at the University of California-Irvine (home of the Anteaters!). You'll find this repository at

```
https://archive.ics.uci.edu/ml/index.php
```

Working with a UCI dataset

Many (but not all) of the UCI datasets are in comma-separated-value (CSV) format: The data are in text files with a comma between successive values. A typical line in this kind of file looks like this:

```
5.1,3.5,1.4,0.2,Iris-setosa
```

This is the first line from a well-known dataset called iris. The rows are measurements of 150 iris flowers — 50 each of three species of iris. The species are
called *setosa*, *versicolor*, and *virginica*. The data are sepal length, sepal width, petal
length, petal width, and species. One typical ML project is to develop a mechanism
that can learn to use an individual flower's measurements to identify that flower's
species.

TECHNICAL
STUFF

What's a sepal? On a plant that's in bloom, a sepal supports a petal. On an iris,
sepals look something like larger petals underneath the actual petals. In that first
line of the dataset, notice that the first two values (sepal length and width) are
larger than the second two (petal length and width).

You can find iris in numerous places, including the datasets package in base
R. The point of this exercise, however, is to show you how to get and use a dataset
from UCI.

So, to get the data from the UCI ML repository, point your browser to

```
https://archive.ics.uci.edu/ml/datasets/Iris
```

Click on the Data Set Description link. This downloads a page called iris.names.
It has valuable information about the data set, including source material, publications that use the data, column names, and more. In this case, this page is particularly valuable because it tells you about some errors in the data (which I show
you how to fix). The page downloads as a text file. To read it (and you should),
open it with a text editor like Notepad.

Next, click on the Data Folder link. This opens a page that shows iris.data — the
data set I use in this chapter.

You have a couple of choices on how to download the data. Whichever way you
choose, you use the read.csv() function.

One way is to read the data set directly from the web page into R:

```
iris.uci <- read.csv(url("https://archive.ics.uci.edu/ml/machine-learning-
    databases/iris/iris.data"), header=FALSE, col.names = c("sepal.
    length","sepal.width","petal.length","petal.width", "species"))
```

REMEMBER

Make sure you have https:// at the beginning of the URL, and /iris.data at
the end.

The first argument is the URL (the web address). The second argument indicates that the first row of the dataset is a row of data and does *not* provide the names of the columns. The third argument is a vector that assigns the column names. The column names come from iris.names. That page gives class as the name of the last column, but I decided that species is correct. (And that's the name in the iris dataset in the datasets package.)

If you think that's a little too much to put in one function, here's another way:

```
iris.uci <- read.csv(url("https://archive.ics.uci.edu/ml/machine-learning-
    databases/iris/iris.data"), header=FALSE)

colnames(iris.uci)<-c("sepal.length","sepal.width","petal.length","petal.
    width","species")
```

Another way is to download the iris.data file and then read it into R. To do this, click the iris.data link.

This downloads the iris data as a file called iris.data.

To import the iris data into R, use this code:

```
iris.uci <- read.csv("C:\\Users\\jschm\\Downloads\\iris.data",header=FALSE,
    col.names=
c("sepal.length","sepal.width","petal.length","petal.width", "species"))
```

If you think that's too much for one function, code it this way:

```
iris.uci <- read.csv("C:\\Users\\jschm\\Downloads\\iris.data",header=FALSE)
col.names=
c("sepal.length","sepal.width","petal.length","petal.width", "species"))
```

The first argument is the file path of the iris dataset on my Windows computer. (I left it in the Downloads folder, although you don't have to.)

Your file path will, of course, be different from mine!

REMEMBER

Also: Note the double slashes in the file path, and the double quotes around the file path.

TIP

If you've downloaded `iris.data` and you want to avoid file paths, here's another way. Open `iris.data` in Notepad (or any other text editor), press Ctrl+A to select everything on the page, and press Ctrl+C to put all the data on the clipboard. Then

```
iris.uci <- read.csv("clipboard", header=FALSE,
col.names=
c("sepal.length","sepal.width","petal.length","petal.width","species"))
```

gets the job done.

Cleaning up the data

Here are the first six rows of the dataframe:

```
> head(iris.uci)
  sepal.length sepal.width petal.length petal.width     species
1          5.1         3.5          1.4         0.2 Iris-setosa
2          4.9         3.0          1.4         0.2 Iris-setosa
3          4.7         3.2          1.3         0.2 Iris-setosa
4          4.6         3.1          1.5         0.2 Iris-setosa
5          5.0         3.6          1.4         0.2 Iris-setosa
6          5.4         3.9          1.7         0.4 Iris-setosa
```

Correcting errors

In `iris.names` under Relevant Information, this message appears (after some other stuff):

> The 35th sample should be: 4.9,3.1,1.5,0.2,"Iris-setosa" where the error is in the fourth feature.

> The 38th sample: 4.9,3.6,1.4,0.1,"Iris-setosa" where the errors are in the second and third features.

Here is the 35th sample:

```
> iris.uci[35,]
   sepal.length sepal.width petal.length petal.width     species
35          4.9         3.1          1.5         0.1 Iris-setosa
```

To change the fourth feature to `0.2`, type this code into RStudio and run it:

```
iris.uci[35,4]=0.2
```

And now it's correct:

```
> iris.uci[35,]
   sepal.length sepal.width petal.length petal.width    species
35          4.9         3.1          1.5         0.2 Iris-setosa
```

The 38th sample is

```
> iris.uci[38,]
   sepal.length sepal.width petal.length petal.width    species
38          4.9         3.1          1.5         0.1 Iris-setosa
```

This code changes the second and third features to 3.6 and 1.4:

```
> iris.uci[38,2:3]= c(3.6,1.4)
```

So the 38th sample is now

```
> iris.uci[38,]
   sepal.length sepal.width petal.length petal.width    species
38          4.9         3.6          1.4         0.1 Iris-setosa
```

Eliminating the unnecessary

In the species column, every entry begins with Iris-. I'd like to eliminate it from every entry. I do that with a function called mapvalues() that lives in the plyr package. Its usage is pretty straightforward:

```
library(plyr)
iris.uci$species <- mapvalues(iris.uci$species, from =
  c("Iris-setosa","Iris-versicolor", "Iris-virginica"), to = c("setosa",
  "versicolor", "virginica"))
```

After running this code, the head of iris.uci is

```
> head(iris.uci)
  sepal.length sepal.width petal.length petal.width species
1          5.1         3.5          1.4         0.2  setosa
2          4.9           3          1.4         0.2  setosa
3          4.7         3.2          1.3         0.2  setosa
4          4.6         3.1          1.5         0.2  setosa
5            5         3.6          1.4         0.2  setosa
6          5.4         3.9          1.7         0.4  setosa
```

Exploring the data

It's a good idea to explore the data and develop a sense of familiarity with it. One quick way to explore the data is to use the summary() function:

```
> summary(iris.uci)
  sepal.length     sepal.width     petal.length     petal.width           species
 Min.   :4.300   Min.   :2.000   Min.   :1.000   Min.   :0.100   setosa    :50
 1st Qu.:5.100   1st Qu.:2.800   1st Qu.:1.600   1st Qu.:0.300   versicolor:50
 Median :5.800   Median :3.000   Median :4.350   Median :1.300   virginica :50
 Mean   :5.843   Mean   :3.054   Mean   :3.759   Mean   :1.199
 3rd Qu.:6.400   3rd Qu.:3.300   3rd Qu.:5.100   3rd Qu.:1.800
 Max.   :7.900   Max.   :4.400   Max.   :6.900   Max.   :2.500
```

This gives you an idea of each variable's range (Max – Min), and central tendency (Median and Mean). You can quickly see that sepals are both longer and wider than petals, as I mention earlier.

The Summary statistics provide information about the distributions. To visualize and compare the distributions of the variables, one strategy is to plot a few histograms together to come up with what you see in Figure 1-1.

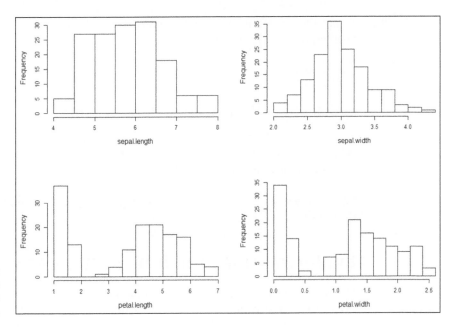

FIGURE 1-1:
The distributions
of the variables in
iris.uci.

Here's how to plot those distributions:

```
par(mfrow=c(2,2))
for(i in 1:4){hist(iris.uci[,i],xlab=colnames(iris.uci[i]), cex.lab=1.2,
    main="")}
```

The par() function is a pretty hot item in base R graphics. It allows me to set (or to find out the values of) the parameters of a plot. It's so rich in possibilities that I could write a chapter or so just on how this function works. Instead, I'll spare you the all the details and show you how I apply this function as needed. Here, the mfrow argument divides the screen into two rows and two columns so that the sepal variables are in one row and the petal variables are in the other. (Think of mfrow as "multiple figures by row.")

The for loop goes through the first four columns of the dataframe and draws a histogram for each one, labelling the x-axis with the column name. The cex.lab argument enlarges the axis labels slightly and the main="" argument eliminates the default title from each histogram.

The histograms show that the petal variables are skewed and the sepal variables are more symmetrical.

TIP

To put the two sepal variables into one column and the two petal variables into another, the par() function is

```
par(mfcol=c(2,2))
```

Quick suggested project: Density plots

Here's a neat little exercise to strengthen your graphics skillset (and your for loop skills): Turn these histograms into density plots. (See Chapter 1 of Book 2 to find out how.) Your finished product should look like Figure 1-2.

The density plots are another way of showing the symmetry and the skewness in the variables.

Exploring relationships in the data

Iris-related ML projects are all about using the relationships among the variables to correctly classify individual flowers. So, in addition to summaries and graphics of each variable, I want to look at the relationships among the variables and how those relationships change across the species.

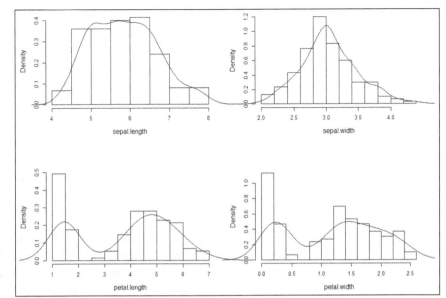

FIGURE 1-2:
Density plots for
the variables of
iris.uci.

Base R graphics

A scatterplot matrix visualizes those intervariable relationships. (See Chapter 1 of
Book 2.) Figure 1-3 shows the base R version of that matrix for iris.uci.

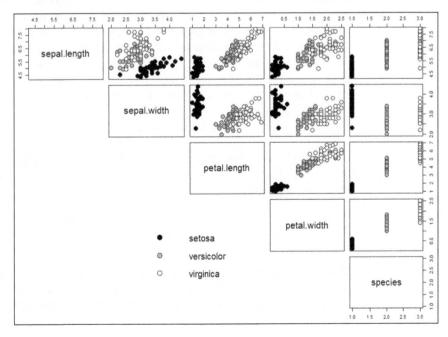

FIGURE 1-3:
Scatterplot matrix
for the iris.
uci dataframe
rendered in
base R.

I eliminated the lower panel of the matrix because it shows the same data as the upper half but with *x* and *y* variables interchanged. I put a legend in that area. The legend indicates that "black" represents "*setosa*," "gray" represents "*versicolor*," and "white" represents "*virginica*." Before I tell you how I did all this, let's take a look at the graph and try to understand what it's saying.

The main diagonal cells, of course, have the names of the variables. Each non-main-diagonal cell represents the relationship between the variable in the cell's row and the variable in the cell's column. So the cell in row 1, column 2 plots the relationship between sepal.length and sepal.width. The cells in column 5 show the relationships between each of the four measured variables and species. In effect, they show the distributions of the measurements within each species.

The cells that plot pairwise relationships among the four numeric variables seem to show that the *setosas* (the black-filled points) are separate and distributed somewhat differently from the other two species. The least amount of overlap in *versicolor* and *virginica* appears (to me, anyway) to be in petal.length versus petal.width. As for the cells in column 5, petal.length and petal.width seem to have the least amount of overlap across the species. By that, I mean that the range of one species has less extension into the range of another. All this suggests that petal.length and/or petal.width might provide a strong basis for a process that has to learn how to assign irises to their proper species.

To create the scatterplot matrix, I use the pairs() function. This function can't work with iris.uci$species in its present format, however. Right now, it's a variable that holds strings like setosa. Instead, we want to use each species as the name of a group, so that we can partition the 150 flowers into three groups. Another way to say this is that we'd like species to be a factor with three levels – setosa, versicolor, and virginica. (I talk about factors and levels in connection with Analysis of Variance in Chapter 4 of Book 3.)

How do I turn iris.uci$species into a factor? Like this:

```
iris.uci$species <- as.factor(iris.uci$species)
```

Now I can create the plot:

```
pairs(iris.uci,lower.panel=NULL,cex=2,pch=21,cex.labels = 2,
    bg = c("black","grey","white")[iris.uci$species])
```

The first argument is the dataframe; the second eliminates the lower panel. The third expands the plot character to twice its size, and the fourth specifies a filled circle as the plot character. The fifth argument doubles the size of the labels in the main diagonal so that you can read them more easily. The final argument is the business end of the whole thing: This one assigns the colors black, gray (excuse me — grey), and white to the three iris species. And bg indicates that those colors are the background colors (the fill colors, in other words) for the plot characters.

Adding the legend is a bit tricky. In effect, it's adding a plot to an existing plot. First, I use par():

```
par(xpd=NA)
```

Think of par() as setting up a region in the center of the scatterplot matrix. It's called the *clipping* region, and it's smaller than the matrix. The xpd argument determines where I can add the next plot — in this case, the legend — to the clipping region. It can take one of three values: TRUE, FALSE, or NA. Without belaboring the point, NA means that I can put the legend anywhere. (For more on clipping, see the nearby sidebar "More on clipping.")

Here's the legend() function:

```
legend("bottomleft", inset=c(-.5,0), legend=levels(iris.uci$species),
       pch=21,pt.bg=c("black","grey","white"),pt.cex=2,
       y.intersp=1.0,cex=1.5,bty="n")
```

The first argument is the location of the legend. The second, inset, is its location relative to the clip region. The negative number for the first argument means that it's to the left of the clipping region, and the 0 means that it's at the bottom. The third argument specifies the terms that appear in the legend. (It's unusual for an argument to have the same name as its function, but there you have it.) I could have used a vector of the species names, but this way is much cooler.

The next three arguments pertain to the symbol in the legend: pch = 21 specifies a filled circle; the pt.bg argument gives the fill colors; pt.cex = 2 doubles the size of the filled circle.

The value of the next argument, y.intersp, shrinks the space between lines of the legend. Without this argument, the legend spreads all over the page. Then cex increases the font size of the text in the legend, and bty="n" means no border around the legend.

Running those three functions produces the plot shown in Figure 1-3. I supplied the values for the arguments based on resolution and screen size, so your plot might look a little different from mine. Feel free to change the values as needed.

MORE ON CLIPPING

Here's an exercise to help you understand clipping, par(), and xpd a little better, but first you have to complete the project in the earlier section "Quick suggested project: Density plots." In that one, I ask you to turn four histograms into four density plots. (See Figure 1-2.) Without totally letting the cat out of the bag, you have to use the lines() function to visualize each density plot after you create each histogram. Inside the for loop, just before you call lines(), insert par(xpd=NA) and note what happens to the ends of the density-plot lines when you run the code. Then change NA to FALSE and note the effects on the line-ends, and, finally, change to TRUE and see what happens.

The ggplot version

As a fan of ggplot, I have to show you how to do all this the ggplot way. Figure 1-4 shows you a ggplot-rendered scatterplot matrix.

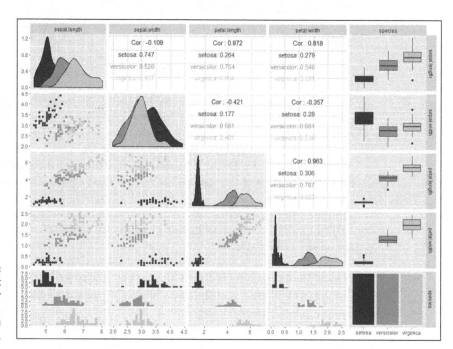

FIGURE 1-4: Scatterplot matrix for iris.uci rendered in ggplot.

Gorgeous, isn't it? Again, before I show you how to create this, I tell you what it all means. The species correspond to black for *setosa*, gray for *versicolor*, and lighter gray for *virginica*. The first four main diagonal cells show density plots for the three species for each variable. The fifth is a histogram of the species. The bottom row presents histograms that correspond to the density plots.

The main diagonal cells and the bottom-row cells clearly show how *setosa* differs from the other two species with respect to the two petal variables. The scatterplots in each cell visualize the relationship between the cell's row variable and the cell's column variable. These relationships also show the difference between *setosa* and the other two species.

Above the main diagonal, each cell in columns 2–4 shows the correlation between its row variable and its column variable. Each cell also shows the correlation for each species. It's instructive to note that the individual correlations can vary greatly from the overall correlation.

The fifth column's first four cells are box plots for the three species with respect to each variable. The box plots show the species overlap for the two sepal variables and little overlap for the petal variables. As is the case with the base R version, the emerging picture is that the petal variables are the stronger indicators of species membership.

On to plot creation. It would be great if `ggplot2` had a function called `ggpairs()` that aesthetically maps `color` to `species` and, like `pairs()` in base R, renders the matrix for you. It doesn't, but a package called `GGally` does, and this package is based on `ggplot2`. To load it, select the Packages tab and click Install. In the Install Packages dialog box, type **GGally**. After it downloads, find `GGally` on the Packages tab and select its check box. Then this code

```
library(ggplot2)
library(GGally)
ggpairs(iris.uci, aes(color = species))
```

creates a perfectly usable scatterplot matrix. It's usable on your *screen,* that is. The default colors wouldn't show up well on the black-and-white page you're reading, so I had to change the color scheme to the grey scale you see in Figure 1-4. If you're interested in how I did this, see the nearby sidebar "Three shades of grey."

TIP

Why is it "grey" and not "gray"? R accepts both, although that wasn't always the case. Originally, R only worked with "grey." To be on the safe side, I use the original spelling because some R function names (like the two in the nearby sidebar) still spell it that way.

REMEMBER

You'll find some of these data exploration techniques in the ML package I show you in the next section. Why did I show them to you here? Two reasons:

>> It's a good idea to know how to use R to explore data.

>> The package I show you uses these R functions to implement some of its exploration techniques. This way, you'll know where these techniques come from.

THREE SHADES OF GREY

To create Figure 1-4 with black, gray, and lighter gray as the species colors, I first have to create the plot matrix:

```
library(ggplot2)
library(GGally)
plot.matrix <-ggpairs(iris.uci,aes(color= species))
```

Why do I assign the plot matrix to the variable on the left? Because I have to go through the matrix, cell by cell, and change the default colors to grey scale. Using the variable name makes it easy to do that.

To go through the matrix. I use a for loop embedded in another for loop. The first loop deals with the rows; the second, with the columns. Thus, the code goes through each cell in the first row, and then each cell in the second, and so on:

```
for(i in 1:5) {
  for(j in 1:5){
     plot.matrix[i,j] <- plot.matrix[i,j] +
      scale_color_grey()  +
      scale_fill_grey()
   }
 }
```

The code inside the embedded for-loop makes the changes. In the cells above the main diagonal, `scale_color_grey()` changes the colors of the correlation coefficients and their associated species names. In the cells below the main diagonal, `scale_color_grey()` changes the colors of the points in each scatterplot. The `scale_fill_grey()` function changes the fill colors of the density plots in the main diagonal, the histograms in the bottom row, and the boxplots in the fifth column.

Finally,

```
plot.matrix
```

puts the plot on the screen.

Introducing the `Rattle` package

R has numerous functions and packages that deal with machine learning. Data science honcho Graham Williams has created `Rattle`, a graphical user interface (GUI) to many of these functions. I use `Rattle` for this book's ML projects.

Much of what Rattle does depends on a package called RGtk2, which uses R functions to access the Gnu Image Manipulation Program (GIMP) toolkit. (GIMP is a widely used open source image editor.) So the first thing to do is download and install this package. In a perfect world, here's how you would have gotten that done: On the Packages tab, you'd click Install. In the Install Packages dialog box, you'd type **RGtk2** and click Install. After the download finishes, you'd find RGtk2 on the Packages tab and click its check box.

In a perfect world, you'd have done the same for Rattle: On the Packages tab, you'd click Install. In the Install Packages dialog box, you'd type **rattle** and click Install. When the download finishes, you'd find rattle on the Packages tab and click its check box.

As I write this, however, the world has become imperfect: RGtk2 no longer resides on CRAN so the usual Install Packages tab procedure doesn't work. For the workaround, see the "Rattle update" sidebar.

Assuming you have the RGtk2 package installed, starting your Rattle chores begin with you typing **rattle** in RStudio's Script panel and then pressing Ctrl+Enter to run. Figure 1-5 shows the window that opens. The window might not be visible at first. (It might open behind other windows.) You might have to hunt around for it, but you'll find it. Expand it to make it look like Figure 1-5.

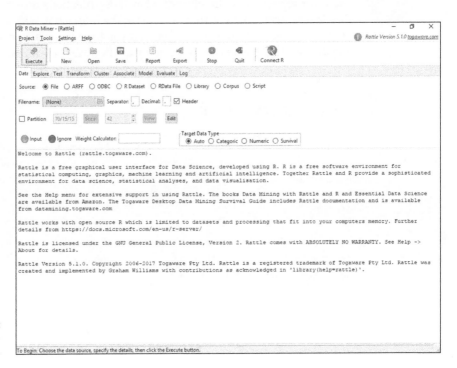

FIGURE 1-5: The Rattle window.

The main panel presents a welcome message and some info about Rattle. The menu bar at the top features Project (for starting, opening, and saving Rattle projects), Tools (a menu of choices that correspond to buttons and tabs), Settings (that deal with graphics), and Help. The row below the menu bar holds icons, the most important of which is Execute. The idea is to look at each tab, make selections, and then click Execute to carry out those selections. (If you're a Trekkie, think of clicking the Execute icon as Captain Picard saying, "Make it so!")

The next row holds the tabs. The first tab (on the left) is for Data. This tab presents the welcome message and, more importantly, allows you to choose the data source. The Explore tab is for — you guessed it — exploring data. The Test tab supplies two-sample statistical tests. If you have to transform data, the Transform tab is for you. The Cluster tab enables several kinds of *cluster analysis* — a type of unsupervised learning. The Associate tab sets you up with association analysis, which identifies relationships between variables. The Model tab provides several kinds of machine learning, including decision trees, support vector machines, and neural networks. The next tab allows you to evaluate your ML creation. The Log tab tracks your interactions with Rattle as R script, which can be quite instructive if you're trying to learn R. I kept the initial caps because that's the way it looks onscreen.

TIP

Remember that Rattle is a GUI to R functions for some complex analyses, and you can't always know in advance what those functions are or which packages they live in. Accordingly, a frequent part of the interaction with Rattle involves a dialog box that opens to first tell you that you have to install a particular package and then asking whether you want to install it. Always click Yes.

RATTLE UPDATE

To run Rattle in Windows, the first objective is to get R Studio running on R version 4.1.3. Fortunately, it's easy to change R Studio's R version. (I know, I know, you went to all the trouble to upgrade to 4.2 or higher. Bear with me.) Download and install version 4.1.3 from https://cran.r-project.org/bin/windows/base/old/4.1.3/R-4.1.3-win.exe.

Next, in R Studio's menu bar select Tools⇨Global Option to open the Options window, and then click the Change button next to the R version box to open the Choose R Installation window. (See the figure below.)

Find and select R-4.1.3 and click OK. Follow the instructions to restart R Studio.

Once it's restarted in version 4.1.3, in the Script panel type and run the following code:

```
install.packages("rattle")
install.packages("https://access.togaware.com/RGtk2_2.20.36.2.zip",
    repos=NULL)
```

The Mac is a little different. For the Mac, you install RGtk2 by typing and running the following:

```
install.packages("https://access.togaware.com/RGtk2_2.20.36.2.tgz",
    repos=NULL)
```

After you've successfully installed Rattle and RGtk2, you're pretty much in business. This is a workaround, so you might get prompted to install additional packages as you work with Rattle. When prompted, always respond Yes or OK.

For latest updates, see `https://rattle.togaware.com/`. (Many thanks to Graham Williams.)

Using Rattle with iris

So I downloaded the iris data set from the UCI ML Repository, cleaned it up a bit, and explored it. Then I installed Rattle. Now I put Rattle to work.

Getting and (further) exploring the data

The first thing to do is bring the dataset into Rattle. On the Data tab, I select the source by clicking the radio button next to R Dataset. This causes the Data Name box to open just below the radio buttons.

Clicking the down arrow on the Data Name box opens a drop-down menu, as shown in Figure 1-6.

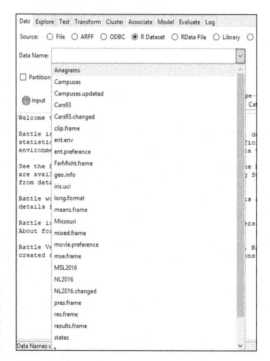

FIGURE 1-6: The drop-down menu in the Data Name box on the Rattle data tab.

On the menu, I click iris.uci. Next, I click the Execute icon. This causes the Data tab to look like Figure 1-7.

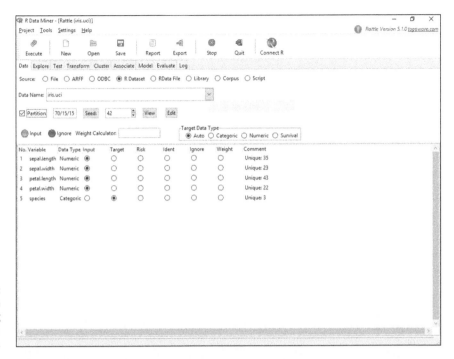

FIGURE 1-7:
The `Rattle` Data
tab, after loading
the `iris.uci`
dataframe.

Notice the check box next to Partition. This partitions the data into a training set, a validation set, and a test set — a division required for many types of machine learning. For what I'm about to do, though, that's not necessary. I'm just quickly showing you some of `Rattle`'s capabilities by doing a hierarchical clustering analysis to look at the structure of the data set. So I deselect that check box.

Notice also the variable names and the selected radio buttons in the main panel. As you can see, `Rattle` has a pretty good idea about the types of data in this data set.

Now for some exploration. Clicking the Explore tab shows the page you see in Figure 1-8.

To explore the distributions of the variables, I click the Distributions radio button, and the tab looks like Figure 1-9.

A `Rattle` plot shows up on the RStudio Plots tab. For an expanded version, click on Zoom.

TIP

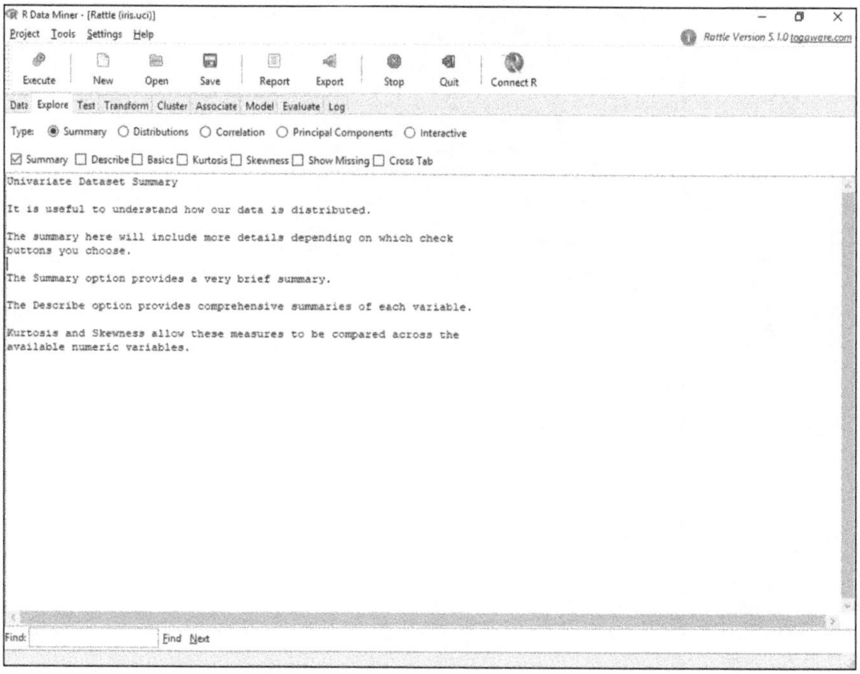

FIGURE 1-8:
The Rattle
Explore tab.

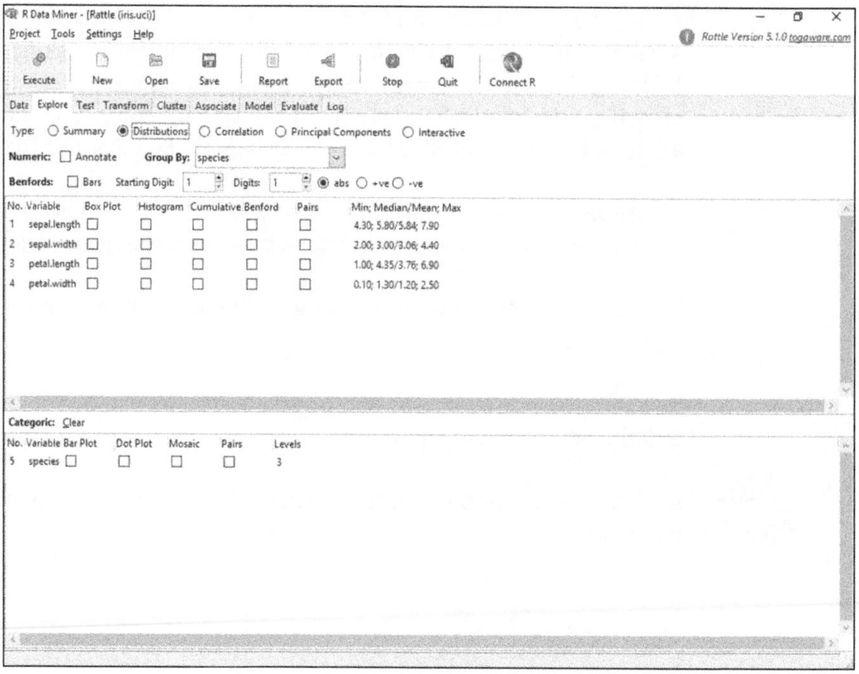

FIGURE 1-9:
The Rattle
Explore tab, with
the Distributions
radio button
selected.

Selecting all Box Plot check boxes (and then clicking Execute) results in the plot shown in Figure 1-10.

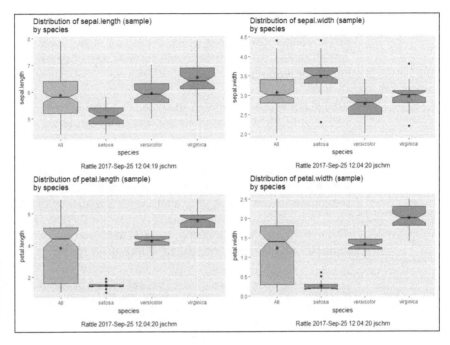

As before, the plots show least variability and least overlap in the petal variables.

If I clear those check boxes and then select the Pairs check boxes and click Execute again, I get a scatterplot matrix that looks very much like Figure 1-4 (but without the fifth row and the fifth column).

I leave it to you to explore the rest of the Explore tab.

Finding clusters in the data

Now for some machine learning. In subsequent chapters, I provide detailed explanations of ML techniques, but here I show you just the superficial aspects of a hierarchical cluster analysis, a type of unsupervised learning that, as I mention earlier, finds the underlying structure in the data set. The analysis reveals the structure as a set of clusters organized in a hierarchy. I'm cheating a bit here because I know the structure: It's three species and, as data exploration suggests, *setosa* somehow is different from *versicolor* and *virginica*.

We might guess, then, that the observations form "clusters" on the basis of their species. So that's three clusters.

What's the "hierarchy"? The overlap between *versicolor* and *virginica* in the scatterplots (and their separation from *setosa*) suggests that they form a "higher-order" cluster, leaving out *setosa*. Then, at a higher level, *setosa* forms a cluster with the other two, resulting in one big cluster that represents the whole data set. That's the hierarchy.

Or, looking at it another way, the data set partitions into two clusters: one consisting of *versicolor* and *virginica* and the other consisting of just *setosa*. The first cluster then breaks down into two clusters, one for each species perhaps.

It's simple for the `iris` data set because everything is pretty much cut-and-dried. With a larger data set that has more variables and more categories, things can get complicated — and this type of analysis can reveal unanticipated structures.

To do the hierarchical clustering, I select the Cluster tab and click the Hierarchical radio button. Clicking Execute makes the Cluster tab look like Figure 1-11.

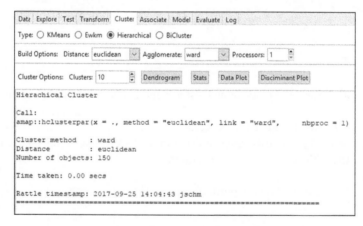

FIGURE 1-11: Performing hierarchical clustering in Rattle.

In the Clusters box, I change the number to 3 and click Execute. (I said I was cheating, remember?) I'd like a picture of the hierarchical clustering I describe earlier, and that appears in a picture called a *dendrogram*. (In Greek, *dendro* means "tree.") So I click Dendrogram and the result, which appears on the Plots tab in RStudio, is shown in Figure 1-12.

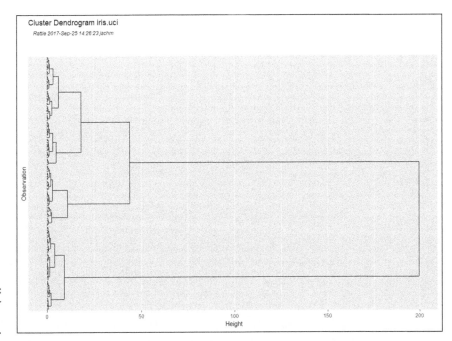

Cluster Dendrogram iris.uci
Rattle 2017-Sep-25 14:26:23 jschm

Observation

Height

FIGURE 1-12: Dendrogram for the `iris.uci` data set.

Think of this as a tree on its side, and then think of the individual observations as the roots. (In my city, which just went through a major hurricane, that's not an uncommon sight!) Two parallel lines joined by a perpendicular line at their ends represents a cluster. At one level, you can see three clusters and numerous clusters below (to the left of) them. Two of the clusters join at a higher (more rightward) level. And then at the highest level, you can see the third cluster joining them.

TIP

With the Cluster box default value of 10, the dendrogram looks similar to Figure 1-12.

It's tempting to say that the three clusters correspond to the three species. But do they really? A quick glance at the dendrogram shows that the three possibly-corresponding-to-the-species clusters don't appear to have equal numbers of observations at their lowest levels. So maybe the cluster-species correspondence isn't exact. Also, see the nearby sidebar "Looking at the `Rattle` log."

Where do the numbers on the Height axis come from? What's the rule for admitting an observation to a cluster? Or for joining one cluster to another? Important questions all, but my objective here is just to acquaint you with `Rattle`.

As was the case with Explore, feel free to look at the remaining options on this tab.

LOOKING AT THE `Rattle` LOG

As I mention earlier in this chapter, the Log tab shows your interactions with `Rattle` as R code. Here's a good example of working with the `Rattle` log.

On the Cluster tab, with the Hierarchical option button selected, click on Data Plot. You see a plot that looks very much like Figure 1-3, from earlier in this chapter. To find the code that produced this plot, select the Log tab and scroll down until you find this:

```
plot(crs$dataset[, c(1:4)], col=cutree(crs$hclust,3))
```

Copy and paste that line into the RStudio Script panel and then press Ctrl+R to run it.

On the Plots tab, you see the same scatterplot matrix, but without the title. The plotting characters aren't filled, and their border colors (black, red, and green) are the colors of the clusters to which `Rattle` has assigned them. (I don't show you this, because the red and green border colors would be hard to distinguish on a black-and-white page.)

To make the matrix look more like Figure 1-3, change `cr$dataset[, c(1:4)]` to `cr$dataset[, c(1:5)]`. This change adds the fifth row and the fifth column.

Add the argument `lower.panel=NULL` to eliminate everything below the main diagonal. Then add plot character arguments so that the code is

```
plot(crs$dataset[, c(1:5)], col=cutree(crs$hclust, 3), lower.panel=NULL,
    pch=21,cex=2,
        bg = c("black","grey","white")[iris.uci$species])
```

Now the border color of each character corresponds to its assigned cluster, and its fill color corresponds to its species. If you run this code, you see that in the scatterplots, some of the plot characters have red borders and are filled with gray and some red-border characters are filled with white. In the fifth column, all points in the rightmost group should have green borders, but some have red borders. What does all this tell us? That the clustering isn't perfect! That is, the three clusters do not correspond exactly with the three species.

Poking around in the `Rattle` log was a pretty good idea!

The `Rattle` Evaluation tab has procedures for evaluating your ML creations, and I discuss them in subsequent chapters.

Chapter **2**

Decisions, Decisions, Decisions

A *decision tree* is a graphical way of representing knowledge. As its name implies, it's a tree-like structure that shows decisions about something, and it's useful in many fields, from management to medicine.

Think of a decision tree as a way to structure a sequence of questions and possible answers. One prominent use of a decision tree is to show the flow of decision-making to a nontechnical audience.

Decision Tree Components

Figure 2-1 shows a decision tree for classifying irises along with decision tree terminology. If you had a chance to look at Chapter 1 in Book 4, you might recall that the `iris` dataset (downloaded from the UCI Machine Learning (ML) Repository and designated as `iris.uci`) consists of 150 rows and 5 columns. The 150 rows represent individual flowers, with 50 each of the *setosa*, *versicolor*, and *virginica* species. The five columns are `sepal.length`, `sepal.width`, `petal.length`, `petal.width`, and `species`.

The decision tree is really an upside-down tree, and it consists of *nodes* and *branches*. Each node presents a question (like petal.length < 2.6, and the question mark is implicit), and branches emanating from the node represent possible answers (yes/no, for example).

(Alternative branches remind me of something the late, great Yogi Berra reputedly said: "When you come to a fork in the road, take it." Not entirely relevant, but I can't write a book without quoting Yogi Berra.)

Roots and leaves

The tree starts from a top-level node called the *root* and ends in bottom-level nodes called *leaves*. (I told you it was upside down.) Each leaf contains a category — in this case, a particular species of iris.

A node that branches to a node below it is the *parent* of the one below. The lower node on a branch is the *child* of the one above it. So a root has no parents and a leaf has no children. An *internal node* has at least one child.

Think of a sequence of branches from the root to a leaf as a *classification rule.* In Figure 2-1, one rule is, "If an iris's petal length is greater than or equal to 2.6 and its petal width is less than 1.8, then the iris is a *versicolor*."

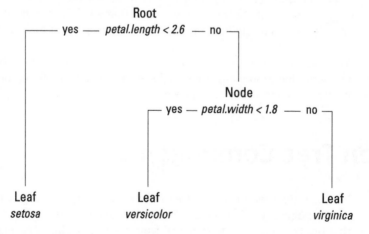

FIGURE 2-1:
A decision tree
for classifying
irises.

REMEMBER

A decision tree with categories in the leaves is called a *classification tree*. A decision tree with numerical values (like "predicted miles per gallon" or "predicted length of hospital stay") in the leaves is called a *regression tree*.

Tree construction

If you had to build a decision tree based on the `iris.uci` data frame, how would you do it? In effect, the job is to create a series of yes/no questions that split the data into smaller and smaller subsets until you can no longer split the subsets.

So you'd examine the variables and find for one of them a value that splits the data into two subsets — perhaps one that has all the *setosa* and the other that has all the rest. Let's call them A and B.

How about splitting them further? If you were careful, you'd find a value such that A had two subsets (A1 and A2), one of which (A1) contained all the *setosa* whereas the other (A2) contained nothing. Because A2 has no members, you can no longer split it. So A is a leaf.

Now look at B. This one holds all the non-*setosa* irises. The same variable (or perhaps another one) might hold the key to a productive split into B1 and B2. That split value (whatever the variable and whatever the value) probably won't put all *versicolor* into B1 and all *virginica* into B2.

Why? You might remember from Chapter 1 of Book 4 that data exploration revealed some overlap between these two species regardless of the variable. So the split won't be perfect, but it might put the vast majority of one species in B1 (along with a tiny group of miscategorized cases) and the vast majority of the other in B2 (again, with a tiny group of miscategorized cases). Ideally, the miscategorizations are so few that you can't split any further. So B1 and B2 are leaves.

This is called *recursive partitioning*, and you could go through the data and do all this manually.

Or you could use R.

Decision Trees in R

R has a package that uses recursive partitioning to construct decision trees. It's called `rpart`, and its function for constructing trees is called `rpart()`. To install the `rpart` package, click Install on the Packages tab and type **rpart** in the Install Packages dialog box. Then, in the dialog box, click the Install button. After the package downloads, find `rpart` in the Packages tab and click to select its check box.

Growing the tree in R

To create a decision tree for the `iris.uci` data frame, use the following code snippet:

```
library(rpart)
iris.tree <- rpart(species ~ sepal.length + sepal.width + petal.length + petal.
    width, iris.uci, method="class")
```

The first argument to `rpart()` is a formula indicating that `species` depends on the other four variables. The tilde (~) means "depends on." (See the section "R Formulas" in Chapter 2 of Book 1.) The second argument is the data frame you're using. The `method = "class"` argument (it's the third one) tells `rpart()` that this is a classification tree. (For a regression tree, it's `method = "anova"`.)

TIP

You can abbreviate the whole right side of the formula with a period. So the shorthand version is

```
species ~ .
```

The left side of the code, `iris.tree`, is called an *rpart object*. So `rpart()` creates an rpart object.

At this point, you can type the rpart object

```
iris.tree
```

and see text output that describes the tree:

```
n= 150

node), split, n, loss, yval, (yprob)
      * denotes terminal node

1) root 150 100 setosa (0.33333333 0.33333333 0.33333333)
  2) petal.length< 2.45 50    0 setosa (1.00000000 0.00000000 0.00000000) *
  3) petal.length>=2.45 100  50 versicolor (0.00000000 0.50000000 0.50000000)
    6) petal.width< 1.75 54   5 versicolor (0.00000000 0.90740741 0.09259259) *
    7) petal.width>=1.75 46   1 virginica (0.00000000 0.02173913 0.97826087) *
```

The first line indicates that this tree is based on 150 cases. The second line provides a key for understanding the output. The third line tells you that an asterisk denotes that a node is a leaf.

Each row corresponds to a node on the tree. The first entry in the row is the node number followed by a right parenthesis. The second is the variable and the value that make up the split. The third is the number of classified cases at that node. The fourth, `loss`, is the number of misclassified cases at the node. Misclassified? Compared to what? Compared to the next entry, `yval`, which is the tree's best guess of the species at that node. The final entry is a parenthesized set of proportions that correspond to the proportion of each species at the node.

You can see the perfect classification in node 2, where `loss` (misclassification) is 0. By contrast, in nodes 6 and 7, `loss` is not 0. Also, unlike node 2, the parenthesized proportions for nodes 6 and 7 do not show `1.00` in the slots that represent the correct species. So the classification rules for *versicolor* and *virginica* result in small amounts of error.

Drawing the tree in R

Now you plot the decision tree, and you can see how it corresponds to the `rpart()` output. You do this with a function called `prp()`, which lives in the `rpart.plot` package.

WARNING

The `rpart` package has a function called `plot.rpart()` which is supposed to plot a decision tree. My version of R can't find it. It can find the function's documentation via `?plot.rpart` but can't find the function. Weird. It's enough to make me *plotz* (which in another language means something like "implode and explode simultaneously").

With `rpart.plot` installed, here's the code that plots the tree shown in Figure 2-2:

```
library(rpart.plot)
prp(iris.tree,type=2,extra="auto",nn = TRUE,branch=1,varlen=0,yesno=2)
```

The first argument to `prp()` is the rpart object. That's the only argument that's necessary. Think of the rpart object as a set of specifications for plotting the tree. I've added the other arguments to make the plot prettier:

>> **type** = 2 means "Label all the nodes."

>> **extra** = **"auto"** tells `prp()` to include the information you see in each rounded rectangle that's in addition to the species name.

>> **nn** = **TRUE** puts the node-number on each node.

>> **branch** = **1** indicates the lines-with-corners style of branching shown in Figure 2-2. These are called *square-shouldered branches,* believe it or not. For slump-shouldered branches (I made that up), try a value between 0 and 1.

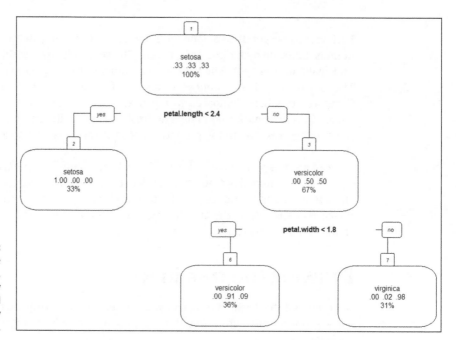

FIGURE 2-2:
Decision tree
for iris.uci,
created by
rpart() and
rendered by
prp().

>> **varlen=0** produces the full variable names on all the nodes (instead of names truncated to 8 characters, the default if you omit this argument).

>> **yesno=2** puts yes or no on all the appropriate branches (instead of just the ones descending from the root, which is the default). Note that each left branch is yes and each right branch is no.

At the root node and the internal node, you see the split. The rounded rectangle at each node shows a species name, three proportions, and the percentage of the data encompassed at that node.

At the root, the proportions are .33 for each species, and 100 percent of the data is at the root. The split (petal.length < 2.4) puts 33 percent of the data at the *setosa* leaf and 67 percent at the internal node. The *setosa* leaf shows the proportions 1.00, .00, and .00, indicating that all the cases at that leaf are perfectly classified as *setosas*.

The internal node shows .00, .50, and .50, which means none of these cases are *setosas*, half are *versicolor*, and half are *virginica*. The internal node split (petal. width < 1.8) puts 36 percent of the cases into the *versicolor* leaf and the 31 percent of the cases into the *virginica* leaf. Already this shows a problem: With perfect classification, those percentages would be equal because each species shows up equally in the data.

On the *versicolor* leaf, the proportions are .00, .91, and .09. This means 9 percent of cases classified as *versicolor* are actually *virginica.* On the *virginica* leaf, the proportions are .00, .02, and .98. So 2 percent of the cases classified as *virginica* are really *versicolor.*

Bottom line: For the great majority of the 150 cases in the data, the classification rules in the decision tree get the job done. But the rules aren't perfect, which is typically the case with a decision tree.

Decision Trees in `Rattle`

`Rattle` provides a GUI to R's tree-construction and tree-plotting functions. To use this GUI to create a decision tree for `iris.uci`, begin by opening `Rattle`:

```
library(rattle)
rattle()
```

I'm assuming that you've downloaded and cleaned up the `iris` dataset from the UCI ML Repository and called it `iris.uci`. I mention that at the beginning of this chapter, and I walk you through all the download and clean-up steps in Chapter 1 of Book 4.

On `Rattle`'s Data tab, in the Source row, click the radio button next to R Dataset. Click the down arrow next to the Data Name box and select `iris.uci` from the drop-down menu. Then click the Execute icon in the upper left corner. Your screen should look like this Book's Figure 1-7.

TIP

If you haven't downloaded the UCI iris dataset and you just want to use the `iris` dataset that comes with base R, click the Library radio button. Then click the down arrow next to the Data Name box and select

```
iris:datasets:Edgar Anderson's iris data
```

from the drop-down menu. Then click Execute.

I recommend downloading from UCI, though, to get the hang of it. Downloading from the UCI ML Repository is something you'll be doing a lot.

Still on the Data tab, select the Partition check box. This breaks down the dataset into a training set, a validation set, and a test set. The default proportions are 70 percent training, 15 percent validation, and 15 percent test. The idea is to use the training set to construct the tree and then use the test set to test its classification rules. The validation set provides a set of cases to experiment with different variables or parameters. Because I don't do that in this example, I set the percentages to 70 percent training, 0 percent validation, and 30 percent test. To do this, I enter **70/0/30** in the Partition text box.

The Seed box contains a default value, 42, as a seed for randomly assigning the dataset rows to training, validation, or testing. Changing the seed changes the randomization.

Creating the tree

Decision tree modeling resides on the Rattle's Model tab. It opens with Tree selected. Figure 2-3 shows this tab.

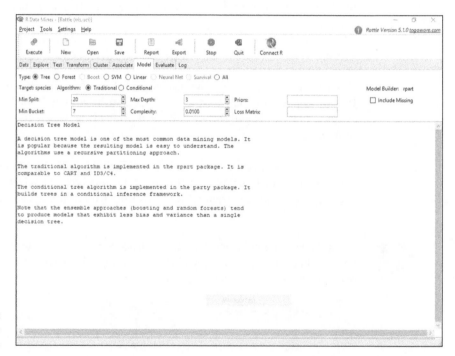

FIGURE 2-3:
The Rattle
Model tab.

A number of onscreen boxes provide access to rpart()'s arguments. (These are called *tuning parameters*.) Moving the cursor over a box opens helpful messages about what goes in the box.

For now, just click Execute to create the decision tree. Figure 2-4 shows what then happens on the Model tab.

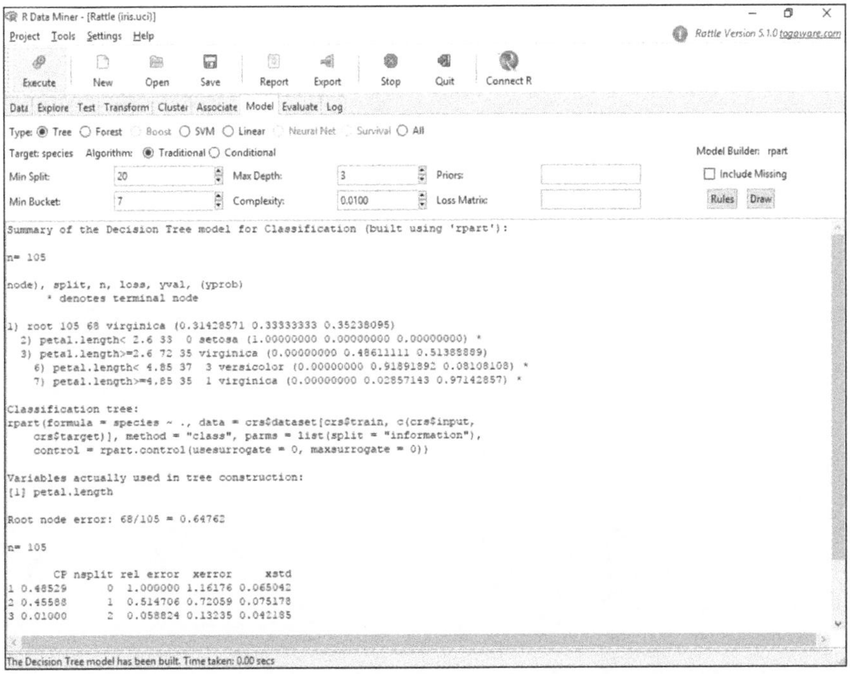

FIGURE 2-4:
The Rattle
Model tab,
after creating a
decision tree for
iris.uci.

The text in the main panel is output from rpart(), with a few more arguments than I use earlier in this chapter. It looks a lot like the output I show you earlier, with some extra info. Note that the tree is based on the 105 cases (70 percent of 150) that constitute the training set. Unlike the tree created earlier, this one uses only petal.length in its splits.

The rest of the output is from a function called printcp(). The abbreviation cp stands for *complexity parameter*, which controls the number of splits that make up the tree. Without delving too deeply into it, I'll just tell you that if a split adds less than the given value of cp (on the Model tab, the default value is .01), rpart() doesn't add the split to the tree. For the most complex tree possible (with the largest number of possible splits, in other words), set cp to .00. (See the section "Quick suggested project: Understanding the complexity parameter," toward the end of this chapter.)

Drawing the tree

Clicking the Draw button produces the decision tree shown in Figure 2-5, rendered by prp() on the RStudio Plots tab. The overall format of the tree is similar to the tree shown earlier, in Figure 2-2, although the details are different and the boxes at the nodes have fill color.

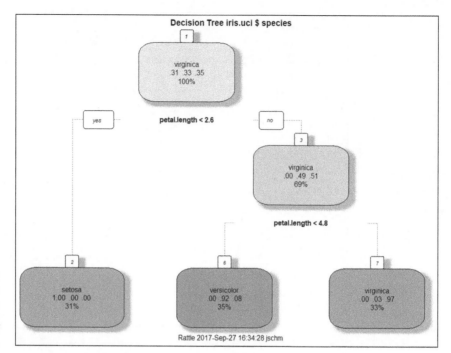

FIGURE 2-5:
A decision tree
for iris.uci,
based on a
training set of
105 cases.

Evaluating the tree

The idea behind *evaluation* is to assess the performance of the tree (derived from the training data) on a new set of data. This is why I divided the data into a Training set and a Testing set.

To see how well the decision tree performs, select the Evaluate tab. Figure 2-6 shows the appearance of the tab after I've clicked Execute with the default settings (which are appropriate for this example).

The results of the evaluation for the 45 cases in the Testing set (30 percent of 150) appear in two versions of an *error matrix*, where each row of a matrix represents the actual species of the flower and each column shows the decision tree's predicted species of the flower. The first version of the matrix shows the results by counts; the second, by proportions.

Correct identifications are in the main diagonal. So, in the first matrix, the cell in row 1, column 1 represents the number of times the decision tree correctly classified a *setosa* as a *setosa* (17). The zeros in the other two cells in row 1 indicate no misclassified *setosas*.

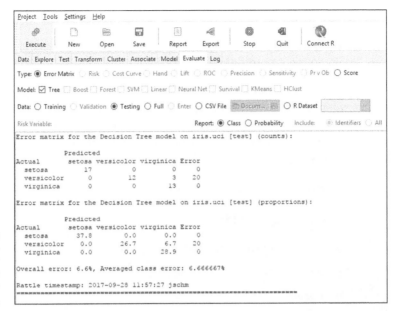

FIGURE 2-6:
The Rattle
Execute tab, after
evaluating the
decision tree for
iris.uci.

The cell in row 2, column 3 shows that the tree incorrectly classified three *virginicas* as *versicolors*. The fourth column shows that the error rate is 20 percent $(3/(12 + 3))$.

Row 3 shows no misclassifications, so dividing the 20 percent by 3 (the number of categories) gives the averaged class error you see at the bottom of the figure. The overall error is the number of misclassifications divided by the total number of observations.

Project: A More Complex Decision Tree

The decision tree for the `iris` dataset is pretty straightforward and yields a relatively low error rate. The following sections lay out a project that results in a more complex tree.

The data: Car evaluation

In the UCI ML Repository, you'll find the `Car Evaluation` dataset. It lives at `http://archive.ics.uci.edu/ml/datasets/Car+Evaluation`.

Click on the `Data Set Description` link to download a text file called `car.names` that describes the data. Open the downloaded `car.names` file in any text editor (like Notepad) to read the description.

As the dataset's description tells you, the designers created the dataset to demonstrate expert system technology, so it's a bit on the "artificial" side. I use it here to give you some practice creating decision trees. The idea is that, given a set of cars' attributes and their values, the decision is whether a specific car is unacceptable, acceptable, good, or very good.

The attributes and their values are

» **buying (the purchase price):** `v-high, high, med, low`

» **maint (the cost of maintaining the car):** `v-high, high, med, low`

» **doors:** `2, 3, 4, more`

» **persons:** `2, 4, more`

» **lug_boot (size of the trunk):** `small, med, big`

» **safety (estimated safety of the car):** `low, med, high`

To get the data set, use any of the methods in Chapter 1 of Book 4. Here's the quickest one.

Click the Data Folder link and, on the new page that appears, click the `car.data` link to download the CSV data file. Open the downloaded `car.data` file in any text editor (like Notepad), press Ctrl+A to highlight the entire page and then Ctrl+C to copy it to the clipboard.

Then the line

```
car.uci <- read.csv("clipboard",header=FALSE)
```

creates the data frame for this project. Now it's time to name the columns:

```
colnames(car.uci) = c("buying","maintenance","doors","persons",
   "lug_boot","safety", "evaluation")
```

The `data.names` file refers to the target as `class`, but I think `evaluation` is more to the point. As a check on what the data looks like, type:

```
head(car.uci)
```

Running that command produces:

```
  buying maintenance doors persons lug_boot safety evaluation
1 vhigh        vhigh     2       2    small    low       unacc
2 vhigh        vhigh     2       2    small    med       unacc
3 vhigh        vhigh     2       2    small   high       unacc
4 vhigh        vhigh     2       2      med    low       unacc
5 vhigh        vhigh     2       2      med    med       unacc
6 vhigh        vhigh     2       2      med   high       unacc
```

With `Rattle` installed,

```
library(rattle)
rattle()
```

opens the `Rattle` screen. On the Data tab, select the R Dataset radio button. Click the down arrow next to the Data Name box and choose `car.uci` from the drop-down menu. Select the Partition check box to partition the data into a training set, a validation set, and a test set. After you click the Execute icon, the Data tab looks like the one shown in Figure 2-7.

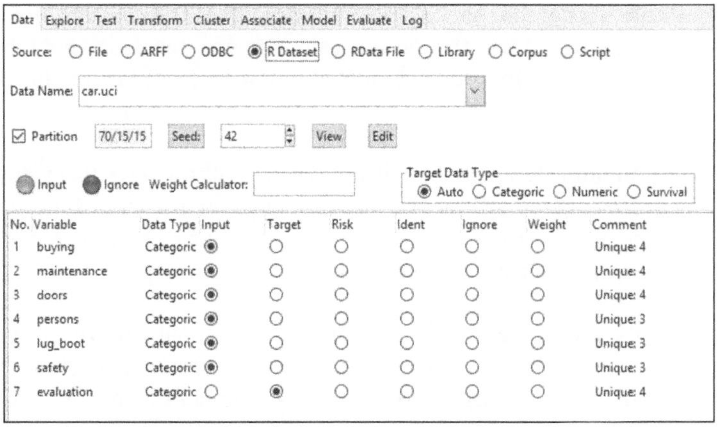

FIGURE 2-7:
The `Rattle`
Data tab, after
acquiring the
`car.uci`
data frame.

Data exploration

Figure 2-8 shows the result of using the Explore tab to show the distribution of the evaluations in `car.uci`. The vast majority of the cars, as you can see, are "unacceptable." The Explore tab allows a variety of data explorations, and I encourage you to examine other aspects of the data.

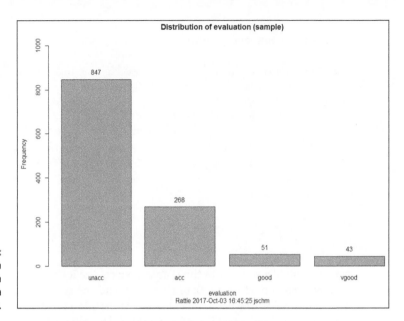

FIGURE 2-8:
The distribution
of evaluations in
the car.uci data
frame.

Building and drawing the tree

On the Model tab, clicking Execute harnesses the rpart() function to create the decision tree. I use the default values in the boxes on this tab. The main panel shows the resulting description of the nodes, similar to what Figure 2-4 shows for iris.uci.

It's all quite detailed, and sifting through all the minutiae would be a real chore. Instead, I draw the tree. In this case, clicking the Draw button results in a lot of nodes, each with a small font that's difficult to read. If I enlarge the font, the whole thing becomes a mishmash.

Here's where the Log tab comes in handy. Selecting the Log tab and scrolling a bit shows that Rattle uses rpart() to create the decision tree in a variable called crs$rpart. Instead of Rattle's function for rendering the tree (it's called fancyRpartPlot()), I use prp(), which is in the rpart.plot package:

```
library(rpart.plot)
prp(crs$rpart, cex=1,varlen=0,branch=0)
```

The result is shown in Figure 2-9.

This is a plainer-looking tree than the Rattle function renders, with no colors and little information in the nodes, but everything is easier to see. The first argument to prp() is the Rattle-created decision tree, and the second enlarges the font. The third argument, `varlen = 0`, prints the full name of each attribute and value (rather than truncating), and `branch = 0` provides the branch style shown in the figure.

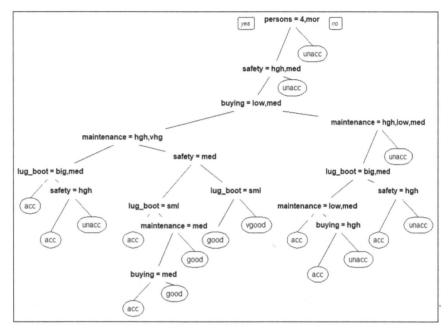

FIGURE 2-9:
The decision tree for car.uci, rendered in rpart().

Evaluating the tree

On the Evaluate tab, click the Testing radio button to evaluate the decision tree against the Testing dataset. Clicking Execute produces the error matrices shown in Figure 2-10.

```
Error matrix for the Decision Tree model on car.uci [test] (counts):

        Predicted
Actual  acc good unacc vgood Error
  acc    57    2     1     0   5.0
  good    0    8     0     3  27.3
  unacc   9    0   169     0   5.1
  vgood   3    0     0     8  27.3

Error matrix for the Decision Tree model on car.uci [test] (proportions):

        Predicted
Actual   acc good unacc vgood Error
  acc   21.9  0.8   0.4   0.0   5.0
  good   0.0  3.1   0.0   1.2  27.3
  unacc  3.5  0.0  65.0   0.0   5.1
  vgood  1.2  0.0   0.0   3.1  27.3

Overall error: 6.9%, Averaged class error: 16.175%

Rattle timestamp: 2017-10-04 10:33:42 jschm
===============================================================
```

FIGURE 2-10:
Error matrices for the car.uci decision tree.

The numbers in the first matrix are counts; the numbers in the second are proportions of the sample. The numbers on the main diagonal are correct classifications, and the others are errors.

The tree does a nice job with the most frequent categories (unacceptable and acceptable), and not quite as well on the other two (good and very good). The overall error rate is 6.9 percent.

Quick suggested project: Understanding the complexity parameter

Rattle is a terrific teaching tool. In this little 2-part project, you can use Rattle to help wrap your brain around the complexity parameter (cp) and what it entails.

The default value of the cp is .01. To tell you how to calculate cp is beyond the scope of this book. To paraphrase what I say earlier in this chapter, just think of cp as the "minimum benefit" that a split must add to the tree. If the split doesn't yield at least that much benefit (the value of cp), rpart() doesn't add it.

What happens if you set cp to .00? You get no restrictions on what a split must add. Hence, you wind up with the most complex tree possible. So here's the first part of this quick project: Set cp to .00 and Execute, and then use

```
library(rpart.plot)
prp(crs$rpart, cex=1,varlen=0,branch=0)
```

to draw the tree. Compare it with Figure 2-9. More complex, right? Evaluate this tree against the Testing set and look at the overall error rate. Compared to the original error rate (6.9 percent), is the extra complexity worth adding?

The second part of this project is to move in the other direction. Set cp to a higher value, like .10. This makes it restrictive to add a split. Click Execute. Then draw the tree. It looks much less complex than with cp = .01, doesn't it? Evaluate against the Testing set. How about that overall error rate?

REMEMBER

On a live tree that grows outdoors in your garden, what do you call the process of cutting branches to make the tree look better? Does *pruning* sound familiar? That's also the name for eliminating splits to make a decision tree less complex (which is what increasing the cp does).

Suggested Project: Titanic

A dataset that's often used to illustrate ML concepts is the information about passengers on the *Titanic*'s disastrous voyage in 1912. The target variable is whether the passenger survived. You can use this data to create a decision tree.

The data resides in an R package called `titanic`. If it's not already on the Packages tab, click Install. In the Install Packages dialog box, type **titanic** and click the Install button. After the package downloads, find it on the Packages tab and select its check box.

In the `titanic` package, you'll find `titanic_train` and `titanic_test`. Don't be tempted to use one as the training set and the other as the test set for this particular application of `Rattle`. The `titanic_test` set doesn't include the `Survived` variable, so it's not usable for testing a decision tree the way I lay out the process here.

Instead, create the data frame like this:

```
library(titanic)
titanic.df <- titanic_train
```

Then use `Rattle`'s Data tab to read in the dataset. Figure 2-11 shows what the Data tab looks like after a few modifications.

No.	Variable	Data Type	Input	Target	Risk	Ident	Ignore	Weight	Comment
1	PassengerId	Ident	○	○	○	◉	○	○	Unique: 891
2	Survived	Numeric	○	◉	○	○	○	○	Unique: 2
3	Pclass	Numeric	◉	○	○	○	○	○	Unique: 3
4	Name	Ident	○	○	○	◉	○	○	Unique: 891
5	Sex	Categoric	◉	○	○	○	○	○	Unique: 2
6	Age	Numeric	◉	○	○	○	○	○	Unique: 88 Missing: 177
7	SibSp	Numeric	◉	○	○	○	○	○	Unique: 7
8	Parch	Numeric	◉	○	○	○	○	○	Unique: 7
9	Ticket	Categoric	○	○	○	○	◉	○	Unique: 681
10	Fare	Numeric	◉	○	○	○	○	○	Unique: 248
11	Cabin	Categoric	○	○	○	○	◉	○	Unique: 148
12	Embarked	Categoric	◉	○	○	○	○	○	Unique: 4

FIGURE 2-11: The `Rattle` Data tab, after modifying the `titanic.df` dataset.

What are those modifications? First, a rule of thumb: If a variable is categoric and has a lot of unique values (and if it's not already classified as an Ident (identifier)), click its Ignore radio button. Also, when first encountering this dataset, `Rattle` thinks `Embarked` is the target variable. Use the radio buttons to change `Embarked` to `Categoric` and to change `Survived` to `Target`.

Good luck!

Chapter **3**

Into the Forest, Randomly

I n Chapter 2 of Book 4, I help you explore decision trees. Suppose a decision tree is an expert decision-maker: Give a tree a set of data, and it makes decisions about the data. Taking this idea a step further, suppose you have a panel of experts — a group of decision trees — and each one makes a decision about the same data. One could poll the panel to come up with the best decision.

This is the idea behind the *random forest* — a collection of decision trees that you can poll, and the majority vote ends up being the decision.

Growing a Random Forest

How does all this happen? How do you create a forest out of a dataset? Well, randomly.

Here's what I mean. In Chapter 2 of Book 4, I discuss the creation of a decision tree from a dataset. I use the `Rattle` package to partition a data frame into a training set, a validation set, and a test set. The partitioning takes place as a result of random sampling from the rows in the data frame. The default condition is that

Rattle randomly assigns 70 percent of the rows to the training set, 15 percent to the validation set, and 15 percent to the test set.

The random row selection proceeds from a seed value, whose Rattle default is 42. This produces the 70 percent of the observations for creating the decision tree. What happens if I change the seed value? The result is a different 70 percent of the sample and (potentially) a different tree. If I change the seed again and again and produce a decision tree each time (and save each tree), I create a forest.

Figure 3-1 illustrates this concept. The trees provide decision rules for the iris. uci data frame, which I show you in Chapter 2 of Book 4. To refresh your memory, the data are measurements of the length and width of petals and sepals in 150 irises. They consist of 50 each of the *setosa*, *versicolor*, and *virginica* species. Given a flower's measurements, a tree uses its decision rules to determine the flower's species. I added .uci to the data frame's name to indicate that I downloaded it from the Machine Language Repository of the University of California-Irvine. A little data cleanup was necessary, which I talk about in Chapter 1 of Book 4.

REMEMBER

After you download and read the UCI iris dataset into R to create iris.uci, an important step is to turn species into a factor:

```
iris.uci$species <- as.factor(iris.uci$species)
```

I discuss this in Chapter 1 of Book 4. This enables important R functions to work with iris.uci.

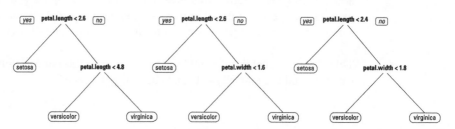

FIGURE 3-1:
Three Rattle-produced decision trees for the iris.uci data frame.

Notice that each tree has its own decision rules and that the splits aren't all based on the same variables. Rather than have only one tree decide a flower's species, I can have all three of them make the determination. If they don't all reach the same decision, the majority rules.

Now imagine hundreds of these trees, all created from the same data frame. In this setup, though, I randomly sample rows from the 70 percent of the rows designated as the training set rather than create a new training set each time, as in the preceding example.

And then I add one more dimension of randomness: In addition to random selection of the data frame rows, suppose I add random selection of the variables to consider for each split of each decision tree.

So, here are two things to consider each time I grow a tree in the forest:

>> For the data, I randomly select from the rows of the training set.

>> For each split, I randomly select from the columns. (How many columns do I randomly select each time? A good rule of thumb is the square root of the number of columns.)

That's a huge forest, with a lot of randomness! A technique like this one is useful when you have a lot of variables and relatively few observations (lots of columns and not so many rows, in other words).

R can grow a random forest for you.

Random Forests in R

R has a package for creating random forests. If you guessed that it's called `randomForest`, you're right. Its function for creating the random forest is called . . . wait for it . . . `randomForest()`.

If this package is already on the Packages tab, select its check box and you're in business. If it isn't on the tab, select the Install tab, and in the Install Packages dialog box, type **randomForest** and click the Install button. When the package finishes downloading, find its check box on the Packages tab and click it.

Building the forest

With the `randomForest` check box selected, here's how to create a 500-tree forest for the `iris.uci` data frame. First, you create a training set consisting of 70 percent of the rows randomly selected from the data frame. For this task, you use the `sample()` function. First, however, you set the *seed* for the randomization, like this:

```
set.seed(810)
```

The `seed` is the number that starts off the randomization in `sample()`. You don't have to do this, but if you want your numbers to come out like mine, set the seed to the same number as mine.

TIP If you want the randomization to take place the same way each time you use `sample()`, you have to set the seed every time.

Now for the sampling:

```
training.set = sample(nrow(iris.uci),0.7*nrow(iris.uci))
```

The first argument of `sample()` is the number of rows in the data frame; the second argument is how many of the rows to randomly sample.

TIP You can use `sample()` with or without `replacement`. "Without replacement" is the default condition. This means that once you randomly select an item for the sample, you don't put it back ("replace it") into the set of items you're sampling from. "With replacement" means that you put it back and you can possibly select it again and again for this sample. For this to happen, add `replacement = TRUE` as an argument.

Then use `randomForest()`:

```
iris.forest <- randomForest(formula =
   species ~ petal.length + petal.width + sepal.length + sepal.width,
              data = iris.uci, ntree = 500, subset=training.set,
              importance = TRUE)
```

In this straightforward example, the first argument is a formula indicating that `species` depends on the other four variables, the second is the data frame, and the third is the number of trees to create. The next-to-last one is the subset of the data for creating each tree. And the last argument, `importance`, tells the function that you want to examine the importance of each variable in creating the forest. (I talk about importance a bit more in the upcoming section "A closer look.")

TIP As is the case with many R functions, this is only the bare minimum. Lots of other arguments are available for `randomForest()`.

Evaluating the forest

Let's take a look at how well the forest does its job. The line

```
print(iris.forest)
```

produces this result:

```
Call:
 randomForest(formula = species ~ petal.length + petal.width + sepal.length +
    sepal.width, data = iris.uci, ntree = 500, importance = TRUE, subset =
    training.set)
               Type of random forest: classification
                     Number of trees: 500
No. of variables tried at each split: 2

        OOB estimate of  error rate: 6.67%
Confusion matrix:
           setosa versicolor virginica class.error
setosa         36          0         0  0.00000000
versicolor      0         32         2  0.05882353
virginica       0          5        30  0.14285714
```

The first few lines, of course, echo the function call and then present descriptive information about the tree. Notice that the default number of variables tried at each split is the square root of the number of independent variables. In this case, that happens to be 2. You can vary this by setting a value for a randomForest() argument called mtry (for example, mtry = 3).

Finally, the confusion matrix (see Chapter 6 of Book 4) shows the actual species of each iris (in the rows) and the species as identified by the forest (in the columns). The numbers of correct identifications are in the main diagonal, and errors are in the off-diagonal cells. The forest mistakenly identified 2 *versicolor* as *virginica* and 5 *virginica* as *versicolor*. The error rate is 6.67 percent. This is the off-diagonal total (5 + 2 = 7) divided by the total number of observations (36 + 32 + 30 + 5 + 2 = 105, and the 105 is 70 percent of 150). So the forest is accurate 93.33 percent of the time — which is pretty good!

Um, what does the OOB represent? OOB stands for *out of bag*. In the random forest world, a *bag* is the part of the training set that went into creating the decision tree. The OOB (out of bag) estimate, then, is based on testing the forest on data not included in the bag.

A closer look

The product of randomForest() is an object, and it has a set of attributes. Here are the attribute names:

```
> names(iris.forest)
 [1] "call"  "type"  "predicted" "err.rate" "confusion" "votes"
```

```
 [7] "oob.times"  "classes" "importance"  "importanceSD" "localImportance"
     "proximity"
[13] "ntree"  "mtry" "forest" "y" "test"  "inbag"
[19] "terms"
```

Some, like `ntree`, are short and sweet and identify inputs to `randomForest()`. Others provide a huge amount of information: `err.rate`, for example, shows the error rates for every tree in the forest. Still others, for this example, are `NULL`.

It's instructive to examine `importance`:

```
> round(iris.forest$importance,2)
              setosa versicolor virginica MeanDecreaseAccuracy MeanDecreaseGini
petal.length   0.31       0.29      0.28                 0.29            30.31
petal.width    0.34       0.30      0.27                 0.30            30.91
sepal.length   0.03       0.01      0.04                 0.03             6.17
sepal.width    0.01       0.00      0.01                 0.01             1.83
```

I rounded to two decimal places so that this example could fit nicely on the printed page. The first three columns show the relative importance of each variable for identifying each species. Without going into exactly how this is calculated, *relative importance* means how much each variable contributes to accuracy for identifying a species. Consistent with the overall impression of the iris data (refer to Chapter 1 of Book 4), the two petal variables add the most.

The measure in the fourth column is based on rearranging the values of a variable and seeing how the rearrangement affects performance. If the variable is not important, rearranging its values does not decrease the forest's accuracy. If it's important, the accuracy does decrease — hence the name, `MeanDecrease Accuracy`. Again, the two petal variables are the most important.

The fifth column looks at importance in a different way: If you don't use the forest, what are the chances that you misclassify an iris if you just select a species for it at random? That's called the *gini* index. The numbers in the fifth column represent the reduction in the gini (that is, in the misclassification) by using the row variable in a split; `randomForest()` measures this for each variable over all the trees in the forest, resulting in the numbers in the fifth column. Once again, the petal variables are the most important: Using them in splits (as variables in a tree, in other words) provides the largest decreases in misclassification.

You get this entire set of importance statistics only if you set `importance=TRUE` when you use `randomForest()`.

REMEMBER

472   BOOK 4 **Learning from Data**

Plotting error

With random forests, one useful plot is to show how the error rates change as the forest encompasses progressively more trees. Sometimes, this plot can give you an idea of the optimal number of trees.

First, I used `plot()`:

```
plot(iris.forest, col = "black")
```

Had I not added `col = black` to `plot()`, the default colors would have been too light and too difficult to distinguish from one another on this black-and-white page.

Then I added `legend()`:

```
legend("topright", legend=c(levels(iris.uci$species),"OOB"),
       lty = c("dashed","dotted","dotdash","solid"), cex=.8,bty = "n")
```

To differentiate among the levels of `species`, I maintained the `plot()` default linetypes (`lty`) and included them as part of the legend. I used the output of `print(iris.tree)` as a guide to match `lty` with `species` (and with OOB).

The last two arguments deal with the legend's overall appearance:

» `cex = .8` contracts the text size and with it the entire legend so that the legend doesn't obstruct the top line in the plot.

» `bty = "n"` removes the border from the legend, which also contributes to the ease of seeing the top line.

The result is shown in Figure 3-2.

With fewer than 100 trees, the plot looks something like a forkful of angel hair pasta. To turn the magnifying glass on the graph between 1 and 100 trees, I added the `xlim` argument to `plot()`:

```
plot(iris.forest, col = "black",xlim = c(1,100))
```

And the result is shown in Figure 3-3.

TIP

To examine the data behind these plots, take a look at the 500 rows of `iris.forest$err.rate`.

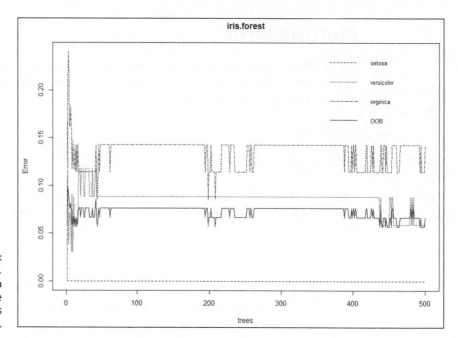

FIGURE 3-2:
iris.forest
error rates as a
function of the
number of trees
in the forest.

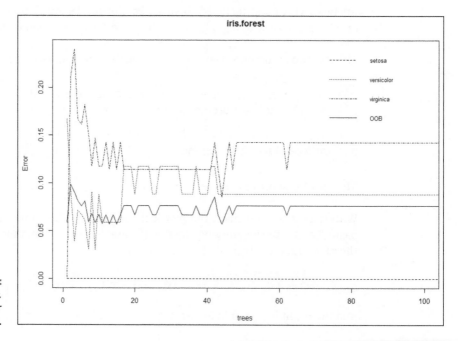

FIGURE 3-3:
iris.forest
error rates for
1 to 100 trees.

LOOKING AT THE RULES

If you want to look at the decision rules for individual trees, a function called print-RandomForests() is the one for you. This function lives in the Rattle package. With Rattle downloaded, these two lines:

```
library(rattle)
printRandomForests(iris.forest, models=c(1,500))
```

print the rules that the first tree and the 500th tree use to decide an iris's species. I don't print the rules here, because each tree uses a lot of them. Give it a try!

Plotting importance

Another useful plot visualizes the MeanDecreaseAccuracy and MeanDecreaseGini of the variables. A ggplot2-based Rattle function called ggvarImp() does this for you:

```
library(ggplot2)
library(rattle)
ggVarImp(iris.forest)
```

The result of this function is the good-looking graph shown in Figure 3-4; it reflects quite well the importance-related numbers I discuss in the earlier section "A closer look."

TIP

In the projects in this chapter and in Chapter 2 of Book 4, the target is a categorical variable. It's also possible for the target to be a numeric variable, (in which case regression is involved), but I don't get into that topic in this book.

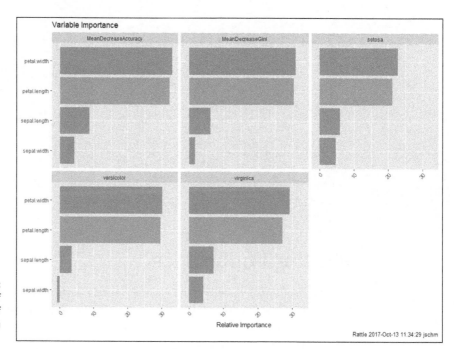

FIGURE 3-4:
The plot of
importance of
the variables in
iris.forest.

Project: Identifying Glass

In this section, I show you how to use the `Rattle` package to grow a random forest for a domain that's more complex than the iris species.

In criminological investigations, it's often important to properly identify glass at crime scenes so that it can serve as evidence. So this random forest identifies where a glass fragment came from (building window, vehicle window, or head-lamp, for example), based on a physical property (refractive index — how much it bends light passing through it) and chemical properties (amount of sodium, magnesium, and aluminum it contains, for example).

The data

The data are in a dataset from the UCI ML Repository. You'll find the data set at

```
https://archive.ics.uci.edu/ml/datasets/glass+identification
```

Click the `Data Set Description` link to download a text file called glass.names that tells you all about the dataset. To read it, open the downloaded glass.names in any text editor (like Notepad).

Next, click the `Data Folder` link. The page that opens has a link called `glass.data`. In Chapter 1 of Book 4, I show you three ways to get the data into R, but here's the one I like best: Click `glass.data` to download a text file of comma-separated variables. Open the downloaded `glass.data` file in a text editor (like Notepad). Press Ctrl+A to highlight everything and then press Ctrl+C to copy it all to the clipboard. Then

```
glass.uci <- read.csv("clipboard",header = FALSE)
```

creates a data frame, and

```
colnames(glass.uci)<-c("ID","RI","Na","Mg","Al","Si","K","Ca","Ba","Fe","Type")
```

assigns the names to the columns. (The names are in `glass.names`.) The first of these names, `ID`, is an identifier for the piece of glass, and the second is the glass fragment's refractive index. The last one, `Type`, is the target variable. All the ones in between are the chemical elements that constitute the glass.

I have one more thing to do before I get down to business. At the moment, the levels of `Type` (the target variable) are numbers. Instead, I want to give them informative names. To do this, I use `mapvalues()`, which lives in the `plyr` library:

```
library(plyr)
glass.uci$Type <- mapvalues(glass.uci$Type, from = c(1,2,3,5,6,7),
     to = c("bldg_windows_float","bldg_windows_non_float",
            "vehicle_windows_float","containers", "tableware","headlamps"))
```

The terms `float` and `non_float` refer to the process of making a window. The "float" process produces near-optical quality glass; "non-float" glass is lower quality.

Notice that the `from` vector does not include 4. This is because the corresponding type (`vehicle_windows_non_float`) is not in the dataset.

Getting the data into `Rattle`

`Rattle` is a graphical user interface (GUI) to many R machine learning functions. With the `Rattle` package downloaded, entering

```
library(rattle)
rattle()
```

Into the Forest, Randomly

opens the `Rattle` Data tab. Notice that `Rattle` (uppercase R) refers to the GUI, and `rattle` (lowercase r) refers to the function.

TIP

`Rattle` might open behind RStudio, which makes it easy to miss if RStudio is full screen.

First, I load the `glass.uci` data frame into `Rattle`. To do this, I click the R Dataset radio button, which opens the Data Name box. Then I click the down arrow next to the Data Name box and select `glass.uci` from the drop-down menu. Next, I click the Execute icon in the upper left corner. Figure 3-5 shows the appearance of the Data tab after I complete these steps.

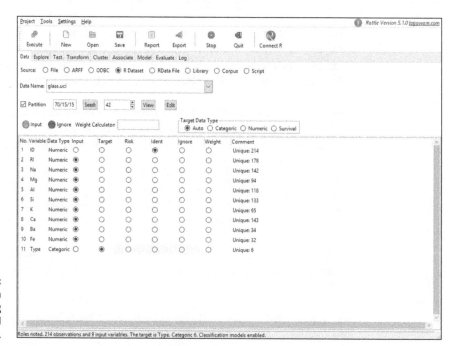

FIGURE 3-5: The rattle Data tab after selecting glass.uci and clicking Execute.

Exploring the data

Next, a little data exploration. To examine the distribution of Type, I click the Explore tab and clear the Group By box (whose default selection is Type), and I click the Distributions radio button. Then I select the Bar Plot check box next to Type, toward the bottom of the window. Figure 3-6 shows how the Explore tab looks after I do this.

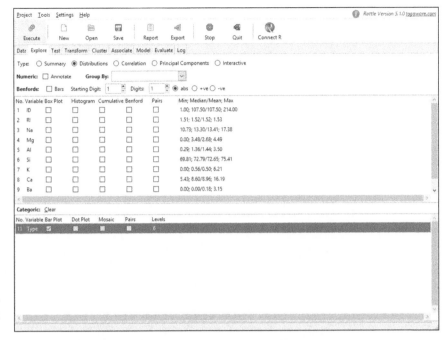

FIGURE 3-6:
The Rattle
Execute tab,
after clearing the
Group By box and
selecting the Bar
Plot check box
for Type.

Clicking Execute produces the bar plot which appears on the Plots tab and is shown in Figure 3-7. As you can see, one of the Type-names (bldg_windows_float) got crowded out of the *x*-axis. The figure shows that the two building window types are the most frequent in the data frame.

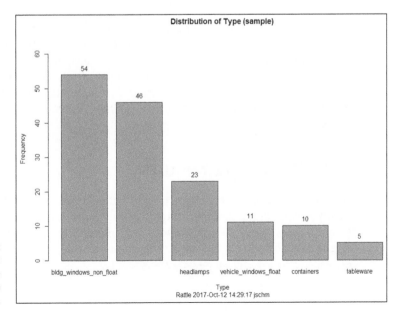

FIGURE 3-7:
The distribution
of Type in the
glass.uci data
frame.

Growing the random forest

On the Model tab, I select the Forest radio button and click Execute. `Rattle` creates the forest and prints the summary shown on the Model tab in Figure 3-8.

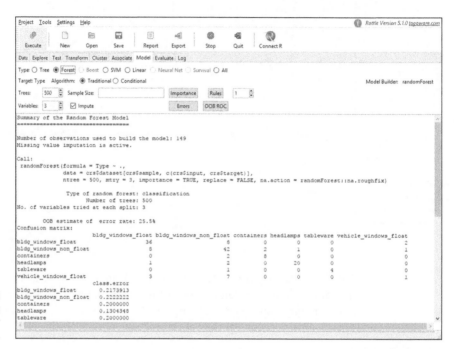

The summary indicates that the random forest has an OOB error rate of 25.5 percent. It identifies headlamps most accurately and does a so-so job on the two types of building windows. The vehicle windows? Not so much. So it would be a good idea to exercise some caution if you use this random forest for glass identification, because its overall accuracy is 74.5 percent. If you select the Evaluate tab and evaluate against the Validation set and then against the Test set, you'll find similar results.

Visualizing the results

To help you visualize the results, I begin with the plot of variable importance. When you click the Importance button on the Model tab, `Rattle` plots what you see in Figure 3-9. As the figure shows, for identifying most types of glass, Mg (Magnesium) content is the most important variable, as is the case for Mean DecreaseAccuracy and for MeanDecreaseGini.

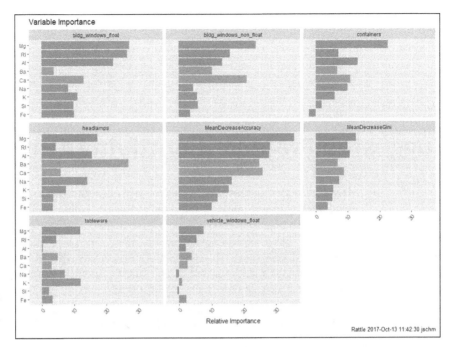

FIGURE 3-9:
The plot
of variable
importance for
glass.forest.

The plot of error rates isn't nearly as easy on the eyes. Pressing the Errors but-ton on the Model tab produces a plot of the error rates with progressively more trees, similar to Figure 3-2. I don't show you this plot, because it's a mishmash. The legend won't help you decipher it, because the legend's linetype colors don't appear to match up with the legend's text colors.

This is one of those extremely rare occasions when looking at the data might be more helpful than looking at a graph. Let's say I want to examine the error rates for the OOB and for the first three variables in the 30th through 35th trees. (Why not all the variables? Because I want the output to fit neatly on this page!)

The Rattle Log tells you that the random forest is in an object called crs$rf. As I mention earlier in this chapter, the error rates for a random forest are in an attrib-ute called err.rate. For all error rates for all trees, I use crsrferr.rate. To round them to two decimal places, it's round(crsrferr.rate, 2). For the 30th to 35th trees, the function call becomes round(crsrserr.rate[30:35,],2). And, to limit the output to just the OOB and the first three variables, I use:

```
> round(crs$rf$err.rate[30:35,1:4],2)
     OOB bldg_windows_float bldg_windows_non_float containers
[1,] 0.28              0.22                   0.28        0.2
[2,] 0.29              0.24                   0.26        0.2
```

[3,]	0.27	0.24	0.24	0.2
[4,]	0.28	0.24	0.22	0.2
[5,]	0.29	0.26	0.26	0.2
[6,]	0.30	0.26	0.28	0.2

Suggested Project: Identifying Mushrooms

If you're the outdoorsy type, you probably encounter mushrooms growing in the wild. As you might know, some mushrooms are edible, and others are most definitely not!

The UCI ML repository has a dataset of mushrooms with lots and lots of instances (8,124 of them) and 22 attributes. The target variable indicates whether the mushroom is edible (e) or poisonous (p). You'll find it at

```
https://archive.ics.uci.edu/ml/datasets/mushroom
```

You create an R data frame by clicking the Data Folder link. On the page that opens click the link to the data file. This downloads the data file. Open the data file in a text editor, and then press Ctrl+A to select all data and Ctrl+C to copy it to the clipboard. Then this line does the trick:

```
mushroom.uci <- read.csv("clipboard", header=FALSE)
```

TIP

A word of advice: The attribute names are long and involved, so for this project *only*, don't bother naming the columns unless you really and truly want to. Instead, use the default V1, V2, and so on that R provides. Also, and this is important, after you put the data into Rattle, you'll see that Rattle makes a guess about the target variable. Its guess, V23, is wrong. The real target variable is V1. So click the appropriate radio buttons to make the changes.

Finally, unlike the datasets I've used so far, this one has missing values. They're all in V12 (2,480 of them), denoted by a question mark. To deal with this, select the Rattle Transform tab and click the radio button for Impute and the radio button for Zero/Missing. Click V12 and then Execute. This substitutes *Missing* for the question mark. (**Spoiler alert:** With this data frame, it doesn't make much difference whether you do this or not.)

When you create the forest, you should have a confusion matrix with just two rows and two columns. You'll be pleasantly surprised by the OOB error rate!

Chapter **4**

Support Your Local Vector

Classification is an important part of machine learning (ML). One important classifying technique is the *support vector machine* (SVM). So, what exactly is an SVM and how does it work?

Some Data to Work With

To introduce the SVM, I use the `iris` data set, which I first discuss in Chapter 1 of Book 4. It provides four measurements on each of 150 irises, with 50 flowers in each of three species.

This data set is useful for examples whose objective is to use the measurements (petal width and length, sepal width and length) as a means of identifying a flower's species. Though one species *(setosa)* is distinct from the other two *(versicolor* and *virginica),* those other two aren't completely distinct from one another.

TIP

In preceding chapters in Book 4, I tell you how to work with `iris.uci`, a data set downloaded from the UCI ML repository and subsequently cleaned up. In this chapter, I describe how to work with the `iris` data set that comes with R.

Using a subset

To make things a bit easier to follow, I start with a subset of the `iris` data set. I call it *set.vers* because it consists of only the *setosa* and *versicolor* species — in other words, everything except *virginica*:

```
set.vers <-subset(iris, Species != "virginica")
```

Figure 4-1 shows a scatter plot of `set.vers` with `Petal.Length` on the *x*-axis and `Petal.Width` on the *y*-axis. Black circles represent *setosa*, and white circles represent *versicolor*.

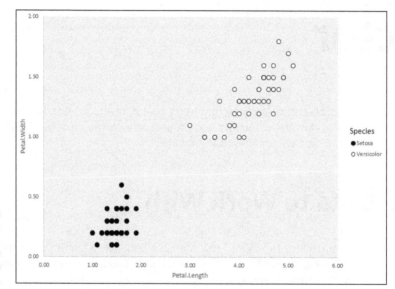

FIGURE 4-1:
`Petal.Width`
versus `Petal.`
`Length` in the
`set.vers` data
frame.

Defining a boundary

The two species shown in Figure 4-1 occupy quite different areas in the plot, don't they? Apparently, it's pretty easy to tell them apart. In fact, you could add a boundary line between the two areas, as shown in Figure 4-2, that nicely divides the plot. Any flower to the right and above the line is a *versicolor*, and any flower to the left and below the line is a *setosa*. The line is called a *separation boundary*.

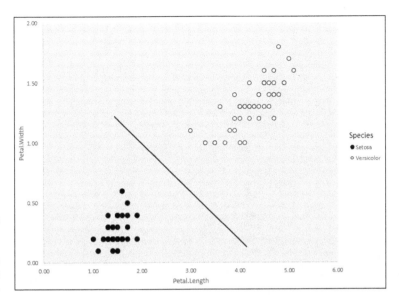

FIGURE 4-2:
Petal.Width
versus Petal.
Length with
a separation
boundary.

When you can draw a line like this one for the separation boundary, the data are said to be *linearly separable*.

Understanding support vectors

Having an infinite number of separation boundaries is possible. Truthfully, I eyeballed this one. But Figure 4-3 shows what the separation boundary is supposed to do. The two dotted lines in the figure represent the *margin*, which is the distance between the separation boundary and its nearest points.

The optimal separation boundary is the one that maximizes that distance. The lines from the two nearest points to the separation boundary are called *support vectors*.

REMEMBER

The term *support vectors* often refers only to the points rather than the lines.

The optimal separation boundary is the one that results in the fewest support vectors. Why? If fewer data points are near the boundary (meaning fewer support vectors), the boundary works better at classifying the data.

In the simple 2-variable case I present here, the separation boundary is a straight line. With more variables, it's a *hyperplane*.

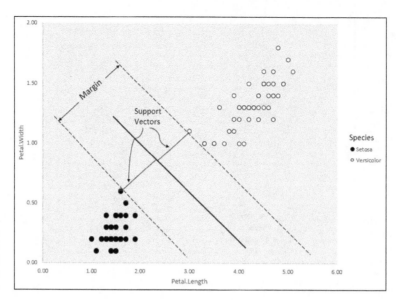

FIGURE 4-3:
Margin and
support vectors
for the separation
boundary.

Whether it's a line or a hyperplane, how do you find this all-important separation boundary, which separates the data into classes? Support vectors get the job done. The idea is to find points, like the two shown earlier in Figure 4-3, that result in support vectors and then use the support vectors to define the separation boundary.

So you have to have something that, in effect, searches for support vectors. That something is the support vector machine. Before I discuss SVMs, I have to tell you a little more about separability, as described in the following section.

Separability: It's Usually Nonlinear

How many data sets are perfectly linearly separable, like set.vers? Not many. In fact, here's vers.virg, the two-thirds of the irises that aren't *setosa:*

```
vers.virg <- subset(iris, Species !="setosa")
```

Figure 4-4 shows the plot of Petal.Width versus Petal.Length for this data frame. You can clearly see the slight overlap between species, and the resulting nonlinear separability.

How can a classifier deal with overlap? One way is to permit some misclassification — some data points on the wrong side of the separation boundary.

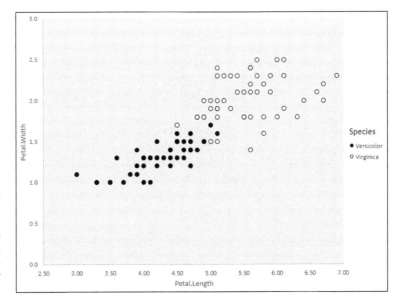

FIGURE 4-4:
Petal.Width
versus Petal.
Length in the
vers.virg data
frame, show-
ing nonlinear
separability.

Figure 4-5 shows what I'm talking about. I've eyeballed a separation boundary with the *versicolor* on the left and (most) *virginica* on the right. The figure shows five *virginica* to the left of the boundary. This is called *soft margin classification*.

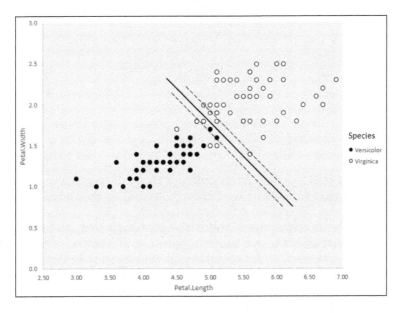

FIGURE 4-5:
Soft margin
classification in
the vers.virg
data frame.

As I eyeballed the boundary, I tried to minimize the miscalculations. As you examine the data points, perhaps you can see a different separation boundary that works better — one that has fewer misclassifications, in other words. An SVM would find the boundary by working with a parameter called C, which specifies the number of misclassifications the SVM is willing to allow.

Soft margin classification and linear separability, though, don't always work with real data, where you can have all kinds of overlap. Sometimes you find clusters of data points from one category inside a large group of data points from another category. When that happens, it's often necessary to have multiple nonlinear separation boundaries, as shown in Figure 4-6. Those nonlinear boundaries define a *kernel*.

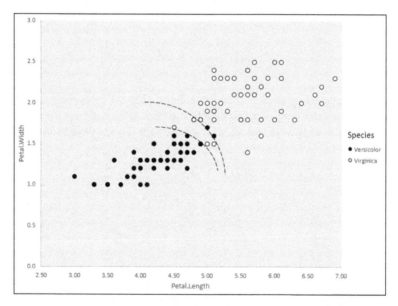

FIGURE 4-6:
A kernel in the
vers.virg data
frame.

An SVM function typically offers a choice of several ways to find a kernel. These choices have names like "linear," "radial," "polynomial," and "sigmoid."

The underlying mathematics is pretty complicated, but here's an intuitive way to think about kernels: Imagine Figure 4-4 as a page torn from this book and lying flat on the table. Suppose that you could separate the data points by moving them in a third dimension above and below the page — say, the *versicolor* above and the *virginica* below. Then it would be easy to find a separation boundary, wouldn't it? Think of *kerneling* as the process of moving the data into the third dimension. (How far to move each point in the third dimension? That's where the complicated mathematics comes in.) And the separation boundary would then be a plane, not a line.

Support Vector Machines in R

Two prominent R packages deal with SVM. One is called e1071, and the other is kernlab. I show you how to work with both of them in this section.

Working with e1071

To get going with the e1071 package, click the Install button on the Packages tab in RStudio. In the Install Packages dialog box, type **e1071** and click Install. After the package downloads, select its check box on the Packages tab.

REMEMBER

Why the cryptic package name? Its authors were in the probability theory group in the department of statistics at the Vienna University of Technology, and e1071 was the university's designation for the group.

The e1071 package provides R functions for a variety of ML techniques, but I only touch on SVM as I create one for the vers.virg data frame.

Creating the data frame

I'll use the data from vers.virg to train an SVM, but I have to take an extra step to create a working data frame.

Wait a sec. A "working data frame?" Isn't vers.virg already a data frame? Yes, it is. But if I don't take an extra step, weird things happen. Specifically, if I train an SVM on vers.virg, it thinks *setosa* is available as a species even though it's not in any row. This can affect the accuracy of the SVM. Apparently, SVM software considers the set (the iris data frame) that the subset came from.

So the plan here is to create a .csv (comma-separated variable) text file and then read that text file back into R and convert it to a data frame. That way, the new data frame has exactly the same data as vers.virg, but it's not the product of subset().

The first step is

```
write.csv(vers.virg,"vvcsv")
```

The second argument is the name of the newly created .csv file.

Next, you navigate to the file. (On my Windows computer, it lands in the Documents folder.) Open the file, and then press Ctrl+A to highlight everything in it. Then you press Ctrl+C to copy it all to the clipboard. This code reads it back into a new data frame called vvx:

```
vvx <-read.csv("clipboard",header=TRUE,sep=",")
```

Here are the first six rows:

	X	Sepal.Length	Sepal.Width	Petal.Length	Petal.Width	Species
1	51	7.0	3.2	4.7	1.4	versicolor
2	52	6.4	3.2	4.5	1.5	versicolor
3	53	6.9	3.1	4.9	1.5	versicolor
4	54	5.5	2.3	4.0	1.3	versicolor
5	55	6.5	2.8	4.6	1.5	versicolor
6	56	5.7	2.8	4.5	1.3	versicolor

In the original vers.virg file, vers.virg$Species is a factor. In vvx, vvs$Species is not a factor. This is important because the upcoming function svm() requires vvx$Species to be a factor. So without further ado —

```
vvx$Species <- as.factor(vvx$Species)
```

Separating into training and test sets

The first thing to do when training an SVM is to split the data frame into a training set and a test set. A neat little function called sample.split() takes care of this, but you first have to install its package, which is called catools. Once it's downloaded and installed, here's how to split the data:

```
set.seed(810)
svm_sample = sample.split(vvx$Species,SplitRatio = .75)
```

TIP

To reproduce my results, set the seed to the same number I did. I set sample.split() so that 75 percent of the observations in vvx are in svm_sample and 25 percent are not. So the training set is

```
training.set = subset(vvx,svm_sample == TRUE)
```

and the test set is

```
test.set = subset(vvx,svm_sample == FALSE)
```

Training the SVM

Now I show you how to use svm() to train the SVM on the training set:

```
svm_model <- svm(Species ~ Petal.Width + Petal.Length, data=training.set,
                 method="C-classification", kernel="linear")
```

The first argument shows that Species depends on Petal.Width and Petal. Length. I did this to stay consistent with Figures 4-1 through 4-6. The next argument specifies the data to use.

The third argument, method, says that this is a classification. The final argument specifies the type of kernel. I mention earlier in this chapter that several types are possible. The one I use here ("C-classification") is the simplest.

After running this code, you examine the SVM:

```
> svm_model

Call:
svm(formula = Species ~ Petal.Width + Petal.Length, data = training.set, method
    = "C-classification", kernel = "linear")


Parameters:
   SVM-Type:  C-classification
 SVM-Kernel:  linear
       cost:  1
      gamma:  0.5

Number of Support Vectors:  16
```

The important item is the last line, which tells you that the SVM found 16 support vectors in its quest to find a boundary that classifies each iris as *versicolor* or *virginica*.

Plotting the SVM

At this point, it's a good idea to visualize the SVM. You can use plot() to do that:

```
plot(svm_model, data = training.set[, c(4, 5, 6)],
               formula= Petal.Width ~ Petal.Length)
```

The first argument is the SVM, and the second supplies the data for the plot: the last three columns of the training set. The last argument, formula, specifies the variables to include in the plot. This formula puts Petal.Width on the y-axis and puts Petal.Length on the x-axis.

The code produces a nice-looking plot, as you can see when you run it. To make everything look nicer on this page, though, I added a couple of touches, and the result is shown in Figure 4-7. (If you're interested, see the following sidebar, "The extra touches for the SVM plot.")

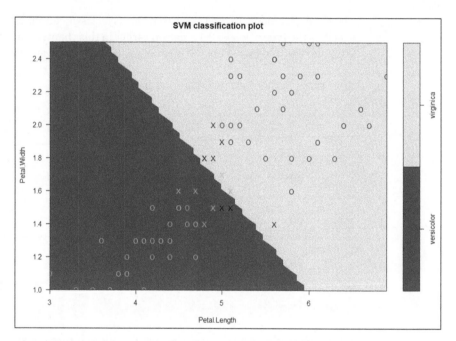

FIGURE 4-7:
Plotting the
SVM for the vvx
training set,
e1071 version.

In the figure, O represents a data point, and X represents a support vector. Points in the darker gray area represent irises classified as *versicolor*, and points in the lighter gray area are irises classified as *virginica*.

The nonlinear separation boundary, as you can see, is a jagged edge. Black points (*virginica*) are predominantly in the lighter area, and gray points (*versicolor*) are predominantly in the darker area. *Predominantly*, of course, doesn't mean "always." Some of the support vector points are misclassified — a few gray Xs are in the lighter area, and a few black Xs are in the darker area.

THE EXTRA TOUCHES FOR THE SVM PLOT

Here's the code that produced what you see in Figure 4-7:

```
plot(svm_model, data = training.set[, c(4, 5,6)], formula=Petal.Width~Petal.
    Length, dataSymbol = "O", svSymbol = "X",
        symbolPalette = palette(c("gray95","gray0")),
        color.palette = gray.colors)
```

The dataSymbol argument specifies an uppercase *O* as the character for the data points, and the svSymbol argument specifies an uppercase *X* as the character for the support vectors. (The defaults are these letters in lowercase.) The symbolPalette argument renders the colors for the symbols, and color.palette renders the colors for the category areas.

Testing the SVM

How does this SVM perform? A function called predict() provides a vector of predicted classifications based on the SVM. First, use predict() to test its classifications of the flowers in the training set:

```
pred.training <-predict(svm_model,training.set)
```

The overall average performance is the mean of the vector of predictions:

```
> mean(pred.training==training.set$Species)
[1] 0.9473684
```

Notice that you have to specify Species in the mean() function.

Okay, and how about the SVM's performance when it comes to the flowers in the test set?

```
> pred.test <-predict(svm_model,test.set)
> mean(pred.test==test.set$Species)
[1] 0.9583333
```

It's highly accurate on both sets.

Quick suggested project 1: Using all the variables

In the earlier section "Training the SVM," the formula I use in the svm( ) function is

```
Species ~ Petal.Width + Petal.Length
```

What happens if you include Sepal.Width and Sepal.Length? The formula then would be

```
Species ~ .
```

The period means "include all the variables."

How many support vectors result? What's the effect on performance?

Quick suggested project 2: Working with kernels

In the earlier section "Separability: It's Usually Nonlinear," I talk about kernels and try to give you an intuitive understanding of what they're about. To get a little more of a feel for kernels, train the SVM with the Polygon, Radial, and Sigmoid options, test each SVM, and then plot the results for each one.

Quick suggested project 3: Classifying all the irises

To simplify the discussion of SVMs, I limited the examples to two classes by taking subsets of the iris data frame. SVMs, however, are not limited to two classes.

Instead of vers.virg, use the entire iris data frame. Remember to split iris into a training set and a test set and then train the SVM on the training set. How many support vectors result? How does the SVM perform on the test set?

Working with kernlab

On the Packages tab, click the Install button. In the Install Packages dialog box, type **kernlab** and click Install. When the package has downloaded, select its check box on the Packages tab.

The kernlab SVM function is called ksvm( ). I show you how to use it here on the training set and then on the test set I already created. Here's the code to train an SVM:

```
kern_svm <-ksvm(Species ~ Petal.Width + Petal.Length, training.set,
    kernel="vanilladot")
```

The first argument is the formula that indicates `Species` is dependent on `Petal.Width` and `Petal.Length` (again, to stay consistent with Figures 4-1 through 4-6). The second argument shows the source of the data (the training set you create in the preceding section). In the third argument, `kernel`, `"vanilladot"` is `kernlab`'s name for a linear kernel.

Running `kern_svm` results in:

```
> kern_svm
Support Vector Machine object of class "ksvm"

SV type: C-svc (classification)
 parameter : cost C = 1

Linear (vanilla) kernel function.

Number of Support Vectors : 16

Objective Function Value : -12.3997
Training error : 0.065789
```

The results (16 support vectors) match up with `e1071`'s `svm()` function.

With respect to performance on the training set, running `predict()` yields this:

```
> pred.test <- predict(kern_svm,training.set)
> mean(pred.test == training.set$Species)
[1] 0.9342105
```

which corresponds to `1-kern_sym$error` (that is, to 1 minus the `Training error` of 0.065789 in the output of `kern_sym`).

The accuracy on the test set is

```
> pred.test <- predict(kern_svm,test.set)
> mean(pred.test == test.set$Species)
[1] 0.9583333
```

You use `plot()` to visualize the SVM:

```
plot(kern_svm,data=training.set, formula=Petal.Width ~ Petal.Length)
```

Figure 4-8 shows the resulting plot. The triangles are *versicolor*, the circles are *virginica*, and the filled-plot characters are the support vectors. Unlike in the `e1071` plot, no legend explains the classification.

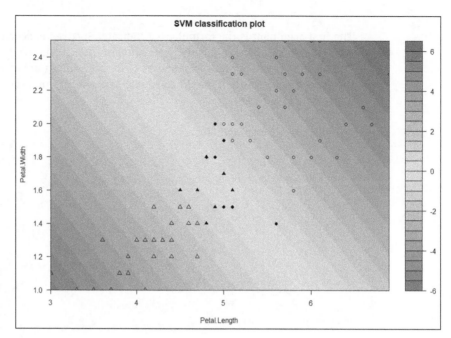

FIGURE 4-8:
Plotting the
SVM for the vvx
training set,
kernlab version.

Project: House Parties

SVMs work well when you have to classify individuals on the basis of many features — usually, many more than in the `iris` data frame. In this section, I tell you how to create an SVM that identifies the party affiliations of members of the 1984 US House of Representatives. The target variable is whether the congressperson is a Republican or a Democrat, based on their votes on 16 issues of that time. The issues range from water-project cost sharing to education spending.

Nine votes are possible, but they're aggregated into the three classes y (yea), n (nay), or ? (vote not registered). (Usually, a question mark [?] signifies missing data, but not in this case.)

Here are a couple of cautions to bear in mind:

>> The name of each issue does not provide enough information to understand the entirety of the issue. Sometimes the associated bill has such convoluted wording that it's hard to tell what a y or n vote means.

>> Nothing here is intended as an endorsement or a disparagement of any position or of either party. This is just a machine learning exercise.

You'll find the Congressional Voting Records data set in the UCI ML repository. The URL is

```
https://archive.ics.uci.edu/ml/datasets/congressional+voting+records
```

Click the Data Set Description link to download house-votes-84.names, a text file that describes this dataset. To read the description, open the downloaded file in any text editor (like Notepad).

Click the Data Folder link. On the page that opens, click the house-votes-84.data link to download the CSV file that contains the data. Open the downloaded house-votes-84.data file in any text editor (like Notepad). Press Ctrl+A to highlight all the data, and then press Ctrl+C to copy it all to the clipboard. Then this code

```
house <- read.csv("clipboard",header=FALSE)
```

turns the data into a data frame. At this point, the first six rows of the data frame are

```
> head(house)
          V1 V2 V3 V4 V5 V6 V7 V8 V9 V10 V11 V12 V13 V14 V15 V16 V17
1 republican  n  y  n  y  y  y  n  n   n   y   ?   y   y   y   n   y
2 republican  n  y  n  y  y  y  n  n   n   n   n   y   y   y   n   ?
3   democrat  ?  y  y  ?  y  y  n  n   n   n   y   n   y   y   n   n
4   democrat  n  y  y  n  ?  y  n  n   n   n   y   n   y   n   n   y
5   democrat  y  y  y  n  y  y  n  n   n   n   y   ?   y   y   y   y
6   democrat  n  y  y  n  y  y  n  n   n   n   n   y   y   y   y   y
```

A look at the variable names (in house-votes-84.names) shows that most of them are pretty long (like anti-satellite-test-ban). Typing them takes a lot of time, and assigning them short abbreviations might not be much more informative than V15 or V16. So just change V1 to Party:

```
colnames(house)[1] = "Party"
```

I use the kernlab package to create the SVM. More specifically, I use the Rattle package, which provides a GUI to kernlab.

Reading in the data

With the Rattle package installed,

```
rattle()
```

opens the Data tab. To read in the data, follow these steps:

1. **Click the R Dataset radio button to open the Data Name box.**

2. **Click that box's down arrow and select House from the menu that appears.**

3. **Click to select the check box next to Partition, and then click the Execute button in the upper left corner of the window.**

4. **Click the Target radio button for Party and the Input radio button for V17, and then click the Execute icon again.**

The Rattle Data tab should now look like Figure 4-9.

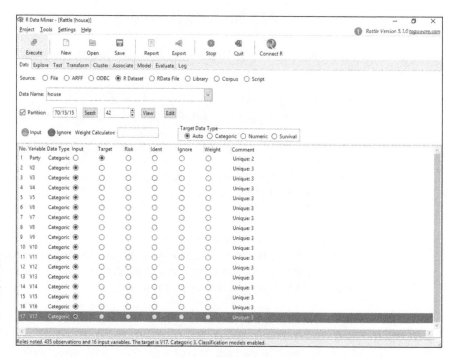

FIGURE 4-9:
The Rattle Data tab, after selecting and modifying the house data frame.

Exploring the data

Next, you'll want to explore the data. The first thing to look at is a distribution of party affiliation. Here's how:

1. **On the Explore tab, click the Distributions radio button and the check box next to Party.**

2. **In the Group By box, select blank (the first choice) so that this box is empty.**

   Figure 4-10 shows what the Explore tab looks like after all this takes place.

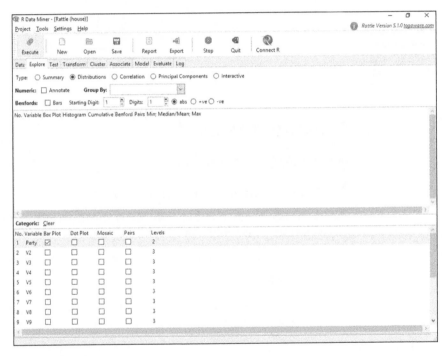

FIGURE 4-10: The rattle Explore tab, set up to plot a distribution of party affiliation.

3. **Click Execute.**

   That last step produces what you see in Figure 4-11, which shows the distribution of Republicans and Democrats in the data frame.

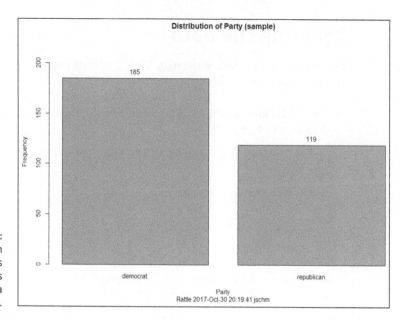

FIGURE 4-11:
The distribution
of Republicans
and Democrats
in the house data
frame.

Creating the SVM

On to the SVM. Follow these steps:

1. **On the Model tab, click the SVM radio button.**

2. **In the Kernel box, click the down arrow and then choose Linear (vanil-ladot) from the menu that appears.**

   Figure 4-12 shows the Explore tab after these choices are made.

3. **Click the Execute icon.**

   Clicking Execute changes the screen to look like Figure 4-13, showing the results of the SVM. The machine found 34 support vectors and produced a Training error of .016447.

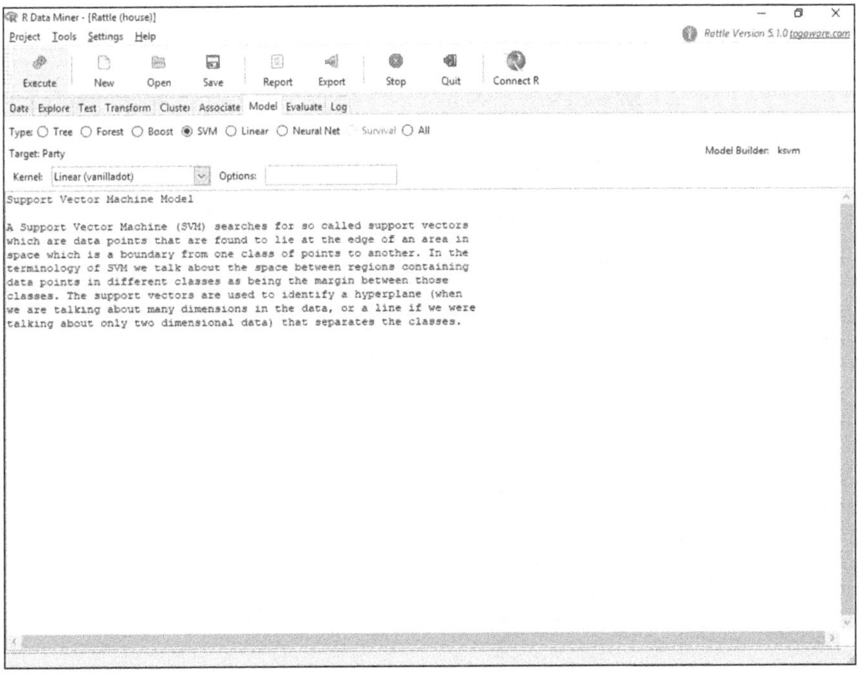

FIGURE 4-12:
The Rattle Model tab, set up to create an SVM for the house data frame.

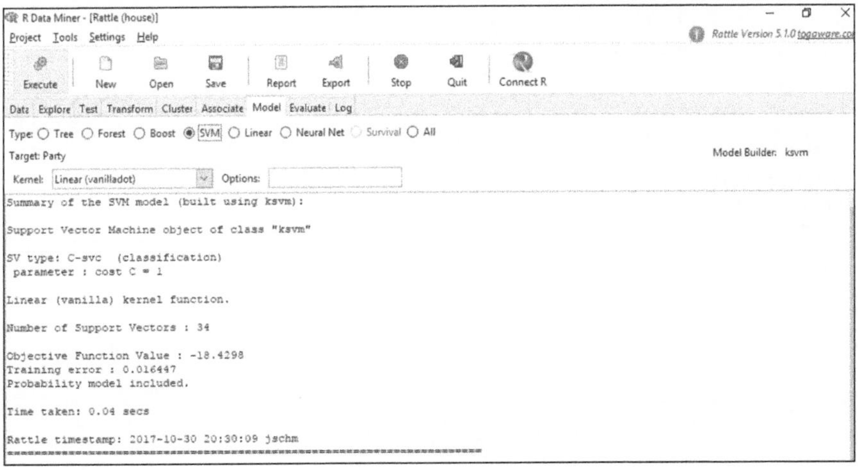

FIGURE 4-13:
The results of the SVM for the house data frame.

Evaluating the SVM

To evaluate the SVM against the Testing set, complete these steps:

1. **Click to select the Evaluate tab.**

2. **For Type, click the Error Matrix radio button.**

3. **For Data, click the Testing radio button.**

4. **Click Execute to produce the screen shown in Figure 4-14.**

   The SVM incorrectly classifies 2 of the 40 Democrats as Republicans, for an overall error rate of 3 percent (2 out of 66 errors) and an average class error rate of 2.5 percent (the average of 5 percent and 0 percent). Pretty impressive.

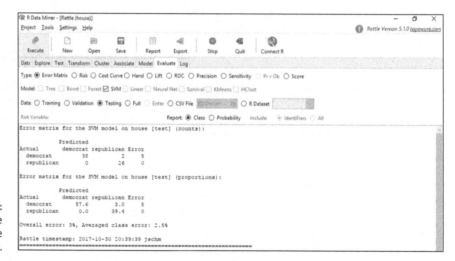

FIGURE 4-14:
Evaluating the
SVM against the
Testing set.

Chapter **5**

K-Means Clustering

I n unsupervised learning, a machine learning (ML) process looks for structure in a data set. The objective is to find patterns, not make predictions. One way to structure a data set is to put the data points into subgroups called *clusters*. The trick is to find a recipe for creating the clusters. One such recipe is called *k-means clustering*.

How It Works

To introduce k-means clustering, I show you how to work with the iris data frame, as I have in previous chapters in this Book. This is the iris data frame that's in the base R installation. Fifty flowers in each of three iris species *(setosa, versicolor,* and *virginica)* make up the data set. The data frame columns are Sepal. Length, Sepal.Width, Petal.Length, Petal.Width, and Species.

For this discussion, you're concerned with only Petal.Length, Petal.Width, and Species. That way, you can visualize the data in two dimensions.

Figure 5-1 plots the iris data frame with Petal.Length on the *x*-axis, Petal. Width on the *y*-axis, and Species as the color of the plotting character. (For the ggplot details, see the later sidebar "Plotting the irises.")

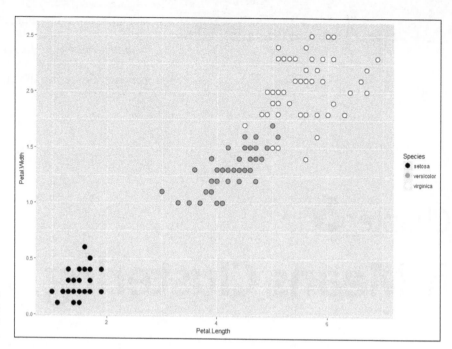

FIGURE 5-1:
Two dimensions
of the iris data
frame.

In k-means clustering, you first specify how many clusters you think the data fall into. In Figure 5-1, a reasonable assumption is 3 — the number of species. The next step is to randomly assign each data point (corresponding to a row in the data frame) to a cluster and then find the central point of each cluster. ML honchos refer to this center as the *centroid*. The *x*-value of the centroid is the mean of the *x*-values of the points in the cluster, and the *y*-value of the centroid is the mean of the *y*-values of the points in the cluster.

The next order of business is to calculate the distance between each point and its centroid, square that distance, and add up the squared distances. This sum-of-squared-distances-within-a-cluster is better known as the *within sum of squares*.

Finally, and this is the crucial part, the process repeats until the within sum of squares for each cluster is as small as possible: in other words, until each data point is in the cluster with the closest centroid.

It's also possible to calculate a centroid for the entire set of observations. Its *x*-coordinate is the average of every data point's *x*-coordinate (Petal.Length, in this example), and its *y*-coordinate is the average of every data point's *y*-coordinate (Petal.Width, in this example). The sum of squared distances from each point to this overall centroid is called the *total sum of squares*. The sum of squared distances from each cluster centroid to the overall centroid is the *between sum of squares*.

THAT DISTANCE THING

"The distance between each point and its centroid"? How do you calculate that?

The most common way to do this is called *Euclidean distance,* and just because you asked, here's how to find it. If the coordinates of a point are x_p and y_p and the coordinates of the centroid are x_c and y_c, the distance d between them is

$$d = \sqrt{\left(x_p - x_c\right)^2 + \left(y_p - y_c\right)^2}$$

With more than two dimensions, the equation gets a little hairier, but the principle is the same. And non-Euclidean distance measures (with names like *Minkowski* and *city-block*) are variations on this theme.

The ratio *(between sum of squares)/(within sum of squares)* is a measure of how well the k-means clusters fit the data. A higher number is better.

TECHNICAL STUFF

If these sums-of-squares ring a bell, then you're recalling the *analysis of variance,* which I describe in Chapters 4 and 5 of Book 3.

K-Means Clustering in R

The R function kmeans() handles k-means clustering. It comes with the base R installation, so no additional package download is necessary.

Setting up and analyzing the data

For k-means clustering with the iris dataset (using Petal.Length and Petal. Width), here's the code:

```
set.seed(810)
```

TIP

If you want to replicate my results, set the seed (for the random selection of sets that kicks off the whole thing) to the same number I did:

```
kmi <- kmeans(iris[,3:4],centers=3,nstart=15)
```

The first argument to kmeans() is the data (Columns 3 and 4 of the iris data frame). The second argument specifies the number of clusters, and the third indicates the number of random sets to choose at the beginning of the process.

Understanding the output

Here are the results:

```
> kmi
K-means clustering with 3 clusters of sizes 52, 50, 48

Cluster means:
  Petal.Length Petal.Width
1     4.269231    1.342308
2     1.462000    0.246000
3     5.595833    2.037500

Clustering vector:
  [1] 2 2 2 2 2 2 2 2 2 2 2 2 2 2 2 2 2 2 2 2 2 2 2 2 2 2 2 2 2 2 2 2 2 2 2 2 2 2
      2 2 2 2 2 2 2 2 2 2 2 2 1 1 1 1 1 1 1 1
 [59] 1 1 1 1 1 1 1 1 1 1 1 1 1 1 1 1 1 1 1 1 1 3 1 1 1 1 1 3 1 1 1 1 1 1 1 1 1 1
      1 1 1 1 1 3 3 3 3 3 3 1 3 3 3 3 3 3 3 3
[117] 3 3 3 1 3 3 3 3 3 3 3 1 3 3 3 3 3 3 3 3 3 3 3 3 1 3 3 3 3 3 3 3 3 3 3

Within cluster sum of squares by cluster:
[1] 13.05769  2.02200 16.29167
 (between_SS / total_SS =  94.3 %)

Available components:

[1] "cluster"      "centers"     "totss"      "withinss"    "tot.withinss"
    "betweenss"    "size"
[8] "iter"         "ifault"
```

The first output line tells you the number of flowers in each cluster. Because not all clusters in fact have 50 — you see 52, 50, and 48 here — they don't match up perfectly with the species.

The Cluster means show you the centroid coordinates for each cluster. The ordering of the clusters is arbitrary: It's based on the random selection at the start of the process. For example, as Figure 5-1 shows, the *setosa* are in the leftmost region of the plot, leading to the expectation that they might be Cluster 1. kmeans() has assigned *setosa* to Cluster 2, however.

You can verify the centroids for Cluster 2 (and that Cluster 2 is the *setosa*) by calculating

```
mean(iris$Petal.Length[iris$Species == "setosa"])
mean(iris$Petal.Width[iris$Species == "setosa"])
```

This doesn't work for the other two species because they don't perfectly correspond to Clusters 1 and 3. (Pretty close, though.)

The next output section, `Clustering vector`, shows the cluster assigned to each flower in the data frame.

The next-to-last section shows the within sum of squares for each cluster and the ratio of the between sum of squares to the total sum of squares. The ratio, 94.3 percent, indicates that the clustering scheme is a good fit with the data.

The final section is a bit more important than it appears at first glance. It shows the names of attributes that are available resulting from this particular k-means clustering. This list tells you how to retrieve the attributes. If, for some reason, you want to retrieve the `Clustering vector` (as mentioned in the later sidebar "Plotting the irises"), that's kmi$cluster. Try it, if you don't believe me. Another important one, as you'll see, is tot.withinss, which is the sum of the withinss for each cluster:

```
> kmi$tot.withinss
[1] 31.37136
> sum(kmi$withinss)
[1] 31.37136
```

How, exactly, do the clusters match up with the species? To answer this question, you have to sum up the data points in each cluster and the data points in each species and cross-tabulate. (For example, how many *versicolor* are in each cluster?) The table() function does all this:

```
> table(kmi$cluster,iris$Species)

  setosa versicolor virginica
1      0         48         4
2     50          0         0
3      0          2        46
```

So kmeans() put 2 *versicolor* in Cluster 3, and 4 *virginica* in Cluster 1.

Visualizing the clusters

How does the clustering look? Figure 5-2 shows you. (For the coding details on how to create this figure, see the later sidebar "Plotting the irises.")

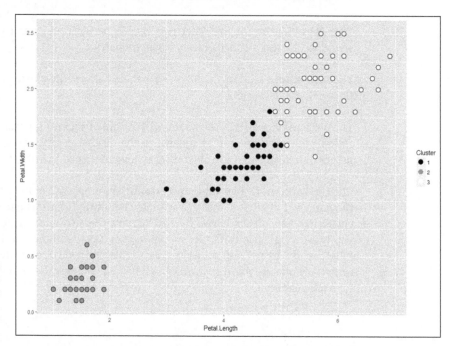

FIGURE 5-2:
K-means
clustering the
iris data frame,
with three
clusters.

It's pretty close to the plot in Figure 5-1, but it's not exact. If you're sharp-eyed, perhaps you can see the six flowers in Figure 5-1 that are classified differently in Figure 5-2. Notice in this figure that no flowers are intermingled with others: The cluster boundaries are pretty clear.

Finding the optimum number of clusters

At the beginning of this discussion, you might have just assumed that 3 was the "best" number of clusters. Three species, three clusters — short and sweet. But is this really the case?

Remember that k-means clustering minimizes the within sum of squares for each cluster. Another way to say this is that k-means clustering minimizes the total of the within sums of squares. So, one way to select the optimum number is to use kmeans() for a range of different values for centers (the number of clusters), retrieve the associated tot.withinss for each one, and compare. (The trivial solution, of course, is to have as many clusters as data points. If each data point has its own, personal cluster, the within sums of squares are all zero.)

To help with the comparison, I'll draw a graph. I'll put the number of clusters on the x-axis and the total within sum of squares on the y-axis. A statistician looking at that graph would look for an "elbow," or a drop in the tot.withinss followed by a leveling-out in which further reduction in the tot.withinss is minimal. That elbow represents the optimum number of clusters.

To run kmeans() on 2 to 15 clusters, you use a for-loop. You begin by creating an empty vector that will eventually hold all total.withinss values:

```
totwss <- NULL
```

The for-loop is

```
for (I in 2:15){
totwss <- append(totwss,kmeans(iris[,3:4],centers=i)$tot.withinss)
           }
```

The loop adds (appends) each new tot.withinss value to the end of the totwss vector.

The code for the plot is

```
plot(x=2:15, y=totwss, type"""", xlab""Cluster"", ylab=""Total Within S"")
```

The type = "b" argument specifies that both lines and points appear in the graph. The plot appears in Figure 5-3.

The graph does show an elbow with three clusters, but after five clusters the graph shows another drop-off. What looks like another elbow appears with six clusters and then total within sum of squares looks pretty stable.

So here's the clustering with six clusters:

```
set.seed(810)
kmi6 <-kmeans(iris[,3:4],centers=6,nstart=15)
```

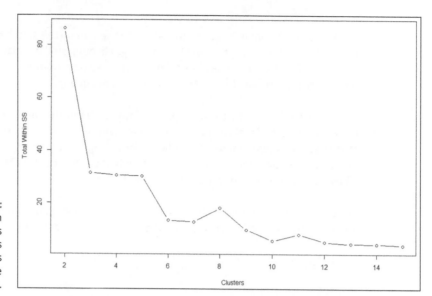

FIGURE 5-3:
Total within sum of squares versus Clusters for k-means clustering of the iris data frame.

Here are some selected results:

```
K-means clustering with 6 clusters of sizes 11, 50, 27, 19, 21, 22

Cluster means:
  Petal.Length Petal.Width
1    6.354545    2.127273
2    1.462000    0.246000
3    4.485185    1.407407
4    3.773684    1.152632
5    5.028571    1.766667
6    5.559091    2.145455

Within cluster sum of squares by cluster:
[1] 1.689091 2.022000 1.232593 2.224211 1.449524 2.407727
 (between_SS / total_SS =  98.0 %)
```

Most of the time, analysts look for the solution with the fewest clusters. Is the almost 4 percent improvement in the between/total ratio (over three clusters) enough to justify the additional three clusters? Hmm. . . .

The answer lies in whether you can make sense of the clusters. Can you attach a meaningful name to each one?

A plot might help. Figure 5-4 shows what the clustering looks like. (Again, coding details are in the later sidebar "Plotting the irises.")

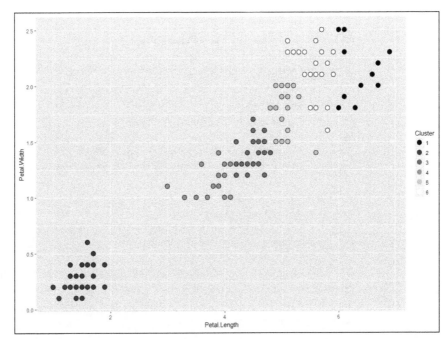

FIGURE 5-4:
K-means
clustering the
iris data frame,
with six clusters.

The clusters are pretty distinct. The *setosa*, as always, form their own group in the lower left area. The cluster in the upper right area consists of *virginica*, but not all the *virginica*. Are these "large" *virginica*? How about the next cluster to the left? Are they "small" *virginica*? Large *versicolor*? A mixture of the two? What about the other three clusters?

A table can be helpful:

```
> table(kmi6$cluster,iris$Species)

    setosa versicolor virginica
1      0          0        11
2     50          0         0
3      0         26         1
4      0         19         0
5      0          5        16
6      0          0        22
```

Most of the *versicolor* are in Clusters 3 and 4, and most of the *virginica* in 1, 5 and 6. And so . . . ?

PLOTTING THE IRISES

If you've read the first sidebar in Chapter 4 of Book 4, "Plotting (two-thirds of) the irises," you're familiar with the ideas explained in *this* sidebar. In fact, this sidebar is that one on steroids. Here, I show you how to plot Figures 5-1, 5-2, and 5-4. For all of them, assume that the package ggplot2 is installed and loaded.

Figure 5-1 plots the iris data frame with Petal.Length on the *x*-axis, Petal.Width on the *y*-axis, and Species as the color of the data points. Here's the code:

```
ggplot(iris, aes(x=Petal.Length,y=Petal.Width,color=Species))+
  geom_point(size=4)+
  scale_color_manual(values=c("grey0","grey65","grey100"))+
  geom_point(shape=1,size=4,color="black")
```

The first line, ggplot( ), specifies the data and maps variables in the data to aspects of the plot. The second line, geom_point( ), adds the data points to the plot and specifies their size. If I just stop here, I get a nice-looking graph whose default colors wouldn't show up well on this black-and-white page.

Instead of the default colors, the third line indicates the colors to use in the data points. The first species is colored in grey0, which is black. The second is in grey65, which is a shade of gray. The third is in grey100, which is white.

The final line, another geom_point( ), is a trick that adds a border to each data point. It superimposes an unfilled data point with a border onto each data point already in the graph.

Figure 5-2 plots the iris data frame in the same way, but this time the data point colors represent the three clusters stored in kmi. So I have to change the color mapping in the ggplot( ) statement. How do I retrieve each flower's cluster from the clustering results? As I point out in the earlier section "Understanding the output," kmi$cluster returns the Clustering vector, which is exactly what I need here.

Does this mean that I just change color=Species to color=kmi$cluster? Not quite. The clusters, remember, are numbers (1, 2, 3). The species are names ("setosa," "virginica", "versicolor"). ggplot( ) thinks that the numbers represent values of a continuous numeric variable, not names, like the species. This doesn't fly with scale_color_manual( ), which maps colors onto category names, not numbers. So I have to somehow turn the cluster numbers into categories. Fortunately, the as.factor( ) function does just that. The change to the code, then, is color = as.factor(kmi$cluster).

One more change: If I change only color and nothing else, the title of the legend is as.factor(kmi$cluster), and no one wants that. So I add the argument name="Cluster" to the scale_color_manual() function to retitle the legend. Here's the code, with the changes in bold:

```
ggplot(iris, aes(x=Petal.Length,y=Petal.Width,color=as.factor(kmi$cluster)))+
    geom_point(size=4)+
    scale_color_manual(name="Cluster",values=c("grey0","grey65","grey100"))+
    geom_point(shape=1,size=4,color="black")
```

You can probably figure out how to plot Figure 5-4. The code is the same as for Figure 5-2, but for Figure 5-4 the results of the 6-cluster k-means clustering are in kmi6. Change the color argument in ggplot() accordingly. The values argument in scale_color_manual() is

```
values=c("grey0","grey20","grey40","grey60","grey80","grey100")
```

The bottom line: Numbers and graphs don't tell the entire story. We can use statistical techniques to suggest possible explanations, but that takes us only so far. Nothing can substitute for knowledge of the content area. A botanist would be able to tell you how to name these clusters in a meaningful way, and perhaps come up with a sensible way of deciding on the number of clusters in the first place.

In my humble opinion, then, this technique works best if you have some knowledge about an area and want to understand more about the structure of a data set in that area.

Quick suggested project: Adding the sepals

In the examples so far in this chapter, I've confined the variables to just Petal. Length and Petal.Width. What happens if the k-means clustering also includes Sepal.Length and Sepal.Width? (To make this happen, change iris[,3:4] to iris[,1:4] in the arguments to kmeans(). And don't forget that first comma in the brackets!)

How does adding the sepal variables affect the clustering for the 3-cluster case? For the 6-cluster case? How about the optimum number of clusters? What do the plots of the 3-cluster case and the 6-cluster case look like with the sepal variables included?

Project: Glass Clusters

In this section, I show you a project that's more complex than clustering irises. The basis for this project is a data set I use in Chapter 3 of Book 4, in the section "Project: Identifying Glass." As a refresher, the data are measurements of chemical and physical properties of 149 pieces of glass. Each piece comes from one of six types (windows or headlamps, for example). Correctly identifying the source of a glass fragment can be a crucial part of a criminal investigation.

The objective here, however, is not identification. The idea is to find structure within the data set: What types of glass are similar to one another? What types are different?

REMEMBER

The distinction between "learning to correctly identify" and "learning the structure of" is the distinction between *supervised* learning and *unsupervised* learning.

The data

As in previous ML projects, the data comes from the UCI ML repository. You'll find this data set at

```
https://archive.ics.uci.edu/ml/datasets/glass+identification
```

Click the `Data Set Description` link to download a text file called `glass.names` that tells you all about the dataset. To read it, open the downloaded `glass.names` file in any text editor (like Notepad).

Next, click the `Data Folder` link. The page that opens has a link called `glass.data`. Click `glass.data` to download a text file of comma-separated variables. Open the downloaded `glass.data` file in a text editor (like Notepad). Press Ctrl+A to highlight everything and then press Ctrl+C to copy it all to the clipboard.

The following command brings the data into R as a data frame:

```
glass.uci <- read.csv("clipboard",header = FALSE)
```

I still need the header, and that's

```
colnames(glass.uci)<-c("ID","RI","Na","Mg","Al","Si","K","Ca","Ba","Fe","Type")
```

The first column, `ID`, is an identifier for the piece of glass, and the second is the glass fragment's refractive index (how much it bends light that passes through it). The last one, `Type`, is unsurprisingly, the type of glass. All the ones in the middle are the chemical elements in the glass.

The levels of Type are numbers. To give them informative names, I use a plyr function called mapvalues():

```
library(plyr)
glass.uci$Type <- mapvalues(glass.uci$Type, from = c(1,2,3,5,6,7),
        to = c("bldg_windows_float","bldg_windows_non_float",
        "vehicle_windows_float","containers","tableware","headlamps"))
```

float and non_float are processes for making a window: "float" produces near-optical-quality glass, and "non-float" glass is lower-quality.

The from vector does not include 4, because the corresponding type (vehicle_windows_non_float) is not in the data set.

REMEMBER

I didn't make up the names for the columns and for the Type levels. They're in the glass.names file.

Starting Rattle and exploring the data

If you've read Chapter 3 of Book 4, you've already seen this part of the movie: Rattle provides a GUI to ML-related functions and enables you to work with those functions in a convenient way. kmeans() is one of those functions.

With the Rattle package downloaded,

```
library(rattle)
rattle()
```

opens the Rattle Data tab. From here on, I summarize the steps. For a fuller exposition, including figures, see the section "Getting the data into Rattle" in Chapter 3 of Book 4.

1. To load the data set into rattle, click the R Dataset radio button on the Data tab and select glass.uci from the Data Name box's drop-down list.

2. Click the Execute button in the upper left corner of the window.

3. Click the Explore tab and select its Distributions radio button to take a look at the data.

    As in Chapter 3 of Book 4, one way to start is to look at the distribution of glass types.

4. **Clear the Group By box and then select the box next to Type.**

5. **Click Execute for the bar plot shown in Figure 3-7 (over in Chapter 3 of Book 4).**

Preparing to cluster

Should I show you how to use all nine numeric variables to form the clusters? I'm going to cheat a bit and ask you to look at the analysis in Chapter 3 of Book 4. Figure 3-9 in that chapter shows how much each variable contributes to the random forest in that example. The plot for MeanDecreaseAccuracy shows that Mg (Magnesium content), RI (refractive index), and Al (Aluminum content) are the three most prominent variables. That sounds like a good starting point.

So, back to the Data tab. After you make the appropriate selections among the radio buttons to ignore all but RI, Mg, and Al, the Data tab looks like Figure 5-5. You click Execute to register these selections.

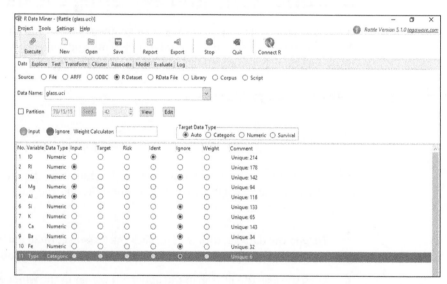

FIGURE 5-5: Setting up the variables for k-means clustering of the glass.uci data frame.

Doing the clustering

On to the Cluster tab. In the Clusters box, I used the arrows to select 6, and I typed **810** into the Seed box, just to be consistent with what I did earlier in this chapter. (Type the same number in that box if you want the same results as mine.) In the Runs box, I used the arrows to select 15 (again, for consistency with what I did earlier). After I made these selections and clicked Execute, the Data tab looks like

Figure 5-6. rattle shows you the cluster sizes (how many observations are in each cluster), the mean of each variable, the cluster centers (the coordinates of each cluster's centroid), and the within sum of squares for each cluster.

FIGURE 5-6:
Setting up the k-means clustering for the glass.uci data frame.

Going beyond Rattle

The Rattle output tells quite a bit about the clusters. Clicking the Data button reveals even more. It's possible to use R functions, as described earlier in this chapter, to find out still more about the k-means clustering that Rattle constructed.

If I click the Log tab, I find that the k-means clustering is stored in a variable called crs$kmeans. This enables me to find out the between-sum-of-squares-to-total-sum-of-squares ratio:

```
> crs$kmeans
```

The relevant line of the output is

```
(between_SS / total_SS = 87.6 %)
```

which is a pretty high ratio.

How about the amounts of the different types of glass in each cluster? That's the province of the `table()` function. Set the first argument to the cluster vector and the second argument to the glass type:

```
> table(crs$kmeans$cluster,glass.uci$Type)

  bldg_windows_float bldg_windows_non_float containers
1                 17                      3          0
2                  0                      1          5
3                  0                      8          1
4                  0                      0          2
5                  0                      4          5
6                 53                     60          0

  headlamps tableware vehicle_windows_float
1         1         0                     5
2        11         4                     0
3         0         0                     0
4        12         0                     0
5         3         5                     0
6         2         0                    12
```

Cluster 6 looks like a `windows` cluster; clusters 2 and 4, like `headlamps` clusters. I can't see any other explanatory labels jumping out, but if I knew more about glass, perhaps I could. Maybe you can.

Chapter **6**

Neural Networks

eural networks are a popular form of supervised machine learning. They're popular because they're widely applied in an array of areas, like speech recognition and image processing. Investors rely on these networks to recognize patterns in the stock market and decide whether to buy or sell. As the name indicates, their design reflects the structure and function of the nervous system.

Networks in the Nervous System

The nervous system consists of cells called *neurons*. Figure 6-1 shows a neuron on the left connected to three neurons on the right. The neuron on the left receives, through its dendrites, messages from other neurons. This neuron processes what it receives, and the result becomes a signal it sends along its axon. Through connections called *synapses* (yes, each one is a tiny gap), the signal passes to the neurons on the right.

Each right-side neuron can receive inputs from several neurons. Each one puts together all its inputs and in turn passes a signal to still other neurons. Ultimately, a message arrives in the brain. The brain interprets the message.

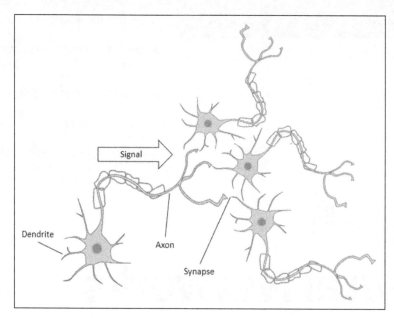

FIGURE 6-1:
Neurons in the
nervous system.

One theory holds that if one neuron continually sends messages to another, the connection between them grows stronger. According to this theory, the adjustment of the connection strengths among neurons is what learning is all about.

Artificial Neural Networks

I've oversimplified the workings of the nervous system. Researchers who uncovered exactly how the neurons process inputs and send messages have won the Nobel Prize.

My description, though, does sketch out the basis for the artificial neural networks in the world of machine learning (ML).

Overview

A machine language neural network consists of simulated neurons, often called *units*, or *nodes*, that work with data. Like the neurons in the nervous system, each unit receives input, performs some computation, and passes its result as a message to the next unit. At the output end, the network makes a decision based on its inputs.

Imagine a neural network that uses physical measurements of flowers, like irises, to identify the flower's species. The network takes data like the petal length and petal width of an iris and learns to classify an iris as either *setosa, versicolor,* or *virginica.* In effect, the network learns the relationship between the inputs (the petal variables) and the outputs (the species).

Figure 6-2 shows an artificial neural network that classifies irises. It consists of an *input layer,* a *hidden layer,* and an *output layer.* Each unit connects with every unit in the next layer. Numerical values called *weights* are on each connection. Weights can be positive or negative. To keep the figure from getting cluttered, I show the weights on the connections only from the input layer to the hidden layer.

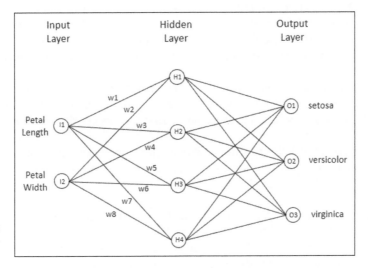

FIGURE 6-2:
An artificial
neural network
that learns to
classify irises.

Input layer and hidden layer

The data points are represented in the input layer. This one has one input unit (I1) that holds the value of petal length and another (I2) that holds the value of petal width. (Refer to Figure 6-2.) The input units send messages to another layer of four units, called a *hidden layer.* The number of units in the hidden layer is arbitrary, and picking that number is part of the art of neural network creation.

Each message to a hidden layer unit is the product of a data point and a connection weight. For example, H1 receives I1 multiplied by w1 (weight 1) along with I2 multiplied by w2 (weight 2). H1 processes what it receives.

What does "processes what it receives" mean? H1 adds the product of I1 and w1 to the product of I2 and w2. H1 then has to send a message to O1, O2, and O3 on the Output layer.

What is the message it sends? It's a number in a restricted range, produced by H1's *activation function*. Three activation functions are common. They have exotic, math-y names: *hyperbolic tangent*, *sigmoid*, and *rectified linear unit*.

Without going into the math, I'll just tell you what they do. The hyperbolic tangent (known as *tanh*) takes a number and turns it into a number between −1 and 1. Sigmoid turns its input into a number between 0 and 1. Rectified linear unit (ReLU) replaces negative values with 0.

By restricting the range of the output, activation functions set up a nonlinear relationship between the inputs and the outputs. Why is this important? In most real-world situations, you don't find a nice, neat linear relationship between what you try to predict (the output) and the data you use to predict it (the inputs).

One more item gets added into the activation function. It's called bias. *Bias* is a constant that the network adds to each number coming out of the units in a layer. The best way to think about bias is that it improves the network's accuracy.

TECHNICAL STUFF

Bias is much like the intercept in a linear regression equation. Without the intercept, a regression line would pass through (0,0) and might miss many of the points it's supposed to fit.

To summarize: A hidden unit like H1 takes the data sent to it by I1 (Petal length) and I2 (Petal width), multiplies each one by the weight on its interconnection (I1 × w1 and I2 × w2), adds the products, adds the bias, and applies its activation function. Then it sends the result to all units in the output layer.

Output layer

The output layer consists of one unit (O1) for *setosa*, another (O2) for *virginica*, and another (O3) for *versicolor*. Based on the messages they receive from the hidden layer, the output units do their computations just as the hidden units do theirs. Their results determine the network's decision about the species for the iris with the given petal length and petal width. The flow from input layer to hidden layer to output layer is called *feedforward*.

How it all works

Where do the interunit connection weights come from? They start out as numbers randomly assigned to the interunit connections. The network trains on a data set of petal lengths, petal widths, and the associated species. On each trial, the network receives a petal length and a petal width and makes a decision, which it then compares with the correct answer. Because the initial weights are random, the initial decisions are guesses.

Each time the network's decision is incorrect, the weights change based on how wrong the decision was (on the amount of error, in other words). The adjustment (which also includes changing the bias for each unit) constitutes "learning." One way of proceeding is to adjust the weights from the output layer back to the hidden layer and then from the hidden layer back to the input layer. This is called *backpropagation* because the amount of error "backpropagates" through the layers.

A network trains until it reaches a certain level of accuracy or a preset number of iterations through the training set. In the evaluation phase, the trained network tackles a new set of data.

REMEMBER

This 3-layer structure is just one way of building a neural network, and it's what I cover in this chapter. Other types of networks are possible.

Neural Networks in R

R has a couple of packages that enable you to create neural networks like the one I describe in the preceding section. In *this* section, however, I deal with the nnet package.

On the Packages tab, click Install to open the Install Packages dialog box. In the dialog box, type **nnet** and click the Install button. When the package finishes downloading, select its check box on the Packages tab.

Building a neural network for the iris data frame

To introduce nnet, I begin with the iris data frame, which comes with R. This data frame consists of 150 rows and 5 columns. Each row provides measurements of sepal length, sepal width, petal length, and petal width of an iris whose species is either *setosa, versicolor,* or *virginica.* Fifty of each species are in the data frame.

In this section, I use the `nnet()` function to build a neural network that does what I describe in the preceding section: It learns to identify an iris's species based on its petal length and petal width.

The first thing to do is create a training set and a test set. I do this with a function called `sample.split()`, which is part of the `caTools` package. So, on the Packages tab, click Install to open the Install Packages dialog box. Type **caTools** in the dialog box and click the Install button. After the package downloads, select its check box on the Packages tab.

Set the seed to this number if you want to reproduce my results:

```
set.seed(810)
```

With `caTools` installed, this line partitions the `iris` data frame into a 70-30 split, maintaining the original proportions of the `Species` in each piece:

```
sample = sample.split(iris$Species, SplitRatio = .70)
```

`sample` is a vector of 150 instances of `TRUE` (the data frame row is in the 70 percent) or `FALSE` (the data frame row is not in the 70 percent).

To create the training set and the test set, use the following:

```
iris.train = subset(iris, sample == TRUE)
iris.test  = subset(iris, sample == FALSE)
```

One of the things I like most about R is its consistency. To create a model, whether it's linear regression, analysis of variance, or k-means clustering — or whatever — the general format is

```
object.name <- function.name(dependent.variable ~ independent.variable(s), data,
                  other stuff)
```

And that's the way to create a neural network with the `nnet` package's `nnet()` function:

```
nni <- nnet(Species ~ Petal.Length + Petal.Width, iris.train, size=4)
```

The first argument to `nnet()` is the formula that relates `Species` to `Petal.Length` and `Petal.Width`. The second argument is the training data, and the third is the number of units in the hidden layer. (Many more arguments are available for this function.)

After running the `nnet()` function, what are the final adjusted weights? To find out, I use the `summary()` function:

```
> summary(nni)
a 2-4-3 network with 27 weights
options were - softmax modelling
 b->h1 i1->h1 i2->h1
-17.92   6.14   6.67
 b->h2 i1->h2 i2->h2
  0.59  -0.09  -0.50
 b->h3 i1->h3 i2->h3
-32.96   1.98  24.58
 b->h4 i1->h4 i2->h4
 11.95  -5.01  -2.53
 b->o1 h1->o1 h2->o1 h3->o1 h4->o1
 20.62 -19.43  39.61 -30.52  27.84
 b->o2 h1->o2 h2->o2 h3->o2 h4->o2
  1.01   2.16  54.41 -13.16   3.25
 b->o3 h1->o3 h2->o3 h3->o3 h4->o3
-20.63  15.79 -93.39  45.34 -30.47
```

After the first two lines of introductory statements, the data for each node in the network is in two rows. For example, these two rows

```
 b->h1 i1->h1 i2->h1
-17.92   6.14   6.67
```

show the information for node h1, the first node in the hidden layer. In Figure 6-2, it's depicted as H1. H1's bias is −17.92. The weight on its connection from I1 (shown in Figure 6-2 as w1) is 6.14, and the weight on its connection from I2 (w2 in the figure) is 6.67.

Plotting the network

To visualize all this, I could go back to Figure 6-2 and add all the weights. Or, I could let R do all the work. A terrific package called `NeuralNetTools` provides `plotnet()`, which does the job quite nicely. To install it, follow the procedure I describe earlier in this chapter: On the Packages tab, click Install to open the Install Packages dialog box. In the dialog box, type **NeuralNetTools** and click the Install button. After the package downloads, select its check box on the Packages tab.

With `NeuralNetTools` installed, this line produces what you see in Figure 6-3.

```
plotnet(nni)
```

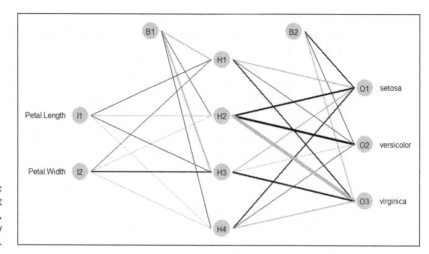

FIGURE 6-3:
The neural net
for iris.train,
rendered by
plotnet().

The figure doesn't show the weights explicitly, but instead represents them graphically. A black line represents a positive weight; a gray line represents a negative weight. The thicker the line, the higher the numerical value. Notice also that the diagram shows B1, which applies the biases to the Hidden units, and B2,which applies the biases to the Output units. (To omit those from the plot, I would add the argument bias=FALSE to plotnet().)

Evaluating the network

How well does the network perform? I use the predict() function (which is in the nnet package) to find out. The line

```
predictions <- predict(nni,iris.test,type = "class")
```

creates a vector of predictions based on the neural network nni, one prediction for each row of the iris.test data frame I created earlier. The type= "class" argument indicates that the neural network decided on a classification for each iris.

Now I use the table() function to set up a *confusion matrix* — a table that shows actual values versus predicted values :

```
table(iris.test$Species,predictions)
```

The first argument is the species of the irises in the test set; the second is the vector of predictions. Here's the matrix:

```
        predictions
          setosa versicolor virginica
```

setosa	15	0	0
versicolor	0	14	1
virginica	0	2	13

The columns are the predicted species, and the rows are the correct species. The numbers in the main diagonal are the correct classifications, whereas the numbers off the main diagonal are errors. The network misclassified one *versicolor* as a *virginica,* and two *virginica* as *versicolor.* The overall error rate is 6.7 percent (3/45), which is quite accurate.

Quick suggested project: Those sepals

As in previous chapters where I use the iris data frame, I used just the two petal variables in the example. And, as in previous chapters, I suggest that you include the sepal variables and create the neural network again. All you have to do is change the formula in the first argument to nnet(). Any effect on the network's performance? How about if you change the maximum number of iterations? What happens to the confusion matrix? What happens if you do it all over again with just the sepal variables?

Project: Banknotes

One popular application of neural networks is image classification. The idea is to represent an image as a set of mathematical characteristics, and each image as a member of a category. The characteristics are inputs to a network; the categories are the outputs. The network learns the relationship between the image characteristics and the image categories and can then classify new images it hasn't trained on.

The data

One area for image classification is the detection of counterfeit currency. A data set in the UCI ML repository provides the opportunity to try out a neural network for just that purpose. It's the banknote+authentication data set, and you'll find it at

```
https://archive.ics.uci.edu/ml/datasets/banknote+authentication
```

For this dataset, the descriptive information is on that web page, not in a separate downloadable text file.

The data are four measures of digital images of 1,372 authentic and fraudulent banknotes.

Three of the four measures are based on some complicated mathematics, called *wavelet transformation,* applied to each image. The transformation produces a distribution of "wavelets." The three measures are the variance, skewness, and kurtosis of each image's wavelet distribution. (If you don't remember what skewness and kurtosis are, take a look at Chapter 5 of Book 2.)

The fourth measure is called *entropy,* which is a measure of how "busy" an image is. A solid black square is a low-entropy image; my cluttered-up desk is a high-entropy image.

Click on the Data Folder link. On the page that opens, click on the data_banknote_ authentication.txt link to download the data file. Open the downloaded file in any text editor (like Notepad). Then press Ctrl+A to highlight the entire file, and press Ctrl+C to copy it all to the clipboard.

These lines of code produce a data frame:

```
banknote.uci <- read.csv("clipboard",header=FALSE)
colnames(banknote.uci) <- c("Variance","Skewness","Kurtosis","Entropy","Class")
```

The last column, Class, indicates whether the banknote is real or fraudulent. The possible values are 0 and 1. The data set's web page doesn't say which is which. (I assume 1 = real, but I could be wrong.)

Taking a quick look ahead

In the iris example, the output layer has three units, one for each species. In this example, two outcomes are possible: 0 and 1. Does this mean we should go with two units in the output layer for this neural network? Nope. In this example, I'll have one output unit that returns a value, and that value represents the network's decision.

At this point, I visualize the data set to get a feel for the numbers I'll be dealing with. I use ggplot techniques that I outline in Chapter 5 of Book 4. (Go over and take a look at the "Plotting the irises" sidebar.) Picking two input variables arbitrarily — Kurtosis and Entropy as the x- and y-variables, respectively, and Class as the color — creates the result shown in Figure 6-4. From this viewpoint, the classes don't appear to be highly separable. Other viewpoints are possible. As an exercise, plot other pairs of variables to see these other viewpoints.

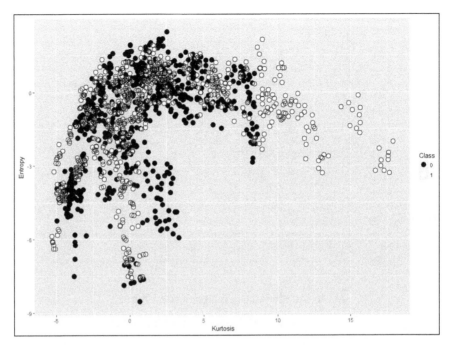

FIGURE 6-4:
Entropy and
Kurtosis in the
banknote.uci
data frame.

Setting up Rattle

Rattle provides a GUI to the nnet package and is useful for creating neural networks of the type I deal with in this example: two possible outputs mapped into one output unit. This is the optimum type of output layer for rattle. Follow these steps:

1. With the Rattle **package installed, type** rattle().

Doing so opens the Rattle Data tab.

2. To read the banknote.uci **data frame into** rattle, **click the R Dataset radio button and then select** banknote.uci **in the Data Name box.**

3. **Click the check box next to Partition and change the accompanying box from 70/15/15 to** 70/30.

This creates a training set of 70 percent of the data and a test set of the remaining 30 percent.

4. **Click Execute.**

The Data tab now looks like Figure 6-5.

5. **On the Model tab, click the Neural Net radio button.**

Neural Networks

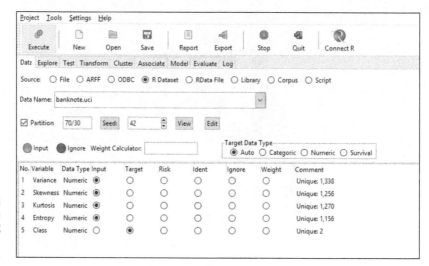

FIGURE 6-5:
The rattle Data tab, after reading in the banknote.uci data frame.

6. **In the Hidden Layer Nodes box, type 3.**

   You can pick a different number, if you like.

7. **Click Execute.**

   The Model tab now looks like Figure 6-6.

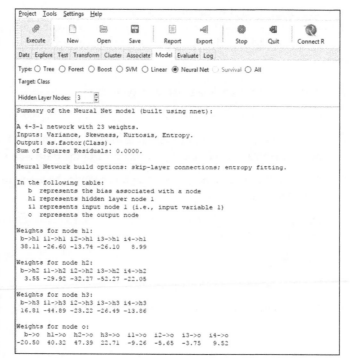

FIGURE 6-6:
The Rattle Model tab, after creating the neural network for the banknote.uci data frame.

I show you this kind of output earlier, in the section "Building a neural network for the `iris` data frame." The table shows the weights for the connections to the Hidden units and to the Output unit, as well as the biases. The exceptionally low sum of squares residual tells you that the network is exceptionally accurate, as you can see in the next section.

Evaluating the network

I click the Evaluate tab and ensure that the Error Matrix radio button is selected as well as the Testing radio button. Clicking Execute creates a confusion matrix based on the Testing set. The output looks like this:

```
Error matrix for the Neural Net model on banknote.uci [test] (counts).

    Predicted
Actual   0   1 Error
     0 225   0   0.0
     1   1 186   0.5

Error matrix for the Neural Net model on banknote.uci [test] (proportions):

    Predicted
Actual   0    1 Error
     0 54.6  0.0   0.0
     1  0.2 45.1   0.5

Overall error: 0.3%, Averaged class error: 0.25%
```

As you can see, the network misclassified just one case. Looks like a pretty good network!

Going beyond `Rattle`: Visualizing the network

My version of `Rattle`, 5.1.0, has no way to plot the network. Perhaps by the time you read this book, a newer version will have that capability.

But that's okay. Designer Graham Williams had the foresight to enable users to tailor `Rattle`'s outputs for their own purposes. To find what I need, I click the Log tab.

Scrolling through the tab reveals that `Rattle` has stored the neural network in an object called `crs$nnet`. To see what the network looks like, I use the `plotnet()` function from the `NeuralNetTools` package:

```
plotnet(crs$nnet)
```

This code produces the neural network shown in Figure 6-7.

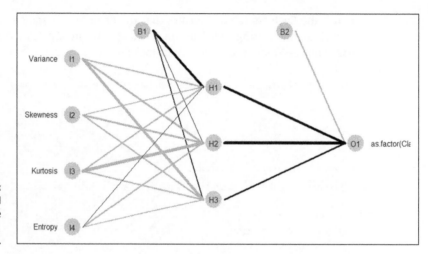

FIGURE 6-7:
The neural network for the `banknote.uci` data frame.

As I mention earlier in this chapter, black lines represent positive connection weights, and gray lines represent negative connection weights. The thickness of a line reflects its numerical value. B1 applies biases to the hidden units, and B2 applies biases to the output units.

Another `NeuralNetTools` tool, `olden()`, plots the importance of each variable. Applying this function to the network

```
olden(crs$nnet)
```

produces what you see in Figure 6-8. Apparently, `Kurtosis` and `Variance` are the most important variables for this neural network.

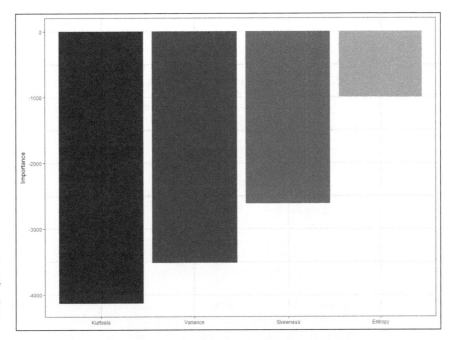

FIGURE 6-8:
Bar plot of the importance of each variable in the neural network.

Suggested Projects: Rattling Around

One benefit of Rattle is that it allows you to easily experiment with whatever it helps you create. Go back to the "Project: Banknotes" section, earlier in this chapter, try varying the number of hidden units, and note the effect on performance. Another possibility is to vary the inputs. For example, the olden() function showed Kurtosis and Variance as the most important variables. Suppose those are the only two inputs. What happens then?

Here's another little project for you. You'll learn more about neural networks if you can see how the network error rate decreases with the number of iterations through the training set.

So the objective is to plot the error rate for the banknote.uci network as a function of the number of iterations through the training data. You should expect to see a decline as the number of iterations increases.

The measure of error for this little project is *root mean square error* (RMSE), which is the standard deviation of the residuals. Each residual is the difference between the network's decision and the correct answer. You'll create a vector that holds the RMSE for each number of iterations and then plot the vector against the number of iterations.

So the first line of code is

```
rmse <- NULL
```

Next, click the Rattle Log tab and scroll down to find the R code that creates the neural network:

```
crs$nnet <- nnet(as.factor(Class) ~ .,
    data=crs$dataset[crs$sample,c(crs$input, crs$target)],
    size=3, skip=TRUE, MaxNWts=10000, trace=FALSE, maxit=100)
```

The values in the data argument are based on Data tab selections. The skip argument allows for the possibility of creating *skip layers* (layers whose connections skip over the succeeding layer). The argument of most interest here is maxit, which specifies the maximum number of iterations.

Copy this code into RStudio.

Set maxit to i and put this code into a for loop in which i goes from 2 to 90.

The residuals are stored in crs$nnet$residuals. The RMSE is sd(crs$nnet$residuals). Use that to update rmse:

```
rmse <-  append(rmse,sd(crs$nnet$residuals))
```

So the general outline for the for loop is

```
for (i in 2:90){crs$nnet <- create the neural net with maxit=i)
                update the rmse vector }
```

(This for loop might take a few more seconds to run than you're accustomed to.)

Finally, use the plot() function to plot RMSE on the *y*-axis and to plot iterations on the *x*-axis:

```
plot(x=2:90, y=rmse, type="b", xlab="Iterations", ylab= "Root Mean Square")
```

Your plot should look like the one shown in Figure 6-9.

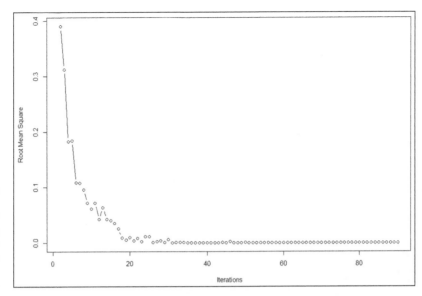

FIGURE 6-9:
Root mean
square error
and iterations
in neural
networks for the
banknote.uci
data frame.

Here's one more suggested project: Take another look at the code for creating crs$nnet. Does anything suggest itself as something of interest that relates to RMSE? Something you could vary in a for-loop while holding maxit constant? And then plot RMSE against that thing? Go for it!

Chapter **7**

Exploring Marketing

I f a business can classify its customers according to how frequently they buy, how recently they bought, and how much they spend, its marketers can target those customers and communicate with them appropriately. A recent customer who buys frequently and spends a lot of money would receive a different type of communication than one who rarely buys, spends little, and hasn't bought anything for a long time.

Analyzing Retail Data

First used in the direct mail industry over 40 years ago, a popular type of marketing analysis depends on *recency* (the date of a customer's most recent purchase), *frequency* (how often the customer purchases), and *money* (how much the customer spends).

Named in order of each element's importance, this is called an *RFM analysis*. Recency is the most important because the more recently a customer has bought, the more likely they will again: The longer it takes for them to return to a business, the less likely they will. And customers who buy more frequently are more likely to again, as are customers who spend more.

One way to proceed is to divide the data into quintiles (fifths) for each variable (R, F, and M), and assign a score from 1 (lowest 20 percent) through 5 (highest 20 percent) to each customer for R, for F, and for M.

With a coding scheme like this one, 125 different RFM scores are possible (555 through 111). RFM analysis segments these possibilities into five classes, with Class 1 as the least valuable customers and Class 5 the most valuable.

TIP

Dividing the data into fifths is an arbitrary (and, apparently, the most popular) way to proceed. A business can divide its data into fifths, fourths, thirds, or whatever suits its purpose. Also, a business can use business rules to create its segments (defining a *high-frequency* customer as someone who has bought at least four times in the past two weeks, for example).

The data

RFM depends on data for individual transactions. The data have to include, at the very least, an invoice number, customer identification number, purchase date, and purchase amount.

The data set for this project holds information for transactions on a British online retail shopping site. The customers are multinational. The transactions occurred between January 12, 2010, and September 12, 2012. It's on the UCI ML Repository, and you can find it here:

```
http://archive.ics.uci.edu/ml/datasets/online+retail
```

After pointing your browser to this URL, follow these steps to read the data set into R:

1. Navigate to the Data folder and download the spreadsheet that contains the data.

2. Open the spreadsheet.

You see that the column names are InvoiceNo, StockCode, Description, Quantity, InvoiceDate, UnitPrice, CustomerID, and Country.

Next, you have to complete a couple of steps to read the data into R. The process is a bit roundabout, but it's reliable and fast, and it gets the job done.

3. Save the spreadsheet as a CSV (comma-separated values) file.

4. Open the CSV file, press Ctrl+A to highlight everything, and then press Ctrl+C to copy to the clipboard.

5. **In RStudio, use the** `read.csv()` **function to read the data into R:**

```
retailonline.uci <- read.csv("clipboard",header = TRUE, sep="\t")
```

The first argument tells the function to take the data from the clipboard, the second one indicates that the first row contains the column names, and the third one shows that the character that separates values is the tab (not the comma, in this case).

TIP

I prefer this method to `read.xlsx()`.

RFM in R

A package called `didrooRFM` provides the function `findRFM()` that works on data like the Online Retail data set. To download the package, click Install on the Packages tab to open the Install Packages dialog box. Type **didrooRFM** into the dialog box and click the Install button.

After the package downloads, select its check box on the Packages tab.

Preparing the data

The function `findRFM()` requires a data frame that has `InvoiceNo`, `CustomerID`, `InvoiceDate`, and `Amount` (in that order). Unfortunately, the `Amount` column is missing from `retailonline.uci`. To create it, I multiply each row's `Quantity` by its `UnitPrice`:

```
retailonline.uci$Amount <- retailonline.uci$Quantity * retailonline.
   uci$UnitPrice
```

Here are the first six rows of the data frame with columns 2 and 3 omitted so that everything fits neatly on the page:

```
> head(retailonline.uci[,-c(2,3)])
  InvoiceNo Quantity     InvoiceDate UnitPrice CustomerID       Country Amount
1    536365        6 12/1/2010 8:26      2.55      17850 United Kingdom  15.30
2    536365        6 12/1/2010 8:26      3.39      17850 United Kingdom  20.34
3    536365        8 12/1/2010 8:26      2.75      17850 United Kingdom  22.00
4    536365        6 12/1/2010 8:26      3.39      17850 United Kingdom  20.34
5    536365        6 12/1/2010 8:26      3.39      17850 United Kingdom  20.34
6    536365        2 12/1/2010 8:26      7.65      17850 United Kingdom  15.30
```

Next, I create a data frame that holds the required columns. The documentation video for `findRFM()` specifies that `InvoiceNo` should be a unique value for each transaction. In this data frame, however, each row represents a purchased item that can be part of a transaction. Accordingly, the InvoiceNo column has duplication: The first six rows, in fact, are all part of the same transaction.

TIP

You can find that findRFM() video by typing **?findRFM**. A link to the video appears in the Help documentation.

In the data frame I'm about to show you how to create, each invoice number covers an entire transaction and the transaction's Amount is the total of the amounts for each item in the transaction.

So you create the data frame in two parts and then merge the two parts. The first part is a data frame that has a unique invoice number associated with the customer ID and the invoice date. The function unique() does the work. It pulls the relevant information from columns 1, 7, and 5 in retailonline.uci:

```
firstPart <- unique(retailonline.uci[,c(1,7,5)])

> head(firstPart)
    InvoiceNo CustomerID      InvoiceDate
1     536365     17850 12/1/2010 8:26
8     536366     17850 12/1/2010 8:28
10    536367     13047 12/1/2010 8:34
22    536368     13047 12/1/2010 8:34
26    536369     13047 12/1/2010 8:35
27    536370     12583 12/1/2010 8:45
```

The second part provides the total of all the amounts in each transaction. For this, you use the helpful aggregate() function. The idea is to *aggregate* all amounts associated with an invoice number by adding them up:

```
secondPart <- aggregate(list(Amount=retailonline.uci$Amount),
    by=list(InvoiceNo=retailonline.uci$InvoiceNo), FUN=sum)
```

The first argument shows what you're aggregating (Amount); the second shows what you're aggregating over (InvoiceNo); and the third specifies that summation is the way you're aggregating. You use list() to create the column names in the aggregation (which is a data frame). Here's what the aggregation looks like:

```
> head(secondPart)
    InvoiceNo Amount
1     536365 139.12
2     536366  22.20
3     536367 278.73
4     536368  70.05
5     536369  17.85
6     536370 855.86
```

To produce the data frame for findRFM(), you merge the two parts:

```
dataRFM <- merge(firstPart,secondPart, by = "InvoiceNo")
```

It looks like this:

```
> head(dataRFM)
  InvoiceNo CustomerID     InvoiceDate Amount
1    536365      17850 12/1/2010 8:26 139.12
2    536366      17850 12/1/2010 8:28  22.20
3    536367      13047 12/1/2010 8:34 278.73
4    536368      13047 12/1/2010 8:34  70.05
5    536369      13047 12/1/2010 8:35  17.85
6    536370      12583 12/1/2010 8:45 855.86
```

One issue remains: InvoiceDate is not in the proper format for findRFM(). It has the date in slash format along with the time in hours and minutes. The function prefers R's date format without the time information.

The easiest way to reformat InvoiceDate appropriately is to use as.Date():

```
dataRFM$InvoiceDate <- as.Date(dataRFM$InvoiceDate, format = "%m/%d/%Y")
```

The second argument to as.Date() lets the function know the format of the date it's operating on. The uppercase Y indicates that the year appears as four digits. (For two digits, as in 12/1/10, it's a lowercase y.)

After the reformat, the data frame looks like this:

```
> head(dataRFM)
  InvoiceNo CustomerID InvoiceDate Amount
1    536365      17850  2010-12-01 139.12
2    536366      17850  2010-12-01  22.20
3    536367      13047  2010-12-01 278.73
4    536368      13047  2010-12-01  70.05
5    536369      13047  2010-12-01  17.85
6    536370      12583  2010-12-01 855.86
```

One more bit of clean-up, and you're done with data prep. It's a good idea to eliminate missing data, so here goes:

```
dataRFM <- na.omit(dataRFM)
```

The data frame is ready for analysis.

Doing the analysis

Now you apply the findRFM() function:

```
resultsRFM <-findRFM(dataRFM,recencyWeight = 4, frequencyWeight = 4,
    monetoryWeight = 4)
```

The first argument is the data frame. The next three arguments are the weights (multipliers) to apply to the Recency score, the Frequency score, and the Monetary score. (Yes, I know: The last argument should be monetary, not monetory. Let it go.) You can use any weights you like to reflect the importance you attach to each variable. I just use the default values (4) here and show you the argument names and their order.

Examining the results

When the findRFM() function finishes its work, it produces Figure 7-1, a histogram that shows the distribution of final weighted scores.

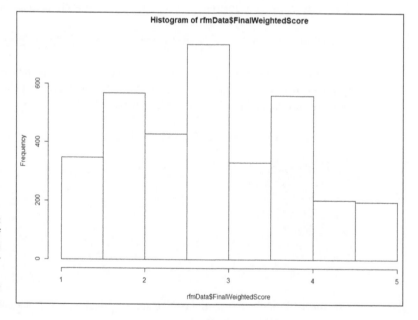

FIGURE 7-1: Distribution of final weighted scores after findRFM() analyzes the online retail data.

How about a look at the data frame that the function creates?

Here are the first four columns (and the first six rows):

```
> head(resultsRFM[,c(1:4)])
# A tibble: 6 x 4
```

```
  CustomerID MeanValue LastTransaction NoTransaction
     <chr>     <dbl>       <date>          <int>
1    12347   592.3920    2011-12-07          5
2    12352   155.5114    2011-11-03          7
3    12353    89.0000    2011-05-19          1
4    12354  1079.4000    2011-04-21          1
5    12357  6207.6700    2011-11-06          1
6    12358   584.0300    2011-12-08          2
```

This is the CustomerID along with the data that lead to the RFM scores: MeanValue (the average amount the customer spent per transaction), the LastTransaction date, and NoTransaction (the number of transactions). The next three columns are the percentiles of each of these pieces of data. I won't show those. (You can take a look on your own, if you like.) These lead in turn to the next three columns: the Monetary, Frequency, and Recency scores. Here they are, along with the FinalCustomerClass, which is in the final column:

```
> head(resultsRFM[,c(1,8:10,16)])
# A tibble: 6 x 5
  CustomerID MonetoryScore FrequencyScore RecencyScore FinalCustomerClass
     <chr>       <dbl>         <dbl>          <dbl>          <chr>
1    12347         5             5              5           Class-5
2    12352         2             5              3           Class-3
3    12353         1             1              1           Class-1
4    12354         5             1              1           Class-2
5    12357         5             1              4           Class-3
6    12358         5             2              5           Class-4
```

For this function, the class is apparently the rounded average of the RFM scores.

The classes represent the RFM segmentation of the customers from most valuable (like Customer #12347) to least valuable (like Customer #12353).

One result of interest is the distribution of classes. To visualize this distribution, you first use the table() function to tabulate the frequency in each class:

```
tblClass <- table(resultsRFM$FinalCustomerClass)
```

The table is

```
> tblClass

Class-1 Class-2 Class-3 Class-4 Class-5
    611    1129     973     603      56
```

And then you use `barplot()`:

```
barplot(tblClass)
```

The result is shown in Figure 7-2, a visualization of the RFM segmentation of the customers. As you can see, Class 5 customers are pretty rare.

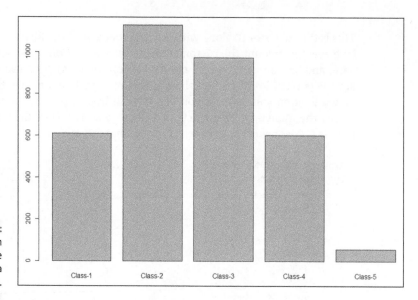

FIGURE 7-2:
The distribution of classes in the `retail.uci` data frame.

TIP

In my discussion of `findRFM()`'s output, I left out columns 5–7 and columns 11–15. Feel free to examine those on your own.

Taking a look at the countries

Most commercial marketing data sets include demographic information about the customers. Combined with RFM analysis, that information can be the basis for some powerful marketing.

The only demographic data in this data set is the customer's country. It might be instructive to see the distributions of the classes in the countries.

To see how the RFM data connect with the countries, you have to add `Country` into the `resultsRFM` data frame. Remember that the `findRFM()` function assigns RFM scores to each `CustomerID`, so each row in `resultsRFM` holds a unique `CustomerID`. To connect `Country` with this data frame, then, you have to create a data frame that connects each `CustomerID` with its `Country` and then merge that data frame with `resultsRFM`.

To create the data frame that associates each CustomerID with its Country, you eliminate the duplicated CustomerID rows in retailonline.uci. You use !duplicated() to do that:

```
retail.nondup<- retailonline.uci[!duplicated(retailonline.
    uci$CustomerID),c(7,8)]
```

Specifying Columns 7 and 8 in c(7,8) limits the new data frame to just Customer ID and Country. Here's what the data frame looks like:

```
> head(retail.nondup)
    CustomerID        Country
1        17850 United Kingdom
10       13047 United Kingdom
27       12583         France
47       13748 United Kingdom
66       15100 United Kingdom
83       15291 United Kingdom
```

Next, merge retail.nondup with selected columns of resultsRFM:

```
RFMCountry <-merge(resultsRFM[,c(1,8:10,16)],retail.nondup, by="CustomerID")
```

I change to shorter column names so that I can show you the data frame on this page:

```
colnames(RFMCountry) <- c("ID","Money","Frequency","Recency","Class","Country")
```

And here it is:

```
> head(RFMCountry)
     ID Money Frequency Recency   Class     Country
1 12347     5         5       5 Class-5     Iceland
2 12352     2         5       3 Class-3      Norway
3 12353     1         1       1 Class-1     Bahrain
4 12354     5         1       1 Class-2       Spain
5 12357     5         1       4 Class-3 Switzerland
6 12358     5         2       5 Class-4     Austria
```

Now you can use table() to examine the distribution of Class for each Country:

```
> table(RFMCountry$Country,RFMCountry$Class)

            Class-1 Class-2 Class-3 Class-4 Class-5
  Australia       2       2       1       2       0
  Austria         2       2       3       2       0
```

Bahrain	1	0	0	0	0
Belgium	4	6	4	3	0
Canada	1	2	0	0	0
Channel Islands	0	3	3	2	0
Cyprus	2	1	2	0	0
Czech Republic	0	0	1	0	0
Denmark	1	5	2	0	0
EIRE	0	0	1	1	1
European Community	0	1	0	0	0
Finland	0	1	2	2	1
France	6	17	30	16	3
Germany	7	24	16	30	1
Greece	0	2	1	0	0
Hong Kong	0	0	0	0	0
Iceland	0	0	0	0	1
Israel	0	1	0	0	0
Italy	1	7	2	2	0
Japan	2	1	1	1	1
Lebanon	0	1	0	0	0
Lithuania	1	0	0	0	0
Malta	0	2	0	0	0
Netherlands	2	2	3	0	1
Norway	0	0	5	1	0
Poland	1	2	1	0	0
Portugal	3	4	3	4	0
Singapore	0	0	0	1	0
Spain	2	6	11	2	0
Sweden	0	3	3	0	1
Switzerland	1	5	9	3	0
United Kingdom	572	1026	869	530	46
Unspecified	0	2	0	0	0
USA	0	1	0	1	0

Obviously, most of the business comes from the United Kingdom. The rest of Europe combines to provide a distant second. It's difficult to make any conclusions from the small non-UK samples, but a quick look shows that the classes seem to be distributed similarly throughout the countries. Perhaps adding post-2011 data would shed some light on intercountry differences.

Enter Machine Learning

Creating classes from RFM scores is one way to segment customers. Another is to use machine learning to discover structure in the data and use that structure as the basis for customer segmentation.

Working with k-means clustering

K-means clustering, which I discuss in Chapter 5 of Book 4, is an applicable machine learning technique. The idea behind k-means clustering is to find subgroups in data. The subgroups are called *clusters*.

Provide a set number of clusters, and a clustering procedure guesses which cluster each data point belongs to. The clustering procedure calculates the distance from each data point to the center of its cluster (known as the *centroid*), squares the distance, and adds up all the squared distances for each cluster. Each cluster thus has its own sum of squared distances, also known as a *within sum of squares*. Adding those up over all the clusters produces a *total within sum of squares*.

The clustering procedure repeats (and potentially reassigns data points to different clusters) until the within sum of squares is as small as possible for each cluster and the total within sum of squares is a minimum. When this happens, each data point is in the cluster with the closest centroid.

How many clusters should you specify? One way to find out is to carry out the clustering procedure on the data and use a range of possibilities for the number of clusters. After each procedure finishes, calculate the total within sum of squares. Generally, the total within sum of squares decreases as the number of clusters increases. The objective is to find the number of clusters above which little or no reduction in total within sum of squares occurs.

That's what I do with the RFM data. Each data point (corresponding to a customer) appears as a Recency score, a Frequency score, and a Monetary score.

I sketch out this procedure in Chapter 5 of Book 4. I begin by showing you how to initialize a vector called totwss, which will hold the values of total within sum of squares:

```
totwss <- NULL
```

A for loop carries out the clustering procedure for cluster amounts from 2 to 15 and appends the resulting total within sum of squares to totwss. The kmeans() function does the clustering:

```
for (i in 2:15){
  totwss <- append(totwss,kmeans(resultsRFM[,8:10],centers=i)$tot.withinss)
}
```

Columns 8–10 in resultsRFM hold the variables of interest. The centers = i argument sets the number of clusters, and $totwithinss holds the total within

Exploring Marketing

sum of squares for a clustering solution. After each k-means procedure ends, append( ) puts the total within sum of squares on the end of the totwss vector.

Finally, you plot total within sum of squares against number of clusters:

```
plot(x=2:15, y=totwss, type="b", xlab="Clusters", ylab= "Total Within SS")
```

The plot( ) function produces Figure 7-3. After 11 clusters, the total within sum of squares seems to not decrease appreciably, suggesting that 11 is a good number of clusters for this data set. This is a judgment call, and you might see it differently. Incidentally, one business analytics website (www.Putler.com/rfm-analysis) advocates for just that many customer segments.

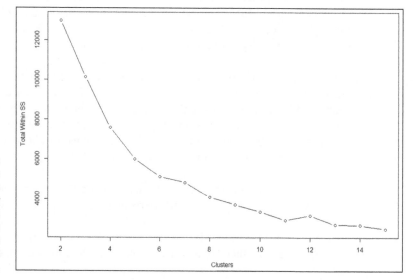

FIGURE 7-3:
Total within
sum of squares
versus number
of clusters
for k-means
clustering of the
resultsRFM
data frame.

Working with Rattle

Rattle provides a GUI to the kmeans( ) function. If you've worked through any of the preceding chapters in Book 4, you have this package downloaded and all you have to do is select its check box on the Packages tab.

This command opens the Rattle GUI Data tab:

```
rattle()
```

Click the R Dataset radio button and then select resultsRFM from the drop-down menu in the Data Name box. You click Execute to read the data frame. When the variable names appear on the Data tab, leave the Ident radio button for CustomerID as is, but select the Ignore radio button for all other variables except MonetoryScore, FrequencyScore, and RecencyScore. If the Partition box is selected, deselect it. Because you clicked those radio buttons, click Execute again. After all this, the screen looks like Figure 7-4.

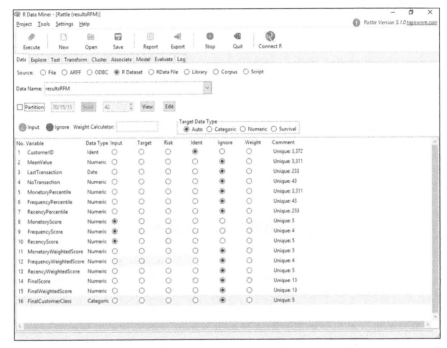

FIGURE 7-4:
The rattle
Data tab,
after selecting
the variables
for k-means
clustering.

Next, you open the Cluster tab and, with the KMeans radio button selected, use the arrow in the Clusters box to set 11 as the number of clusters. Make sure that the Re-Scale box is deselected. Then click Execute. Figure 7-5 shows the appearance of the Cluster tab after all these actions.

The first couple of lines show the number of data points in each of the 11 clusters. The next lines present the mean for each variable. The table shows the centroids for each cluster.

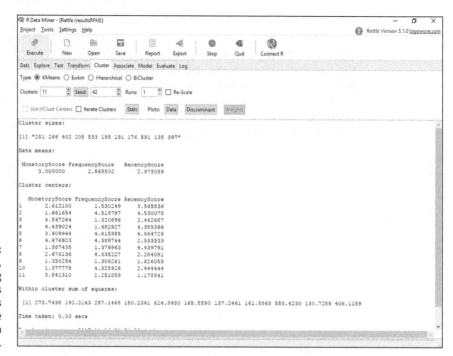

FIGURE 7-5:
The Cluster tab, after executing the selections for *k*-means clustering of the resultsRFM data frame.

Digging into the clusters

The Log tab reveals that `Rattle` stores the results of the k-means clustering in an object called `crs$kmeans`. Working with attributes of this object allows you to go beyond the `Rattle` results.

For example, you can treat the table of centroids as the R, F, and M values of each cluster. That table is in `crs$kmeans$centers`. It's easier to work with those values if you round them off and turn the table into a data frame. Strictly speaking, you first have to turn the table into a matrix and then into a data frame. The function `as.data.frame.matrix()` does all that in one fell swoop:

```
rounded.clusters <- as.data.frame.matrix(round(crs$kmeans$centers))
> rounded.clusters
  MonetoryScore FrequencyScore RecencyScore
1             3              2            4
2             2              5            5
3             5              1            2
4             4              1            4
5             4              5            5
6             4              4            3
7             1              1            4
```

8	3	4	2
9	1	1	2
10	1	4	2
11	4	1	1

With the numbers in a data frame, I can manipulate them and get a sense of what the clusters mean. The cluster numbers are arbitrary: The customers in cluster 1 aren't necessarily more valuable than the customers in cluster 11. So you can use some rules of thumb to reorder them and see what shakes out.

As I mention earlier, experience indicates that recency is most important (a more recent customer is more likely to repeat), followed by frequency (a frequent customer is more likely to repeat), followed by money.

Here's how to sort the clusters by recency, and then by frequency, and then by money:

```
with(rounded.clusters, rounded.clusters[order(-RecencyScore,-FrequencyScore,
    -MonetoryScore),])
```

I suggest using `with()` so that in the `order()` function you don't have to use arguments like `rounded.clusters$RecencyScore`. The `order()` function specifies the order of the rows. The minus sign (−) in front of each argument means "in descending order." Running that code produces this:

	MonetoryScore	FrequencyScore	RecencyScore
5	4	5	5
2	2	5	5
1	3	2	4
4	4	1	4
7	1	1	4
6	4	4	3
8	3	4	2
10	1	4	2
3	5	1	2
9	1	1	2
11	4	1	1

With this ordering, the most valuable customers are in Cluster 5, and the least valuable are in Cluster 11. Cluster 5 customers are apparently frequent and recent buyers whose spending is at the second-highest level. Cluster 11 customers spend as much as Cluster 5 customers, but not recently and not frequently. How would marketers communicate with each group?

I leave it to you to interpret the other clusters.

The clusters and the classes

I'm curious to know how the RFM analysis compares with the clustering. How do the clusters line up with the classes?

Each customer's assigned cluster is in `crs$kmeans$cluster`, and the assigned class is in `resultsRFM$FinalCustomerClass`. So this table tells the tale:

```
> table(Cluster=crs$kmeans$cluster,Class=resultsRFM$FinalCustomerClass)
       Class
Cluster Class-1 Class-2 Class-3 Class-4 Class-5
     1        0     214      67       0       0
     2        0       0     205      61       0
     3        0     239     163       0       0
     4        0       0     185      20       0
     5        0       0      47     430      56
     6        0       0     103      92       0
     7        0     169      22       0       0
     8        0      52     124       0       0
     9      528      63       0       0       0
    10        0      78      57       0       0
    11       83     314       0       0       0
```

The table shows Class 5 customers all in Cluster 5, which ranked highest among the clusters. (That they're both "5" is a coincidence.) Cluster 11 (the lowest-ranked) consists entirely of Class 1 and Class 2 customers.

So it looks like the two segmentation schemes are related. To get a definitive answer (instead of "looks like"), you'd need a statistical analysis.

Is this a good time for statistical analysis? It's *always* a good time for statistical analysis! For a table like this, I show you how to use a statistical test to see whether the clusters and the classes are independent of one another. Recapping what I tell you in Book 3, statisticians call this the *null hypothesis*. A statistical test tells you how likely it is that "independence" can explain the data in the table. If that probability turns out to be very small (less than .05, by convention), you reject the independence explanation.

Here's another way to look at it: If the clusters and the classes were independent of one another, the numbers in the table would look different. They would still add up to the same number of customers and to the same row totals and column totals, but the numbers inside the table would be distributed differently. The question is, does the arrangement we have differ significantly from the independence-based arrangement?

The appropriate statistical test is called *chi squared*. Here's how to use it:

```
> chisq.test(table(Cluster=crs$kmeans$cluster, Class=resultsRFM$FinalCustomer
  Class))

  Pearson's Chi-squared test

data:  table(Cluster = crs$kmeans$cluster, Class = resultsRFM$FinalCustomer
  Class)
X-squared = 6261.6, df = 40, p-value < 2.2e-16
```

The exceptionally low p-value indicates that you can reject the idea that Cluster and Class are independent of one another. Independence is highly unlikely.

Quick suggested project

If you'd like to explore the Clusters versus Classes table a bit further, download and install the vcd (visualizing categorical data) package. One function, assocstats(), provides some additional statistics you can apply. Another function, assoc(), produces a nice-looking graphic that spotlights deviations from independence in the table.

Suggested Project: Another Data Set

If you're interested in trying out your RFM analysis skills on another set of data, this project is for you.

The CDNOW data set consists of almost 70,000 rows. It's a record of sales at CDNOW from the beginning of January 1997 through the end of June 1998.

You'll find it at: https://raw.githubusercontent.com/rtheman/CLV/master/1_Input/CDNOW/CDNOW_master.txt

Press Ctrl+A to highlight all the data, and press Ctrl+C to copy to the clipboard. Then use the read.csv() function to read the data into R:

```
cdNOW <- read.csv("clipboard", header=FALSE, sep = "")
```

Here's how to name the columns:

```
colnames(cdNOW) <- c("CustomerID","InvoiceDate","Quantity","Amount")
```

The data should look like this:

```
> head(cdNOW)
  CustomerID InvoiceDate Quantity Amount
1          1    19970101        1  11.77
2          2    19970112        1  12.00
3          2    19970112        5  77.00
4          3    19970102        2  20.76
5          3    19970330        2  20.76
6          3    19970402        2  19.54
```

It's less complicated than the Online Retail project because Amount is the total amount of the transaction. So each row is a transaction, and aggregation isn't necessary. The Quantity column is irrelevant for our purposes.

TIP

Here's a hint about reformatting the InvoiceDate: The easiest way to get it into R date format is to download and install the lubridate package and use its ymd() function:

```
cdNOW$InvoiceDate <-ymd(cdNOW$InvoiceDate)
```

After that change, here's how the first six rows look:

```
> head(cdNOW)
  CustomerID InvoiceDate Quantity Amount
1          1  1997-01-01        1  11.77
2          2  1997-01-12        1  12.00
3          2  1997-01-12        5  77.00
4          3  1997-01-02        2  20.76
5          3  1997-03-30        2  20.76
6          3  1997-04-02        2  19.54
```

Almost there. What's missing for findRFM()? An invoice number. So you have to use a little trick to make one up. The trick is to use each row identifier in the row-identifier column as the invoice number. To turn the row-identifier column into a data frame column, download and install the tibble package and use its rownames_to_column() function:

```
cdNOW <- rownames_to_column(cdNOW, "InvoiceNumber")
```

Here's the data:

```
> head(cdNOW)
  InvoiceNumber CustomerID InvoiceDate Quantity Amount
1             1          1  1997-01-01        1  11.77
2             2          2  1997-01-12        1  12.00
3             3          2  1997-01-12        5  77.00
4             4          3  1997-01-02        2  20.76
5             5          3  1997-03-30        2  20.76
6             6          3  1997-04-02        2  19.54
```

Now create a data frame with everything but that Quantity column and you're ready.

See how much of the Online Retail project you can accomplish in this one.

Happy analyzing!

Chapter **8**

From the City That Never Sleeps

n airline flight generates a lot of data. The data includes identification of the plane (airline, tail number), identification of the flight (flight number, date, time, origin, destination), characteristics of the flight (distance, time in the air, departure delay, arrival delay), and more. For a budding data analyst, a data set of airline flights presents a treasure trove of opportunities. And that's what I show you how to work with in this chapter.

Examining the Data Set

The data set is called `flights`, and it lives in a package called `nycflights13`. It has the data on all domestic flights out of New York City in 2013. On the Packages tab, click Install to open the Install Packages dialog box. In the dialog box, type **nycflights13** and click the Install button. After the package downloads, select its check box on the Packages tab. Additional data sets are in this package, and I show you how to work with them, too.

A number of other packages are important for data manipulation, and they're part of a bigger package called `tidyverse`. To download this package, follow the procedure in the preceding paragraph (and type **tidyverse** in the dialog box). Select the tidyverse check box on the Packages tab and you're ready for business.

Warming Up

Before I start you out on the project, I walk you through some fundamental skills. Let me begin with a look at the data.

Glimpsing and viewing

The `flights` data set has 19 columns, so `head(flights)` won't be much help. Instead, a `tidyverse` function called `glimpse()` flips the script, by showing you the column names in a column and the first few values of each column in a row:

```
> glimpse(flights,width=50)
Observations: 336,776
Variables: 19
$ year          <int> 2013, 2013, 2013, 2013...
$ month         <int> 1, 1, 1, 1, 1, 1, 1, 1...
$ day           <int> 1, 1, 1, 1, 1, 1, 1, 1...
$ dep_time      <int> 517, 533, 542, 544, 55...
$ sched_dep_time <int> 515, 529, 540, 545, 60...
$ dep_delay     <dbl> 2, 4, 2, -1, -6, -4, -...
$ arr_time      <int> 830, 850, 923, 1004, 8...
$ sched_arr_time <int> 819, 830, 850, 1022, 8...
$ arr_delay     <dbl> 11, 20, 33, -18, -25, ...
$ carrier       <chr> "UA", "UA", "AA", "B6"...
$ flight        <int> 1545, 1714, 1141, 725,...
$ tailnum       <chr> "N14228", "N24211", "N...
$ origin        <chr> "EWR", "LGA", "JFK", "...
$ dest          <chr> "IAH", "IAH", "MIA", "...
$ air_time      <dbl> 227, 227, 160, 183, 11...
$ distance      <dbl> 1400, 1416, 1089, 1576...
$ hour          <dbl> 5, 5, 5, 5, 6, 5, 6, 6...
$ minute        <dbl> 15, 29, 40, 45, 0, 58,...
$ time_hour     <dttm> 2013-01-01 05:00:00, ...
```

The `width` argument controls how much of each row to show. If you leave it out, the output fills out the whole screen (and wouldn't translate well to this page).

Another function, called `View()`, presents a spreadsheet-like (spreadsheetesque?) look at the data on a new tab in the RStudio Script window:

```
View(flights)
```

It produces what you see in Figure 8-1.

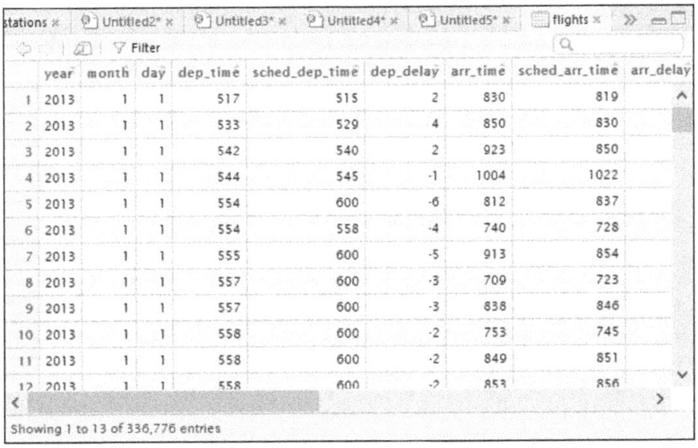

stations | Untitled2* | Untitled3* | Untitled4* | Untitled5* | flights

Filter

	year	month	day	dep_time	sched_dep_time	dep_delay	arr_time	sched_arr_time	arr_delay
1	2013	1	1	517	515	2	830	819	
2	2013	1	1	533	529	4	850	830	
3	2013	1	1	542	540	2	923	850	
4	2013	1	1	544	545	-1	1004	1022	
5	2013	1	1	554	600	-6	812	837	
6	2013	1	1	554	558	-4	740	728	
7	2013	1	1	555	600	-5	913	854	
8	2013	1	1	557	600	-3	709	723	
9	2013	1	1	557	600	-3	838	846	
10	2013	1	1	558	600	-2	753	745	
11	2013	1	1	558	600	-2	849	851	
12	2013	1	1	558	600	-2	853	856	

Showing 1 to 13 of 336,776 entries

FIGURE 8-1: `View(flights)` puts this view into the RStudio Script window.

Piping, filtering, and grouping

Dealing with a data frame often calls for putting multiple commands and functions together. To make that easy to do, the `tidyverse` provides the `pipe` operator, which looks like this: `%>%`. (It's part of the `magrittr` package that installs along with `tidyverse` — no doubt named after Belgian artist René Magritte whose famous painting of a smoker's pipe includes the French translation of the phrase "This is not a pipe!")

You use `%>%` to connect one function to the next.

Suppose that I'm interested in the mean and standard deviation of how long flights from Newark lasted (`air_time`) in the first five days of January. That's

```
Newark_January <- flights %>%
  filter(origin == "EWR" & month == 1 & day <= 5) %>%
  group_by(day)%>%
  summarize(mean=mean(air_time,na.rm=TRUE),
            std_dev=sd(air_time, na.rm=TRUE))
```

The first line, of course, assigns `flights` to `Newark_January`. Read the `%>%` operator as "then."

So *then* the second line uses `filter()` to extract just the flights out of Newark (`"EWR"`) and only in January (`month == 1`) and just the first five days (`day <= 5`).

Then the third line uses `group_by()` to group the data by `day`.

And *then* the fourth line provides the statistics, omitting the missing data.

From the City That Never Sleeps

TIP

The %>% operator works a lot like + does in ggplot.

To render this little structure nicely onscreen, you use the kable() function (which lives in the knitr package, so make sure you download and install knitr):

```
> kable(Newark_January,digits=2)


| day|   mean| std_dev|
|---:|------:|-------:|
|   1| 166.89|   97.46|
|   2| 159.20|   93.47|
|   3| 151.36|   83.44|
|   4| 143.39|   84.37|
|   5| 157.10|   95.34|
```

Before going any further, you should know about another statistic: the *standard error of the mean*. It's the standard deviation divided by the square root of the number of scores that go into calculating the mean. Why is the standard error important? Think of the air times in Day 1 as a sample drawn from a large population. The standard error is a measure of how accurately the sample mean estimates the population mean: The larger the sample, the more accurate the estimate.

Given the importance of the standard error of the mean, you'd think that base R would provide a function to calculate it. But it doesn't. A function called std. error() is in the plotrix package. Follow the usual steps to download and install this package. With plotrix loaded and installed, you can get the standard error of the mean by adding a line to summarize():

```
Newark_January <- flights %>%
   filter(origin == "EWR" & month == 1 & day <= 5) %>%
   group_by(day)%>%
   summarize(mean=mean(air_time,na.rm=TRUE),
             std_dev=sd(air_time, na.rm=TRUE),
             std_err=std.error(air_time, na.rm=TRUE))
```

and then use kable() once again:

```
> kable(Newark_January,digits=2)


| day|   mean| std_dev| std_err|
|---:|------:|-------:|-------:|
|   1| 166.89|   97.46|    5.63|
|   2| 159.20|   93.47|    5.06|
```

```
|   3| 151.36|    83.44|    4.59|
|   4| 143.39|    84.37|    4.60|
|   5| 157.10|    95.34|    6.19|
```

Visualizing

Next, you graph the data, which is always a good thing to do. Figure 8-2 shows the graph of Newark_January, complete with bars for the standard errors.

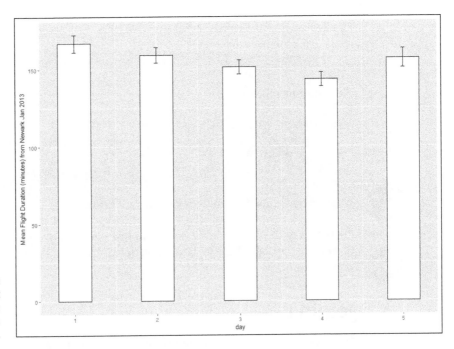

FIGURE 8-2:
Mean flight
duration
versus day in
Newark_January.

You use ggplot() to draw this graph. The first line specifies where the data comes from and maps day to the x-axis and mean to the y-axis:

```
ggplot(Newark_January, aes(x=day, y=mean)) +
```

Next, you add the bars to the plot:

```
geom_bar(stat="identity", color="black", fill = "gray100",width=0.4)+
```

The geom_bar() function usually plots frequency counts. It tries to count frequencies in the data unless you tell it otherwise. Here, the first argument tells geom_bar() to not count frequencies, and instead use the statistic in the table (mapped to *y*) to plot the bars. The `color` argument sets the border, and `fill = "gray100"` fills each bar with white. The last argument, unsurprisingly, sets the width of each bar.

Next, you add the bars that represent the standard error of the mean:

```
geom_errorbar(aes(ymax = mean + std_err, ymin = mean - std_err), width=.05)+
```

The aesthetic mappings show how high each error bar ascends and how low it descends.

Finally, you give the *y*-axis an informative label:

```
labs(y="Mean Flight Duration (minutes) from Newark Jan 2013")
```

The whole megillah is

```
ggplot(Newark_January, aes(x=day, y=mean)) +
  geom_bar(stat="identity", color="black", fill = "gray100",width=0.4)+
  geom_errorbar(aes(ymax = mean + std_err, ymin = mean - std_err), width=.05)+
  labs(y="Mean Flight Duration (minutes) from Newark Jan 2013")
```

REMEMBER

Whenever you plot a mean, plot its standard error.

TIP

Another way to plot the error bars is to just show them coming out of the top of each bar rather than in both directions. To do that in this example, set `ymin = mean`.

Joining

If you've ever flown in the United States and you've checked your baggage, you'll see what might look like a strange abbreviation on your baggage tag. Fly to Chicago's O'Hare International Airport, for example, and the tag says *ORD* (which might confuse you if you've ever been to Fort Ord in California).

Assigned by the Federal Aviation Administration (FAA) and other agencies, some abbreviations are pretty easy to figure out — like JAX, for Jacksonville, Florida, or JFK, for New York's John F. Kennedy International Airport. But would you know off the top of your head that PDL is Hartford, Connecticut? Or that INT is Winston-Salem, North Carolina? Me, neither.

Airport abbreviations are in the `origin` and `dest` columns of `flights`. With only three origins — EWR (Newark), LGA (LaGuardia), and the aforementioned JFK — these are easy to remember. What about the destinations?

```
> glimpse(flights$dest, 60)
 chr [1:336776] "IAH" "IAH" "MIA" "BQN" "ATL" "ORD"...
```

IAH? BQN? If I have to look up airport abbreviations whenever I want to explore data about origins and destinations, I'd waste a lot of time.

Instead, I can let R do the work. One of the data frames in nycflights13 is called airports, and it holds the abbreviations along with other information about the airports:

```
> glimpse(airports,60)
Observations: 1,458
Variables: 8
$ faa   <chr> "04G", "06A", "06C", "06N", "09J", "0A9",...
$ name  <chr> "Lansdowne Airport", "Moton Field Municip...
$ lat   <dbl> 41.13047, 32.46057, 41.98934, 41.43191, 3...
$ lon   <dbl> -80.61958, -85.68003, -88.10124, -74.3915...
$ alt   <int> 1044, 264, 801, 523, 11, 1593, 730, 492, ...
$ tz    <dbl> -5, -6, -6, -5, -5, -5, -5, -5, -5, -8, -...
$ dst   <chr> "A", "A", "A", "A", "A", "A", "A", "A", "...
$ tzone <chr> "America/New_York", "America/Chicago", "A...
```

The abbreviations are in the faa column, and the corresponding names are in the name column. I don't know about you, but I would have never guessed that 04G refers to Lansdowne Airport (Youngstown, Ohio).

But I digress. To let R do the work of finding out which airports correspond to which abbreviations, you can *join* the flights data frame with the airports data frame. Joining takes place by matching a *key* variable in one data frame with the corresponding *key* variable in the other. (It's something like merge(), which I describe how to use in Chapter 7 of Book 4.) In this case, the key variables have different names (dest in flights, faa in airports).

So here's how to join the flights data frame with the airports data frame. Without belaboring the point, several types of *join* operations are possible, but the *inner join* best suits our purposes:

```
flites_dest_names <- flights %>%
  inner_join(airports, by = c("dest" = "faa")) %>%
  rename(dest_airport=name)
```

The by argument in inner_join() sets up the equivalence between dest and faa. The rename() function substitutes a more informative label for name.

To see the new data frame, use the `View()` function:

```
View(flites_dest_names)
```

Running this code produces Figure 8-3. I've scrolled to the right so that you can see the relevant information that the `join` adds.

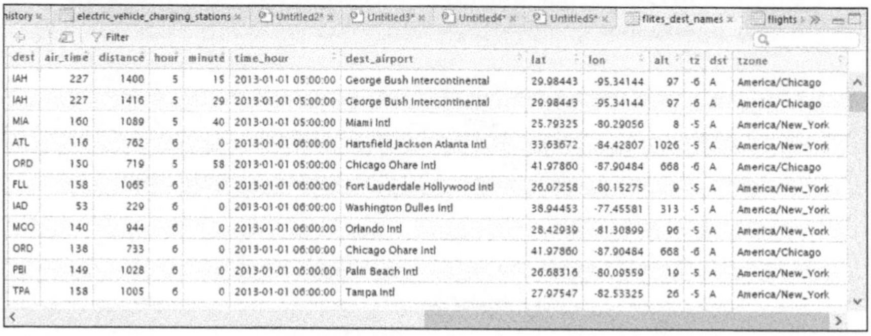

FIGURE 8-3:
The result of
joining `flights`
with `airports`:
`flites_dest_
names`.

dest	air_time	distance	hour	minute	time_hour	dest_airport	lat	lon	alt	tz	dst	tzone
IAH	227	1400	5	15	2013-01-01 05:00:00	George Bush Intercontinental	29.98443	-95.34144	97	-6	A	America/Chicago
IAH	227	1416	5	29	2013-01-01 05:00:00	George Bush Intercontinental	29.98443	-95.34144	97	-6	A	America/Chicago
MIA	160	1089	5	40	2013-01-01 05:00:00	Miami Intl	25.79325	-80.29056	8	-5	A	America/New_York
ATL	116	762	6	0	2013-01-01 06:00:00	Hartsfield Jackson Atlanta Intl	33.63672	-84.42807	1026	-5	A	America/New_York
ORD	150	719	5	58	2013-01-01 05:00:00	Chicago Ohare Intl	41.97860	-87.90484	668	-6	A	America/Chicago
FLL	158	1065	6	0	2013-01-01 06:00:00	Fort Lauderdale Hollywood Intl	26.07258	-80.15275	9	-5	A	America/New_York
IAD	53	229	6	0	2013-01-01 06:00:00	Washington Dulles Intl	38.94453	-77.45581	313	-5	A	America/New_York
MCO	140	944	6	0	2013-01-01 06:00:00	Orlando Intl	28.42939	-81.30899	96	-5	A	America/New_York
ORD	138	733	6	0	2013-01-01 06:00:00	Chicago Ohare Intl	41.97860	-87.90484	668	-6	A	America/Chicago
PBI	149	1028	6	0	2013-01-01 06:00:00	Palm Beach Intl	26.68316	-80.09559	19	-5	A	America/New_York
TPA	158	1005	6	0	2013-01-01 06:00:00	Tampa Intl	27.97547	-82.53325	26	-5	A	America/New_York

I use the new data frame to answer the question, "How many flights left JFK for Miami or Orlando in February?" Here's the code:

```
JFK_Miami_Orlando <- flites_dest_names %>%
    filter(origin == "JFK" &
            (dest_airport == "Miami Intl" | dest_airport == "Orlando Intl")
            & month == 2) %>%
    group_by(carrier) %>%
    summarize(number_of_flights = n())
```

The `filter()` function is a bit more complicated than the one I show you earlier in this chapter. This is due to the "Miami or Orlando" part. The vertical line inside the parentheses (the ones inside `filter()`, to be more specific) means *or*. I group the results by `carrier`. The `summarize()` function uses `n()` to count the number of flights.

Here are the results:

```
> kable(JFK_Miami_Orlando)


|carrier | number_of_flights|
|:-------|-----------------:|
|AA      |              228|
|B6      |              252|
|DL      |              196|
```

Quick Suggested Project: Airline Names

It would be more helpful to show the names of the airlines instead of the abbreviations in the `carrier` column. The `nycflights13` data set has another data frame called `airlines` that shows each abbreviation along with the full name of the carrier. Join this data frame with `flites_dest_names` and redo what I just did, showing the carrier names instead of the abbreviations.

Suggested Project: Departure Delays

I don't know about you, but I'm not a big fan of hustling to the airport to make a flight, only to find that it's delayed. So, in this project, I address my pet peeve (and maybe yours) by taking a look at departure delay data.

Adding a variable: weekday

On which day of the week are the delays longest? To find out, you have to add a variable that indicates the weekday of a departure. The `time_hour` column has the calendar date and the hour for each flight in the data frame. To extract the weekday, you use the `lubridate` package's `wday()` function.

Here's an example of how it works on one entry from `time_hour`:

```
> wday("2013-01-01 05:00:00")
[1] 3
```

This function considers Sunday as Weekday 1, so January 1, 2013, was a Tuesday.

You create a new data frame by adding a variable called `weekday` to `flites_dest_names`. To add the variable, you use the intriguingly named `mutate()` function:

```
flites_day <- flites_dest_names %>%
    mutate(weekday = wday(time_hour))
```

This results in a column of numbers with `1 = Sunday`, `2 = Monday`, and so forth. To turn those numbers into the appropriate weekdays, you treat the weekday numbers as levels of a factor and provide substitute labels for the numbers:

```
flites_day$weekday <- factor(flites_day$weekday,
                    labels = c("Sunday", "Monday", "Tuesday",
                        "Wednesday", "Thursday", "Friday", "Saturday"))
```

TIP

The wday() function takes an argument called label. If you set label=TRUE, the function supplies the weekday names and you don't have to complete this last step. I couldn't get it to work. Maybe you can.

Just to verify:

```
flites_per_weekday <- flites_day %>%
  group_by(weekday) %>%
  summarize(number_of_flights = n())
```

```
> kable(flites_per_weekday)

|weekday   | number_of_flights|
|:---------|-----------------:|
|Sunday    |             45240|
|Monday    |             49626|
|Tuesday   |             49362|
|Wednesday |             49016|
|Thursday  |             49147|
|Friday    |             49221|
|Saturday  |             37562|
```

Quick Suggested Project: Analyze Weekday Differences

It looks like you have far fewer flights to choose from on Saturday and Sunday than on any other day. Are the differences among days significant? Another way of asking this question: Is number_of_flights independent of weekday? Looking at it still another way: If the two were independent, you would expect an equal number of flights for each weekday. Does the data differ significantly from that pattern?

In this Book's Chapter 7, I use chisq.test() to help you answer a similar question. Use that function here. Remember that what you're analyzing is flites_per_weekday$number_of_flights. What can you conclude?

Delay, weekday, and airport

Does weekday delay vary with airport of origin? To find out, you create a data frame called summary_dep_delay:

```
summary_dep_delay <- flites_day %>%
  group_by(origin, weekday) %>%
  summarize(mean = mean(dep_delay, na.rm = TRUE),
            std_dev = sd(dep_delay, na.rm = TRUE),
            std_err = std.error(dep_delay,na.rm=TRUE))
```

Applying `kable()` gives an okay-looking table (try it!), but a graphic shows the results more clearly. Figure 8-4 shows what I mean.

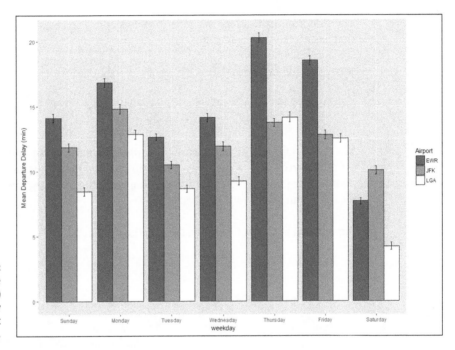

FIGURE 8-4:
Mean departure
delay (min)
versus weekday
and airport
of origin.

This bar plot shows that the shortest delays (in 2013) were out of LaGuardia (LGA), and shortest on Saturdays.

Here's how to use `ggplot()` to draw it. You begin as always by specifying the source of the data and the aesthetic mappings:

```
ggplot(summary_dep_delay, aes(x=weekday, y=mean, fill=origin)) +
```

Next, you add the bars:

```
geom_bar(position="dodge", stat="identity", color="black")+
```

The first argument (`position = "dodge"`) means that the bars aren't stacked on top of one another. Instead, they "dodge" each other and line up side by side. As I mention earlier in this chapter, `stat = "identity"` tells `geom_bar()` to use the numbers in the table to plot the bars and to not try to count frequencies in the data. The `color` argument sets the border color of each bar.

Now you add some artistic effects to the bars:

```
scale_fill_manual(name="Airport",values=c("grey40","grey65","grey100"))+
```

The first argument attaches a title to the legend. The second is a vector of colors that associate with each origin.

Next, you add the error-bars:

```
geom_errorbar(aes(ymax=mean+std_err,ymin=mean-std_err), width=.1,
              position=position_dodge(.9))+
```

The first argument, as in the earlier example, sets the upper and lower boundaries of the error bars. A little experimenting led me to the numbers for the second and third arguments. With the wrong number in the third argument, the error bar locations can be way out of whack.

Finally, you add an informative label to the y-axis:

```
labs(y="Mean Departure Delay (min)")
```

Here's the whole thing:

```
ggplot(summary_dep_delay, aes(x=weekday, y=mean, fill=origin)) +
  geom_bar(position="dodge", stat="identity",color="black")+
  scale_fill_manual(name="Airport",values=c("grey40","grey65","grey100"))+
  geom_errorbar(aes(ymax=mean+std_err,ymin=mean-std_err), width=.1,
                position=position_dodge(.9))+
  labs(y="Mean Departure Delay (min)")
```

Another way to visualize the data is to create a separate plot for each airport of origin and show them one above the other. In this kind of arrangement, each plot is called a *facet*. (I discuss facets in Chapter 2 of Book 2 and Chapter 5 of Book 3.) Figure 8-5 is a prime example.

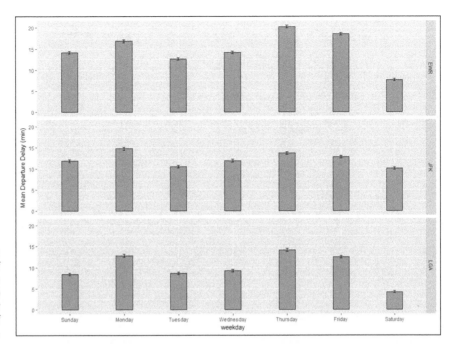

FIGURE 8-5:
A facets plot of mean departure delay (min) versus weekday and airport of origin.

No new conclusions; just a different way of plotting the data. The code is

```
ggplot(summary_dep_delay, aes(x=weekday, y=mean)) +
  geom_bar(stat="identity", color="black", fill = "gray65",width=0.3)+
  geom_errorbar(aes(ymax=mean+std_err,ymin=mean-std_err), width=.05)+
  facet_grid(origin ~ .)+
  labs(y="Mean Departure Delay (min)")
```

The code is a bit different from the earlier plot. Color doesn't differentiate the origins in this plot (facet does), so the ggplot() function doesn't need an aesthetic mapping for color. The geom_bar() function is pretty much the same, except for the addition of a fill and a slight change to the width. Feel free to modify those, if you like. geom_errorbar() is the same as before, but in this plot, you don't have to use the position argument. And you change the width.

I added the facet_grid() function. Its argument arranges the facets vertically. To arrange them horizontally, the argument would be . ~ origin, but that would look terrible. Try it, if you don't believe me. As before, the final line adds the label for the y-axis.

ANALYZING THE WEEKDAY AND AIRPORT DIFFERENCES

Are those differences among weekdays significant? How about those differences among airports of origin? And what about the combination of the two? Does that have any effect? One way to answer these questions is with an analysis of variance (ANOVA). The function that performs the ANOVA is called aov( ), and here's how to apply it:

```
wkdyorgin <- aov(dep_delay ~ weekday * origin, data=flites_day)
```

To see the results, use summary( ):

```
> summary(wkdyorgin)
                   Df    Sum Sq Mean Sq F value Pr(>F)
weekday             6   2268319  378053  233.26 <2e-16 ***
origin              2   1310239  655120  404.21 <2e-16 ***
weekday:origin     12    405916   33826   20.87 <2e-16 ***
Residuals      320939 520164045    1621
---
Signif. codes: 0 '***' 0.001 '**' 0.01 '*' 0.05 '.' 0.1 ' ' 1
8214 observations deleted due to missingness
```

The relevant columns here are F value and Pr(>F). If it's the case that weekday means are about the same, the F value for weekday would be around 1.00. As you can see, the F value is much larger than that. It's always possible that in reality all the weekday means are about the same and this data set is a fluke. The Pr(>F) value indicates that probability, and that probability is microscopically small. Same story for origin. For more on ANOVA, see Chapter 4 of Book 3.

Figures 8-4 and 8-5 suggest that the pattern of means across weekdays is different from EWR to JFK to LGA. The weekday:origin row in the summary table verifies this. The large F value and small Pr(>F) in that row tell you that weekday and origin are not independent of one another. This non-independence is a statistical characterization of the difference in appearance across the facets of Figure 8-5.

Delay and flight duration

Can the duration of the flight (air_time in the data frame) somehow influence departure delay? Why might that happen? With a longer flight duration, is departure delay likely to be longer or shorter?

First, take a look at some summary statistics for dep_delay and for air_time:

```
> summary(flites_day$dep_delay)
   Min. 1st Qu.  Median   Mean 3rd Qu.    Max.   NA's
 -43.00   -5.00   -2.00  12.71   11.00 1301.00   8214
```

```
> summary(flites_day$air_time)
   Min. 1st Qu.  Median   Mean 3rd Qu.   Max.   NA's
   20.0    81.0   127.0  149.6   184.0  695.0   9365
```

Looks like they're on two very different playing fields. One way to reduce the discrepancy is to subtract the mean of dep_delay from each dep_delay and then divide by dep_delay's standard deviation. Then follow the same procedure for each air_time. This is called *scaling* the data. (If you've had a statistics course, you might remember *z*-scores, also known as standard scores.)

The scale() function handles the scaling. I use it in a moment.

To address the questions about air_time and dep_delay, you create a regression line that summarizes the relationship between them (or, more accurately, between their scaled versions). Regression analysis has a lot of ramifications that I don't go into here. That would require a whole separate chapter.

Just for descriptive purposes, I'm concerned about the slope of the regression line. If that line has a positive slope, departure delay increases as flight time increases. It the line has a negative slope, departure delay decreases as flight time increases.

Here's how to construct the regression line between scale(air_time) and scale(dep_delay):

```
dlyat <-lm(scale(dep_delay) ~ scale(air_time), data=flites_day)
```

And here's how to retrieve the slope of the line:

```
> dlyat$coefficients[2]
scale(air_time)
    -0.02165165
```

Yes, it's a small number, but the negative slope suggests that longer flight durations are associated with shorter departure delays.

Why might that be?

Suggested Project: Delay and Weather

It's conceivable that weather conditions could influence flight delays. How do you incorporate weather information into the assessment of delay?

Another `nycflights13` data frame called `weather` provides the weather data for every day and hour at each of the three origin airports. Here's a glimpse of exactly what it has:

```
> glimpse(weather,60)
Observations: 26,130
Variables: 15
$ origin     <chr> "EWR", "EWR", "EWR", "EWR", "EWR", "...
$ year       <dbl> 2013, 2013, 2013, 2013, 2013, 2013, ...
$ month      <dbl> 1, 1, 1, 1, 1, 1, 1, 1, 1, 1, 1, 1, ...
$ day        <int> 1, 1, 1, 1, 1, 1, 1, 1, 1, 1, 1, 1, ...
$ hour       <int> 0, 1, 2, 3, 4, 6, 7, 8, 9, 10, 11, 1...
$ temp       <dbl> 37.04, 37.04, 37.94, 37.94, 37.94, 3...
$ dewp       <dbl> 21.92, 21.92, 21.92, 23.00, 24.08, 2...
$ humid      <dbl> 53.97, 53.97, 52.09, 54.51, 57.04, 5...
$ wind_dir   <dbl> 230, 230, 230, 230, 240, 270, 250, 2...
$ wind_speed <dbl> 10.35702, 13.80936, 12.65858, 13.809...
$ wind_gust  <dbl> 11.918651, 15.891535, 14.567241, 15....
$ precip     <dbl> 0, 0, 0, 0, 0, 0, 0, 0, 0, 0, 0, 0, ...
$ pressure   <dbl> 1013.9, 1013.0, 1012.6, 1012.7, 1012...
$ visib      <dbl> 10, 10, 10, 10, 10, 10, 10, 10, 10, ...
$ time_hour  <dttm> 2012-12-31 19:00:00, 2012-12-31 20:...
```

So the variables it has in common with `flites_name_day` are the first six and the last one. To join the two data frames, use this code:

```
flites_day_weather <- flites_day %>%
  inner_join(weather, by = c("origin","year","month","day","hour","time_hour"))
```

Now you can use `flites_day_weather` to start answering questions about departure delay and the weather.

What questions will you ask? How will you answer them? What plots will you draw? What regression lines will you create? Will `scale()` help?

And, when you're all done, take a look at arrival delay (`arr_delay`). . . .

5

Harnessing R: Some Projects to Keep You Busy

Contents at a Glance

Chapter **1**

Working with a Browser

A s I emphasize throughout this entire book, R is rich with opportunities for visualizing data. In this chapter, I show how to create R applications whose visualizations depend on user input. I also show how to present these applications in a browser so that web users can interact with them. Putting an R application in a browser is a helpful way to share data and analyses. And you don't have to know HTML or JavaScript to get the job done!

Getting Your Shine On

A creation of RStudio honchos, shiny is the package that enables interactive, browser-based R applications. Use RStudio to install it in the usual way. On the Packages tab, click Install and then type **shiny** into the Install Packages dialog box. After the package finishes downloading, select the check box next to shiny on the Packages tab, or type

```
> library(shiny)
```

A couple of words about architecture before I move on and show how to create your first shiny project. Behind any web page with a shiny app is a computer that serves that page. The computer is running the R code (also known as a *script*) that creates the page. Though the computer can be a server that operates via the cloud, for the apps I show you in this chapter, the server is your laptop.

Creating Your First shiny Project

A shiny application is a directory that contains a file with R code. So, in your working directory, create a new directory called shinydir1.

RStudio gives you an easy way to do this: With the shiny package installed, choose File ➪ New File ➪ Shiny Web App.

This menu command opens the New Shiny Web Application dialog box, shown in Figure 1-1.

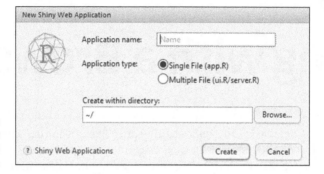

FIGURE 1-1:
The New Shiny
Web Application
dialog box.

In the Application Name box, I enter a descriptive name for the app I'm about to create. I'm creating an interactive histogram that shows random sampling from a uniform distribution, so I type **UniformRandom** (no spaces!).

For the Application Type option, I leave the Single File (app.R) radio button selected.

Finally, I create the directory. I click the Browse button to open the Choose Directory dialog box, which you see in Figure 1-2.

In this dialog box, I create a new folder called shinydir1 and click Select Folder. This closes the Choose Directory dialog box. Back in the New Shiny Web Application dialog box, I click Create.

After you complete these steps, you'll notice that the tab in the Scripts pane is now titled app.R. Every shiny app tab is labeled app.R. (Different app.R applications reside in different directories.) You'll also notice that an R script for a sample shiny app appears in the pane. Figure 1-3 shows you what I mean.

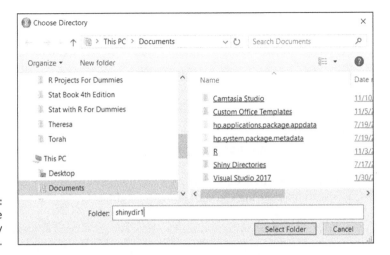

FIGURE 1-2:
The Choose Directory dialog box.

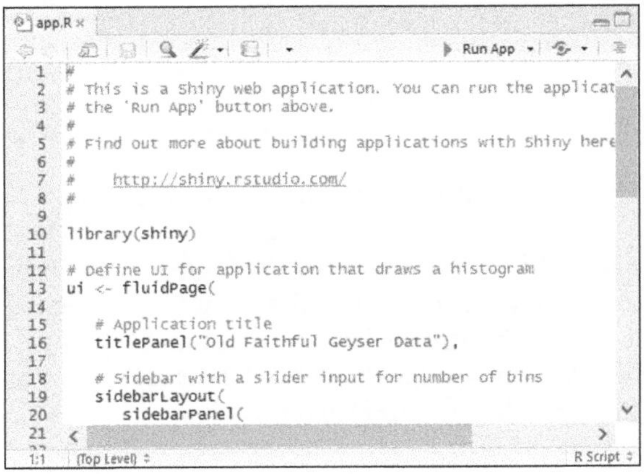

FIGURE 1-3:
The Scripts pane after clicking Create in the New Shiny Web Application dialog box.

As the comment lines in the Scripts pane tell you, you can run this sample app by clicking the Run App button at the top of the pane. I'll leave it to you to run this application and see how the application reflects the code.

In this section, however, I delete the sample code and develop a similar (but somewhat more elaborate) application that teaches you some additional R skills as I explore shiny's capabilities. With the Scripts pane active, I press Ctrl+A and press Delete. Now I have an empty Scripts pane.

The code for a shiny app has two main components: a *user interface* and a *server.*

The first order of business is to create a function that defines the *user interface* —
the page that the user sees and interacts with. The fundamental structure of this
script is

```
ui <- type_of_page()
```

Several types of pages are possible. Arguments in the parentheses determine the
appearance and functionality of the page.

Then you create a set of instructions for the server to execute when the user interacts with the user interface. One way to begin is

```
server <- function(input,output){}
```

Inside the curly brackets, put the instructions you create.

Finally, the function

```
shinyApp(ui=ui, server=server)
```

ties together the ui and the server into a shiny application.

In the early days of shiny, it was necessary to create one file for the user interface
and another for the server (including the shinyApp() function) and to store both
in the directory. You can still do that (by choosing the Multiple File radio button in
the New Shiny Web Application dialog box). Nowadays, only one file is necessary,
and that's the way I do it in this chapter.

Figure 1-4 shows what your first shiny project looks like when all the pieces are
in place.

It's a simple app, and it's typical of first projects with this package. The user
manipulates a slider to determine the number of values to sample in a uniform distribution. The minimum value of the distribution is 0, and the maximum value is 1.

The histogram shows the results of the sampling. The minimum number of values
is 25, the maximum number is 1,000, and the default is 500. Figure 1-4 shows the
app in a window that RStudio opens.

To see the app in a browser, click Open in Browser in the upper left corner. (Spoiler
alert: It looks pretty much the same.) As we proceed, I show you shiny apps in
RStudio windows because they look better in the confines of the pages you're
reading. Just bear in mind that it's easy enough to see the browser version by
clicking Open in Browser.

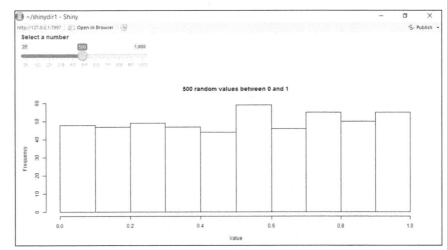

FIGURE 1-4:
Your first shiny project.

The user interface

First things first. To define the user interface, I specify the type of page. For this application, I want a page that changes with the width of the browser: If I make the browser narrower, for example, I want the appearance of the page to change accordingly. This type of page is *fluid*, so the function that creates it is called `fluidPage()`:

```
ui <- fluidPage()
```

And that's the beginning of the user interface.

Next, I need a function that defines the slider and the input (the result of moving the slider) and another function that sets up the output. I put those two functions inside the parentheses.

For the slider, it's

```
sliderInput(inputId = "number",
            label = "Select a number",
            value = 500, min = 25, max = 1000)
```

The first argument establishes an identifier for the number the user selects by moving the slider. In the upcoming `server()` function, I refer to it as `input$number`.

The second argument adds the instruction above the slider. The remaining arguments set the default number, the minimum number, and the maximum number of values to sample from the uniform distribution.

Finally, I reserve an area for the output:

```
plotOutput("hist")
```

At this point, the app doesn't know what kind of output to plot. All it knows is that "hist" is the name of the output.

The user interface code is

```
ui <- fluidPage(
    sliderInput(inputId = "number",
                label = "Select a number",
                value = 500, min = 25, max = 1000),
    plotOutput("hist")
)
```

Think of sliderInput() as an input function and plotOutput() as an output function.

TECHNICAL STUFF

What does this code actually do? In the Scripts pane, highlight fluidPage() and all its arguments (don't include ui <- in your highlighting). Then press Ctrl+Enter to run the highlighted code. The result? A lot of HTML in the Console pane. This shows you that the user interface code generates a web page.

The server

As I point out earlier in this chapter, the starting point for the server is

```
server <- function(input,output){}
```

The first thing to put in the curly brackets is an R expression that represents the output. In the user interface, the name of the output is "hist". Here in the output, I refer to it as output$hist.

That expression receives the value of a function called renderPlot(), which, unsurprisingly, renders the plot.

A word about renderPlot(). The syntax of this function is

```
renderPlot({})
```

Inside renderPlot's curly brackets, you add as many lines of code as necessary to, well, render the plot. In this application, the base R graphics function hist() does the honors, as described in Chapter 1 of Book 2:

```
server <- function(input, output) {
   output$hist <- renderPlot({ hist(runif(input$number,min=0,max=1),xlab="Value",
main=paste(input$number,"random values between 0    and 1"))
   })
   }
```

That first argument to `hist()` is `runif()`. Do *not* pronounce it "run if"! It's not a *run* statement combined with an *if* statement or anything like that. Instead, think of the *r* as *random* and *unif* as *uniform*. This is R's way of saying, "Randomly sample from a uniform distribution." (The correct pronunciation is "r unif.") How would R say, "Randomly sample from a normal distribution"? If you guessed `rnorm()`, you're absolutely right.

The first argument to `hist()` indicates that the data for the histogram comes from a random sample of values from a uniform distribution. How many values are in the sample? `input$number`, that's how many. The next two arguments to `runif()` set the distribution's minimum value to 0 and its maximum value to 1.

Now for the remaining arguments for `hist()`. If you've completed the examples in Chapter 1 of Book 2, you'll remember that `xlab` labels the *x*-axis, and `main` provides a title. Within `main`, I use the `paste()` function to add the value of `input$number` to the beginning of the title. The result is that the histogram title (as well as the histogram) changes each time the user moves the slider to a new number.

Final steps

To tie the user interface to the server, I add

```
shinyApp(ui = ui, server = server)
```

The entire script (including the `library()` function at the beginning) is

```
library(shiny)
ui <- fluidPage(
   sliderInput(inputId = "number",
               label = "Select a number",
               value = 500, min = 25, max = 1000),
   plotOutput("hist")
)
server <- function(input, output) {
   output$hist <- renderPlot({      hist(runif(input$number,min=0,max=1),xlab="Va
               lue",main=paste(input$number,"random values between 0 and 1"))
   })
   }
shinyApp(ui = ui, server = server)
```

Save the code (press Ctrl+S or choose File⇨Save) and then click the Run App button. That opens the display shown earlier, in Figure 1-4, and puts this in the Console pane:

```
> runApp('shinydir1/UniformRandom')

Listening on http://127.0.0.1:3328
```

The second line means that R is waiting for the user to do something. (Move the slider, in other words.) The URL on your machine will no doubt be different from the one on mine.

To end the session with the application, press Esc or close the RStudio window that shows the page. You can also click the little red stop sign in the upper right corner of the Console pane.

Getting reactive

I can write the server in a different way. Instead of this:

```
server <- function(input, output) {
  output$hist <- renderPlot({ hist(runif(input$number,min=0,max=1),xlab="Value",
main=paste(input$number,"random values between 0    and 1"))
  })
  }
```

I can write this:

```
server <- function(input, output) {
  histdata <- reactive({
    runif(input$number,min=0,max=1)
    })

  output$hist <- renderPlot({
    hist(histdata(),xlab="Value",
    main=paste(input$number,"random values between 0 and 1")
  )
  })
}
```

It accomplishes the same thing. Why bother setting a variable called histdata for the runif() function? And what's that reactive({}) deal? And, finally, why do I have parentheses after histdata in the first argument to the hist() function?

Creating the `histdata` variable enables me to use the results of sampling from the uniform distribution for additional outputs — not just for the histogram. For example, I might want to add the data's mean, median, and standard deviation to the `shiny` app. I show you how to do that in just a moment.

What about `reactive({})`? To make the `shiny` app responsive to user input, I have to create `histdata` in a *reactive context* so that the variable can *react* to the input (when the user moves the slider to change the value of `input$number`, in other words). Accordingly, `reactive({})` provides that context.

"But wait a second," you might exclaim. "In the original version, I was able to explicitly use `runif()` in `renderPlot({})`. Why is that?" Because `renderPlot({})` is a reactive context. (The curly brackets are a giveaway.) For that reason, changes in `input$number` show up as changes in the histogram plot. If `renderPlot({})` is the only reactive context I use, it's not necessary to have another reactive context and create `histdata`.

In `shiny`, **every** `render` function is a reactive context.

TIP

Now for the parentheses next to `histdata` in `hist()`. When I create a reactive variable like `histdata`, I create an object I can *call* to see whether changes have occurred (in this case, to `input$number`), and it returns the changes. If it's callable and it returns something, it's a function, and to indicate that, I add the parentheses. So `histdata` is the reactive variable I define here, and when I use it again, it's `histdata()`. Got it?

I can't emphasize this enough: When you create a variable in a reactive context, *you must add the parentheses whenever you use it.* Forgetting to do that is the biggest roadblock when you're starting out with `shiny`.

TIP

Now my objective is to create a `shiny` app that shows not just the histogram of the sample from the uniform distribution but also the sample mean, median, and standard deviation. The app will look like Figure 1-5. The mean, median, and standard deviation are below the histogram, to the left.

In the user interface, I have to create space for those three items. Each one is a `textOutput`, so I add these three lines to the user interface:

```
textOutput("mean"),
textOutput("median"),
textOutput("sd")
```

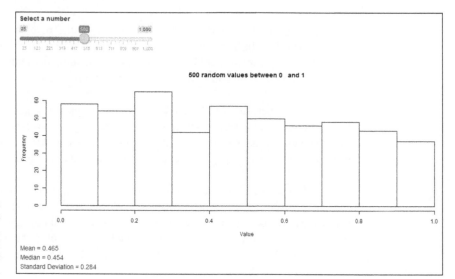

FIGURE 1-5:
The shiny app
with the mean,
the median, and
the standard
deviation.

Of course, I also have to make changes to the server. Remember, I add

```
histdata <- reactive({
    runif(input$number,min=0,max=1)
    })
```

at the beginning of the server code.

For the textOutputs, I add

```
output$mean <- renderText({paste("Mean =",round(mean(histdata()),3)
  )
  })

output$median <- renderText({paste("Median =",round(median(histdata()),3)
  )
  })

  output$sd <- renderText({paste("Standard Deviation =",round(sd(histdata()),3)
  )
  })
```

The whole thing is

```
library(shiny)
ui <- fluidPage(
  sliderInput(inputId = "number",
              label = "Select a number",
```

```
                value = 500, min = 25, max = 1000),
    plotOutput("hist"),
    textOutput("mean"),

    textOutput("sd")
)
server <- function(input, output) {

    histdata <- reactive({
        runif(input$number,min=0,max=1)
        })

    output$hist <- renderPlot({
        hist(histdata(),xlab="Value",
        main=paste(input$number,"random values between 0    and 1")
    )
    })

    output$mean <- renderText({paste("Mean =",round(mean(histdata()),3)
    )
    })

    output$median <- renderText({paste("Median =",round(median(histdata()),3)
    )
    })

    output$sd <- renderText({paste("Standard Deviation =",round(sd(histdata()),3)
    )
    })
}
shinyApp(ui = ui, server = server)
```

Working with ggplot

By now, you likely know that I'm a huge fan of the ggplot2 package. After reading this book, I hope you become one, too. In this section, I show you how to use ggplot functions to create the first version of the app from the preceding section. When it's done, it will look like Figure 1-6. (As in the preceding section, I show the app in an RStudio window. Click Open in Browser to see it in your browser.)

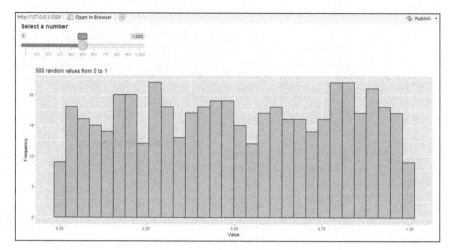

FIGURE 1-6:
The first version
of the shiny
app from
the preceding
section, rendered
in ggplot2.

To get started, I follow the steps in the preceding section to create a new application called UniformRandomggplot in a new directory called shinydir2. Again, I delete the sample code and begin the coding with these two lines:

```
library(ggplot2)
library(shiny)
```

The user interface code remains the same as in the preceding section's first version:

```
ui <- fluidPage(
  sliderInput(inputId = "number",
              label = "Select a number",
              value = 500, min = 1, max = 1000),
  plotOutput("hist")
)
```

Changing the server

The function that does the plotting has to change. Instead of a base R function, I'm going to put ggplot() into renderPlot()'s curly brackets. Recall from Chapter 1 of Book 2 that ggplot() has to have a data frame as its first argument. So I can't just pass runif(input$number, min = 0, max=1) as an argument to ggplot().

Instead, I have to turn the sample of `input$number` values into a data frame, and here's how I do it:

```
df <- data.frame(runif(input$number, min=0,max=1))
```

That would be the first line of code I put into `renderPlot()`'s curly brackets.

The second argument to `ggplot()` is `aes()`, which maps the values in the data frame into the *x*-axis of the histogram. This means I have to have a name for the column of values in the `df` data frame:

```
colnames(df)<-c("Value")
```

That's the second line of code in the curly brackets.

Now I can start on the plot:

```
ggplot(df,aes(x=Value))+
```

And I can add the histogram

```
geom_histogram(color = "black", fill = "grey80")+
```

and some landscaping:

```
labs(y="Frequency",title = paste(input$number,"random values from 0 to 1"))
```

Altogether, the code for the server looks like this:

```
server <- function(input, output) {
output$hist <- renderPlot({
    df <- data.frame(runif(input$number, min=0,max=1))
    colnames(df)<-c("Value")
    ggplot(df,aes(x=Value))+
            geom_histogram(color = "black",fill="grey80")+
            labs(y="Frequency",
title = paste(input$number,"random values from 0 to 1"))
    })
}
```

Remember to add

```
shinyApp(ui = ui, server = server)
```

With the code for the user interface (including the two library() functions) and the server (and shinyApp()) saved in shinydir2, click the Run App button to produce what you see in Figure 1-5.

A few more changes

In the Console pane, this line appears each time you move the slider:

```
`stat_bin()` using `bins = 30`. Pick better value with `binwidth`.
```

This indicates that R has taken a guess about how to render the appearance of the histogram. Specifically, R takes a shot at the binwidth — the width of each bar. Some modifications eliminate the guesswork.

First, I want to add a slider that enables the viewer to set the binwidth. To do that, I add the following lines to the user interface code, placing them between the first sliderInput() and plotOutput():

```
sliderInput(inputId = "binwidth",
            label = "Select a binwidth",
            value = .05, min = .01, max = .10),
```

The first argument sets the identifier for this particular input, and the second puts a label above the slider. The third gives the starting binwidth, the fourth gives the minimum binwidth, and the fifth gives the maximum binwidth.

TIP

The (approximate) number of rendered bars is the range of values (1.00) divided by the selected binwidth. So the starting value (.05) produces 20 (ish) bars.

Changes to the title argument in the labs() function in the server add the binwidth information to the histogram title:

```
labs(y="Frequency",
title = paste(input$number,"random values from 0 to 1 with binwidth =",
    input$binwidth))
```

The whole megillah is shown here:

```
library(ggplot2)
library(shiny)
```

```
ui <- fluidPage(
  sliderInput(inputId = "number",
              label = "Select a number",
              value = 500, min = 1, max = 1000),
  sliderInput(inputId = "binwidth",
              label = "Select a binwidth",
              value = .05, min = .01, max = .10),
  plotOutput("hist")
)
server <- function(input, output) {
  output$hist <- renderPlot({
    df <- data.frame(runif(input$number, min=0,max=1))
    colnames(df)<-c("Value")
    ggplot(df,aes(x=Value))+
           geom_histogram(binwidth=input$binwidth,
                          color = "black",fill="grey80")+
           labs(y="Frequency",
title = paste(input$number,"random values from 0 to 1 with binwidth
  =",input$binwidth))
    })
}
shinyApp(ui = ui, server = server)
```

Press Ctrl+S to save it all in the `shinydir2` directory, and then run the app to produce the display in Figure 1-7.

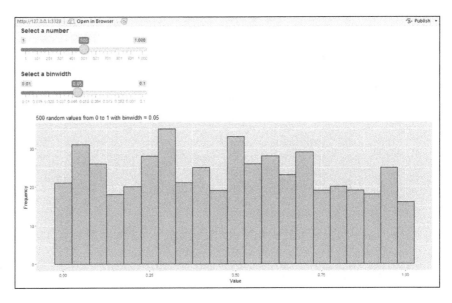

FIGURE 1-7:
Adding a slider
to enable the
selection of
binwidth.

Getting reactive with ggplot

To add the mean, median, and mode to the display you see in Figure 1-7 — the idea here is that it should match what you see in Figure 1-5 — I first add the `textOutput`s to the user interface, as before:

```
textOutput("mean"),
textOutput("median"),
textOutput("sd")
```

Things start to get a bit tricky in the server because I have to do two things: Use `reactive({})` to create a variable for `runif()`, and create a data frame for `ggplot()`. Why is this tricky? Because in the simpler version with just the plot and not the statistics, I was able to accomplish both at one time inside the reactive context of `renderPlot()`:

```
df <- data.frame(runif(input$number, min=0,max=1))
```

In this version, however, I have to create the variable in a reactive context outside `renderPlot({})` (so that I can use that variable to calculate the mean, median, and standard deviation) and the data frame inside `renderPlot({})` so that `ggplot()` can use it.

Here's the variable (`histdata`) in `reactive({})`:

```
server <- function(input, output) {
  histdata <- reactive({(runif(input$number, min=0,max=1))

})
```

And here's the data frame (`df`) inside `renderPlot({})`:

```
output$hist <- renderPlot({
  df <-data.frame(histdata())
  colnames(df)<-c("Value")
  ggplot(df,aes(x=Value))+
    geom_histogram(binwidth=input$binwidth, color = "black",fill="grey80")+
    labs(y="Frequency",
         title = paste(input$number,"random values from 0 to 1 with binwidth
             =",input$binwidth))
```

And finally, here are the `output$`s:

```
output$mean <- renderText({paste("Mean =",round(mean(histdata()),3)
    )
    })

  output$median <- renderText({paste("Median =",round(median(histdata()),3)
    )
    })

  output$sd <- renderText({paste("Standard Deviation =",round(sd(histdata()),3)
    )
    })
```

TIP

Yes, I'm going to harp on this: Notice that after I define `histdata` in reactive(`{}`), it's `histdata()` whenever I use it again.

HOW DOES ALL THIS WORK, REALLY?

When you drive, do you have to know the inner workings of your car's engine? Do you have to know exactly how your refrigerator keeps your food cold? If you answered yes to at least one of those questions, this sidebar is for you. Even if you didn't, you might still want to read it.

I hate to break this to you, boys and girls, but like computer animation, reactivity is an illusion. In computer animation, nothing moves across the screen: Instead, one pixel turns off, another turns on, and the illusion is that the pixel has moved from the first pixel's location to the second.

Likewise, in reactivity, it is *not* the case that the app only monitors the user and that when the user makes a change to the input (like moving the slider to change `input$number`), the output (like the plot in `output$hist`) changes accordingly. Instead, the server constantly recomputes everything in the app every few microseconds. So if the user moves the slider, for example (or changes the input in some other way), within microseconds the output updates.

Wait a (micro) second. Suppose the user doesn't make a change. Then what? Recomputation takes place anyway. It's just that everything recomputes its previous results, and it looks like the app hasn't changed at all. Bear in mind that whether or not the user does anything, recomputing is always going on in the background.

The illusion is that the user's action immediately causes the app's reaction. And, like computer animation, that's a pretty useful illusion!

Make those changes and run the app. It should look like Figure 1-8:

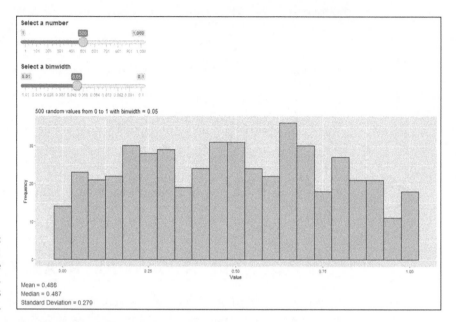

FIGURE 1-8:
The ggplot2
version of the
first shiny app,
with statistics
added.

Another shiny Project

In this section, I move from a shiny app based on random sampling to an app based on data. The data that forms the basis of this project is in the data frame airquality, which lives in the datasets package.

As I mention in Chapter 2 of Book 2, this data frame holds data for temperature, wind velocity, solar radiation, and ozone for New York City for May–September 1973. To refresh your memory, here are the first six rows of the data:

```
> head(airquality)
  Ozone Solar.R Wind Temp Month Day
1    41     190  7.4   67     5   1
2    36     118  8.0   72     5   2
3    12     149 12.6   74     5   3
4    18     313 11.5   62     5   4
5    NA      NA 14.3   56     5   5
6    28      NA 14.9   66     5   6
```

The objective is an app that shows a scatterplot of two user-selected variables (excluding Month and Day) along with statistical summaries (correlation and regression) of the relationship between the variables. I show you how to create two versions: one in base R graphics and the other in ggplot.

The base R version

Figure 1-9 shows the finished product. The user selects an *x*-variable from one drop-down menu, and a *y*-variable from the other. The application then produces a scatterplot, which contains the regression line that summarizes the relationship between the two variables. The first line of the scatterplot title includes the selected variables. The second line shows the correlation coefficient (r) between the two, along with the equation of the regression line in the plot.

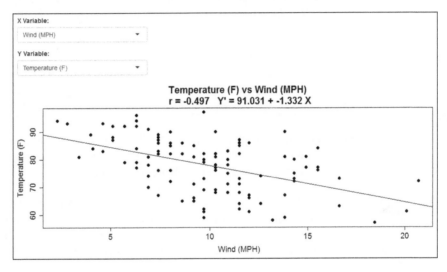

FIGURE 1-9:
A shiny app for
the airquality
data frame.

I begin by choosing File⇨NewFile⇨Shiny Web App to create a new app called AirQuality in a new directory called shinydir3. I then delete the sample code.

For the new code, the first thing I do is to attach the library that contains the data frame:

```
library(datasets)
```

I'll have to clean up the data by eliminating missing values. The function that does that, drop_na(), lives in the tidyr package, so I add

```
library(tidyr)
```

I describe `drop_na()` in Chapter 2 of Book 1.

One more package, `tibble`, supplies a useful function called `rownames_to_column()`, which I also describe in Chapter 2 of Book 1. I use it here in a moment, so I add its package:

```
library(tibble)
```

Next, I delete the missing values from `airquality`:

```
aq.no.missing <-drop_na(airquality)
```

The newly created data frame `aq.no.missing` is the one I use going forward.

The next task is to provide a set of options for the *x*-variable menu and for the *y*-variable menu. The options, of course, are the same for both variables. I create the vector:

```
options <- c("Ozone (parts per billion)" = "Ozone",
             "Solar (Langleys)" = "Solar.R",
             "Wind (MPH)" = "Wind",
             "Temperature (F)" = "Temp")
```

Each term of the vector is a pair. The first element of each pair is the label that appears on the drop-down menu. The second element is the name of the variable in `aq.no.missing` that the first element connects to.

TECHNICAL STUFF

What is a langley? Used as a measure of solar radiation, one langley is one small calorie per square centimeter of irradiated area. What's a small calorie? The amount of energy required to raise 1 gram of water by 1 degree Celsius. (A thousand of them make up each calorie you count in food.) Aren't you glad you asked?

Take another look at Figure 1-7. Notice that the names in the plot title and on the axes are the labels from the drop-down menus, not variable names from the data frame. I think this makes the whole thing more informative. How do I get this done?

First, I turn the `options` vector into a data frame:

```
df.options <-data.frame(options)
```

Here's what that data frame looks like:

```
> df.options
                                options
Ozone (parts per billion)   Ozone
Solar (Langleys)            Solar.R
Wind (MPH)                     Wind
Temperature (F)                Temp
```

For this data frame to be useful, the row names on the left have to constitute a data column, so

```
df.lv <-rownames_to_column(df.options)
```

makes that happen. I use lv in the new data frame name to denote label (the name that appears on the menu) and value (the corresponding variable name in the data frame). To complete this data frame, I name its columns:

```
colnames(df.lv) <- c("label","value")
```

This data frame now looks like this:

```
> df.lv
                          label     value
1 Ozone (parts per billion)   Ozone
2           Solar (Langleys) Solar.R
3               Wind (MPH)    Wind
4           Temperature (F)    Temp
```

On to the user interface:

```
ui <- fluidPage(
  selectInput("X", "X Variable:",
              options),
  selectInput("Y", "Y Variable:",
              options),
  plotOutput("scatter")
)
```

Once again, it's a fluid page. Each selectInput() is a drop-down menu. The first argument is its name, the second argument is its onscreen label, and the third is the options vector that presents the choices. And plotOutput() sets aside the space for the plot.

Now for the server. The overall structure of the server, remember, is

```
server <- function(input,output) { }
```

The first item between the brackets assigns the user selections input$X and input$Y to a data frame I call selections. I do this in a reactive context (see the earlier section "Getting reactive"):

```
selections <- reactive({
    aq.no.missing[, c(input$X, input$Y)]
})
```

Here I go again: I've created selections in a reactive context (within reactive({}), in other words), and the next time I use it, I have to refer to it as selections().

The comma within the square brackets means "all rows in the aq.no.missing data frame." The second expression c(input$X, input$Y) limits those rows to just the variables the user has selected. The result is that I can now refer to all rows in the first selected variable as

```
selections()[,1]
```

and to all the rows in the second as

```
selections()[,2]
```

which I will do almost immediately. Stay tuned.

The next item in the server is the output function, whose overall structure is

```
output$scatter <- renderPlot({})
```

The code for rendering the output goes between the curly brackets.

And now, as promised, I use those references to the two selected variables. I assign the first user selection to a variable called x_column:

```
x_column <- selections()[,1]
```

and the second to y_column:

```
y_column <- selections()[,2]
```

The correlation coefficient is

```
correlation <-cor(x_column,y_column)
```

and the regression is

```
regression <- lm(y_column ~ x_column)
```

To put the equation of the regression line into the title, I have to know its inter-cept (where the line meets the *y*-axis) and its slope (how slanted it is). In base R graphics, I also have to have those pieces of information to plot the regression line.

The result of a regression analysis is a list. For a regression analysis of Temp dependent on Wind, for example, part of that list looks like this:

```
Coefficients:
            Estimate Std. Error t value Pr(>|t|)
(Intercept)  91.0305    2.3489  38.754  < 2e-16 ***
Wind         -1.3318    0.2226  -5.983 2.84e-08 ***
---
```

To retrieve the intercept from the list, the expression is

```
intercept <- regression$coefficients[1]
```

And to retrieve the slope, it's

```
slope <- regression$coefficients[2]
```

Two more pieces of information and I'm ready to plot. So far, the R code has worked with the variable names that correspond to the user selections, like Wind and Temp. In the plot, remember, I want to use the names on the menus — Wind (MPH) and Temperature (F) — for the title and for the axis labels.

So I'm looking for the label names that correspond to the selected variable names. Here's where that df.lv data frame comes into play. For the label for the *x*-variable, I'm looking for

```
X_Label <- df.lv$label[whose corresponding df.lv$value matches input$X]
```

Fortunately, R provides a neat little trick that fills the bill. It's a function called which(), and here's how to use it:

```
X_Label <- df.lv$label[which(df.lv$value == input$X)]
```

And for the label for the y-variable, it's

```
Y_Label <- df.lv$label[which(df.lv$value == input$Y)]
```

And now, here's the `plot()` function:

```
plot(x=x_column,y=y_column,xlab = X_Label,ylab = Y_Label,
        cex.axis = 1.5,cex.lab = 1.5, pch = 20, cex = 2,
        main = paste(Y_Label,"vs",X_Label, "\n r =",round(correlation,3),"
            Y' =",round(intercept,3),"+",round(slope,3),"X"), cex.main=1.8)
```

The first two arguments, x and y, are the variables to plot. The next two, `xlab` and `ylab`, are the titles for the axes. The `cex.axis` argument specifies the size of the numbers on the axes, and `cex.lab` is the size of the axes labels. The value 1.5 means "1.5 times the normal size of a character." The next argument, `pch`, means that the plot character is a filled circle, and its size, `cex`, is 2.

The argument `main` is the title. I use `paste()` to put Y_Label and X_Label into the title. \n means to continue on the next line, where I paste the rounded `correlation` (rounded to three places) as well as the rounded `intercept` and the rounded `slope` into the regression equation. The size of the title, `cex.main`, is 1.8.

One more function draws the regression line:

```
abline(intercept,slope)
```

Here's the whole thing, including the `shinyApp()` function at the end:

```
library(datasets)
library(tidyr)
library(tibble)


aq.no.missing <-drop_na(airquality)

options <- c("Ozone (parts per billion)" = "Ozone",
            "Solar (Langleys)" = "Solar.R",
            "Wind (MPH)" = "Wind",
            "Temperature (F)" = "Temp")
df.options <-data.frame(options)
df.lv <-rownames_to_column(df.options)
colnames(df.lv) <- c("label","value")

ui <- fluidPage(
```

```r
    selectInput("X", "X Variable:",
                options),

    selectInput("Y", "Y Variable:",
                options),

  plotOutput("scatter")


)
server <- function(input, output) {
  selections <- reactive({
    aq.no.missing[, c(input$X, input$Y)]

  })


  output$scatter <- renderPlot({

    x_column <- selections()[,1]
    y_column <- selections()[,2]

    correlation <-cor(x_column,y_column)
    regression <- lm(y_column ~ x_column)
    intercept <- regression$coefficients[1]
    slope <- regression$coefficients[2]

    X_Label <- df.lv$label[which(df.lv$value == input$X)]
    Y_Label <- df.lv$label[which(df.lv$value == input$Y)]

    plot(x=x_column,y=y_column,xlab = X_Label,ylab = Y_Label,
         cex.axis = 1.5,cex.lab = 1.5, pch = 20, cex = 2,
         main = paste(Y_Label,"vs",X_Label,
                   "\n r =",round(correlation,3),"
            Y' =",round(intercept,3),"+",round(slope,3),"X"),
         cex.main=1.8)
    abline(intercept,slope)
  })


}

shinyApp(ui = ui, server = server)
```

Save the file and run the app!

The ggplot version

Rendered in ggplot(), this app looks like Figure 1-10.

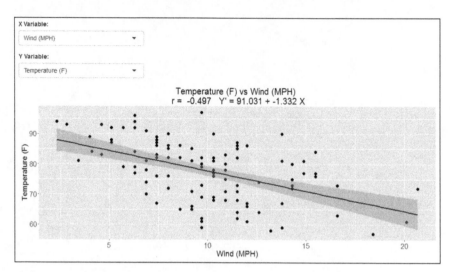

FIGURE 1-10:
The app from
the preceding
section, rendered
in ggplot.

The code is the same as in the base R version, except that I have to add

```
library(ggplot2)
```

to the beginning, and of course I have to change the plotting function in output$scatter.

Instead of plot(), I begin with ggplot():

```
ggplot(selections(),aes(x=x_column,y=y_column))+
```

The first argument is the data frame that supplies the data; aes() then maps the first selected variable to x and the second selected variable to y.

Next, I add geom_point() to specify that I want points to appear in the plot:

```
geom_point(size=3) +
```

and the argument shows how big the points should be.

Adding a `labs()` function renders the *x*-axis, *y*-axis, and title:

```
labs(x = X_Label,y = Y_Label,
       title = paste(Y_Label,"vs",X_Label,
       "\n r = ",round(correlation,3),"                    Y'
            =",round(intercept,3),"+",round(slope,3),"X"))+
```

To set the sizes of the fonts, I use a `theme()` function:

```
theme(axis.title.x = element_text(size=18),
       axis.text.x = element_text(size=17),
       axis.title.y = element_text(size=18),
       axis.text.y = element_text(size=17),
       plot.title = element_text(hjust = 0.5,size=20))+
```

In `plot.title, hjust =0.5` centers the title.

Finally, `geom_smooth()` plots the regression line:

```
geom_smooth(method="lm",col="black")
```

The first argument specifies a linear model (linear regression, in this example), and the second makes the line black. Notice that, unlike in base R, it's not necessary to specify the slope or the intercept.

The shadow around the regression line in Figure 1-10 represents the *standard error of estimate* — a measure of variability around the line. The tighter the shadow, the better the fit of the line to the data. (Note what happens when the *x*-variable and the *y*-variable are the same.). To eliminate the shadow, add `se=FALSE` as an argument to `geom_smooth()`.

Here's the entire set of functions for the `ggplot` version:

```
ggplot(selections(),aes(x = x_column,y = y_column))+
     geom_point(size=3) +
     labs(x = X_Label,y = Y_Label,
          title = paste(Y_Label,"vs",X_Label,
          "\n r = ",round(correlation,3),"
          Y' =",round(intercept,3),"+",round(slope,3),"X"))+
     theme(axis.title.x = element_text(size=18),
          axis.text.x = element_text(size=17),
          axis.title.y = element_text(size=18),
          axis.text.y = element_text(size=17),
          plot.title = element_text(hjust = 0.5,size=20))+
     geom_smooth(method="lm",col="black")
```

Substitute this set of functions for the `plot()` function and `abline()` in the base R version, save, and run the application.

Suggested Project

Feeling adventurous? Take what you learned in this last project and try it out on a different data frame. It's a great way to build up your skill set.

I suggest `Cars93`, which lives in the `MASS` package. This data frame provides information on a number of variables (way more than four!) for 93 models of cars from 1993.

Good luck!

Chapter **2**

Dashboards — How Dashing!

A *dashboard* is a collection of graphics that make it easy for a user to access and understand information. Think about the dashboard in a car: It shows how fast the car is moving, how much gas is in the tank, the temperature, and a number of other pieces of information that help a driver understand the state of a car at any given moment.

In this chapter, I show you how to use R to create dashboards that show multiple pieces of information about data.

The shinydashboard Package

In Chapter 1 of Book 5, I introduce you to `shiny`, a package for creating interactive applications in R. Like `shiny`, the `shinydashboard` package is a creation of the same folks who brought us RStudio. As its name indicates, it has all the elements of `shiny` (like user interface, server, and reactivity), and you use it to create dashboards. If, as you work with this package, you get the idea that a dashboard is a `shiny` app on steroids, you've pretty much got it.

Here's what I mean. Figure 2-1 shows a dashboard I created in shinydashboard. It shows a random sample from a uniform distribution with values between 0 and 1, and it shows the mean, median, and standard deviation of the sample. The user moves a slider to set the sample size. It's the same example I use to introduce shiny in Chapter 1 of Book 5. Compare this figure with Figure 1-5 and you'll see that this app presents the same information, but in a snazzier way.

How do you create something like this? Read on.

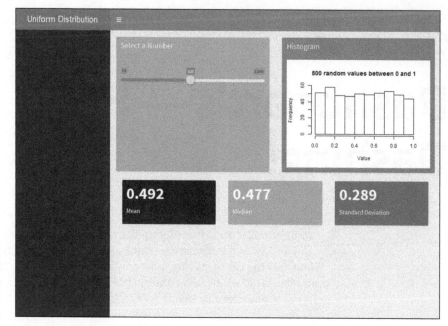

FIGURE 2-1:
First shiny app
from Chapter 1
of Book 5
rendered in
shinydashboard.

Exploring Dashboard Layouts

The first step in creating a dashboard is to install the shinydashboard package. On the Packages tab in RStudio, click Install. In the Install Packages dialog box, type **shinydashboard** and then click Install.

After the package installation is finished, select its box on the Packages tab. Make sure that the box next to shiny on the Packages tab is selected as well.

Choose File ➪ New File ➪ Shiny Web App from the main menu.

Doing this opens the New Shiny Web Application dialog box. Type **Dashboard-Development** (or another descriptive title) in the Application Name box. Use the

Browse button to open the Choose Directory dialog box and create a new directory for the app. In the new file, clear out all the sample code.

Getting started with the user interface

A dashboard user interface consists of a header, a sidebar, and a body. In shinydashboard code, that looks like this:

```
library(shinydashboard)

ui <- dashboardPage(
  dashboardHeader(title = "This is the Header"),
  dashboardSidebar(),
  dashboardBody()
)
```

I add a server

```
server <- function(input, output) {}
```

and the shinyapp() function:

```
shinyApp(ui, server)
```

With all this code typed into the new DashboardDevelopment file, clicking the Run App button creates the screen you see in Figure 2-2.

Building the user interface: Boxes, boxes, boxes . . .

The user interface so far, of course, doesn't allow a user to do anything. In shinydashboard, you use *boxes* to build the user interface. I add them inside a fluidRow (something like fluidPage in a shiny app; see Chapter 1 of Book 5) in dashboardBody() — one box for the slider and one box for the plot:

```
dashboardBody(

  fluidRow(

    box(
      title = "Select a Number",
      sliderInput(inputId = "number",
                  label = "",
```

```
                    value = 500, min = 25, max = 1000)),

        box(
        title = "Histogram",
            plotOutput("hist", height = 250))
        )
    )
```

FIGURE 2-2:
The
beginning of a
shinydashboard
dashboard.

TIP

Notice the `label` argument to `sliderInput()`. I don't want a label in the slider, but omitting the argument results in an error message.

TIP

The `height` argument in `plotOutput()` sets a height for the graph inside the box, not for the entire box.

I also have to add code to the server to render the plot:

```
server <- function(input, output) {
    output$hist <- renderPlot({})
}
```

Running this app produces the elements for the screen shown in Figure 2-3.

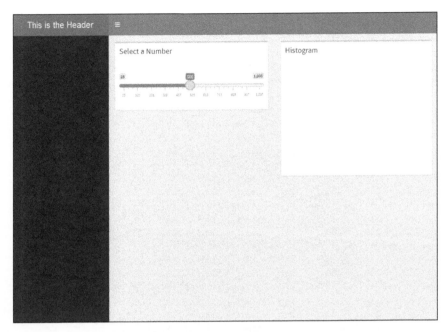

FIGURE 2-3:
Adding a slider
and a plot.

The app still doesn't do anything. If you've read Chapter 1 of Book 5, you know what's coming next in the way of code.

I use reactive({}) to set a variable (histdata) for the results of random sampling from a uniform distribution whose values are between 0 and 1:

```
histdata <- reactive({runif(input$number,min=0,max=1)})
```

And, in order to draw the graph of the sample, I add hist() and appropriate arguments to renderPlot({}):

```
output$hist <- renderPlot({
    hist(histdata(),xlab="Value",
    main=paste(input$number,"random values between 0 and 1"))
  })
```

The first argument in hist is the variable I just set within reactive({}) (along with parentheses!), and the next two add the x-axis title and the main title.

Here's all the code at this point:

```
library(shinydashboard)

ui <- dashboardPage(
  dashboardHeader(
    title = "Uniform Distribution"
    ),
  dashboardSidebar(),
  dashboardBody(

    fluidRow(

  box(
        title = "Select a Number",
        sliderInput(inputId = "number",
                    label = "",
                    value = 500, min = 25, max = 1000)),

      box(title = "Histogram",
          plotOutput("hist", height = 250))
      )
    )
)

server <- function(input, output) {

  histdata <- reactive({runif(input$number,min=0,max=1)})
  output$hist <- renderPlot({

    hist(histdata(),xlab="Value",
         main=paste(input$number,"random values between 0 and 1"))
  })

  }

shinyApp(ui, server)
```

Notice that in `dashboardHeader()` I changed the `title` to "Uniform Distribution". This code produces the functionality shown in Figure 2-4. Moving the slider now changes the histogram and the heading just above it.

Each box can have a `status`. Although it's not strictly necessary, I assign a `warning` status to the slider and a `primary` status to the plot:

```
box(title = "Select a Number",
        status="warning",
```

```
        sliderInput(inputId = "number",
               label = "",
               value = 500, min = 25, max = 1000)),
    box(title = "Histogram",
        status="primary",
        plotOutput("hist", height = 250))
    )
```

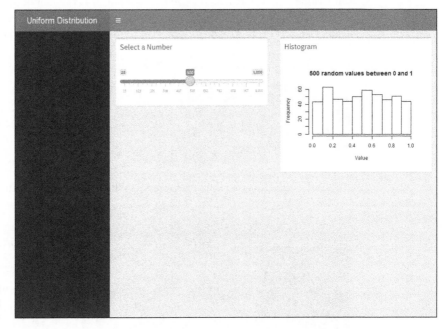

FIGURE 2-4:
Adding
functionality.

Each status is associated with a color, so this change adds a little color to the box
edges: yellow for the slider (although it looks more like gold) and light blue for
the plot.

TIP

The other possible statuses and their associated colors are success (green), info
(aqua), and danger (red). (No shades of gray here. Sorry.)

I add more color to those boxes by setting the background argument for each box:

```
    box(title = "Select a Number",
        background ="yellow",
        status="warning",
        sliderInput(inputId = "number",
               label = "",
               value = 500, min = 25, max = 1000)),
```

```
box(title = "Histogram",
                    background ="light-blue",
        status="primary",
        plotOutput("hist", height = 250))
)
```

I'd like the two boxes to be the same height. (It's good user interface design.) I've already set the height of the plot to 250 (pixels). Do I set the height of the slider to 250? Nope. The value of height in plotOutput() is the height of the plot, not the height of the box that contains it. The box adds an extra 62 pixels (discovered via trial-and-error), so if I set the height of the slider to 312, the two boxes match up:

```
box(title = "Select a Number",
        background ="yellow",
        status="warning",
                height = 312,
        sliderInput(inputId = "number",
            label = "",
            value = 500, min = 25, max = 1000)),
```

After all these changes, the developing dashboard looks like Figure 2-5.

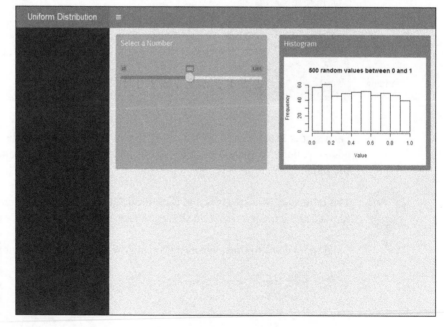

FIGURE 2-5:
The dashboard,
after adding
status and
background and
changing the
height of the
slider.

All that's left is to add the boxes for the mean, median, and standard deviation. In shinydashboard, boxes that show values are called, appropriately enough, value-Boxes. So in the user interface, I add

```
valueBoxOutput("meanBox"),
valueBoxOutput("medianBox"),
valueBoxOutput("sdBox")
```

And in the server, I add functions that render the valueBoxes. Just as render-Plot() provides the reactive context for rendering the plot, you can probably guess that renderValueBox() provides the reactive context for rendering the val-ueBox, and valueBox() does the rendering:

```
output$meanBox <- renderValueBox({
  valueBox(
    round(mean(histdata()),3),"Mean",
    color = "navy"
  )
})

output$medianBox <- renderValueBox({
  valueBox(
    round(median(histdata()),3),"Median",
    color = "aqua"
  )
})

output$sdBox <- renderValueBox({
  valueBox(
    round(sd(histdata()),3), "Standard Deviation",
    color = "blue"
  )
})
```

For each valueBox(), the first argument is the value in the box (the statistic rounded to three decimal places) which appears as a kind of title, the second is the subtitle, and the third, of course, is the color.

The whole code chunk is shown here:

```
library(shinydashboard)

ui <- dashboardPage(
  dashboardHeader(
    title = "Uniform Distribution"
    ),
```

```
    dashboardSidebar(),
    dashboardBody(

      fluidRow(
        box(
            title = "Select a Number",

            background = "yellow",
            status="warning",
            height = 312,
          sliderInput(inputId = "number",
                      label = "",
                      value = 500, min = 25, max = 1000)),

        box(title = "Histogram",
            background = "light-blue",
            status="primary",
            plotOutput("hist", height = 250))
        ),
        valueBoxOutput("meanBox"),

        valueBoxOutput("medianBox"),

        valueBoxOutput("sdBox")

    )
)

server <- function(input, output) {

  histdata <- reactive({runif(input$number,min=0,max=1)})

  output$hist <- renderPlot({ hist(histdata(),xlab="Value",main=paste(input$
               number,"random values between 0 and 1"))
  })

  output$meanBox <- renderValueBox({
    valueBox(
      round(mean(histdata()),3),"Mean",
      color = "navy"
    )
  })

  output$medianBox <- renderValueBox({
    valueBox(
      round(median(histdata()),3),"Median",
      color = "aqua"
    )
  })
```

```
output$sdBox <- renderValueBox({
  valueBox(
    round(sd(histdata()),3), "Standard Deviation",
    color = "blue"
  )
})



}

shinyApp(ui, server)
```

Click Run App and you'll see a dashboard that looks just like the one in Figure 2-1.

Lining up in columns

So the dashboard in Figure 2-1 shows two rows of boxes. How about arranging the boxes in columns? I can put the slider and the plot in one column and the statistics boxes in another. Figure 2-6 shows what I mean.

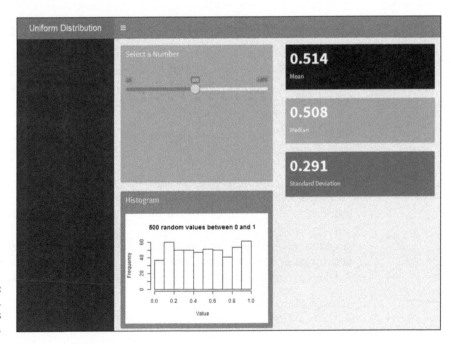

FIGURE 2-6:
The dashboard,
with the boxes
in columns.

To get this done, I keep everything in a `fluidRow()`, and within the row I add a `column()` that encompasses the boxes for that column. Here's the overall structure, with some lines of code omitted for clarity:

```
fluidRow(
    column(

     box( ... This is the slider ... ),

     box( ...  This is the plot ...)

     ),

    column(

     valueBoxOutput("meanBox"),

     valueBoxOutput("medianBox"),

     valueBoxOutput("sdBox")
     )

     )
```

Column-based layouts require specifications for `width`. I have to specify the width of each column and the width of each box in that column. Remember when I specified `height` (of the slider and the plot) in pixels? When I specify `width`, it's measured in columns.

Wait. What? I'm dealing with columns and the measurement unit of their width is . . . columns?

Yes, it's a bit confusing. Keep in mind that the `dashboardBody` is divided into 12 "columns." Each column I *create* can take up a number of those 12 `dashboardBody` columns.

For example, if I want the first column (the one with the slider and the plot) to take up six of those columns, and the second column (with the statistics boxes) to take up four of those columns, I add the `width` argument to each one:

```
fluidRow(
    column(width = 6

     box( ... This is the slider ... ),

     box( ... This is the plot ... )
```

```
  ),

  column(width = 4

    valueBoxOutput("meanBox"),

    valueBoxOutput("medianBox"),

    valueBoxOutput("sdBox")
  )

)
```

But wait — there's more: I also have to specify the width of each box. For each box, I add `width=NULL`:

```
fluidRow(
    column(width = 6

      box(...This is the slider ... width = NULL),

      box( ... This is the plot ... width = NULL )

    ),

    column(width = 4

      valueBoxOutput("meanBox", width = NULL),

      valueBoxOutput("medianBox", width = NULL),

      valueBoxOutput("sdBox", width = NULL)
    )

)
```

TIP

Why didn't I specify `width` in the first (row-based) layout? I could have, but default values kicked in very nicely. In the first row, each of the two boxes takes up half the 12 columns (so each `width` is 6). In the second row, each of the three boxes takes up one third of the 12 columns (so each `width` is 4). If I add another box to the second row . . . it goes into the next row.

So the code for the `dashboardBody()` is

```
dashboardBody(

    fluidRow(
      column(width=6,
```

```
     box(
         title = "Select a Number",
         solidHeader = TRUE,
         background = "yellow",
         status="warning",
         width = NULL,
         height = 312,
         sliderInput(inputId = "number",
                     label = "",
                     value = 500, min = 25, max = 1000)),

     box(title = "Histogram",
         solidHeader=TRUE,
         background = "light-blue",
         status="primary",
         width = NULL,
         plotOutput("hist", height = 250))
     ),

   column(width = 4,

     valueBoxOutput("meanBox",width = NULL),

     valueBoxOutput("medianBox",width = NULL),

     valueBoxOutput("sdBox",width = NULL)
     )

   )
 )
```

This code, along with the rest of the user interface and everything else, produces the screen you see in Figure 2-6.

A nice trick: Keeping tabs

Another type of dashboard box acts like a box full of tabbed documents. It's called tabBox and I show how to use it in Figure 2-7. I've put the mean and the median valueBoxOutputs in separate tabs in a tabBox called Central Tendency. In this context, a tabbed document is called a tabPanel. I've put the standard deviation valueBoxOutput and a new variance valueBoxOutput in separate tabPanels in a tabBox called Variability. Clicking a tabPanel reveals its associated statistical value.

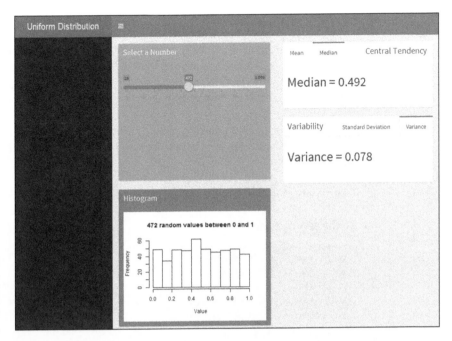

FIGURE 2-7:
The dashboard,
with tabBoxes
labeled Central
Tendency and
Variability.

As you can see in the figure, the statistical values are in text rather than in valueBoxes. So I work with textOutput() in the user interface and renderText() in
the server.

To construct this version, I add this code to the user interface:

```
tabBox(
        title = "Central Tendency",
        id = "tabs1", height = 150, width = NULL,
        tabPanel("Mean",
h2(textOutput("meantext")),width = NULL),
        tabPanel("Median", h2(textOutput("mediantext")),width = NULL)
        ),

    tabBox(
        title = "Variability",
        id = "tabs2", height = 150, width = NULL,
        side = "right",
        tabPanel("Variance",
h2(textOutput("vartext")),width = NULL),
        tabPanel("Standard Deviation", h2(textOutput("sdtext")),width = NULL)
```

Each tabBox has a title, an id, a height, and a width. The important action is in
the tabPanels. Each one has a textOutput and each textOutput has an id (like
"meantext") so that the server can track it.

Pay close attention to a particular aspect of each tabPanel — the h2() that surrounds each textOutput(). The h2() comes from HTML. It sets the font size of its argument by declaring the argument to be a "level 2 heading." So it's a nice, quick way to increase the font size of the textOutput. If I don't do this, the font is very small. You might try experimenting with h1() and h3().

TIP

In the second tabBox, I added side = "right" to show you an alternative layout for the title and the tabPanels. I recommend that you pick one tabBox layout and stick to it.

I won't be using the valueBoxOutputs, so I delete them.

To the server, I add

```
output$meantext <-renderText({
paste("Mean =",round(mean(histdata()),3))})

output$mediantext <-renderText({
paste("Median =",round(median(histdata()),3))})

output$vartext <-renderText({
paste("Variance =",round(var(histdata()),3))})

output$sdtext <-renderText({
paste("Standard Deviation =",
round(sd(histdata()),3))})
```

And I delete all the renderValueBox({}) functions.

Do I also need render({}) functions for the tabBoxes? Not in this case. If each tabPanel in the first tabBox, for example, just contains some unique text that I want to show, I'd add that text as an argument in each tabPanel and add

```
output$tabs1Selected <- renderText({
    input$tabs1
  })
```

to the server. But that's not necessary here.

Just to clarify, the whole set of code is shown here:

```
library(shinydashboard)

ui <- dashboardPage(
```

```
dashboardHeader(
  title = "Uniform Distribution"
  ),
dashboardSidebar(),
dashboardBody(

  fluidRow(
    column(width=6,
      box(
        title = "Select a Number",
        solidHeader = TRUE,
        background = "yellow",
        status="warning",
        width = NULL,
        height = 312,
        sliderInput(inputId = "number",
                label = "",
                value = 500, min = 25, max = 1000)),

      box(title = "Histogram",
        solidHeader=TRUE,
        background = "light-blue",
        status="primary",
        width = NULL,
        plotOutput("hist", height = 250))
      ),

    column(width = 6,

      tabBox(
        title = "Central Tendency",
        id = "tabs1", height = 120, width = NULL,
        tabPanel("Mean",
h2(textOutput("meantext")),width = NULL),
        tabPanel("Median",
h2(textOutput("mediantext")),width = NULL)
      ),

      tabBox(
        title = "Variability",
        id = "tabs2", height = 120, width = NULL,
        side = "right",
        tabPanel("Variance",
h2(textOutput("vartext")),width = NULL),
        tabPanel("Standard Deviation", h2(textOutput("sdtext")),width = NULL)
      )
```

```
          )
        )
      )
    )

server <- function(input, output) {

  histdata <- reactive({runif(input$number,min=0,max=1)})

  output$hist <- renderPlot({

  hist(histdata(),xlab="Value",
main=paste(input$number,"random values between 0 and 1"))
  })

  output$meantext <-renderText({
paste("Mean =",round(mean(histdata()),3))})

  output$mediantext <-renderText({
paste("Median =",round(median(histdata()),3))})

  output$vartext <-renderText({
paste("Variance =",round(var(histdata()),3))})

  output$sdtext <-renderText({
paste("Standard Deviation =",
round(sd(histdata()),3))})


  }

shinyApp(ui, server)
```

Click Run App for a dashboard that looks (and acts) like the dashboard shown in Figure 2-7.

Suggested project: Add statistics

One way to sharpen your `shinydashboard` skills is to extend this tabbed version. Add a `tabBox` that provides statistics for the appearance of the histogram. The statistics are called *skewness* (how weighted the histogram is to the left or the right), and *kurtosis* (how peaked or how flat the histogram is). Functions for these statistics live in a package called `moments`.

When you're done, your dashboard should look similar to Figure 2-8.

FIGURE 2-8:
The dashboard,
with a tabBox
for statistics
that describe
the histogram's
appearance.

TIP

Move the slider and check the resulting values for skewness and kurtosis against the appearance of the histogram. You might just get a feel for what those two statistics are all about!

Suggested project: Place valueBoxes in tabPanels

It's possible to render the statistics in the tabPanels in a different way. Instead of textOutput you can use valueBoxes, as in the original, nontabbed version. The idea is to move each valueBox inside a tabPanel. Your finished product should look like Figure 2-9. If you're feeling ambitious, add the Appearance tabBox from the suggested project in the previous section, "Suggested project: Add statistics."

FIGURE 2-9:
The dashboard,
with statistics
presented in
valueBoxes in
the tabPanels.

Working with the Sidebar

In this section, I show you some more shinydashboard features, beginning with the sidebar. Similar to the tabbed boxes I show you earlier, the sidebar is a way of navigating through content. Click a sidebar menu item, and its corresponding content appears.

I create a dashboard with two content-screens. The first is a repeat of the first version of sampling from a uniform distribution, with statistics presented in valueBoxes. The second involves sampling from a standard normal distribution (mean = 0, standard deviation = 1). In this one, the statistics appear in another kind of box: the infoBox. Clicking icons in the sidebar navigates between the sections.

The first screen, shown in Figure 2-10, looks very much like Figure 2-1. The only difference is in the sidebar. The sidebar has a Square icon that represents the uniform distribution, and a Bell icon that represents the standard normal distribution. (See what I did there?) Also, I changed the title of the whole thing to Sampling.

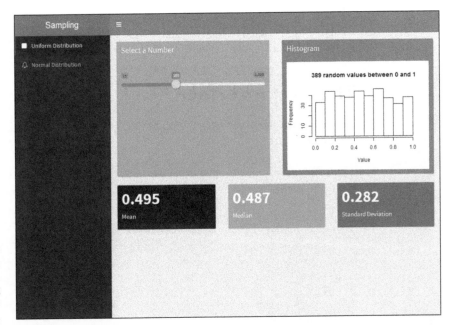

FIGURE 2-10:
The first screen
of the dashboard,
showing sampling
from a uniform
distribution.

Figure 2-11 shows the second screen. The slider is a bit different, and the graph is
a density plot rather than a histogram. (See Chapter 1 of Book 2.) The statistics, as
I mention earlier, are in `infoBox`es.

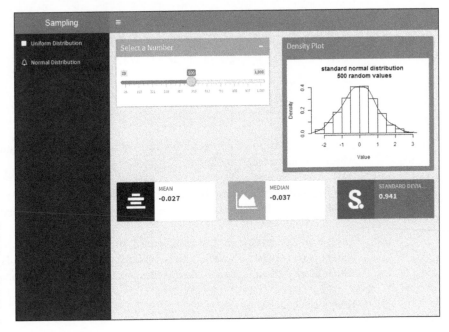

FIGURE 2-11:
The second
screen of the
dashboard,
showing
sampling from a
standard normal
distribution.

I begin the project by choosing File ⇨ New File ⇨ Shiny Web App from the main menu in order to create a new file called sidebarDevelopment in a new directory.

The user interface

The best way to get you started with building the user interface is to show you its overall structure:

```
ui <- dashboardPage(
 dashboardHeader(
   title = "Sampling"
 ), # dashboardHeader
 dashboardSidebar(
   sidebarMenu(
     menuItem( ... Uniform distribution stuff .1 . . ),
     menuItem( ... Standard Normal Distribution stuff ... )

   ) # sidebarMenu

 ), # dashboardSidebar

 dashboardBody(
   tabItems(

     tabItem( ... Uniform distribution stuff ... ),

     tabItem( ... Standard Normal Distribution stuff ... )

     ) # tabItems

   ) # dashboardBody

 ) # dashboardPage
```

The close parentheses can get a bit confusing (trust me!), so I added comments where I thought they'd help.

The first difference from the earlier projects in this chapter, of course, is the sidebarMenu() in dashboardSidebar(). The sidebarMenu consists of menuItems.

The second difference is the tabItems() in dashboardBody(). As you can see, tabItems() consists of, well, tabItems. Each tabItem corresponds to a menuItem, which is why clicking a menuItem causes tabItem content to appear.

Here's the sidebarMenu():

```
sidebarMenu(
    menuItem("Uniform Distribution", tabName = "uniform", icon = icon("square")),
    menuItem("Normal Distribution", tabName = "normal", icon = icon("bell-o"))
  )
```

For each menuItem, the first argument is the text that appears on the menu, the second is the name that will also appear in the corresponding tabItem, and the third is the icon() function that renders the icon on the menu. These icons (like "square" and "bell-o") are special characters that you can find at http://fontawesome.io/icons.

Here is tabItems(), along with its component tabItems:

```
tabItems(

    tabItem(
tabName = "uniform",

        fluidRow(

          box(
            title = "Select a Number",
            solidHeader = TRUE,
            background = "yellow",
            status="warning",
            height = 312,
            sliderInput(inputId = "number",
                        label = "",
                        value = 500, min = 25,
                        max = 1000)),

          box(title = "Histogram",
            solidHeader=TRUE,
            background = "light-blue",
            status="primary",
            plotOutput("hist", height = 250)),

          valueBoxOutput("meanBox"),

          valueBoxOutput("medianBox"),

          valueBoxOutput("sdBox")

        )

      ),
```

```
tabItem(tabName = "normal",

        fluidRow(
            box(title = "Select a Number",
                solidHeader = TRUE,
                collapsible = TRUE,
                status="warning",
                sliderInput(inputId = "normnumber",
                            label = "",
                            value = 500, min = 25,
                            max = 1000)),

            box(title = "Density Plot",
                solidHeader=TRUE,
                background = "light-blue",
                status="primary",
                plotOutput("density", height = 250)),

            infoBoxOutput("meanInfoBox"),

            infoBoxOutput("medianInfoBox"),

            infoBoxOutput("sdInfoBox")

        )

    )
```

The first tabItem (tabName = "uniform") is just a rehash of the first project: the slider, histogram, and statistics in valueBoxes.

The second tabItem (tabName="normal") shows some new features. First, notice collapsible = TRUE in the box that creates the slider. This creates the little minus sign in the upper right corner of the Select a Number slider box. (Refer to Figure 2-11.) Clicking it collapses the slider and turns the minus sign into a plus sign. And this tabItem features infoBoxes rather than valueBoxes.

The server

The server code begins with reactive({}) functions for the uniform distribution and for the standard normal distribution:

```
histdata <- reactive({runif(input$number,min=0,max=1)})
densitydata <- reactive({rnorm(input$normnumber)})
```

Next are the functions for rendering the histogram:

```
output$hist <- renderPlot({
  hist(histdata(),xlab="Value",
    main=paste(input$number,
    "random values between 0 and 1"))
  })
```

and for rendering the density plot:

```
output$density <- renderPlot({
  hist(densitydata(),xlab="Value",
    main=paste("standard normal distribution \n",
    input$normnumber,"random values"),
    probability=TRUE)
  lines(density(densitydata()))
```

If the `hist()` function for the density plot looks strange to you, go back and reread the first section of Chapter 1 of Book 2. The `probability=TRUE` argument puts density on the *y*-axis, and the `lines()` function adds the line for the density plot.

Next, I add the `render({})` functions for the `valueBox`es:

```
output$meanBox <- renderValueBox({
    valueBox(
      round(mean(histdata()),3),"Mean",
      color = "navy"
    )
  })

  output$medianBox <- renderValueBox({
    valueBox(
      round(median(histdata()),3),"Median",
      color = "aqua"
    )
  })

  output$sdBox <- renderValueBox({
    valueBox(
      round(sd(histdata()),3), "Standard Deviation",
      color = "blue"
    )
  })
```

and add the render({}) functions for the infoBoxes:

```
output$meanInfoBox <- renderInfoBox({
    infoBox("Mean",
       round( mean(densitydata()),3),
  icon=icon("align-center"),
       color = "navy")
})

  output$medianInfoBox <- renderInfoBox({
    infoBox(icon=icon("area-chart"), "Median",
       round(median(densitydata()),3),
       color = "aqua")
})

  output$sdInfoBox <- renderInfoBox({
    infoBox("Standard Deviation",
       round(sd(densitydata()),3),icon=icon("scribd"),
       fill = TRUE,
       color = "blue")
})
```

In the third infoBox, I show what happens if fill=TRUE.

I'm not sure that the icons I used are the most appropriate ones. Perhaps you can find some better ones.

It's okay to use icons in the valueBoxes. I just chose not to.

Putting all this code between the curly braces in

```
server <- function(input, output) {}
```

and adding

```
shinyApp(ui, server)
```

at the end, and adding

```
library(shinydashboard)
```

at the beginning produces the framework for Figures 2-10 and 2-11 when I click Run App.

Suggested project: Relocate the slider

The sidebar can have more than just `menuItems`. For example, you can put a slider or other kinds of input in the sidebar, and that's what this suggested project is all about.

Suppose the objective is to see what a specific sample size looks like from a uniform distribution and compare that with a standard normal distribution. The user selects a number from a slider in the sidebar and then uses the sidebar menu to see the uniform distribution results or the standard normal distribution results. The dashboard (with Uniform Distribution selected) looks like Figure 2-12.

FIGURE 2-12: The dashboard, with the slider in the sidebar and Uniform Distribution selected.

Figure 2-13 shows the dashboard with Normal Distribution selected.

Give it a try. You'll have to come up with values for `width` and `height` for the sidebar and its slider, and for each plot, to make your dashboard look like Figures 2-12 and 2-13. You'll also have to adjust some aspects of the slider's appearance.

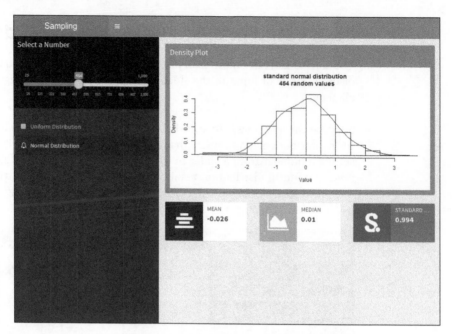

FIGURE 2-13:
The dashboard,
with Normal
Distribution
selected.

Interacting with Graphics

In the projects I've shown you so far in this chapter, plot changes follow user interactions with components like sliders or drop-down menus. In this section, I reverse the process: When the dashboard opens, a plot appears, the user interacts with the plot, and other user interface components change.

As you learn how to make this happen, you'll see some additional dashboard and graphics capabilities along the way.

Clicks, double-clicks, and brushes — oh, my!

Up to this point in the chapter, all I've done with `plotOutput()` is set the `height` and `width` of the plot. The `plotOutput()` function offers more possibilities: It takes arguments called `click`, `dblclick`, `hover`, and `brush`.

TIP

Brush? What's that? If you've ever dragged the mouse while you pressed and then released the left mouse button (and I know you have!), you've brushed. A joke about doing this after every meal suggests itself, but I won't pursue it.

I can set the `click` argument to a value like `"single_click"`. When I click the plot, the plot sends the xy-coordinates of the click to the server. The values of those coordinates are stored in `input$single_click`. The `dblclick` argument works the same way: If I set dblclick to "double_click" and click a point twice in rapid succession, the plot sends the coordinates to the server, and the values are stored in input$double_click. You can probably figure out how hover works.

The brush argument works a bit differently. When you brush across the plot, you create, in effect, a box. Four pairs of xy-coordinates define the box: xmin, ymin (the lower left corner), xmax, ymax (the upper right corner), xmin, ymax (the upper left corner), and xmax, ymin (the lower right corner). Setting brush to "brushed" and dragging the mouse and then releasing the mouse button sends xmin, xmax, ymin, and ymax to the server. I get to those values via input$brushed.

To show you all this in action, I work with a data frame called UScereal in the MASS package. This data frame holds nutritional information (and some other stuff) about 65 brands of cereal sold in the United States. The initial of each cereal manufacturer (Kellogg's, Post, General Mills, Quaker Oats, Ralston Purina, and Nabisco) represents the manufacturer's name.

Figure 2-14 shows a dashboard with a plot that presents Calories versus Proteins (gm) of each cereal. The measurements are per portion, and a portion is 1 cup (240 ml). I thought it would add pizazz to the graph if each data point identifies the manufacturer — hence, all the letters inside the plot.

Below the plot is a box that shows the coordinates for the different types of mouse interactions. Here's how to do it:

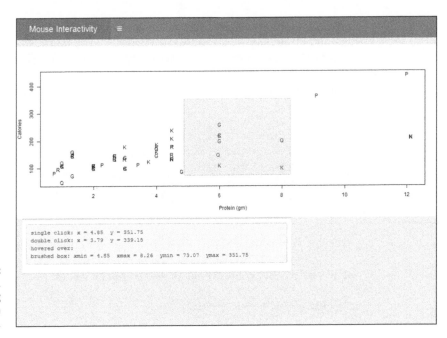

FIGURE 2-14: Data on U.S. cereals, showing interaction with the plot.

As usual, I begin the project by choosing File⇨New File⇨Shiny Web App to create a new file called mouseActions in a new directory.

I start with the libraries:

```
library(shinydashboard)
library(MASS)
```

Next comes the user interface:

```
ui <- dashboardPage(
  dashboardHeader(title="Mouse Interactivity"),
  dashboardSidebar(collapsed=TRUE),
  dashboardBody(
    fluidRow(
                plotOutput("CerealPlot",
                click = "single_click",
                dblclick = "double_click",
                hover = "hovering",
                brush = "brushing"
  ),

                box((verbatimTextOutput("coords")),width =8)
  )
  )
  )
```

The box toward the end of the code holds the coordinates for the mouse actions. Its output method — verbatimTextOutput — is a quick way of presenting the values. This saves me from putting the values in valueBoxes or in infoBoxes.

And finally, the server, which begins with the function for rendering the plot:

```
server <- function(input, output) {
  output$CerealPlot <- renderPlot({
    plot(x=UScereal$protein, y=UScereal$calories,
         xlab="Protein (gm)",
         ylab="Calories",
         pch=as.character(UScereal$mfr))
  })
```

The last argument, pch, puts those manufacturer initials in the plot.

The next reactive context renders the coordinate values:

```
output$coords <- renderText({})
```

The `renderText({})` function is for rendering character strings, like the coordinate values.

Three functions are placed between the curly brackets of `renderText({})`. The first is for the coordinates that `click`, `dblclick`, and `hover` return:

```
xy_points <- function(datapoints) {
    if(is.null(datapoints)) return("\n")
    paste("x =", round(datapoints$x, 2), " y =", round(datapoints$y, 2), "\n")
}
```

If the user hasn't performed a particular action, the function returns a newline character. Ultimately, the function outputs rounded values of the x-coordinate and the y-coordinate.

The second function is for the four coordinates that `brush` produces:

```
xy_points_range <- function(datapoints) {
    if(is.null(datapoints)) return("\n")
    paste("xmin =", round(datapoints$xmin, 2),
          " xmax =", round(datapoints$xmax, 2),
          " ymin =", round(datapoints$ymin, 2),
          " ymax =", round(datapoints$ymax, 2))
}
```

The third function puts the coordinate values on the screen:

```
paste0(
    "single click: ", xy_points(input$single_click),
    "double click: ", xy_points(input$double_click),
    "hovered over: ", xy_points(input$hovering),
    "brushed box: ", xy_points_range(input$brushing)
)
```

TIP

For the third function, `paste0()` works a little better than `paste()`, since `paste0()` manages to concatenate strings without adding a space between each one.

With those three functions inside the curly brackets of `renderText({})`, and with the close curly bracket for `server({})` and `shinyApp(ui = ui, server = server)` at the end, clicking Run App produces the dashboard shown in Figure 2-15. You can click, double-click, hover, and brush to watch the effects on the coordinate values. One helpful feature is that the coordinates are in terms of the units on the axes, not in terms of pixels.

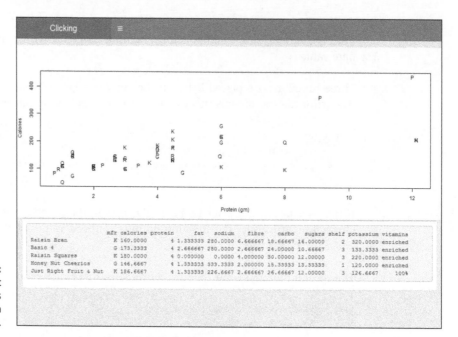

Why bother with all this?

Interacting with the data points on a plot is a useful way to select data points and then render the rows of selected data in a table. Figure 2-15 shows a dashboard that presents data resulting from a single click on the plot. The click was on the cluster of data points above the 4 on the x-axis.

The coding for this is, believe it or not, easier than for the immediately preceding section. What makes the data row rendering possible is a neat little function called nearPoints(). This function takes the coordinates of the click and finds the rows in the associated data frame.

I'll tell you all about it, but first here's the beginning of the code for the dashboard in Figure 2-15:

```
library(shinydashboard)
library(MASS)
ui <- dashboardPage(
  dashboardHeader(title="Clicking"),
  dashboardSidebar(collapsed=TRUE),
  dashboardBody(
    fluidRow(
              plotOutput("CerealPlot",
          click = "single_click"
                ),
```

```
                    box((verbatimTextOutput("coords")),width =12)
    )
  )
)
```

The server code is

```
server <- function(input, output) {
  output$CerealPlot <- renderPlot({

  plot(x=UScereal$protein, y=UScereal$calories,
       xlab="Protein(gm)",ylab="Calories",
       pch=as.character(UScereal$mfr))
  })

  output$coords <- renderPrint({
    nearPoints(UScereal, input$single_click,
        xvar = "protein", yvar = "calories", threshold=20)
  })
}
```

The `renderPrint({})` function is for printable output, like the rows of the data frame.

The first argument to `nearPoints()` is the name of the data frame. The second is the user input. Next come the names of the *x*- and *y*-variables in the plot. The final argument, `threshold`, specifies the maximum number of pixels from the click to include:

Add

```
shinyApp(ui = ui, server = server)
```

and that's all there is to it.

TIP

The `nearPoints()` function also works with `dblclick` and `hover`.

Brushing proceeds in a similar way. The only difference is that brushing requires `brushedPoints()`, which works very much like `nearPoints()`.

For a dashboard like the one shown in Figure 2-16, the only changes I make to the code are

```
dashboardHeader(title="Brushing"),
```

and

```
plotOutput("CerealPlot",
           brush = "brushing"
),
```

in the user interface, and

```
brushedPoints(UScereal, input$brushing, xvar = "protein", yvar = "calories")
```

in the renderPrint({}) function in the server.

Figure 2-16 shows the result, including a brush box and the selected data.

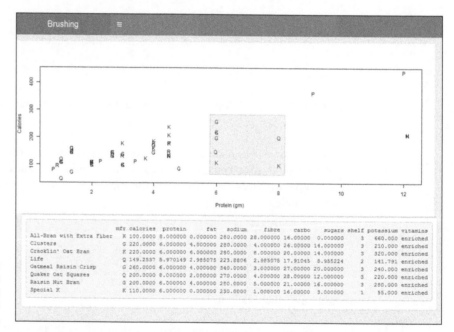

Suggested project: Experiment with airquality

The airquality data frame, which you find in the datasets package, provides a nice data set to experiment with. I've used it before. Just to refresh your memory, here are the first six rows:

```
> head(airquality)
  Ozone Solar.R Wind Temp Month Day
1    41     190  7.4   67     5   1
2    36     118  8.0   72     5   2
3    12     149 12.6   74     5   3
4    18     313 11.5   62     5   4
5    NA      NA 14.3   56     5   5
6    28      NA 14.9   66     5   6
```

For a dashboard with brushing capability, your project should look like Figure 2-17.

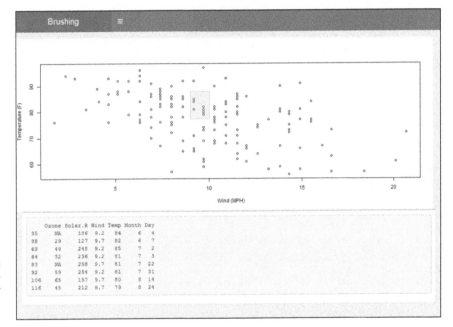

FIGURE 2-17:
A brush-capable
dashboard for
the airquality
data frame.

Index

Symbols and Numerics

A

functions *(continued)*

  append( ), 27, 548

  arrow( ), 231

  as.data.frame.matrix( ), 550

  as.Date( ), 541

  as.factor( ), 512

  assoc( ), 553

  assocstats( ), 553

  attach( ), 97

  auto.arime( ), 366

  barplot( ), 63, 544

  binom.test( ), 411, 414

  boxplot( ), 73

  brushedPoints( ), 635

  c( ), 22–23, 26

  cat( ), 141, 189, 213

  cbind( ), 34, 274

  chisq.test( ), 201–202, 566

  choose( ), 373, 401

  cochrane.qtest( ), 385

  colnames( ), 78

  column( ), 614

  combinations( ), 402

  combn( ), 401

  cor( ), 324–326, 390

  corrgram( ), 328

  cor.test( ), 324–325, 388

  for counting rules, 401–403

  cumsum( ), 136

  dashboardBody( ), 605, 615, 624

  dashboardHeader( ), 608

  dashboardSidebar( ), 624

  datadensity( ), 143

  data.frame( ), 32

  dbinom( ), 407

dchisq( ), 202–205

decompose( ), 362

density, 403–405

describe( ), 143

df( ), 227–229

dim( ), 28

dnbinom( ), 409–410

dnorm( ), 149, 150, 162

drop_na( ), 44, 593–594

dt( ), 179, 191–192

!duplicated( ), 545

element_blank( ), 86

empirical cumulative
   distribution, 138

exp( ), 341, 345, 350

facet_grid( ), 569

factor( ), 32, 34

factorial( ), 401

filter( ), 47, 559, 564

findRFM( ), 539–542, 544, 554

fivenum( ), 123–124

fluidPage( ), 579

fluidRow( ), 614

forecast( ), 365

friedman.test( ), 385

gather( ), 46

geom, 93, 196–197, 295, 297

geom_bar( ), 79, 219, 221, 408, 561–562,
   568, 569

geom_boxplot( ), 90

geom_dotplot( ), 78

geom_errorbar( ), 264, 569

geom_histogram( ), 76, 171

geom_jitter( ), 90

geom_line, 196–197,
   205–206

numerical variables, 134–142

numerical vectors, 26–27

O

objects, 15

olden() function, 532

one-sample hypothesis testing

  about, 181

  errors, 181–183

  hypotheses, 181–183

  sampling distributions and, 183–185

  t-distributions, 189–200

  testing variances, 200–202

  tests, 181–183

  t.test() function, 190–191

  visualizing chi-square distributions, 203–206

  visualizing t-distributions, 192–200

  working with chi-square distributions, 202–203

  working with t-distributions, 191–192

  z-scores, 185–187

  z.test() function, 188–189

one-tailed hypothesis test, 186–187, 207–208

order() function, 551

ordinal data, 10

outliers, 98–99

output function, 596

output layer, 522

outputs, 425, 506–507

overplotting, 90

P

packages

  about, 43

  car, 302–303

datasets, 37–39, 592

e1071, 490–495

ggplot

  data relationships and, 436–437

  working with, 585–592

  installing, 37–39

knitr, 559

magrittr, 559

plotrix, 559

Rattle

  about, 438–440

  decision trees in, 455–459

  getting data into, 477–478

  log, 448

  running, 440–441

  setting up for Banknotes project, 529–531

  starting, 515–516

  using with iris, 442–447

  working with, 548–550

rgl, 302–303

scatterplot3d, 301–302

shiny, 575

shinydashboard, 603–604

tidyr, 593

tidyverse, 44–47, 557

paired samples

  hypothesis testing for, 222–223

  t-testing in R, 224

pairs() function, 71, 73, 86, 434, 437

par() function, 432, 435, 436

parameters

  about, 8

  of normal distribution, 147–148

partial correlation, 331

Pascal distribution, 407

paste() function, 581, 598, 633

vectors
  about, 25–26
  numerical, 26–27
  working with two, 216
versions, R, 15
vertical line (|), 398
View() function, 558, 564
visualizing
  chi-square distributions, 203–206
  clusters, 508, 518
  correlation matrices, 326–328
  data, 558–561
  data points, 518
  neural networks, 531–533
  results from logistic regression, 421–422
  t-distributions, 192–200

W

Warning icon, 4
wday() function, 565–566
websites
  Cheat Sheet, 4
  Comprehensive R Archive Network (CRAN), 15
  R packages and functions, 47
  RStudio, 15
  University of California (UCI) ML Repository, 426
which() function, 597
whiskers, 59
Wickham, Hadley (E expert), 73, 74
wide format, 45
Wilcoxon matched-pairs signed ranks, 379–380
Wilcoxon rank-sum test, 372–375
wilcox.test() function, 380
Wilkinson, Leland (author), 73–74

Williams, Graham (designer), 531
with() function, 34, 96–97, 110–111, 551
within sum of squares, 505, 547
within-subjects analysis, 251
working directory, 18–19
write.table() function, 50

X

x^2 (chi-square)
  about, 200–201
  distributions
    visualizing, 203–206
    working with, 202–203
  plotting
    in base R graphics, 203–205
    in ggplot2, 205–206
x-coordinate, 58
x-variable (independent variable), 280

Y

y-coordinate, 58
ymd() function, 554
y-variable (dependent variable), 280

Z

zero
  about, 10
  correlation coefficient greater than, 321–322
z-score (standard score)
  about, 114–116, 160–161
  central limit theorem and, 211–212
  hypothesis testing and, 185–187
z.test() function, 188–189
z-testing, for two samples in R, 212–213

About the Author

Joseph Schmuller is a veteran of over 25 years in the field of information technology. He is the author of several books on computing, including *Statistical Analysis with R For Dummies*, *R Projects For Dummies*, and all five editions of *Statistical Analysis with Excel For Dummies* (all from Wiley), and the three editions of *Teach Yourself UML in 24 Hours* (SAMS).He has created and delivered online coursework on statistics and Excel for LinkedIn Learning. Over 100,000 people around the world have taken these courses.

For seven years, Joseph was the editor-in-chief of *PC AI* magazine, and he has written numerous articles on advanced technology.

A former member of the American Statistical Association, he has taught statistics at the undergraduate and graduate levels. He holds a BS from Brooklyn College, an MA from the University of Missouri-Kansas City, and a PhD from the University of Wisconsin, all in psychology.

He and his family live in Jacksonville, Florida, where he works on the Digital Cloud & Enterprise Architecture Team at Availity.

Dedication

In loving memory of Jason Edward Sprague, as wonderful a nephew as an uncle could have hoped for.

Author's Acknowledgments

I've written a number of *For Dummies* titles, but this is my first *All-in-One*. It's a bit daunting to write a book that's all-encompassing, but I thoroughly enjoyed the journey.

Adding to the enjoyment was the opportunity to work again with the Wiley team. No author can write a book without a great team, and Wiley always provides one. Executive editor Steve Hayes conceived the idea for this book and got the band back together to bring it to life.

After our work on previous titles, my teammates are all now my friends. As always, project editor Paul Levesque monitored my writing, improved it where necessary, and kept all the moving parts in motion. I've said it before, and I'll say it again: Coordinating all the components is way harder than it sounds, and not nearly as easy as my friend Paul makes it look. Copyeditor Becky Whitney sharpened my prose and made it easier to read the book you're holding (and to hold the book you're reading). Technical editor Guy Hart-Davis made sure the code and the technical aspects were correct. I am the owner and sole proprietor of any errors that remain.

Speaking of indispensable individuals, many thanks to my longtime agent and friend David Fugate of Launchbooks.com for representing me in this effort.

My mentors in statistics in college and graduate school shaped my knowledge and my thinking, and thus influenced this book: Mitch Grossberg (Brooklyn College); Al Hillix, Jerry Sheridan, the late Mort Goldman, and the late Larry Simkins (University of Missouri-Kansas City); and Cliff Gillman and the late John Theios (University of Wisconsin-Madison). I hope my books are an appropriate testament to my mentors who have passed on.

As always, my thanks to Kathy for her inspiration, her patience, her support, and her love.

Publisher's Acknowledgments

Acquisitions Editor: Steve Hayes
Senior Project Editors:
    Paul Levesque
Copy Editor: Becky Whitney

Technical Editors: Guy Hart-Davis
Production Editor: Saikarthick Kumarasamy
Cover Image: © Nmedia/Adobe Stock Photos